M000234834

INTRODUCTION TO
PHENOMENOLOGY

For years philosophers have been looking for a clear, engaging, accurate introduction to phenomenology to recommend to students and read themselves. This is the book. *Introduction to Phenomenology* is a pleasure to read, yet it provides deep insights into what is surely one of the most important philosophical movements of the twentieth century.

Charles Guignon, University of Vermont

This book is genuinely impressive. It provides the most accessible, the most scholarly, and philosophically the most interesting account of the phenomenological movement yet written.

David Bell, University of Sheffield

This long-awaited introduction is a work of admirable care and concision. Moran has an innovative sense of the scope of phenomenology, and the construction of the overall context within which to place each thinker is masterly. Written in a clear, succinct style, it will soon become a standard reference work in the field.

Joanna Hodge, Manchester Metropolitan University

Not since Spiegelberg's *The Phenomenological Movement* has one author covered so many phenomenological figures so well between two covers. Moran's solid and straightforward presentations will greatly help faculty as well as students who are seriously interested in this century-old movement.

Lester Embree, Florida Atlantic University,
Editor in Chief, *Encyclopedia of Phenomenology*

Dermot Moran is Professor of Philosophy at University College Dublin and Editor of the *International Journal of Philosophical Studies*.

INTRODUCTION TO PHENOMENOLOGY

Dermot Moran

London and New York

First published 2000
by Routledge
11 New Fetter Lane, London EC4P 4EE

Simultaneously published in the USA and Canada
by Routledge
29 West 35th Street, New York, NY 10001

Reprinted 2000

Routledge is an imprint of the Taylor & Francis Group

© 2000 Dermot Moran

Typeset in Times by Taylor & Francis Books Ltd
Printed and bound in Great Britain by Clays Ltd, St Ives plc

All rights reserved. No part of this book may be reprinted or
reproduced or utilised in any form or by any electronic,
mechanical, or other means, now known or hereafter
invented, including photocopying and recording, or in any
information storage or retrieval system, without permission in
writing from the publishers.

British Library Cataloguing in Publication Data
A catalogue record for this book is available from the British Library

Library of Congress Cataloging-in-Publication Data
Moran, Dermot.
Introduction to Phenomenology / Dermot Moran.
Includes bibliographical references and index.
1. Phenomenology.   I. Title
B829.5.M647   1999   99-042071
142'.7–dc21

ISBN 0–415–18372–3 (hbk)
ISBN 0–415–18373–1 (pbk)

FOR MY FAMILY
AND
ESPECIALLY IN LOVING MEMORY
OF
MY NEPHEW TRISTAN MORAN
(1978–1999) R.I.P.

CONTENTS

CONTENTS

CONTENTS

ix

CONTENTS

CONTENTS

PREFACE

This book is an introduction to *phenomenology*, a movement which, in many ways, typifies the course of European philosophy in the twentieth century. Writing at the close of this era, the extent of this contribution can now be more clearly articulated, appreciated, and, inevitably, criticised. Phenomenology was announced by Edmund Husserl in 1900–1901 as a bold, radically new way of doing philosophy, an attempt to bring philosophy back from abstract metaphysical speculation wrapped up in pseudo-problems, in order to come into contact with the matters themselves, with concrete living experience. As Husserl originally envisaged it, phenomenology had much in common with William James' radical empiricism, but more than anything else it was stimulated by Franz Brentano's ground-breaking work in *descriptive psychology*, the a priori science of the acts and contents of consciousness. Somewhat later, Husserl came to realise the connection between his conception of phenomenology and Descartes's project of providing a secure edifice for knowledge. Husserl eventually came to see that his own project had much in common with Neo-Kantianism, and thus his phenomenology became a form of transcendental idealism. But his studies of consciousness also led him to pursue investigations into our awareness of time, and history, which led to his development of the concept of the life-world, and to investigations of the evolution of culture reminiscent of Hegel's phenomenology of spirit.

Husserl constantly pushed his thought in new directions, and each new phase in his thinking was developed further by the various generations of students who worked with him. Phenomenological description of things just as they are, in the manner in which they appear, the central motif of phenomenology, meant that phenomenologists were free to engage with all areas of experience. So long as one rendered faithfully the experience of the matters themselves, there was no limit put on what could be examined. Thus phenomenology blossomed into an extraordinarily diverse set of projects, "a set of infinite tasks", as Husserl put it. Husserl envisaged his students as carrying out the task of mapping out the entire phenomenological domain.

However, phenomenology cannot be understood simply as a method, a project, a set of tasks; in its historical form it is primarily a set of people, not just Husserl and his personal assistants, Edith Stein, Martin Heidegger, Eugen Fink, Ludwig Landgrebe, but more broadly his students, Roman Ingarden, Hedwig Conrad-Martius, Marvin Farber, Dorion Cairns, Alfred Schütz, Aron Gurwitsch, and many others, including Max Scheler and Karl Jaspers, who developed phenomenological insights in contact and in parallel with the work of Husserl. Thus phenomenology as a historical movement is exemplified by a range of extraordinarily diverse thinkers.

Phenomenology also translated into different philosophical climates, most notably in France, where Emmanuel Levinas began a tradition of exploration of phenomenology which was developed in brilliant, idiosyncratic fashion by Jean-Paul Sartre, Simone de Beauvoir, Maurice Merleau-Ponty, Michel Henry, Paul Ricoeur, and many others. But phenomenology also provided a platform for the exploration of other possibilities, including a revolt against phenomenology. In Germany, Rudolf Carnap reacted against Heidegger's view of metaphysics; Theodor Adorno, Max Horkheimer, and the Frankfurt school criticised the limitations of phenomenology from the standpoint of Marxism. Hans-Georg Gadamer developed phenomenological hermeneutics, and Hannah Arendt brought her phenomenological mode of viewing to bear on the nature of human action in the modern world. Jacques Derrida's deconstruction, too, finds its origin in certain worries about the nature of signification and of presence at the centre of Husserl's work, as well as drawing on Heidegger's conception of the destruction of the history of philosophy.

In this book, therefore, I have tried not only to provide accessible, critical introductions to the original precursor, Brentano, and the founders, Husserl and Heidegger, but also to indicate something of the range of the later development of the movement in Sartre, Levinas, and Merleau-Ponty, on the one hand, and in Heidegger's students, Hans-Georg Gadamer and Hannah Arendt, on the other. Perhaps the most unusual feature of the book is that I have decided to include both Gadamer and Arendt as important phenomenologists in their own right, but I believe that their inclusion is fully justified and rectifies an earlier neglect of their roles in the evolving story of phenomenology. The inclusion of Derrida, which may strike some phenomenological purists as odd, is justified, I believe, on the basis of his long engagement with phenomenological texts.

While phenomenology never came to be a movement in the sense Husserl intended, it still presents the most coherent philosophical alternative to the project of naturalising consciousness. Phenomenology's emphasis on examining the structures of consciousness from within still presents a challenge to all third-person attempts to explain consciousness in terms of natural science. For this reason, as well as for its complex conception of the nature of the historical and cultural elements of human experience, phenomenology will continue to challenge other schools of philosophy well into the twenty-first century.

I have endeavoured to write this book in an accessible, jargon-free manner. I have tried to explain technical terms as they are introduced, and to connect phenomenological discussion with more traditional philosophical vocabulary and concerns. Above all else, I have tried to show the *development* of phenomenology from its origins in Brentano to its critique in Derrida. Because of the singular importance of Edmund Husserl and Martin Heidegger, I have devoted approximately half of the book to their visions of phenomenology. I have principally restricted my references to the primary sources and their translations, because I want to point those interested in the subject towards the actual texts themselves. Too often, students have been discouraged from exploring these texts by their sheer difficulty and complexity. I have made every effort here to attempt to demystify these texts and to clarify their complex mode of expression. If erring on the side of clarity leads students to read the original works, I shall be more than pleased. I also hope that this book may serve as a reliable guide for students primarily schooled in the analytic tradition, who are seeking an accessible introduction to the central strand of twentieth-century European philosophy. Hopefully, the common threads connecting the traditions will become apparent even where they are not explicitly treated.

This book makes no claims to offer a survey of contemporary Continental philosophy in general, a task far too ambitious to be undertaken in a single book. In fact, I want to present phenomenology in its own right, and for this reason, I have not treated the connections of phenomenology with the thought of Nietzsche or especially emphasised the connection of phenomenology with existentialism. I believe that phenomenology is a mode of doing philosophy which should first be appreciated in its own terms. At the same time, I hope there will be sufficient detail and philosophical content to interest the professional philosopher attempting to understand the nature of twentieth-century philosophy. It is my hope that this study will contribute in some way to the understanding of Continental philosophy among analytic philosophers and will also serve as the basis for the construction of teaching courses in phenomenology.

ACKNOWLEDGEMENTS

I have been reading and lecturing on phenomenology for almost thirty years, so it would be impossible here to give thanks to all the people who have helped me on my way in exploring this fascinating subject. As a graduate student at Yale University, I attended the courses of Karsten Harries on Heidegger, where I came to read Heidegger's later essays on language and on poetry in a new light. I also benefited from Edward Casey's "Phenomenology and Imagining" course, and came to understand the relation between Hegel's *Phenomenology of Spirit* and later phenomenology in the seminars of the late George Schrader.

In the course of researching this book, I owe a debt of gratitude to people too numerous to mention, but I would specifically like to thank Robin Rollinger, Otto Pöggeler, Jan Wolenski, Peter Simons (for discussion of Brentano), Kevin Mulligan (for much help in clarifying the early Husserl), Ullrich Melle, Rudolf Bernet, Sebastian Luft, Ingrid Lombaerts, all of the Husserl Archiv, Leuven, Belgium, and Jos DeCorte, William Desmond, and Carlos Steel of the Higher Institute of Philosophy there, for the hospitality afforded during my several visits. I would also like to thank Michael Kober, Klaus Jacobi, Philip Buckley, John J. Cleary, Claire Ortiz Hill, Lester Embree, Jeffrey Barash, Hubert Dreyfus, Robert Sokolowski, Jean Greisch, Ed Casey, William Hamrick, Mark Dooley, Tim Mooney, and Brian O'Connor, for conversation, comments, and insights. I wish to thank my colleagues at UCD and especially Richard Kearney for providing me with the necessary departmental support to complete the writing of this book, and for his critical but encouraging comments on earlier drafts of some chapters. Of course, all errors and misinterpretations must remain my sole responsibility.

I would like to record my thanks to UCD for a President's Fellowship which enabled me to research the project in 1996–1997, and Tony Bruce of Routledge, for his unfledging enthusiasm for the project. Maurice Larkin, Tim Crowley, Nardene Berry, and Ryan Clancy were of enormous assistance with the bibliography and the proof-reading; Mary Buckley provided invaluable secretarial support. Last of all I would like to thank my mother for arriving with the confectionery to accompany my (too frequent) coffee breaks, my brothers and sisters for their support, my wife Loretta for her patience, and our three children, Katie, Eoin, and Hannah, for the necessary interruptions and distraction. Finally, I would like to dedicate this book to the memory of my nephew, Tristan Moran (1978–1999).

Dublin
October 1999

ABBREVIATIONS

BN	Sartre, *Being and Nothingness*
BPP	Heidegger, *Basic Problems of Phenomenology*
Briefwechsel	Husserl, *Briefwechsel*
BT	Heidegger, *Being and Time*
Chronik	Schuhmann, *Husserl-Chronik*
CM	Husserl, *Cartesian Meditations*
COP	Twardowski, *On the Content and Object of Presentations*
CPP	Levinas, *Collected Philosophical Papers*
Crisis	Husserl, *The Crisis of European Sciences*
DP	Brentano, *Descriptive Psychology*
EE	Levinas, *Existence and Existents*
EI	Levinas, *Ethics and Infinity*
EIJ	Arendt, *Eichmann in Jerusalem*
EJ	Husserl, *Experience and Judgement*
EW	Husserl, *Early Writings in the Philosophy of Logic and Mathematics*, trans. Willard
FCM	Heidegger, *Fundamental Concepts of Metaphysics*
FTL	Husserl, *Formal and Transcendental Logic*
GA	*Gesamtausgabe* (Heidegger)
Gramm.	Derrida, *Of Grammatology*
HAHA	"Hannah Arendt on Hannah Arendt", in M. Hill, ed., *Hannah Arendt: The Recovery of the Public World*
HAKJ	*Hanna Arendt–Karl Jaspers, Correspondence 1926–1969*, trans. R. and R. Kimber
HC	Arendt, *The Human Condition*
HCT	Heidegger, *History of the Concept of Time*
HSW	Husserl, *Shorter Works*
Hua	Husserliana series (Husserl)
Ideas I	Husserl, *Ideas* I
Ideas II	Husserl, *Ideas* II
Ideas III	Husserl, *Ideas* III
ILI	Husserl, *Introduction to Logical Investigations*, ed. Fink

IM	Heidegger, *Introduction to Metaphysics*
IP	Husserl, *Idea of Phenomenology*
KPM	Heidegger, *Kant and the Problem of Metaphysics*
LI	Husserl, *Logical Investigations*
Margins	Derrida, *Margins of Philosophy*
OBBE	Levinas, *Otherwise Than Being or Beyond Essence*
OG	Derrida, *Origin of Geometry*
OSS	Brentano, *On the Several Senses of Being in Aristotle*
OT	Arendt, *Origins of Totalitarianism*
OTB	Heidegger, *On Time and Being*
Pathmarks	Heidegger, *Pathmarks*
PDE	Gadamer, *Plato's Dialectical Ethics*
PES	Brentano, *Psychology from an Empirical Standpoint*
Phen. Psych.	Husserl, *Phenomenological Psychology*
Phil. App.	Gadamer, *Philosophical Apprenticeships*
Phil. Herm.	Gadamer, *Philosophical Hermeneutics*
PI	Sartre, *Psychology of the Imagination*
PLT	Heidegger, *Poetry, Language and Thought*
Pos.	Derrida, *Positions*
PP	Merleau-Ponty, *Phenomenology of Perception*
Prol.	Husserl, *Prolegomena, Logical Investigations*
PRS	Husserl, *Philosophy as a Rigorous Science*, trans. Lauer
Richardson	Richardson, *Heidegger. Through Phenomenology to Thought*
RW	Brentano, *On the Origin of Our Knowledge of Right and Wrong*
SB	Merleau-Ponty, *Structure of Behavior*
SN	Brentano, *Sensory and Noetic Consciousness*
SNS	Merleau-Ponty, *Sense and Non-Sense*
SP	Derrida, *Speech and Phenomena*
TE	Sartre, *Transcendence of the Ego*
The True	Brentano, *The True and the Evident*
THI	Levinas, *The Theory of Intuition in Husserl's Phenomenology*
TI	Levinas, *Totality and Infinity*
TM	Gadamer, *Truth and Method*
TO	Levinas, *Time and the Other*
Trans. Phen.	Husserl, *Psychological and Transcendental Phenomenology and the Confrontation with Heidegger (1927–1931)*, trans. Palmer and Sheehan
VI	Merleau-Ponty, *Visible and Invisible*
WD	Derrida, *Writing and Difference*

INTRODUCTION

Phenomenology and twentieth-century European philosophy

Phenomenology, as the movement inaugurated by Edmund Husserl (1859–1938), is now a century old. It was one of several strong currents in philosophy prominent at the outset of the twentieth century, alongside, for example, *Neo-Kantianism* in its various schools (e.g. Rickert, Natorp, Cassirer, Windelband, Lotze), *idealism* (Green, Bradley, McTaggart), *logicism* (Frege, Russell), *hermeneutics* (Dilthey, Bultmann), *pragmatism* (Dewey, Peirce, James), *Lebensphilosophie* (Bergson, Simmel), *Existenz* philosophy (Kierkegaard and Nietzsche), as well as the *empiricism* of Hume's followers (e.g. J. S. Mill), and the *positivism* and *empirio-criticism* of Comte, Mach, Avinarius, and, somewhat later, of the Vienna Circle. In one form or another, phenomenology engaged with all these philosophical currents.

Though important precursors of phenomenology can be found in the work of Immanuel Kant, Georg Wilhelm Friedrich Hegel, and Ernst Mach, phenomenology, as a new way of doing philosophy, was first formally announced by Edmund Husserl in the Introduction to the Second Volume of the First Edition of his *Logische Untersuchungen* (*Logical Investigations*, 1900–1901), when, in discussing the need for a wide-ranging theory of knowledge, he speaks of "the phenomenology of the experiences of thinking and knowing".[1] After these words, in the 1913 Second Edition of the same work, Husserl immediately adds:

> This phenomenology, like the more inclusive pure phenomenology of experiences in general, has, as its exclusive concern, experiences intuitively seizable and analysable in the pure generality of their essence, not experiences empirically perceived and treated as real facts, as experiences of human or animal experients in the phenomenal world that we posit as an empirical fact. This phenomenology must bring to pure expression, must describe in terms of their essential concepts and their governing formulae of essence, the essences which directly make themselves known in intuition, and

1

the connections which have their roots purely in such essences. Each such statement of essence is an *a priori* statement in the highest sense of the word.

(LI, Intro. § 1, p. 249; Hua XIX/1 6)

This added paragraph neatly illustrates how Husserl's earlier project of 1900, concerned with the clarification of epistemological concepts, had grown, by 1913, into an a priori transcendental science of pure consciousness as such. As Husserl's conception of phenomenology deepened and broadened, he came to see himself as the founder of a new movement, and through his subsequent efforts and those of his students, phenomenology gradually developed to become the most important current of European thought throughout the century as a whole.

Husserl saw himself as founder of an entirely new discipline, a self-styled 'radical beginner', engaged in the constant act of radical founding (*Letztbegründung*). He frequently cast himself in the role of pioneer, an explorer in the new domain of consciousness, a Moses leading his people to the new land of transcendental subjectivity. He gathered students, planned ambitious research projects, and sought to promote the phenomenology of the various sub-divisions of the field of consciousness, aware always that phenomenology was a 'set of infinite tasks'. But above all else, in his mature years, Husserl thought phenomenological practice required a radical shift in viewpoint, a *suspension* or *bracketing* of the everyday natural attitude and all 'world-positing' intentional acts which assumed the existence of the world, until the practitioner is led back into the domain of pure transcendental subjectivity. Without this leading back, this *reduction*, genuine phenomenological insight would be impossible in Husserl's eyes; at best it would be no more than a naturalistic psychology of consciousness, which treated consciousness as just "a little tag-end of the world" (*ein kleines Endchen der Welt*).[2] Few of Husserl's students, however, were convinced of the value of this reduction, or indeed of the possibility of carrying it out; many felt that Husserl had lapsed back into the very Neo-Kantian idealism from which phenomenology had originally struggled to free philosophy.

As his former colleagues struck out on their own independent paths of investigation, Husserl, in later years, saw himself more and more as a 'leader without followers' (*als beruferer Führer ohne Gefolge, Briefwechsel* II 182), and in 1931 declared himself the greatest enemy of the so-called 'phenomenological movement' (*Briefwechsel* IX 79). As a result, the phenomenological movement understood in its broadest terms includes not just the work of Husserl, but also the work of many original practitioners of phenomenology, who did not feel bound to Husserl's methodology, the most prominent of whom were Max Scheler (1874–1928) and Martin Heidegger (1889–1976). Indeed, the French philosopher, Paul Ricoeur, has justly remarked that phenomenology is the story of the deviations from Husserl; the history of phenomenology is the history of Husserlian heresies.[3] After the publication of Heidegger's *Being and Time* (1927), phenomenology came to be understood almost exclusively in terms of the *combined* contribution of both Husserl and Heidegger, and so it appeared to Levinas, Sartre, Merleau-Ponty, and Derrida.

It is important not to exaggerate, as some interpreters have done, the extent to which phenomenology coheres into an agreed *method*, or accepts one theoretical outlook, or one set of philosophical theses about consciousness, knowledge, and the world. Indeed, as we shall see, the philosophers who in some sense identified with the practice of phenomenology are extraordinarily diverse in their interests, in their interpretation of the central issues of phenomenology, in their application of what they understood to be the phenomenological method, and in their development of what they took to be the phenomenological programme for the future of philosophy. Thus, Martin Heidegger, who fully acknowledged the importance of phenomenological seeing for philosophy, at the same time declared, in his 1927 lecture course on *Basic Problems of Phenomenology*, "there is no such thing as *the one* phenomenology" ("Die *Phänomenologie gibt es nicht*").[4] True philosophy, following phenomenology's inspiration, followed the matters themselves, and therefore, for Heidegger, phenomenology simply became identified with the essence of philosophy as such and its ways were as diverse as the matters themselves. Heidegger's way of attending to the things themselves was explicitly followed by Hans-Georg Gadamer who located the manifestation of the matters themselves in living dialogue, in speech.

Perhaps because of this very diversity, phenomenology, despite its pervasive influence in European philosophy, is, both as a method and a general movement, now little understood outside a narrow circle of specialists, eclipsed on the European mainland and in North America by various subsequent movements, including structuralism, post-structuralism, deconstruction, and more recently, concerns with multi-culturalism and postmodernism generally, as well as by analytic philosophy, which has developed into the main way of doing academic philosophy in English-speaking countries and, increasingly, elsewhere. The purpose of this book, then, is to provide both an understanding of phenomenology as a way of doing philosophy and also an introduction to the philosophies of some of its most able practitioners. I have chosen to introduce the themes of phenomenology through an account of the work of a number of philosophers who are, in my opinion, the key figures in European thought.

I have portrayed phenomenology as a thoroughly *modernist outlook* which has its beginnings in the efforts of Franz Brentano (1838–1917) to supply a philosophical foundation for the newly emerged science of psychology and to tie it to the Cartesian discovery of consciousness as the domain of apodictic self-evidence. Having considered Brentano's contribution, namely

3

his rediscovery of the intentional structure of consciousness and his project of scientific description of consciousness, the central focus of the first half of the book will be on Husserl and Heidegger as, respectively, founder and transformer of phenomenology. Unfortunately, for reasons of space, I have been forced to exclude many of Husserl's and Heidegger's students and followers, for example Edith Stein, Roman Ingarden, Aron Gurwitsch, Alfred Schütz, Eugen Fink, and Herbert Marcuse (1898–1979), to name but a few.[5] Furthermore, I have, reluctantly, omitted consideration of Max Scheler (1874–1928) from this study, though a case could be made for him as one of the earliest practitioners of phenomenology. However, he was always something of a philosophical rival to Husserl, and after 1911 had moved away from phenomenology generally. Moreover, when he died in 1928, Heidegger's *Being and Time* was just on the point of transforming phenomenology for good, and thus Scheler was quickly eclipsed in its future development. After Husserl and Heidegger, the phenomenologists included in this book – Hans-Georg Gadamer, Hannah Arendt, Emmanuel Levinas, Jean-Paul Sartre, Maurice Merleau-Ponty, and Jacques Derrida – all became familiar with a phenomenological movement in which the different philosophical perspectives of Husserl and Heidegger were already inextricably interwoven. This book, then, is not strictly speaking a history of Husserlian phenomenology *tout court*, but is rather an exploration of the intellectual climate and philosophical significance of phenomenology as an enterprise *begun* and *elaborated* by Husserl and then radically *transformed* by Heidegger. The further metamorphoses of phenomenology in the work of French philosophers constitutes the second half of this book. Again, for reasons of space, I have had to leave to one side discussion of some French phenomenologists who deserve consideration in their own right, for example, Paul Ricoeur, Mikel Dufrenne, Michel Henry, and others.

What is phenomenology?

Though there are a number of themes which characterise phenomenology, in general it never developed a set of dogmas or sedimented into a system. It claims, first and foremost, to be a *radical* way of doing philosophy, a *practice* rather than a system. Phenomenology is best understood as a radical, anti-traditional style of philosophising, which emphasises the attempt to get to the truth of matters, to describe *phenomena*, in the broadest sense as whatever appears in the manner in which it appears, that is as it manifests itself to consciousness, to the experiencer. As such, phenomenology's first step is to seek to avoid all misconstructions and impositions placed on experience in advance, whether these are drawn from religious or cultural traditions, from everyday common sense, or, indeed, from science itself. Explanations are not to be imposed before the phenomena have been understood from within.

Freedom from prejudice means overcoming the strait-jacket of encrusted traditions, and this also means rejecting the domination of enquiry by externally imposed methods. Most of the founding figures of phenomenology emphasised the need for a renewal of philosophy as radical enquiry not bound to any historical tradition; and they advocated a rejection of all dogmatisms, a suspicion of a priori metaphysical premises and earlier accounts of the nature of knowledge, especially as found in Neo-Hegelianism and in positivism, and a steady directing of attention to the things themselves. Phenomenology was seen as reviving our living contact with reality, and as being remote from the arid and academic discussion of philosophical problems found in nineteenth-century philosophy, for example in the Neo-Kantian tradition.

In particular, the programme of phenomenology sought to reinvigorate philosophy by returning it to the life of the living human subject. Thus, the readers of Husserl's *Logical Investigations* reported that it approached traditional logical and epistemological problems in a new, fresh, and exciting manner. Similarly, Heidegger's students of the 1920s claimed the experience of thinking came to life in their classes, as both Arendt and Gadamer have confirmed. This call to renew philosophy went hand in hand with an appeal to return to *concrete*, lived human experience in all its richness. In the 1930s, both Sartre and Merleau-Ponty saw phenomenology as a means of going beyond narrow empiricist, psychological assumptions about human existence, broadening the scope of philosophy to be about everything, to capture life as it is lived. Thus, Sartre's encounter with phenomenology through Raymond Aron allowed one to philosophise about a wineglass.[6] Sartre sees phenomenology as allowing one to delineate carefully one's own affective, emotional, and imaginative life, not in a set of static objective studies such as one finds in psychology, but understood in the manner in which it is meaningfully lived. Sartre's account of experiences of shame and self-deception are classics of phenomenological description. Similarly, Emmanuel Levinas's phenomenology is closely attentive to the way in which other human beings inhabit the horizons of my experience and present themselves as a *demand* to me, a call on me to get outside the sphere of my own self-satisfaction, my own preoccupations.

Phenomenology also claimed to have overcome the impasse reached in the treatment of many traditional philosophical problems. Thus both Husserl and Heidegger believed that the real philosophical issue in the traditional sceptical worry about the existence of the external world was not the need to find rational grounds to justify our natural belief in this world, but rather to explain how this kind of worry could have arisen in the first place. Both Husserl and Heidegger rejected the traditional representationalist account on knowledge, the Lockean way of ideas, which explained knowledge in terms of an inner mental representation or copy of what exists outside the mind. Phenomenology rejects this entire representationalist account of knowledge as absurd. Our experience properly described must acknowledge that it presents itself as the experience of engaging directly with the world. Any philosophical account of knowledge has to remain faithful to the deepest experiential evidence. Above all else, phenomenology must pay close attention to the nature of consciousness as actually experienced, not as is pictured by common sense or by the philosophical tradition. Thus, for instance, we must not think that experiences in consciousness are like objects in a box. As Husserl objects in *Formal and Transcendental Logic*:

> But experience is not an opening through which a world, existing prior to all experience, shines into a room of consciousness; it is not a mere taking of something alien to consciousness into consciousness...Experience is the performance in which for me, the experiencer, experienced being "is there", and is there *as what* it is, with the whole content and the mode of being that experience itself, by the performance going on in its intentionality, attributes to it.[7]

Phenomenology must carefully describe things as they *appear* to consciousness. In other words, the way problems, things, and events are approached must involve *taking their manner of appearance to consciousness into consideration.*

The origins of the term 'phenomenology'

Husserl was not the first to employ the term 'phenomenology'; in fact it first began to appear in philosophy texts in the eighteenth century, in Lambert, Herder, Kant, Fichte, and Hegel.[8] Johann Heinrich Lambert, a follower of Wolff, employed the term 'phenomenology' in the title of the fourth section in his *Novus Organon* to signify a *science of appearance* (*Schein*) which allows us to proceed from appearances to truth, just as optics studies perspective in order to deduce true features of the object seen. Lambert inspired Immanuel Kant (1724–1804), who infrequently used the term 'phenomenology' in several early letters. For instance, in a letter to Lambert of 2 September 1770, Kant says that "metaphysics must be preceded by a quite distinct, but merely negative science (*Phaenomenologica generalis*)".[9] Similarly, in his letter to Marcus Herz of 21 February 1772, Kant spoke of "phenomenology in general" (*die Phänomenologie überhaupt*), which eventually developed into the Transcendental Aesthetic section of the *Critique of Pure Reason*. Kant used the term in his mature treatises also. Thus, in his *Metaphysical Foundations of Natural Science* (1786), he has an entire section labelled "Phenomenology", dealing with the area of motion or rest in relation to their appearances to our external senses. *Phenomenology*, for Kant, then, is that branch of science which deals with things in their manner of appearing to us, for example, relative motion, or colour, properties which are dependent on the human observer. Kant's enquiry into the conditions for the possibility of objectivity – as seen from the subjective side – was criticised by G. W. F. Hegel (1770–1831) for failing to develop a conception of mind other than as consciousness. For this reason, Hegel said that Kantian philosophy remained "only a *phenomenology* (not a *philosophy*) of mind".[10] Johann Gottlieb Fichte (1762–1814) also made use of the term 'phenomenology' in his *Wissenschaftslehre* of 1804 to refer to the manner of deriving the world of appearance, which illusorily appears to be independent of consciousness, from consciousness itself.[11]

Hegel himself made the most prominent use of the term 'phenomenology' when it featured in the title of his 1807 *Phänomenologie des Geistes* (*Phenomenology of Spirit*),[12] but this work was largely eclipsed during the nineteenth century and had little influence. It was only in the 1920s and 1930s, after Husserl's inauguration of phenomenology, that, especially in France, Alexandre Kojève, Jean Hyppolite, Jean Wahl, Merleau-Ponty, and others began to look to Hegel as the true progenitor of the phenomenological method.

Despite these prior occurrences of the term 'phenomenology', the immediate inspiration for Edmund Husserl's use of the term was neither Kant nor Hegel, but Franz Brentano, who first employed the term in 1889. Soon after, in 1894, Brentano's friend, the physicist Ernst Mach, proposed a "general physical phenomenology" which would *describe* our experiences of physics as a basis for a more general physical theory. Mach, for example, wanted to describe electricity in terms of the sum of experiences we have of it. Husserl was familiar with Mach's use of the term 'phenomenology' even at the beginning of his career, but later on, in his Amsterdam lectures of 1929, he explicitly acknowledged Mach as a forerunner of phenomenology, and he characterised himself as involved in "a certain radicalizing of an already existing phenomenological method".[13]

Phenomenology in Brentano

Phenomenology as initially understood by Edmund Husserl in the First Edition of the *Logical Investigations* meant *descriptive psychology* and had its origins in the project of Brentano. From Brentano, Husserl took over the conviction that philosophy is a rigorous science, as well as the view that philosophy consists in *description* and not causal explanation. Husserl also adopted from Brentano a general appreciation of the British tradition of empiricism, especially Hume and Mill, along with an antipathy towards Kantian and Hegelian idealism. In a manner not dissimilar to the positivists, Husserl went on to reject Neo-Kantian and Hegelian problematics as 'pseudo-problems' (*Scheinprobleme*) and pseudo-philosophy. For Husserl, as for Brentano, philosophy is the description of what is given in direct 'self-evidence' (*Evidenz*).

Husserl's phenomenology has its first anticipation in Brentano's attempt to rethink the nature of psychology as a *science*. Brentano had proposed a form of descriptive psychology which would concentrate on illuminating the nature of inner self-aware acts of cognition without appealing to causal or genetic explanation. In other words, Brentano was proposing a kind of philosophical psychology, or philosophy of mind. In his *Psychology from an Empirical Standpoint* (1874), Brentano sets out to do 'empirical psychology' by descriptively identifying the domain of the mental in terms of intentionality.[14] Brentano contrasts empirical psychology with 'genetic psychology'. *Genetic psychology* studies the material substrate of psychic acts – the nature of the sense organs, the patterns of the nerves, and so on – and is essentially committed to causal explanation. Empirical psychology is to be a descriptive, classificatory science, offering a taxonomy of mental acts. Later, in his lectures on *Descriptive Psychology* (1889), Brentano employed the phrase 'descriptive psychology or descriptive phenomenology' to differentiate this science from genetic or physiological psychology.[15] Descriptive psychology is conceived of as an a priori science of the laws of the mental, identifying universal laws on the basis of insight into individual instances.

Following Descartes, Brentano believed in the self-evidence of our grasp of inner mental life – inner perception – as opposed to the fallible nature of outer perception. It must be stressed that Brentano thought of inner perception as quite distinct from introspection or what he called 'inner observation'. We are not able to observe our mental acts while occupying them but we can reflectively grasp them as they occur. They can be grasped *en parergo*, 'by the way' (*nebenbei*), a conception Brentano borrowed from Aristotle and Aquinas. There is no act without an object; an empty act cannot be conscious of itself. Given the presence of the intentional content or object awakening the intentional act, then the act is directed primarily on the object. However, acts can have a secondary moment whereby they become conscious of themselves. This accompanying secondary act of reflection is so built into the original act that it cannot be wrong about the nature of the act upon which it is reflecting. Following Aristotle's analysis in his *De anima*, Brentano holds that, in sensing, I am aware that I am sensing. The awareness is not an act of the sensing itself whose proper object is always the sensible as such, rather there is a common inner sense which is aware of the operation of the primary act. But, for Brentano, the apodicticity of this reflective act is severely limited to the act itself and the immediate memory of it.

From such empirical instances of inner perception general laws could be extracted by reflection. Such a law of the mental, for Brentano, is, for example, that there can be no mental act which is not either a presentation or based on a presentation. Brentano went on to think of the relation between the object and the act in terms of the relation between *part* and *whole*. When we are aware of a complex phenomenon, awareness of the part is present in the awareness of the whole though it may not be explicitly noticed. Thus when I see a red patch, it is a part of that presentation that it is also a presentation of extension, but this part-presentation may not be explicitly noticed. Like Sartre and John Searle, Brentano explicitly denies the possibility of purely unconscious mental acts.[16] Acts of that kind are simply not mental. A mental act must be at least a possible object of inner reflection for the Brentanian tradition.

Brentano envisaged his new science of descriptive psychology as providing the conceptual foundation for the *Geisteswissenschaften*, that is all the sciences which employ mental acts in their formulations, for example, the law, politics, economics, sociology, aesthetics, religion, etc. Descriptive psychology will provide clear, evident truth about the mental acts employed in these sciences. This became Brentano's overall project of philosophy as a rigorous science. Husserl went on to develop this descriptive *psychology* into the most general descriptive science of consciousness, underlying not only the *Geisteswissenschaften*, but all forms of scientific knowledge.

The presuppositionless starting point

Right from the outset, Husserl laid great stress on phenomenology's *principle of presuppositionlessness* (*Prinzip der Voraussetzunglosigkeit*, LI, Intro. § 7, p. 263; Hua XIX/1 24); that is, the claim to have discarded philosophical theorising in favour of careful description of phenomena themselves, to be attentive only to what is *given* in intuition.

Husserl first extended the application of descriptive psychology to the clarification of concepts of the exact sciences in his *Philosophy of Arithmetic* (1891). Then, ten years later, in his 'breakthrough work' (*Werk des Durchbruchs*), *Logical Investigations*, he went on to develop the application of descriptive psychology, now also called *phenomenology*, to the epistemological clarification of the essential concepts in logic. Phenomenology, at this stage, is a kind of conceptual clarification which is to form part of a wider 'critique of reason'. But the key feature of this conceptual analysis was not that it engaged in an examination of the role of concepts in a language, but rather that it relied on the self-evident givenness of insights in intuition. The clarion cry of phenomenology, "back to the things themselves" (*zu den Sachen selbst*, LI, Intro. § 2, p. 252; Hua XIX/1 10), first announced in Husserl's *Logical Investigations*, summed up this dependence on intuition. Indeed, this emphasis on the importance of 'intuition' in philosophy was, of course, in line with the mood of the times. Many philosophers at the turn of the century, including Wilhelm Dilthey, Henri Bergson, and William James, were one in emphasising the role of intuition, though they differed in their accounts of it. Thus, Henri Bergson had claimed in his *An Introduction to Metaphysics*:

> By intuition is meant the kind of intellectual sympathy by which one places oneself within the object in order to coincide with that which is unique in it and consequently inexpressible.[17]

Indeed, the prevalence of notions of intuition as a kind of spiritual sympathy with the object of knowledge has often led to phenomenology being widely misunderstood as a form of irrational mysticism. At least in the vision of its founder, Edmund Husserl, nothing could be further from the truth.

Husserl's understanding of phenomenology grew out of his attempt to understand the nature of mathematical and logical truths, and from his more general concern with a critique of reason whereby all the key concepts required for knowledge would be rigorously scrutinised as to their essential meanings, their validity, and justification. Intuitions are the highest stage of knowledge and as such are hard-won insights, akin to mathematical discoveries. When I *see* that '2 + 2 = 4', I have as clear an intuition as I can have. Husserl thought, however, that similar intuitive fulfilments occurred in many types of experience, and were not just restricted to the truths of mathematics. When I see a blackbird in the tree outside my window under normal conditions, I also have an intuition which is fulfilled by the certainty of the bodily presence of the blackbird presenting itself to me. There are a wide variety of different kinds of intuitive experience. Husserl was led by reflection on these kinds of experience to attempt to develop a classification of all conscious experiences, with an eye to considering their essential natures and the kinds of intuitive fulfilment which were proper to them.

In his mature works, Husserl called these intuitions 'originary giving' or 'presentive' intuitions. Thus, even after his transcendental turn, first publicly announced in *Ideas* I (1913), Husserl retained the primacy of intuition. In *Ideas* I, he announces his *principle of all principles*:

> *that every originary presentive intuition is a legitimizing source of cognition*, that *everything originarily* (so to speak in its "personal" actuality) *offered* to us in "*intuition*" *is to be accepted simply as what it is presented as being*, but also *only within the limits in which it is presented there*.[18]

Every act of knowledge is to be legitimised by "originary presentive intuition" (*originär gebende Anschauung*). This concept of *originary presentive intuition* is at the core of Husserl's philosophy. Indeed, he criticises traditional empiricism for naively dictating that all judgements be legitimised by experience, instead of realising that many different forms of intuition underlie our judgements and our reasoning processes (*Ideas* I, § 19, p. 36; Hua III/I 36).

What does Husserl mean here by 'givenness' (*Gegebenheit*), the term which Heidegger characterised in his 1920 Freiburg lectures as the 'magic word' (*Zauberwort*) of phenomenology, which, nevertheless, stands as a 'stumbling block' (*Stein des Anstoßes*) to others?[19] 'Givenness' sums up the view that all experience is experience *to someone*, according to a particular manner of experiencing. There is a 'dative' element in the experience, a 'to whom' of experience. Intuitions, for Husserl, occur in all experiences of understanding; but in cases of genuine certain knowledge, we have intuition with the highest kind of fulfilment or evidence.

The suspension of the natural attitude

In works written subsequent to the *Logical Investigations*, Husserl came to believe that the scrutiny of the structure and contents of our conscious experiences was inhibited and deeply distorted by the manner of our engagement with experience in ordinary life, where our practical concerns, folk assumptions, and smattering of scientific knowledge all got in the way of a pure consideration of experience as it is given to us. In order to ensure against theoretical stances creeping back in to the phenomenological viewing of the phenomena, Husserl proposed a number of steps, most notably *the phenomenological epoché*, or *suspension of the natural attitude*, as well as a number of methodological reductions and alterations of viewpoint (including the so-called '*eidetic*' and '*transcendental reductions*'), in order to isolate the central essential features of the phenomena under investigation. This bracketing meant that all scientific, philosophical, cultural, and everyday assumptions had to be put aside – not so much to be negated as to be put out of court (in a manner not dissimilar to that of a member of the jury who is asked to suspend judgements and the normal kinds of association and drawing of inferences in order to focus exclusively on the evidence that has been presented to the court). Thus, in considering the nature of our conscious acts, we should not simply assume that the mind is some kind of a container, that memories are like picture images, and so on. Nor should we assume any scientific or philosophical hypothesis, for example that conscious events are just brain events. Indeed, in genuine phenomenological viewing, we are not permitted *any* scientific or philosophical hypotheses. We should attend only to the phenomena in the manner of their being given to us, in their *modes of givenness*. Later, many phenomenologists will appeal to our different way of approaching art works as paradigmatic for revealing the different modes of givenness of phenomena, for example Heidegger's reflection on the art work or Merleau-Ponty's account of the experience of looking at Cézanne's paintings. The mode of givenness is best approached when assumptions about the world are put out of account.

For Husserl the suspension of the natural attitude, and the development of theoretical manoeuvres for excluding distortion in order to gain insight into the nature of the conscious processes themselves, are at the centre of his understanding of the practice of phenomenology. Thus he always stressed that his greatest discovery was the reduction. The reduction led Husserl in two directions simultaneously. On the one hand, it led him in a Neo-Kantian and Cartesian direction towards the transcendental ego as the formal structure of all self-experience; while on the other hand, it led him towards the manner in which consciousness is always wrapped up in its intentional correlate, completely caught up in a world. This intuition of the worldliness of consciousness led to Husserl's investigations of the environment and of the *life-world*.

The life-world and being in the world

Focusing on what is given intuitively in experience led Husserl, in his late writings such as *Experience and Judgment* (1938),[20] to focus on what he termed "prepredicative experience" (*die vorprädikative Erfahrung*), experience *before* it has been formulated in judgements and expressed in outward linguistic form, before it becomes packaged for explicit consciousness. As Husserl put it, all cognitive activity presupposes a domain that is passively pregiven, the existent world as I find it. Returning to examine this pregiven world is a return to the *life-world* (*Lebenswelt*), "the world in which we are always already living and which furnishes the ground for all cognitive performance and all scientific determination" (EJ § 10, p. 41, 38). Husserl claims that the world of our ordinary experience is a world of formed objects obeying universal laws as discovered by science, but the foundational experiences which give us such a world is rather different: "This experience in its immediacy knows neither exact space nor objective time and causality" (EJ § 10, p. 43, 41). Returning to the life-world is to return to experience before such objectifications and idealisations (EJ § 10, p. 45, 44).

In attempting to rethink the life-world, one has to understand the impact of the scientific world-view on our consciousness. Phenomenology has to interrogate the supposedly objective view of the sciences, what has been termed the 'God's eye' perspective, or the 'view from nowhere'. Husserlian phenomenology did not dispute the possibility of our gaining a 'view from nowhere', understood as the aperspectival, theoretical, 'objective' understanding of things. This indeed was the traditional ideal of knowledge. Husserl in particular was very anxious to give full credit to this view, which is the view adopted in mathematics and in the exact sciences. But he saw this as an *idealisation*, as a special construction of the theoretical attitude, one remote from everyday experience. This view from nowhere is constructed on, and abstracted from, our ordinary experiences which take place in time and space. One must not think of objects as existing exactly in the manner in

12

which they are given in the view from nowhere. All objects are encountered perspectivally; all conscious experience occurs in a temporal flow, the nature of which must be recalled in any analysis of human perception. The positing of entities outside experience is ruled out as meaningless.

Besides rejecting rationalist and idealist accounts of reality, phenomenologists in general were also critical of the narrow, reductionist models of human experience found in varieties of nineteenth-century empiricism, positivism, and sensationalism. Phenomenology was understood to have challenged traditional epistemology in so far as it had oscillated back and forth between the alternatives of *rationalism* and *empiricism*. Phenomenology claimed to have overcome the basis of this opposition between rationalism and empiricism and indeed to have rejected the subject–object distinction altogether. Phenomenologists claimed that both the traditional concepts of subject and of object were philosophical constructions which in fact distorted the true nature of the human experience of the world. Phenomenology claimed instead to offer a *holistic* approach to the relation between objectivity and consciousness, stressing the mediating role of the body in perception, for example. Phenomenology's success came in calling attention to aspects of experience neglected by empiricism, in particular the horizons and background assumptions involved in all acts of understanding and interpreting.

Martin Heidegger, who claimed Husserl remained too Cartesian and intellectualist in his account of human engagement with the world, decided that the only way to avoid what he regarded as sterile epistemological formulations was to abandon the use of the terms 'consciousness' and 'intentionality' altogether. Humans are always already caught up in a world into which they find themselves thrown, which reveals itself in moods, the overall nature of which is summed up by Heidegger's notion of 'Being-in-the-world' (*In-der-Welt-sein*). When Levinas attended Heidegger's lectures in 1928 he was captivated by Heidegger's attempts to understand Being-in-the-world. Both Sartre and Merleau-Ponty followed Heidegger in reading intentionality as naming an irreducible ontological relation with the world.

Drawing on Husserl's investigation of the manner in which consciousness is both enabled and inhibited by its corporeality, Merleau-Ponty explored the relation of consciousness to the body, arguing for the need to replace these categories with an account of embodied human being in the world. Adopting Husserl's and Scheler's distinction between a material body (*Körper*) and a living, animate body (*Leib*), Merleau-Ponty further explores the manner my experience of my own body differs from my experience of inanimate physical objects. My whole mode of being in regard to my body is very different from my relation to other things, and phenomenology must be attentive to describing that mode of being as accurately as it can.

Merleau-Ponty maintained that the whole scientific edifice is built upon the world as directly perceived, and that science is always a second-order expression of that world. He was deeply suspicious of scientific naturalism which treats human beings as an outcome of evolution and material processes. This ignored the nature of consciousness and myself as the 'absolute source' (*la source absolue*, PP ix; iii). Merleau-Ponty of course claims that this return to the self as absolute source of all meaning is not a kind of renewal of idealism. Idealism, whether in its Cartesian or Kantian forms, had, for Merleau-Ponty, detached the subject from the world.

Phenomenology as the achievement of knowing

While Brentano saw phenomenology as rooted in Aristotle's description of psychological acts in the *De anima*, and Husserl saw it as a radicalisation of empiricism, phenomenology has often been portrayed by its critics as an appeal to a long-refuted form of introspectionism, or to mystical, irrational intuition, or as promoting an unregulated rhapsodising on the nature of lived experience, or as seeking to repudiate science and the scientific view of the world, and so on. These views do not just come from those practising analytic philosophy, but are often held by the followers of structuralism and deconstruction, movements which have grown out of phenomenology itself. Indeed, as much as one has to defend phenomenology from various misinterpretations current among analytic philosophers, there is equally a growing need to distinguish the more disciplined practice of phenomenology from some of the more baroque elements present in current Continental theorising, which seem to regard unregulated assertion as the fundamental mode of philosophising. Even some of the best practitioners of phenomenology have been guilty of sloppy talk in relation to the phenomenological approach. For instance, Maurice Merleau-Ponty in his ground-breaking *Phenomenology of Perception* (1945), having stated correctly that phenomenology describes rather than explains ("It is a matter of describing, not of explaining or analysing"[21]), then casts the Husserlian bracketing of scientific explanation as if it were a *repudiation* of science. Thus, he writes, phenomenology is "from the start a rejection of science" (*le désaveu de la science*, PP viii; ii). This suggests that Merleau-Ponty sees phenomenology as replacing science, whereas in fact both he and Husserl thought of it as supporting and clarifying science in its fullest sense.

The problem of clarifying accurately the nature of phenomenology has been exacerbated by the application of the term to any vaguely descriptive kind of philosophising, or even to justify proceeding on the basis of hunches and wild surmise. For example, the term 'phenomenology' is also increasingly often encountered in analytic philosophy to mark off any zone or aspect of experience which cannot be fully articulated. For example, Owen Flanagan speaks of "the phenomenology of our mental life"[22] and Colin McGinn talks of the "technicolour phenomenology" our brains produce.[23] Here the term is used to stand for the flow of psychic life itself. But the term is also used for the mode of access to this subjective life, for the *first-person experience* of conscious states. Thus contemporary philosophy of mind in the analytic tradition has been engaged in a long-running debate as to whether phenomenological description has a place in the investigation of consciousness and intentionality; that is, whether close attention to the actual qualitative features of our conscious experience (those features which Bertrand Russell termed 'qualia') are illuminating for the scientific study of consciousness. Daniel Dennett talks about the need to replace impotent first-person "auto-phenomenology" with a properly objective, third-person "heterophenomenology".[24] Gregory McCulloch and Christopher Peacocke debate the issue of whether there is a non-conceptual *content* to sensory experience, or whether these experiences are completely colourless or 'transparent'.[25] In analytic terms this is usually referred to as the problem of 'qualia' or of 'first-person truths', or of the 'how' of experiences, the what-it-is-like to have the experience.[26] Though analytic philosophy of mind in general does recognise the need to provide some account of this qualitative aspect of experience, it rarely concedes that the methods of traditional Husserlian phenomenology are adequate to this task. Husserlian phenomenology is seen as a kind of *introspectionism* and as such is vulnerable to all the criticisms of introspection which emerged in experimental psychology and cognitive science.

It is indeed true that central to phenomenology, and indeed part of its continuing appeal, is its attempt to provide a rigorous defence of the fundamental and inextricable role of subjectivity and consciousness in all knowledge and in descriptions of the world. But phenomenology attempts to recognise and describe the role of consciousness in the achievement (*Leistung*) of *knowledge* and is not a wallowing in the subjective domain purely for its own sake. Indeed, the whole point of phenomenology is that we cannot split off the subjective domain from the domain of the natural world as scientific naturalism has done. Subjectivity must be understood as inextricably involved in the process of constituting objectivity. Thus, for Husserl, the central mystery of all philosophy, the "mystery of mysteries" is the question: *how does objectivity get constituted in and for consciousness*? There is only objectivity-for-subjectivity. Heidegger's own development of phenomenology was motivated by a deep unhappiness with the inescapably Cartesian metaphysical overtones of Husserl's concept of consciousness. He resorted instead to a description of the manner in which Being appears, which speaks of human beings as the site of that appearing, using the German word *Dasein*, existence, or literally 'there-being'. But despite the radical differences in these accounts, both philosophers are struggling to express the manner in which the world comes to appearance *in and through* humans. Phenomenology's conception of objectivity-for-subjectivity is arguably its major contribution to contemporary philosophy.

The structure of intentionality

The basic insight which allowed Husserl to explicate this conception of objectivity-for-subjectivity was his radical understanding of the intentional structure of consciousness. Franz Brentano had retrieved an earlier Scholastic conception of the intentional inexistence of the object of consciousness in order to characterise the essential nature of psychic acts. Husserl took this basic structure of intentionality and, having stripped it of its metaphysical baggage, presented it as the basic thesis that all conscious experiences (*Erlebnisse*) are characterised by 'aboutness'. Every act of loving is a loving *of* something, every act of seeing is a seeing *of* something. The point, for Husserl, is that, disregarding whether or not the object of the act exists, it has meaning and a mode of being for consciousness, it is a meaningful *correlate* of the conscious act. This allowed Husserl to explore a whole new domain – the domain of the meaning-correlates of conscious acts and their interconnections and binding laws – before one had to face ontological questions concerning actual existence, and so on. Phenomenology was to be true *first philosophy*. While it is true, then, that phenomenology turns to consciousness, it is proposing above all to be a science of consciousness based on elucidating the intentional structures of acts and their correlative objects, what Husserl called the noetic–noematic structure of consciousness.

Sometimes, as we have mentioned, phenomenology's emphasis on the mutual belonging of the notions of subjectivity and objectivity is expressed as an overcoming of the subject–object divide. But this overcoming, at least in Husserl, is really a retrieval of the essential radicality of the Cartesian project. Husserl saw intentionality as a way of reviving the central discovery of Descartes's *cogito ergo sum*. Instead of proceeding to an ontological account of the *res cogitans* as a thinking substance as Descartes himself did, one can focus on the intentional structure which Husserl describes as *ego-cogitatio-cogitatum*, the self, its acts of consciousness, and its objective correlate. We have overcome the subject–object divide only by finding a deeper meaning within subjectivity itself. There is, therefore, a central paradox in Husserl's thought which sought to overcome a certain crude kind of Cartesianism by a radical rethinking of the Cartesian project itself.

After Husserl, phenomenologists such as Heidegger and Levinas saw Husserlian phenomenology as the apotheosis of modern subjective philosophy, the philosophy of the *cogito*, and rebelled against it. Heidegger and others proposed a more radical phenomenology which broke with the metaphysical assumptions still underpinning Husserl's enterprise. Levinas wanted to orient phenomenology on the basis of the founding experience of the other and hence to overcome self-centred subjectivity from the outset. Sartre, on the other hand, still tended to see phenomenology as a carrying out of Cartesian philosophy. One way or another, phenomenology is always in a tension with Descartes and hence with the subjective turn of modern philosophy – either radicalising it or seeking to overcome it.

After Heidegger, both Levinas and Sartre interpreted the thesis of intentionality as expressing the manner in which consciousness comes into direct contact with the world and with being, and thus in a sense creatively misunderstood Husserl. This misunderstanding led both Levinas and Sartre to an ontological intuition of being in itself as something impassive and all encompassing, something which resists consciousness. Levinas's response is to seek to identify ways to evade this all-encompassing being, ways of achieving a kind of transcendence, a kind of 'exteriority', a preservation of the experience of the unlimited and *infinite* against the *totality*. Sartre, beginning from a very similar thesis about the relation of being and consciousness, understands consciousness in terms of its unending attempts to seek to become pure being and its failure to achieve that status. Merleau-Ponty, on the other hand, regards the relation of human consciousness to being in itself as so intertwined and interwoven that there is no possibility of even attempting to conceptualise one without the other. The challenge of Merleau-Ponty's philosophy, then, is to describe what he terms the 'chiasmic' intersection between humans and the world, a relation which comes to be in the personal lived body (he is employing the term 'chiasm' both in its rhetorical sense as an inversion of phrases and in its physiological sense as an intertwined nerve in the eye – the sense, as applied to the body–world relation, is of a mutual intertwining that cannot be undone).

Philosophy and history

Despite its initial open antipathy towards history, phenomenology, like all philosophical movements, was shaped by the particular historical and cultural circumstances of its foundation. It was unavoidable, therefore, that phenomenology's fortunes should become tangled up in the history of the twentieth century and the impact of the world wars. These upheavals claimed the lives of Husserl's own son, as well as of some of his most gifted students, for example Adolf Reinach, who died on the front during the First World War, and Edith Stein, who died in a Nazi concentration camp during the Second World War. Similarly, the lives of Heidegger, Gadamer, Arendt, Levinas, Sartre, and Merleau-Ponty were all, in one way or another, seriously affected by the war. Difficult times disrupted studies, closed avenues of intellectual exploration, and forced whole schools of philosophers to flee Germany. Levinas and Arendt grieved both for their loss of family and home, and, more generally, for the destruction of Jewish intellectual culture in Europe. From an entirely different perspective, Heidegger's controversial espousal of National Socialism led to his suspension from teaching at Freiburg after 1945 and thereafter permanently cast a shadow on his reputation. Sartre said the war split his life in two, and

Merleau-Ponty's reflections on the manner in which war compromised everyone are strikingly evoked in his essay, "The War Has Taken Place" (1945), published in *Les Temps modernes*.

Events such as the founding of the New School for Social Research in New York, and the refoundation of the Frankfurt school after the Second World War, led to a transformation of the nature of European philosophy, and also had their impact on phenomenology. Both Max Horkheimer (1895–1973) and Theodor Adorno (1903–1969) began their philosophical careers with critical studies of Husserl. Adorno's first work in philosophy, his 1924 doctoral dissertation, written at Frankfurt under Hans Cornelius, treated critically of Husserl's theory of the object from the standpoint of Neo-Kantianism.[27] Later Adorno wrote several studies critical both of Husserlian phenomenology and of Heideggerian mysticism. Hannah Arendt considered the phenomena of totalitarianism, moral evil, violence, and human action, even love, from her unique perspective without allowing her thought to be academised or dominated by the shadow of her early mentor, Heidegger. Phenomenology, then, is in many ways inextricably linked with the twentieth century. It is a fractured movement, and its inspiration often appears to run like an underground stream enriching the ground rather than as an explicit and self-confident movement in its own right.

Phenomenology in France

A number of Husserl's students, including Jean Héring, Raymond Aron, and others, brought phenomenology to France.[28] But the most prominent of Husserl's French interpreters was Emmanuel Levinas who was responsible for making available a French translation of Husserl's *Cartesian Meditations* some twenty years before the German text was published. Similarly, Heidegger's thought first entered France through Levinas and through the translations of Henri Corbin, but later, crucially, through Jean Beaufret and Jean Wahl. Husserl's work entered a French philosophical tradition dominated by René Descartes, Auguste Comte, Henri Bergson, and Léon Brunschvicg. Indeed, Husserl explicitly played to this Cartesian heritage when he gave his lectures in Paris in 1929. In the French context especially, phenomenology was understood as a radical Cartesianism, a Cartesianism which ignored substance dualism in order to probe more carefully the manner of appearances of entities in consciousness and the structure of transcendental consciousness itself. Phenomenology developed in France in a distinctive manner through Emmanuel Levinas, Maurice Merleau-Ponty, Jean-Paul Sartre, Paul Ricoeur, Julia Kristeva, Gilles Deleuze, and Jacques Derrida, all of whom began their philosophical careers by writing careful studies of Husserl.

Emmanuel Levinas studied with both Husserl and Heidegger in Freiburg in the late 1920s and returned to France to become a major force in nascent

French phenomenology through his 1930 study *The Theory of Intuition in Husserl's Phenomenology*, as well as through his part in translating the *Cartesian Meditations*. Levinas wrote a number of phenomenological reflections on the nature of moral experience before producing *Totality and Infinity* (1961), a major study of human intentionality and its limits. Levinas's contribution consists in orienting phenomenology towards ethics, specifically towards the appearance of the other in our subjective sphere. Though Husserl was interested in, and lectured on, the phenomenology of value and on ethical theory (understood as the attempt to achieve universal rational community), especially in the period from 1910 onwards, the first published phenomenological treatment of ethics came from Max Scheler whose *Formalism in Ethics* appeared in Husserl's *Jahrbuch für Phänomenologie* in 1913.[29] Scheler's concept of the person had a formative influence on the thought of the early Heidegger, who was drawn towards Scheler's treatment of the concrete person over Husserl's more abstract discussions of the self. But ethical matters did not receive favourable treatment in Heidegger's conception of fundamental ontology, as it was laid out in *Being and Time* (1927). Subsequently Scheler had an influence on Gabriel Marcel and on Merleau-Ponty. Sartre's ethical focus, on the other hand, at least as it appeared in published essays after *Being and Nothingness* (1943), for example, when he was defending his existentialism against charges of amoralism and nihilism, relied heavily on a Kantian appeal to universalism. In fact, the influence of Heidegger, and of structuralism, on Continental philosophy in general was such that there was little to say on the subject of ethics, and it is in the light of this dearth of ethical theory that Levinas's ethical explorations must be viewed.

Jean-Paul Sartre was initially very taken with the possibility for extracting philosophy from phenomenological description, and, in his early studies of the 1930s, embraced the key concept of intentionality while offering thoughtful criticisms of Husserl's conception of the transcendental ego and his account of the nature of perceiving and imagining. By the time of *Being and Nothingness* (1943), Sartre had inserted his phenomenological accounts of human behaviour into a vast metaphysical edifice, and in his later writings he moved more in the direction of political philosophy. Sartre was hugely influential in wedding phenomenology to existentialism, a union which, however, had a detrimental effect on the understanding of phenomenology as it tended to link it with irrationalism. In fact, Sartre's portrayal of Heidegger as an existential thinker led directly to Heidegger's *Letter on Humanism* which explicitly repudiated Sartre's interpretation of his philosophy.

Around the same time as Sartre was writing *Being and Nothingness*, Merleau-Ponty was engaged in writing a major critique of behaviourism in psychology and exploring Husserl's discussions of the nature of the living body and his critique of scientism in the unpublished manuscripts *Ideas* II and the *Crisis*, which were available in the newly opened Husserl Archives in Leuven. Reacting against naive empiricism, positivism, and behaviourism, and strongly influenced by Aron Gurwitsch, Merleau-Ponty applied Gestalt psychology to Husserl's researches in phenomenology. In his first book, *The Structure of Behavior*, Merleau-Ponty was a major critic of the mechanistic stimulus/response mode of explanation as applied to human beings. His second book, *Phenomenology of Perception* (1945), is regarded by many as the most important phenomenological study of perception. Here Merleau-Ponty recognises that there is a basic form of intentionality already present in the body which cannot be explained in merely mechanistic terms. There seemed to be a symbiotic relationship between the act of perception and the environment of the perceiver, which Merleau-Ponty sought to describe in dialectical terms. Thus he pioneered the study of the relations between consciousness and embodiment which are now the subject of major debate. In later writings, Merleau-Ponty wrote on language, combining Heidegger's views on language with insights drawn from the semiotic and structuralist tradition.

Jacques Derrida (b. 1930) studied Husserl with Jean Hippolyte and Paul Ricoeur. Although he went on to develop the movement or style of thinking known as *deconstruction*, he drew his inspiration from problems in Husserl's theory of signification in general and even in his later work he remains a radical interpreter of Husserl. Derrida's deconstruction itself arose from considerations of certain aspects of the problem of presence and absence, sameness and difference in Husserl, Hegel, Heidegger, and the Swiss linguist Ferdinand de Saussure (1857–1913).

Conclusion

Phenomenology has been subjected to an internal critique (by, for example, Heidegger, Merleau-Ponty, Gadamer) as well as an external critique. The most important internal critique came from Heidegger. Heidegger rejected three central facets of Husserlian phenomenology. On the one hand, Husserl, especially in his 1911 *Logos* essay, *Philosophy as a Rigorous Science*, had been explicitly opposed to life philosophy and the philosophy of world-views, whereas Heidegger, though deeply critical of both these movements, nevertheless adopted the central claim that phenomenology must be attentive to *historicity*, or the *facticity* of human living; to *temporality*, or the concrete living in time; and furthermore it must not remain content with description of the internal consciousness of time. Secondly, from Friedrich Schleiermacher and the tradition of theological hermeneutics, Heidegger claimed that all description involves *interpretation*, indeed that description was only a derivative form of interpretation. Husserl's project of pure description, then, becomes impossible if description is not situated inside a radically historicised hermeneutics. Thirdly,

Heidegger rejected Husserl's concept of transcendental idealism and first philosophy as an 'egology', and instead proclaimed that phenomenology was the way to raise the question of Being, leading Heidegger to state publicly, from 1925 onwards, that only as phenomenology is ontology possible. Though Heidegger changed his manner of doing philosophy in the years that followed *Being and Time*, he never repudiated the essence of the phenomenological approach, the phenomenological attention to the things themselves. Thus in his 1962 letter to William Richardson he proclaims that he is moving *through* phenomenology to thinking (*Denken*), if one accepts phenomenology to mean "the process of letting things manifest themselves" (*als das Sichzeigenlassen der Sache selbst*).[30]

The external critique of phenomenology came from positivism and from the members of the Vienna Circle. Thus Moritz Schlick (1882–1936) criticised Husserl's reliance on intellectual intuition, Carnap criticised Heidegger for promoting a meaningless pseudo-metaphysics, and A. J. Ayer popularised the critique of all forms of phenomenology. Another line of critique came from Marxism, which, in general, saw phenomenology as the apotheosis of bourgeois individualism. Thus Horkheimer, the founder of the Frankfurt school, saw Husserl's phenomenology as exemplifying what he termed 'traditional theory' against which he opposed his own critical theory, which was not the product of an isolated ego thinking on its own.[31] Adorno also subjected phenomenology to an immanent critique in a number of important publications, notably in *Negative Dialectics*.[32] In France, the stucturalism of Althusser, Lévi-Strauss and others also repudiated phenomenology for maintaining a naive trust in the evidence of consciousness, generally defending a humanist perspective, whereas structuralism wished to argue that invariant unconscious structures underlie our experiences of conscious, free, meaning-intending. Derrida's deconstruction, by deliberately attacking the assumption of the possibility of the full presence of the meaning in an intentional act, and by emphasising the displacement of meaning, led to the collapse of phenomenology as a method.

What then is the enduring influence of phenomenology? It is frequently argued that the main contribution of phenomenology has been the manner in which it has steadfastly protected the subjective view of experience as a necessary part of any full understanding of the nature of knowledge. Phenomenology will continue to have a central role in philosophy because of its profound critique of *naturalism* as a philosophical programme. From the beginning, Husserl's phenomenology initially set itself against *psychologism* and more generally against all forms of *naturalism*. Husserl and his followers see naturalism as self-defeating because it consciously excludes consciousness, the very source of all knowledge and value. Today, it is quite clear that phenomenology shared much with Neo-Kantianism, in particular the critique of naturalism and positivism. Husserl himself also criticised relativism and especially its cultural version, typified in historicism. However, Heidegger immediately reintroduced the historical and relative into phenomenology, and Merleau-Ponty was a self-conscious relativist while proclaiming to practise a version of the phenomenological method. It is this very diversity and conflict among the practitioners of phenomenology that leads one from an interest in the general considerations of phenomenology to the study of the thought of the individual phenomenologists themselves.

1

FRANZ BRENTANO

Descriptive psychology and intentionality

Introduction: exact philosophy

Franz Brentano's project for reviving exact scientific philosophy, and, specifically, his project for *descriptive psychology* (*deskriptive Psychologie*), provided the first and most important intellectual stimulus for Husserl's development of phenomenology. At first glance, Franz Brentano (1838–1917) seems an unlikely forerunner to Husserlian phenomenology, and indeed phenomenology is by no means an inevitable outgrowth of Brentano's efforts. But Husserl was in fact deeply inspired by Brentano's overall vision of philosophy as an exact science, and by Brentano's reformulation of Aristotle's conception of intentionality, as well as by his account of the peculiar kind of self-evidence of mental states which could yield apodictic truths, and thereby found a descriptive science of consciousness.

Of aristocratic birth, Brentano combined a grounding in Aristotelian and Thomistic philosophy – over his life, he would publish *five* monographs on Aristotle – with a strong interest in the fledgling science of psychology, a science which he understood as a renewal of the enquiry regarding the nature of the soul first undertaken in Aristotle's *De anima*, an enquiry which, he felt, was continued in Aquinas's and in Descartes's accounts of the soul. Following his mentor Aristotle, Brentano's approach was problem oriented rather than historical, characterised by the careful study of empirical instances and by the drawing of subtle distinctions. Brentano read Aristotle as the first empiricist, whose enquiries had more in common with the empiricist tradition of Hume and Mill than with the decadent tradition of German metaphysics. Throughout his life, Brentano constantly referred back to Aristotle, though he eventually abandoned the conviction that philosophy could be founded on the Aristotelian system. Brentano always drew more on Aristotle than on the medieval Neo-Aristotelians such as Thomas and Suarez, presumably because he had completed his studies on Aristotle *before* the rise of Neo-Thomism. He planned a major collection of his writings on Aristotle which he never managed to complete. He did, however, publish one short monograph, *Aristotle and His World View*, in 1911.[1]

An admirer of Comte and positivism, Brentano believed that philosophy was continuous with the natural sciences. He is recognised, along with Wilhelm Wundt, as one of the founding fathers of scientific experimental psychology. His emphasis on the importance of dispelling ambiguities in scientific language led, in his later work, to a kind of linguistic analysis not dissimilar to that being separately developed by Bertrand Russell, and which was developed in its own way by Brentano's pupil, Anton Marty. On account of his friendship with Ernst Mach and others, his insistence on the empirical method, and his interest in distinguishing logical from grammatical form, Brentano was even cited as a formative influence in the *Manifesto* of the Vienna Circle, in which he is praised for his interest in Bolzano and Leibniz.[2] Brentano's view of philosophy as a rigorous science put him at a considerable intellectual distance from his contemporaries who were proponents of idealism, existentialism, and life philosophy. Indeed he especially disdained Nietzsche as a practitioner of bad philosophy.[3]

The Brentano school

The works that appeared in Brentano's lifetime (many on the history of philosophy) do not adequately portray either the richness of his philosophical insights or the charismatic influence he exerted over the gifted students attracted wherever he taught. Better evidence of his originality as a thinker is to be found in the *Nachlass*. But it is clear that Brentano himself was an inspiring, original thinker, who stimulated his students to develop in many different philosophical directions. These students were sufficiently united in their attachment to their teacher, and their desire to emulate his methods, such that one can speak loosely of a 'Brentano school'. Besides Edmund Husserl, the membership of this 'school' included Anton Marty (1847–1914), who pioneered a form of linguistic analysis; Carl Stumpf (1848–1936), who developed descriptive psychology, especially of sensory experience (e.g. audition); Kasimir Twardowski (1866–1938), the so-called 'father of Polish philosophy' whose interests included both metaphysics and linguistic philosophy; Alexius Meinong (1853–1920), who developed the theory of objects (*Gegenstandstheorie*) against which Bertrand Russell reacted; Alois Höfler (1853–1922), an influential logician and descriptive psychologist who also taught at Vienna; Christian von Ehrenfels (1859–1932), the founder of Gestalt psychology; and Thomas Masaryk (1850–1937), philosopher and nationalist, who went on to become President of Czechoslovakia, and was supportive of Husserl to the end. Though not a member of the Brentano school, Sigmund Freud (1856–1939), the founder of psychoanalysis, attended Brentano's lectures between 1874 and 1876, the only philosophy courses Freud took as part of his medical training. Members of the Brentano school contributed to realist metaphysics, Gestalt psychology, and the reform of Aristotelian logic and were clearly extremely influential in the birth of both phenomenology and logical positivism.[4] But here, however, we are interested chiefly in the intellectual motivation which Brentano's researches and teachings provided for Edmund Husserl in his development of phenomenology.

Husserl's two years (1884–1886) of studying with Brentano were crucial for his intellectual development, and he gratefully acknowledged Brentano's influence throughout his subsequent career. Having completed his doctorate in pure mathematics, Husserl was drawn to Brentano's lectures, curious to learn more about this renowned teacher of whom his friend, Thomas Masaryk, had spoken so highly. Masaryk himself had completed his doctorate under Brentano in 1876, and had taught as *Privatdozent* in the University of Vienna from 1876 until 1882, when he moved to the University of Prague.[5]

Brentano's lectures provided Husserl with his first serious introduction to traditional philosophy. He passed on to Husserl a conviction concerning the self-critical and serious life of the philosopher, and, within a short time, had influenced Husserl's decision to transfer from a career in mathematics to philosophy. Husserl adopted Brentano's view that any worthwhile philosophy must be rigorously scientific, not speculatively generating arbitrary opinions. In his first decade of research (1890–1900), Husserl saw himself as advancing Brentano's programme of 'descriptive psychology', taking Brentano's account of *intentionality* as the key concept for understanding and classifying conscious acts and experiential mental processes (*Erlebnisse*). Brentano's philosophy of *Evidenz*, 'evidence' or, more accurately, 'self-evidence', had an enormous impact on Husserl's conception of philosophy as the winning of genuine insights which can be held with justifiable certainty.[6] Husserl also adopted and developed Brentano's distinction between 'authentic' and 'inauthentic' presentations, a distinction which plays a key role in Husserl's first publication, the *Philosophy of Arithmetic* (1891), and, subsequently, in Husserl's phenomenological account of the difference between 'empty' and 'filled' intuitions, between symbolic thought and mental acts, which takes place in the full presence of the object. Brentano also inspired Husserl's initial impetus to investigate time consciousness as a kind of original association or synthesis distinct from memory. Over the years, Husserl became more critical of aspects of Brentano's teaching, and eventually came to see that he had progressed far beyond his teacher in the study of consciousness and in his conception of philosophy generally, until, finally, Husserl came to reject entirely Brentanian 'descriptive psychology' as a proper characterisation of his own phenomenology. Husserl, though he developed Brentano's theory of wholes and parts, does not appear to have ever been attracted to, or influenced by, Brentano's more metaphysical interests, for example his Aristotelianism, or, indeed, his later turn to *reism*, the doctrine which holds that only individual things exist, denying the existence of universals, species, and even properties.[7]

In contrast to Brentano's effect on Husserl, Husserl had little influence on his teacher. Brentano never could understand Husserl's enthusiasm for phenomenology and seemed genuinely perplexed by Husserl's claims for phenomenology as an eidetic science. Overall, though they remained in personal contact and corresponded until Brentano's death in 1917, Brentano did not follow Husserl's subsequent philosophical development with any great interest, nor did he actually read Husserl's books in any depth. Husserl's gift of a copy of the *Philosophy of Arithmetic* remained unopened, though some passages from the *Logical Investigations* may have been read to Brentano, when his eyesight was failing. Nor did Brentano sympathise with Husserl's critique of psychologism in the *Prolegomena* (1900) to the *Logical Investigations*. Brentano retained the classical view of logic as a 'technique' (*Kunstlehre*) for correct reasoning, and even suspected that he himself was the target of Husserl's crusade against psychologism. In general, he tended to see Husserl as akin to Meinong in pursuing avenues of research (e.g. the theory of ideal 'objectivities', *Gegenständlichkeiten*), which he himself had already discarded, or indeed which he claimed were a distortion of his own position.

Brentano: life and writings (1838–1917)

Because of Brentano's monumental influence, it is worth briefly charting his life and philosophical development. On the personal level, Franz Clemens von Brentano was an engaging, warm-hearted, conversationalist, a lover of songs and word-play. He even composed a book of riddles, *Aenigmatias*.[8] He was born in Marienberg-am-Rhein in Germany on 16 January 1838 into a wealthy, well-connected, Catholic, but politically liberal, aristocratic family which originally had come from Italy.[9] Soon after his birth, the family moved to Aschaffenburg, Germany.[10] He graduated from the Royal Bavarian Gymnasium there in 1855, and, after a year at the Lyceum, also in Aschaffenburg, in 1856 he enrolled in the Philosophy Faculty at the University of Munich, where he spent three semesters,[11] followed by one semester studying theology at the University of Würzburg. He then went to Berlin, where he studied for one semester under the great logician and Aristotle scholar Friedrich August Trendelenburg (1802–1872), attending his lectures on psychology.

The encounter with Aristotle

Because he wished to specialise in medieval philosophy, Brentano moved to Münster to study for two semesters with one of the earliest advocates of Thomism in Germany, Franz Jacob Clemens (1815–1862), a vigorous Catholic polemicist. Brentano proposed a doctoral dissertation on Suarez, but, when Clemens died, Brentano changed to a different doctoral thesis, entitled *On the Several Senses of Being in Aristotle*, submitted to the University of Tübingen. This work, published in 1862, and dedicated to Trendelenburg,[12] was, much later in 1907, to be Martin Heidegger's first introduction to philosophy and to the meaning of Being.[13] This doctoral thesis is a fairly standard, systematic study of Aristotle's metaphysics which defends Aristotle's account of the categories and argues, against Kant, Trendelenburg, and others, that Aristotle's presentation is not haphazard, but rather offers a complete and systematic account of the ways in which something can be predicated of a first substance (OSS 130).

Trendelenburg had completed an edition of Aristotle's categories and published *A History of the Doctrine of the Categories*[14] in 1846, which argued that Aristotle's categories should be construed *grammatically* as a classification of the way things can be *said* to be. Against Trendelenburg, Brentano argues that Aristotle's account of the categories is a genuine *metaphysical* contribution and not just an essay in grammar or logic. The categories are all the ways in which a being can be, and are all dependent on the manner of being of the first category, substance. Brentano, elucidating Aristotle's claim in *Metaphysics* Book IV that "being is said in many ways" (*to de on legetai men pollakos*, OSS 3), reviews Aristotle's different accounts of being, identifying four main senses which he then proceeds to discuss in detail: accidental being (*on kata symbebekos*), being according to the categories, potential and actual being (*on dynamei kai energeia*), and being in the sense of being true or false (*on hos alethes*). Brentano finds that the chief meaning of 'being' for Aristotle is given by the category of substance, meaning thereby an individual thing, but credits Aristotle with the important discovery that 'being true' is another equally important meaning for 'being'. Sometimes to say 'is true' is to do no more than affirm that something 'is', but there is a particular and proper sense of truth which belongs solely to judgements. Something is true if we judge it correctly. In later essays, dictated between 1907 and 1917, and collected as *The Theory of the Categories*, Brentano proposed a revision of Aristotle's account of substance and accident, reversing the priority of these principles so that, instead of an accident being *in* a subject as Aristotle held, Brentano saw the subject as contained in the accidental unity and defended the view that accidents could supervene on accidents and not only on substances.[15]

On the Several Senses of Being in Aristotle testifies to Brentano's early interest in metaphysics, and especially the theory of substances, accidents, and relations, an interest consciously suppressed in *Psychology from an Empirical Standpoint* in order to concentrate on the presuppositionless description of psychical phenomena. Nevertheless, a metaphysical approach underpins much of his later work, and elements of his later 'reism' can already be found in this thesis, for example in his tendency to understand 'substance' as always meaning an individual entity (e.g. a man, a horse).

Having completed his doctorate in 1862, Brentano entered the Dominican house in Graz, the order to which his friend, Heinrich Denifle (1844–1905), later a renowned medievalist, belonged, but he soon left to become a seminarian in Munich. He was ordained a priest on 6 August 1864. In 1866 he completed his *Habilitation* at the University of Würzburg with a thesis entitled *The Psychology of Aristotle, In Particular His Doctrine of the Active Intellect.*[16] This *Habilitation* thesis shows Brentano's careful reading of Aristotle's psychology, but it also lays down the basis for his later account of psychical acts. In particular, Brentano claims that when we perceive 'cold' then cold is 'objectively' in us. Furthermore, Brentano endorses Aristotle's view that the mind grasps itself accidentally, *per accidens*, in its thinking of other objects. In this work, Brentano sought to defend Aristotle's psychology against charges of inconsistency levelled by the critic Eduard Zeller, which led to a protracted controversy with Zeller. In particular, Brentano controversially argued, and continued to defend, the view that Aristotle maintained *both* the immortality of the soul *and* the doctrine of the creation of the world. Brentano interprets the Aristotelian God, that is, thought thinking itself, as also thinking of itself as governor of the universe, as a Creator.

On 15 July 1866, as part of his *Habilitation* defence, Brentano presented twenty-five theses in philosophy for discussion at the University of Würzburg. These theses, which included questions on the existence of God, issues of logic, aesthetics, and the general nature of philosophy and theology, are an interesting early indication of Brentano's philosophical breadth of interests and offer a programmatic outline of his later development. Among the theses he defended was one proposing the complete separation of philosophy and theology, and another stating that the "the true method of philosophy is none other than that of natural science" (*Vera philosophiae methodus nulla alia nisi scientiae naturalis est*).[17] In this *Habilitation* defence, Brentano criticised Kantian transcendental philosophy and German idealism, as he would continue to do throughout his career, and defended the claim that philosophy was continuous with natural science.[18]

Immediately following his *Habilitation*, Brentano became *Privatdozent* at the University of Würzburg. Würzburg had been set up specifically as a Catholic University and Brentano was held in high esteem as an up-and-coming Catholic philosopher, seemingly destined for the Chair of Philosophy. Many of his Würzburg students were Catholic seminarians at that time, including Marty, Stumpf, and Denifle. He was required to lecture mainly on the history of philosophy, but he also developed lectures in metaphysics, which were not well received by the Faculty. Brentano's independence of spirit was manifesting itself and he was now strongly drawn to empiricism, lecturing on Auguste Comte and positivism.[19] Brentano's career at Würzburg was soon disrupted by a momentous event. In 1870, when the First Vatican Council officially declared the doctrine of papal infallibility, Brentano vigorously opposed this doctrine on the grounds that it was contrary to reason, Scripture, and the tradition of the Church. He prepared a paper on it for Bishop Ketteler, one of the opponents of infallibility in Germany, which was favourably received when presented to a meeting of the German bishops in Fulda. Brentano's opposition to infallibility led him to doubt other Church doctrines, including, according to Stumpf's recollections, the dogmas of the Trinity and Incarnation, propelled by general worries about the metaphysical theory of substance underlying these doctrines.[20] Brentano first withdrew from teaching to a monastery in Munich. But, in the spring of 1872, he began a series of travels, first to England to acquaint himself with the latest philosophy, meeting with Herbert Spencer and, in Liverpool, with John Henry Cardinal Newman. In 1873 he resigned from the priesthood, and on 11 April of that year officially renounced his faith, henceforth remaining religious, but proclaiming a rationalistic theism of the Aristotelian variety. Indeed, Brentano never lost his belief in the existence of God and in the immortality of the individual soul.

As a result of his resignation from the priesthood, Brentano also felt obliged to resign his lectureship in Würzburg, where he had been teaching for seven years. He resumed his travels, going to Paris and then to Avignon with the intention of visiting the ailing John Stuart Mill, but unfortunately Mill had passed away before Brentano arrived. Brentano was now intent on pursuing his interests in contemporary psychology, a subject on which he had been lecturing since 1871 and on which he was planning a book. Thus he took the opportunity to visit Leipzig, a centre of psychology, to meet Fechner, Drobish, Windelband, and others engaged in pioneering this new science.[21]

The Vienna years and the programme for psychology

On 22 January 1874, partly due to the support of the influential German philosopher Hermann Lotze, Brentano was appointed by the Ministry to a full professorship, *professor ordinarius*, at the University of Vienna, a somewhat more liberal institution than Würzburg. Some months later, in May 1874, he published the First Edition of *Psychology from an Empirical Standpoint*.[22] This ground-breaking work of 'empirical psychology' appeared in the same year as Wilhelm Wundt's *Principles of Physiological Psychology*, both now seen as foundational texts of the new discipline of empirical psychology.[23] Brentano adopts Friedrich Lange's slogan of 'psychology without the soul' (*Psychologie ohne Seele*). Whereas traditionally, Brentano says, psychology studied the soul as "the substantial bearer of presentations" (*der substantielle Träger von Vorstellungen*),[24] here all metaphysical speculation on the nature of soul substance is to be avoided,[25] so that psychological processes can be studied on their own, without raising the issue of the nature of the ego in which they are enacted, or the causal physiological processes which engender and support them. Indeed, on the nature of the self Brentano takes a broadly Humean line; we experience only psychic processes themselves, not an ego. Brentano went on to revise and expand *Psychology from an Empirical Standpoint* in subsequent years, without ever bringing the project to completion.[26] A Second Edition, containing part of Book Two, eventually appeared more than thirty years later in 1911 as *The Classification of Mental Phenomena*. A further, greatly expanded edition, compiled by his student Oskar Kraus, was published posthumously in 1924. This 1924 edition, which is the basis of the English translation, must be used with caution as it draws together texts from across Brentano's career, tending to mask his development.

Brentano quickly attracted another circle of brilliant students at the University of Vienna, including Meinong, Husserl, Freud, Höfler, Twardowski, Ehrenfels, Masaryk, and Kraus. But his academic career suffered another reversal when he decided to marry Ida von Lieben, the daughter of a colleague in the Philosophy Faculty. Though the University of Vienna had tolerated a former Catholic priest on the staff, the Austrian Concordat with the Catholic Church meant that Austrian law did not recognise the marriages of former clerics. His marriage was not considered valid, causing some scandal in the University. He was forced to resign the Chair in 1880, but was allowed by the University to continue teaching at the lowest rank of *Privatdozent* while his case was under review. Brentano and his students, including Meinong, were interested in and carried out psychological experiments. Brentano had originally planned to open a psychology laboratory in the University, but plans were shelved and it was eventually opened only on condition that it would be run by Brentano's pupil, Franz Hillebrand, Brentano himself being considered a threat to morals.

This period of turbulence, however, proved to be a very active period in Brentano's own intellectual development, though it did not produce significant publications. In *Psychology from an Empirical Standpoint*, Brentano had drawn a contrast between empirical psychology and physiologically-based psychology, but, between 1887 and 1891, he developed his programmatic lectures on 'descriptive psychology' (also termed 'psychognosy' or 'phenomenology'), which sharpened the contrast between this descriptive and apodictic science and all 'genetic psychology'. These lectures would have a strong influence on Stumpf and Marty, and on Husserl who read them in manuscript.[27]

In 1889 Brentano delivered a number of important public lectures. In January he gave a lecture to the Vienna Law Society, published as *The Origin of Our Knowledge of Right and Wrong*,[28] and he also delivered a lecture to the Vienna Philosophical Society, published posthumously, "On the Concept of Truth", a crucial essay for understanding the conceptions of

30

truth found in Husserl and Heidegger.[29] In this lecture, Brentano criticised several contemporary interpretations of the traditional view of truth as correspondence, *adequatio rei et intellectus*. Correspondence requires a further judgement which compares the initial judgement with reality, and this is impossible as we have no access to reality independent of our judgements. As a result of these problems with the *adequatio* account of truth, Brentano offered a reinterpretation of 'correspondence' in terms of the notion of 'evidence' (*Evidenz*). Some judgements are evidently true, self-evident. They assert *what is*. Judgements do not 'combine' or 'separate' elements, as the traditional Aristotelian account maintains, rather they affirm something as *existing*, as being the case. In this lecture as elsewhere, Brentano, in line with Aristotle and Descartes, emphasised the necessity of founding knowledge on judgements which are *evident* or certain in themselves. Truth is recognition of what is asserted, and the correspondence is between the thing given and its 'self-givenness' (*Selbstgegebenheit*).[30] Brentano, however, thought that Descartes himself had not grasped the true significance of the 'evident' since he thought of *ideas* as the bearers of evidence rather than *judgements* (RW 78). Furthermore, when we grasp some judgement as evident, we see it as evident *for everyone*; we also grasp that its negation cannot be evident to anyone else (RW 80). Judgements can be given with evidence or without (i.e. they are 'blind'). This point is crucial for understanding Husserl's concept of evidence. If given with evidence, then the matter judged on is characterised by a 'self-givenness'. To judge correctly is to assert something as one with evidence would assert it.

This lecture has a crucial significance for the interpretation of Brentano's theory of intentionality as here he appears to posit *irrealia*, 'unreal things', or, to use Husserl's and Meinong's language, 'states of affairs' and 'objectivities' as the objective correlatives of true judgements, a position which influenced Marty, Kraus, Husserl, and Meinong to posit objective correlates of judgement contents (*The True*, xii; 23). Brentano needed to posit these correlates of judgements in order to defend the correspondence theory of truth. However, in his later writings, he rejected these *irrealia* along with the notion of correspondence. Thus, in his Foreword to the 1911 *Classification of Mental Phenomena*, he states: "I am no longer of the opinion that mental relation can have something other than a thing (*Reales*) as its object" (PES xx). We shall return to these important concepts of 'evidence' and of 'states of affairs' in later chapters, but we should simply note here that this lecture signals that Brentano did hold, at least for a short time, the view that judgements asserted certain states of affairs as existent. Even in his 1889 lecture, Brentano thought of truth not so much as correspondence, but as a 'harmony', 'fittingness', or 'appropriateness' between the thing as it appears and the manner of judging about it (RW 74), a conception which will influence Husserl's Sixth Investigation and Heidegger's *Being and Time* § 44.

Brentano in Italy

Brentano remained in Vienna, teaching as a *Privatdozent*, until 1895. The Austrian authorities refused to reappoint him to the Chair of Philosophy, even after the death of his first wife in 1893. He was forced to retire and, in April 1895, he left Austria for good, but not before publishing *My Last Wishes for Austria*, a catalogue of the indignities he had suffered, including the manner his plan for a psychology laboratory had been turned down.[31] After a short spell in Rome and Palermo, he settled in Florence, becoming an Italian citizen in 1896, and came into contact with Italian philosophers including Giovanni Vailati in Sicily, and Mario Puglisi in Palermo. In 1897 he married again, to Emilie Ruprecht. He remained active, attending psychology conferences, including the International Congress of Psychologists in Munich in 1896, where he delivered a paper "On the Theory of Sensation". Brentano had an abiding interest in the nature of sensory perception, a topic which was significantly developed by his oldest student Carl Stumpf as well as by Husserl. Brentano's researches on sensation were eventually published as *Investigations in Sense Psychology* in 1907.[32]

Though he bracketed the question of the nature of the soul in *Psychology from an Empirical Standpoint*, Brentano in fact defended the unity, indivisibility, and immortality of the soul in subsequent writings, and gave his fullest account of the soul as an individual substance in his later reist period. His later years were taken up with metaphysical investigations, including the nature of space and time, possibility and necessity, and an argument for the existence of God.[33] Brentano kept up with contemporary developments in physics and mathematics including the work of Poincaré, Dedekind, and Cantor, and he even proposed an anti-Cantorian account of the continuum.[34] In his arguments for the existence of God, he opposed Kant's criticisms of the cosmological and ontological proof, and also defended a strong conception of divine omniscience, one which entailed that God existed in time.

In his last ten years Brentano went blind, but he continued writing, dictating much of his work. Since he could not read over his work, many of his manuscripts repeat earlier drafts.[35] Brentano – like Husserl – carried out voluminous correspondence in which he elaborated in detail on his doctrines (1400 letters exchanged between himself and Marty alone!). He left behind a large number of unpublished manuscripts, including lectures on the history of philosophy. Many of his works were also edited by his pupils, sometimes with considerable rewriting. He entrusted the publication of his manuscripts to two of his students, Alfred Kastil and Oskar Kraus, both of whom had also been students of Marty. With the support of Masaryk, Kraus set up the Brentano-Archiv in Prague but, when Czechoslovakia was invaded in 1938, the Archive was damaged and the *Nachlass* was taken out of the country by Georg Katkov, first to Oxford. It is now preserved in Houghton Library,

Harvard University, and there are also archives in Würzburg and Graz.[36] Brentano had opposed the rising militarist nationalism in Germany, and later opposed Italy's incursions into Libya. When Italy entered the First World War, Brentano moved to Switzerland in May 1915. He died in Zurich on 17 March 1917.

Brentano's philosophical outlook: empiricism

What aspects of Brentano's prodigious philosophical output most influenced Husserl? Husserl himself claimed to have been chiefly influenced by Brentano's interest in the reform of logic. More generally, Husserl admired Brentano's demand for *exactitude* in philosophy and his account of the apodictic nature of descriptive psychology. Furthermore, Husserl accepted Brentano's view – crucial both for the subsequent development of phenomenology and for Marty's linguistic philosophy – that primacy must be given to *description* over *explanation*.

Brentano's understanding of philosophy as a rigorous science is partly explained by his view of the cyclical progress of philosophy. From his earliest days in Würzburg, Brentano promulgated the theory that philosophy progressed in four phases, including alternating phases of abundance and different stages of decline.[37] Brentano diagnosed his own age as a period of decline, and hence he advocated a renewal of philosophy as rigorous science. According to his periodisation, all great periods of growth in philosophy are characterised by the preponderance of the *purely theoretical interest* (*ein reines theoretisches Interesse*) and develop a method proper to the subject matter.[38] In this stage philosophy is pursued as a theoretical science. Thus, in the period from Thales to Aristotle, there was the steady growth of pure *theoria* (similarly, with Aquinas in the thirteenth century, and Bacon and Descartes in the modern period). After a while, there comes an inevitable weakening of theoretical activity and *practical interests* begin to dominate, for example the Stoics and Epicureans in the post-Aristotelian period, nominalism in the medieval era. This phase of applied philosophy is in turn followed by a third phase when *scepticism* grows, counterbalanced by the construction of sects and dogmatic philosophies (among which he included Kant). Finally, in a fourth phase, *mysticism*, intuitionism and irrationalist world-views, 'pseudo-philosophy', and religious *Schwärmerei* start to proliferate (e.g. Plotinus at the end of classical philosophy; Eckhart and Cusanus in the Middle Ages; Schelling and Hegel in recent times with their defence of intellectual intuition), leading to a moral and intellectual collapse.[39] Then the cycle begins again.

In the aftermath of the collapse of speculative German idealism, Brentano wanted to reawaken the theoretical attitude of scientific philosophy associated with the first phase. His fierce criticism of the prevailing German idealism, which he regarded as kind of speculative mysticism, irrationalism, and promotion of arbitrary opinion, carried over to Husserl. He had a particularly negative view of Kant. In contrast with Hume's subtle psychological analyses, Brentano maintained that "Kant possessed only a modest capacity for psychological observation",[40] and even proclaimed:

> I consider Kant's entire philosophy a confusion, and one which gave rise to even greater mistakes, and which, finally, led to complete philosophical chaos. I do believe that I learned a great deal from Kant; I learned, however, not what he wanted to teach me, but, above all, how seductive for the philosophical public, and how deceptive, is the fame which the history of philosophy has tied to names.
>
> (*The True*, 10)[41]

Brentano's negative view of Kant was echoed by the early Husserl, for example, in his first lecture course of 1887–1888 on "Epistemology and Metaphysics", where he speaks of the "mystical pseudo-philosophy which at first attracted itself to Kant".[42] It was many years before Husserl was able, freeing himself from Brentano, to appreciate Kant's transcendental philosophy.

Against this mysticism, Brentano championed the British empiricists, especially Hume and Mill (notably his *System of Logic*, 1843),[43] and the French positivists, especially Auguste Comte. Brentano regarded Comte as the greatest contemporary philosopher, though he disagreed with Comte's complete rejection of metaphysics.[44] He also had a high regard for Ernst Mach's empirio-criticism and had even supported Mach's candidature for a chair in Vienna.[45] Brentano's emphasis on 'presentations' (*Vorstellungen*), as the basis of judgements and other intellectual acts, is his version of the Humean thesis that ideas must be related to impressions. Brentano was, however, critical both of the crude *associationism* of Humean and subsequent British psychology and the view of the mind as passively receiving impressions. He also opposed the prevailing introspectionism in empirical psychology and sought to replace it by what he called 'inner perception' (*innere Wahrnehmung*). We shall have more to say about inner perception, but for the moment it is important to grasp Brentano's conception of descriptive psychology, the science which specifies the laws governing the succession and nature of our psychic experiences.

Brentano had proposed to reconstruct philosophy on the basis of psychology, and strongly argued that the nature of psychic acts had been misunderstood by much contemporary philosophy. For him, the domain of psychical phenomena possessed 'actual existence' (*eine wirkliche Existenz*), whereas the purely physical world had merely phenomenal existence: "Our mental phenomena are the things which are most our own" (PES 20).

34

Furthermore, our mental acts are as they appear to be (PES 20), para-phrasing Berkeley, their *esse* is *percipi*. Brentano takes this to be an Aristotelian doctrine also; the mind can grasp itself as it is, even if it does so in acts which are directed at other objects. Because psychic acts can be grasped immediately with absolute certainty, with what Brentano calls *Evidenz*,[46] self-evidence, we can make real discoveries about the nature of the mental which have the status of a priori universal laws though they are grasped with insight on the basis of even a single instance. Evidence is not to be equated with a psychological intensity or force of conviction (PES 204), a view he associated with Mill and Herbert Spencer. He remarks that if a judgement were a case of intensity of feeling, then doctors would warn people against mathematics, as mathematical judgements would carry dangerously high levels of intensity (*The True*, 35). We can grasp necessary laws connecting items which are given in experience. Descriptive psychol-ogy, then, for Brentano, will be the apodictic science of inner perception, studying the elements of psychic acts and their relations. This will have huge consequences for Husserl's understanding of phenomenology. Brentano himself, at least in his earlier years, saw descriptive psychology as providing the scientific basis for aesthetics, economics, and other disciplines dependent on human judgements. Husserl would generalise to see phenomenology as the basis of all sciences. But both Brentano and Husserl see science as the securing of insights which are given with evidence.

As we have seen, Brentano developed a taste for metaphysical description in his early studies of Aristotle. Over his life, his conception of metaphysics began to change, and, in particular, he rethought the relation between accidents and substance such that he reversed the priority and argued that accidental unities of subjects and accidents are the prime existents. In his later writings, he developed the view that only particular things existed, a doctrine later known as *reism*.[47] Although he acknowledged, with Aristotle, that the word 'is' is used in many senses, only one sense is *genuine* or *authentic* (*eigentlich*), namely actual existence as a concrete being, a concretum (*Seiend, ein Reales*). In his earlier writings Brentano had postulated that, besides real things (*Realia*), there were various kinds of unreal entities corresponding to our true judgements, simple and complex, positive and negative, real and ideal, and even states of affairs, though Brentano himself did not develop a proper account of *Sachverhalte*, states of affairs, of the kind to be found in Husserl and Reinach.[48] Brentano was not entirely clear how these *Irrealia* related to the judgements made about them.[49] In his later writings, especially after 1905, he maintained that the only true objects were concrete, individual entities such as a 'soul', a 'person', a 'judger', a 'thinking thing' (*ein Denkendes*). For the later Brentano, to describe a 'thinking man' correctly in metaphysical terms, we should not speak of a substance ('man') to which an accident ('thinking') is added, but rather speak of a new concrete whole ('man-thinking-x'), wherein both the accident and the substance are to be construed as dependent parts of the new complex whole. Thus '*Socrates standing*' is a different individual thing from '*Socrates sitting*'. On this view, temporary whole objects are constantly coming into being and disappearing. Husserl was especially influenced by Brentano's account of wholes and parts.

Brentano's theory of wholes and parts

In order properly to formulate his rethinking of the relation between substance and accident, Brentano, drawing on Aristotle, developed the outlines of a theory of the relations between parts and wholes in general. Brentano saw the Aristotelian theory of the categories as really containing a theory of wholes and parts, now called '*mereology*', from the Greek term for 'part', *meros*. In his *Descriptive Psychology* lectures (1887–1891) and in the essays in *The Theory of the Categories*, he laid the foundations for such a mereology. Brentano's scattered remarks on this subject were later taken up by Carl Stumpf, by Edmund Husserl in the Third Logical Investigation, as we shall see in a later chapter, and by Lesniewski who developed a formal system.[50] Already in his doctoral dissertation, Brentano had criticised Aristotle's account of parts.[51] For Aristotle, a whole and its proper part are not both actual at the same time; only the whole is actual, the parts only potentially exist. For example, before the orange is sliced, its segments are potential not actual; when it is sliced, the whole is no longer actual. Leibniz, on the other hand, in his *Monadology*, maintained that only objects without parts exist. For Brentano, both Aristotle and Leibniz are incorrect: wholes have real parts upon which they depend. In his lectures, published as *Descriptive Psychology*, Brentano developed an important distinction, which would become especially significant for Husserl, between 'dependent' and 'independent' or 'separable' parts. Brentano further distinguishes between different kinds of parts, between the physical, and the metaphysical and logical parts of a whole. Husserl will distinguish between concrete and abstract, independent and dependent parts. Thus if 'red' is a real part of a piece of cloth, then 'being coloured' is an abstract, dependent part of the cloth. For Brentano, especially in his lectures on *Descriptive Psychology*, psychic acts relate to one another as parts to whole, objects are parts 'nested' inside presentations, and presentations in turn are 'nested' inside the corresponding judgements, and so on. This nested, mereological account of mental acts will have enormous influence on Husserl's *Logical Investigations*. Before discussing Brentano's account of psychological acts in more detail we need to examine his views on the reform of logic, as Husserl later claimed that he was chiefly impressed by Brentano's efforts in this area. We need to understand the role of judgement in Brentano before we can consider its central importance in Husserl.

36

Brentano's reform of logic

When Husserl attended Brentano's lectures in 1884–1885, he said he was especially drawn to Brentano's lectures on logic. Indeed, although Husserl rejected Brentano's anti-Aristotelian account of judgement, he himself saw his *Logical Investigations* (1900–1901) as, in part, an effort to pay tribute to Brentano's logical insights. As early as his Würzburg lectures of 1870–1871, Brentano had proposed various reforms of traditional Aristotelian predicate logic, some of which are contained in the 1874 *Psychology from an Empirical Standpoint*. Through Kasimir Twardowski, Brentano's logical innovations had some influence on the first generation of Polish logicians, especially Jan Lukasiewicz (1878–1956) and Stanislaw Lesniewski (1886–1939). Brentano's reforms, however, were quickly overshadowed by the logical revolution of Frege, Russell, and others, and Brentano's influence was limited as he could not absorb the importance of mathematical logic and hence was unable to clarify the notion of logical form.[52] Thus, it is not surprising that he failed to appreciate the logical contributions of Frege and even of Husserl. Brentano clung to the traditional view of logic as an art or 'technique' (*Kunstlehre*) and rejected Husserl's call for a 'pure logic' as the study of purely theoretical objects and the ideal laws that bind them. Moreover, he regarded mathematical logic as a mere calculus, and his own reluctance to employ symbolism leads to a degree of ambiguity in his formulation of central axioms.

For Brentano, logic is the doctrine of correct judgement, and his main contribution was to offer a new account of the nature of judgement which rejected the classical Aristotelian view of judgement as a *combination* or *separation* of a subject (*hypokeimenon*) and a predicate, or that which is asserted about the subject.[53] Mere *combination* or *separation* is just association of ideas and is not yet judgement; rather, for Brentano, the central form (or 'quality') of a judgement is the *assertion* (*Anerkennung*) or *denial* (*Leugnen*) of an object. A theist simply affirms 'God' not 'the *existence* of God'. Judgements, then, are primarily assertions of existence and need not take the subject–predicate form; for example, 'it is raining' is a judgement of existence which ostensibly lacks a subject in the traditional sense. Nothing is being *combined* or *separated* in the judgement 'it is raining'. Furthermore, Brentano also accepted – as Husserl also did – Kant's view that existence is not a real predicate, it adds nothing to what is asserted. Assertion itself is always the asserting of existence, and no combination is involved in the judgement 'God exists'. All judgements are already existential judgements in form. For Brentano, philosophers have been misled by the subject–predicate grammatical form of judgements to think that judgements themselves have this form rather than being assertions or denials of the existence of particulars. Moreover, what is asserted, the propositional content, is also only a mirage of grammar, as we shall see.

Since all judgements are existential in form, Brentano reduces the four categorical forms (A, E, I, O) of traditional logic to the existential judgement (PES 214; 295).[54] In a sense, then, Brentano abandons quantification altogether. For example, the I-proposition, 'some man is sick', (some a are b) really has the form of asserting 'a sick man [exists]' (an ab exists, PES 213). Similarly, universal affirmations (A-propositions) may be rewritten as negative existential propositions: the assertion 'all men are mortal' is really the *existential denial*, 'there is no non-mortal man'. Indeed, Brentano will interpret the universal laws of descriptive psychology as really negative singular propositions. To support his account of the relations between categorical forms, Brentano proposed some amendments to traditional logic, amendments which have been generally recognised as valid in contemporary logic. Thus, contrary to classical logic, A-propositions do not imply I-propositions, since universal propositions do not have existential import. 'All unicorns have one horn' does not imply 'some unicorn has one horn' since unicorns do not exist (PES 304). Similarly, E-propositions do not imply O-propositions. Brentano further, and idiosyncratically, wants to rewrite negative assertions as positive ones. The judgement "No S is P" is to be replaced by the judgement: "Someone who judges 'No S is P' does so incorrectly".

While Brentano adopted the traditional distinction between the *quality* of a judgement and its *matter*, he did not accept the traditional account of the nature of propositional content or 'judgement content' (*Urteilsinhalt*). For him, the *matter* of a judgement is always a 'presentation' (*Vorstellung*), and 'every content of an experience is individual' (DP 149). Acts of judging assert the existence of particulars, that is individual objects, they do not posit or deny *contents* at all (PES 292). For Brentano (PES 221), since the presentation can also be made the object of a judgement, what is given to be judged is the object presented and not the propositional content.[55] Brentano does not seem to have been able to distinguish between the meaning-content of the judgement itself and the state of affairs which holds if the judgement is true. Brentano did not fully understand the distinction between the *content* and the *object* of a judgement, even when such a distinction was proposed by his students (chiefly by Twardowski). In his later reist phase, Brentano modified this view of content to hold that what is asserted is not a *content* but the existence of the individual substance, the one who judges.

The overall effect of Brentano's revision of Aristotle's syllogistic is to highlight the central act of judging as the locus of truth. To emphasise the role of judging so strongly, of course, can leave Brentano open to the view that truths as such *depend* on the mental acts of humans, a view Husserl would later describe as *psychologism*, though without explicitly implicating his revered teacher Brentano. Brentano himself repudiated psychologism as a subjectivism.[56]

Descriptive psychology

Brentano held, against Kant (PES 65), that psychology can be established as a rigorous science, whose function is to identify and classify in the right order mental acts and their essential parts. Psychology, then, is the descriptive study of our 'psychical realities' (DP 137), the 'ultimate mental elements' (PES 45). Brentano compared the resulting taxonomy of the mental with the identification of the alphabet, and saw psychology as a possible basis for realising Leibniz's dream of a *characteristica universalis* (PES 369). *Psychology from an Empirical Standpoint* (1874) was his first systematic attempt to delimit this new subject area of a scientific, empirical but non-physiological, *psychology*, but it was written hurriedly in order to achieve the position in Vienna. Although he lectured extensively on psychology, years went by before he published anything else on this topic, specifically his *The Origin of Our Knowledge of Right and Wrong* in 1889. Indeed, the title of the lecture course for 1888–1889 was '*Deskriptive Psychologie oder beschreibende Phänomenologie*', 'descriptive psychology or descriptive phenomenology'. According to Brentano, descriptive psychology will provide the necessary grounding for genetic or causal psychology and for other sciences, including logic, aesthetics, political economy, sociology, and so on (DP 78). He conceives of it as an *exact* science, like mathematics (DP 5), 'independent' of (DP 156), 'prior' to (DP 8), and indeed 'providing a basis for' (DP 78) 'genetic' or physiological psychology, such as was being developed by Gustav Theodor Fechner (1801–1887) and others.[57] Unfortunately, Brentano had little to say about how psychology would perform this grounding function, but Husserl took over the vision of descriptive psychology as a foundational science, as we shall see.

For Brentano, genetic or physiological psychology studies causal relations between the physical and the mental, specifically the laws governing the succession of these states. Genetic psychology may ultimately discover that intentional phenomena have a physico-chemical substratum, but this does not affect the description of mental states which are accessible from within by the experiencing subject him- or herself, nor can genetic psychology explain the co-existence of different mental states at the same time. For Brentano, in psychology, as in other sciences, description must precede causal explanation; we must know the contours of the phenomenon before we seek to explain it (PES 194). Descriptively at least, then, the psychological domain stands on its own. In fact, his view in 1874 was that it was undeniable that mental processes *depend* on the physiological processes (PES 48), and specifically on occurrences in the brain (PES 61–62), but the physical does not *explain* the mental, which Brentano holds must be understood on its own terms (a point on which Husserl's phenomenology agrees). Brentano dismisses the possibility that laws governing the mental could be deduced from physiological laws and ultimately from physical and chemical laws (PES 47). He believed that subjective experiences of colour and other sensations could never be explained just in terms of the physiological conditions which are necessary in order that they occur. One reason for believing this is essentially Cartesian: our ideas of sensation are not like anything in bodies themselves (PES 60). He also suspected that the basic assumption of physiological psychology, that to every physical process only one mental effect can be linked, was untenable. The multiplicity of mental effects of the same physical process militated against explaining the psychical in terms of the physical. Furthermore, this kind of psychology cannot explain how one psychological state gives rise to another. In *Descriptive Psychology*, he strengthened this claim: it is "a confusion of thought" (DP 4) to think that consciousness can be explained by physico-chemical events. Different orders of enquiry are involved.

Brentano envisaged this new science of descriptive psychology as a combination of *empirical* and *a priori* factors. At the outset, Brentano characterised his approach as purely empirical: "My psychological standpoint is empirical; experience alone is my teacher" (PES xv). In this sense, Brentano understood psychology to proceed by empirical observation and careful classification of results. According to Brentano:

> just as the natural sciences study the properties and laws of physical bodies, which are the objects of our external perception, psychology is the science which studies the properties and laws of the soul, which we discover within ourselves directly by means of inner perception.
>
> (PES 5)

In *Psychology* he initially accepted that psychological laws were arrived at by the inductive method (PES 70), though he was already pointing to flaws in inductive reasoning and the fact that it produced only generalisations not universal truths.[58] He does not rule out the inclusion of 'a certain ideal intuition' (*eine gewisse ideale Anschauung*, PES xv) in his descriptions, and, although he never satisfactorily clarified what he means by this, it is obvious that he thought it possible to make some kind of idealisation to a universal law from a *single* empirical instance, yielding necessary truth.[59] Brentano believed that psychology, through inner perception with evidence, could secure certain knowledge and identify universal laws governing the psychic realm. Brentano characterised these universal psychological laws as 'a priori' and 'apodictic'. The concepts themselves arise from experience but the laws governing them are arrived at by reflection and have the character of *necessity*.[60] He constantly rejected Kant's account of the a priori as a confusion leading only to 'blind', non-evident judgements, and he certainly would not have approved of Husserl's characterisation of truths governing this domain as 'synthetic a priori'. Brentano thought that the claim that descriptive psychology yielded universal and necessary truths was essentially an Aristotelian claim.[61] He invoked Leibniz's distinction between 'truths of fact' (*vérités de fait*) and 'truths of reason' (*vérités de raison*) to declare that the laws of descriptive psychology, along with the laws of mathematics and logic, belong to the latter. Strictly speaking, for Brentano, a priori universal laws have a negative form (PES 370), they list impossibilities, and as such are not existential claims, as Brentano's editor, Kraus, explained (PES 372). We are compelled by the evidence for the judgement to recognise that it would be impossible for anyone to deny it.

Inner perception

Descriptive psychology proceeds through inner perception. Though their terminology is not in exact agreement, both Brentano and Wundt distinguish between *outer perception* (*außere Wahrnehmung*) and *inner perception* (*innere Wahrnehmung*).[62] Since Brentano believed that psychological processes and their parts, unlike phenomena studied in the natural sciences, cannot be observed, he maintained that they are disclosed in 'inner perception'. Inner perception is the key to the discovery of our psychic states. Inner *perception* is evident, while inner *observation* (*innere Beobachtung*), or introspection, is highly fallible and subjective.

Most nineteenth-century psychology proceeded by introspection and offered training in this 'armchair' self-observation.[63] Indeed, many philosophers today consider the method of phenomenology to be a kind of trained introspection.[64] However, both Brentano and Husserl repudiated traditional introspective psychology (e.g. PES 29). Brentano, in particular, accepted Hume's view that we can never catch the self in any of its states in introspection. We cannot *observe* our own mental states while occupying them. Introspection can only distort the phenomena it seeks to study, we cannot *observe* our anger without modifying it in some way (PES 30). This failure of introspection can be rewritten as a something with the status of a fundamental psychological law: "It is a universally valid psychological law that we can never focus our *attention* upon the object of inner perception" (PES 30). Brentano thought of inner perception in an essentially Aristotelian manner. When the intellect is actualised in thinking of some object, it perceives itself accidentally, *per accidens*, at the same time.[65] The phenomena of 'inner perception' (*innere Wahrnehmung*) or 'inner sense' are absolutely given, in a manner which makes them self-transparent or self-conscious, self-evident. It is this self-evidence of psychic acts which, Brentano thinks, makes the framing hypotheses and the use of induction to arrive at generalities inessential to psychological method. I have direct acquaintance of my psychic acts and, furthermore, they present themselves as they are in themselves.

Of course, for Brentano, this apodictic knowledge is severely restricted, specifically to my own acts and then only when they are attended to

41

properly. I know only my own thoughts directly (PES 92); I have only indirect awareness of the inner perceptions of others (PES 37), a point which Husserl will develop. Descriptive psychology can claim universal validity only if my own grasp of the psychical is a perfect mirror of the psychic life of others. This emerges as a central problem in Husserl's analyses of intersubjectivity and empathy. Husserl sees the unity of psychic life as something not properly treated in Brentano.

Psychology, in the first instance, studies what is given in immediate reflection on our self-conscious acts. Since psychology has direct and certain awareness of its subject matter, Brentano held that, as a science, it was in advance of physics, which could only postulate entities and formulate hypotheses about the putative laws governing them. For Brentano, the objects studied by physics lie outside consciousness, and as such are unknown in themselves. Or, as Brentano puts it, they are 'unintuitable' (*unanschaulich*, DP 4). We do not know things in themselves. Brentano retains this view all his life, writing, for example, in 1915:

> On one occasion, in the presence of Lord Kelvin, someone said how it might be preferable not to speak of such a thing as the ether, since we know virtually nothing about it. To this, he replied, that however much in the dark we may be about the nature of ether, we are even more so in the case of the nature of matter. Actually, psychology, in so far as it is descriptive, is far in advance of physics. The thinking thing – the thing that has ideas, the thing that judges, the thing that wills – which we innerly perceive is just what we perceive it to be. But so-called outer perception presents us with nothing that appears the way it really is. The sensible qualities do not correspond in their structure to external objects, and we are subject to the most serious illusions with respect to rest and motion and to figure and size.[66]

In propounding his view of the physical, Brentano is sympathetic to the phenomenalism of Mach and Comte: all we know are the effects of these physical things on our sense organs:

> We have no experience of that which truly exists, in and of itself, and that which we do experience is not true. The truth of physical phenomena is...only a relative truth.
>
> (PES 19)

Indeed, even the assumption of the existence of an external world is 'initially hypothetical' (DP 163). According to Brentano, the physical sciences study the causal relations ('forces') between these real objects and our sense organs (PES 48–49). Spatio-temporal objects are not experienced directly, they are posits, theoretical constructs placed in a world which 'resembles' or is 'similar to' one which has three spatial dimensions and flows in one direction in time. The objects we infer appear to have three-dimensional existence or are best treated as so having (PES 100). Our knowledge of physical phenomena is always fallible. We *infer* the existence and nature of physical objects, whereas, in contrast, we are directly acquainted with our own experiences. "Our mental phenomena are the things which are most our own" (PES 20).

Inner perception as additional awareness

Though he rejected *introspection*, Brentano believed he could achieve direct knowledge of his inner mental states, by catching these states *reflectively* while engaged in acts of outer perception. All consciousness of an object is accompanied by a consciousness of itself as act, though this need not be explicit. There is no perceiving without the possibility of apperception (DP 171; PES 153) and hence, for Brentano, there can be no unconscious mental acts. Brentano drew on Aristotle and Thomas Aquinas[67] for a description of the nature of this accompanying, concomitant, or 'additional conscious-ness' (*Bewußtseinsnebenbei*), whereby the essential features of the primary act are grasped 'by the way', 'incidentally' (*per accidens, en parergo*, PES 276). In *De anima* III, 2 425b 12ff., Aristotle considers whether the sense of sight may also be said to have itself as object. Is it through the sense of sight that we see that we are seeing? Aristotle recognised that there was a way in which the senses appeared to communicate what they were doing, but the seeing itself could not be the proper object of the sense of sight, since the proper object of sight is the visible, the coloured. Aristotle's solution is to say that sight knows that it is seeing, *per accidens*.[68] In Brentano's language, we *apperceive* ourselves having perceptions, we cannot *observe* these perceptions directly.

Brentano's conception of inner perception was hugely influential among the members of his school and was defended by Alois Höfler and others, but it obviously has deep flaws, many of which Husserl would later catalogue in the *Logical Investigations* (LI VI, Appendix § 6, pp. 864–867; Hua XIX/2 767–771). In a sense, Brentano weds the Aristotelian account to the Cartesian–Leibnizian view that inner perception is apodictic, given with certain 'self-evidence' (*Evidenz*).

It is important to realise how restrictive descriptive psychology is. Our immediate infallible knowledge is restricted to the present moment, to the now.[69] We do not have infallible awareness of a stream of consciousness and hence we cannot really *perceive* temporally extended phenomena. Brentano thinks we can supplement what we learn in our now-perception with the observation of earlier mental acts in immediate memory (PES 34), though he acknowledges this memory is unreliable. In so far as it draws on memory, descriptive psychology is not apodictic. In later years, especially during his Italian sojourn, Brentano softened his claims about inner perception and acknowledged that it required an extended present in time (as William James and Wundt held), and that it was inherently complex since it included moments of comparing, distinguishing, and noticing. Brentano treats temporality as a mode of apprehending the object rather than as a feature of the object itself. Our main mode of apprehending is the *modus praesens*, in the present moment, but we can also grasp things obliquely in memory and in expectation though to a more limited degree and without apodicticity. We shall have more to say on these psychic modes below.

Though it is a feature of psychic acts that they present with certainty, this certainty can be overlooked and obscured for various reasons. In line with the Cartesian tradition, Brentano believes that something can be *perceived* without being explicitly *noticed*.[70] Something can be given with apodictic certainty while all its parts may not be distinctly noticed. Thus, in the case of hearing a chord (PES 277), some people can distinguish and hear separately the individual notes making up the chord, while others cannot. For Brentano, if the chord is heard at all, then all the notes of the chord must be 'really apprehended' but they need not be individually distinguished or noticed by everyone (DP 26). Similarly, when I grasp a complex inner psychological state, I may not at the same time attend to all the component parts of that state, but nevertheless they are all psychologically *presented* and perceived, even if not explicitly noticed, a point also made by Twardowski. Furthermore, they may, with training, be discovered, which is the whole task of descriptive psychology. Furthermore, Brentano recognised, as did Descartes, that our apprehension of psychic states may be confused even if the states themselves are presenting the objects clearly and distinctly. Although our inner psychic states in inner perception have the character of certain evidence, what we perceive may be confused (PES 277) and suffer from 'incompleteness', 'unnoticeability', 'misinterpretability' (*Misdeutlichkeit*, DP 10; 156). This incompleteness, nevertheless, does not affect its evidence and universal validity (PES 277). In agreement with Descartes, we can – through lack of attention – take one thing for another,[71] but careful, trained inner perception can yield necessary truth. Unfortunately, Brentano never effectively clarifies these distinctions between 'perceiving' and 'noticing' (*Bemerken*), and other modalities such as 'attending to', 'taking note of', 'being struck by', 'being absorbed by' (DP 37), and so on, all of which belong to inner perception. Husserl made much more headway in this realm. Husserl, as we shall see, will attempt to clarify some of the confusions inherent in Brentano's account of descriptive psychology. Carl Stumpf, and then Edmund Husserl, took on board this distinction between *perceiving* and explicitly *noticing* the parts or elements of a psychic act in their discussion of the apprehension of fused unities, such as hearing a chord, seeing a flock of sheep or a collection of objects to be counted, as we shall see.

The tripartite structure of mental life

A fundamental plank of Brentano's descriptive psychology is his acceptance of a traditional classification of mental acts into three 'fundamental classes' (*Grundklassen*, PES 45) or 'modes' (PES 276),[72] namely 'presentations' (*Vorstellungen*), 'judgements' (*Urteile*), and the 'phenomena of love and hate', or 'relations of feeling', (*Gemütstätigkeiten*, PES 276; RW 55), or 'phenomena of interest' (*Interessephänomene*). He thought this classification was given its first complete and accurate statement by Descartes in Meditation Three (RW 15), but suggested a similar classification could also be traced back to Aristotle and Aquinas.[73] Brentano understands these three basic sets of acts as grouped around each other in a certain way. The fundamental principle of Brentano's descriptive psychology is that all mental processes are either presentations or founded on presentations (PES 80). This, for Brentano, is a psychological law, and as such is a priori and necessary and formulated in the negative: no mental act without a presentation. For Brentano, "it is impossible for conscious activity to refer in any way to something which is not presented" (PES 198). Mental acts are, as it were, incomplete functions unless they contain a presentation. When I hear a tone, I have a *presentation* of a tone; when I see a red patch, I have a *presentation* of red.

Brentano uses the term 'presentation' much as Locke and Hume used the term 'idea'. There are as many kinds of presentations as there are mental contents. I can have a presentation of a 'triangle' or of 'colour', or even 'the thinking of a general concept' (PES 79). The term 'presentation' refers to that part of any mental process which brings something before the mind: "We speak of a presentation whenever something appears to us" (PES 198). A presentation in general is an act of mental seeing or mental entertaining of an individual object or concept, or even of a complex relation as in the entertaining of a state of affairs. Husserl and Meinong (in his *On Assumptions*, 1902) will both later interpose a new class of 'assumptions' between presentations and judgements, thus allowing for a more complex sentential content to be entertained without being explicitly affirmed or denied.[74] But, for Brentano, something which is merely before the mind, whether it is a sensation or a thought, and which is not explicitly affirmed or denied or willed, is a *presentation*. A presentation provides the basic 'object' or 'content' (terms which Brentano employs indiscriminately) around which other kinds of mental act crystallise. This is the core of Brentano's account of intentionality, as we shall see.

Although Brentano sometimes, like William James, suggests that simple presentations can occur on their own without judgements,[75] elsewhere he says that our mental life employs all three levels: "there is no act in which all three are not present" (PES 265). He thinks of psychic activity as layered or nested sets of acts whose parts combine into new wholes. I *see* something, I *judge* it to be a violin, I *enjoy* it, and so on. All other mental acts *presuppose* and are 'founded' on these presentations. Every presentation is *of* something.[76] When I *judge* that this is a musical note, and I *am pleased* by the sound, the judgement and the emotion of pleasure are founded on the initial presentation *of the tone*.

Presentations and modifications of presentations

No judgement can occur without some presentation; for example, my decision to go on a journey requires the presentation of the journey (DP 90; PES 181). Brentano did not manage to specify the modes of appearing with the same phenomenological accuracy as Husserl later did, but he did allow that presentations have different 'modes of presentation', the same object may appear in different ways in thinking, desiring, or fearing (PES 181). Each kind of act has its own mode of presentation (PES 278). Different kinds of act don't necessarily take special objects but are "distinguished according to the different ways they refer to their content" (PES 197–198). As we have seen above, Brentano recognises that *remembering* and *perceiving* involve presentations of the object under different temporal *modes*, specifically a direct mode, *modus rectus*, and an indirect mode, *modus obliquus*. When I am remembering making a mistake, I am not performing the error over again. In remembering the error, the 'error' is presented but now under a different, non-active mode of presentation (SN 57).[77] Similarly, remembering being angry is not the same as being angry. Or, to use a favourite example of Husserl's, to have an aesthetic experience of a painting is not the same as to judge that the painting is aesthetically pleasing, without personally living through the pleasure. Temporal differences (e.g. perceiving *versus* remembering) are not to be construed as differences in the *object* of the act, but in the *mode of presentation* of the act itself or a mode of an associated judgement.[78] In his 1883 lectures, Brentano began to distinguish between sensory and more abstract presentations, and, soon after, between perceptual and phantasy presentations, where the perceptual are given with greater 'genuineness' or 'authenticity' (*Eigentlichkeit*).[79] In his later writings, possibly under pressure from Husserlian phenomenology which recognised a plurality of mental forms, Brentano recognised the need to posit more and more diverse modes of presenting; he saw the need to "multiply the modes of mental reference" (PES 386) beyond the three basic kinds. Beliefs and desires consider the same object under different modes or manners (DP 143). There are also many subsidiary modes of presentation. Brentano even controversially distinguished affirming and denying as two different kinds of acts with distinct psychological modes, whereas Frege held that to affirm *p* is to deny not-*p*. Similarly, loving and hating, for Brentano, present the object under different modes.

As a descriptive psychologist, Brentano claims to be interested in the *presentative act* rather than the object of the act, for example the *act of perceiving* and not in the *thing* perceived. Hence he was not particularly interested in specifying the ontological nature of the object of a presentation. Rather he was interested in the act of presenting as the basis of the psychical domain itself. Brentano's assumption concerning the fundamental role of presentations in our mental life leads directly to his account of the intentional relation.

The intentional relation

Intentionality is the doctrine that every mental act is related to some object. Brentano understood the mind's awareness of an object, or content, in terms of the traditional Scholastic doctrine of intentionality, though he himself did not use the term 'intentionality', despite its currency in late Scholasticism.[80] Rather he speaks of the *intentional object* or the *intentional relation*. In *Psychology from an Empirical Standpoint*, Brentano states:

> Every mental phenomenon is characterized by what the Scholastics of the Middle Ages called the intentional (or mental) inexistence of an object [die *intentionale (auch wohl mentale) Inexistenz eines Gegenstandes*], and what we might call, though not wholly unambiguously, reference to a content, direction towards an object (which is not here to be understood as meaning a thing) [*die Beziehung auf einen Inhalt, die Richtung auf ein Objekt (worunter hier nicht eine Realität zu verstehen ist)*] or immanent objectivity (*oder die immanente Gegenständlichkeit*). Every mental phenomenon includes something as object within itself, although they do not all do so in the same way. In presentation something is presented, in judgement something is affirmed or denied, in love loved, in hate hated, in desire desired and so on.
>
> (PES 88)[81]

Some years later, in his 1889 lecture *The Origin of Our Knowledge of Right and Wrong*, Brentano writes:

> The common feature of everything psychological, often referred to, unfortunately, by the misleading term "consciousness", consists in a relation that we bear to an object. The relation has been called *intentional*; it is a relation to something which may not be actual but which is presented as an object. [Brentano adds in a footnote: A suggestion of this view may be found in Aristotle; see especially

Metaphysics, Book V, Chapter 15, 1021a 29. The expression "intentional", like many other terms for our more important concepts, comes from the Scholastics.] There is no hearing unless something is heard, no believing unless something is believed; there is no hoping unless something is hoped for...and so on, for all the other psychological phenomena.

(RW 14)

It makes no sense to have a process of judging where nothing is judged, loving without something loved, and so on.

In his initial phase of expressing this relation, Brentano emphasised it was possible to be intentionally related to all kinds of objects, imagined, possible, impossible, and so on. Roughly from 1874 to 1904, Brentano frequently expresses intentionality in terms of the intentional inexistence of the object. 'Inexistence' (*Inexistenz*) is, in fact, Brentano's translation of the Latin term *in-esse*, the verb meaning 'to be in', which was used by the Scholastics to characterise the manner in which an accident is said to be *in* a substance (e.g. knowledge is *in* a man), and specifically with regard to epistemology, the manner in which a form is in the mind. By 'inexistence' Brentano does seem to intend that the object of an act of consciousness is something *immanent* in consciousness, whether or not there is also a real object or 'reality' (*Realität*) outside of consciousness. Clearly, as a follower of Descartes and Aristotle, Brentano believes there is something in the mind when it thinks, and, furthermore, what the mind thinks about may or may not have any actual existence outside the mind. It may be a real entity (*ein Reales*) or something 'unreal'. Thus I can see a dog, or think of a 'golden mountain' or a 'round square'. The early Brentano tends to speak of the intentional object as a 'non-real' entity (*Nicht-Reales*), something 'insubstantial' (*unwesenhaft*), 'some internal objective [thing]' (*ein innerlich Gegenständliches*), something 'in-dwelling' (*inwohnendes*, DP 24),[82] 'mentally immanent' (*geistiges inhaben*, DP 155), which "need not correspond to anything outside" (DP 24). Brentano's student, Twardowski, is therefore correctly interpreting Brentano when he explains 'intentional inexistence' as 'phenomenal existence', the kind of existence possessed by an intentional object in consciousness.[83]

Later, in his 1911 *Classification of Mental Phenomena*, the revised edition of Book Two of *Psychology from an Empirical Standpoint*, reissued at the request of his students, Brentano admitted his use of the phrase 'intentional inexistence' (PES 180 n.) had been misunderstood and he would have been better to have avoided it altogether. He says he even considered replacing the term 'intentional' with another Scholastic term 'objective', but this would have given rise to more misunderstandings by those who did not appreciate the Scholastic meaning of *esse objectivum*, the manner in which things are 'objectively' in the mind.[84] Brentano is referring to the Cartesian distinction between 'formal' and 'objective reality' in the Third Meditation, where Descartes distinguished the meaning-content (*realitas objectiva*) which belongs to the *idea* of God from the 'formal reality' (*realitas formalis*) of the cause of the idea, namely the actual being, God. According to Brentano's employment of this distinction, when I believe something actively, or when I am actually making an error, the belief or error is *formally* in me; when I *remember* believing something or making an error, then that belief or error is *objectively* in me (*The True*, 15–16). These distinctions between the 'presented object' and the 'mode of presentation', the formal and the objective, are efforts by Brentano to accommodate a conceptual distinction which his students were forcing on him, namely the distinction between the *content* and the *object* of the act.

In Brentano's earlier interpretation of intentionality, he understood the intentional object to be a mentally immanent object and the intentional relation to be an immanent relation between the mind and its contents, and he did not distinguish between the characteristic of 'directedness towards an object' (*die Richtung auf ein Objekt*), and 'relation to a content' (*die Beziehung auf einen Inhalt*). Brentano's earliest formulations treat the intentional object as purely immanent and as non-real. However, as Brentano examined further this class of unreal entities (*Irrealia*, as he dubbed them), and specifically as he contemplated the content of judgements as opposed to presentations, he appears to have postulated some kind of intermediary objects between the mind and external things. Though it is hard to find straightforward assertions of these entities in Brentano himself, his students, Marty, Kraus, and Meinong, all developed theories about them. What Brentano called 'judgement contents' (*Urteilsinhalte*) became Marty's *Sachverhalte* and Meinong's *Gegenständlichkeiten*. Husserl, similarly, identified different kinds of objectivities in his *Logical Investigations*. In his theory of objects, Alexius Meinong postulated baroque typologies of 'objectives' or 'objectivities' which has been variously called an ontological jungle and an ontological slum (Quine). In particular, Meinong felt we had to overcome 'a prejudice in favour of the actual' to allow there to be 'objectives' standing for all our intentional acts. Meinong sought to explain thought's ability to refer to all kinds of things, from actual things to non-existent *possible* things (e.g. gold mountains), ideal things (e.g. numbers, ideal laws) or even *impossible* things (e.g. square circles), by positing these entities as having various special kinds of being distinct from actual existence.[85] Thus Meinong maintained that a 'square circle' had a kind of being, 'being-thus' (*Sosein*), which meant that it truly had the properties of being circular and square even if it could never be actually existent. In correspondence with Meinong, Russell wondered if an 'existent square circle' meant that it also existed. Meinong replied that indeed it did have the property of existence but this was not the same as asserting that it actually existed. Marty, similarly, defended the concept 'the non-being of A' as a genuine object of thought. It is clear that Meinong and others were developing what they took to be a genuine Brentanian doctrine.

In later writings, however, after the so-called 'crisis of immanence' (*Immanenzkrisis*) of 1904 or 1905, Brentano denied trying to give any special kind of existence to the intentional object and explicitly repudiated the efforts of Meinong, Marty, Husserl, and others. As he puts it in his letter to Marty of 17 March 1905, when one thinks of a 'horse', one is thinking of an actual horse, not the 'thought-about horse' (*gedachtes Pferd*, *The True*, 78). For Brentano, furthermore, it is the height of absurdity to think that, if I promise to marry someone, I commit myself to an *ens rationis* and not to an actual person.[86] In many letters to Marty and others, Brentano forcefully rejected all positing of '*entia rationis*', beings of reason, which was his name for these Platonic entities. Brentano emphasised that he had always taught a more Aristotelian interpretation of intentionality, whereby the mind is directly related to an object, receives the form of the object intentionally, and is not related to the immanent mental thought of the object (*The True*, 79). The confusion, however, lies in Brentano's espousal of *both* Aristotle and Descartes without recognising the tension between Aristotle's direct realism and Descartes's representationalism.

The rejection of the conception of the intentional object as a kind of 'object', or 'objectivity', possessing a certain kind of being, is connected with Brentano's later metaphysical turn. Though not possible to date with precision, Brentano gradually moved to a position which later became known by Kotarabinski as 'reism', namely that 'nothing is ever made an object of thinking but a real thing'.[87] Only concrete individuals (*Realia*) exist, and the intentional object is now construed as a part or accident of an individual concrete substantial whole, which may be only a temporary accidental unity, for example 'Socrates sitting', 'someone-thinking-x'.[88] Leaving aside this later reism, in most of Brentano's formulations, including the later, a certain terminological indecisiveness prevails: the term 'object' (*Objekt*) can refer either to the content of the act or to the external object. Consider the following passage from a letter to Marty dated 17 March 1905:

> But by an *object* of thought I meant what it is that the thought is about, whether or not there is anything outside the mind corresponding to the thought. It has never been my view that the *immanent* object is identical with the "*object of thought*" (*vorgestelltes Objekt*). What we think about is *the object* or *thing* and not the "object of thought".
>
> (*The True*, 77)[89]

Rather than making a distinction between object and content, Brentano's strategy for handling this ambiguity of the term 'object' was to declare that terms like 'object' gain their meaning from their position in the sentence and have no meaning on their own, what Brentano in his late works calls, borrowing the term from Anton Marty, *'synsemantic'* (*synsemantike, misbedeutende*, PES 332) as opposed to an *'autosemantic'* term whose meaning remains fixed in all contexts.[90] Some terms, that is 'names', possess meanings on their own; other terms gain their meanings solely from their contexts (e.g. prepositions, conjunctions, and so on). Terms like 'the non-being of A' appear to be names but are really *synsemantic* terms.

The later Brentano developed various logical and linguistic techniques for dispelling the embarrassing ontological commitment to these 'irrealia' or 'objectivities' or 'states of affairs'. The supposed intentional objects are to be considered as linguistic fictions, rather like the 'fictions' (*Fiktionen*) employed by mathematicians.[91] Apparent affirmations of non-existent objects are to be rephrased as existential denials. 'Perceiving *a lack of money*' really means 'denying money'. Here, Brentano's assumption that a judgement is not a relation between a subject and a predicate, but is rather an act of assertion or denial of a singular entity, comes to the fore. In his reist period, there is only the subject whose act of judgement produces a new temporary whole – in this case, 'money-denying man'. Husserl will take issue with this non-propositional account of judging in the Fifth Logical Investigation (§§ 20–43).

As we saw above, Brentano also developed a distinction between direct and oblique modes of reference, a distinction meant to sort out the problem of the apparent positing of intentional objects as somehow having real existence. Modes of reference, for the later Brentano, do not have ontological commitment: when I think of *someone who loves flowers*, the person is presented directly *in modo recto* and the flowers are presented indirectly *in modo obliquo* (PES 374). Neither the direct nor the oblique mode here implies an existing object. Similarly, thinking about something in the past or future is thinking under a special mode, a non-positing mode, which is distinct from a present perception. Irreal entities do not exist, rather their mode of being is that they are modifications of the intending mind.

Besides talking of mental objects or contents, Brentano also speaks of the 'intentional relation' (*die intentionale Beziehung*). As both Husserl and Heidegger saw, intentionality cannot be a relation between two extant things, that is, a subject and a physical thing. As Heidegger says, intentionality is not a relation between two things that first arises when the two things are put together, as spatial distance arises when two objects are placed near each other.[92] Nor is the relation that between a mental act and its own immanent content (BPP § 9, p. 61; GA 24, p. 86). Brentano often talks as if this is the relation – that the mental act of hearing is related to a heard sound which itself is caused by something (sound waves) in the outer world.[93] Indeed Heidegger criticises as a Cartesian misinterpretation of intentionality the characterisation of the question as:

How can this ego with its intentional experiences get outside of its
sphere of experience and assume a relation to an extant world?

(BPP § 9, p. 61; GA 24, p. 86)

What is the nature of this supposed intentional relation? What relation can
hold between two things when one of them need not exist at all? Brentano
himself shifted from saying it was a *genuine* relation to something 'relation-
like' (*etwas Relativliches*), quasi-relational. It has the general character of a
relation which makes one of the *relata* an *object*, something over and
against a subject. For Brentano, the intentional relation is a kind of relating
where only one of the terms, the fundament, is real.

Distinction between physical and psychical phenomena

Before proceeding, we need to take time to dispel one confusion surrounding Brentano's account of intentionality, a confusion generated by
Brentano's peculiar use of the term 'physical' to refer to certain real parts of
mental processes. A version of this distinction has entered contemporary
analytic philosophy of mind through Roderick Chisholm, where intentionality has been interpreted as that feature of the mental which shows that the
mental is really distinct from the physical.[94] This is a misunderstanding of
Brentano's distinction. In fact, as we shall see, Husserl, and phenomenology
in general, paid no attention to this distinction, since they correctly
understood it to be merely a consequence of Brentano's more fundamental
distinction between inner and outer perception. *Phenomenology* is interested
in the fact that every mental act intends an object, not that there is a
fundamental distinction between the physical and psychical domain, which
later phenomenologists, including both Husserl and Heidegger, took to be a
remnant of Cartesian metaphysics still operative in Brentano.

To make more precise the domain of psychology, Brentano distinguished
the 'appearances' (*Erscheinungen*) or 'phenomena' (*Phänomene*) of consciousness into two kinds:

All the appearances of our consciousness are divided into two great
classes – the class of physical and the class of mental phenomena.

(PES 77)[95]

In attempting to make his distinction between psychic phenomena and
physical phenomena, Brentano considers a number of possible criteria.
Thus, according to classical criteria invoked by Descartes, Spinoza, and
even by Kant, *extension* and spatial location characterise the physical,
whereas the mental is considered to be unextended (PES 85). Brentano does
not consider this criterion to be satisfactory, as some mental phenomena
appear to have extension, for example I *locate* anger in the lion (PES 87), a

pain *in* my foot, and so on. Similarly, some physical phenomena appear without extension, for example hearing a noise, experiencing a smell. Another criterion which Brentano considers is the claim that mental phenomena have serial as opposed to simultaneous presentation (PES 94). But, Brentano thinks, several mental phenomena can appear simultaneously (PES 95). Other criteria are somewhat closer to the truth, for example the claim that physical phenomena belong to outer as opposed to inner perception, or that mental phenomena are characterised by a special kind of unity, and so on. All these characteristics are more or less unsatisfactory, however, in the light of the chief and only truly reliable characteristic for distinguishing mental from physical phenomena, namely the intentional relation of the object, the object's immanence in the act. No physical phenomena possess intentionality; they do not refer beyond themselves intrinsically.

But what does the expression 'physical phenomena' mean for Brentano? Unfortunately, Brentano's account of the physical is ambiguous. Here he is referring to physical phenomena as the manifest or phenomenal properties or objects – a tone, a colour, and so on – *as these are grasped in the mind*:

> Examples of physical phenomena...are a color, a figure, a landscape which I see, a chord which I hear, warmth, cold, odor which I sense; as well as similar images which appear in the imagination.
> (PES 79–80)

Brentano also speaks of physical objects (which he calls *Realia*) as the posits of empirical science, spatially extended things out there, the objects of science. He wavers between referring to sense qualities (tastes, colours, sensations of touch) and external objects (e.g. his reference to 'a landscape') as *physical* phenomena. When, in the Table of Contents of *Psychology*, Brentano makes the claim that "physical phenomena can only exist phenomenally" (PES 401), he appears to mean that our evidence for the existence of extra-mental or extra-perceptual objects is in the first instance their occurrence in perception. We cannot always infer directly from our perceptual experience to what lies beyond it, although Brentano also dismisses Berkeleyan and Humean phenomenalism. Brentano says that we make no mistake if in general "we deny to physical phenomena any existence other than intentional existence" (PES 94). That is to say, we must first treat of the physical domain that enters into our perception as has a purely perceptual and intentional existence. Brentano withholds judgement about whether colours and sounds have a real, extra-perceptual existence, since, as we have already seen, he holds we do not know the world as it is, rather we know it through our sensory impressions. Physical phenomena then are the phenomenal occurrences of external objects in our acts of perception.

The *acts* of perceiving a colour, or the *act of hearing* a tone, belong to inner perception, and as such have 'actual existence' (*eine wirkliche Existenz*), which means they present themselves with indubitable, self-evident givenness. The contents of these mental acts, the tones I hear, the colours I see, have only 'a phenomenal and intentional existence' (PES 92). They appear only in and through the mental act and have no relationships between themselves; they are 'physical phenomena'. Brentano's distinction between physical and psychical phenomena, then, is directed at distinguishing what is given in outer perception from what is given in inner perception. Since physical phenomena in the strict sense only occur as components, dependent parts, of psychic acts, Brentano can say that, strictly speaking, "all phenomena should be called 'inner' " (DP 137) and again, "everything psychical falls under inner perception" (DP 129). Since any act of outer perception (e.g. seeing) is capable of grasping itself (realising that I am seeing), then, as an act, it belongs to inner perception. Outer perception, then, is just a special case of inner perception.

Elaborating on his account of the intentional object, Brentano distinguishes between the *primary* and *secondary* object of a mental act (PES 127–128). The *primary object* is what is immediately presented in the act, for example the colour I see, the sound I hear; the secondary object is the *act of seeing* or hearing itself (or, as Brentano prefers to phrase it in his later reist period, myself performing the act, SN 41). This act is grasped *en parergo*, 'additionally' (*nebenbei*). Secondary objects only appear because primary objects do, though the primary object is not to be thought of as temporally prior to the additional consciousness. Both objects belong to the one act, there are not two acts (this would open up an infinite regress, PES 127). Perhaps Brentano intended to retain the term 'physical phenomenon' solely for the primary object as immediately given in *sensory* experience, but he complicates the matter by declaring: "the mental as well as the physical can become a primary object" (PES 278). When I attend to the mental life of others, for example 'I know what you are thinking', the act belongs to outer perception not inner. And of course in thinking of a 'triangle', which we might consider to be a mental object *par excellence*, for Brentano, the triangle is a 'physical' phenomenon, though it may seem to have little sensory make-up (aside from spatial extension). Elsewhere, he says that "the presentation which accompanies a mental act and refers to it is part of the object on which it is directed" (PES 128), suggesting that 'object' refers both to the appearing physical phenomenon *and the act itself*. The *physical* phenomenon now belongs to the content of the secondary act and hence is contained within the mental phenomenon. The secondary object contains the primary object as a part. As Twardowski interprets Brentano, the primary object is the physical phenomenon and the secondary object is "the act and content taken together" (COP 16), now both considered as belonging to inner consciousness. The relation between an intentional act and the accompanying consciousness of it became a theme for both

Husserlian phenomenology and for Sartre, who, perhaps, offers the clearest discussion of the relation between the original 'thetic' or 'positional' act and its accompanying 'non-thetic' act in *Being and Nothingness* (BN xxvii–xxx).

Twardowski's modification of Brentanian descriptive psychology

As we have seen, Brentano did not clearly distinguish between the *content* of an act and its *object*; indeed he seemed to reject such a distinction if he appreciated it at all. Of course, Brentano himself had employed the term 'content' in a broad sense for the *matter* as opposed to the *quality* of a judgement. For Brentano: "If one speaks of the content of a presentation, of a judgement or of an emotional relation, one is thinking of what is enclosed in it" (DP 160). However, Brentano had explicitly acknowledged the term 'content' as ambiguous (PES 88), or 'synsemantic' (PES 294), varying with the context (like the term 'object'). In Brentano's distinction of the three fundamental classes of psychical acts, each class has its own particular kind of content. Brentano thus distinguished between presentational content (including, perhaps, perceptual content), judgeable content or judgement-content (*Urteilsinhalt*), and emotional content. But the judgeable content did not necessarily take a subject–predicate form. For Brentano, a judgement did not have a proposition as its content. Brentano thought of the content as what is psychologically available for inspection. He acknowledges a certain depth in mental content, however, when he distinguishes between the *explicit* and *implicit* content. The explicit content is the whole which is presented. When I see a tree, the tree is the explicit content but the leaves are implicitly the content (DP 160). Unfortunately, Brentano never distinguished between the psychologically apprehended elements, and the 'real', logical, or ideal components in the content of the act. He is thus never able to distinguish between what belongs to the thought as a mental episode, and what in the thought supports and conveys the objective, ideal meaning, a recurrent problem in the Cartesian tradition within which he situated himself.[96]

The later Brentano sometimes appeared to be acknowledging the need to insert a *sense* or *meaning* between the mental act and its object, especially when he talked of a 'mode of presentation', but in fact he explicitly repudiated the distinction between content and object, in so far as he can be said to have understood it at all (PES 293). Brentano thought that to acknowledge 'content' must in some sense lead to acknowledging the independent existence, even an ideal state of affairs, which the content names. Thus to judge "there are no centaurs" is to assert or deny something about the "being of centaurs". For Brentano, it is entirely wrong to admit as content of a judgement something like the "being of centaurs". However, some of his students went on to make an explicit distinction between the *content* and the *object* of an intentional act. In 1890, Alois Höfler and Alexius Meinong, in their introductory textbook on logic, pointed out that a distinction must be made between the 'content' (*Inhalt*) which is in the mind and "lies wholly in the subject" ("*liegt ebenso ganz innerhalb des Subjektes*") on the one hand, and the object (*Objekt oder Gegenstand*) on the other.[97] Höfler and Meinong go on to point out that the term 'object' is ambiguous since it can mean the really existent thing or it can mean the presentation or picture in us. Soon after, in 1894, Kasimir Twardowski (1866–1938)[98] in his *Habilitation* thesis, *On the Content and Object of Presentations*, citing Höfler and Meinong, as well as Austro-German logicians such as Bolzano, Kerry, Zimmermann, and others, argued for the need to distinguish between the immanent content (or mental picture) of an act and its extra-mental object (COP 7). For Twardowski, "What is presented *in* a presentation is its content; what is presented through a presentation is its object." (COP 16). The content, according to Twardowski, is purely a vehicle to the object.

Twardowski thought that making a distinction between content and object was crucial to saving Brentano's descriptive psychology. Twardowski began by accepting the principle that all psychic phenomena are either presentations or based on presentations. Moreover, every presentation presents an object; there are no 'objectless presentations'. But Twardowski thinks that the notion of presentation as employed by Brentano is ambiguous. To clarify the concept, Twardowski invoked a grammatical distinction between the *attributive* and *modifying* functions of adjectives. In the phrase 'yellow gold' the adjective 'yellow' is *attributive*; we are attributing a property to the substance, *gold*. But if we speak of 'false gold', the adjective 'false' is *modifying*, since it transforms the object; the term it qualifies is not really gold at all. Similarly, a 'false friend' is a modifying use of the adjective since 'false' here means that the person is not a friend at all (COP 11).

Now, applying a version of this grammatical distinction to psychic acts, we can clarify the term 'presentation'. It can mean the *act of presenting* itself, what *is actually presented* in the act, or the *object* presented, or referred to, by the act. Twardowski drew an analogy with painting a picture, since, for him, having a presentation is much like seeing a picture (COP 12). Consider, for example, the expression a 'painted landscape'. The term 'painted' here can function as *attributive*, adding meaning to the object, in this case a painting, not a sketch or charcoal drawing, but a *painting* of a landscape. The term 'painted' can be *modifying* when applied to the landscape; we are talking of a painting, a 'painted' landscape, and not a *real* landscape. Thirdly, a painting of a landscape *depicts* the landscape, so here, to say that this landscape was 'painted' by X, is to determine the landscape and not to modify it, since the real landscape is not changed by being painted. With these careful distinctions in mind, Twardowski could articulate clearly the ways in which the content and the object are presented. Thus he stressed, as did Husserl, that we must distinguish the properties of the *content* from the properties of the *object*. When we think of a *red square*, the presentation itself (its content) in the mind is neither red nor square, but the object intended is intended as having both those properties. The content is a *real* part of the act and really exists. Furthermore, as such, it possesses properties which are not in contradiction with one another. Whereas Brentano held a model of the intentional relation which may be illustrated as follows:

Brentano

psychic act – intentionally relates to – immanent objectivity

(may or may not be real thing)

Twardowski proposed an amended version which may be illustrated as:

Twardowski

psychic act – *content* – object – (real thing)

act relates *through* content to object

For Twardowski, the 'object' is not necessarily an actual, existent, external thing. He separates the intentional 'objectivity' (*Gegenständlichkeit*) which every intentional act possesses from the existence of the object in reality (COP 35). Thus, for Twardowski as for Meinong, a 'square circle' can be the genuine object of a representation; that is, it possesses a genuine 'meaning' (*Sinn*) which can be given in a presentation, even though the meaning includes contradictory properties. The object posited may have contradictory properties and hence can never exist, but it is nonetheless a genuine object of an act of presentation. It will simply be the case that true judgements will deny it existence. By these moves, Twardowski believes he has dissipated the ontological problem of the status of the intentional objectivities. Unfortunately, he has not specifically addressed the problem of the nature of the object intended.

Husserl had already begun to refine the Brentanism of his *Philosophy of Arithmetic* (1891) through his reading of German logicians, Ernst Schröder, Bernard Bolzano, Hermann Lotze, etc., as well as through his correspondence with Gottlob Frege.[99] But his diagnosis of the importance of the distinction between concept and object was confirmed by reading Twardowski's treatise, which came into his hands in 1894. Indeed, Husserl deals with this topic in his unpublished review of Twardowski's book (*c.* 1896), as well as in drafts of an unpublished 1894/1896 article on "Intentional Objects". There is also his extended discussion of 'content', including criticisms of Twardowski, in the *Investigations* themselves (e.g. LI I, § 13, p. 290n.).[100] Husserl wished to review Twardowski's work as an important development of Brentano's ideas in Natorp's journal. However, as Paul Natorp had already reviewed it, he suggested that Husserl rewrite his piece as a critical notice.[101] For some reason, Husserl's draft review remained unpublished. Husserl was generally impressed by Twardowski's distinctions but thought the whole account still too *immanentist* in its understanding of the notion of content. Twardowski had tried to solve the problem of *sameness of reference* by distinguishing two aspects of the content, both immanent in the act, one of which pointed to the transcendent object and the other of which Husserl calls the 'presenting' or 'representing content' (*der gegenwärtige Inhalt*). Thus, I may think of a *tree* and represent a *fir* tree, while another person may think the same thought but represent an *oak*. Husserl wants to contend that Twardowski's account cannot really explain the *sameness* or *identity* of meaning which our different acts share: we are both thinking of a *tree*, each through our own 'subjective presentation' (Bolzano) or 'phantasm' as Husserl calls it. Husserl agrees with Twardowski that the act has what Husserl calls a '*real psychological content*'. There is a real psychic act which has real ('*reell*' in Husserl's early vocabulary) temporal parts.[102] For Husserl, the real psychic act is an event in the natural world, subject to psycho-physical laws. Its content is also a genuine, though dependent, part of the act; that is, it cannot survive on its own apart from the act, it swims in the act, as it were. The act's 'parts' and 'moments' can be identified and studied by psychology, though the content is not immediately apprehended, as Twardowski thought, in the act itself, but, for Husserl, is reached only by special reflection on the act.

The crucial thing, for Husserl, is that meanings are *identities* which can be accessed again and again by the same speaker, or shared between speakers. As such, these non-individuated, transtemporal identities are *idealities*, for Husserl. Furthermore, the analysis of the real constituent parts of a psychic process will not reveal the structure the act has, its specific 'act quality', the way it relates to its content or given, the manner it endows meaning and expects fulfilment. These structures are of a different kind. They reach to and instantiate *idealities*. The *ideal, logical* content, then, is what is expressed by, or *tokened* in, the psychological content, and it is the *ideal* content which guarantees sameness of reference, reiteration of the same meaning over a number of acts. Husserl makes a distinction between two roles of the content (or two features of the content – at this stage of Husserl's development, 1896, his vocabulary is not fully refined). Whereas Twardowski speaks of the content moving in two directions, one giving meaning and the other giving the object, for Husserl, this threatens the identity of the object intended (see LI I, § 13, p. 290n.).

In his review of Twardowski, Husserl promises further distinctions in a future study, which turned out to be the *Logical Investigations* (1900–1901). By the time of *Ideas* I (1913) § 129, Husserl, though still praising Twardowski, now regards the content/object distinction as having become a tired slogan which fails to elucidate, since it is not based on a proper phenomenological elucidation of the act (such as Husserl will provide with his concepts of *noesis* and *noema*). In this review, Edmund Husserl distinguishes the 'psychological' – or what he calls the 'real' – content (*Gehalt*) from the 'ideal content' (*Inhalt* or *ideales Gehalt*) or 'meaning content' (*Bedeutungsinhalt*). On this account, the *psychological* content is individual, a temporally delimited slice of the living stream of consciousness, but the meaning content is not 'real' in that sense at all. Meanings are shared, accessible by many. The meaning cannot be a real component of the act. As the *Logical Investigations* (1900–1901) will make clear, Husserl considers meanings as the *ideal* contents of acts, alternatively called *intentional* contents (LI V, § 11). Moreover, for Husserl, as for Twardowski, ordinarily our psychic acts go directly to the object, are about the object, not the content. It takes a special act of reflection to make the 'content' of an act into its object. While commentators in the main have sided with Husserl in his criticism of Twardowski as compromising the ideality and identity of the meaning content, it is not entirely clear if this does full justice to Twardowski's contribution. Personal tensions between the two men may have contributed. It has even been claimed, in a recent study by Jens Cavallin, that Twardowski was familiar with Frege's distinction between sense and reference and may not have been as immanentist as Husserl alleges.[103]

Brentano and Husserl

Husserl's phenomenology takes its beginnings from a certain project of describing mental acts and their parts initiated by Brentano, his *descriptive psychology*. Brentano's account of mental acts emphasised an intentional structure whereby acts are in intentional relations to their objects. The earlier Brentano's efforts, to specify the nature of the intentional relation and intentional object, provoked much discussion among his students. Twardowski, Höfler, and Meinong all saw the need to distinguish between the psychological content of the mental act as actual mental process and some kind of ideal meaning-content which was graspable by different acts. In trying to specify the nature of these ideal meanings Twardowski and Husserl turned to the logic of Bolzano and the tradition of Lotze and others. In so doing, Husserl was led to a critique of psychologism, and this critique led to the founding of phenomenology as a science separate from both psychology and logic. We must now turn to Husserl as the founder of phenomenology proper.

2

EDMUND HUSSERL
Founder of phenomenology

Introduction: an overview of Husserl and his philosophy

Though Brentano anticipates many of the themes of phenomenology, it is with Edmund Husserl that phenomenology, conceived of as a *science* of the essential structures of pure consciousness with its own distinctive *method*, begins. Husserl first announced his allegiance to phenomenology in the *Logical Investigations* (1900–1901). While writing the last two Investigations in particular he came to see the need for a more general 'phenomenological' approach to consciousness. Phenomenology, as Husserl conceived it, would be theory of science, a 'science of science' (*Wissenschaftslehre*), a rigorous clarification of what essentially belongs to systematic knowledge as such. Later, in *Ideas* I and elsewhere, Husserl talked of the need for a wide-sweeping 'critique of reason',[1] and 'a complete reform of philosophical knowledge'.[2] Phenomenology gradually grew to be a project of 'ultimate grounding' (*Letztbegründung*) which finally, in Husserl's vision, came to encompass the whole of philosophy.

Husserl's central problem: the mystery of subjectivity

In common with many other researchers working at the end of the nineteenth century, for example William James and Henri Bergson, Husserl was fascinated both by the ever-changing stream, the 'perpetual Heraclitean flux', of conscious experience (*Bewußtseinsstrom, der Erlebnisstrom, Ideas* I § 34), and by its apparent seamless unity.[3] Furthermore, consciousness is the basis of all experience and its mode of appearing seemed to be inextricably linked to the nature of time itself. Indeed, no experience would be possible *without* time consciousness; it enters into every experience. Somehow, out of this living flux of consciousness come the 'achievements' (*Leistungen*) of ideal, timeless meanings, the graspings of transcendent objects and truths. For Husserl, objectivity was always a particular 'achievement of consciousness' (*Bewußtseinsleistung*) and he was fascinated by the miracle of this process. Furthermore, consciousness was always particularised as someone's consciousness and so the process of investigating this 'originary sphere'

(*Originärsphär*) of meaning-origination must begin with oneself, with the rigorous self-examination which Husserl characterised as the standpoint of "transcendental solipsism" in the *Cartesian Meditations* (CM § 13, 30; Hua I 69). Husserl also recognised, however, a point that is often forgotten in the consideration of his philosophy, that this methodological solipsism could not be the whole of philosophy, but merely its beginning.

From the beginnings, Husserl recognised the intersubjective communal grounding of the knowing activity and focused more on the ethical dimensions of this intersubjectivity, how the 'I' stands in the 'we'. From early on, and most emphatically from about 1912, he came to see objectivity as the achievement of intersubjective confirmation and acceptance. His phenomenology also began to concentrate more and more on the assumed context of human experience, and he pioneered the description of the 'environment' (*Umwelt*) and the conception of a human world that received expression in his notion of *Lebenswelt* or 'life-world'. Besides this 'constitutive' phenomenology, and the description of phenomenology as a transcendental science in Kantian idealist terms, Husserl carried out what he termed 'genetic' and 'generative' phenomenological investigations, charting the historical evolution of cultural concepts in an almost Hegelian manner. Both forms of phenomenology are represented in his 1936 work, *The Crisis of European Sciences and Transcendental Phenomenology*.[4]

Underneath the diversity of themes and approaches adopted by Husserl there lies a deep unity of project, the project of 'first philosophy': the relation between being (*das Seiendes*) and reason (*Vernunft*). Thus in the *Crisis*, he asks: "Can reason and that-which-is be separated, where reason, as knowing, determines what is?" (*Crisis* § 5, p. 11; Hua VI 9). The relation between being and thinking leads Husserl to a thorough exploration of the mystery of subjectivity and the question of the *constitution of objectivity*; that is, how does consciousness attain to objective knowledge? Indeed, this fundamental guiding question took many shapes throughout his life.[5] As Eugen Fink (1905–1975), Husserl's loyal assistant from his later Freiburg years, put it, Husserl's concern was not so much with the problem of objectivity as with the constitution of the world (*Briefwechsel* IV 292), leading Husserl to endorse the transcendental, critical turn taken in modern philosophy by Descartes, Hume, and Kant. Philosophy which is defined as the "knowledge of what is" must pursue its goal by methodological reflection on how our knowledge is constituted. Indeed, so great was Husserl's interest in the conditions of knowledge that he has been accused of having no interest at all in the factual existent world.

Husserl's central insight was that consciousness was the condition of all experience, indeed it constituted the world, but in such a way that the role of consciousness itself is obscured and not easy to isolate and describe. Husserl therefore constantly sought to explain how to overcome *prejudices* which stood in the way of the recognition of the domain of pure consciousness, leading to a new beginning in philosophy. To this end, over his career, he wrote many introductions to phenomenology, each of which sought to articulate the essential insights of phenomenology from different perspectives.[6] These programmatic statements emphasise the originality and radicality of the phenomenological method, often interpreted in terms of the Cartesian programme of renewal.

Husserl as perpetual beginner

Husserl, in a sense, bridges two different worlds. As a university professor, he was a grave, imposing figure, fully at home in the austere world of German academia at the turn of the century.[7] He exemplified the nineteenth-century bourgeois world with its high seriousness, solid confidence in science, rationality, and human progress through knowledge.[8] But he was also acutely aware of the threat of cultural fragmentation and relativism, brought about by deep uncertainties about the nature and project of reason in the twentieth century. Husserl saw himself as a visionary pioneer, approaching his themes with an almost religious fervour, even comparing himself to a Moses leading his people to the promised land.[9] Indeed, he believed his own decision to opt for a life of philosophy was propelled by a deep religious conviction. He perceived himself as a ground-breaking explorer in the domain of the a priori science of pure consciousness and transcendental subjectivity.

A self-styled perpetual 'beginner' in philosophy, Husserl was a radical, self-critical thinker, constantly struggling to clarify his insights and to articulate the method by which he arrived at them and which he thought justified them. He frequently changed his mind, criticising inadequacies in his own earlier formulations, and thus leading his work in different and new directions, often returning to discuss earlier problems from a new angle. This constant reworking of his philosophical writings makes it very difficult to portray his intellectual and philosophical development in linear fashion, and the sequence of his publications is not in itself a guide to his thought directions. Moreover, Husserl was often beset with a sense of failure and frustration. Indeed he thought that someone who never experienced contradictions and paradoxes was no philosopher (*Briefwechsel* VI 239). From his diaries and letters we know that he suffered long periods of philosophical despair and depression (which he described as "the evil demon of nervousness") leading to illness,[10] interspersed with short periods of great creativity and furious composition. During these bouts of *Arbeitsfieber*, he worked "as in a trance" (*wie in Tranze, Briefwechsel* IV 413; IV 210), composing books in a *furor philosophicus* (*Briefwechsel* III 47), "a paroxysm of work" (IV 269). Thus *Ideas* I (1913) was written hurriedly in a period of about three months, and *Formal and Transcendental Logic* (1929) was composed in a similar rush. Such work was intellectually salutary, and he credited writing *Logical Investigations* with ridding him of the depression of his Halle years. But he also abandoned works shortly before they would have gone to the printer for publication and hence his published books represent only a small proportion of his actual researches. Much of his surviving research papers consists of sheets where he would write out a problem until he came to an insight which he would then develop. There is therefore a great deal of overlap and repetition in the surviving papers. Most of his research work remained unpublished at the time of his death, and over 45,000 pages of hand-written manuscripts, composed in an obsolete form of German shorthand, the Gabelsberger system (further modified by Husserl himself to include philosophical terms), are now preserved in the Husserl Archives established in the Catholic University of Leuven, Belgium, in 1939.[11] The full extent of Husserl's research programme is only now being uncovered as researchers carefully transcribe and edit Husserl's *Nachlass* for publication in the complete edition, *Husserliana*, which now runs to over thirty volumes, with a further ten volumes of correspondence. Husserl had begun the process of classifying his work before he died, and his obsessive cataloguing efforts mean that we possess countless folders of his lectures and personal notes, as well as his library, including extensive marginal comments on books such as Heidegger's *Being and Time* (1927).[12]

Although Husserl was capable of writing clearly and incisively, his published works tend to be abstract, technical discussions, stylistically dense and tortuous, and, notoriously, given the project of *descriptive* phenomenology, lacking in concrete examples. Concentration on these published statements of *method* tends to obscure the fact that Husserl and his devoted assistants carried out a vast range of concrete phenomenological investigations – *descriptions* of different areas of conscious experience, such as perception, imagination, spatial and temporal awareness (e.g. his 1907 so-called '*Dingvorlesung*' – lectures on *Thing and Space*), and later investigations of the body and the life-world.[13] Few of Husserl's own phenomenological investigations were published in his lifetime, the exception being *On the Phenomenology of the Consciousness of Internal Time*, a series of lectures given over many years (1893–1917), originally transcribed and edited by his assistant, Edith Stein, and eventually brought to press in 1928 by Martin Heidegger, though in an unsatisfactory, truncated form which left Husserl himself dissatisfied.[14]

Husserl is a paradoxical figure. He thought of phenomenology as a collaborative enterprise, a *symphilosophein* (philosophising together), yet he normally worked entirely on his own, writing his daily 'meditations', which he only interrupted when he was being pressed to publish a book. Indeed, Husserl often spoke of carrying out his enquiries as a *solus ipse*, as a lone researcher (*Briefwechsel* V 137). Husserl even characterised the philosophical process as curiously anonymous and even remarked that, if he had the choice, he would publish his research anonymously (*Briefwechsel* III 26), reacting against the kind of popular adulation received by Scheler and Bergson. He promoted the conception of the philosopher as a kind of faceless functionary or civil servant, serving humanity, "pure functionaries of the absolute" (*als reiner Functionär des Absoluten, Briefwechsel* III 218; see also *Crisis* § 7, p. 17; Hua VI 15). He rarely attended philosophical conferences and communicated best in writing; indeed he seemed able to think only by writing things out.[15]

Husserl's lectures were careful and methodical, but often quite abstruse, leading his students through a maze of subtle distinctions. These students, including both Helmut Plessner and Emmanuel Levinas, described him as a "monologist" *par excellence*.[16] Another student, Johannes Daubert (1877–1947), reported that Husserl never appeared to understand anyone else; and Gadamer recalls that a friend of his came away from Husserl's lectures with the impression that Husserl's small hand gestures were reminiscent of a "watchmaker gone mad".[17] From Brentano, Husserl retained the view that identifying a new distinction was to see something others had not observed. Thus, as one of Husserl's North American students from the early Göttingen days, William Ernest Hocking, recalled: "his teaching was a succession of important and difficult distinctions, conveyed with intense care and scruple".[18] In the *Cartesian Meditations*, for example, Husserl refers to "seemingly trivial nuances" (CM § 14, 32; Hua I 71) which can make the difference between right and wrong paths in philosophy. On the other hand, Husserl, despite his careful conceptual distinctions, was often quite careless in linguistic expression and did not always observe the distinctions he had made. In his Göttingen days, students recalled that it was Adolf Reinach (1883–1917) who was the real star teacher, developing phenomenology in a much clearer and more succinct manner than Husserl. Later, in Freiburg, Gadamer had a negative impression of Husserl's seminars: they were not without a certain elegance, but "what he presented sounded in all ways like refinements of already known analyses" (*Phil. App.* p. 35).

Husserl was initially not well trained in philosophy; indeed he continued to see himself as something of an 'autodidact' in this area (*Briefwechsel* VI 460). His main contact with the philosophical tradition was through Brentano. Thus he relied more on the etymological meanings of philosophical terms than their meanings as rooted in the historical tradition with which he was, initially at least, relatively unfamiliar. In his earlier years he mostly read material in mathematics and logic though he came to admire Hume and Kant. His reviews of logic, in the period from 1890 to 1905, show him to be familiar with contemporary developments, including the work of Frege and Russell. He owned all Frege's early works and also Russell's *Principles of Mathematics* (1903). Indeed, over the years, Husserl kept in touch with Russell's developing views through his correspondence with a former student, Winthrop Bell. Husserl thought Russell was becoming too naturalistic and sceptical about the possibility of a rigorously scientific value theory and morality (*Briefwechsel* I 115). In turn, Russell wrote to Husserl in 1920 recalling that he had taken the *Logical Investigations* to prison with him, with the intention of reviewing it for *Mind*, but the review never appeared. Russell, incidentally, also possessed a copy of Husserl's *Philosophy of Arithmetic*.[19]

Since his qualities as a lecturer and as a literary stylist were mediocre, he must have possessed some personal charisma to be able to attract such bright minds. Husserl had an extraordinarily long career as a teacher and researcher during which he came into contact with several generations of students, including some of the brightest minds of his time. On a personal level, Husserl was quite approachable, though lacking in humour, in contrast to the vibrancy of his teacher, Brentano. Dispensing with formality, he regularly invited students to his house for evenings of discussion, and, in his Freiburg years, he took daily walks on the Lorettoberg with his students and held Saturday morning philosophy sessions at his home. The originality and bold sweep of the *Logical Investigations* inspired small groups of researchers at Göttingen and Munich to apply his realistic phenomenology to philosophical problems, and later his transcendental phenomenology attracted support in Freiburg, though it alienated students from the Göttingen days such as Roman Ingarden (1893–1970) and Hedwig Conrad-Martius (1888–1966), who had been attracted by the realism of the *Logical Investigations*. Especially in his later Freiburg years, many great philosophers visited Husserl, including thinkers as diverse as Rudolf Carnap (1891–1970), Gilbert Ryle, William Kneale, Herbert Marcuse (1898–1979), Charles Hartshorne (who attended Husserl's seminars from 1924 to 1926), Ernst Cassirer, and, in November 1934, Ortega Y Gasset.[20] Others such as Ludwig Binswanger, Max Scheler (1874–1928), Alfred Schütz (1899–1959), and Roman Ingarden developed phenomenology in the direction of psychiatry, social philosophy, and aesthetics.

The stages of Husserl's development

Given Husserl's writing habits, there is no simple story of progress, nor is there evidence of a major reversal or turning. What we have is a huge body of original researches, approaching the same topic over and over again from a variety of perspectives. These manuscripts were composed at different times, taken up, and dropped at intervals, and Husserl was also, unfortunately, rather lax about dating his writings. Nevertheless, some attempt at periodisation of his life's work is useful. Husserl's assistant, Eugen Fink, has offered a convenient way of approaching Husserl's development, proposing three stages: the first he labels *psychologism* (1887–1901), though, more accurately, it represents Husserl's *struggles* with psychologism; the second Fink labels *descriptive phenomenology* (1901–1913); and the third phase, *transcendental phenomenology* (1913–1938).[21] These three stages roughly correspond to Husserl's stays at Halle, Göttingen, and Freiburg. In Halle, Husserl wrote the *Philosophy of Arithmetic* (1891) and some essays on logic. In the Göttingen period his major publications were the essay *Philosophy as a Rigorous Science* (1910–1911) and *Ideas* I (1913); while in his Freiburg period he produced the *On the Phenomenology of the Consciousness of Internal Time* (1928), *Formal and Transcendental Logic* (1929), the *Cartesian Meditations* in their French version (1931), and finally Part One of *The Crisis of European Sciences* (1936). *Experience and Judgement* (1938), written in collaboration with Ludwig Landgrebe, was in press when Husserl died. It is helpful to divide the Freiburg period (1916–1938) into two phases separated by his retirement from teaching in 1928. Husserl's middle period from 1905 to 1928 is marked by his development of the concept of *reduction* and his elaboration of a purely a priori analysis of transcendental subjectivity. This period, however, also contains the research for his later discussions of intersubjectivity and the life-world prominent in his last years.

In Husserl's earliest researches he sought the foundations of mathematics and logic employing elements taken from Brentano's method of descriptive psychology, especially as elaborated by Carl Stumpf, his *Habilitation* director. Thus, in the First Edition of the *Logical Investigations* (1900–1901), the major published text of the Halle years, Husserl characterised his approach as '*descriptive psychology*' or '*descriptive phenomenology*'. Around 1904–1905, however, he began more self-consciously to characterise his methodology in terms of a Cartesian or Kantian transcendental approach, as is evident in the recently published Göttingen lectures from 1905 to 1907. A major reason for the new direction in his thinking was that the analyses of conscious acts in the *Logical Investigations* were relatively static and did not take into account their temporal nature and their underlying foundation in the unity of an individual consciousness. Husserl felt obliged to rethink the nature of the pure ego which he had excised from the *Logical Investigations*, where he had pursued a more Humean approach to the self, following Brentano. Husserl was, at this stage, beginning to see phenomenology not just as a new method for clarifying logic and epistemology, but as a whole new approach to the sciences as such. After 1907 Husserl's phenomenology became allied to transcendental idealism.

After his retirement in 1928, partly in response to what he regarded as the mistaken direction of Heidegger's phenomenology of concrete, historical human existence in *Being and Time*, Husserl began to offer his own version of the themes of historicity and the finitude of human understanding and began to emphasise the manner in which human consciousness is always caught within the context of the 'life-world' (*Lebenswelt*). While this third phase is termed 'transcendental' by Fink, we ought, however, to recognise that Husserl's interest in Kant dates from early in his Göttingen years, and, furthermore, that his research on the human life-world began early in his Freiburg years. Indeed Husserl's researches into transcendental phenomenology, drawing on Kant and Descartes, developed side by side with his interest in intersubjectivity and the embodied subject. For Husserl, these were complementary modes of access to the one domain of transcendental subjectivity and intersubjectivity. Husserl's development, then, is best seen as an ongoing clarification of the same set of initial problems, probed more and more deeply from different angles. In particular, it is necessary to reject the widespread view that Husserl moved from a vital, creative period of descriptive psychology and exact philosophical discrimination to adopt a rather idiosyncratic and somewhat outlandish transcendental idealism in his later work.

Husserl: life and writings (1859–1938)

Edmund Husserl was born on 8 April 1859, the same year as Henri Bergson and John Dewey, in Prossnitz, Moravia, then part of the Austrian Empire, now Prostejov not far from Brno in the Czech Republic.[22] Husserl's family were assimilated Jews who had lived for centuries in the area. His father, Adolf Abraham, was a draper who apparently reared the family in an atmosphere indifferent to matters of religion. Seemingly, they did not mix with the local Jewish population and there is even some evidence that the father hid the fact of their Jewishness from the children for some years. Edmund first attended the local school, and then at the age of 9 was enrolled in the *Realgymnasium* in Vienna (1868/1869). In 1869 he transferred to the *Staatsgymnasium* in Olmütz (Czech: Olomouc), completing the Austrian *Matura*, or school-leaving certificate, there in June 1876. According to his wife Malvine's later reminiscences, he was a somewhat disinterested schoolboy, who did not achieve good grades and was given to falling asleep in class, but who, nevertheless, displayed an aptitude for mathematics.[23] Classmates were reportedly surprised when he announced an interest in studying astronomy at university. It appears, however, that Husserl had an early preoccupation with detail and exactitude. Emmanuel Levinas recounted a tale that Husserl had told him: as a schoolboy the young Husserl had been given a penknife as a present, which in his opinion was not sharp enough, so he pared and pared it away, until in the end no blade at all was left (*Chronik*, p. 2). Seemingly, the adult Husserl felt this episode symbolised his philosophical endeavours. In the autumn of 1876 he enrolled in the University of Leipzig, taking three semesters of astronomy, and attending lectures in mathematics and physics, including philosophy lectures given by the elderly Wilhelm Wundt from whom he reputedly gained little. Here he befriended a philosophy student, Thomas Masaryk (1850–1937), the self-educated son of a blacksmith, and an admirer of Brentano. Masaryk interested Husserl in modern philosophy, including Descartes and Leibniz, but especially in British empiricism, which Masaryk, following his mentor Brentano, considered an antidote to the otherworldliness of German speculative idealism.[24] Husserl became particularly interested in Berkeley whose system he often defended in colloquy against other students.[25]

Husserl's teachers: Weierstrass and Brentano

At the beginning of the summer semester of 1878 Husserl moved to Berlin where he took six semesters of mathematics and philosophy, attending the lectures of the great mathematicians Karl Weierstrass (1815–1897) and Leopold Kronecker (1823–1891). Weierstrass was particularly influential, and, throughout his life, Husserl would cite Weierstrass and Brentano, presumably on account of their personalities and ways of doing research, as his great formative influences. Weierstrass interested Husserl in the project of arithmetising analysis and introduced him to Bolzano's work on numbers. Later Husserl would write that he hoped to do for philosophy what Weierstrass had done for arithmetic – that is, set it on a single foundation. During his Berlin stay Husserl became somewhat more interested in philosophy, attending the lectures of Friedrich Paulsen (1846–1908), an exponent of Kantian idealism, but he did not progress very far in the subject at this time.

Husserl thought that possession of an Austrian degree might improve his chances of gaining employment,[26] so he transferred from Berlin to the University of Vienna at the beginning of the summer semester of 1881, attending lectures in mathematics. He was awarded his doctorate in October 1882 for a dissertation supervised by Leo Königsberger (1837–1921), a disciple of Weierstrass, entitled "Contributions to the Theory of the Calculus of Variations" (*Beiträge zur Theorie der Variationsrechnung*), a work of pure mathematics – on differential calculus. Here he renewed contact with Thomas Masaryk, now *Privatdozent* in Vienna. It was Masaryk who advised Husserl to attend Brentano's lectures, and interestingly, also encouraged Husserl to study the New Testament. Much later, in 1919, Husserl wrote to his student Arnold Metzger about his early years:

> I still lived in an almost exclusive dedication to my theoretical work – even though the decisive influences, which drove me from mathematics to philosophy as my vocation, may lie in overpowering religious experiences and complete transformations. Indeed the powerful effect of the New Testament on a 23-year old gave rise to an impetus to discover the way to God and to a true life through a rigorous philosophical inquiry.[27]

In later recollections of his youth, Husserl claimed to have been drawn to philosophy by his interest in religious questions of a non-dogmatic kind, such as the question of the existence of God. On 26 April 1886, under the influence of Masaryk, Husserl was baptised in the Lutheran Christian Church in Vienna (*Chronik*, p. 15) and, many years later, in 1919, he characterised himself to Rudolf Otto as a "free Christian", an undogmatic Christian (*Briefwechsel* VII 205–208). Indeed, Husserl continued to read the New Testament in later years, though in general he characterised his philosophical approach as "atheological" (*Briefwechsel* VII 237).[28]

In the summer of 1883 Husserl moved back to Berlin as Weierstrass's assistant, helping him to write his lectures, but, by then, he had little enthusiasm for the work and, when Weierstrass became ill, Husserl decided to undergo military service (as a "Freiwilliger" or volunteer) in Olmütz and Vienna in 1883–1884, presumably to gain a period of reflection on his future career (*Chronik*, p. 11). While in the military, his father died on 24 April 1884. On completion of his military service, he remained in Vienna to attend Franz Brentano's lectures for two years, from 1884 to 1886. In the summer of 1886 Husserl accompanied Brentano on his holidays near St Gilgen in the Wolfgangsee for a period of three months (during which time Brentano's wife completed a portrait of Husserl, now lost). Martin Heidegger later wrote of Husserl's formation:

> Husserl himself was originally a mathematician. He was a student of Weierstrass and wrote a mathematical dissertation for his degree. What he heard of philosophy did not go beyond what any student picked up in lecture courses...It was only after he graduated that Husserl attended the courses of the man who was then much discussed. Brentano's passion for questioning and reflection impressed Husserl so strongly that he remained with Brentano for two years from 1884–6.[29]

With Brentano he read the British empiricists, especially David Hume (attending Brentano's seminar on Hume's *Inquiry*) and John Stuart Mill, as well as the work of the physicist and philosopher of science, Ernst Mach. Husserl shared Brentano's admiration for Hume, whom he always saw as a genuine transcendental philosopher and a practitioner of phenomenology, who questioned the naive manner we attribute causality to the world without reflecting on how it is constituted by us. Husserl also acquired from Brentano and Masaryk a dislike of bombastic German romanticism and a distaste for the 'unscientific' philosophy of Hegel, which, he thought, denied the Principle of Non Contradiction.[30] As he later admitted, it took some considerable time before he came to appreciate the German idealist contribution as essentially a continuation of Descartes's transcendental subjectivity, and an immature version of the ideal of philosophy as rigorous science (HSW 344–5; Hua XXV 309).

According to Husserl, "Brentano's pre-eminent and admirable strength was in logical theory" (HSW 345; Hua XXV 309). As we saw in the last chapter, Husserl was particularly drawn to Brentano's project for a reform of Aristotelian logic, proposed in Brentano's 1884–1885 lecture course "Elementary Logic and its Necessary Reform". Indeed, Husserl saw his own *Logical Investigations* as an attempt to do justice to the extraordinary genius of Brentano.[31] Through Weierstrass, Husserl had already encountered Bernard Bolzano's work on infinite sets, the *Paradoxes of the Infinite*, but Brentano introduced him to Bolzano's *Wissenschaftslehre*.[32] Bolzano (1781–1848) was in relative obscurity at the time owing to his suspect religious heterodoxy and radical political liberalism.[33] Indeed, Husserl was partly responsible for his revival, adopting Bolzano's notions of a 'theory of science' and 'pure logic', developed in the *Logical Investigations* (see *Prolegomena* § 61 and *Briefwechsel* I 39). Husserl never abandoned the Bolzanian inspired vision of mature science as a coherent intermeshing system of theoretical truths, 'truths-in-themselves' (*Wahrheiten an sich*) and 'propositions-in-themselves' (*Sätze an sich*). Brentano, on the other hand, wrote to Husserl that he had no time for the notion of truths in themselves.

Husserl attended Brentano's lectures on 'practical philosophy', which struck him as dogmatic, but he was very taken with Brentano's dialectical style, his Socratic method of discussion, and his prophetic sense of mission. As Husserl himself later recalled, in his posthumous tribute to his former teacher in 1919, Brentano "expressed the consciousness of a great mission in each trait...in his entire way of behaving".[34] Husserl never ceased to worship him as a teacher but, as he put it in his "Recollections", he was not destined to remain a member of the 'Brentano school'. Nevertheless, Husserl was quickly recognised as a "new star" in Brentano's circle.[35]

Even after his stay in Vienna, Husserl diligently continued to collect Brentano's lecture notes, including the transcripts of Brentano's lectures on descriptive psychology (1887–1891), his investigation of the senses, as well as his studies of fantasy and memory. In subsequent years, Husserl would occasionally visit with Brentano and continued to send him his publications and to correspond with him, often on technical issues in mathematics and geometry, until Brentano's death in 1917.[36] Brentano himself was not enamoured with the direction Husserl's researches took. He did not agree with Husserl's attempts in the *Prolegomena* to distinguish pure logic as a theoretical discipline from logic as an art of reasoning, a *Kunstlehre*, since, for Brentano, logic had been since Aristotle a technique for thinking correctly. Brentano, furthermore, harboured suspicions that Husserl linked him with logical psychologism (e.g. his letter to Husserl of 17 November 1911), though Husserl (possibly out of respect for his revered teacher) denied any such imputation. It took Husserl many years to extract himself from under the shadow of Brentano. In a late letter to Marvin Farber, he concedes that:

> Even though I began in my youth as an enthusiastic admirer of
> Brentano, I must admit that I deluded myself, for too long, and in a
> way hard to understand now, into believing that I was a co-worker
> on his philosophy, especially, his psychology. But in truth, my way
> of thinking was a totally different one from that of Brentano, al-
> ready in my first work, namely the *Habilitation* work of 1887.[37]

When Brentano was forced to resign his professorship in Vienna, he was
reduced to the status of *Privatdozent*, which meant that he no longer had
the legal right to supervise *Habilitation* theses. He therefore referred Husserl
to a former student of his, Carl Stumpf (1848–1936), who was developing
descriptive psychology.[38] Stumpf was pursuing careful studies of sense
perception, especially hearing tones, as well as studying the psychological
origin of the sense of space.

With Stumpf in Halle (1886–1901)

Husserl moved to Halle in 1886 with Stumpf supervising his *Habilitationsschrift*. He attended Stumpf's lectures on psychology and, fourteen
years later, dedicated his *Logical Investigations* to him. In fact, his
relationship with Stumpf remained cordial even after his thought took a
transcendental turn which Stumpf criticised. Stumpf was critical of
Husserl's idealism in *Ideas* I, while recognising his project for seeking the
grounding notions of science. Stumpf was sympathetic to the project of
studying the essences of consciousness but regarded the Husserlian idea of
'pure' phenomenology as a contradiction in terms, phenomenology without
phenomena. Stumpf, a close friend of, and correspondent with, William
James, recommended James' *Principles of Psychology* to Husserl in 1894. As
Husserl admitted, James played a formative role in his own thinking on the
nature of consciousness as a living seamless flux, with contents which are in
central focus surrounded by a 'halo' of less focused contents. Unfortunately, James was less enthusiastic about Husserl, being responsible for a
proposed project to translate the *Logical Investigations* into English being
rejected by the publishers in 1910.[39]

During his two-year sojourn with Brentano, from 1884 to 1886, Husserl
had become increasingly interested in the relations between mathematics
and formal logic, and was conscious of the need for a clarification of the
fundamental concepts of mathematics. His 1887 *Habilitation* thesis, *On the
Concept of Number, Psychological Analyses*, directly addressed this topic.
This thesis was printed, but not publicly distributed, in 1887.[40] The
mathematician Georg Cantor, a former student of Weierstrass, sat on
Husserl's examination committee. By 'psychological analyses' Husserl
means descriptive psychology and is proposing a psychological clarification
of arithmetic, through the analysis of how we form the concept of number.

Husserl follows Weierstrass in conceiving of the cardinal number as the central concept of mathematics and the basis of arithmetic. Husserl traces the formation of the concept of number to a set of psychic acts of distinguishing multiplicities and the relations which pertain among the constituents of these multiplicities.

On completion of his *Habilitation* Husserl married Malvine Steinschneider, the daughter of a prominent Hebraist, on 6 August 1887. She herself had been baptised a Christian a little earlier, on 8 July 1887. Together they had three children: a daughter, Elizabeth (Elli), born in 1892, followed by two sons, Gerhart born in 1893, and Wolfgang, born in 1895. In the autumn of 1887 Husserl was appointed to the Philosophy Department in Halle as *Privatdozent* and on 24 October 1887 he delivered his inaugural lecture, "The Aims and Tasks of Metaphysics". He would remain in Halle for the next fourteen years, until the publication of the *Logical Investigations* occasioned a move to the University of Göttingen. In Halle he began lecturing on geometry (including Riemann and Helmholtz) and on the history of philosophy, on logic, ethics, and psychology. He developed close friendships with his colleagues, the mathematician Georg Cantor (1845–1918),[41] the philosopher Erdmann, and the philologist Hans von Arnim. However, he was never happy at Halle, feeling isolated and unrecognised. When he moved to Göttingen, he wrote to Meinong that he found the scientific community there highly stimulating after his somewhat depressing time at Halle, where he had remained at the lowest teaching rank of *Privatdozent*.

While at Halle, Husserl published his first real book, the *Philosophy of Arithmetic: Psychological and Logical Investigations, Book I* in 1891, dedicated to Brentano.[42] The first four chapters of this work contained his 1887 thesis *On the Concept of Number* almost verbatim. He planned a second volume on the nature of the calculus and including a new philosophical theory of Euclid's geometry, but almost as soon as the first volume was published in 1891 Husserl had recognised that the project was flawed, though he did not formally renounce it until 1894.[43] By the time Husserl was preparing the volume for publication, he had already abandoned its central assumption. As he indicated in a letter to Stumpf, he realised that the negative, irrational, and imaginary numbers were not based on the cardinal numbers and he could not explain the whole of arithmetic in the manner he originally intended. He now saw that arithmetic was really a segment of formal logic.[44] During the decade from 1890 to 1900, Husserl wrote a number of articles which included powerful criticisms of prevailing conceptions of logic, not just psychologistic tendencies but also formal mathematical approaches, including those (e.g. Ernst Schröder) which purported to develop an extensionalist logic based on the emerging set theory. These essays pursue themes later developed in the *Logical Investigations*. Husserl also wrote on the nature of geometry and the theory of manifolds (*Mannigfaltigkeitslehre*), a topic to which he frequently returned in his later logical researches.

Through the 1890s Husserl corresponded with Frege, Meinong, Brentano, Stumpf, Natorp, Anton Marty, and Ernst Mach, and many other scientific researchers. Gottlob Frege and Husserl discussed logical problems and compared their views on sense and reference. Frege, however, reviewed Husserl's *Philosophy of Arithmetic* very critically in 1894, and his searching criticisms may have been partly responsible for Husserl's change of focus[45] which resulted in the lengthy *Logical Investigations*, published in 1900–1901 but in preparation since 1890. Frege accused Husserl of having no way of distinguishing between a *presentation* (*Vorstellung*) and the *object* of a presentation, for example between the idea of the moon and the moon itself, and, again, between the *presentation* and the *concept* (*Begriff*). He condemns Husserl as a psychologistic logician – one who has not distinguished 'true' from 'taken for true' (playing on the meaning of the German word for perceiving, *wahrnehmen*). As W. R. Boyce Gibson, the translator of *Ideas* I, who studied with Husserl in Freiburg, later recorded in his diary, Husserl felt Frege's criticism had hit the nail on the head. Frege had truly understood his work, whereas the revered Brentano, on the other hand, appears never to have read the *Philosophy of Arithmetic*. However, Husserl was not moved to follow Frege in the direction of symbolic logic. Rather it seems that Frege's influence for Husserl was in helping him appreciate the true dangers of psychologism.

Another important turning point in Husserl's development was an article entitled "Intentional Objects", written possibly between 1894 and 1896, but never published. This draft essay was an attempt to clarify the nature of so-called "objectless presentations" (e.g. the thought of 'nothing', or a 'centaur', a 'round square', a 'green virtue' or a 'gold mountain') originally discussed by Bolzano in his *Wissenschaftslehre* Book I § 67, and subsequently taken up by Brentano, Twardowski, Marty, Meinong, and Russell, among others.[46] In this article, as in his unpublished review of Twardowski's book, which we discussed in the last chapter, Husserl introduces a crucial distinction between the *real* psychological content and the *ideal* logical content, or meaning, of the act, and also between the whole notion of content and the intentional object of the act. These distinctions, reworked in subsequent publications, including *Ideas* I, enabled Husserl to separate the psychological components of a mental process (part of the proper object of the science of psychology) from the unchanging ideal meanings which are manipulated in logic, and again to distinguish both of these from the phenomenological features of the act as meaning-constituting, crucial for understanding the true domain of phenomenology.

There came a moment during his years at Halle, as Husserl recalled much later to his friend Leo Schestow, when he found himself at the lecture podium expounding the epistemological ideas of his contemporaries, and he realised he himself had nothing to say (*Chronik*, p. 331). The failure of traditional epistemology to illuminate the issues he was addressing led him to embark on new investigations of logic and epistemology. The outcome of these reflections, *Logical Investigations*, appeared in two volumes: the first, *Prolegomena to Pure Logic*, was published in 1900, followed by a second volume of six 'Investigations' on "Phenomenology and the Theory of Knowledge", published in two parts in 1901. The *Prolegomena* to the *Logical Investigations* was a devastating critique of logical psychologism, and was originally given as a lecture series in Halle in the summer and autumn of 1896 (LI, Foreword to Second Edition, p. 47; Hua XVIII 12). On 21 January 1897 Husserl had written to Jaspers telling him he was composing a work directed against the "subjective-psychologising tendency" of modern logic, a tendency which he himself, as a student of Brentano, had originally followed (*Briefwechsel* V 43). The *Prolegomena* in particular was influenced by Husserl's reading of Leibniz, Lotze, and Bolzano, as well as by his constant preoccupation with Hume. In the Foreword to the First Edition of the *Logical Investigations* Husserl ruefully invokes Goethe's remark: "One opposes nothing more strongly than errors one has just abandoned" (LI, Foreword, p. 43; Hua XVIII 7, translation modified).

As Husserl composed the *Investigations*, the Sixth Investigation grew in size and complexity, such that he came to realise that the whole book needed reworking, especially as the conception of truth employed in the earlier Investigations had now been superseded by his discoveries in the Sixth Investigation, leaving the entire work unbalanced. According to Malvine's recollection, which may not be entirely reliable, in the end, Stumpf was apparently forced to remove physically the manuscript of the *Logical Investigations* from Husserl's desk to give to the printers (*Chronik*, p. 58). The First Investigation is a study of the nature of acts of expression, the Second Investigation examines the nature of universals and species and contains searching criticisms of Locke, Berkeley, and Hume and their conceptions of ideas and of the process of abstraction; the Third Investigation is a study of wholes and parts, while the Fourth applies this theory to working out a formal grammar of language. The Fifth Investigation is an extended critique of Brentano's conception of intentionality, while the Sixth develops Husserl's account of judgement and its relation to truth. In general the Investigations do not claim to be a work of speculation or of philosophical critique. Rather, Husserl proposes to abandon old ways of doing philosophy in favour of a return to the careful description of the 'things themselves', that is the ideal objectivities which constitute meanings. Thus, originally, phenomenology was a kind of conceptual analysis.

Husserl's demand to overturn tradition and to return to the matters themselves struck a chord with a whole generation of philosophers at the dawn of the twentieth century. It was the *Logical Investigations* which impressed senior philosophers such as Wilhelm Dilthey and Paul Natorp, and attracted students such as Daubert, Reinach, Stein, Ingarden, and Heidegger. Brentano, on the other hand, was, as we have seen, taken aback by Husserl's onslaught on psychologism, and was convinced he himself was one of the targets of Husserl's criticism. Brentano interrogated Daubert on the matter on a visit to Munich in 1907.[47] Brentano suspected Husserl of Platonism as regards the existence of ideal truths. For Brentano, truth belonged to judgement, but for Husserl, truth was independent of any human judgement; for example, Newton's laws of motion were true irrespective of whether anyone judged them or not. Husserl, on the other hand, acknowledged the influence of Lotze's interpretation of Platonic ideas in helping to understand Bolzano's 'propositions-in-themselves' (*Sätze an sich*) as the senses of statements and not as mysterious kinds of things,[48] and thus came closer to a reading of Neo-Kantian idealism which Brentano would have repudiated.

Before discussing Husserl's Göttingen days, we should mention a significant event for the future development of phenomenology which occurred in Halle. In 1901 Husserl first met Max Scheler at a Kant conference in Halle. He would afterwards maintain close contact with Scheler, at least until the outbreak of the Great War. Scheler was in many ways the co-founder of phenomenology, and was much admired by a whole generation of German phenomenologists including, and most especially, Heidegger. Scheler was an early admirer of the *Logical Investigations* but was critical of Husserl's conception of philosophy as a rigorous science and his later turn towards idealism. Husserl, in return, had little time for the philosophy of life (*Lebensphilosophie*) which Scheler admired. Nevertheless, they co-operated in the production of the *Year Book for Philosophy and Phenomenological Research*, founded in 1913, though some letters from Husserl to Scheler suggest that Husserl was less than impressed with Scheler's laconic attitude towards his editing and proofing duties. Husserl, who was rather prudish in moral terms, was also shocked by Scheler's personal conduct in the area of amorous relations, and he was less than sympathetic with what he took to be the irrational emotional sentiments articulated by Scheler. He was therefore somewhat dismayed by Scheler's huge popular success as a writer and public lecturer in the post-war years (whereas Heidegger, in his eulogy on the occasion of Scheler's death in 1928, characterised him as one of the leading philosophers of his generation).

The Göttingen period (1901–1916) and the rise of transcendental phenomenology

In September 1901, as a result of his recent publication, *Logical Investigations*, Husserl was appointed by the Prussian ministry as Professor Extraordinarius at Göttingen University, against the wishes of the

Philosophy Faculty.[49] He remained there until 1916, becoming Professor Ordinarius in 1906, again opposed by the philosophers in the Faculty, who thought his work lacked scientific distinction. By this time, however, Husserl was beginning to attract larger numbers of students to his lectures, including the American Harvard student William Hocking (1873–1966) who studied with Husserl in 1902–1903 on the recommendation of Paul Natorp. Indeed, after the *Logical Investigations* Husserl's name came to be known largely through the recommendations of influential figures such as Natorp and Dilthey. In his review of the *Prolegomena* Natorp praised the work, though he claimed Husserl underappreciated the role of Kant.[50] Indeed, much of Husserl's knowledge of Kant in the early days come from his engagement with Natorp. The two remained in correspondence, although Natorp was rather critical of Husserl's *Ideas* I when he reviewed it in 1919. Dilthey would later claim that Husserl's work allowed him to achieve a breakthrough in his own researches.

At Göttingen Husserl became an active member of a renowned circle of scientists which included the mathematicians David Hilbert (1862–1943), Felix Klein, Richard Courant (1888–1972) and Erhard Schmidt. Hilbert, who had already formulated his axiom of completeness for arithmetic, had envisaged Husserl as playing a vital role in advancing the cause of *formalism* in mathematics and logic, but Husserl himself already suspected that the imaginary numbers would prove an obstacle to such completeness.[51] In fact, Husserl was also being drawn away from mathematics towards *epistemological* issues concerning perception and conscious awareness. Though he continued to read logical and mathematical studies, even addressing the Göttingen Mathematical Society in 1901, his interests were gradually being drawn to traditional philosophy, including Descartes and Kant.

Outside of the critique of psychologism, Husserl's *Logical Investigations* were beginning to have an impact for their treatment of intentional experiences. Of considerable importance for the future development of phenomenology was a visit paid during the summer semester of 1902 to Husserl by Johannes Daubert (1877–1947), a student of Theodor Lipps in Munich, who himself had been criticised as a psychologistic thinker by Husserl in the *Prolegomena*.[52] Daubert had been so impressed by the *Logical Investigations* that, reputedly, he cycled all the way from Munich to Göttingen to seek out its author (*Chronik*, p. 72). Through Daubert,[53] and under the influence of Lipps, an informal 'school' of Husserlian phenomenologists began to form at Munich, which included Alexander Pfänder (1870–1941),[54] Adolf Reinach (1883–1917), and, from 1906, Max Scheler. Husserl enthusiastically supported this group, travelling to Munich in 1904 to lecture to them. In 1905 many of Lipps's Munich students travelled to Göttingen to study with Husserl. Reinach, in particular, was highly regarded by Husserl, writing his *Habilitation* with him and acting as a teaching assistant for Husserl at Göttingen. When

Reinach lost his life in the Great War in 1917, Husserl wrote several moving obituaries.[55]

The Munich school saw phenomenology as a realist philosophy of pure description of objects and emphasised the objective truth discoverable through close description. An elegant expression of this outlook can be found in Reinach's "Concerning Phenomenology?" essay of 1914 and in Roman Ingarden's later study, *On the Motives Which Led Husserl to Transcendental Idealism.*[56] These students did not follow Husserl in his reductions and transcendental idealism, a position Husserl later characterised as "empirical phenomenology" as opposed to his own "transcendental" phenomenology.[57] In 1907 a group of students at Göttingen founded a similar circle of phenomenology, the Göttingen Philosophy Society, led by Theodor Conrad and including Hedwig Conrad-Martius, the French student Jean Héring,[58] Fritz Kaufmann, the Canadian Winthrop Bell, the Pole Roman Ingarden, the Russian Alexandre Koyré,[59] and Edith Stein.[60]

Whereas the First Edition (1900–1901) of the *Logical Investigations* had equated phenomenology with descriptive psychology, by 1903 Husserl began to have reservations about describing his own work as 'psychology' (Hua XXII 206) and more and more began to utilise the term 'phenomenology' exclusively. Indeed, in later years, right up to his death, Husserl constantly and very explicitly sought to distinguish radically between his phenomenology (later 'transcendental phenomenology') and every kind of psychology, including both empirical psychology of the quantitative, inductive, experimental kind and Brentanian descriptive psychology.[61] For Husserl, psychology, an entirely legitimate positive science, always studies psychic processes as events in nature, and therefore misunderstands consciousness, whereas phenomenology disregards and excludes the physiological nature of acts and their causal location in nature, in order to focus exclusively on their meaning-constituting function. Phenomenology proceeds by a pure 'intuiting' (*anschauen*) and 'reflection' (*Reflexion*) which "precludes any copositing of objects alien to consciousness".[62]

Around 1905, Husserl began to characterise his phenomenology in transcendental terms and embarked on a serious re-reading of Kant. His researches on time consciousness brought him to the realisation that he had neglected the structural features which unified conscious acts over time. In particular, he realised that his treatment of the ego in the *Logical Investigations* had been seriously inadequate. He had originally accepted the Brentanian view that the source of psychic acts could be bracketed in order to describe the nature of the acts themselves, their structure, and their real and ideal contents, but he came to realise that the ego played a crucial role not only in generating these acts and stamping its unifying syntheses upon them, but in structuring the meaning-constituting functions of the acts themselves. Of course, Scheler, Dilthey, and Natorp had all criticised

Husserl's thin Humean account of the ego in the *Logical Investigations*, arguing for the need to postulate the person as the 'performer of acts'.

Around the same time as Husserl came to see the need to rethink his position on the transcendental ego, he also introduced the notion of the 'reduction' (*Reduktion*) in his lecture courses, probably first publicly announced in his 1906–1907 lecture course on *Logic and the Theory of Knowledge*.[63] In April and May 1907 Husserl delivered five lectures at Göttingen, later published as *The Idea of Phenomenology*, which focused on the reduction as a way of moving from the psychological to the truly epistemological domain.[64] Over the rest of his life Husserl struggled to articulate the nature of the breakthrough afforded by the phenomenological reduction and what he also called 'eidetic' and 'transcendental' reductions (we shall return to these in a later chapter). Husserl felt that the nature of consciousness could only be properly grasped if persistent naturalistic distortions can be removed. These distortions are produced not just by our incorrect *theories* about the nature of the world but also by the very object-positing thetic structure of consciousness itself. Thus Husserl wanted to 'put out of action' the 'natural attitude' (*die natürliche Einstellung*), bracket it, with the aim of purifying consciousness of all intrusion from "objective actualities" – including "the actuality of all material nature" and of psychic experiences. The aim of the initial 'phenomenological' reduction is to individuate correctly the domain of pure consciousness as the domain of meaning-constitution.

Not only do we need to put to one side all naturalistic and speculative theories about consciousness, but also we need to shift focus from the empirical and factual to the *essential, necessary* features of experience. This is achieved by what Husserl terms the 'eidetic' reduction. There still remains a whole domain of 'reduced' phenomena, the realm of "pure consciousness", understood richly as the site of the a priori structures (which he terms 'essences') of acts of meaning. The 'transcendental' reduction serves to relate these essential meaning-structures to their source in the pure ego. A Kantian element is also absorbed by Husserl in that pure consciousness must be understood as at least encompassing the set of ideal a priori conditions which any objectivity has to meet. However, Husserl saw himself as pushing far beyond Kant in his investigation of the meaning-fulfilling elements in cognitive acts. We shall return to these reductions in a subsequent chapter.

The mature Husserl saw phenomenology as dealing with what is left over when the preoccupation with actuality was removed. This absolute insistence on the necessity of bracketing the actual world in order to proceed phenomenologically remained problematic for many of his students. In *Ideas* I (1913), Husserl even went so far as to characterise the 'reduction' as acting under the hypothesis of the very 'annihilation' or 'nullification' of the world (*Weltvernichtung*), a formulation he regretted in later years as he attempted to shake off comparisons with subjective idealism. Indeed, as we shall see, attempting to think how being remains somehow residually present in consciousness as other than consciousness was one of the motivations which led Heidegger to attempt his own account of the nature of being. Husserl himself never saw his reduction as a moving away from the richness of the given world, rather he saw it as bringing the richness of our insertion into the world to light in a new manner.

Meanwhile, Husserl had extended his attack on *psychologism* to include all varieties of *naturalism*. He also found a new target for critique in the increasingly influential historical hermeneutics of Wilhelm Dilthey. At the invitation of Rickert, Husserl wrote his famous programmatic essay, *Philosophy as a Rigorous Science*, which appeared in Rickert's journal *Logos* in 1910–1911 and which Walter Biemel has described as Husserl's *Kampfschrift*, his critique of naturalism and historicism as leading to relativism.[65] Husserl singled out Dilthey's philosophy of world-views, *Weltanschauungsphilosophie*, as denying the objective validity of cultural formations. This led to a correspondence with the elderly Dilthey who claimed to have been misunderstood. Dilthey insisted he was most conscious of the need to protect the human sciences from naturalism, and declared himself also to be involved in the struggle against relativism and scepticism, and to be defending the possibility of objective knowledge in the human sciences. Furthermore, Dilthey agreed with Husserl's views on the need to ground philosophy as a rigorous science. Husserl seemed to have been won over by Dilthey's protestations and agreed to write a correction, but unfortunately Dilthey died on 1 October 1911 and the correction never appeared.[66] Later, in his 1925 lectures on *Phenomenological Psychology*, Husserl returned to the critique of Dilthey, this time for his absence of conceptual rigour, though he now acknowledged the importance of Dilthey's 1894 work on descriptive psychology as a first assault on naturalism.[67] In these lectures, however, Husserl continued to criticise Dilthey's descriptive psychology for failing to establish universal psychological laws.

In 1913 the first volume of the newly founded *Jahrbuch für Philosophie und phänomenologische Forschung* appeared, jointly edited by Husserl and his 'school' associates, Pfänder, Reinach, Geiger, and Scheler. Husserl wanted a major organ for the new phenomenology,[68] and had been planning such a journal since 1907 (see his letter to Daubert 26 August 1907, Hua XXV xv), but the plan was revived when a *Festschrift* was written for Lipps in 1911 containing many phenomenological contributions. Husserl seemed worried that Lipps rather than himself would be seen as phenomenology's originator. The *Jahrbuch*, when it finally appeared, quickly became a repository of brilliant phenomenological studies. The first volume contained Husserl's new essay in transcendental phenomenology, *Ideas* I, as well as the first book of Scheler's *Formalism in Ethics*. The fifth volume (1922) contained works by Edith Stein and Roman Ingarden, whereas Volume VIII (1927) contained Heidegger's *Being and Time* together with a work by another Freiburg phenomenologist, Oskar Becker, on the nature of mathematical objects. Volume X was Husserl's own *Formal and Transcendental Logic* and Volume XI his Postface to *Ideas* I. The *Jahrbuch* eventually ceased publication in 1930.

Ideas I was Husserl's first major publication in thirteen years, and the medium through which his transcendental vision of phenomenology came to be more broadly known. Complementing *Ideas* I, Husserl published a Second Edition of the *Logical Investigations*, revised to bring it into line with the transcendental framework of *Ideas* I. The Second Edition explicitly repudiates the identification of phenomenology with descriptive psychology and introduces the idea of the reduction from the natural to the transcendental features of consciousness. Moreover, whereas in the 1901 edition he had treated the ego as merely a bundle of acts, he now puts the doctrine of the transcendental ego centre stage, claiming in a textual note to have "found" this ego. The revision of the text was, however, incomplete, as Husserl found revising the Sixth Investigation too daunting a task. Over the next decade, and again in retirement, he worked on revising the Sixth Investigation without ever completing it.[69]

Ideas I was written in a period of eight weeks in the summer of 1912, and, immediately after it went to press, Husserl, still in a 'fever of work' (*Arbeitsfieber*), in three months hurriedly scribbled in pencil a manuscript, the original draft for what would become the posthumously published *Ideas* II and *Ideas* III. In 1915 Husserl rewrote the manuscript of *Ideas* II, planning to publish it in the *Jahrbuch*, but he held back and continued revising it until 1928 when he finally abandoned it, in part because he felt he had not worked out the problem of constitution. As Husserl later explained to Schütz, he felt the problem of intersubjectivity had not been properly addressed.[70] Edith Stein, who herself was interested in the phenomenology of intersubjective empathy and personal embodiment, closely collaborated with Husserl on the drafting and organisation of the work, which was finally published in 1952. In its unpublished draft form, *Ideas* II influenced both Merleau-Ponty and Heidegger.

Ideas II, a set of studies in "the phenomenology of constitution", is one of Husserl's most original and successful works. It begins with the discussion of the "idea of nature" in general and then goes on to discuss material, animal, and human nature, the last being the realm of personhood and spirit. In discussing the nature of the personal "I" Husserl discusses the manner in which we relate to our bodies and to the surrounding world.[71] Husserl lectured on the relation of nature to spirit in the first years at Freiburg. The work on social constitution and on the human personal world was carried out at the same time as the work on transcendental subjectivity, showing that Husserl did not believe these two approaches conflicted. Indeed, for him, both were necessary to the full understanding of the constitution of the objective world, including the domains of nature and culture.

Soon after writing the various manuscripts of *Ideas* and re-editing the *Logical Investigations*, Husserl again hit a spiritual low, and, during the war years from 1914 to 1918, he found he did not have the heart to engage deeply in the phenomenology of logic or epistemology, but instead concentrated on "the most general philosophical reflections" focusing mainly on the idea of a phenomenological philosophy as such (see his remarks in the 1920 Foreword to the Second Edition of the Sixth Logical Investigation, LI VI, p. 661; Hua XIX/2 533). The outbreak of the First World War led to Husserl's sons being called up, and his daughter Elli volunteered to work in a field hospital. Like most Germans of his time, Husserl saw the war in mainly patriotic terms; God was on Germany's side (*Briefwechsel* III 402).[72] Indeed, right to the end of his life, he associated himself proudly with the great accomplishments of German culture – Beethoven, Herder, Schiller, Goethe (letter to Eduard Baumgarten of 22 December 1936, *Briefwechsel* VII 27) – and even saw phenomenology as part of this German contribution to world culture. However, he became deeply depressed by the loss of so many of his students, including the gifted Reinach. On 8 March 1916 his 20-year-old son Wolfgang, bearer of the Iron Cross, was killed at Verdun, and his eldest son Gerhart was badly wounded. Though grieving deeply, Husserl remained proud of his own family's role in the war effort and wrote encouraging letters to Heidegger when he too was stationed on the front.

In political outlook, Husserl was something of an old-style Bismarckian nationalist, who was ennobled by the "magnificent stream of national will" running through everyone involved in the war effort.[73] Husserl felt deeply betrayed when the USA joined the war on the side of the French, though he remained aloof from the propaganda efforts in which many of his fellow academics engaged. Indeed in 1919, he wrote to Metzger that he was glad he had not written patriotic books during the war, as had Scheler and Natorp and other German intellectuals. He was sufficiently unworldly and politically naive that, as late as 1918, according to Malvine Husserl (*Briefwechsel* IX 348), he was still predicting a German victory. By 1920, however, he had come to the view that the old idea of a just war was now without ethical force (*Briefwechsel* X 20).

Late in the war, in November 1917, and again in January and in November 1918 just before the armistice, Husserl delivered a series of three lectures to serving soldiers in Freiburg, on "Fichte's Ideal of Humanity". These lectures earned him the Iron Cross for his assistance to the military effort. They cannot be seen as supportive of militant nationalism though they portray Germany as a nation threatened from without.[74] Husserl admired Fichte as the essence of the genuine German idealism, "indigenous to our people". Fichte is the philosopher of the absolute world-creating ego, "the world as the teleological product of the world creating I". Fichte also is the philosopher who put Kant's philosophy on the secure footing by genuinely uniting theory and practice and ridding it of obscure 'things in themselves'. Going beyond Kant's formalism, Fichte understood the essence of higher morality as a free embrace of the universal. Husserl himself, looking to a universal moral community beyond any narrow national self-interest, cites Fichte's hope for a "total rebirth of humanity". Later, in the twenties, his *Kaizo* articles would emphasise the necessity of cultural renewal through a surpassing of narrow nationalisms in order to found true community in shared interests.

In the midst of this political turmoil and family tragedy, in 1916 Husserl was appointed Professor Ordinarius to *Lehrstuhl* I of the Philosophy Seminar at the Albert-Ludwigs University of Freiburg, succeeding Heinrich Rickert (1863–1936) who moved to Heidelberg.[75] Husserl was attracted to Freiburg in part because of its association (through Rickert and, earlier, Windelband) with Neo-Kantianism, which he had now come to appreciate more and more.

The Freiburg years (1916–1938)

Husserl took up his lecturing duties at Freiburg on 1 April 1916. He would continue to live in Freiburg, at his second-floor apartment at 40 Lorettostraße, until 1937, when his deteriorating financial circumstances and declining health forced him to move to a house in Schöneckstraße further out from the old town. On 3 May 1917, he delivered his Inaugural Lecture (*Antrittsrede*) entitled, "Pure Phenomenology: Its Research Domain and Method".[76] In this programmatic lecture he claimed that the present era was one of flux wherein traditional forms have to be re-examined, as had happened with the reconstruction of the fundamentals of mathematics. In philosophy too such reconstruction was required:

> Most recently, the need for an utterly original philosophy has re-emerged, the need of a philosophy that...seeks by radically clarifying the sense and the motifs of philosophical problems to penetrate to that primal ground on whose basis those problems must find whatever solution is genuinely scientific.
>
> (HSW 10; Hua XXV 69)

Husserl here expressed his concern for the "spiritual life of mankind" (*das Geistesleben der Menschheit*) and went on to claim that philosophy is possible as a rigorous science only through phenomenology: "all philosophical disciplines are rooted in pure phenomenology" (HSW 10; Hua XXV 69). Phenomenology is defined as "the science of every kind of object", where 'object' simply means whatever is encountered in consciousness:

> To every object there correspond an ideally closed system of truths
> that are true of it and, on the other hand, an ideal system of possi-
> ble cognitive processes by virtue of which the object and the truths
> about it would be given to any cognitive subject.
>
> (HSW 10–11; Hua XXV 69)

These ideal processes of grasping the object and the truths about it are what
phenomenology studies, or, in other words, they are the modalities of
intentionality. He went on to claim that Descartes had been poised on the
point of discovering the genuinely phenomenological domain. Husserl ends
his lecture with the hope that philosophers would not dismiss phenomenology with ill-conceived criticisms from on high (which he compared with
Berkeley's criticisms of infinitesimal calculus), but would instead attempt to
apply the methods themselves.

Husserl's phenomenology now began to attract students in great
numbers. These students who came to Freiburg after the First World War
ended in 1918 had different interests to the earlier generation Husserl had
taught at Göttingen. They had a distinct sense of the failure of the
project of rationalism, and thus in spirit differed very much from Husserl,
who retained his rather old-fashioned faith in rationalism.[77] They were
now more attracted by Kierkegaard's and Nietzsche's existential *Angst*
and spiritual turmoil, by Scheler's account of the emotional, personal life,
and by Spengler's analysis of cultural crisis, as outlined in his popular
The Decline of the West.[78] Gadamer recalls that phenomenology was even
being mentioned as a possible remedy for the crisis of civilisation known
generally, and referred to by Husserl also, as the "decline of the West".[79]
German and foreign students were attracted to phenomenology because
of its theme of renewal, a renewal of humanity itself through the practice
of philosophy.[80] Indeed, inspired by a somewhat similar mood, in
1923/1924 Husserl himself contributed three articles, on the role of a
renewal of philosophy and science in the creation of a universal moral
order, to a Japanese intellectual journal, *The Kaizo* ('Renewal') to which
Rickert and Russell had also contributed.[81] Husserl, echoing the mood of
many Germans, here bemoaned the appalling state of affairs in the
Weimar Republic where "psychological tortures" and economic humilia-
tion had replaced war. Husserl saw the only hope for overcoming
Realpolitik and rebuilding the confidence of a people was through a
spiritual retrieval of the human sense of purpose, a renewal of the ideals
of the European Enlightenment (which culture, in his opinion, Japan had
recently joined). Of course, this renewal consisted in philosophy as a
rigorous science, but now a science of the human spirit was needed to
complement and give moral purpose to the exact sciences. Husserl
proposes "the a priori science of the essence of human spirituality" (HSW
329; Hua XXVII 9).

Husserl now attracted students from the USA such as the Harvard students Dorion Cairns and Marvin Farber, sent by Hocking, and also students from Japan. Among the students from his Freiburg period were Karl Löwith, Aron Gurwitsch, Hans-Georg Gadamer, Günther Stern (who later married Hannah Arendt), Herbert Marcuse, Eugen Fink, Ludwig Landgrebe, and Alfred Schütz. Rudolf Carnap spent the year 1924–1925 living near Freiburg and attending Husserl's seminars, while working on his own *Logische Aufbau der Welt*. As an indication of his growing international reputation, from 6 to 12 June 1922, Husserl gave a series of four lectures at University College, London, at the invitation of Professor George Dawes Hicks, entitled "The Phenomenological Method and Phenomenological Philosophy".[82] The fourth lecture was chaired by G. E. Moore, then Editor of *Mind*. In a letter to his student Winthrop Bell, Husserl described his London lectures as part of a new spirit of international co-operation. In the same year, Husserl was elected corresponding member of the Aristotelian Society.

Returning to his theme of the nature of phenomenology, Husserl delivered an important series of lectures, *First Philosophy*, in 1923/1924 (Hua VII). In 1925 he lectured on *Phenomenological Psychology*, which stressed the distinction between phenomenology and psychology and the need for a phenomenological clarification of basic concepts in psychology.[83] These lectures provide a valuable rethinking of the *Logical Investigations* and a restatement of his own position regarding the descriptive psychology of Brentano and Dilthey. Indeed, in lectures from 1925 to 1929 (including his Amsterdam lectures), Husserl focused on the distinctions between transcendental phenomenology and all psychology and anthropology which operate under the natural attitude.

Husserl's encounter with Martin Heidegger

Undoubtedly the most important philosophical event of his Freiburg years was his encounter with Martin Heidegger. Soon after his arrival in Freiburg in 1916, Husserl became aware of the student Heidegger, who had recently received his *Habilitation*, which undoubtedly was being talked about, prompting Husserl to write to Heidegger asking for a copy of the thesis. Indeed, Husserl was instrumental in getting the thesis published later in 1916, and Heidegger thanked Husserl in the dedication to the published version. The two obviously discussed philosophy during the period from 1916 to 1917, and kept in contact when Heidegger was called up for military service, but they did not have a close relationship until after the end of the First World War when Heidegger returned to lecture as *Privatdozent* in the Philosophy Department at Freiburg, commencing during the Emergency War semester which ran from January to April 1919. On 21 January 1919, Heidegger became Husserl's salaried assistant and remained in Freiburg until he moved to Marburg as Professor Extraordinarius in 1923, at which time Ludwig Landgrebe took over as Husserl's assistant.

Husserl's initial allotted role for Heidegger in the great domain of phenomenology was as someone who would develop a phenomenology of religion, but he soon came to see Heidegger's genius and his devotion to philosophy as singling him out as someone with great promise. At Freiburg Heidegger conducted regular lecture series and seminars on phenomenology.[84] Having initially taken Heidegger for a rather dogmatic Catholic philosopher, Husserl in a letter to Natorp on 11 February 1920 expressed some relief that the young Heidegger had "freed himself from dogmatic Catholicism" (*Briefwechsel* V 139). Indeed, Husserl marvelled that his influence on his students was such that Catholics became Protestants and vice versa (Edith Stein, who was originally Jewish, became Catholic, for example).

Right from his earliest lecture courses in Freiburg, however, Heidegger was critical of Husserl's ideal of philosophy as a rigorous science and equally critical of Dilthey's and Jaspers' philosophy of world-views, *Weltanschauungsphilosophie*. In his Freiburg lecture courses, Heidegger criticised Husserl's notion of the transcendental ego, his prioritising of theoretical knowing and cognitive acts over practical living experiences, his notion of certainty and evidence, his lack of historical understanding, and so on. Heidegger was quite open about these criticisms but Husserl seemed oblivious to them, and continued to promote Heidegger as his future successor.[85] Husserl had even stayed with Heidegger in Todtnauberg during the Easter break of 1926, in order to assist Heidegger in the preparation of the proofs of *Being and Time* (1927), which itself was originally dedicated to Edmund Husserl, "in admiration and friendship" (*in Verehrung und Freundschaft*) – the same terms of dedication as Husserl had used for Stumpf in the dedication to the *Logical Investigations* – though this dedication was dropped in later editions. In late 1927 Husserl was invited to write the 'Phenomenology' article for the 14th edition of the *Encyclopaedia Britannica*. He wrote a first draft and asked Heidegger for his help in revising it, and, although they eventually worked through several drafts together from September 1927 through to February 1928, their views diverged too much and, in the article that was finally submitted, Husserl had excised much of Heidegger's contribution, especially Heidegger's introductory paragraph locating phenomenology within fundamental ontology.[86] Heidegger and Edith Stein edited and published Husserl's lectures on internal time consciousness in 1928. Initially Husserl was satisfied but he quickly came to find fault with the truncated form in which the lectures were published, for which he later blamed Heidegger.

Husserl retired on 31 March 1928. Eventually Heidegger, with no publications in the ten years leading up to *Being and Time*, but with an excellent reputation as a teacher and original thinker, succeeded Husserl to the Chair of Philosophy in 1928. Heidegger had Husserl's full support (against some opposition in the Faculty), succeeding even over Husserl's more senior student Alexander Pfänder, who had been teaching at Munich for many years, and also the prominent Neo-Kantian, Ernst Cassirer. Later, in 1931, Husserl wrote a letter to Pfänder acknowledging his "blindness" in not seeing through Heidegger, but pointing out that Heidegger had been an excellent assistant and had followed the later development of Husserl's transcendental phenomenology, which, in his opinion, none of his earlier Munich followers had done.[87]

Husserl's initial retirement produced another burst of frenetic activity, during which, in a space of some months, he wrote the *Formal and Transcendental Logic*, published in 1929 in the *Jahrbuch*. This work is a very successful, sustained attempt to revisit issues first discussed in the *Logical Investigations*, namely the objectivity of truth and meaning and the phenomenological structures which constitute it. In the summer of 1929 Heidegger presented a copy of *Being and Time* and of *Kant and the Problem of Metaphysics* to Husserl, who finally found time to carefully read and annotate them. Husserl was shocked by the extent of Heidegger's departure from his phenomenology.[88] By this time, Husserl was an international figure of great renown, and also something of an elder statesman of German philosophy, travelling extensively and attracting huge crowds to his lectures. Having visited Berlin on the occasion of Stumpf's 80th birthday, he travelled to Amsterdam in April 1928 to deliver two public lectures on "Phenomenology and Psychology", a development of his views as laid out in the recently completed *Encyclopaedia Britannica* article.[89] Levinas attended Husserl's and Heidegger's seminars in the summer semester of 1928 and the winter semester of 1928–1929, and actually assisted Husserl's wife, Malvine, with French lessons in preparation for their forthcoming trip to Paris.[90] In February 1929 he gave two lectures in Paris (published as the *Paris Lectures*, 1935) which were attended by L. Lévy Bruhl, Jean Héring, Alexandre Koyré, Emmanuel Levinas, Gabriel Marcel, and, according to Maurice de Gandillac, Maurice Merleau-Ponty. These lectures served formally to inaugurate the phenomenological tradition in France. In 1931, a French translation of the *Cartesian Meditations* was published, edited by Levinas and Gabrielle Peiffer, assisted by Alexandre Koyré. Husserl held back the German edition for further revisions and it was not published until 1950. On 10 June 1931 he gave an invited talk to the Kant Society in Frankfurt on "Phenomenology and Anthropology", and gave further lectures in Berlin and Halle to huge audiences.

In 1929 a *Festschrift* was prepared for Husserl's 70th birthday and published as a special issue of the *Jahrbuch*. Many of his students were in attendance for the presentation on 8 April including Heidegger. In his acceptance speech, Husserl laid special emphasis on the influence of his teachers Brentano and Weierstrass (*Chronik*, pp. 344–345). Heidegger's contribution was the essay "On the Essence of Ground",[91] and in his own speech, Heidegger stated that, though Husserl's students had tried to follow their master, they had not always succeeded. Many philosophers visited Husserl in retirement. In 1929 he was visited in Freiburg by Gilbert Ryle, with whom he spent an hour discussing phenomenology (*Chronik*, p. 340), and by the Czech philosopher Jan Patočka. Alfred Schütz first met Husserl in 1932.[92] In 1935 he corresponded with the French anthropologist Lucien Lévy-Bruhl (*Briefwechsel* VI 161–164), attesting to his interest in the historical development of human mentality. International honours came: he was made an Honorary Member of the American Academy of Arts and Sciences in 1928, and in 1932 he was elected *Correspondant* to the Académie des Sciences Morales et Politiques in Paris. In 1930 Husserl was invited to visit Oxford on the occasion of the International Congress of Philosophy but he declined (*Chronik*, p. 364). In 1936 he became a Corresponding Fellow of the British Academy. But this international recognition was in inverse proportion to his situation at home.

Husserl under the Nazis

Early in 1933 the Nazis came to power in Germany and, on 7 April 1933, a new law on "the re-establishment of a permanent civil service" was promulgated which prohibited non-Aryans from holding positions in the state service. Heidegger, in his capacity as Rektor of Freiburg University, countersigned this official decree of enforced leave of absence ('*Beurlaubung*') which affected many Freiburg academics, including emeritus professor Edmund Husserl.[93] Husserl was shocked by this move. He always considered himself a German nationalist, whose sons had served Germany in the military, and whose daughter had worked with the war wounded in a field hospital during the Great War (*Chronik*, p. 428). The effect of the decree on Husserl is well put by Hannah Arendt, who later wrote to Jaspers that Heidegger's action against Husserl was virtual 'homicide'. Arendt also alleged that Heidegger as Rektor was responsible for banning Husserl from the faculty[94] but this account has been disputed by Jaspers in his reply to Arendt.[95]

The initial decree against non-Aryans in public service was rescinded on 28 April 1933 (Husserl was exempted because of his family's contribution to the war effort in the Great War), but not before Husserl's surviving son Gerhart had lost his position in the Law Faculty at Kiel. Gerhart left Germany for the USA and eventually secured a position in the Washington College of Law; his sister Elli married a Harvard professor. In September 1935 a new law was promulgated and Husserl had his teaching licence withdrawn and, finally, his German citizenship revoked. Husserl's letters from this period witness his attempts to get his son a job, writing to many of his former students, including Dorion Cairns and Marvin Farber, on his son's behalf. As an official non-German, Husserl was then refused a position on official delegations of German philosophers to the conferences in Belgrade in 1936 and the Ninth International Philosophy Congress in Paris in 1937. From 1936 his name was dropped from the Freiburg faculty lists and, though his published works were not banned, he was not allowed to publish anything else in Germany. The National Socialists denounced his philosophy for promoting an ideal of universal rationality for all men, since this meant including '*Unmenchen*' such as Jews and Negroes. For the Nazis, Husserl represented "a barren spirit without blood lineage or race" which did not understand "the attachment to the soil of genuine spirituality (*Erdverbundenheit echter Geistigkeit*)".[96]

The crisis of the European sciences

Husserl himself continued his research work, focusing increasingly on genetic phenomenology and on the problem of what he called "generativity", that is the manner in which historical becoming takes place. He lived in relative isolation, visited only by a few loyal friends, notably Fink and Landgrebe. Life became increasingly difficult for him and his family, but, though he was offered a professorship in the University of Southern California, he did not take it up, partly because he could not secure a place for his assistant, Eugen Fink, or for Dorion Cairns, and partly because, at his advanced age, he could not see himself as a professor in another country; he was German and would live and die there.

Because he was forbidden to teach, he was forced to develop his later philosophy in a series of foreign lectures, including a lecture, "Philosophy in the Crisis of European Humanity", delivered in Vienna in May 1935, and two lectures in Prague on 14 and 15 November 1935. These lectures would later form part of the *Crisis of the European Sciences* which Husserl had to arrange to have published in Belgrade in the yearbook *Philosophia* in 1936. Alfred Schütz attended these lectures and recalls that at a separate invited seminar he talked to students of the importance of the Greek breakthrough in asking why things are as they are and went on to talk about the theoretical attitude.[97] The *Crisis* was originally planned as a work in five sections, but Husserl wrote to Jan Patočka in 1936 that the work was already becoming too big. Only the first two parts appeared in 1936, with the third part completed but not published. Husserl died before completing the *Crisis*, which was eventually published in 1954, edited by Walter Biemel (in 1993, some preparatory drafts of the *Crisis* were published as *Husserliana* Volume XXIX).

Husserl was sick for most of his last year and died on 27 April 1938. No one from the Freiburg Philosophy Faculty, except Gerhard Ritter, attended his funeral; Heidegger was in bed, sick. Some months after Husserl's death, on 15 August 1938, a Belgian Franciscan priest, Fr Hermann Van Breda, who had just completed his licentiate in philosophy in the Catholic

University of Leuven, arrived in Freiburg with the intention of researching Husserl's later manuscripts. Van Breda met with Husserl's widow, Malvine, and Husserl's assistant Eugen Fink, and they soon embarked together on a plan to secure the future of the extensive *Nachlass*, which they feared the Nazis planned to destroy. Husserl had spent his last years trying to order his manuscripts with the help of his assistants, and he had tentatively planned with Landgrebe to locate a Centre for Phenomenology in Prague, but the German invasion of Czechoslovakia made that impossible. Van Breda had offered to relocate the *Nachlass* in Leuven, on the strength of a vague promise of help from the President of the Higher Institute of Philosophy at Leuven. Following an unsuccessful attempt to smuggle the manuscripts out through Switzerland, in September 1938 Van Breda convinced the Belgian embassy in Berlin to send them to Leuven using the diplomatic courier service.[98] Van Breda and others hid the manuscripts in Belgium during the German Occupation. They were then given to the University of Leuven, where they now form part of the Husserl Archives (where Levinas, Merleau-Ponty, and Derrida all studied).[99] Van Breda also arranged for Husserl's widow to move to safety in Belgium, where she hid in a convent during the Nazi years, eventually travelling to the USA in 1946 to join her two surviving children, who had emigrated there in 1933–1934. It is assumed that Husserl's ashes were also taken to Belgium during the war for fear his grave would be desecrated. These remains were later buried in the cemetery in the Franciscan Abbey in Günterstal outside Freiburg, where Malvine is also buried.[100] Eugen Fink (1905–1975), who had become Husserl's private assistant in 1928 and had refused all offers of university employment after 1933 in sympathy with Husserl's plight, and Ludwig Landgrebe (1902–1991), a former assistant who had a university position in Prague until the German invasion, continued to transcribe Husserl's manuscripts, but they too came to Leuven in 1939. However, when Germany invaded Belgium, Fink and Landgrebe were interned by the Germans, sent to a transit camp in France, and then back to Germany. After 1929, Husserl's earlier assistant, Edith Stein (1891–1942), who had become preoccupied with reconciling phenomenology and Thomism, eventually converted to Catholicism and entered a Carmelite convent. She was arrested in Holland and died in a Nazi concentration camp in 1942. She has recently been canonised by Pope John Paul II.

A leader without followers

Though Husserl had many dedicated followers who went on to pioneer their own work in phenomenology, and was well served by his loyal assistants, for example Edith Stein, Eugen Fink, and Ludwig Landgrebe, he felt himself increasingly intellectually isolated, convinced that his work was being undermined and his discoveries credited to other philosophers.

Husserl's early hope Adolf Reinach had fallen in the Great War; Pfänder and the Munich phenomenologists did not accept Husserl's reduction and idealism. After 1928 Heidegger, too, was a bitter personal disappointment to him. Husserl spent his last years attempting to rescue the true meaning of the science of phenomenology from Heidegger who had turned it into anthropology, just as earlier Scheler had weakened it into a form of life philosophy. Indeed Husserl even remarked in a letter to his friend Gustav Albrecht in 1931 that he felt so isolated and separated from his students that he could now even count himself as the greatest enemy of the famous "Husserlian Phenomenological Movement".[101] Husserl's sense of betrayal was deepened by the rise of the National Socialist movement in Germany. An indication of his isolation was that he felt compelled to write to Landgrebe at one point, asking him if he was a member of the Nazi Party. Husserl was acutely aware that he had no genuine successor (expressed in letters to Ingarden and Pfänder) – he referred to himself as a "leader without followers" (als beruferer Führer ohne Gefolge, Briefwechsel II 182) – and that the scientific conception of phenomenology which he had promoted had now dissipated into many separate styles of enquiry in many diverse areas. For better or worse, phenomenology in Germany in the 1930s and 1940s came to be associated with the name of Martin Heidegger, and after the war, in France, with the existential phenomenology of Sartre and Merleau-Ponty.

3

HUSSERL'S *LOGICAL INVESTIGATIONS* (1900–1901)

Introduction

Husserl's *Logical Investigations* has been one of the most influential works of philosophy of the twentieth century, though more for its announcement of phenomenology than for its logical discoveries, which though original and important were largely ignored, and subsequently discovered independently of Husserl's own efforts. *Logical Investigations* is a huge, unmanageable book in two volumes. Husserl rarely signifies in advance where he is going, and rarely considers the views of other philosophers. Husserl himself was among the first to acknowledge its defects, speaking of its "internal unevenness and fragmentary nature" (ILI, p. 17; Fink, p. 110). It was the product of ten years of research from 1890 onwards, but Husserl singles out the Halle lectures of 1896 on logic as the proximate source of the book. Its roots, however, lie much deeper in studies on logic, signification, and meaning, which Husserl was carrying out from the time of the publication of *Philosophy of Arithmetic*. Furthermore, Husserl was still revising the work when the manuscript, according to the tradition, was wrested from his hands by Carl Stumpf for publication. It remains, then, a work-in-progress, a 'patchwork' of different themes. It would be wrong to conclude, however, that because the *Logical Investigations* is, as David Bell says, "badly written, poorly organised, and not always obviously consistent", that it is without philosophical merit.[1] The work is a *tour de force* of philosophical thought in process, full of conceptual clarifications of lasting significance, and, even more importantly, providing a living demonstration of the practice of phenomenology as conceptual clarification. In this chapter, I shall try to provide a basic sense of the book's aims and achievements.

The composition of the *Logical Investigations*

In his Foreword to the First Edition, Husserl says the book was the outcome of his critical reflections on the nature of mathematics and logic (LI, Intro. § 1, p. 41; Hua XVIII 5). Through the 1890s, Husserl had come to realise that the logic of his time was not adequate to address the problems he had uncovered in attempting to provide a clarification of the basic concepts of arithmetic. Husserl complains that mathematics and logic were utilising concepts and meanings not fully analysed within those disciplines themselves, and, consequently, countless equivocations were being tolerated (LI, Intro. § 2, pp. 252–253; Hua XIX/1 11). Mathematicians (e.g. the French mathematician Augustin-Louis Cauchy (1789–1857) in analysing imaginary numbers) were employing different and even conflicting theories to justify the same insights (EW 168; Hua XXII 121). Moreover, these theoretical confusions were not confined to mathematics and logic but infected all formal deductive systems, all of which seemed in need of the same kind of philosophical clarification, as they all relied on the same kind of mental operations and employed the same kinds of concepts (LI, Intro. § 1, p. 41; Hua XVIII 5). The *Logical Investigations*, then, is a sustained attempt to sort out these theoretical difficulties by providing epistemological and logical clarifications of fundamental notions which belong to the form of science as such, notions such as 'content', 'sense', 'truth', and so on. In particular, the *Investigations* offers a clarification of the proper object of logic; logic studies the necessary relations between ideal contents of expressions, what gets expressed, senses, propositional contents. In later life, Husserl would revisit these basic logical problems, most notably in *Formal and Transcendental Logic*, in which, almost thirty years later, he describes the earlier *Investigations* as trapped in a kind of 'transcendental psychologism' or 'eidetic psychology'.

In the *Selbstanzeige*, self-advertisement or published announcement, for the Second Volume of the *Investigations*, Husserl says that he is conducting a phenomenological clarification of knowledge and not a 'genetic psychological' investigation (Hua XIX/2 779). In 1901, Husserl thought of phenomenology as a taxonomy of epistemic and cognitive acts, which would serve 'empirical psychology' (LI, p. 249; Hua XIX/1 7). He also characterised phenomenology in terms of *epistemology*. Thus, the Second Volume of *Investigations* is subtitled "Investigations in Phenomenology and the Theory of Knowledge" (*Theorie der Erkenntnis*). Of course, Husserl employs the term 'epistemology' here, not to refer to the kinds of epistemic justification usually marshalled to overcome the threat of scepticism, but rather, more in the Kantian sense of an a priori investigation into the nature of those acts which yield cognition (*Erkenntnis*), and chiefly the central acts Brentano had specified, namely presentations, judgements, acts of knowing in general (LI, p. 249; Hua XIX/1 7). Furthermore, as Husserl emphasises *ad nauseam*, his account was to be 'pure', that is to abstract from different applications of cognition in different fields and study its conceptual nature as such, though this emphasis is much stronger in the reworked text of the Second Edition of 1913. Husserl understands phenomenology then as the exploration of the conceptual foundations required for any kind of knowing or cognising, without invoking or grappling with traditional philosophical theories or positions. However, as it is impossible to carry out such a critique of

Erkenntnis without employing basic epistemological terms, he must proceed in a 'zig-zag' manner (*im Zick-Zack*), first using concepts and then tracking back later to clarify them (LI, Intro. § 6, p. 261; Hua XIX/1 22).

Husserl also distinguishes his interest in mental acts from the pure logician. The pure logician has no interest in the epistemological processes at work but solely in the *meanings* or *senses* which are asserted and the necessary, formal connections between them. But logic does not have the last word on our cognitive life. As distinct from both empirical psychology and pure logic, phenomenology is concerned with concrete *acts of meaning*, meaning-intendings, not as empirically occurring facts in the world or in terms of the ideal meanings they articulate, but in so far as they have essential, intentional, a priori structures. Furthermore, the clarification of pure logic as a science of pure meanings cannot simply rely on the meanings of words as ordinarily used, but must secure these meanings in concrete intuitions: "we must go back to the things themselves" (*Wir wollen auf die "Sachen selbst" zurückgehen*, LI, Intro. § 2, p. 252; Hua XIX/1 10). Once these meanings are secured in pure intuition, it will be a straightforward, though undoubtedly difficult, task to fix conceptually all the meanings required in logic, and then all the meanings required by scientific knowledge as such. Phenomenology fixes these meanings by going back to the a priori connections between acts which intend meanings and those acts which confirm meanings, meaning-fulfilments (LI, p. 252; Hua XIX/1 11). It is only through such a phenomenological fixing of meanings that we are able to keep the psychological distinct from the logical: "psychologism can only be radically overcome by pure phenomenology" (LI, p. 253; Hua XIX/1 11–12). The refutation of psychologism *requires* phenomenology; Husserl is now a long way removed from Frege's project.

As Husserl later recalled, in his *Phenomenological Psychology* lectures of 1925, looking back at the task and significance of the *Logical Investigations*:

> In 1900–01 my *Logical Investigations* appeared as the result of ten-year long efforts for a clarification (*Klärung*) of the pure idea of logic by a return to the bestowing of sense (*Sinngebung*) or the performance of cognition (*Erkenntnisleistung*) which occurs in the nexus of lived experiences of logical thinking. More accurately speaking, the single investigations of the second volume [i.e. the Six Investigations themselves] involved a turning of intuition back towards the logical lived experiences which take place in us whenever we think but which we do not see just then, which we do not have in our noticing view whenever we carry out thought activity in a naturally original manner. The thinker knows nothing of his lived experiences of thinking (*Denkerlebnissen*) but only of the thoughts (*Gedanken*) which his thinking engenders continuously. The point was to bring this obscurely occurring life of thinking into one's grip

by subsequent reflection and to fix it in faithful descriptive concepts (*in getreuen deskriptiven Begriffen zu fixieren*); further, to solve the newly arising problem, namely, to make intelligible how the forming of all those mentally produced formations takes place in the performance of this internal logical lived experiencing, formations which appear in assertively judicative thinking as multiply formed concepts, judgments, inferences, etc., and which find their generic expression, their universally objective mental stamp in the fundamental concepts and axioms of logic.

(*Phen. Psych.* § 3, p. 14; Hua IX 20–21)

A similar formulation of this aim can be found in the Introduction to the *Investigations* themselves where Husserl puts his problem as follows:

We have, on the one hand, the fact that all thought and knowledge have as their aim *objects* or *states of affairs*, which they putatively "hit" in the sense that the "intrinsic being" (*An-sich-sein*) of these objects and states is supposedly shown forth, and made an identifiable item, in a multitude of actual or possible meanings, or acts of thought. We have, further, the fact that all thought is ensouled by a thought-form which is subject to ideal laws, laws circumscribing the objectivity or ideality of knowledge in general. These facts, I maintain, eternally provoke questions like: How are we to understand the fact that the intrinsic being (*das "an-sich"*) of objectivity becomes "presented", "apprehended" in knowledge, and so ends up by becoming subjective? What does it mean to say that the object has "intrinsic being" (*"an-sich"*), and is "given" (*gegeben*) in knowledge? How can the ideality of the universal *qua* concept or law enter the flux of real mental states and become an epistemic possession (*Erkenntnisbesitz*) of the thinking person? What does the *adequatio rei et intellectus* mean in various cases of knowledge, according as what we apprehend and know, is individual or universal, a fact or a law etc.?

(LI, Intro. § 2, pp. 253–254; Hua XIX/1 12–13)

The ideal of science as a system of evident cognitions

Husserl begins the *Investigations* with an account of the 'Idea of science in general' (LI, *Prol.* § 11), what belongs to science as such, every kind of science, including sciences of the possible, the ideal, and so on. He calls this 'theory of science' (*Wissenschaftslehre*), following Bolzano, and he further agrees with Bolzano that logic provides the essence of this science. The conceptual requirements of the discipline of logic also supply the requirements for science in general.[2] Indeed it is not a paradox that logic which investigates the *form* of science should also investigate its own nature (LI, *Prol.* § 42, p. 173; Hua XVIII 165); pure logic is a set of self-evident truisms (*Selbstverständlichkeiten*).

Husserl holds, moreover, that the set of logical truths, and hence scientific truths, are all interrelated, and thus, he, like Carnap, is committed to the ideal of the unity of science: science is the body of true propositions linked together in a systematic way (LI, *Prol.* § 10). All theoretical research, no matter how it is conducted, eventually comes to expression in a body of *statements* (*Aussagen*, LI, Intro. § 2, p. 250; Hua XIX/1 7) or propositions. Logic, then, studies propositions. What is important for logic and science is the inferential connections between what is stated, between the propositional contents themselves, which has nothing to do with the contingent acts of assertion and judgements which gave rise to them. Logic, as any other theoretical science, is "an ideal fabric of meanings" (*eine ideale Complexion von Bedeutungen*, LI I § 29).

Science is concerned with the possession of truth, with *knowing* (*Erkennen*) or *cognition* (*Erkenntnis*) in a systematic, coherent sense, which means having grounds for one's knowing, possessing truths with evidential insight (LI, *Prol.* § 6, p. 62; Hua XVIII 30). Knowledge in the strictest sense requires *evidence* (*Evidenz*), cognitions given with insight (*Einsicht*), a certainty to be sharply distinguished from blind belief and all mere feelings of conviction, a point on which Husserl agreed with his mentor Brentano. For Husserl, "the most perfect 'mark' of correctness is inward evidence" (*Evidenz*, LI, *Prol.* § 6, p. 61; Hua XVIII 29). All genuine knowledge rests on *Evidenz*, which had been variously rendered as 'inner evidence' (Findlay), or 'self-evidence', but which we shall simply call 'evidence'. An act of knowing is evident when it displays or 'gives' itself with all the requirements necessary for knowledge, or when it has self-evidence, in the sense that one is fully warranted in holding the belief. Evidence, here, is not to be understood as a psychological feeling of some kind, or as a kind of mysterious, irrational hunch, but is "immediate intimation of truth itself" (LI, *Prol.* § 6, p. 61; Hua XVIII 29) and one which is not verified by further acts, though, of course, these may act as subsequent confirmations of the original truth-grasping. Indeed, evidence is achieved only after long and hard endeavours.[3] Crucially, self-evidence should not be thought of as occurring solely in the mathematical or logical domains, as when I see that 'A = A' is evident or self-evident. Husserl's standard examples of self-justifying evident acts are our normal perceptual acts; for example, acts of seeing which normally present the object with all the accompanying evidence necessary to warrant a judgement of the form "I see x". To get someone else to see requires drawing their attention to it, nothing more.[4] Evidence is not just to be encountered in rarified disciplines such as mathematics and logic but rather it is an on-going, everyday 'achievement' (*Leistung*) in all cognitions where the object is given in a satisfactory form, with 'intuitive fullness' (*anschaüliche Fülle*) or as Husserl prefers to say, in which the object gives itself, though, of course, always under an aspect.

In fact, evidence is more difficult to achieve in the mathematical sciences than in everyday life. As Husserl will say, our cognitive acts (*Erkenntnisse*) and 'lived experiences' or 'thought processes' (*Erlebnisse*) can become knowledge only when they are confirmed or illuminated by fulfilling intuitions. Truth involves identity between meaning intention and fulfilment. Ordinarily, we still speak of knowledge in a looser sense to include experiences where this evidence is no longer present: for example, I can say, "I believe Pythagoras's theorem is true, but I have forgotten the demonstration." But, in principle, to have knowledge is to be able to access or repeat the steps through to the original evidence. To know something is to be able to verify it, by tracing it back to some evident experiences which ground it fully. Thus, Husserl was captivated by Descartes's project of securing science on the basis of evident cognitions, cognitions given 'clearly and distinctly' (*clare et distincte*), the project of founding all deductions in intuitions. Indeed, even in the First Edition of the *Investigations*, Husserl invokes Descartes's phrase in speaking of the need to achieve 'clarity and distinctness' (*Klarheit und Deutlichkeit*, LI, p. 252; Hua XIX/1 10) in our concepts.

Husserl, however, recognised that Descartes's specifications of the nature of certainty were too theoretical. In the end, all acts of knowing possess a degree of fulfilment and can be fulfilled adequately if imperfectly (FTL § 106, p. 281; Hua XVII 287). In most of our knowledge, we have evidence only of the relative probability of the proposition being true. Discussions of *Evidenz* are scattered through the *Investigations* but the most comprehensive discussion is to be found in the Sixth Investigation. The important point here is that, in the *Investigations*, Husserl is producing, for the first time, a phenomenological account of evidence, an account of how our acts of cognition, *Erkenntnisse*, turn into genuine knowledge. How do acts of cognition achieve not just meaning intentions but fulfilments of meaning? How is objective knowledge possible in a knowing subject? This is the overall question of the *Investigations*.

Our acts of consciousness may, of course, be studied just as occurrent psychological occurrences, real events in nature, causally connected with other events, but in order to grasp the manner in which these acts become bearers of truth, we need to understand them as acts of intending meaning, 'significative acts' (*Akte des Bedeutens*), or what Husserl will call in the First Investigation, 'sense-bestowing acts' (*sinnverleihende Akte*, LI I § 9), acts which intend meanings, acts which purport to be *about* something, even when these acts are not expressed linguistically and hence are not aiming at propositional meaning. It is this extraordinary feature of our conscious life which was first properly expressed by Brentano, namely that we are, through psychic acts, able to intend entities beyond the psychic acts themselves. Normally, we are focused on external things or on our purposes and tasks, passing over those meaning contents which belong to the acts of intention. We look out and see *that it is raining*, and we focus on the fact or state of affairs itself, not on the meaning which we constituted in order that this be grasped as a fact for us. Husserl now wants to catalogue and analyse how, in the process of intending objects or states of affairs, we instantiate *meanings*. The difficulty of focusing on these meanings is due to the entirely 'unnatural' direction (*in der widernatürlichen Anschauungs- und Denksrich- tung*) of this kind of reflection (LI, Intro. § 3, p. 254; Hua XIX/1 14). Instead of becoming absorbed in the objectivating acts, we must reflect on them. In the revised Second Edition, Husserl inserts the reduction at this point as that methodology which allows us to move from natural reflection to phenome- nological reflection. Natural reflection needs to be purified by the applica- tion of the reduction in order to grasp these meaning structures without reifying them or naturalising them as the natural attitude is wont to do.

Already in numerous essays of the 1890s Husserl had in fact been carry- ing out such careful phenomenological descriptions (understood by him at the time in terms of Brentanian *descriptive psychology*) of these acts of meaning-intending. As early as 1893, for example, he was carefully distinguishing the kind of 'presentation' (*Vorstellung*) of an object experienced in an act of visual perception from the kind of 'representation' (*Repräsentation*) of the object in acts of fantasy or symbolisation, or, for example, when we intuit the sides of a cube not given directly in perception.[5] In a sense, this problem had grown out of an earlier distinction Husserl made in the *Philosophy of Arithmetic* between the manner in which the lower numbers are presented to us immediately or 'authentically' in intuition, whereas thinking of higher numbers involved an 'inauthentic' grasp of them through symbols. Husserl now recognises this as a particular form of a more general distinction which occurs in all forms of knowing, between the empty presentation and the various forms of 'filling' (*Erfüllung*) it can undergo. Husserl recognised the importance of being able to have empty significations; the possibility of symbolic thought founds the very possibility of science as such. On the other hand, seeing something before me right now in its bodily presence is the paradigm of the kind of bodily filling of our experience. A different form of presencing of the object occurs in acts of recalling that entity in its absence, whether in memory or imagination or expection.

Through the 1890s, Husserl became more interested in carefully describ- ing how objects present themselves in sensory intuition, in memory, fantasy, symbolic thinking, and so on. These studies show careful attention to the actual experience of seeing an object, focusing on it, letting one's gaze wander over it, having one's perceptual experience fulfilled in a definite way. Husserl distinguishes between the centrally attended to object in the perceptual act and the 'halo' or 'fringe' (a concept taken from William

James' *Principles of Psychology*, EW 326; Hua XXII 283) of relatively unfocused perceptions around it, the background against which the perception of the object is set off (EW 322; Hua XXII 278–279). Husserl is interested not only in the nature of the perceptual act performed but in the kind of 'content' yielded, distinguishing between *psychological* and *semantic* content, and between the *concrete* part or moment and the *abstract* part of the act. From the beginning to the end of the glance at the object (e.g. an inkwell), the content appears as a unity and yet it is 'modified' as its different parts come into view. Moreover, "the intuitive sequence is a temporal sequence" yet the experience of time plays no apparent role in the experience of the physical object (EW 323; Hua XXII 280).

In all these studies, Husserl explicitly distinguished between the psychological real *mental process* with its sensory and imaginative accompaniments and the *ideal mental content*, the meaning that the mental process enacts. One of his most careful studies at this time was his discussion of "Intentional Objects", dating from 1894–1895, which directly addresses the nature of intention and the problem, deriving from Bolzano, of 'objectless presentations', presentations whose contents were not or could not be realised in actuality (e.g. 'square circle', 'present King of France', 'centaur', 'square root of minus one', and so on). Husserl dismisses any solution which would claim these are merely mental images which do not exist in reality. When we intend these objects, we really intend them as objective and not as subjective creations of the mind. Husserl for this reason also rejects Twardowski's solution which separates these 'immanent' contents from the object. Part of Husserl's solution is to distinguish the immanent content from the ideal 'objective content' (*objektive Gehalt*, EW 373; Hua XXII 333). The recognition of the importance of that distinction led Husserl to devote the separately published *Prolegomena* (1900) of the *Logical Investigations* to the explicit repudiation of all forms of psychologism.

In the First Edition of the *Logical Investigations*, Husserl characterises the study in which he is engaged, namely the description of the processes which engender the ideal objectivities of logic, as a form of 'descriptive psychology' (LI, Intro. § 6, p. 262; Hua XIX/1 23). This led critics to claim that Husserl had refuted psychologism in the *Prolegomena*, the first book, only to fall back into it in the second book of the Six Investigations themselves, since here Husserl returns to the 'thought processes' or 'lived experiences' (*Erlebnisse*) which constitute the ideal meanings studied by logic. Partly to clarify that this was not the case, in the Second Edition of the *Logical Investigations*, Husserl emphatically rejects the view that the phenomenogical description of pure consciousness was in any way to be confused with psychology. Husserl will devote a great deal of the rest of his life to accepting the critique of psychologism and at the same time studying the a priori structures which make grasp of these objective meanings possible. Husserl saw this, in general terms, as the attempt to distinguish between naturalistic psychology in its various forms and transcendental phenomenology. Turning now to the *Logical Investigations*, let us first examine the *Prolegomena*, which was published separately, and came to have something of a separate life in German philosophy.

The *Prolegomena* (1900)

Husserl's long *Prolegomena* to his *Logical Investigations* was published first as a separate book at the end of 1899, and rather quickly had widespread impact among philosophers in Germany, being praised by Natorp, Dilthey, and others. Strictly speaking, the *Prolegomena* is propaedeutic to phenomenology. Indeed, only the First, Fifth and Sixth Investigations are genuinely phenomenological, to the extent that they fill out the kind of meaning-constituting acts which are required in order to constitute the ideal objectivities required by science.

The main purpose of the *Prolegomena* is to revive the old idea found in Leibniz and Bolzano of a 'pure logic' (*reine Logik*) and to defend the need for positing ideal objectivities (*Gegendständlichkeiten*), not just in mathematics and logic, but in all sciences which posit and operate with ideal laws. These ideal 'objectivities' are to be sharply distinguished from the psychological acts through which they are thought, otherwise many conceptual confusions arise, which can be gathered under the heading of 'psychologism'. *Psychologism* leads to conceptual absurdities and to relativism: psychologism, in fact, is the same as relativism (*Prol.* § 38).

The *Prolegomena* does not enquire into how we come to be in contact with the ideal realm; its purpose is to justify the need to posit ideal entities and to explain logic as the science of these entities. As Husserl put it:

> The reader of the *Prolegomena* is made a participant in a conflict between two motifs within the logical sphere which are contrasted in radical sharpness: the one is the psychological, the other the purely logical. The two do not come together by accident as the thought-act on the one side and the thought-meaning (*Denkbedeutung*) and the object of thought on the other. Somehow they necessarily belong together. But they are to be distinguished.
>
> (ILI, p. 20; Fink, p. 113)

Husserl is at pains to stress that we must recognise, besides real existent things in the world, such as stones and horses, with their causal powers and interactions, another domain of objecthood, which contains such 'irreal' or 'ideal' objectivities as the 'Pythagorean theorem' or the number '4'.

> Such irreal, or as one also says, ideal objects are, in their numerically identical singularity, substrates of true or false judgments just

99

as real things are; conversely "object" in the most universal logical sense means nothing else than anything at all concerning which statements can be made sensefully and in truth.

(*Phen. Psych.* § 3, p. 15; Hua IX 22)

Husserl then is postulating different kinds of objects, not all of which are spatio-temporal or sensibly grasped. In the *Logical Investigations*, he makes an attempt to clarify the different kinds of objectivities and how they relate to one another, and thus anticipated by two years Meinong's own attempts at a 'theory of objects' (*Gegenstandstheorie*), in his *On Assumptions* (1902). Husserl thought Meinong's theory of objectivities was defective (ILI, p. 44; Fink, p. 323), and even suspected him of plagiarism. For Husserl, the idea of an a priori 'rational ontology' of objects in general was an old philosophical idea, which he had revived despite the opposition from Kantianism and empiricism.

As Husserl never tires of stressing, we must distinguish particular, existent things (usually physical things, but including also occurrent psychological acts understood as psycho-physical entities) from the sets of ideal meanings which those acts grasp and the objectivities to which those meanings refer. Thus, for example, we encounter a particular object which has a particular red colour. The actual particular red which exists is, in Husserl's terms, a 'moment' (*Moment*) of red, that is the particular red is a *dependent* (*unselbstständige*) part of the object and would not exist unless the object did, but in seeing the colour as 'red', we also grasp 'redness' and 'colour'. That is, we intuit the species *red* and even the species *colour*. These *species* are instantiated in the particular red moment of the object. These *species* are, using the language of the Brentano school, 'objects of a higher order'. They differ from the individual, temporal particular in that they do not change over time, they have strict identity conditions, and yet they are multiply instantiable:

A red object stands before us, but this red object is not the Species Red. Nor does the concrete object contain the Species as a "psychological" or "metaphysical" part. The part, the non-independent moment of red (*dies unselbständige Rotmoment*), is, like the concrete whole object, something individual, something here and now, something which arises and vanishes with the concrete whole object, and which is *like*, not identical, in different objects. Redness, however, is an ideal unity (*eine ideale Einheit*), in regard to which it is absurd to speak of coming into being or passing away. The part (moment) red is not Redness, but an instance of Redness (*ein Einzelfall von Röte*). And, as universal objects differ from singular ones, so, too, do our acts of apprehending them.

(*Prol.* § 39, p. 149; Hua XVIII 135)

Furthermore, here Husserl distinguishes between individual entities and their parts and moments, and these ideal species and the ideal 'states of affairs' (*Sachverhalte*) and the 'situations' (*Sachlage*) which underlie them; for example, that *the square on the hypotenuse is equal to the sum of the squares on the other two sides of a right-angled triangle* which are said to 'obtain' (*bestehen*) as opposed to existing.[6] We grasp these identities in acts of ideation quite distinct from sensory perception, and we are able to express meanings which correspond to those idealities. These meanings have relations to other meanings and form a network of ideal relations. Husserl actually distinguishes ideal objects from *meanings* which are also idealities. For Husserl, different expressions in the same language may express the same *meaning*. Meanings are ideal self-identical unities which are the correlates of the expressive acts. As such they are to be distinguished from the objects referred to *through* our expressive acts of meaning. Or to put it another way, meanings are not ontological items in the manner in which ideal objects are.[7] Husserl's phenomenology in the *Investigations* has been interpreted as nothing more than conceptual analysis, or as the analysis of the meanings of words. Indeed, Husserl's earlier descriptions of his method tends to support this interpretation: for example, in his 1907 lectures on *Thing and Space* he begins with the everyday meaning of the word 'perception'. But in his 1913 draft *Introduction to the Investigations* Husserl rejects the interpretation of phenomenology as 'meaning-analysis' (*Bedeutungsanalyse*, ILI, p. 49; Fink, p. 328). Of course, phenomenology is concerned with meanings, but its real focus is on the a priori manner in which these meanings are related together and the structural nature of all kinds of acts, including acts of perception, imagining, and so on.

Psychologism

The main function of the *Prolegomena* is to demonstrate that science, at least as an ideal, as a set of ideal truths, requires positing meaning-unities and other ideal entities, which are irreducible to the factually occurrent entities of the physical world. The great enemy is *psychologism* which confuses these domains. In his Foreword to the First Edition of the *Investigations* Husserl stated that he had originally began with the "prevailing assumption that psychology was the science from which logic in general, and the logic of the deductive sciences, had to hope for philosophical clarification" (LI, p. 42; Hua XVIII 6), but he soon realised that the "logical unity of the thought content" could not be treated satisfactorily from the psychological standpoint. He ends the Foreword by invoking Goethe's dictum that there is nothing upon which one is more severe than the errors one has just abandoned, thus conceding that, in his eyes at least, his earlier work in the *Philosophy of Arithmetic* had been tainted by *psychologism*.

Psychologism is a philosophical label, usually pejorative, for a whole set of different positions not all of which are easily definable, but which may be said to hold, at least in some sense, that logic and arithmetic reduce to, or are explained by, the psychological acts wherein logical and mathematical concepts operate and originate.[8] The term 'psychologism' had been coined by the German philosopher J. E. Erdmann. A psychologistic tendency was evident among many nineteenth-century logicians, and Husserl, in his *Selbstanzeige* to the *Prolegomena*, refers to psychologism as the 'dominant' position in Germany. The English philosopher John Stuart Mill (1806–1873), who, in his *A System of Logic* (1843), defined logic as "the science of the operations of the understanding, which are subservient to the estimation of evidence", was extremely influential on the European tradition of logic.[9] Psychologistic philosophers included Theodor Lipps, in his *Grundzüge der Logik* (1893), as well as Erdmann, Sigwart, and others. Psychologism also had its opponents in the older Austro-German logical tradition stemming from Bernard Bolzano who had most clearly distinguished the thinking process from the thought. In this tradition must be situated Hermann Lotze in his *Logik* (1874), and his student, Gottlob Frege, in the *Begriffschrift* (1879), *Foundations of Arithmetic* (1884), and *Grundgesetze* (1893). For Frege, in particular, psychologism involves a "psychological falsification of logic". But the Neo-Kantians, including Hermann Cohen, Heinrich Rickert, Windelband, and Paul Natorp, also opposed psychologism. The Neo-Kantian position saw logic as dealing with judgements of 'validity' (*Geltung, Gültigkeit*) rather than with anything factual, the domain of 'facticity' (*Faktizität*). Husserl himself was deeply influenced by Natorp who features frequently in the *Prolegomena*, and despite his criticisms of certain kinds of Neo-Kantianism, was clearly more influenced by this tradition than he was willing to admit. Husserl sides with those (such as Hermann Lotze) who argue for the independence of logic as a purely theoretical science of ideal objectivities and the relations between them. In any event, in Germany, Husserl and Frege offered the strongest arguments against psychologism, but, since Frege's work was largely in obscurity, it was Husserl's *Prolegomena* which produced the strongest counterblast to psychologism.

Psychologism is a catch-all label for a whole bundle of theses and tendencies. Some take it to be an ontologically reductionist thesis about the nature of the entities which logic studies: that is, they are in fact psychological entities within the mind. Others see it as a thesis about the nature of logic as a practical discipline: that is, that logic is an art of organising one's reasoning processes to generate sound conclusions, a view held by Brentano himself. From around 1896 Husserl had opposed this tendency to think of logic as an art of reasoning. While Husserl was aware that Brentano subscribed to the traditional view of logic as a *Kunstlehre*, he himself understood logic as a pure a priori science of ideal truths and ideal laws, these laws then grounding the normative rules which are prescribed in different disciplines (*Phen. Psych.* § 3, p. 24; Hua IX 33–34). Furthermore, Brentano thought the locus of truth was the act of judgement, whereas Husserl thought of objective propositions as the bearers of truth. Husserl's concept of a pure science of ideal laws, a pure logic, came from Lotze and Bolzano and was originally inspired by Leibniz's conception of a *characteristica universalis* (LI, *Prol.* § 61, pp. 221–224; Hua XVIII 225–229). Thus Husserl's problematic was "a clarification of the essential aims of a pure logic". Yet, paradoxically, in his own mind at the time, Husserl also saw the *Investigations* as a development of Brentano's suggestions concerning logic, though Brentano is mentioned only once in the *Prolegomena* (*Prol.* § 13, p. 78; Hua XVIII 48).

In the *Prolegomena*, however, Husserl is concerned only with the *ideal* of science, and the nature of the ideal objectivities and ideal laws which relate them. Normative sciences rest on a theoretical science of ideal truths (*Prol.* § 16) which are expressed in general propositions, laws descriptive of this ideal domain of eternal truths. In agreement with Frege, Husserl wants to make a sharp distinction between ideal *theoretical laws* and *norms* of reasoning, and criticises the Neo-Kantians for having confused these two domains. Indeed Husserl's distinction between the *ideal* and the *normative* is an important distinction which is often ignored. Husserl himself simply took over the distinction from Lotze – logic deals with ideal "validities" (*Geltungen*) and the laws which hold between them. Ideal laws of this kind are ideal truths and are to be distinguished from 'rules' which, as procedures, do not demonstrate the inner connections which validly hold between these ideal entities. Logical entities have their own 'being-in-itself' (*Ansichsein*), though it cannot be said that Husserl explicates this notion in any systematic manner.

Psychologism is a betrayal of the very essence of logic as a science. To secure understanding of this ideal domain of truths, it is necessary to distinguish the objects of logic, thoughts, from all factually occurring psychic processes. Furthermore, even those who have criticised psychologism have expressed their own anti-psychologistic arguments in a confused manner (*Prol.* § 20). Thus Husserl brings a two-pronged attack to bear on both psychologism and even varieties of anti-Kantianism which opposed it. Some supposedly anti-psychologistic logicians have proposed that psychology be understood as dealing with thought *as it is*, while logic deals with thought *as it ought to be*. But Husserl argues that this initial formulation is too crude, since even psychologism's supporters argue that logic is about thinking as it *should* be carried out, "good thinking", as Mill calls it. The real problem is that psychologistic theorists understand this normative science to be only a division of thinking as it is, and hence logic is to be a part of psychology. Husserl, on the other hand, wants to sharply distinguish *psychological* from purely *logical* laws. Psychology is a factual, empirical science of consciousness and its so-called 'psychological laws' (e.g. the so-called law of association of ideas) are quite vague, being merely generalisations from experience (LI, *Prol.* § 21, p. 98; Hua XVIII 72), laws limited by *ceteris paribus* clauses, expressible only as probabilities, at best mere approximations to the ideal laws. The laws of logic, on the other hand, are exact, universal, and ideal. Furthermore, logic is an a priori science, and hence it cannot be based on a science of fact. Logic makes no assumptions about the existence or nature of mental states, it knows nothing of presentations or judgements (*Prol.* § 23). Logical laws are not about the "facticities of mental life" (*Tatsächlichkeiten des psychischen Lebens, Prol.* § 23, p. 104; Hua XVIII 81). Of course, traditional logic understood logical laws like *modus ponens* as norms for reasoning, but *modus ponens* itself tells us nothing about mental phenomena or reasoning processes, but rather states necessary relations between propositions. Thus Husserl is here articulating Frege's view that logic has as little to do with psychology as it has with star gazing. Perhaps the most classic example of the confusion between psychology and logic is the Law of Non-Contradiction, which is often stated as a kind of rule of reasoning or even as a factual limit on human conceptualising: that is, that we cannot posit a proposition and its negation as both true at the same time. Mill, for instance, interpreted this law as a generalisation from human experience: we cannot entertain together a belief and its contradictory. In fact, however, the Law of Non-Contradiction states solely that a proposition and its negation cannot both be true, and makes no reference to what is actually, subjectively thinkable. Husserl then rejects all empiricist attempts to locate logical laws in actual mental activity.

Though Husserl's repudiation of empiricist views of logic agrees in general with the Neo-Kantian view, Husserl, nevertheless, also criticises certain Neo-Kantian interpretations of logic, as having been seduced by a psychologising tendency in that they understand logic as a set of a priori psychological structures which every human possesses. Indeed, Husserl thinks Kant himself had been guilty of treating his transcendental psychology precisely as a psychology, an account of structures factually possessed by the human species. Neo-Kantians such as Friedrich A. Lange have tried to claim a kind of 'double status' for logical laws: on the one hand, they are *natural laws* determining actual reasoning; on the other hand they are *normative laws* (*Prol.* § 28). For Husserl, however, the laws governing the two domains are radically different in kind. Natural laws are generalisations whereas logical laws are ideal and exact.

Having criticised empiricist and Neo-Kantian misunderstandings of logic, Husserl goes on to a general repudiation of psychologism, which, for him, turns out to be a kind of *relativism* and *subjectivism* (*Prol.* §§ 34–38), and hence collapses into 'absurdity' (*Widersinn*). Husserl sees psychologism as leading to a subjectivism which may be either individualist or specific in form. Protagorean relativism ("man is the measure of all things") is one possible consequence of psychologism, whereby truth is relative to human nature, whether relative to each individual or relative to the species as a whole. Treating the logical laws as describing the thinking of human beings as such leads to a kind of 'species relativism' (*der spezifische Relativismus*) or 'anthropologism' (*Anthropologismus, Prol.* § 36), a kind of subjectivism which extends to the whole human species.

Anthropologism maintains that truth is relative to the human species and hence, without humans, there would be no truth. Husserl understands Kant's account of knowledge as a kind of anthropologism in this sense. He accuses Kant of misunderstanding the subjective domain as if it were something natural, and hence of construing the a priori as if it were an essential part of the human species (*Prol.* § 38). But Husserl maintains this is a contradition, since 'there is no truth' would then be true. Truth as such does not depend on any facts, including facts of human nature. The law of non-contradiction is not merely a law governing the species *Homo sapiens*. If there were no minds to think them the logical laws would still hold, though as ideal possibilities unfulfilled in actuality (*Prol.* § 39, p. 149; Hua XVIII 135–136). Furthermore one should not confuse a *true judgement*, one made in conformity with truth, with the *truth* of the judgement, the objective true content of the judgement (*Prol.* § 36, p. 142; Hua XVIII 126). For Husserl, logic emerges from considering the essential necessary relations between basic concepts:

> Anyone can see from my statements up to this point that for me the pure truths of logic are all the ideal laws which have their whole foundation in the "sense" (*Sinn*), the "essence" (*Wesen*) or the "content" (*Inhalt*) of the concepts of Truth, Proposition, Object, Property, Relation, Combination, Law, Fact, etc.
>
> (*Prol.* § 37, p. 144; Hua XVIII 129)

The six Investigations and the 'breakthrough' to pure phenomenology

Though the *Prolegomena* was enthusiastically received, Husserl later regretted that the second volume, which contained the six Investigations themselves, met with bemused puzzlement, where it was noticed at all. Natorp and Dilthey had welcomed the anti-psychologistic *Prolegomena*, but reviewers of the second volume assumed either that Husserl, with all his talk of 'lived experiences' (*Erlebnisse*), had relapsed back into psychologism, or that he was merely substituting a rationalistic, scholastic account of ideal meanings (ILI, p. 22; Fink, p. 115). In the six Investigations Husserl is attempting to describe the domain of mental processes precisely in so far as they are the original sources from which the meaning-unities analysed by logic are distilled.

In the First Edition (1901) version of the Introduction to the Second Book of the *Logical Investigations*, Husserl explicitly states that phenomenology is epistemological critique or 'descriptive psychology':

> Phenomenology is descriptive psychology. Epistemological criticism is therefore in essence psychology, or at least capable of being built on a psychological foundation.
>
> (LI, p. 262; Hua XIX/1 24)

Thus, in 1901, Husserl publicly identified with Brentano's and Stumpf's project of descriptive psychology; indeed the *Logical Investigations* is dedicated to Stumpf. But even in 1901 Husserl recognises the apparent paradox: if pure logic rests on psychology, what was the point of the critique of psychologism in the *Prolegomena*? Husserl's answer in the First Edition is that logic and psychology are two sciences which depend on the same preparatory field of the pure description of the phenomena on which both logic and psychology are based. Phenomenology then is a description of the concrete acts from which logic draws its essential ideal meanings. Clearly this account of phenomenology was not satisfactory to Husserl. In the revised Introduction in the Second Edition of 1913, Husserl repudiated the label 'descriptive psychology' and in much of his subsequent writing (e.g. the lectures on *Phenomenological Psychology* of 1925 and the Amsterdam lectures of 1929) was concerned to distinguish phenomenology from all kinds of psychology as traditionally understood, including Brentanian descriptive psychology. Psychology is now seen as describing mental processes as events and real facts in nature, whereas phenomenology is understood as contemplation of pure essences on the basis of exemplary individual intuitions of experiences (including freely imagined experiences). Phenomenology is a 'viewing of essences' (*Wesenserschauung*) which examines the essence of perception, judging, feeling, as such, not as in this or that animal organism (LI, p. 262; Hua XIX/1 23). Thus Husserl opens up the field of phenomenology as that science which maps the a priori essential possibilities of knowledge in general, entirely distinct from the different kinds of factual embodiments of cognition in humans, animals, and even imagined beings such as angels or Martians. Moreover, Husserl believed such essential forms could be intuited through imaginative variation and rotation of possibilities in consciousness. This would eventually lead to him espousing a form of transcendental idealism where all meanings and essences are already embedded somehow in the transcendental ego.

In both editions of the *Logical Investigations*, phenomenology is characterised as a pure *descriptive* science of consciousness in general, consciousness as such, which presupposes nothing about what it is describing other than what is directly given in intuitive evidence. As such, phenomenology is primarily a *concrete* science foregoing abstract speculative theorising of the kind associated with traditional metaphysics. Phenomenology wants to trace acts of cognition to their ground in acts of clarifying and fulfilling intuition. Thus in the Introduction to the Second Volume (i.e. the six Investigations themselves), Husserl emphasises the absolute generality of phenomenology:

> we are concerned here with discussions of a most general sort which cover the wider sphere of an objective *theory of knowledge*, and closely linked with this last, the *pure phenomenology of the experiences of thinking and knowing*. This phenomenology, like the more inclusive *pure phenomenology of experiences in general* (*reine Phänomenologie der Erlebnisse überhaupt*) has, as its exclusive concern, experiences intuitively seizable and analysable in their pure essential generality (*in reiner Wesensallgemeinheit*), not experiences empirically perceived and treated as real facts, as experiences of experiencing humans or animals in the phenomenal world that we posit as an empirical fact. This phenomenology must bring to pure expression (*zu reinem Ausdruck*), must *describe* in terms of their essential concepts and their governing formulae of essence, the essences which directly make themselves known in intuition, and the connections which have their roots purely in such essences. Each such statement of essence is an *a priori* statement in the highest sense of the word.
>
> (LI, Intro., p. 249; Hua XIX/1 6, trans. slightly altered)

The nature of this description of phenomenology is problematic. How can there be a description of the a priori? Surely, if the a priori forms the conditions of experience, the transcendental domain, it cannot itself be experienced and descriptively characterised. This, in the main, was the charge the Neo-Kantians, especially Natorp, levelled against phenomenology.[10] Husserl's response was to argue that he had fixed the concept of the a priori which was loosely understood in Kantian philosophy and, in his later writings, claimed that the reduction allows us access to a transcendental domain of experience. Only constant employment of the reduction allows us to access the transcendental field of pure experience and prevents us from the lapsing back into psychologism and naturalism about the psychic.

In fulfilling the aim to clarify the basic concepts of logic and of formal knowledge generally, Husserl claimed it was necessary to go back 'to the things themselves' (*Wir wollen auf die 'Sachen selbst' zurückgehen*, LI, Intro. § 2, p. 252; Hua XIX/1 10). Husserl does not mean that we must bring philosophy back to a concern with factual, empirical things, such as physical objects in space and time. Indeed, Husserl has no interest in the factual or individual as such. Nor is Husserl invoking the Kantian opposition between 'phenomena' and 'things in themselves'. By going back to the things themselves, Husserl means we cannot be satisfied with employing concepts whose evidential basis has not been properly clarified by being brought back to their original sources in intuition. The 'things themselves', then, are the immediately intuited essential elements of consciousness, viewed not as psychological processes, but in terms of their essential natures as meaning-intentions (*Bedeutungsintentionen*) and their interconnected meaning-fulfilments (*Bedeutungserfüllungen*), essential structures involved in all understanding (LI, Intro. § 2, p. 252; Hua XIX/1 11). Husserl's 'things themselves' are the pure a priori *essences* of the acts constituting ideal objectivities, as Husserl's Göttingen assistant, Adolf Reinach, insisted.[11] Husserl wants phenomenology to address the given, the phenomena, the things themselves, in the sense of whatever immediately appears to consciousness in the manner that it so appears. As Husserl never ceased to emphasise, this was the true meaning of positivism and of radical empiricism, not going beyond the evidence that is yielded in the experiences as they manifest themselves to be.

In the Investigations, of course, Husserl is primarily concerned with analysing our 'logical experiences' (*logische Erlebnisse*) and phenomenology is the disciplined attempt to describe and clarify their essential nature and structure. But he was already conceiving phenomenology in its widest sense as the clarification of meaning-formations in all aspects of cognition. It is important to note too, that, by 'cognition' (*Erkenntnis*), Husserl means the experiences in which something comes to be grasped as known. He is not primarily dealing with theoretical knowledge, a criticism which Heidegger levels against him; rather he includes all forms of knowing-how and emotional states wherein something can be intuited and fulfilled – for example, what it means to be in love, and so on.

The six Investigations are concerned with analysing the most basic elements which are required for any form of knowledge whatsoever: "the pure phenomenology of the experiences of thinking and knowing" (*Denk-und Erkenntniserlebnisse*, LI, Intro. § 1, p. 249; Hua XIX/1 6). These experiences are to be studied not as factually occurring psychological entities but in terms of their necessary structure as acts of their kind. In other words, Husserl is asking the question: what is the essence of an act of perception as such, an act of thinking, and so on? Essences are the web of ideal possibilities and relationships that constitute a particular domain of experience. Husserl is also emphatic that he is not interested in treating the logical contents of the acts as the logician is. Phenomenology paves the way for logic and other formal sciences, by elucidating the manner concepts are 'constituted' in concrete experiences. This particular way of uniting the subjective and the objective is the essence of phenomenology. Husserl conceives of phenomenology as a realm of a priori ideal meaning structures which provide the necessary structural links between empirical psychological acts on the one hand and the realm of ideal entities, objectivities and states of affairs on the other.

It has, of course, been much disputed whether phenomenology does in fact access an a priori domain distinct both from the psychological and the purely logical. But it is precisely Husserl's point that distinguishing the psychological correctly from the logical is the first step to bringing into proper view the essential processes of meaning-intending and meaning-fulfilling that unite these two areas. This is the proper domain of phenomenology. Indeed, Husserl himself seems not to have been fully aware of the exact nature of this domain until he began writing the Fifth and Sixth Investigations which dealt directly with the intentional structures of consciousness and the nature of evidence and truth. As we shall see in the next chapter, by the time of the Second Edition of the *Investigations* in 1913, Husserl was characterising the outlook of phenomenology as 'transcendental', explicitly aligning himself with the transcendental turn in Descartes and Kant. Indeed, he considered himself to have clarified the nature of the a priori much better than Kant. Husserl wants to distinguish the phenomenological a priori from the more traditional ontological a priori.

In the 1913 Second Edition of the *Investigations*, Husserl inserts the notion of the 'reduction' (*Reduktion*) as the proper way of gaining access to this realm of transcendental subjectivity. This partial revision of the *Investigations* in the light of Husserl's transcendental turn, makes the composite text quite confusing and complex. We shall have more to say about this later in this chapter, but for now we shall turn to a brief survey of the six Investigations themselves.

A brief survey of the six Investigations

The six Investigations are in-depth meditations on certain key concepts which Husserl thinks are required in any formal science, for example the nature of signification in general, the relation of individual to universal, part to whole, the a priori rules determining the pure form of meaning in general, the structure of intentional acts and the nature of presentation, and finally the nature of the modes of fulfilment of intentional acts which relate to the manner in which truth is understood.

Since mature science is expressed in sentences, Husserl thinks we must begin with an examination of the nature of expression as such. Hence in the First Investigation, Husserl carefully describes the nature of acts of signification in general, discriminating between their different functions, and concentrating on those sign-complexes which relate to their designated objects through *meanings*. The Second Investigation considers various aspects of the formal relations between the individual instance and the universal, including a reflection on the nature of traditional accounts of reaching the universal through abstraction. The Third Investigation generalises from the relation between instance and universal to produce a general formal theory of the necessary a priori relations specifiable between parts and wholes in general. The Fourth Investigation applies the theory of parts and wholes to explicate the relations between the parts of speech in any language, hence producing a formal grammar. The Fifth Investigation goes behind language to the nature of mental acts and their contents, understanding mental acts as having an intentional structure and offering a careful account of the nature of mental repesentation in general. The Sixth Investigation examines the nature of the experience of truth and evidence as elements in a phenomenological elucidation of knowledge. We shall now discuss in more detail three of the Investigations – the First, Fifth, and Sixth – as these, by Husserl's own admission, were the most important Investigations for developing his concept of phenomenology.

The First Logical Investigation

Knowledge takes place in deliberately intended expressive acts (e.g. written or uttered sentences). Every sign (*Zeichen*) signifies something, but Husserl makes a distinction between signs which operate purely as 'indications' (*Anzeichen*), and simply point beyond themselves to something else, and signs which function as 'expressions' (*Ausdrücke*) which require a *meaning* (*Bedeutung*) and whose purpose is to communicate: "it is part of the notion of an expression to have a meaning" (LI I § 15, p. 292; Hua XIX/1 59). Indications include such types of signification as smoke indicating fire, or a fossil as a sign of a mammal, or a flag standing for a nation, or a knot in a handkerchief serving as a reminder, where no intrinsic 'meaning' or 'content' links sign and signified and the 'indicative relation' between sign and the signatum is causal or conventional, that is external (LI I § 2). Indications as such do not *express* meanings. *Expressions*, for Husserl, are primarily parts of speech, and he excludes gestures and facial expressions which signify only by indicating. Expressions, of course, also serve as indications in that they indicate to someone that a meaning is being communicated; that is, they motivate the hearer to believe that the speaker is undergoing a mental process, entertaining a content and seeking to communicate something (LI I § 7). This is what Husserl calls the 'intimating function' (*die kundgebende Funktion*) of the sign: when someone is speaking, I listen to them as someone thinking, recounting, etc. But these kinds of indication, which are often found 'interwoven' (*verflochten*) with expressive acts, differ sharply in essence from the nature of expression as such. Logic is interested only in expression, in the expressed meanings and their formal interconnections (e.g. relations of inference), their essential kinds and differences (LI I § 29). Expressions express meanings, they carry as it were an ideal expressive meaning or sense. A meaningless (*bedeutungslos, sinnlos*) expression is, strictly speaking, not an expression at all. Husserl rejects the traditional view of expressions which accounted for them solely in terms of the set of physical sounds or written marks, on the one hand, and a sequence of mental states, on the other. This account ignores the role of the ideal sense. A set of sounds (a chain of noises) only becomes a communicable meaning when it is endowed with an intention by the speaker, when it is animated by an intention (LI I § 7). Husserl holds that this is true, even in our 'solitary mental life' (*im einsamen Seelenleben*, LI I § 8); that is, in one's private mental thinking to oneself, even here expressions continue to function as they do in public communication though this time without the intimating function being operative. The words (whether a phrase or a sentence) still express meanings (*Bedeutungen*). But there is no need for a private thinker to have to signal to him- or herself that he or she is having such a thought. Expression of meaning then is essentially different from 'intimation' (*Kundgabe*), though of course the different functions are usually found operating in the one speech act. Moreover, we normally experience an expression as a set of words and meanings which are so unified that they cannot be separated. They have fused in a whole. Husserl wants to describe this whole phenomenologically in terms of the physical phenomenon (sounds, marks) and the "acts which give it meaning and possibly intuitive fulness, in which its relation to an expressed object is constituted" (LI I § 9, p. 280; Hua XIX/1 44). At this point Husserl introduces two crucial distinctions. On the one hand, he distinguishes between the sense-giving and sense-fulfilling acts, between meaning-intentions (*Bedeutungsintentionen*) and their fulfilment (LI I § 9). He will return to give a fuller account of these acts and their interrelation in the Sixth Investigation. Secondly, he distinguishes between an expression's meaning or sense and its objective correlate, the 'objectivity' (*Gegenständlichkeit*) to which it refers. An expression "*means* something, and in so far as it means something, it relates to what is objective" (*Er meint etwas, und indem er es meint, bezieht er sich auf Gegenständliches*, LI I § 9, p. 280; Hua XIX/1 44). The relation between an expression and its meaning is an ideal relation, meanings are ideal, self-identical unities (e.g. 'that the three perpendiculars of a triangle intersect in a point') which do not come into being or pass away, and which may be shared between speakers (LI I § 11). Moreover, a meaning is entirely different from the mental images which may accompany an act of thinking, and Husserl derides the retarded state of descriptive psychology which has confused the two (LI I § 17).

Expressions not only express meanings, they express these meanings *of* something. An expression *refers* to (*bezieht sich auf*, LI I § 12) an object. Expressions, then, not only have a 'meaning' (*Bedeutung*) but also have a 'reference' (*Beziehung*). Furthermore, different expressions may pick out the same object through different *meanings*; thus 'the vanquished at Waterloo' and the 'victor at Jena' both designate the same entity, Napoleon (LI I § 12).

111

Similarly two expressions with the same meaning can actually refer to different objects, for example when I use the word 'horse' to refer to two different horses. Expressions not only refer to, or name, individual objects (like 'Napoleon' or 'a horse') but may also refer to more complex situations or states of affairs (e.g. 'the cat is on the mat'). At this point Husserl maintains that two different propositional senses ('a > b' and 'b > a') actually pick out the same state of affairs (*Sachlage, Sachverhalt*, LI I § 12).[12] This account of sense and reference, though it uses different technical language, is more or less the same as that of Frege with which Husserl had been familiar since the early 1890s. For both, the reference is made *through* the meaning (*mittels seiner Bedeutung*, LI I § 13). Husserl, of course, disagrees with Frege's idiosyncratic terminological distinction between *Sinn* and *Bedeutung* and continues to use the two interchangeably (LI I § 15). Of course, Frege held the strange view that all true sentences have the same reference, namely *the true*, whereas for Husserl the references of sentences will be the state of affairs that they affirm as holding. For Husserl, expressions in so far as they have senses also have intended references, but these intended references may be quite vague and general until they are specified by context, and for some expressions (e.g. 'round square') the reference is incapable of being fulfilled. In general a meaning has a 'range of possible fulfilment' (LI I § 13). Expressions like 'round square' do not lack meaning, they are not meaningless, but they lack referential fulfilment. They are absurd or counter-sensical rather than non-sensical. 'The present King of France' likewise is a meaningful expression, which at one time had a genuine object to which it referred. Not all uses of the phrase then fail to refer.

Husserl's analysis of states of affairs is worth noting. States of affairs were a distinctive feature of Austrian philosophy, discussed in the Brentano school by Meinong, Marty, Husserl, and Reinach, through whom they entered into Wittgenstein's *Tractatus*. These are ideal complex, non-linguistic unities, the ontological counterparts of propositional contents, which may contain as their parts individual things. They can be said to 'hold' (*bestehen*) or not to hold; when they hold, the proposition expressing this state of affairs is said to be true. States of affairs, then, are what they are whether we assert their validity or not (LI I § 11). A state of affairs is a 'unity of validity' (*Geltungseinheit*). States of affairs are the objective correlates of complex intentional contents. When I believe that it is raining, then I am intending the state of affairs that *it is raining*. Written in that format they were often confused with the contents of judgements, or with the contents of sentences. But states of affairs are rather that which is said to be the case or to hold if a sentence is true. Sentences are truth bearers, whereas 'states of affairs' are truth makers, that which makes the sentences true. It is part of their nature that they can be expressed as nominalisations or as infinitives, for example the *rose's redness*, the *being red of the rose*.

States of affairs combine objects with objects or objects with predicates. Indeed it is a structural feature of a state of affairs that anything can be a part of it, including real spatio-temporal objects.

It is not possible here to discuss Husserl's rich account of sense and reference in relation to earlier theories such as those of Mill (who distinguished *connotation* from *denotation*), or indeed to more recent theories of signification. Suffice to say that Husserl proposed a carefully differentiated account which can be seen as a challenging alternative to the Fregean account which has achieved currency in contemporary philosophy. However, one part of Husserl's discussion deserves mention here. In the First Investigation, Husserl offers a treatment of expressions whose reference varies with the occasion of their use. Husserl calls these 'essentially occasional expressions' (*wesentlich okkasionelle Ausdrücke*, LI I § 26) and sees their meaning as tied to the circumstances of utterance, unlike mathematical expressions which mean the same thing in every context. These occasional expressions would now be termed 'indexicals', for example personal pronouns, demonstratives, 'I', 'here', 'now', 'this', 'the President', and so on. Thus 'I' picks out whoever is speaking that phrase. His treatment of these occasional expressions (which he later admitted was still wholly inadequate) is quite general, and includes proper names in an account which runs directly counter to that developed by Mill and later by Russell and is now thought to be close to the theory developed by Gareth Evans.[13] Husserl rejects Mill's view that a proper name (e.g. 'Socrates') is merely a mark which directly picks out the object it denotes (LI I § 16). Mill has confused expression and indications. Proper names are fully expressions and hence they have a sense. They are, however, not disguised descriptions either. A proper name picks out a person or object, and has a meaning or represents some kind of content. Every time we use the name we directly refer to the person but we may also have different presentational contents.

The First Logical Investigation has been subjected to intense critical scrutiny by Derrida, especially in *Speech and Phenomena* (1967) where, in a long critique of Husserl's concepts of signs, Derrida accuses Husserl of prioritising spoken speech, claiming that Husserl's notion of expression is indelibly tied to the notion of spoken language (SP 18) and prioritising the relation of presence between sign and signified. We shall discuss Derrida's criticisms in a later chapter, but here we shall simply notice that Derrida generally speaking has misunderstood the thrust of Husserl's distinctions, for example the nature of different functions of expression and indication.

The Fifth Logical Investigation

The Fifth Logical Investigation, entitled "Intentional Experiences and Their Contents", engages in a long meditation on the nature of intentional acts, particularly the act of presentation, which takes its general orientation from

Brentano's descriptive psychology though it offers careful refinements of Brentano's concepts, and provides a particularly careful differentiation of the different meanings of 'representation' (*Vorstellung*) and 'content' (*Inhalt*). Husserl emphasises the fundamental importance of the concept of intentionality for analysing consciousness, but he regards Brentano's situation of intentionality within the project of attempting to distinguish between mental and physical phenomena as profoundly misleading as to the true nature of intentionality. Moreover, Husserl is particularly unhappy with Brentano's terminology of 'psychic acts', 'presentations', 'immanent contents', as well as his description of 'inner perception', all of which was, for Husserl, shot through with ambiguities of a fatal kind. Husserl wants to drop talk of the 'psychical' as too loaded with preconceptions and instead proposes to talk broadly of our 'intentional experiences' (*Erlebnisse*), or intentional 'acts' (*Akte*), which does not necessarily refer to any conscious activity on the part of the subject or make any claims about the nature of the physical. An act of perception, for example, may be a passive act, as when I cannot help hearing a sound.

According to Husserl's interpretation of Brentano, intentionality yields the essence of psychic acts: "In perception something is perceived, in imagination, something is imagined, in a statement something stated, in love something loved, in hate hated, in desire, desired, etc." (LI V § 10, p. 554; Hua XIX/1 380). Whereas, as we have seen, Brentano recognised only three basic forms (*Grundklasse*) of psychical acts, namely presentations, judgements, and phenomena of love and hate, Husserl recognises myriad forms and never set a limit to the number of possible intentional structures. The main point is to recognise that "there are essentially different species and sub-species of intention" (LI V § 10, p. 555; Hua XIX/1 381) and that there is no other way to express them than in the language of commonsense psychology:

> To represent an object, e.g. the Schloss at Berlin, to oneself, is, we said, to be minded in this or that descriptively determinate fashion. To *judge* about this Schloss, to delight in its architectural beauty, to cherish the wish that one could do so, etc. etc., are new experiences, characterized in novel phenomenological terms. All have this in common, that they are modes of objective intention, which cannot be otherwise expressed than by saying that the Schloss is perceived, imagined, pictorially represented, judged about, delighted in, wished for etc. etc.
>
> (LI VI § 11, pp. 559–560; Hua XIX/1 388)

Intentional *Erlebnisse* can be simple, like having presentations, or more complex, where we have nested clusters of intentional acts, for example when I *remember feeling angry* about something. Indeed, most of our experiences involve complex structures which need to be carefully distinguished. A favourite example of Husserl's is the difference between aesthetic approval and theoretical assessment of an aesthetic object, a distinction which he again discusses in *Ideas* II, to show the difference between living in an experiential act and taking a more detached contemplative view of it. These complex acts are best understood as part–whole structures, where the wholes are 'founded' on the parts. In the case of intentional acts such as suppositions, judgements, and so on, which are non-objectivating acts, Husserl believes they must be founded on what Brentano called 'presentations' and Husserl prefers to call 'objectivating acts', that is acts which present an object.

In speaking of the parts of a mental process, we must distinguish between the *real* psychical process, which is an actual event in time and which possesses distinguishable constituent *real* parts, on the one hand, from the intentional, abstract, ideal elements which are instantiated in the act. Husserl attempted to articulate this distinction as the difference between '*reell*' and '*reall*' parts of the act, but he is not always consistent in this terminological distinction; he seemed to settle for the distinction between real parts of the act and the intentional or ideal parts of the act. The point is that there are different kinds of parts depending on the manner in which we approach the *Erlebnis*.

Husserl accepts Brentano's view that in inner perception, in those acts whereby our conscious acts are reflexively aware of themselves in the act (e.g. when I see something, I am also aware that I am seeing), the object (in this case, the act itself) is given wholly whereas our outer perceptions always only reveal 'adumbrations', 'aspects', or 'profiles' (*Abschattungen*) of the object. This allows Husserl to be able to get access to the essential structures of our conscious acts. But, in talking of an intentional object, Husserl wishes to avoid all talk of containment or of objects immanent to consciousness (LI V § 11, p. 560; Hua XIX/1 388). In a sense, all objects of thought are mind-transcendent and the intentional act is directly focused on the object, not on its own contents. Even a fictional concept like the god Jupiter is *transcendent* in Husserl's sense: for example, if I think of the god Jupiter and dismantle this thought, the god Jupiter will not be found *inside* the thought. Husserl wants to emphasise that in our intentional experience we are always "transcending" consciousness towards the object. Aron Gurwitsch and Jean-Paul Sartre will make this the defining feature of consciousness, with Sartre offering many evocative descriptions of how the emptiness of consciousness seeks to be filled by the object itself. Husserl conceives of the object as the "totality" or "unity of the series" generated from thinking about the infinite sweep of profiles, *Abschattungen*. But he denies that we experience the series; we always experience just the object.

In describing the intentional structure of an act, we abstract from everything empirically real. Husserl goes on to stress the difference between the contents of experience and the properties of the mind-transcendent object.

When I see an object, I only ever see it from one side, in a certain kind of light, from a certain angle, and so on. As I walk around the box, for example, I see different 'profiles' (*Abschattungen*) of the box, and yet I know I am getting glimpses of the same object in the different perceptual acts. Husserl is insistent that what we actually see is the box and not a certain set of visual sensations. I do not see colour sensations but coloured things and these are always given under a certain 'mode of presentation'. Thus I don't just hear a bare sound, but I hear a door closing. I hum a few bars and you immediately grasp what song I am humming. I can hear the same concert music in the hall or muffled through the walls when I am listening from outside, but no matter how different those aural sensations are, I am convinced I am listening to the same concert. It is the same object for me.

Furthermore, Husserl, adopting a traditional distinction drawn from classical logic, introduces a new and important distinction between the *matter* and the *quality* of intentional acts (LI V § 20). Here Husserl is introducing a technical term 'act quality' to mark out that *abstract* part of the intentional act which carries the content – it could be a perception, a remembering, a questioning, and so on. This is equivalent to the contemporary distinction between the propositional attitude and the propositional content. Thus when I judge that '2 + 2 = 4', the *act-quality* is one of judgement and the *matter* of the act is the propositional content '2 + 2 = 4'. Furthermore, the act quality is thought by Husserl to be an *abstract moment* of the intentional experience; it makes no sense to talk of the occurrence of an act of judgement which is not a judgement of a particular, determinate content (LI V § 20, p. 589; Hua XIX/1 430). Act-quality and matter are mutually dependent parts of the *Erlebnis*. The matter is what makes the act determinate.

For Husserl, it is the act's matter that determines the intentional reference to the object and also the manner in which the object is grasped:

> The matter, therefore, must be *that element in an act which first gives it reference to an object, and reference so wholly definite that it not merely fixes the object meant in a general way, but also the precise way in which it is meant.*
>
> (LI V § 20, p. 589; Hua XIX/1 429)

The content which provides reference to the object is not to be understood as a kind of formless matter of sensations, as in the Kantian account of the relation of form to content. For Husserl, the content of an act already contains a certain 'interpretative sense' (*Auffassungssinn*), which is then manipulated by the act-quality, be it a question, a judgement, a wish, or whatever. Husserl wants to refine Brentano's dogma that every psychic act is either a presentation or based on a presentation. Presentations are not the only kinds of content which Husserl envisages. Certainly, Husserl believes it would be wrong to identify contents with raw sensations.

Not all content should be construed propositionally as far as Husserl is concerned. Not all aspects of our mental processes or lived experiences are intentional in the sense of presenting something to our attention. Sensations are part of the 'matter' whereas the *act-quality* provides the form of the act. According to Husserl, *sensations* are not intentional, rather they accompany the intentional act as experiences simply undergone. The sensations are a non-intentional real part or 'moment' of the act. For Husserl sensations are part of every perceptual act but they are not what makes the act intentional. The sensations fill out the act as it were but it is the act character which determines what is actually understood. Furthermore, for Husserl, it is the "act character which as it were ensouls sense" (LI V § 14, p. 567; Hua XIX/1 399). It is a function of the act character which determines whether we see a patch of red as an instance of 'red', or of 'colour', and so on. It is noteworthy that Husserl thinks of the organisation or synthesis of sense in the initial act of interpretation (*Auffassung*) as a non-conceptual act, distinct from conceiving and from naming an object. There is, for Husserl, pure sensuous perception of physical objects and this is not necessarily mediated by language. In later works, Husserl will spend more time trying to account for the nature of this receptive experience of objects through his paradoxical concept of 'passive synthesis'.

In analysing the intentional structure of an act, it makes no difference at all to the phenomenological nature of the experience whether or not the object exists, is fictitious, or is perhaps completely absurd (LI V § 11, p. 559; Hua XIX/1 387). Husserl took this position long before the *Investigations* were published. He had already seen that the content of what is given in a presentation is what it is regardless of whether the presentation comes in perception or in fantasy. This is an essentially Cartesian insight. The content of consciousness is given *as it is*, regardless of its causal origin, whether it comes from contact with an outer object or an inner act of the mind. However, in the Second Edition of the *Logical Investigations* Husserl at various points inserts references to the need to suspend the natural attitude and to reduce to the pure essential structures of consciousness.

An extremely important element of Husserl's analysis of intentional modalities is his distinction between the various ways in which the object is presented or given. Husserl had already mentioned in the First Investigation that, in perception, we have direct awareness of the intentional object *in propria persona*, in the flesh, with full 'bodily presence' (*leibhaftig*). In the depictive recall (*Vergegenwärtigung*) of memory and fantasy, we still have a full intuition of the object but no longer presented with bodily presence. In language we have merely a form of signification of the object which can be a kind of 'empty intending' (*Leermeinen*).

117

Husserl's distinctions here between the object grasped and the particular mode of presentation or *Abschattung* under which it is grasped are very similar to Frege's distinction between sense and reference. The sense is the mode of presentation of the reference. Much has been written on this relation between Husserl and Frege, but we shall postpone discussion to the next chapter when discussing the theory of the *noema* first articulated in *Ideas* I (1913) §§ 87–96. However, we should note the basis for Husserl's distinction between object and *noema* was already laid in the Fifth Logical Investigation where, especially in § 17, Husserl distinguishes between "the object which is intended" (*der Gegenstand, welcher intendiert ist*) and "the object as it is intended" (*der Gegenstand, so wie er intendiert ist*, LI V § 17, p. 578; Hua XIX/1). To use Husserl's own example, we can think of the German Emperor (object which is intended) as "the son of Emperor Frederick III" or as "the grandson of Queen Victoria". Two people may make the same judgement and employ the same matter and still end up with two distinct and differing meaning conceptions. To articulate this, Husserl makes a distinction between the *semantic essence* and the *ideal meaning* of the act: the "ideational abstraction of this [semantic] essence yields a 'meaning' in our ideal sense" (LI V § 21, p. 590; Hua XIX/1 431). The semantic essence is a unity of the act's quality and matter. Two people can have the same thought of Greenland, for example, whereby the semantic essence differs considerably. Husserl's method in this Investigation is to peel back layer upon layer of complexity in the intentional act, leading him to a complete break with the earlier Brentanian conception of intentionality, and providing him with the initial set of tools to develop his phenomenology of consciousness.

In summary, Husserl sees our mental processes as, normally speaking, object-directed acts. When directed at a material object, the act is always only a partial view of the object; nevertheless, it has the sense of grasping the object as it is. This sense of reaching to the object and grasping it as what it is is enabled by the sensuous given substratum, the non-intentional experience undergone, being grasped and shaped through an act of interpreting which yields up the "interpreting sense". This sense in turn is acknowledged in one form or another by the act-quality, be it a judgement, a wish, and so on.

The Sixth Logical Investigation

Husserl regarded the Sixth Logical Investigation as his most mature discussion of the central issues of logic, specifically offering a phenomenological clarification of the nature of judgement and the manner in which judgements relate to truth. Husserl spent so much time on this Investigation that it threatened to dwarf the others in length. Furthermore, it was while writing this Investigation that Husserl got his first full appreciation of the nature of the phenomenological field he was uncovering. He spent much longer over its attempted revision, in the end never bringing it to publication, though he worked on it in 1913 and again in the mid-1920s. Here Husserl develops a phenomenological account of truth in terms of adequation or fulfilment; that is, he modelled his account of the relations between thought and its object on the relation between perception and its fulfilment. It is in this Investigation that Husserl proposes a *categorial intuition* (*kategoriale Anschauung*) side by side with sensory intuition, and it was to this Investigation that Martin Heidegger was drawn, when he sought the conceptual groundwork for his own attempt to understand the question of the Being of beings. The Sixth Investigation and Husserl's account of categorial intuition subsequently played an important role in the philosophy of logic of Kurt Gödel. But in general, it has been neglected, eclipsed by Heidegger's account of truth in *Being and Time*.

Whereas the Fifth Investigation had concentrated on the intentional structure of meaning-intending acts, the Sixth Investigation wants to focus in on the manner in which such acts achieve their 'fulfilment'; that is, achieve the accomplishment (*Leistung*) of winning an intuition of an objectivity. As we have seen, Husserl sees the paradigmatic form of a fulfilled intentional act as an act where the meaning intended is actually fulfilled by the bodily *presence* of the object thought about. This is an act of 'adequate self-presentation' (*adäquate Selbstdarstellung*) which is the paradigm for all genuine knowledge. Thus when I *see* the bridge, I have a fulfilled intuition of the bridge. The experience presents the bridge "bodily" (*leibhaftig*), *in propria persona*. Later, I can relive this intuition, but now only as a memory – still oriented to the actual bridge but this time the bridge is not presented with the same sense of presence and immediacy. Similarly, if I idly daydream about a bridge, see it in my mind's eye with certain specific features, the bridge is given in an intuition which presents itself in ways different to either a perception or a memory. The sense that the bridge is really there is now absent. These different forms of psychological relation have different essential structures. There are other forms of intending which are merely 'empty', for example when I use words in a casual way without really thinking about what I am saying, when I talk about the bridge without really thinking about it, and so on. Here I am caught up mostly in operating with the sign standing for the thing. For Husserl, signitive or empty intending is a basic feature of human intentionality through which we grasp things not 'authentically' (*eigentlich*) as in the paradigmatic case of sense perception, but 'inauthentically' (*uneigentlich*) or 'symbolically', such as when we are doing calculations in mathematics. Indeed, as we saw in the last chapter, it was Husserl's puzzles about these forms of thinking which led him to the *Logical Investigations* in the first place. Most forms of thinking, by their very nature, are required to perform operations with things taken merely as signs. If, for example, I am counting the number of people killed in road accidents in a year, my focus is on the number, not on the felt experience of what it is to die in an accident. Heidegger himself would develop the notion of 'empty intending' into a central aspect of our being in the world: that is, when we are involved in 'idle talk' (*Gerede*), where we dwell on meanings which have been passed on to us and which we pass along without authentically making our own.

Now, in perceptual acts, when I see an object, the object is there before me in its full bodily presence. I have a sensuous intuition of a blackbird out in the garden, for example. Now Husserl realises that not all acts of immediate givenness are of this kind, namely that they present a thing straightforwardly and 'in one blow' (*in einem Schlage*, LI VI § 47, p. 788; Hua XIX/2 676). Besides seeing sensuous objects, I also see facts, and grasp states of affairs. Husserl argues, against the empiricists and against Kant, that we have a direct immediate intuition, akin to sensory perception, not only of concrete sensory entities but also of ideal meanings, objects and states of affairs. I see *that the bird is black, that the house is large*, and so on. My intuition of a 'state of affairs' (*Sachverhalt*), for example 'I see *that the paper is white*', involves what Husserl calls 'categorial intuition', an intuition that something is the case. Categorial intuition is the intuition of essences and it was to become the centrepiece of Husserl's transcendental phenomenology. For Husserl, it is crucial to appreciate and be able to account for the difference between the expression 'this white paper' and 'this paper is white' (LI VI § 40).

According to Kant, our experience has two components: a receptive element of sensory intuition and an element of reflective conceptuality (which Kant called 'spontaneity'). But Kant explicitly denied that humans had the capacity to *intuit* intellectual concepts; we do not have intellectual intuition. Intuitions without concepts are blind, concepts without intuitions are empty. Husserl agrees with Kant that there is no purely intellectual intuition; on the other hand, he believes that we have a graded series of intuitions of higher levels of categoriality which, though based on sensuous intuition, have less and less of the sensory in them.

> Acts of straightforward intuitions we called 'sensuous': founded acts, whether leading back immediately or mediately to sense, we called 'categorial'. But it is worth our while to draw a distinction, within the sphere of categorial acts, between those acts that are *purely categorial*, acts of 'pure understanding', and *mixed acts of understanding that are blended with sense*. It lies in the nature of the case that everything categorial ultimately rests upon sensuous intuition, that a 'categorial intuition', an intellectual insight, a case of thought in the highest sense, without any foundation of sense, is a piece of nonsense.
>
> (LI VI § 60, pp. 817–818; Hua XIX/2 712)

All intuition has its accompanying sensuousness. There is an 'apprehension' (*Auffassung*) of the sensory matter, as Husserl had already outlined in the Fifth Investigation, but the sensuous content *underdetermines* the range of assertible meanings to which the perception can give rise. The same sensuous apprehension can ground quite different judgements. I look out and see the blackbird in the garden and can formulate many judgements based on that perception: 'I see a blackbird flying', 'that bird is black', and so on. In other words, the perceptual meaning of the act of seeing cannot be strictly identified with any one of the judgements based on it. The sense underdetermines the meaning. We have a quasi-perceptual intuition of a non-linguistic state of affairs when we look and see the blackbird. Now, we can make judgements with higher degrees of abstraction from the sensuous. We have purely sensuous acts, mixed acts (e.g. acts which grasp geometrical concepts still have a residual sensuousness), and pure higher order categorial acts which grasp logical categories such as unity, plurality, and existence. These do not retain any sensuous element in their meaning.

Categorial intuitions grasp the being of the entity (*that* this apple *is* red) and not just the individual properties (redness). It was this feature of categorial intuition which was instrumental in reawakening the problem of being in Heidegger's philosophy. Husserl comments on Kant's claim 'existence is not a predicate' and argues that, while correct, it misses the fact that we have another mode of intuiting facts, the being of states of affairs. Husserl agrees that I *see* a colour, but that I cannot see the state of *being-coloured* (LI VI § 43, p. 780). Nevertheless, I do immediately grasp the state of being coloured, when I grasp the meaning of the judgement, 'this is coloured'.

Saying that something 'is' does not give us an intuition of a new property in a manner similar to learning 'something is red'. But this shows for Husserl that assertion of the category of being does not involve grasping a property of the object. Nor does it emerge from reflecting on the act of consciousness – being is no part of the act either. Rather the categorial structure belongs to the ideal structure of the object – to objectivity as such, which Husserl distinguishes from objects.

Realism and idealism in the *Logical Investigations*

As we shall see in more detail in the next chapter, in his later years Husserl moved more and more in the direction of idealism. In the *Logical Investigations*, however, he was somewhat ambivalent about questions of realism and idealism. In part, this is because Husserl is claiming to be involved merely in the project of pure *description* (*Deskription*; *Beschreibung*) of what is presented in conscious acts precisely as they are so presented. Husserl makes numerous assertions about perception that can be construed in realist terms. In particular, he emphatically asserts that we grasp the actual object directly and 'straightforwardly' (*schlichte*) in perception, and repeats this position in *Ideas* I even after his turn to transcendental idealism (*Ideas* I § 43, p. 93; Hua III/1 79). This appears to be a commitment to direct, empirical realism. Furthermore, Husserl rejects all traditional representationalist accounts of perception which require the mediation of an idea, an image, or a sensuous appearance. It is simply not the case that we are aware directly only of our own sensations, rather we grasp the thing directly. Only in specific, willed, reflexive acts do we specifically attend to and notice our sensations. Husserl also emphasises that, even though each perception is only of an aspect or profile of the thing, nevertheless we clearly perceive the thing itself and not merely one part of it, nor do we think of the thing as made up of the set of profiles or the series of perceptions present and anticipated. We don't have to articulate the thing, "each single percept in this series is already a percept of this thing" (LI VI § 47, p. 789; Hua XIX/2 677). We grasp the whole object through the part; we don't grasp the part and infer the whole.

On the other hand, Husserl also makes claims that many have thought to amount to a Platonic realism, whereby abstract objects are treated as 'real' or 'actual' (*wirklich*): that is, possessing genuine – albeit non-temporal – existence. Indeed, Husserl had problems with Brentano's account of intentional objects precisely because it invoked an idea of 'inexistence' (*Inexistenz*) which seemed to suggest that objects in thought have a shadowy kind of existence separate from their existence in reality. In fact, he had similar problems with various traditional forms of Platonism precisely because he thought that Platonists did not distinguish between an object and a fact. At times Husserl asserts that there was only one kind of existence: "For us temporality is a sufficient mark of reality" (LI II § 8, p. 351; Hua XIX/1 129). Real existence or actuality or some relation to temporality suffices for existence. Real being and temporal being are identical in their extensions while not being exactly the same concepts. However, towards the end of the Sixth Investigation, he is already talking of the 'real object' as the correlate to the act of perception: "we define a real object as the possible object of a straightforward perception" (LI VI § 47, p. 791; Hua XIX/2 679).

When Husserl revised the *Investigations* in 1913 much had changed. He now admits to being dissatisfied with the conception of truth operative in the earlier Investigations, and he also thinks he has not fully distinguished between psychology and phenomenology and therefore still retained a residual psychologism. In particular, he felt that the characterisation of phenomenology as descriptive psychology could be read as tainted by a certain "psychologising of the eidetic" (*Ideas* I § 61, p. 139; Hua III/1 116), a transformation of the genuine into something of another kind, *metabasis in allo geno*. Indeed Husserl felt that the first five Investigations vacillated on this issue and did not perceive the eidetic in properly transcendental terms. The *Prolegomena* had made a sharp separation between the psychological and the ideal and showed that the realm of objectivity, truth, and validity belonged to the ideal not the real. Though logic itself could choose to focus solely on the ideal entities and the laws connecting them, phenomenology has to deal with the fact that logical knowledge, even in its purity, is still a form of *knowing*. Just as the ideal objects of mathematics can be studied so too can the essential natures of the knowing acts. Originally Husserl misconstrued this study as 'descriptive psychology'.

In the Second Edition, Husserl also thought his treatment of the ego in the First Edition was severely inadequate. In the First Edition, Husserl had excluded all talk of a 'pure ego' as something unexperiencable (following Hume and Brentano) and had even explicitly criticised Natorp for retaining this notion. In the 1913 revision, he now claims to have 'found' the pure ego. Indeed Natorp in his incisive review of the *Investigations* had predicted that Husserl would move in a Kantian direction. Finally, Husserl tries to conceive the whole movement of the *Investigations* in terms of his newly discovered concept of reduction. A sweeping suspension of the natural attitude is now required to grasp the essential nature of knowledge. Husserl's commitment to bracketing of the original acts of positing a world, the acts which inhabit the natural attitude, suggests that he is withdrawing from his earlier commitment to realism.

4

HUSSERL'S DISCOVERY OF THE REDUCTION AND TRANSCENDENTAL PHENOMENOLOGY

Introduction

The *Logical Investigations* constituted Husserl's first "breakthrough" into phenomenology, though at the time he was somewhat unclear about the exact nature of this supposed new way of doing philosophy. In the years that followed, at the Universities of Göttingen (1901–1916) and Freiburg (from 1916 until his death in 1938), Husserl set about elaborating the full programme of phenomenology, not just as the epistemological clarification of logic and mathematics, or even as the a priori science of the essential features of consciousness, but rather as a pure eidetic science, a 'science of essences' (*eine Wesenswissenschaft, Ideas* I § 18) which would also provide the essential grounding for all scientific knowledge, and would finally, in Husserl's mature vision, become co-extensive with philosophy itself, *phenomenological philosophy* as such. Everything which appears to consciousness could be studied by phenomenology.

Husserl came to see the whole of philosophy as somehow encompassed in, or founded on, this new science of phenomenology. Whereas, in 1901, he had conceived of phenomenology specifically in relation to problems of logic and epistemology, gradually he came to conceive of the field of phenomenology as encompassing all conscious experiences, their correlates, and their essential structures, as a science of all essential possibilities. As Husserl worked his way through the *Investigations*, he appears to have been genuinely amazed by the richness of the phenomenological field he had uncovered. He realised that phenomenology could contribute not just to the region of conscious experiences, but to all material regions of being, every field of 'material essences' (*Ideas* I § 10) from geometry to morality. Phenomenology would illuminate the necessary laws governing such essences as are possessed by colour, sound, extension, time, as well as the more formal essences of identity, unity, plurality, difference, whole and part, individual and species, and so on (Hua XXIV 231). Of necessity, as phenomenology grew it also became a co-operative enterprise, indeed, a set of 'infinite tasks'. This phenomenology of infinite tasks would be the focus of the remainder of his life's work.

After 1903 Husserl's thinking also began to take a *transcendental* turn. Phenomenology must explore not just the essential structures of all conscious experiences and their intentional objects, but the rootedness of these essences and objects in a transcendental realm and in the transcendental ego as their "absolute source". As Husserl pushed his phenomenology more and more in the direction of a transcendental grounding of all possible meanings and essences, he realised that phenomenology had no special link with either logic or psychology. The fact that he had entered phenomenology through the philosophy of logic struck him as merely accidental, a contingent fact of his own biography, rather than the sole mode of access into the phenomenological domain. Secondly, Husserl came to suspect that his attempt to study the essential features of consciousness in the *Logical Investigations* still harboured certain *naturalistic presuppositions* about consciousness, such that he eventually came to realise that even phenomenological psychology itself is not the whole of phenomenology. The true turn to the transcendental brings phenomenology deeper than any psychology, even phenomenological psychology, and returns us to the realm of transcendental, world-constituting subjectivity. Transcendental phenomenology became a parallel discipline to phenomenological psychology, constantly rethinking the phenomena purified of all naturalistic tendencies. Early in his Freiburg period, beginning in the 1920s but especially in the 1930s, for example in the *Crisis*, Husserl began to recognise that 'static' constitutive phenomenology needed to be supplemented by a phenomenological study of the historical genesis of all meaning, not just cultural meanings but scientific meanings also. Besides 'constitutive phenomenology' Husserl came to recognise the need for a 'genetic phenomenology', a project which came to the fore in the *Crisis* but which existed in subterranean form in his manuscript researches for many years prior to the publication of that work.

In this chapter we shall take on the extremely challenging task of trying to gain a fuller understanding of Husserl's phenomenological method as elaborated in his mature period from 1901 to 1929, approximately. That is, from his rethinking of the results of the *Logical Investigations* to his visit to Paris to deliver the lectures on transcendental phenomenology interpreted in terms of Descartes's project. Inevitably, we shall be drawing a composite picture, trying to get at the essentials of Husserl's mature transcendental phenomenology, as he proposed it in his main publications of this period: *Philosophy as a Rigorous Science* (1911), *Ideas* I (1913), *Formal and Transcendental Logic* (1929), and *Cartesian Meditations* (1931). We shall, for the purposes of exposition, assume that Husserl more or less consistently set out the same view of phenomenology in his mature years, although it is now obvious from the publication of his lectures and research notes that he was exploring many different directions at once and the structure of his mature thought was not confined to the method he elaborated in his few published works of the period. Nevertheless, it is generally true that Husserl advanced through the different stages of phenomenology by his progressive application and refinement of the central methodology of 'reduction' which emerged as a philosophical instrument around 1905 and continued to be applied as a tool to refine his understanding of phenomenology as a transcendental science. The nature of the reduction (*Reduktion*), then, will be our central focus in this chapter.

Phenomenology as a presuppositionless science

Already in the First Edition of *Logical Investigations*, Husserl presented phenomenology as a pure, *presuppositionless* science of consciousness. The claim, as we have seen, means first of all that phenomenology cannot assume or utilise the results of any other science in its investigations. It cannot even take for granted the *ideal* of the scientific project itself, or any specific meaning of the concept of *philosophy*. Husserl made more and more radical claims about the nature of this freedom from presuppositions. In the *Cartesian Meditations*, for instance, he claims that everything the enquirer needs, he or she must discover within him- or herself, including the very meaning of his or her philosophical terms. The phenomenologist must begin "in absolute poverty, with an absolute lack of knowledge" (CM § 1, 2; Hua I 44). Thus, in his 1930 Preface to W. R. Boyce Gibson's English translation of *Ideas* I, Husserl says that he can help no one who has not realised, being confronted with the profusions of different philosophical systems, that in fact they offer no choice at all, since none "has taken care to free itself from presuppositions and none has sprung from the radical attitude of autonomous self-responsibility which the meaning of a philosophy demands".[1]

Since Hegel, many philosophers have argued that it is impossible for a science to be completely presuppositionless. But Husserl does not mean that we cannot begin from our ordinary experience, or using our ordinary language and thought processes; rather he believes that we should not assume any philosophical or scientific *theory*, and furthermore must avoid *deductive* reasoning (which presupposed logic) and mathematics as well as any other empirical science or speculative theory of psychology and philosophy, in order to concentrate on describing what is given directly in *intuition* (*Anschauung*). Initially this meant refraining from preconceived ideas drawn from philosophy and the sciences, but gradually it came to mean the most radical form of *self-questioning*, involving a kind of Cartesian overthrow of all previous assumptions to knowledge, and a questioning of many of our 'natural' intuitions about the nature of our mental processes or the make-up of the objective world. Nothing must be taken for granted or assumed external to the lived experiences themselves as they are lived.

Phenomenology is a return to 'phenomena'. Husserl understands *phenomenon* as 'what appears as such'; in other words, everything that appears, including everything meant or thought, in the *manner* of its appearing, in the 'how' (*Wie*) of its manifestation.[2] Heidegger will capture this meaning well in his discussion of phenomenology as the science of that which appears as it appears:

> Thus "phenomenology" means *apophainesthai ta phainomena* – to let that which shows itself be seen from itself in the very way in which it shows itself from itself.
>
> (BT § 7, 58; 34)

But Husserl had already made this claim as early as his 1907 lectures on *The Idea of Phenomenology*. Phenomenology must return to what is directly given in exactly the manner in which it is given. It must begin with intuitions which are self-validating. The claim for phenomenological knowledge to be *presuppositionless* is, then, essentially tied to the notion that we are limited to what is intrinsically given in our intuitions, provided we attend to our intuitions in the proper way. Phenomenology focuses totally on what is given in intuition and is not meant to rely on logical inferences, or mediate knowledge of any kind. Husserl wants to explore experience in a pure manner, unsullied by assumption. Thus when Husserl proclaims himself, in the manner of William James, to be a *radical empiricist*, that is, to count only what is given in experience and all of what is given in experience, it is because Husserl claims to have identified far richer resources for evident cognition in experiences than any philosopher hithertofore. Though classical empiricism correctly acknowledged the importance of experience, it had misconstrued the nature of our grasp of universals and concepts, even to the extent of denying this genuine feature of our experience.

Husserl's principle of principles

The return to pure intuition leads Husserl to formulate his famous 'principle of principles' expressed in *Ideas* I § 24:

> Enough now of absurd theories. No conceivable theory can make us err with respect to the *principle of all principles: that every originary presentive intuition is a legitimizing source of cognition*, that *everything originarily* (so to speak in its "personal" actuality) *offered* to us *in "intuition" is to be accepted simply as what it is presented as being*, but also *only within the limits in which it is presented there*.
>
> (*Ideas* I § 24, p. 44; Hua III/1 43)

Or, as Husserl says in his 1911 essay, *Philosophy as a Rigorous Science*: "What has been grasped from an intuitive point of view can be understood and verified only from an intuitive point of view" (*nur in schauender Haltung*, PRS 119; Hua XXV 39). As we have seen in the last chapter, Husserl took over from Descartes and Brentano the idea that the kind of insight which science seeks is evident insight, cognition given self-evidently, with *Evidenz*. According to the *Cartesian Meditations*, *Evidenz* is "in an *extremely broad sense*, an '*experiencing*' of something that is and is thus; it is precisely a mental seeing of something itself" (*ein Es-selbst-geistig-zu-Gesicht-Bekommen*, CM § 5, 2; Hua I 52). For Husserl, intuitions with *Evidenz* were normal, everyday occurrences, and indeed his constant example of a typical evident intuition or cognition is our ordinary perceptual acts where the object of the act is presented as it is, there in the flesh, *in propria persona*. I see a tree in a garden, I hear the sound of a violin, and so on. The most adequate case is when the object is perceived 'bodily' (*leibhaftig*), in the flesh, in its full presence, rather than merely imagined or thought about, or referred to in a more abstract, symbolic way. For example, when I *hear* a musical tone actually being played or *see* a yellow station wagon there before me, this tone or object is given with the *Evidenz* proper to sensory perception, there is a fulfilment of my meaning expectation in the fullest possible sense appropriate for that kind of experience. I cannot expect a higher kind of fulfilment of my meaning intention. In contrast to Brentano, ordinary sense perception is Husserl's paradigmatic case of evident intuition, because, as he says in *Ideas* I, it is always available to us for inspection. Whereas anger may evaporate or its content may be modified by reflection on it, perception is a steady and repeatable source of insights not just about the world, as in factual discovery, but also for revealing truths of a phenomenological kind (*Ideas* I § 70, 158; Hua III/1 130). Normally, our sense perceptions are not clouded, nor do they evaporate when reflected on. They come to grips with things in full bodily presence.

While the manner of presence of the perceived object in occurrent sensuous perception is Husserl's paradigm case of evident intuition, all other forms of experience set up their own 'conditions of satisfaction', to use John Searle's term, and have their own kinds of coming to evidence. Thus, in mathematics, when I grasp that the three angles of a triangle are equal to two right angles, I have an object which is given with *Evidenz*. I experience this simple truth not just as something that can be validated or which has been validated, but as validated right now. Furthermore, intuitions can be grasped as not possible otherwise, that is not just as adequate but as apodictic. Already in the 1900 *Prolegomena* to the *Logical Investigations* Husserl had commented on the 'originary givenness' of the evident judgement. He had rejected all empiricist accounts of *Evidenz* as inner feeling or as something psychic attached to the judgement. Rather, evidence is the experience of truth (*das "Erlebnis" der Wahrheit, Prol.* § 51, p. 194; Hua XVIII 193), the instantiation of truth itself in the judgement:

> *The experience of the agreement* (*Zusammenstimmung*) between the meaning and what is itself present, meant, between the actual *sense of an assertion* and the self-given *state of affairs*, is inward evidence; the *Idea* of this agreement is truth, whose ideality is also its objectivity.
>
> (*Prol.* § 51, p. 195; Hua XVIII 193–194)

In an evident judgement, we experience an accord between our expectation and its fulfilment. Furthermore, for Husserl, this evident cognition of the agreement itself is an intuitional experience in its own right. It is not to be cashed out as a sensory experience accompanied by a belief, as in many epistemological accounts. Rather the evident intuition is the basis and motivation for the accompanying, justified beliefs. Indeed, when we have an evident insight, we know that it is impossible for anyone else to think otherwise.

In *Ideas* I and in all his subsequent work, Husserl maintains essentially the same account of evidence as originary self-givenness. Following Descartes, Husserl held that deductions are founded on evident intuitions. Unless there were such evident cognitions, Husserl maintains, we could have no success in reasoning. Furthermore, the idealists misunderstood the nature of *Evidenz* in terms of a 'feeling of evidence', a mystical pointing to the truth, *index veri* (*Ideas* I § 21). The rationalists or idealists sought to deduce all truths from a small body of such evident insights, such as the Cartesian *cogito*, or the a priori truth that something must be identical with itself, but Husserl thought such rationalistic thought-constructions were inadequate simply because they ignored the enormous, indeed infinite, diversity of such evident insights. Thus, for Husserl (and Merleau-Ponty will follow him closely here), phenomenology must steer a path between traditional empiricism and forms of idealism or rationalism.

The absolute self-givenness of our mental acts

Husserl always fully accepts the legitimacy of Descartes's argument leading to the discovery of the *cogito*. For Husserl, when I try to doubt everything, I come up against the bedrock fact that I cannot doubt that I am doubting, I cannot doubt or wish away my very conscious act of doubting. Not only is the "I am", as experienced by me, always immediately certain, but so also is any mental experience just as it is experienced (LI V § 6). In general, I cannot deny the stream of my thoughts (*cogitationes*) just in the manner in which they are given. My conscious experience is given in an absolute sense:

> If we inquire into the essence of cognition, then whatever status it and our doubts about its reaching the object may have one thing is clear: that cognition itself is a name for a manifold sphere of being which can be given to us absolutely, and which can be given absolutely each time in the particular case.
>
> (IP, p. 23; Hua II 30)

In other words, whether I am imagining or perceiving, if I disregard the veridical claims of the act (i.e. whether it gives me true knowledge about the world), I can at least be certain that I am engaging in an act of consciousness and that the act, together with its contents just in the manner in which they appear, is given absolutely. Husserl maintains that "to doubt what is immanent, and is meant as such, as it is, would be evidently irrational" (LI VI Appendix, § 6, p. 864; Hua XIX/2 768, translation altered; see also IP, p. 24; Hua II 31). Husserl thinks that every mental process is given and can be viewed *as it is* (*wie es ist*). It is "absolutely given". These thoughts have "*absolute* and *clear givenness, self-givenness in the absolute sense*" (IP, p. 28; Hua II 35).

Originally, Husserl conceived of this self-certainty and incorrigibility in Brentanian terms, namely that the acts of inner perception, the acts whereby I identify my own mental acts (i.e. I know that I am imagining), are absolutely given, are apodictic. But already in the *Logical Investigations* Husserl thought that the Brentanian distinction which made acts of inner perception apodictic while acts of outer perception are fallible, did not do justice to the proper distinction between evident and non-evident perceptions. Husserl thinks that evidence does not attach only to inner acts, rather evidence attaches to all mental processes, all *Erlebnisse*, considered just as they are experienced, just as they are given to us. As Husserl writes in the *Logical Investigations*: "It is absolutely clear that the conceptual pairs of inner and outer, and of evident and non-evident perception, need not coincide at all" (LI VI Appendix). Similarly, in *Ideas* I Husserl rejects entirely Brentano's terminology of *inner perception* (*Ideas* I § 38).

Already in the *Logical Investigations*, Husserl took the kind of evident givenness of our mental processes in an actual perception as 'adequate' givenness, as opposite to the kind of 'inadequate' givenness of an object which is merely supposed. In inadequate perception there is a separation between the intention and its object, whereas in an adequate perception these fall into line: "I cannot doubt an adequate purely immanent perception, since there are no residual intentions in it that must yet achieve fulfilment. The whole intention, or the intention in all its aspects, is fulfilled" (LI VI Appendix, § 6, p. 866; Hua XIX/2 770). Fallibility is possible in all perception when we go beyond what is immanently given as it is immanently given. If I have a toothache and I feel it in a certain tooth (which in fact is healthy), I have misperceived. But if I attend purely to the feeling of the toothache I have an evident and adequate perception. Thus, Husserl does acknowledge that phenomenology in one sense is fallible – we can come up with the wrong data – but he maintains that this occurs through some kind of mis-identification, lack of attention, or misdescription. Husserl never seems to have seriously entertained that we could be absolutely misled by what appeared in consciousness, provided we attend only to what is given as it is given, although he did think phenomenology could be very helpful in clarifying the notion of error, illusion, misperception, and the like. Like Brentano, he believed that the evidence of inner certainty was absolute evidence, evidence of the very best kind. Husserl's rhetoric overemphasises the manner in which eidetic insights are 'absolute', 'certain', 'apodictic', and so on, whereas in fact he saw this as a regulative ideal which will only ever be partially achieved. From the *Logical Investigations* to the *Cartesian Meditations* Husserl clearly distinguishes between 'adequate' evidence and 'apodicticity'. Adequacy is a normal achievement but he never renounces apodicticity as a goal.

Husserl wants to admit only these intuitions and experiences into phenomenology, that is, intuitions which are given with absolute apodictic *Evidenz*. In the *Logical Investigations* the way to get at the pure features of consciousness is called 'reflection' (*Reflexion*), but Husserl gradually came to be aware that he was still carrying a lot of psychological and naturalistic baggage in his notion of reflection and, while still retaining the notion of reflection in *Ideas* I, he invoked the idea of reduction to get away from anything that might reify consciousness. Transcendental reflection is the most radical form of thinking possible. Phenomenological attention which employs transcendental reflection is not just a continuation of ordinary philosophical analysis, as Gilbert Ryle, for example, has claimed. Thus, when he emphasises transcendental reflection, Husserl moves away from his earlier determination of phenomenology as conceptual analysis.

Working within the reduction and focusing on self-given intuitions, results are achieved by focused attention and reflection. The reduction has removed reliance on logic and mathematics. Even the law of non-contradiction cannot be assumed but must first be secured by evident insight. Intuitions are immediate presentations of experience, but they can only be admitted to his science when they have been purged of everything empirical and naturalistic. Intuitions must be clarified and reduced, and they then reveal new contents which were not available to ordinary consciousness and even ordinary reflection. Furthermore, they are "verified" by others, but only by those people carrying out the observations themselves. Intersubjective validation is really based on each individual performing acts of reflection on the immanent contents of his or her own psychic processes.

Phenomenology an eidetic not a factual science

Sciences as such, for Husserl, are always focused on the sphere of essential validity, the necessary laws and structures governing the realm of phenomena they study. Phenomenology, similarly, is to be a science of pure essences. It must abstract from the merely contingent, factual features of our experience in order to isolate what is essential to all experiences of that kind. Phenomenology must overcome all 'contingency' (*Zufälligkeit*) and 'factualness' or 'factuality' (*Tatsächlichkeit, Ideas* I § 2, 7; Hua III/1 9). While Husserl already understood phenomenology in the *Logical Investigations* (1901) as the project of gaining essential eidetic insights in the realm of the a priori, he gradually came to the view that this domain could not be clearly viewed in ordinary forms of reflection but would require a specially purified way of regarding. Thus Hans Jonas recounts his early experiences of Husserl's approach to phenomenology:

> In 1921, when, at the age of eighteen, I went to the University of Freiburg to study philosophy, the leading figure there was the already graying Edmund Husserl. "Phenomenology" which he so passionately preached, was a program of self-examination of consciousness as the site of the appearance of all things possibly present to thought. A "pure" phenomenology of "pure" consciousness was to become the basis of all philosophy. "Pure" of what? Of the adventitious nature of factual and individual elements, whereby inner awareness of essences is deemed able to extract that which is valid for all subjects in equal measure. A Platonizing element is unmistakable here, but – what is novel – it is applied to the field of subjectivity. The method, correspondingly, involves observation and description, not causal explanation as in psychology.[3]

Though it is probable that, already in 1901, Husserl was convinced that one could gain access to the essential features of all phenomena manifest to consciousness, regardless of their actuality (*Wirklichkeit*) or non-actuality, without regard to the consequences of their being actual entities in the real world, this claim became prominent in the Second Edition (LI V § 14, pp. 565–566; Hua XIX/1 396). In other eidetic sciences, such as geometry, the actual existence of triangles, or diagrams on paper, is of no essential import to the scientific discoveries themselves. Similarly, one can gain essential insight into the nature of sensuous experience as much through entertaining these supposed experiences in fantasy as through observing them in reality (*Ideas* I § 4). In fact, the observation of experiences in their worldly setting often leads to difficulties in grasping their essences. Husserl, therefore, after 1905 especially, proposes some measures explicitly to suspend our assumption about the 'existence' (*Dasein*) or 'actual being' (*wirkliches Sein*) of the world in order to allow the essential structures of our experience and their intentional contents manifest themselves.

Husserl began to pay more attention to the manner in which a certain change of orientation can bring about a clearer vision of the field to be examined. *Scepticism*, as practised by the ancients and by Descartes, provided a model of how to suspend our natural commitment to our epistemic beliefs in order to bring to light the fundamental features at work in belief as such. Descartes's hyperbolic doubt which puts in question the very existence of the world is the most radical of these forms of suspension of belief. Similarly, for Husserl, phenomenology must be able to cope with the most radical denial of the world, with the challenge of the most radical hyperbolic doubt which sees the whole world as a dream or even as non-existent, what Husserl calls 'empty seeming' or the 'nullifying illusion' (*Phänomenologie des nichtigen Scheins*). The objects focused on in phenomenological viewing must be neutralised with respect to the question of actuality (*Ideas* I § 151, 364; Hua III/1 318). In these formulations, which are numerous in his writings, Husserl is expressing the belief that phenomenology can continue its discoveries *even if the world ceased to exist*, because we are uninterested in factual existence and want to isolate solely the meaning-constituting structures which make consciousness possible, understood as the "invariant structural systems" (*die invarianten Wesensgehalten*; *Trans. Phen.*, p. 165; Hua IX 284) which make these conscious experiences possible.

Husserl designates phenomenology as a 'pure' science, by which he means, following Kant, one stripped of all empirical content, one which provides essential knowledge of the invariant structures at work in all knowing, perceiving, imagining, and so on, irrespective of what goes on in the actual world, irrespective of the existence of that world. How can a science which claims to remain true to experience, to the phenomena themselves, seek to be a pure a priori science stripped of all experiential elements? Brentano's descriptive psychology achieved genuine insights with apodictic validity on the basis of singular experiences, but Brentano never thought to bracket the very existence of this singular occurrence. Husserl wants to affirm both that phenomenology is attention to the phenomena and that its insights yield truths of a purely a priori character. The phenomena themselves must be accessible, independent of questions of existence or non-existence, and must be viewed solely as correlates of consciousness, as being immanent in consciousness but in such a way that the kind of transcendence of the object comes across in this immanence. That is, my experience of an object often contains, as part of that very experience, my sense that the object actually is beyond or outside the experience, and has aspects other than the ones I am now apprehending. The notion of grasping the essence is to grasp something which has transcendence in immanence (Hua XXIV 231).

133

Eidetic seeing (*Wesenerschauung*)

The phenomenological intuition of essences requires a move from the here-and-now individual experience, the occurrent *Erlebnis*, to the contemplation of its essence. Like Brentano, Husserl thought that a singular experience, appropriately regarded, could yield absolutely evident insight and *universal* truth. Husserl, however, will go to considerable lengths to specify the manner in which the experience is to be appropriately regarded, namely from within the immanence of the experience, disregarding the issue of actuality. Thus, in *The Idea of Phenomenology* he says:

> I have a particular intuition of redness, or rather several such intuitions. I stick strictly to the pure immanence; I am careful to perform the phenomenological reduction. I snip away any further significance of redness, any way in which it may be viewed as something transcendent, e.g., as the redness of a piece of blotting paper on my table, etc. And now I grasp in pure "seeing" the meaning of the concept of redness in general, redness *in specie*, the *universal* "seen" as *identical* in this and that. No longer is it the particular as such which is referred to, not this or that red thing, but redness in general...Could a deity, an infinite intellect, do more to lay hold of the essence of redness than to "see" it as a universal?
>
> (IP, pp. 44–45; Hua II 56–57)

Here Husserl claims that the universal is *seen* in the individual. The move from the individual intuition to the grasp of the universal is a move to grasp the essence; this is what Husserl terms *eidetic intuition*. Husserl believed that the route from the individual to the universal is actually installed in our conscious act itself. In other words, the essence in a certain sense is already instantiated in our sensuous intuition of the individual patch of red. Whereas initially, in the First Edition of the *Logical Investigations*, Husserl had seen the recognition of the essence of red to arise through a kind of abstraction from the sensuous experience, by the time of *Ideas* I, Husserl claims that there is a spontaneous intuition of the species itself, an 'ideation' of the species. Husserl now sees the so-called 'theories of abstraction' as a false epistemological move leading us away from the requirement to posit essences and essential seeing (*Ideas* I § 22).

Husserl believed that it was possible to have an insight into the essential natures of things, that these could be 'seen' in a manner analogous to perceptual seeing of a physical object. This eidetic seeing is what Husserl calls 'seeing essence' (*Wesensschau*) or 'essential seeing' (*Wesenserschauung*, *Ideas* I § 3, 8; Hua III/1 10), though he always emphasised that this was a complex act (*Ideas* I § 23). It is arguable that Husserl never developed a full critical understanding of the notion of essence (indeed Ingarden attempted to remedy defects in Husserl's account) and that his constant emphasis on

134

seeing essences led to phenomenology being misunderstood as a kind of Platonism (as Jonas acknowledges in the quotation above), or as promoting a kind of mystical intuition. But Husserl always rejected the accusation of Platonism (e.g. *Ideas* I § 22) just as he rejected empiricist, abstractionist accounts of the universal. Both accusations exhibit a blindness to the true nature of the ideal.

Phenomenology, then, is to be an eidetic science. The only fully worked-out existent eidetic sciences were the mathematical sciences. Husserl thought that working with essences was precisely what scientists did; geometers work with essential shapes, arithmeticians with the essential nature of numbers, and so on. Indeed traditional positivism had allowed itself to be blinded by its faith in a narrow empiricism so much that it ignored the fact that the sciences themselves operate with essences and eidetic insights (*Ideas* I § 25). There is an essence of motion, of sound, of the musical note, and so on, material essences belonging to the different regional ontologies (*Ideas* I § 7). Furthermore, these essences are not generated in our thinking, but are grasped, 'framed', in our acts of thinking (*Ideas* I § 23). Similarly a geometer does not draw insights about the essential features of shapes from an empirical diagram. Nothing factual need exist at all for the geometer who is concerned only with essential possibilities.

Training ourselves to look on essences is especially difficult according to Husserl and we need to be constantly vigilant that we don't allow naturalistic assumptions about the world to slip back in and colour our viewing. The important step in the eidetic reduction is to realise that what is given in seeing a red patch *as* red, is not an individual datum, but a grasp of the essence itself. I understand pure redness and indeed from there I can move to recognising the pure phenomenon of colour itself. Now central to Husserl's claim about seeing these essences is that I can grasp the essence of colour not just from an actual perception of a red patch, but from an imagined red patch or a remembered one. The science of essences has nothing to do with actual existence, but moves in the sphere of pure possibilities. Eidetic sciences have nothing factual about them, while, on the other hand, every factual science depends on eidetic insights (*Ideas* I § 8, p. 17; III/1 18). Husserl emphasised the importance of moving from the merely factual to the level of essential truths, of universal laws, of essences. Husserl saw phenomenology as the viewing of essences (*Wesensschau*) and "fixing" them conceptually and then linguistically (*Ideas* I § 66, 151; Hua III/1 124).

In *Philosophy as a Rigorous Science*, Husserl poses the problem as one concerning how we rise from the temporally flowing, unified whole of a concrete, monadic, conscious life to grasping the meaning-essences that constitute valid scientific knowledge. This meant overcoming a naturalistic prejudice which confuses phenomenological viewing of essences (*phänomenologische Schauung*; *Wesensschau*) with a more naturalistic psychological self-observation or introspection (PRS 115; Hua XXV 36). Here, as elsewhere, Husserl vigorously rejects the view that phenomenological viewing involves introspection. Introspection belongs to natural processes as a way of grasping them in inner intuition. *Wesensschau*, on the other hand, is a slow, hard-won procedure of evident insight acquired by reflection (*Reflexion*). Geometry, for example, is an a priori science of essences but its evident insights do not arise from introspection.

Gradually Husserl began to think that this realm of ideal meanings and meaning-generating acts, and their structures, could be studied independently only through a special method of approach. This method involves 'bracketing' or 'suspending' all our natural attitudes towards the objects in the world and towards our psychological acts, suspending all our theories about these matters, and leading back our attention to these pure essences of consciousness. This led Husserl to postulate a number of *phenomenological* and, later, *transcendental reductions*, according to which all our assumptions and prejudices belonging to our normal worldly consciousness (or 'natural attitude', *die natürliche Einstellung*) need to be bracketed, put aside, suspended, or to use a term taken from the Greek Sceptics, to put under an *epoché* (meaning a 'cessation' or 'suspension'), in order to be led back to the unprejudiced sources of experience. Husserl compared this bracketing with Descartes's methodical doubt in the *Meditations* (*Ideas* I § 31). The aim of both is to expose the transcendental structures of consciousness itself. Husserl began to see more parallels between his investigations and Descartes's new science and Kant's critique of pure reason.

Husserl's transcendental turn

In 1901, immediately after the publication of the *Logical Investigations*, Husserl moved to his new post in the University of Göttingen, where he continued his researches into logic but now took a new interest in epistemological problems. He offered lecture courses and seminars on modern philosophy, including Locke, Leibniz, Hume, Berkeley, Kant, Mach, and Fichte.[4] By 1903 Husserl was beginning to have misgivings about the extent to which his new phenomenology could really be equated with the *descriptive* psychology of the Brentano–Stumpf variety. Though he had overcome psychologism, Husserl came to believe that he was still trapped in a kind of *naturalism* regarding the nature of mental acts. He now saw that it was impossible to grasp the essential epistemological nature of cognition if we continued to think of cognitive *Erlebnisse* merely as factual processes occurring in nature. Consciousness has an absolute existence not akin to the existence of things in nature. As he will argue in *Ideas* I (1913), without consciousness there would not be a world at all.

But consciousness is, as it were, saturated with world-positing tendencies which masked its true nature. In order to access the realm of pure consciousness and to study the essential formations found there, a new methodology was required, one which involved 'suspension' of our natural attitude towards the world, and the application of various phenomenological and transcendental 'reductions' in order to uncover the peculiar act–object structure, which, in *Ideas* I, is called the "noetic–noematic structure" of intentional acts. It was not sufficient to reflect in naturalistic terms on the achievements of cognitive acts, he needed to purify transcendentally his own mode of access to the domain of consciousness itself. Phenomenology, as the science which reveals the essence of science as such, must be distanced from all natural sciences, and even from the inherently naturalistic outlook woven into our cognitive processes themselves. Phenomenology must now become, to invoke a term taken up by Merleau-Ponty, the 'science of origins' (*Ideas* I § 56, 131; Hua III/1 108), an investigation into how meanings are constituted in and for consciousness.

Husserl considered the failure of his earlier researches, and indeed, as we shall see, the parallel failure by Locke and others to maximise upon Descartes's discovery of transcendental subjectivity, to have been due to a strong tendency to *naturalise* the activities of consciousness. Phenomenological description of phenomena was hindered by the inherent human tendency to interpret, to apply our everyday preconceptions and practical interests, to the pure experience. Phenomenology needs "an entirely new point of departure and an entirely new method" (IP, p. 19; Hua II 24) to distinguish it from all forms of natural science. After 1901, Husserl never tires of insisting that phenomenology is "remote from natural thinking" (*Ideas* I xvii; Hua III/1 1). In the reduction, there is a radical 'upheaval' (*Umsturz*) and consciousness even "ceases to be human", loses all connection to the empirical, natural human ego and its psychological states (*mein natürliches menschliches Ich und mein Seelenleben*).[5] As Paul Ricoeur has perceptively remarked: "It is in conquering oneself as man that the pure subject inaugurates phenomenology."[6]

This new direction in Husserl's thought was prompted by a number of realisations: he realised he had been too much in debt to *naturalism* in his descriptive psychological approach to *Erlebnisse* in the *Logical Investigations*. He would settle his debt with naturalism in the *Philosophy as a Rigorous Science* essay of 1911. His reflections on logic in 1906–1907 and 1907–1908 led him to abandon his earlier Lotzean account of meanings as universal species instantiated in individual acts of experience. Indeed in 1906 this new interest in meanings led him to renew correspondence with Frege. He now came to the view that meanings are special kinds of entities in their own right, what he will soon call *noemata*. We shall return to this topic later in this chapter.

Besides rejecting naturalism, Husserl was also uncomfortable with the way he had ignored the role of the ego as synthesising our mental experiences into a single life in the *Logical Investigations*, because he had followed Brentano's more or less Humean treatment of the ego as a bundle of acts.

137

The *Logical Investigations* had conceived of mental processes (*Erlebnisse*) more or less as isolated, individual occurrent events and had not examined how they are united together in the life of an individual ego or soul. In 1902–1903 he was still insisting that the phenomenologist is not interested in the ego to which mental processes appear but only in the appearing. He even spoke of the need for "exclusion of the ego" (*Ausschaltung des Ich*). His recognition that this neglect of the ego itself was distorting the understanding of the nature of the mental processes themselves came during his analyses of the nature of our conscious experience of time and the manner in which ordinary acts of perception carry along with them moments of the past (retentions) as well as anticipations of the future (protentions). Husserl's meditations on their temporal structure of retentions and anticipations, together with his strong sense of the unity of psychic life, prompted him to revise his approach to the ego. Now he recognised the need to focus on the unifying factor underlying the temporal spread of consciousness. Return to the ego inevitably meant a return to Descartes and to the legacy of German idealism.

More and more, he articulated his methodology in terms of the radical foundationalist project of Descartes's *Meditations*, understood as the grounding of objectivity in subjectivity. Influenced by both Descartes and Kant, Husserl's philosophy took an *idealistic, transcendental turn* from 1905 to 1906, a turn he first revealed in lectures given at Göttingen University in 1906–1907 and thereafter.[7] This new commitment to a form of idealism was first announced in print in *Ideas* I (1913), much to the dismay of many of Husserl's Göttingen students, for example Roman Ingarden and Hedwig Conrad-Martius, who had been attracted by the direct realism and logical objectivism of the *Logical Investigations*.[8] Nevertheless, Husserl maintained the thrust of interpreting phenomenology as transcendental idealism and regularly interpreted his philosophy in terms of the Cartesian project, for example in his 1917 *Inaugural address (Antrittsrede)* in Freiburg, in the 1923–1924 lectures on *First Philosophy*, and, of course, in the *Cartesian Meditations* where Husserl begins by saying that transcendental phenomenology may be termed a 'neo-Cartesianism', though one which takes up Descartes's attitude rather than any of the doctrinal content of his philosophy.

Like Descartes, Husserl, in his search for the ultimate grounding of meaning-constituting acts, was constantly seeking an Archimedean point from which to begin, a point from which he could move the world, as it were. Husserl always credited Descartes with the first discovery of this new transcendental domain of the pure ego. Thus, in his *First Philosophy* lectures of 1923–1924, Husserl states: "Historically we find the seed of transcendental philosophy in Descartes" (*Erste Philosophie*, Hua VIII 4). Husserl says that we must – like Descartes's doubter – put all our naturalistic beliefs into *suspension* in order to grasp the special mode of givenness of the fundamental truth of the *cogito ergo sum*. For Husserl, the clarity and distinctness with which the *cogito* is disclosed is the key to understanding Descartes's essential breakthrough; all other sciences are to be measured by the way in which philosophy itself achieved its clarification as a science. This is why, as Husserl says, phenomenology is "the secret nostalgia of all modern philosophy" (*Ideas* I § 62, 142; Hua III/1 118). Of course, Descartes himself had failed to understand the true significance of the *cogito* and misconstrued it as *thinking substance* (*res cogitans*), thus falling back into the old metaphysical habits, construing the ego as a "little tag-end of the world" (*ein kleines Endchen der Welt*, CM § 10, 24; Hua I 63), *naturalising* consciousness as just another region of the world, as indeed contemporary programmes in the philosophy of mind deliberately seek to do. True phenomenology will grasp the original givenness of consciousness precisely as *modes of self-givenness* rather than as entities in any naturalistic sense.

It was not until much later in his life that Husserl began to criticise his own too ready assumption of a Cartesian starting point for phenomenology, as we shall see in the next chapter. Thus, in the *Crisis* in particular, he recognised that the "Cartesian way" of *epoché* and reduction brought the ego into view in one bound, as it were, but, in so doing, revealed it as "apparently empty of content" and, hence, passed over the whole apparatus which constituted the 'life-world' (*Crisis* § 43, p. 155; Hua VI 158). Husserl realised that the modelling of his reduction on the Cartesian model bypassed all the complex ways in which human subjectivity is already located in the world and tied to it.

David Hume as a transcendental philosopher

Husserl's recognition of Descartes as *discoverer* of the transcendental sphere went side by side with a radical interpretation of Hume as the first *practitioner* of genuine transcendental philosophy (e.g. FTL § 100, pp. 255–260; Hua XVII 262–267). Husserl understood the transcendental approach to be a radicalisation of the empiricist project, and, in the *Crisis* and elsewhere, treats Hume as an important *transcendental* philosopher, who took seriously the Cartesian requirement of focusing purely on what lies inside (*die reine Inneneinstellung*, FTL § 100, p. 256; Hua XVII 263). On Hume's account, causality, once considered to be an objective feature of the world, comes to be immanently constituted in consciousness out of the experiences of temporal and other relations. This, for Husserl, is a paradigm of transcendental–phenomenological philosophy, albeit one motivated by sceptical considerations (*Crisis* § 24, pp. 88–90; Hua VI 91–93).[9] Hume had the essentially phenomenological insight of "the life of consciousness as a life of *accomplishment*" (*daß Bewußtseinleben leistendes Leben ist, Crisis* § 26, p. 90; Hua VI 93). In other words, Hume discovered the problem of constitution, the immanent genesis in subjectivity of transcendent objectivities.

Hume was limited by his adherence to "naturalistic sensualism, which could see only a collection of data floating in an insubstantial void", as well as by an inability to understand the meaning of intentionality (FTL § 100).

Husserl's intellectual reconstruction of the history of modern philosophy tended to conflate together the efforts of Descartes, Berkeley, Hume, and Kant, in his analysis of transcendental subjectivity. Or rather, Husserl steadfastly uncovered his own unique account, which, nonetheless, he often reported as an achievement of modern philosophy and, specifically, in terms of comparisons with these philosophers of modernity (Husserl admitted that he could find no trace of the transcendental in Leibniz). Furthermore, for Husserl, John Locke is always the villain of the piece who interpreted Descartes's transcendental subjectivity in naturalistic terms and turned it into a psychology of inner experience. Locke is, for Husserl, the father of psychologism.

Husserl's recognition of phenomenology as ineluctably transcendental philosophy forced him to confront Kant whom he had been reading seriously since the late 1890s.[10] But the precise nature of his debt to Kant is rather difficult to specify. He agreed with Kant's general view that the profusion of different philosophical systems was testimony that philosophy had failed to live up to its aspiration to be a science. Like Kant, he believed that toleration of competing systems would lead eventually to *relativism* and *scepticism*. Furthermore, Husserl, like Kant, believed that philosophy could only become a genuine science after it had embarked on a radical critique of its claim to be able to be a science at all. This involved a critique of the instrument of knowledge. Husserl sees Kant as correctly seeing the need for a transcendental critique of the sciences, one which saw them as subjective cognitive accomplishments. But Kant remained focused on the objective side, on the "ontological", and did not see the need to examine the concrete intuitive performances of subjectivity.[11] Husserl is Kantian in the sense that *the conditions for the possibility of* knowledge in general are now sought. But Husserl conceived of this problem in a markedly different way from Kant. As his assistant Eugen Fink has justly remarked, Husserl's concern was not so much the constitution of objectivity as the constitution of the world, world being understood here in phenomenological terms which we shall attempt to clarify in this chapter. Husserl wants to get at consciousness in its "own essentiality" (*Eigenwesentlichkeit*) through very close descriptive accounts of the conscious acts and their contents and objects, but also by focusing on the mystery of the manner in which meanings and objects arise in consciousness, leading to his concerns with the notion of "originary givenness", with coming to grips with the essential nature of consciousness.

Husserl praised Kant for identifying the domain of transcendental philosophy and the role of *temporalisation* (*Zeitigung*) in meaning constitution, but criticised him for lapsing back into naturalism, faculty psychology, and into 'mythical constructions'[12] in his attempt to study consciousness. Thus Husserl rejected Kant's metaphysical construction of the "thing in itself"; all objectivity is objectivity for consciousness. Similarly Husserl dismissed Kant's conception of transcendental logic as a misunderstanding of the transcendental realm (FTL § 100). Kant never grasped the peculiar sense in which logic is ideal. Kant, then, never grasped the problem of going back from the ideal objectivities of pure logic to "the consciousness that constitutes them phenomenologically", which is essentially the purpose of Husserl's *Formal and Transcendental Logic* (FTL § 100, p. 263; Hua XVII 270). Kant did not appreciate the need for a proper study of all forms of sense bestowal. Furthermore, Kant's grasp of the a priori was naive; he did not recognise that every region of being has synthetic a priori truths. On the positive side, Husserl saw the earlier or 'A-version' of Kant's transcendental deduction as "operating inside the realm of phenomenology" (*Ideas* I § 62, 142; Hua III/1 119), an insight later developed by Heidegger in his *Kantbuch* (1929).

Husserl took over Kant's language of the 'transcendental' and talked of the need to adopt the transcendental standpoint, though Husserl was, as with all his technical terms, quite loose in his application of the term 'transcendental':

> I myself use the word "transcendental" *in the broadest sense* for the original motif...which through Descartes confers meaning on all modern philosophies...It is the motif of inquiring back (*das Motiv des Rückfragens*) into the ultimate source of all the formations of knowledge, the motif of the knower's reflecting upon himself and his knowing life in which all the scientific structures that are valid for him occur purposefully, are stored up as acquisitions, and have become and continue to become freely available...it is the motif of a universal philosophy which is grounded purely in this source and thus ultimately grounded (*letztbegründeten Universalphilosophie*). This source bears the title *I-myself*, with all of my actual and possible knowing life and, ultimately, my concrete life in general.
> (*Crisis* § 26, pp. 97–98; Hua VI 100–101)

Husserl's sense of the transcendental, then, is not dependent on Kant's formulations, but rather is seen by Husserl as a kind of discovery of a new realm, the realm of "transcendental experience", a realm which must be explored and criticised (CM § 13).

In *Ideas* I (1913), phenomenological philosophy appears as an explicitly *transcendental* philosophy, a science of subjectivity as an entirely self-contained realm which in some strong sense is 'absolute'. Genuine philosophy wants to uncover the source of the meanings we encounter in the world, and to do this it must adopt a new attitude, one which abandons, disables, or neutralises our normal, 'natural attitude' (*die natürliche Einstellung*). This is not an easy task, as Husserl never tires of reminding us;

141

it requires special trained vigilance not to let the natural attitude creep back in at some stage in our enquiries. The natural attitude is our way of belonging to the surrounding world (*Umwelt*) in an everyday sense where there is always a general commitment to the existence of that world (*Ideas* I § 30).

The critique of naturalism

Soon after writing the *Logical Investigations*, as we have seen, Husserl came to the view that his earlier researches had not completely escaped *naturalism*. After that Husserl constantly set his face against naturalism, but his most cogent critique is to be found in his 1911 essay, *Philosophy as a Rigorous Science*. Husserl thinks that all traditional philosophy, including Descartes and Kant, had treated consciousness as something having a completely natural being, a mere part of nature, and a dependent or epiphenomenal part at that. Even Kant had misunderstood transcendental psychology as a psychology. Husserl regards naturalism both as the dominant *theoretical* outlook of his age and also as deeply embedded in our ordinary assumptions about the world surrounding us. In other words, our pre-theoretical engagement with the world has an inbuilt bias towards naive naturalism. This is fine in our ordinary practices in the world, but when naturalism is elevated into an all-encompassing *theoretical* outlook, it actually becomes far removed from the natural attitude and in fact grossly distorts it. Husserl's critique of naturalism is that it is a distorted conception of the fruits of scientific method which in itself is not inextricably wedded to a naturalist construal.

Husserl's conception of naturalism relates to his understanding of the projects of John Locke, David Hume, and J. S. Mill, as well as nineteenth-century positivists, especially Comte and Mach. *Naturalism* is the view that every phenomenon ultimately is encompassed within and explained by the laws of nature; everything real belongs to physical nature or is reducible to it. There are of course many varieties of naturalism, but Husserl's own account in his 1911 essay more or less correctly summarises the naturalistic outlook:

> Thus the naturalist...sees only nature, and primarily physical nature. Whatever is is either itself physical, belonging to the unified totality of physical nature, or it is in fact psychical, but then merely as a variable dependent on the physical, at best a secondary "parallel accomplishment". Whatever is belongs to psychophysical nature, which is to say that it is univocally determined by rigid laws.
> (PRS 79; Hua XXV 8–9)

As *naturalism* has again become a very central concept primarily in contemporary analytic philosophy, largely due to W. V. O. Quine's call for a *naturalised epistemology*, it is worth taking time here to elucidate further Husserl's conception of naturalism.[13] Indeed, precisely this effort to treat consciousness as part of the natural world is at the basis of many recent studies of consciousness, for example the work of Daniel Dennett or Patricia Churchland. Compare Husserl's definition with that of David Armstrong for example:

> Naturalism I define as the doctrine that reality consists of nothing but a single all-embracing spatio-temporal system.[14]

In *Philosophy as a Rigorous Science*, Husserl explicitly identifies and criticises the tendency of all forms of naturalism to seek the *naturalisation* of consciousness and of all ideas and norms (*die Naturalisierung des Bewußtseins*, PRS 80; Hua XXV 9).

Naturalism as a theory involves a certain 'philosophical absolutising' of the scientific view of the world (*Ideas* I § 55); "it is a bad theory regarding a good procedure" (PRS 105; Hua XXV 28). Certain characteristic *methodological* devices of the sciences, chiefly *idealisation* and *objectification*, have been misunderstood such that their objects are thought to yield the natural world as it is in itself, for example that nature is treated as a closed system of physical entities obeying laws, and everything else is squeezed out and treated as psychical, possibly even epiphenomenal. Indeed, a new science of psychology, with laws modelled on the mechanical laws of the physical domain, was then brought in to investigate this carved off sub-domain, but it was guilty of reifying consciousness and examining it naively. Husserl constantly points out that such a division of the world into physical and psychical makes no sense. For Husserl, naturalism is not just only partial or limited in its explanation of the world, it is in fact *self-refuting*, because it has collapsed all value and normativity into merely physical or psychical occurrences, precisely the same kind of error made by *psychologism* when it sought to explain the normativity of logic in terms of actual, occurrent psychological states and the empirical laws governing them. The whole picture is absurd or 'counter-sensical' (*ein Widersinn*) in that it denies the reality of consciousness and yet is based on assuming the existence of consciousness to give rise to the picture in the first place (*Ideas* I § 55). Or as Husserl says in the 1911 essay: "It is the absurdity of naturalizing something whose essence excludes the kind of being that nature has" (PRS 107; Hua XXV 29).

In contrast to the outlook of naturalism, Husserl believed all knowledge, all science, all rationality depended on conscious acts, acts which cannot be properly understood from within the natural outlook at all. Consciousness should not be viewed naturalistically as part of the world at all, since consciousness is precisely the reason why there was a world there for us in the first place. For Husserl it is not that consciousness *creates* the world in any ontological sense – this would be a subjective idealism, itself a consequence of a certain *naturalising* tendency whereby consciousness is cause and the world its effect – but rather that the world is opened up, made meaningful, or disclosed through consciousness. The world is inconceivable apart from consciousness. Treating consciousness as part of the world, reifying consciousness, is precisely to ignore consciousness's foundational, disclosive role. For this reason, all natural science is naive about its point of departure, for Husserl (PRS 85; Hua XXV 13). Since consciousness is *presupposed* in all science and knowledge, then the proper approach to the study of consciousness itself must be a *transcendental* one – one which, in Kantian terms, focuses on the *conditions for the possibility of* knowledge, though, of course, Husserl believes the Kantian way of articulating the consciousness–world relation was itself distorted since it still postulated the thing in itself.

Husserl's critique of naturalism in science is implicitly bound up with his recognition of the central role of the natural attitude in daily life. The naturalistic outlook is in fact a species of the more general natural attitude, as is the personalistic attitude also. As Husserl states in 1924: "The natural attitude is the form in which the total life of humanity is realized in running its natural practical course."[15] The natural attitude is our normal, taken for granted way of approaching the world, its 'general thesis' (*Generalthesis*) of an existent world is always running as it were. Moreover, as Husserl says in his 1911 *Logos* essay:

> We do not easily overcome the inborn habit of living and thinking according to the naturalistic attitude, and thus of naturalistically adulterating the psychical (*das Psychische naturalistisch zu verfälschen*).
>
> (PRS 109; Hua XXV 31)

In his earliest public formulations of his new approach, namely his early Göttingen lectures published posthumously as *The Idea of Phenomenology*, Husserl contrasts the *natural attitude* with what he calls here the *philosophical attitude* (which is co-terminous with the *phenomenological* outlook for Husserl):

> What is *taken for granted* in natural thinking is the possibility of cognition. Constantly busy producing results, advancing from discovery to discovery in newer and newer branches of science, natural thinking finds no occasion to raise the question of the possibility of cognition as such...Cognition is a fact in nature. It is the experience of a cognising organic being. It is a psychological fact.
>
> (IP, p. 15; Hua II 19)

On the other hand, philosophy arises when we first question the very possibility of cognition, when we raise theoretical questions concerning the manner in which thinking is able to refer to its object and the connection between this intentional object and the external world. We are now no longer interested in consciousness and cognition as occurrent facts or episodes in the world. Nor are we interested in sceptical questions as to whether cognition is possible or whether it reaches its object. Husserl furthermore rules out two traditional ways of thinking of the relation of consciousness and world. On the one hand, one can become an idealist and deny the existence of anything outside thought. On the other hand, one can take Hume's approach and claim that the objective world is constructed through habit, inductive generalisation, mechanically linked chains of association, as determined by the nature of the sense organs, and so on. Husserl rejects both approaches: both are conditioned by naturalistic assumptions concerning knowledge which must be refuted. Thus, in *The Idea of Phenomenology*, Husserl says that we should put aside metaphysical worries about cognition and

> confine ourselves purely to the task *of clarifying the essence of cognition and of being an object of cognition, then this will be phenomenology of cognition and of being an object of cognition* and will be the first and principal part of phenomenology as a whole.
>
> (IP, p. 18; Hua II 23)

Phenomenology is a science of the essences of consciousness and of the ideal essences of the objective correlates of conscious acts. How to arrive at these essences without construing them psychologistically is the function of the *epoché* and the phenomenological and eidetic reductions. The general thesis of the natural attitude, if left unbracketed, will inevitably distort our more theoretical consideration of consciousness itself: for instance, we will inevitably think of consciousness as something 'immanent' and objects as something 'transcendent'. Instead of being drawn into this traditional epistemological way of proceeding, we must operate the *epoché*, assign to everything transcendent 'the index zero', as Husserl says (IP, p. 4; Hua II 6), and we now operate with a new 'reduced' concept of immanence. Immanence does not now mean being within something factual, but that all claims of validity have been disowned. Similarly the transcendent is not understood as existent but as that which stands as object apart from the experience, regardless of questions of existence or non-existence (IP, p. 7; Hua II 9). As Husserl investigates more in this realm, reality comes to be treated more and more as a *correlate* of consciousness, which led Ingarden to protest that Husserl was replacing his earlier *realism* with an *idealism*.[16] In the mature Husserl of his Freiburg years, questioning the natural attitude and placing it in brackets became the very essence of transcendental philosophy, construed now as *transcendental idealism* (a position which is first argued for but not explicitly named in *Ideas* I §§ 39–49). Furthermore, the transcendental is thinkable only through the reduction, in Husserl's eyes the most radical method of philosophising. In the *Cartesian Meditations* Husserl claims that the nature of the transcendental must be discovered within the domain of the reduction itself (CM § 11).

The *epoché* and the reductions

Given the difficulty of doing philosophy (i.e. escaping from the natural attitude which constantly seeks to reassert itself), it is necessary to employ a set of procedures which Husserl generally labels as the 'reduction' (from the Latin *reducere*, 'to lead back'). Husserl's so-called discovery of the reduction took place in the summer of 1905,[17] but, in subsequent years, Husserl wrote many programmatic accounts concerning its nature and purpose.[18]

Husserl had a number of different theoretical reasons for introducing the notion of reduction. First it allowed him to detach from all forms of conventional opinion, including our commonsense psychology, our accrued scientific consensus on issues, and all philosophical and metaphysical theorising regarding the nature of the intentional. We must put aside our beliefs about our beliefs, as it were. Secondly, it allowed him to return to and isolate the central structures of subjectivity. By putting aside psychological, cultural, religious, and scientific assumptions, and by getting behind or to one side of the meaning-positing or thetic acts normally dominant in conscious acts, new features of those acts come to the fore. Most of all, the reduction is meant to prevent what we have won by insight being transformed or deformed into an experience of another kind, a change from one kind to another, a '*metabasis in allo geno*' (*Ideas* I § 61). There is an almost inevitable tendency to 'psychologise the eidetic'. Husserl thought there would be no need for the reduction were there a smooth transition from the factual to the eidetic, as there is in geometry, when the geometer moves from contemplating a factual shape to its idealisation (*Ideas* I § 61, p. 139; Hua III/1 116). In other areas, however, especially in grasping consciousness, the move to the eidetic is difficult to achieve – hence the need for the vigilance of the *epoché*.

In his earliest public discussion of reduction, the 1907 lectures series delivered in Göttingen, entitled *The Idea of Phenomenology*, Husserl introduces a 'phenomenological reduction' (IP, p. 4; Hua II 5) to exclude everything posited as transcendently existing, but he goes on to speak of an 'epistemological reduction' (*erkenntnis-theoretische Reduktion*) as necessary in order to focus on the pure phenomena of conscious acts as *cogitationes*, and to avoid misleading assumptions about the nature and existence of the *sum cogitans* (IP, p. 33; Hua II 43). Husserl has in mind the specific bracketing of a psychological interpretation of what is given in the acts of knowing. In so far as it relates to the nature of psychic states Husserl refers to a "psychological reduction".[19] In general, however, it is not clear how to distinguish the different stages and grades of reduction. He distinguishes at various times between different kinds of reduction: indeed in *Ideas* I he speaks of phenomenological reduction*s*; that is, in the plural (*Ideas* I § 56). Husserl often speaks indifferently of *phenomenological* and *transcendental* reductions. In the *Cartesian Meditations*, Husserl runs these together into a 'transcendental–phenomenological reduction' (CM § 8, 21; Hua I 61). In the *Crisis*, as many as eight different forms of reduction have been catalogued.[20] Iso Kern has argued that Husserl had different models of the reduction – a Cartesian way, a way from intentionality, a way through critique of the natural sciences, and through ontology (i.e. through questioning the grounds of pure logic as in the *Formal and Transcendental Logic*, or through searching for the pregiven elements of the life-world in the *Crisis*).[21] However, Husserl is not so well organised. Although he did talk about the need for a "systematic theory of phenomenological reductions" (*Ideas* I § 61, 139; Hua III/1 115), in practice he was quite lax about distinguishing between the different ways of approaching the one domain.

Husserl characterised the practice of *epoché* in many different ways: 'abstention' (*Enthaltung*), 'dislocation' from, or 'unplugging' or 'exclusion' (*Ausschaltung*) of the positing of the world and our normal unquestioning faith in the reality of what we experience. He speaks of 'withholding', 'disregarding', 'abandoning', 'parenthesising' (*Einklammerung*), 'putting out of action' (*außer Aktion zu setzen*), and 'putting out of play' (*außer Spiel zu setzen*) all judgements which posit a world in any way as actual (*wirklich*) or as 'there', 'present at hand' (*vorhanden*). But the essential feature is always to effect an alteration or 'change of attitude' (*Einstellungänderung*), to move away from naturalistic assumptions about the world, assumptions both deeply embedded in our everyday behaviour towards objects and also at work in our most sophisticated natural science. The change of orientation brings about a 'return' (*Rückgang*) to a transcendental standpoint, to uncover a new transcendental domain of experience. The *epoché* then is part of the reduction. Above all else, the transcendental must not be thought to be simply a dimension of my own mind, reached through psychological reflection. Husserl always regarded his formulation of the reductions as the real discovery of his philosophy and as necessary in order to reveal non-psychologically the essence of intentional consciousness and of subjectivity as such. To experience the reduction is to experience an enrichment of one's subjective life – it opens infinitely before one.

Husserl is always insistent that reduction provides the only genuine access to the infinite subjective domain of inner experience, and that he who misunderstands reduction is lost:

> But in the final analysis everything depends on the initial moment of the method, the phenomenological reduction. The reduction is

the means of access to this new realm, so when one gets the meaning of the reduction wrong, then everything else also goes wrong. The temptation to misunderstandings here is simply overwhelming. For instance, it seems all too obvious to say to oneself: "I, this human being, am the one who is practicing the method of a transcendental alteration of attitude whereby one withdraws back into the pure Ego; so can this Ego be anything other than just a mere abstract stratum of this concrete human being, its purely mental being, abstracted from the body?" But clearly those who talk this way have fallen back into the naive natural attitude. Their thinking is grounded in the pregiven world rather than moving within the sphere of the *epoché*.

> ("Phenomenology and Anthropology", *Trans. Phen.*, p. 493; Hua
> XXVII 173)

The reduction leads to the domain of the transcendental ego which must be kept distinct from the psychological domain of the empirical self. The transcendental ego is at work constituting the world for me, in consciousness, though not in a manner graspable by naive reflection. For Husserl, one must put the thumbscrews not on *nature*, as Francis Bacon had said, but on transcendental *consciousness* itself, to get it to yield up its secrets as to how the world and its meanings are constituted (*Trans. Phen.*, p. 497; Hua XXVII 177).

The *epoché* and scepticism

When introducing the reduction according to "the Cartesian way", Husserl often refers to a first procedure of 'bracketing' (*Einklammerung*) or *epoché*. He took his term *epoché* from the Sceptics where it means a 'cessation'.[22] As we have seen, Husserl reacted against the tradition of modern philosophy which had prioritised epistemology, and had construed the problem of knowledge as the problem of how subjectivity transcends itself to reach the objective world. Traditionally, sceptical moves had been employed (e.g. by Descartes) to lay bare the basis of this epistemological project. Both Descartes and Kant had in their own way been highly conscious of the necessity to refute scepticism. Though Husserl himself never took seriously sceptical worries about the existence of the external world, indeed he regarded this as a counter-sensical problematic; and though he attributed the steady progress of modern science to the fact that it did not allow itself to be diverted by sceptical arguments (*Ideas* I § 26), nevertheless, like Descartes, he appreciated the usefulness of sceptical considerations for sharpening focus on what was essential to knowledge. Thus, in his lectures on *First Philosophy*, Husserl interpreted his task as "redeeming in a higher sense the truth of the radical subjectivism of the sceptical tradition" and doing so by way of *transcendental subjectivism* (*Erste Philosophie, Vorlesung* § 9, Hua VII 61). Thus the reduction is understood in relation to a manoeuvre for defusing the force of sceptical worries. In other words, scepticism's own lack of commitment to assertion could prove to be the very tool needed in the phenomenological researches Husserl was undertaking.

The ancient Sceptics recommended suspending judgement when faced with conflicting arguments, each of which appeared to carry the same weight, to be *equipollent* – that is, supported by the same degree of evidence. This left the person judging facing both alternatives with a certain 'undecidability'. The Sceptic recommendation in these cases was to refrain from judgement, to practise abstention from judgement, *epoché*. As Sextus Empiricus explains in his *Outlines of Pyrrhonism*:

> Suspension of intellect is a standstill of the intellect, because of which we neither reject nor accept anything.[23]

For the ancient Greek Pyrrhonian Sceptics, this attitude was meant to lead to tolerance and openmindedness.[24] With a rather different purpose in mind (i.e. not seeking the equanimity of the ancient Sceptics), Husserl recommends his 'phenomenological' *epoché* in order to suspend the thesis of the natural standpoint. We need to *bracket* certain fundamental structures in order to allow more basic objectifying acts of consciousness to become visible in themselves. Husserl used various mathematical analogies to articulate his sense of the *epoché*: it is like putting brackets round an expression in an equation (e.g. $2 + 2 = (8 \div 4) + 2$) which allows one to employ an expression without subjecting what is inside the brackets to the operations going on outside the brackets. Husserl offers another analogy: *epoché* is like 'changing the value' (*Umwertung, Ideas* I § 31, 59; Hua III/1 55) on a mathematical expression (e.g. putting a minus sign in front of some formula), or putting an index on it which changes radically the way we view it (e.g. we can think of 27 as 3^3). In one sense this does not change anything, but in another sense an essential feature of the number 27 has been exhibited as 3 to the power of 3.

This is what Husserl thinks will happen with all conscious acts when their thetic world-positing character is bracketed. We can never switch off this thetic character of our acts but, by a free act of will, we can refuse to be drawn in the direction of the positing, and instead focus on the structure of the act and its intentional correlate, without thinking of it in terms of the existent world. Husserl believes this is a first step to laying bare the essence of the act, for example what precisely it *means* to perceive something, remember something, imagine something, and so on.

The natural attitude always employs a *thetic act* (German *Thesis*, from the Greek *thesis*, a proposal, proposition), an act of positing (*Setzung*), 'position taking' (*Stellungnahme*). Disconnecting the natural standpoint means making a conscious decision not to rely on any beliefs which involve the spatio-temporal world (*Ideas* I § 27). The aim is to "inhibit the acceptance of the objective world" (CM § 11, 25; Hua I 64). Moreover, Husserl often emphasises that the suspension of the natural attitude, like the entertaining of Cartesian methodic doubt, is based on a free act of the mind; we can freely choose to alter our standpoint. We need not be drawn by the assumption that there really exists a world independent of us, nor do we assume anything about the composition of that world, or about the relationship between mind and world. The very *positing* aspect of our intentional experiences (beliefs and desires) has to be put out of operation, though this does not mean taking up the orientation of actually doubting it or even of remaining undecided. Rather the positing undergoes a modification (*Ideas* I § 31, 58–9; III/1 54). The core of this reduction involved isolating the very world-commitment, or positing of being, which seemed to be contained in all our normal intentional experiences. Through the phenomenological reduction we strip away the actual character of the experience and grasp it as *pure phenomenon*:

> Thus at this point we speak of such absolute data; even if these data are related to objective actuality via their intentions, their intrinsic character is *within* them; nothing is assumed concerning *the existence or non-existence of actuality*.
>
> (IP, p. 35; Hua II 45)

Under the natural standpoint we believe that things are genuinely present in space and we are aware of time passing and of ourselves as in some sort of continuity with the world. When we effect the phenomenological bracketing, all that disappears and, according to Husserl, we are left with a *residuum* of pure consciousness, consciousness as absolute existence, whose objects are always correlates of consciousness. Husserl insists that this is the real significance of Descartes's methodology of universal doubt. Except that now, instead of the world disappearing or being entirely disregarded, it appears in a wholly new light, not as something absolutely existent, there in itself, but rather as the 'correlate of consciousness' (*Bewußtseinskorrelat*, *Ideas* I § 47), as something which has a peculiar mode of being of its own, a peculiar mode of 'self-givenness' (*Selbstgegebenheit*). Consciousness consists here of the acts of the ego, what Husserl calls *cogitationes*, and the correlates of those acts, the unities that are thought, the *cogitata*, whether these refer to the adumbrations of physical objects or to ideal objectivities and states of affairs. Furthermore, this world of correlated meanings is the one world for all possible beings. Whatever is a possible intuition for me is also a possible intuition for everyone else (*Ideas* I § 48). Although Husserl later came to regret this formulation, in *Ideas* I he thought that one could radicalise thinking about the nature of consciousness to such a degree that one could even undertake the thought experiment of imagining the very destruction of the world, 'world-annihilation' (*Weltvernichtung, Ideas* I § 49), which would show that consciousness survived as pure, absolute being. The existence of objects is revealed as contingent, whereas consciousness is shown as absolute.

The aim of the suspension of the natural attitude is to uncover the inner core of our subjectivity. The reduction leads directly to transcendental subjectivity. Elsewhere he says:

> Subjectivity, and this universally and exclusively, is my theme. It is a purely self-enclosed and independent theme. To show that this is possible and how it is possible is the task of the description of the method of phenomenological reduction.[25]

Initially, Husserl thought of the reduction in terms of the move from the natural psychic life of an empirical individual ego to the self-certain domain of inner perception (e.g. LI V § 6). Here it is a matter of an attention shift from the object given in consciousness to the *contents* of consciousness itself which are usually not noticed, because we attend to the objects of our acts. The reduction moves from mere empirical judgements to ones which by their nature are self-certain and are grasped "adequately". This early reduction is not primarily a bracketing of the world so much as a redirection of attention away from the objects given in perception to the contents: the parts of consciousness which are the genuine parts (both real and ideal) of that consciousness. However, the real focus is not the individual parts of consciousness, but the ideal intentional structures and essences required by conscious processes in order to be knowledge yielding. The reduction uncovers our psychic "stream of pure lived experiences with both their real and ideal contents" (*Phen. Psych.* § 37, p. 147; Hua IX 192). There are the *cogitationes* and their correlative objectivities or *cogitata*, called such in order to distance ourselves from the factual psychical processes and contents which instantiate them and are their counterparts in the real world. In his drafts for the *Encyclopaedia Brittanica* article, Husserl suggests that the *epoché* which excludes the thetic positing of the world is a first step in the reduction aiming to bring the proper phenomenological domain into view, the second being the identification, comprehension, and description of the ideal unities of sense that now appear, these being the *noemata* and *noeses* which we shall shortly discuss (*Trans. Phen.*, p. 185). In later writings, Husserl continued to see the reduction as the move from the ordinary empirical ego to the transcendental ego (CM § 11). Thus in the *Cartesian Meditations*, Husserl explains the workings of reduction as follows:

> By phenomenological *epoché* I reduce my natural human Ego and psychic life – the realms of my *psychological self-experience* – to my

transcendental phenomenological Ego, the realm of *transcendental-phenomenological self-experience (Selbsterfahrung)*.

(CM § 11, 26; Hua I 65)

Here, as in *Ideas* I, the *epoché* is seen as questioning the "basis of validity" (*Geltungsgrund*) of the objective world, seeking to suspend our natural tendency to validate what is presented in experience.

Gradually Husserl gave more content to the notion of the transcendental domain and of the ego as the focal centre of that domain. He also came to worry that the Cartesian way of describing the reduction both bracketed the world from the ego, thus emptying out the ego, and also lost hold of the genuinely intersubjective character of experience. The Cartesian attempt to treat the world as a complete illusion, while methodologically useful, served to obscure the deep way in which the world is always there as a horizon for all our experiences, and, moreover, the manner in which our experiences of meaning are always experiences which, as we are aware, are confirmable by others. Other ways of performing the reduction had to remedy this distortion, and one such method is given in the *Crisis* where the reduction consists in leading the self back to considering the original pregivenness of the world in all our acts. But Husserl does seem to suggest, with his many warnings, that even in our reduction back to the transcendental ego, it is easy to confuse this special domain and our special access to it as just another way of thinking about our existent world and our existent psychic states, and thus to fall back into naturalism.

Breaking with actuality

A crucial aspect of the reduction, as Husserl applies it, is that all features of conscious experience must be taken as they appear, without our attempting to categorise them as 'false', 'illusory', and so on, without assessing their 'validity' (*Geltung*) as such. The reduction removes reference to the real world of existent entities, and all appearances are taken as genuine in their own right. Husserl takes this to be an essentially Cartesian move. Descartes, for instance, could examine the content (what Descartes called 'objective reality', *realitas objectiva*) of his experiences without worrying whether they represented actual perceptions or were merely dreams or illusions. For Husserl too, experiences can be examined with regard to their evidence, regardless of whether they are experiences of perception or fantasy. Indeed, in phenomenology as in the eidetic sciences in general, as we have seen, factual experience has no claim to priority. Memory, fantasy, and other forms of attention can disclose as many acts of perception as factual experience. Whether I am dreaming or am awake, I am experiencing *cogitationes*, 'thoughts' in the widest sense, and these can be examined so that the essential structures of both the acts and the objects of the acts can be disclosed. The whole world becomes for the reduced consciousness a field of *possible* experiences. Husserl drops reference to the actual world, to factuality.

What matters, however, is not whether experience is actual or fictional but the essential structure and contents of the experiences and the manner in which we live through them. In this case, we don't seek for external criteria to distinguish between different categories of our experience, but simply attend to how our experiences are discriminated by us from within, as it were. Our mental experiences have a peculiar kind of self-givenness. Husserl thought Descartes was right to acknowledge the peculiar self-givenness of the *cogito*. But, on close investigation of the stream of mental processes, Husserl recognises that there are myriad modes of givenness and not all psychic acts are given with the same degree of conviction and certitude: "It becomes clear that in the Cartesian sphere itself different types of objectivity are 'constituted'" (IP, p. 56; Hua II 71). Perceptions, for example, posit the existence of their objects in a way in which fantasies don't. In fact, fantasy presents itself with the conviction that it is not real, not fully present, but only has an "as if" fictional presence. A mathematical judgement gives itself as a judgement about mathematics and not about the weather. How are these differences produced? How are the forms of givenness constituted? Husserl is very critical of the common view that mental acts of cognition are pure form, like an empty box into which we put contents (IP, p. 56; Hua II 71). Rather we have different kinds of *schauen*, different kinds of manifestation.

Phenomenology is to proceed by careful attention to the dimensions of the experience itself. In *Ideas* I §35 Husserl gives a famous example (indeed one of the few examples in the whole book) of looking at and touching a sheet of white paper. He is trying to articulate how the application of the *epoché* uncovers aspects of an experience not obvious in the naturalistic viewpoint. Husserl is trying to give a very careful, scrupulous account of just what his perception is actually like, avoiding importing any assumptions. When I hold a sheet of paper in my hands and I specifically focus on it, I am directed towards it, I single it out, and seize it in a special manner. I see it surrounded by a more marginal field of vaguer experiences, for example as surrounded by books, pencils, and so on. Each perception of the white sheet has "a halo of background intuitions" (*ein Hof von Hintergrundsanschauungen, Ideas* I § 35, 70; III/1 62) of the entities and also of other conscious acts. Moreover, I grasp it as a visual perception and not as a hallucination, and I am aware that I can vary the modality of my grasp of the object, I can remember it, and so on. We know that, even if the sheet of paper doesn't exist, it is still referred to; something of the very essence of a mental process is being grasped. This example shows how Husserl moves from a concrete factual experience to try to uncover something essentially about the structure of an act of consciousness or a series of acts and the peculiar consciousness that accompanies them. Thus Husserl believes that we are distinctly aware in a different way when we perceive something than when we imagine. We just intuitively attend to the object in a structurally different manner (and this is not a matter of the meanings of the words we use but a feature of the mental acts themselves). Furthermore, in grasping the white sheet of paper, I am aware of being directed towards the object (the paper) in a fundamentally different way than that in which I am aware of the whiteness. My sensation of white forms part of the experience, but is not the object of my experience as the paper is. From this kind of example, we learn how Husserl intended the phenomenological method to be applied.

Imaginative free variation

In order to grasp an essence more clearly, Husserl thought it useful to perform what he called 'imaginative free variation' where we take aspects of our original intuition and substitute parts in a manner which allows the essence to come into view and anything merely contingent to drop away. The whole point of free variation is to open up new aspects of the experience and especially those invariant aspects – aspects which belong to the essence of the experience. Something like imaginative free variation was practised by Descartes in his famous wax example in Meditation Two. There Descartes asks us to imagine a piece of wax – with a certain shape, colour, consistency, smell, and so on. Then we heat the wax until all these properties alter – it no longer has the same shape, colour, smell, or consistency, yet we judge it to be the same piece of wax. For Descartes this was evidence that the essence of the wax was grasped by the mind and not by the senses. Now, Husserl wants us to perform a similar thought-experiment or set of experiments. The act of imaginative variation is connected with the notion of reduction. In a sense, by staying within the realm of imagination and fantasy we avoid the pitfalls associated with naturalistic positing. Indeed, Husserl points out that geometers proceed by a kind of fantasy.

Suppose we are seeking the essence of an act of perception itself, an example Husserl gives in the *Cartesian Meditations*. We can take any current perception, for example *seeing* a table, and then seek to alter its constituent parts, while retaining the perceiving element in the act. The essential features are those which cannot be varied in our imagination. Imaginative free variation plays a helpful role in allowing the *eidos* or essence of the phenomenon to manifest itself as the structure of its essential possibilities. As Husserl says:

> Starting from this table perception as an example, we vary the per-
> ceptual object, table, with a completely free optionalness, yet in
> such a manner that we keep perception fixed as perception of some-
> thing, no matter what. Perhaps we begin by fictionally changing the

154

shape or the colour of the object quite arbitrarily...In other words: Abstaining from acceptance of its being, we change the fact of this perception into a pure possibility, one among other quite "optional" pure possibilities – but possibilities that are possible perceptions. We so to speak, shift the actual perception into the realm of non-actualities, the realm of the as-if.

(CM § 34, 60; Hua I 104)

Husserl thought that through techniques such as we have described the essence of the phenomenon can come to be grasped and understood (note: it is one thing to intuit an essence and quite another to express that intuition in words). Indeed he was sure everyone was already familiar with the eidetic domain in their ordinary encounters with mathematics. Husserl merely wanted us to become aware that there was an important eidetic core in all acts of knowledge – not just when mathematics is involved. There is an essence to perceiving, to remembering and so on, there is an essential kind of objectivity belonging to physical objects and a different kind of objectivity belonging to ideal objects such as numbers. This is Husserl's "new eidetics" as he calls it in the *Formal and Transcendental Logic*. Indeed grasping the *eidos* was at the heart of reason itself, and the basis of all linguistic conceptualisation (CM § 34).

The noetic–noematic structure of experience

In his writings from 1907 to 1913 Husserl gradually unveiled his new thinking about the nature of intentional experiences in general, seeking to identify the "eidetic moments" of intentional acts and their objects. In order to get away from all psychologistic and naturalistic misconceptions, including those of descriptive psychology, he introduced a new terminology, drawing on the ancient Greek terms for the 'act of thinking', *noesis*, and 'what is thought', *noema*, terms which carried less philosophical baggage than traditional terms for the intentional structure, for example 'act', 'content', 'meaning', and so on. For Husserl, the most important thing to emphasise is that *noesis* and *noema* are correlative parts of the structure of the mental process.

In *Ideas* I, Husserl claims that grasping and mastering the doctrine of the *noema* are "of the greatest importance for phenomenology, are indeed decisive for the legitimate grounding of phenomenology" (*Ideas* I § 96, 233–234; Hua III/1 200). Elsewhere, Husserl says that the account of the intentional object provides a 'transcendental clue' to the entire multiplicity of possible *cogitationes* (CM § 21) leading to a theory of the transcendental constitution of any object whatsoever. Husserl's analysis of the *noesis* and *noema* has given rise to a huge discussion concerning the nature of the phenomenological theory of meaning and the nature of the intentional object.

The *noesis* is "the concretely complete intentive mental process" approached in such a way that its noetic components are clearly emphasised (*Ideas* I § 96, 233; Hua III/1 199). The *noesis* includes what Husserl formerly called the 'quality' of the act, that which all acts of hoping, or remembering, have in common. But the *noesis* has a larger function in that it is responsible for bestowing sense, for constituting the meaning of what it grasps.

Although Husserl's first published discussion of *noema* and *noesis* occurred in *Ideas* I, he was already formulating the concept of the 'noetic' in his 1906–1907 lectures on *Introduction to Logic and the Theory of Knowledge* (Hua XXIV § 27, 134), and developing the theory of the *noema*, though without using the term, in his summer semester 1908 *Lectures on the Theory of Meaning* (*Vorlesungen über Bedeutungslehre*, Hua XXVI). The term 'noema' is first used in the pencil draft of *Ideas* I in 1912.[26] Husserl's interest in the *noema* came through a reconsideration of the relation between the individual experiential act and its acts of grasping a meaning and referring to an object. Husserl is rethinking the nature of the intentional object, now under the bracketing of existence. He is in a sense meditating on the kind of relation between sense and reference which Frege had proposed in his famous article in 1891, but, with the *epoché*, all questions regarding the true referent of an expression are excluded. He is interested, then, not in *actual* reference but only in the act of referring and the *intended* reference of the act. With the *noema* Husserl is positing a single complex entity which will take care both of what Frege includes under the term sense, and the referential function of the act. In this sense, Husserl is not simply restating the Fregean conception in his own terms, but essentially rethinking the relation between the act of giving meaning and the meaning and object intended.

The fundamental distinction which underlies the doctrine of *noema* was already present in the Fifth Logical Investigation, where Husserl distinguished between the *object which is intended* and the *object as it is intended* (LI V § 17, p. 578; Hua XIX/1 414), for example the Emperor of Germany may be understood as the son of Frederick III or the grandson of Queen Victoria. In the 1906–1907 *Lectures on Logic and Theory of Knowledge*, Husserl speaks of grasping this intended object immanently, as it is given, without regard to existence (Hua XXIV § 38, 232). As usual, Husserl contrasts the real temporal living act of intending with the ideality or non-real nature of the object grasped as it is grasped. The problem is whether the *noema* as an immanent entity in consciousness is a part of the occurrent thought, or whether it refers to the object beyond the thought, or whether it is the abstract ideal meaning (*Sinn*) through which the object is given.

In our everyday natural attitude we focus just on the object, but the function of suspending the natural standpoint is to focus on the *noema* by a kind of reflection which Husserl acknowledges is 'unnatural'. Husserl thought that a special kind of phenomenological or philosophical reflection was required to focus on the *noema* rather different from our ordinary act of reflection, as when, for example, we reflect on the meaning of the sentence we have just uttered.[27] If these forms of reflection were the same, then phenomenology would not differ from semantic or conceptual analysis. But, for Husserl, the reason for applying the reduction is to be able to generate a new kind of reflection, one which is self-consciously 'unnatural', as Husserl puts it. I am not normally conscious of the *noema* in my acts of perception, rather I see the objects directly and the *noema* itself can only be grasped by a special act of transcendental reflection. Our consciousness always has *directedness*; it is always directed as if there were an object. An intentional act is normally directed to the real or "transcendent" object; if I am thinking of a box, it is the real box that my thought is directed on. Similarly, when I am fantasising about a holiday on Paradise Island, it is the imagined place, Paradise Island, that I am focusing on (whether or not it exists in reality). The *noema* is not the object towards which the act is directed, but rather provides the vehicle which connects my occurrent thought to the intended object. The *noema* is that *through* which the object is grasped; it is the route to the object. Husserl always emphasises that we are at first naive realists in perception; we see the tree out there, we do not see the *noema*. But we see a tree because our perceptual act has a noetic–noematic constitution, *because* our act has a *noema*.

Husserl's main discussion of the *noema* occurs in *Ideas* I §§ 87–96, where he introduces it in terms of a fundamental rethinking of the components proper to the intentional process. The *noesis* is considered in its essence to contain within it something like a 'sense' (*Ideas* I § 88). Correlative to the noetic element of the act there is the 'noematic content' (*noematische Gehalt*) or *noema*, and even perceptual acts have a 'sense' in this wide sense. In the natural attitude, when I see an apple tree in the garden I treat it as a transcendent really existing thing. But now the reference to the outside world is suspended: "now the real relation (*das reale Verhältnis*), previously meant as actually existing, is destroyed" (*Ideas* I § 88, 215; Hua III/1 182). There remains left over a *perceiving* and a *perceived*. To examine the structure of this 'perceived as perceived' is to examine the *noema*. The bracketing has changed our relation to this object. As Husserl says, the object, the apple tree, can be destroyed but the *noema* cannot be destroyed:

> The *tree simpliciter*, the physical thing belonging to Nature, is nothing less than this *perceived tree as perceived* which, as perceptual sense, inseparably belongs to the perception. The tree simpliciter can burn up, be resolved into its chemical elements, etc. But the sense – the sense *of this* perception, something belonging necessarily to its essence – cannot burn up; it has no chemical elements, no forces, no real properties.
>
> (*Ideas* I § 89, 216; Hua III/1 184)

This 'perceived' entity contains nothing in itself but what appears and precisely as it appears, 'in the mode of givenness' appropriate to it. Even the non-existence of the actual object cannot remove the sense from the intending act, but Husserl does not want to speak of the sense as merely 'intentional' or 'immanent' in the Scholastic or Brentanian sense. Husserl would talk of the intentional object as opposed to the actual object if this were not to bring in a false dichotomy. There is no second immanent tree besides the real tree in the garden which I perceive. In the phenomenological reduction the whole point of distinguishing between the internal, intentional object and the external object has been annulled, and Husserl is concerned more to account for the manner in which the tree-object as perceived appears in consciousness.

Husserl distinguishes this one-sided sense in the perception from the 'full *noema*' (*das volle Noema*; *Ideas* I §§ 90–91) which consists of a 'complex of noematic moments' around a 'central core' (*Kern*). There is a certain noematic meaning (*noematische Sinn*) which anchors the object so that it remains the same through different intentional acts about it, but there is also a varying element in the *noema*, what Husserl terms the 'mode of givenness' (*die Gegebenheitsweise*). Husserl characterises this as a 'determinable X', a subject of predications, and as a set of further determinations. Furthermore, because *noesis* and *noema* are correlative, the *noema* can be said to include 'thetic moments' which are the meaning modifications correlated to the noetic act qualities (believing, desiring, etc.). The problem with Husserl's analysis is that he is not greatly advancing our understanding by saying that the unity of various acts of intending the same object is explained by a 'determinable X'. Nevertheless, we can see what he is talking about if we think of attending to a musical note, now directly hearing it, now recalling it as it slips into memory. There clearly is something which makes these notes the *same*, even if the acts of intending differ, and further, if the actuality of the tone itself is left aside. What we experience is the *same* tone under different modifications. What makes this possible is the *noema*.

Furthermore, though every act has a *noema* not every act has an object: for example, in thinking of a unicorn, my act has a *noema* but there exists nothing corresponding to this *noema*. Different acts of attention by the ego in fact present the *noema* under different modifications. Logic, which studies propositional contents, is interested only in the objective noematic core and is not interested in the fuller noemata of judgements – that which makes one judgement evident and another blind, for example (*Ideas* I § 94), the 'how' of its givenness. Similarly when I see a tree, the perceived as perceived includes the properties of being 'lovely', 'admired', 'to the left of the window', and so on. The noematic core is to be distinguished from the determinations which are often thought of as more 'subjective'.

Dagfinn Føllesdal has argued that the *noema* is an intensional entity, rather like Frege's notion of *sense* (*Sinn*), but now generalised from linguistic assertions to cover all intentional acts including, for example, visual perception.[28] Føllesdal quotes Husserl's remark in *Ideas* III that "the noema is nothing but the generalisation of the idea of meaning (*Bedeutung*) to the field of all acts".[29] The *noema* is to be found in all acts, not just linguistic acts. Indeed linguistic comprehension is founded on the grasp of the *noema* in perceptual and other acts of cognition. In his famous distinction between sense (*Sinn*) and reference (*Bedeutung*), Frege had given an example to help clarify his meaning. He pointed out that one can think of or refer to the planet Venus by thinking of it either as the Morning Star or as the Evening Star. When one thinks of the Evening Star one is referring to the planet, but under the *mode of presentation* of the star which appears in the evening. Thus it becomes clear that two people can be referring to the same thing without realising it, because each is grasping it under their own *mode of presentation*. Now here the *mode of presentation* (Morning Star, Evening Star) should be taken as having the role of what Frege calls *Sinn* (sense, meaning, connotation) whereas what is being referred to, the planet Venus, is the *Bedeutung* (referent, denotation). Frege gives another example: looking at the moon through a telescope. The moon is the referent but the moon is seen through the inverted image in the lens of the telescope, and this latter can be understood as the sense. Føllesdal emphasises that on his reading the *noema* is an abstract entity. Husserl does indeed consider the *noema* to be abstract, but Husserl had many senses of abstract. It is true that the *noema* is *ideal* in that it has no spatial or temporal existence. It is transtemporal, timeless. The *noema* is also not perceived in the usual sense.

Føllesdal wants to define *noema* as "all those features of the act in virtue of which it has the object it has".[30] Every intentional act has an object, but the object strictly speaking is not the same as the *noema*. Moreover, in each mental act there is only one *noema*. When we think of something in different ways the *noema* supports changes in the mode of givenness, and thus guarantees that our experiences are of the same object. Husserl speaks here of a "noematic nucleus" which is what allows 'the victor at Jena' and the 'vanquished at Waterloo' to refer to the same object.

Husserl in *Ideas* I § 96 admitted to having great difficulties regarding the 'mode of being' (*die Seinsweise*) of the *noema*, the manner of its immanence in the noetic act, and the mode of its intending of the object. In his earlier discussion in 1908 he characterised his new thinking of meaning as 'ontic' and this has also led critics to worry about the *ontological status* of the *noema*. Husserl himself never addressed this problem in a clear way. These difficulties have been bequeathed to subsequent commentators. Føllesdal, Smith and McIntyre, Mohanty, among others, have taken it to be an ideal, abstract, intensional object associated with the act, an extension of the

Fregean doctrine of sense. Others understand it as a linguistic meaning.[31] David Bell has argued that it is not a sortal notion at all, but rather a "ragbag concept" covering different items which are there to condition or produce the meaningfulness of the noetic act.[32] As such, Bell thinks Husserl's notion is incoherent; Husserl is assuming that there is a single entity – the *noema* – responsible for making intentional acts meaningful, but for Bell this is a misunderstanding. Furthermore, Bell holds that Husserl, in having a notion of a determinable X at the centre of the *noema*, is simply assuming what he is setting out to explain, namely how the intentional act achieves reference.

In all external perception, there is always more to the object than is contained in the *noema*. There is an excess, as it were. Thus Aron Gurwitsch interpreted the *noema* as the object itself, the object itself as seen from a certain perspective, or perhaps a part of the object, for example the *tree as perceived*. Gurwitsch tends to think of the object as an assembly of noemata; thus when we grasp a *noema* we grasp the object in part, as it were. For Gurwitsch, the object is a *series* of noemata and nothing more. Robert Sokolowski, on the other hand, argues that the *noema* is the object as it is intended in the act, and hence it is not the same as a *Sinn* or meaning. We cannot here sort out these difficulties. Husserl clearly thought his account of the noetic–noematic structure of intentionality to have radical repercussions in terms of how we are to think of science. Before addressing issues concerning the actual existence of objects, Husserl thinks phenomenology has the task of clarifying their noetic–noematic structures. At stake is how consciousness coheres together and how the object achieves its ideal unity.

Problems with the reduction

Husserl claimed that anyone who failed to grasp the reduction was doomed to misunderstand phenomenology. The reduction allows the true structure of intentionality to be understood, now stripped of naturalistic misconceptions. This intentional structure thus reduced is then understood by Husserl in terms of the concepts of *noesis* and *noema*. As we have seen, he believed he had achieved a significant advance by employing this terminology. But many philosophers, including many of Husserl's own followers, have rejected the possibility of carrying out the reduction. Both Heidegger and Merleau-Ponty denied the possibility of carrying out a *complete* reduction, insisting that we can only think back to our being-in-the-world, and attempting to go behind this phenomenon makes no sense. At best, and here he is taking his orientation from the late Husserl, Merleau-Ponty thought we could hold on to the idea of reduction as a 'leading-back' to the well-springs of our experience, to the pre-reflective element in our consciousness. We cannot reduce our dependence on the world, we can only make the

160

transcendence of the world more visible. Thus, in the Preface to his *Phenomenology of Perception*, Merleau-Ponty claims that "the most important lesson which the reduction teaches us is the impossibility of a complete reduction" (PP xiv; viii). We should note here that Husserl himself held what Merleau-Ponty subsequently asserted, namely the impossibility of a complete reduction.

More recently, David Bell has rejected Husserl's account of the reduction as an appeal to an "esoteric experience":

> There is something dismal and dogmatic about a philosophy whose utility, cogency and plausibility depend essentially, not on objective arguments, rational analysis, or the critical consideration of evidence available to all, but rather on the individual philosopher's having undergone some esoteric experience.[33]

There is no doubt that Husserl constantly underscores the radicality and critical importance of the reduction. Thus, in the *Crisis*, Husserl says that the reduction will lead to "a complete personal transformation (*Wandlung*) comparable in beginning to a religious conversion, which then, however, over and above this, bears within itself the significance of the greatest transformation which is assigned as a task to mankind as such" (*Crisis* § 35, p. 137; Hua VI 140). Despite this rhetoric, Husserl thought of the reduction rather as a change of standpoint which led from our everyday immersion in the natural attitude to the uniquely philosophical viewpoint, one which puts behind all reliance on empirical data and focused purely on what is given a priori in intuition, which grasped all forms of givenness as precisely givenness-to-consciousness. Husserl believed that by careful acts of a priori reflection, or *transcendental reflection* as he calls it, we can arrive at the precise meaning of the essential features of our conscious life. Many philosophers today believe this to be radically misguided, arguing that we have no access to many of the most important acts upon which our conscious life rests, these acts taking place in the brain and being strictly speaking not available to consciousness at all. Husserl, however, thought of the transcendental turn as leading us into a realm of pure essential possibilities which could be mapped scientifically in the manner in which geometry maps the domain of pure space.

The horizon

Husserl recognised that in all grasping of objects, there are aspects of the objects which are not directly grasped. Husserl calls this the 'horizon' (*Horizont*) and it became a crucial element in his account of phenomenology. The 'horizon' is constituted by those aspects of a thing that are not given in perception but rather are possibilities which can be given in further acts of perception or reflection. As Husserl says in the *Cartesian Meditations*:

> There belongs to every genuine perception its reference from the "genuinely perceived" sides of the object of perception to the sides "also meant" – not yet perceived but anticipated.
>
> (CM § 19, 44; Hua I 82)

Traditional empiricism or sensationalism had attempted to describe the actual nature of our perception in terms of the presence of sensual data but had ignored the manner in which all perception takes place under a number of horizons which are implicit structural aspects of our original experience itself. When I see a pen, I also, in that very act, see it as something which could be handled, which could be picked up. I grasp its *graspability*, as it were. Various 'horizonal' layers of reference are contained in the very experience itself – and of course they can be either confirmed or denied in subsequent experiences: for example, if I seek to pick up the pen and find it is glued to the desk. The horizon then maps out a set of expectations, and seeks confirmations or disconfirmations consistent with the original given in the experience. If I pick up an apple, I have the expectation that I can bite into it. This is disconfirmed if it is a wax apple in a waxworks museum (as in one of Husserl's favourite examples).

Husserl recognises not only that in any perceptual act there is present the actual side of the object perceived, but also that each act of perception takes place within a horizon of anticipations. I know I will be able to see other sides of a table if I walk around it; it will be resistant to touch, I may not be able to lift it, and so on. Subsequent perceptions either confirm these anticipations or else set up a whole new domain of anticipations. In our ordinary experience we are interested in the confirmations themselves; in phenomenology we are attempting to delimit the nexus of expectations etc. which are enabled by the perceptual act as such. Husserl is particularly aware that perception is a temporal process; it does not take place wholly in the present but is oriented towards future experiences and at the same time is an experience of enduring or continuing from past experiences. There is also a "horizon of the past" (*Vergangenheitshorizont*), the potential to awake recollections (CM § 19, 44; Hua I 82). Crucially, for phenomenology, Husserl was alert to the fact that many of these unrealised possibilities, which are given 'horizonally' in any experience, are given in the form of possibilities which I myself can carry out. They have the character of "I can", as Husserl says.

In his later philosophy, Husserl became more and more concerned to clarify the way in which the horizons of our experience overlap and interrelate so that they produce our experience of a world as such. These lead to Husserl's reflections on the nature of the life-world and the manner in which temporal experience congeals into historical and cultural consciousness, which will be the focus of the next chapter.

5

HUSSERL AND THE CRISIS OF THE EUROPEAN SCIENCES

Introduction

We must now turn to some of the most interesting and also most difficult aspects of Husserl's mature philosophy: his conception of constitution, the role of the ego, and the problem of intersubjectivity, culminating in his last reflections on the nature of the life-world and the evolution and fate of Western rationality.

The notion of constitution

'Constitution' (*Konstitution*) is a central notion in Husserl and one of the least explained, being one of what Eugen Fink termed Husserl's 'operative concepts' as opposed to his 'thematic' concepts; that is, it is a concept he employs rather than elucidates.[1] In a sense, the whole problem of phenomenology comes down to the problem of constitution. The term 'constitution' itself has a pre-history in Kantian philosophy, and, though rare in Kant's own writings, is commonly found among Neo-Kantians, including Paul Natorp, who had an important influence on the early Husserl. In the Kantian sense, 'constitution' refers to the manner in which objects are 'built up' for consciousness out of a synthesis of sensory intuitions and various categories which are applied according to rules, a meaning which continues in Husserl (he emphasises the rule-governed nature of the transcendental sphere in the *Cartesian Meditations*). As early as *Philosophy of Arithmetic*, Husserl had already employed the term 'constitution', and he subsequently interpreted this first work as a study in the constitution of mathematical entities. In the *Logical Investigations* 'constitution' referred to the manner in which non-intentional sensations are interpreted and brought into objectifying intentions so as to produce objects for consciousness. The term has a major role in Husserl's mature transcendental writings. The performance of the *epoché* and the reduction leaves us with the intentional structures which show how objectivity is constituted out of subjectivity.

For Husserl, 'constitution' expresses the manner in which objects of consciousness come to have the kinds of 'sense and being' that they do, the manner in which subjectivity carries out its function of giving sense. Husserl's notion of constitution should perhaps be thought as a kind of setting out or 'positing' (*Setzung*), as a giving of sense, 'sense-bestowing' (*Sinngebung*).[2] Husserl uses words like 'manifesting' and 'exhibiting' as equivalent to 'constituting'. 'Constitution', as Eugen Fink recognised, can mean 'putting together' (*Zusammenstellung*) in the sense of 'constructing', 'producing', 'making', or even 'creating'. Very frequently in Husserl's mature writings, constitution is spoken of as a kind of 'production' of objectivities, though he distinguishes between a kind of passive production (in the case of natural objects) and production which presupposes "genuine activity, an operation" *(Ideas* II § 10, 23; Hua IV 21). Thus, in the *Cartesian Meditations*, Husserl speaks of new objects being constituted for consciousness as 'products' (*Erzeugnisse, Leistungen*): that is, in acts of collecting, I am faced with a collection; in acts of division I am faced with a part, and so on (CM § 38, 77; Hua I 111). The grasping of something as 'collectivity' or 'part' is produced by an act of synthesis.

Some commentators (e.g. Robert Sokolowski) have argued that constitution should not be read as meaning that the entire *being* of the world is produced from consciousness. Husserl would have regarded this viewpoint as subjective idealism, which he associated with Berkeley and dismissed as naive. On the other hand, Husserl does actually speak of transcendental consciousness giving both meaning and *being* to the world, but 'being' here means the manner in which beings appear to consciousness, being-for-us as opposed to being-in-itself (terms Husserl himself employs). Husserl's later view of this is that even in the most extreme performance of the reduction, the *correlation* of consciousness to world remains intact. There is no question of escaping the world. The world remains as a horizon in all our mental processes, it is always 'pregiven'. In the *Formal and Transcendental Logic* (1929) Husserl clearly sets out the claim that the relation of consciousness to the world is not a haphazard event produced either by God or by the evolution of the world itself, but rather that the world is always the product of a constituting ego. In the same vein, Heidegger, in his 1925 lectures on the *History of the Concept of Time*, interprets Husserl's meaning: " '*Constituting*' does not mean producing in the sense of making and fabricating; it means *letting the entity be seen in its objectivity*" (HCT § 6, 71; 97). Heidegger, furthermore, claims that it is misleading to think of constitution as the mind's imposition of form upon sensuous material elements given by the world; the form/matter analogy is inappropriate for the structure of constitution. The kind of objectivity which entities have is bestowed by consciousness and the object is unthinkable apart from consciousness, but the being of entities is experienced in consciousness as *other than* consciousness. In this sense, Husserl always emphasises the *transcendence* of being with regard to consciousness, being is other than consciousness, though both Sartre and Levinas, as we shall see, interpret Husserl here in a more extreme manner than his own complex and ambiguous comments on the subject warrant. Thus Husserl's stress on constitution does not rule out the recognition of the facticity of the world, and the manner in which contents appear in consciousness over which it has no control. Constitution includes a kind of passive construction of all the meanings found in consciousness. Rather the whole object as such is experienced as *given from the world.*

Constitution is a universal feature of conscious life; all meanings are constituted in and by consciousness. Everything experiencable in both the natural and cultural world is constituted, as Husserl argues in *Ideas* II. In the first part of *Ideas* II Husserl is especially interested in the constitution of natural, physical things, or sense objects (*Ideas* II § 10). How does it come about that physical things of nature present themselves to us as being in space and time and having the kind of properties they do? Husserl builds up from a sketch of how physical things appear to consciousness in terms of a sensory grasping to a discussion of animate nature, which includes features like mobility, alterability, and, at the higher levels, personhood. Husserl speaks of the living body being constituted by its kinaesthetic functions. In *Ideas* II also, he talks of the constitution of social and cultural entities. This last is more familiar, particularly since, throughout the twentieth century, there has been much talk of the 'socially constructed' nature of social entities such as families, institutions, banks, money, and so on.[3] In this sense, constitution can be considered as similar to social construction. However, Husserl goes much further than social constructionists in that, for him, even things of nature are constituted.

Static and genetic constitution

Around the time he was writing *Ideas* Husserl also began to distinguish different forms of 'constitution' and began to distinguish within phenomenology between 'static' and 'genetic' constitution. Static constitution considers the noetic and noematic structures which make it possible for objects to be intuited in consciousness, whereas genetic constitution examines the manner in which objects appear within the temporal flow of our experience, the temporal approach being crucial to our understanding of human beings and cultural objects. Thus in the draft of *Ideas* III Husserl distinguishes between 'ontology' which treats objects as fully formed, fixed identities, and the 'phenomenological–constitutive consideration' which follows up the flow within which such unities are constituted. This approach is, Husserl says, "in certain measure kinetic or 'genetic': a 'genesis' that belongs to a totally different transcendental world than does the natural and natural-scientific genesis" (*Ideas* III, p. 117; Hua I 129).

In these earlier attempts to distinguish a genetic moment within constitutive phenomenology, Husserl does not see the genetic element as constituting a distinct discipline. Husserl made stronger efforts to distinguish the genetic element from around 1917 onwards, especially in his studies on the relation between nature and spirit. He now saw genetic phenomenology as a much larger field, required in order to study the constitution of essentially historical entities such as social and cultural objects and institutions, what Husserl calls 'personalities of a higher order'. The 1930s for Husserl were largely taken up with genetic phenomenological accounts which bear strong similarity to Hegel's claims for the *Phenomenology of Spirit*. In *Experience and Judgement* he even uses the term 'genealogy', a term usually associated in its philosophical sense with Nietzsche.

Husserl believed static constitutional analysis did not fully capture the diachronic layering of our experience of objects and of ourselves as historical beings. Husserl believes that the basis of our experience of objects in perception is a process he calls "passive genesis". How this is to be understood will require phenomenological reflection. *Passive genesis* must be distinguished from another Husserlian concept, *passive synthesis*. Passive synthesis refers to the manner in which we experience sense-contents already structured and laid out before us. Thus we encounter formed objects against a horizon of intentions which are already there for us. Our experience is passive and yet it is structured. Passive genesis on the other hand refers to the structuring of objects in layers sedimented upon one another. Husserl discusses active and passive genesis in the Fourth Cartesian Meditation (CM § 38). Whereas static constitution sees things in their types and arranges them in a synchronic hierarchical order, genetic constitution examines the structuring in a temporal manner. Genetic constitution may be active as in practical reasoning where new objects are constituted by the ego (just as new collectivities are generated in the act of counting, CM § 38, 77; Hua I 111). But objects are also encountered as already made up – as cultural objects, for example hammers, tables, works of art, and so on. How is it that we experience things as objects immediately and in a single grasp? The passive reception of these objects has its own constitutional history, and this is what is covered by the term 'passive genesis'. Passive genesis is, as it were, the history of a series of acts of passive synthesis. Thus, before we had an adult perception of things in the world we saw them as children. The child's way of experiencing these objects is somehow layered in with our adult way of seeing. Therefore, for Husserl, it is possible to grasp how an infant grasps objects, not by doing third-person psychology but by uncovering in oneself the layering of acts which show up the passive genetic acts which must have occurred (CM § 38, 79; Hua I 112). Husserl is quite qualified in his claim here. We cannot put ourselves back into the pure passivity of the infant's experiencing, nor do we have to rely on child psychology, for instance, but we can repeat these experiences in ourselves through the discovery of the eidetic laws which constitute them:

> Everything known to us points to an original becoming acquainted; what we call unknown has, nevertheless, a known structural form: the form "object" and, more particularly, the form "spatial thing", "cultural Object", "tool", and so forth.
>
> (CM § 38, 80; Hua I 113)

The basic eidetic law or principle of passive genesis is what Husserl calls 'association' (*Assoziation*), which he thinks is a genuine transcendental phenomenological principle, one identified by Hume and others but misconstrued as a naturalistic psychological principle (CM § 39). *Association* is a general name for a set of laws determining why it is that one experience points forward to something similar. It is, then, a primitive feature of all sense-bestowal.[4] Husserl had discussed association as early as the *Logical Investigations* (LI I § 4, pp. 273–274; Hua XIX/1 35–37) where he noted that its key characteristic was to produce a sense of felt belongingness between the two contents which are connected together. Husserl never changes his view of 'association' as an irreducible, primitive feature of our intentional life, itself constituted according to a priori laws. But it was only in the late 1920s that he saw a means of exploring this area phenomenologically.

Is there anything which is not constituted? For Husserl all objects experienced in consciousness, all meanings, and the very nature of consciousness itself are always constituted. Thus the ego, too, is self-constituted, as we shall shortly see. Husserl does think that all constitution has its source in what he calls 'the absolute ego' (a very difficult and obscure notion in Husserl) and the ego itself is only understandable through 'the phenomenology of genesis' (CM § 39). On the other hand, there appear to be some elements in the ego, its self-presence, its self-givenness in the present, which are for Husserl absolutely originally given and hence not constituted.[5] In the last phase of his career Husserl came closer and closer to life philosophy, and to the philosophy of Bergson in particular, in emphasising the organic unity of the life process itself, and he even began to think of the ego as the source of all temporality and hence as escaping temporality in some manner, as having a living present which acted to found all temporality. Temporality itself is constituted genetically, a claim which sounds circular if genesis itself is understood as having a temporal element. Certainly the self is experienced as something constantly being generated in a temporal manner.

The transcendental ego

The successive application of this method of phenomenological reductions eventually led Husserl to locate the source of all meaning in *transcendental subjectivity*, leading to a commitment to a form of transcendental *idealism*, a commitment he retained until his death. Husserl understood phenomenology essentially as 'egology', the study of the ego and its 'self experience'

(*Selbsterfahrung*), the continuation of the programme first set out with Descartes's discovery of the *cogito*. The whole of the world, in all its meanings, had to be rethought as an accomplishment of subjectivity, of the ego. The true focus of philosophy too is the region of self-experience, the transcendental ego.

But what is the transcendental ego? Husserl made many pronouncements on the nature of the transcendental ego. At times, he spoke as if empirical consciousnesses may come and go, but that the transcendental ego is a necessary condition not just for the possibility of experience, but for the possibility of a world at all. The transcendental ego can survive the destruction of the world. Indeed, Alfred Schütz recalls that Husserl, in their last conversations together as Husserl lay dying, talked about the fact that he would die but his transcendental ego would live on.[6] Thus, in *Cartesian Meditations*, Husserl says the transcendental ego is responsible, not just for meaning or sense, but for the being of the world (CM § 28, 62; Hua I 97; see also CM § 41, 84; Hua I 117). The transcendental ego constitutes the world as a world of meanings and as a world of objects. The transcendental ego is the absolute subject as understood by German idealism, though Husserl's transcendental ego is reflectively observable and not deduced as a condition for the possibility of objects. Husserl credits Fichte in particular for recognising the task of a transcendental science of subjectivity; nevertheless he believes Fichte misunderstood the task because of a groundless speculative outlook. Husserl himself believes the ego must be understood as the source of all validations of sense. The turn to the transcendental ego is not, Husserl insists, a turning away from the world, rather it is the condition for the possibility of understanding the world at all. For Husserl it is the discovery of an infinitely rich field.

The transcendental ego was not a feature of Husserl's early writings.[7] As we have already seen, Husserl had, from the very beginning, difficulties conceiving the nature of the ego, the source of all cognitive acts. Initially, in the First Edition of the *Logical Investigations*, he followed Brentano and Hume in methodologically treating the ego merely as a bundle of acts, a collection of *Erlebnisse*.[8] He did not attempt to analyse the unity which the ego placed on the bundle of *Erlebnisse*. In a note added to the Second Edition, Husserl acknowledges that "in the First Edition the name 'phenomenological ego' was given to the stream of consciousness as such" (LI V § 4, p. 541; Hua XIX/1 363). However, he tended to think of the ego itself as an empirical object which transcends consciousness, an account which greatly influenced Sartre in his 1936 essay, *The Transcendence of the Ego*. Sartre, in particular, followed Husserl's student Aron Gurwitsch in interpreting the ego as itself constituted, as itself a transcendent entity out there in the world, a product of impersonal, non-egological consciousness, Sartre's *néant*.[9]

However, even in 1913 the 'phenomenologically reduced ego' is identified with the unity of the set of structures which cause the various acts of consciousness to glue together into a single self-related stream (LI V § 4, p. 541; Hua XIX/1 363–364): "The phenomenologically reduced ego is therefore nothing peculiar, floating above many experiences: it is simply identical with their own interconnected unity." The empirical ego is intentionally constituted out of the phenomenological ego (LI V § 6, p. 545; Hua XIX/1 370). Husserl had originally held a Kantian position that the "I think" which can accompany all experiences plays a purely formal role. But by the time of the Second Edition, he maintained that the reduction had to leave behind a *residuum* which was the pure ego itself. At this point in his development, Husserl was somewhat perplexed by the Kantian notion of the transcendental ego, for information about which he turned to the Marburg Neo-Kantian, Paul Natorp. All psychology, according to Natorp, needed to postulate a pure ego which was subject but never object to itself; in Kantian terms, a formal condition for the possibility of experience. Husserl says that, contrary to Natorp, he is unable to find this pure ego, "this primitive necessary centre of relations" (*Beziehunszentrum*, LI V § 8, p. 549; Hua XIX/1 374). By the time of the Second Edition of 1913, he adds a footnote to this sentence, admitting ruefully that he has now found the very pure ego he had repudiated in his First Edition: "I have since managed to find it, i.e. have learnt not to be led astray from a pure grasp of the given through corrupt forms of ego-metaphysic" (LI V § 8, p. 549; Hua XIX/1 374). Having performed the reduction, Husserl believed that one could actually intuitively grasp the pure ego as distinct from the empirical, natural ego. Nevertheless, he continued to do a kind of 'ego-less' phenomenology. Thus in *The Idea of Phenomenology* (1907) Husserl thought he could proceed to the examination of *Erlebnisse* only by leaving the ego out of account (IP, p. 34; Hua II 44). The reduction brackets the empirical ego; "the ego as a person, as a thing in the world" is treated as transcendent. What I am left with is experiences as my experiences but no reduced ego is in sight. In other words, at this time, Husserl thought the very notion of a pure ego surviving the reduction to be a reimporting of a naturalistic conception back into the phenomenological viewing. Phenomenology would be a description of consciousness, purified of personal ownership, "no one's thought". There is just the stream of consciousness unified precisely as a *stream*, in the same way a herd of cows is unified as a *herd*.

After 1905, Husserl turned to Descartes and Kant with new eyes, seeking for philosophical conceptions which he could employ in his egological investigations. Descartes correctly recognised that I exist for myself and am always given to myself in a radically original way. I am a structure of *ego-cogito-cogitatum*. According to Husserl, as we have seen, Descartes's mistaken metaphysical move was to think of this *ego* as a part of the natural world – as *res cogitans*, a thinking *substance*. I am not a part of the world, and neither is the world a part of me. When we perform the reduction we shed everything to do with our bodily and psychological experiences as an individual incarnate human, a psycho-physical natural being, and I discover the nature of consciousness in general, consciousness in its essence, in its pure possibility. That is, we enter into the domain of meaning, not the consciousness of an individual human, but the essence of all meaning-making. In fact, even in the *Logical Investigations* Husserl was emphatic that we don't discover an empirical ego in our reflections, rather we encounter something like the 'subject pole' of a set of acts. Our thoughts are oriented around this subjective 'pole of identity' (*Identitätspol*), though Husserl is not particularly clear about what this means. The notion suggested is similar to a magnetic pole that draws things towards it. However, the ego does more than simply identify thoughts as its own: in some way it is a generative source of thoughts, a *terminus a quo*, from which thought and emotions irradiate (*Ideas* II § 25, 112; Hua IV 105). In the First Edition of the *Logical Investigations* Husserl recognises that the Cartesian *ego sum* is not the experiencing of an empirical 'I', but his account of the phenomenologically experienced self stopped there. In the Second Edition he recognises that the unity of the flow of psychic experiences was crucial to understanding the ego, but he still concentrated on the structure of the temporal protentions and retentions rather than on the ego itself. We should recall here that in the *Logical Investigations* Husserl had an account of the use of the word 'I' as an 'essentially occasional expression'. The term 'I' means whoever is speaking now, but this sense cannot be substituted in all contexts. The 'I' has a double sense as it were: it also picks out 'me'. I am able to identify myself by using the word 'I'. The term, then, has both a sense and a reference. The reference is in part constituted by the occasion of its occurrence, and in part it picks out the essence of what it is to be me.

By the time we get to *Ideas* I, Husserl wants strictly to separate the natural, worldly psychic life of the ego and its psychological experiences from the spectator-like pure ego which is uncovered as absolute source of all meaning-giving. This consciousness is a 'residuum' which resists all reduction.[10] This pure ego peers through each of its *cogitationes*; it is a 'ray of regard' which shines through each *cogito*. It is not a part of any mental process but is a necessary condition of these processes (*Ideas* I § 57, 132; Hua III/1 109). Husserl quotes Kant: "The 'I think' must be capable of accompanying all my presentations" (*Ideas* I § 57, 133; Hua III/1 109). It is a source of self-identity. Husserl often talks of this ego in Kantian language as providing a formal condition for the unity of inner experiences. As such, this pure ego is essentially "empty of content", it is certainly not any phenomenologically purified conception of a person. In *Ideas* I, Husserl does not yet speak of the transcendental ego as such, rather he posits a distinct pure ego for each separate stream of living conscious experience. On the other hand, he continues to see this pure ego as having a transcendency of a peculiar kind – a "transcendency within immanency". He finds it hard to think of this ego other than as a part of the *Erlebnis* itself. As Elizabeth Ströker has put it, for Husserl in *Ideas* I it was consciousness which possessed an ego, rather than an ego which was generating consciousness.[11] However, as Husserl himself admits in *Ideas* I, he had postponed difficult questions concerning the ego to *Ideas* II. At this point, Husserl did not see how the ego and its self-identity could be understood phenomenologically and the whole focus of his work was turned towards the individual experiences themselves. Furthermore, in all the accounts of the structure of consciousness in *Ideas* I, the noematic–noetic structure of *Erlebnisse* for example, the consciousness under consideration is the essence of consciousness in general. Husserl is not yet explicating consciousness as having its source in my ego, since he is dealing with the essence of consciousness as such, something which is by definition ownerless.

Ideas II, initially written just after *Ideas* I but revised over many years by Ludwig Landgrebe and Edith Stein, with little direction from Husserl, and published posthumously, concentrates on the unity of the self as person and on the self as an embodied, spatially oriented, and temporally located subject, thus providing a corrective to the rather disembodied idealist standpoint of *Ideas* I. The ego now is a 'bodily I' (*leiblicher Ichlichkeit, Ideas* II § 41, 166; Hua IV 158). Roman Ingarden thought that this embodied ego fitted in well with Husserl's realist phase, and Edith Stein employed conceptions of the incarnate self as a person which she thought to be deeply in sympathy with the thought in *Ideas* II. In *Ideas* II Husserl says

> the ego is the identical subject functioning in all acts of the same stream of consciousness; it is the center whence all conscious life emits rays and receives them, it is the center of all affects and actions, of all attention, grasping, relating, connecting.
>
> (*Ideas* II § 25, 112; Hua IV 105)

The self is a 'zero point' (*Nullpunkt*), a centre of reference and orientation, from which distances, times, etc., radiate outwards. Something is over there, to the left, on top, far away, near, all as mapped out taking myself as the centre of space (*Ideas* II § 41). As such the ego requires a bodily orientation and spatial location. The transcendental ego becomes embodied in a living body.

The ego also can be passively affected by its experiences. Husserl now thinks the characterisation of the ego as a purely formal 'pole of identity' needs to be revised. The ego is not a purely formal notion, empty of content, as it is for Kant; rather, the ego is full of attitudes, beliefs, it has a character made up of 'convictions' and 'habitualities' that have accrued to it (i.e. I am a person who hates racism, or is in favour of democracy and so on), stances which are not necessarily articulated in occurrent acts of belief (*Ideas* II, Supplement II, 324; Hua IV 311). Husserl calls these states of belief convictions (*Überzeugungen*).[12] They come together into layers to form the 'spiritual ego' which has its free moments and its moments of being caught up in habitual modes of behaviour (*Ideas* II § 61). The ego also has a set of abilities, of "I can's" as both Levinas and Merleau-Ponty are fond of emphasising. The embodied ego is a particularisation of the general transcendental ego. Husserl recognises that there is a problem maintaining the self-identity of the ego, while also recognising that an ego can shed its habitualities, change its convictions, be in bad humour, and so on. Husserl raises many questions in *Ideas* II about the nature of the person, the embodied self.

In later works, Husserl saw the ego as built up from habitualities which attach to it in a manner which can only be investigated by genetic phe-nomenological analysis. Thus when I come to have a conviction, that conviction becomes part of myself, of my character, even if I am not consciously alluding to it. The ego, Husserl says in the *Cartesian Medita-tions*, is not merely an empty centre or pole of identity, it acquires abiding properties (CM § 32, 66; Hua I 100). Husserl came to recognise that he had spent too much of his early work treating *Erlebnisse* as individual mental acts or processes which are occurrent. He now recognised that he needed to treat of dispositional mental states as well as occurrent mental acts, to have an account of how the ego comes to have contentful personal character, to be an ego which believes that the earth is round, and so on. When I decide something, that act-process of deciding quickly vanishes but the decision persists, attaches to the ego, even in sleep. I am in a state of being 'thus and so decided', which should not be misunderstood as a stream of decisions actively going on. There is actually no process at all going on, for Husserl; rather the ego by his own active generating constitutes himself as a fixed and abiding personal ego (CM § 32, 67; Hua I 101). In a sense, the constitution of the ego is a *self-constitution* (*Selbstkonstitution*), an active genesis of the stable, abiding ego on the basis of its own convictions. Though Husserl does not explicitly acknowledge Max Scheler's influence, he did turn more to acknowledging the need to talk about 'persons' and about intersubjective communal groupings, which have the character of 'persons of a higher order', akin to the objects of a higher order spoken about by Meinong and the Brentano school.

It was not until the 1920s that Husserl began to face squarely the prob-lem of articulating the nature and role of the transcendental ego. His deepest account will emerge at the end of the 1920s in the Fifth Cartesian Meditation. More and more Husserl saw the problem of the constitution of the ego as deeply related to the source of time consciousness. In his later writings, the ego is thought in terms of the flow of time: not merely as a connected series of *cogitationes*, but as "*a connectedness that makes the unity of one consciousness*" (CM § 18, 41; Hua I 79). In his earlier writings, Husserl had recognised the self-presence of the *cogito* and had stressed that one's intuitive grasp of inner mental processes was apodictic and full, unlike the grasp of external entities which was always one-sided and given in 'profiles' or 'adumbrations' (*Abschattungen*). But Husserl gradually came to see that the ego is given in *temporal* profiles. "Time is the universal form of all egological genesis", Husserl says in the Fourth Cartesian Meditation § 37. There are different essential structures involved in the ego understood in temporal terms; the mentality of childhood, for example, needs to be distinguished from the mentality which produces mature scientific reasoning. Husserl began to see the necessity of speaking about the 'history' of the ego.

As Husserl developed he distinguished not just the natural psychological ego, and the phenomenologically reduced ego, or the pure ego and the transcendental ego, respectively. He also paid attention to the pre-egological founding stages of consciousness. From around 1910 Husserl also began to articulate the notion of the ego in terms of the Leibnizian notion of the 'monad', a term which appears in *Philosophy as a Rigorous Science* (1910–1911), and in *Ideas* II §§ 26, 29, but is fully articulated in the *Cartesian Meditations*. The 'monad' is Husserl's name for the whole concrete conscious life of an ego taken as the full set of all its intentional experiences, both actual and possible (CM § 33, 68; Hua I 102). It is the complete draft of a life as it were. Husserl speaks of 'monadisation' of the transcendental ego and of the self as a 'monad with windows'.

It is not possible for us here to follow Husserl through each of these distinctions. We shall attempt a simplified and no doubt necessarily distorted summary of Husserl's mature account. Is there one transcendental ego or many? Does each person have a single transcendental ego? These questions Husserl probably would regard as misguided. In a sense, the transcendental ego is a set of anonymous eidetic structures within which individual consciousnesses come to have their experience of meaning, but what is inhabited and lived is a single individual life. Furthermore, Husserl often talks about the transcendental ego as *my* transcendental ego. In the *Crisis* he says that the transcendental ego is just a way of regarding the human ego revealed in the worldly sphere (*Crisis* § 27, 264). Yet one cannot help thinking that perhaps Husserl thought of the transcendental ego as having a life of its own.

Husserl's later works tend to operate with a sharp contrast between the naive everyday ego and the transcendental ego. The naive everyday ego can be explored by psychology and anthropology; the transcendental domain requires the *epoché* and the reduction, and hence is purely phenomenological. Husserl stressed the absolute *parallelism* between the two domains. He admits that it is indeed possible to have an intentional psychology within the natural attitude; indeed many had been misled into thinking that phenomenology was precisely a kind of descriptive psychology. Husserl himself had come to realise the need for a radical change of viewpoint to avoid falling into all kinds of psychologistic errors. Thus his later works are constantly a defence of transcendental phenomenology of the ego against various deviant forms. This distinction in Husserl is difficult to understand. For Husserl there can be an eidetic intentional psychology of the natural human ego and parallel to this a transcendental phenomenological exploration of the transcendental ego (CM § 35, 73; Hua I 107).

Intersubjectivity and the experience of the other (*Fremderfahrung*)

Husserl came to believe that since the self-constitution of the ego is the source of all constitution, then all phenomenology really coincided with the phenomenology of the self-constitution of the ego (CM § 33, 68; Hua I 103). Connected with the focus on the ego necessarily comes the problem of the experience of other egos, of alter egos, the experience of the 'foreign', the 'strange', the 'other' (*Fremderfahrung*) in general. Husserl seems to have become more worried about the constitution of our intersubjective life around the same time as he began the close explorations of the natural attitude, that is from around 1911. Our natural life is a life in community, living in a world of shared objects, shared environment, shared language, shared meanings. Moreover, this is something I can read off the world at first glance. I see a tree in the garden and know it is a publicly accessible object, a tree others can also see, not just as a physical object but indeed precisely as a *tree*. In other words, my perception of the tree already indicates to me that it is a tree *for others*. In the *Cartesian Meditations*, Husserl says I even experience the reduced world of experiences as an intersubjective world (CM § 43, 91).

Initially in the *Logical Investigations* there are no references to our knowledge of other persons except in terms of the ideality of meanings which are shareable between people and the intimating function (*kundgebende Funktion*) of speech whereby, when I make a statement, besides expressing a *meaning*, I intimate to another that I am undergoing a particular mental process. Husserl's new approach after 1901 led him to a Cartesian methodological solipsism but it also pointed up the problem of escaping from enclosed subjectivity. Husserl later claimed to have overcome the problems of solipsism as early as his Göttingen lectures of 1910–1911 (FTL § 96d, p. 243 n. 1; Hua XVII 250 n. 1).

Husserl's treatment of intersubjectivity at first employed a conception of *empathy* with others, the manner I am able to read into another's actions, as an expression of inner states analogous to my own. Husserl adopted the term 'empathy' (*Einfühlung*) from Lipps and the Munich school, but he gave it a different emphasis and was always worried that it carried the wrong connotations. Husserl's first Freiburg assistant, Edith Stein, had earlier written her doctoral dissertation on the problem of empathy, published in

1917, and this represents a reliable guide to Husserl's thinking on this problem at the time, his own thinking being expressed in the manuscripts of *Ideas* II.[13] For Stein, empathy is the source of our experiences of 'the foreign' (*das Fremde*). She gives examples: I see someone blush and know she feels ashamed of herself; a friend tells me of the loss of his brother and I become aware of his pain. Stein argues that one can never get an orientation from which one can perceive the other's pain directly, just as in similar fashion there are aspects of my awareness of an object which are not given in the perception of the profile I am now experiencing. I can *live in* the other's experience in an intuitive manner but I don't undergo that experience myself in an original fashion. Empathy is, for Stein as for Husserl, a non-primordial experience which reveals a primordial experience. Empathy is not a matter of judgement, reasoning, or ideation in general. It is a *founded* experience.

On the basis of this, Husserl differentiated various forms of primordiality and originality. I cannot experience the other person's pain in full bodily presence, *leibhaftig*. Rather it is given to me much as objects are given to me in memory, in a kind of non-full calling to mind or representation, *Vergegenwärtigung*, rather than 'presencing' (*Gegenwärtigung*), having something directly present. In his 1923–1924 lectures on *First Philosophy* Husserl acknowledged the failure to gain access to the proper being of others (Hua VIII 174n.). Husserl even concedes that for many years he did not see how the reduction could give access to the being of the other. Thus Husserl remarks in his 1924 lecture on Kant:

> Finally, one must pay attention to the fact that a possible transcendental subjectivity in general is not merely understood as a possible singular but rather also as a possible communicative subjectivity, and primarily as one such that purely according to consciousness, that is to say, through possible intersubjective acts of consciousness, it encloses together into a possible allness a multiplicity of individual transcendental subjects. To what extent a "solipsistic" subjectivity is at all possible in thought, outside of all community, is itself one of the transcendental problems.[14]

Husserl especially dealt with this topic in the Fifth Cartesian Meditation which expanded to become as long as the other Meditations put together. Here Husserl radicalises the problem. The problem is not: how do I understand the other? Rather Husserl's problem is: how is the other *constituted* for me? How does the other enter into my consciousness? The experience of the other is a natural and inextricable part of my consciousness. Yet the other is not given in the manner in which objects are given. There is always a certain apprehended gap and emptiness in my experience of the other. Other humans are given to me only through 'indications' or 'appresentations'. For Husserl, appresentations have their own form of verification, since the experience of the other is not given *originaliter*, though the experience of his body is originarily given (CM § 52, 114; Hua I 143). In the experience of the other, we have an experience that presents itself as genuinely unfulfillable by me, but nevertheless within which something is indicated. The experience of the other is based on a kind of verifiable accessibility of what is not originally accessible:

> The character of the existent "other" has its basis in this kind of verifiable accessibility of what is not originally accessible (*bewährbarer Zugänglichkeit des original Unzugänglichkeit*). Whatever can become presented, and evidently verified, originally – is something I am; or else it belongs to me as something peculiarly my own. Whatever, by virtue thereof, in that founded manner which characterises a primordially unfulfillable experience – an experience that does not give something itself originally but that consistently verifies something indicated – is "other".
>
> (CM § 52, 114–115; Hua I 144)

The other then is a phenomenological modification of myself, for Husserl, grasped only "within my ownness". This grasping is on the basis of something like analogy. Just as a primary givenness is experienced in perception, memory affords a kind of secondary givenness. Similarly, the experience of the other is not unlike the experience of memory, it is an experience of a kind of givenness which is always marked as non-original, that is as not lived through in a primordial fashion by myself. It is characterised by secondary or indeed tertiary givenness.[15]

Similarly, as we know, Husserl treats one's own body as the zero point of orientation in space, an account which is taken over more or less unaltered by Merleau-Ponty. I experience where I currently am as 'here' and recognise other places as 'there' – places where I can be by locomotion and where I will have a different viewpoint on the world. My own experience gives me the possibility of understanding that there are other possible viewpoints on experience. When I experience another person, I *apperceive* them as having the kind of experiences I would have if I was over there (CM § 53, 117; Hua I 146). On the basis of these kinds of "pairing" experiences (*Paarung*, CM § 51) I experience the other as another body like myself. But Husserl always believed that when I perceive another person, I primarily perceive them in sensuous manner as living animate bodies, and I also realise that their bodies are expressive of their psychic selves. But Husserl did not appear to think I could grasp the other self or person immediately and fully, in an originary manner. Husserl thinks that a natural person reflecting on their ego will in normal circumstances think of their body or of the stream of their remembered experiences. In other words, the ego itself is not grasped except through some kind of experience of an objectivity. In the end, Husserl will argue that seeing another person *as* a person is itself no greater a mystery than any other form of constitution. Levinas will dissent radically from Husserl on this very point.

Husserl does have an interest in describing the possibility of genuine communication and communion between persons, for "specifically personal acts of the ego that have the character of acts of mine directed to you" (CM § 57, 132; Hua I 159), and also for the development of a communal life, the personalities of a higher order, which even have a kind of animate corporate bodiliness, *Leiblichkeit*, of their own. But the nature of these graspings eluded him.

Though Husserl was by instinct a 'methodological solipsist', someone who began his enquiry as a '*solus ipse*' (CM § 42), nevertheless, as we have repeatedly stressed, he was always at pains to deny that his philosophy ended in Berkeleyan idealism or a 'transcendental solipsism'. In *Formal and Transcendental Logic* § 96, Husserl directly addresses the *illusion* that phenomenology must end in a 'transcendental solipsism': if everything is constituted by the ego, then everything that exists appears to be merely a moment of that ego (FTL § 96b, p. 241; Hua XVII 248). For Husserl, this does not do justice to the multiplicity of forms in which objects are constituted in consciousness and indeed ignores the nature of self-constitution itself (CM § 41, 83; Hua I 117). It is entirely nonsensical to conceive of the world as divided into two domains, a subjective and an objective domain, lying outside of each other. The only meaning of the world is as world for consciousness.

Husserl acknowledges the intersubjective nature of our experience but always grounds it on the subjective: "the world is continually there for us, but in the first place it is there for *me*" (FTL § 96b, p. 242; Hua XVII 249). Merleau-Ponty frequently cites a passage from the *Crisis* whereby Husserl claims that transcendental subjectivity is an intersubjectivity, but this quotation is not actually found in the *Crisis* and, in fact, represents something of a distortion of Husserl's actual position. His position seems to have been that we belong contingently and factually to an intersubjective world. Others give me my name, teach me my native language, and acculturate me to the world of my society. There is what Husserl calls 'communalisation' (*Vergemeinschaftigung*). But all this is possible only because I, as ego, can make sense of these directions, encouragements, pointings, and so on. Nothing comes from outside into the ego; rather everything outside is what it is already within the inside, as Husserl says cryptically in the *Formal and Transcendental Logic* (§ 99, p. 250; Hua XVII 257). As he puts it in his 1931 lecture:

> It is from out of myself as the one constituting the meaning of being within the content of my own private ego that I attain the transcen-

dental other as someone just like me; and in this way I attain the open and endless whole of *transcendental intersubjectivity*, precisely as that which, within its communalized transcendental life, first constitutes the world as an *objective* world, as a *world that is identical for everyone*.[16]

Husserl sees the ground for understanding of the mental life of the other (*das Fremdpsychische*) as lying in one's own self-understanding, as exemplified "when I perceivingly reflect on my perceiving".[17] The constitution of the other comes about through a kind of splitting of the self. The difficulty with this view is that my own factual experience of being an animate body must play a role in my self-constitution, each transcendental I "must necessarily be constituted in the world as a human being" (*Crisis* § 54b, 186; Hua VI 189). Fact and essence are entwined in my own self-relation in a manner in which Husserl never satisfactorily resolved and which, in fact, strained the whole project of his phenomenology.

The Crisis of European Sciences: the investigation of the life-world

All through his Freiburg period, Husserl never tired of asserting that phenomenology could not be separated from transcendental idealism. Yet his complex understanding of transcendental idealism did not rule out consideration of the constitution of the lived world of personal, social, and historical processes, and the whole human cultural world in general. Whereas earlier he had been fascinated by the constitution of mathematical entities, he came to realise that the manner in which cultural and social objects are constituted in many ways offers a better model for understanding the nature of constitution in general. Meanings are experienced, lost, and recovered. Other meanings become sedimented into attitudes and into a cultural outlook. These in turn seem to be instituted in a temporal manner and needed to be approached as such. Thus, in late writings like the *Crisis of European Sciences*, Husserl shows a much greater appreciation of historical, or what he called 'historico-genetic', explanation. Husserl became more urgently aware that the condition of the natural attitude and indeed the scientific attitude were not merely static universal states of humankind but were historically constituted. Husserl in particular began to recognise the nature of our current outlook as a product of modernity and he started to read history as a shaping of modernity, such that the constitution of our life needs also to be investigated historically, since we are essentially historical beings, oriented teleologically (*Crisis* § 15). Husserl proposed nothing less than a critical investigation of the whole of history, of history approached from the inside and as a unity:

179

> Our task is to make comprehensible the *teleology* in the historical becoming of philosophy, especially modern philosophy, and at the same time to achieve clarity about ourselves, who are the bearers of this teleology, who take part in carrying it out through our personal intentions. We are attempting to elicit and understand the unity (*die Einheit*) running through all the projects of history that oppose one another and work together in their changing forms.
>
> (*Crisis* § 15, 70; Hua VI 71–72)

As we have seen, Husserl was already criticising historicism in 1911 and was preaching the need for a spiritual renewal of the West, a theme which became more urgent with his turn to Fichte at the end of the First World War. It is not true, then, as Paul Ricoeur has suggested, that Husserl's interest in history was provoked by the terrible political circumstances in Germany in the 1930s. Nevertheless, the rise of the National Socialist movement in Germany during the late 1920s was seen by Husserl as one more dreadful symptom of a turn towards irrationalism which seemed to be engulfing Western civilisation. Husserl interpreted the threat of National Socialism as part of a larger deformation of our understanding of the world, brought on by a one-sided understanding of the new framework of modern science.[18] Despite the great personal and professional difficulties imposed on him by the anti-Jewish laws in force in the mid-1930s, Husserl embarked on writing *The Crisis of European Sciences* in an attempt to alert the world to the increasing danger of the collapse of the genuinely scientific and philosophical outlook which had marked out the progress of the West since the time of the Greeks. Husserl was here diagnosing and opposing what he considered to be the disastrous social consequences of a science which espoused reductive scientism and naive empiricism. He also opposed what he regarded as the misguided, deformed rationalism, a consequence of the Enlightenment, which naturalised the spirit and settled for a naive objectivism, and did not notice the very subjectivity which made genuine rational objectivity possible. Husserl's late writings attempt to explicate the guiding ideals of objectivity and rationality by charting the emergence of these concepts in history, and particularly by a kind of *re-establishment* (*Nachstiftung, Crisis* § 15) of the original establishment of the scientific mentality among the ancient Greeks. In early writings, Husserl had deliberately bracketed historical causal–genetic explanation, but it had become increasingly a subject of his interest from 1919 onwards. Now he believed that the phenomenon of European reason could only be appreciated by tracing its historical evolution in a conceptual manner, as Hegel had earlier tried to do in the *Phenomenology of Spirit*. For Husserl, as for Hegel, it was phenomenology which could chart the transformations of the basic concepts of human culture. Thus in the Vienna lecture Husserl says:

> It is my conviction that intentional phenomenology has made of
> spirit qua spirit for the first time a field of systematic experience
> and science and has thus brought about the total reorientation of
> the task of knowledge...Only through it [intentional phenomenol-
> ogy] do we understand, and from the most profound reasons, what
> naturalistic objectivism is and understand in particular that psy-
> chology, because of its naturalism, had to miss entirely the accom-
> plishment, the radical and genuine problem, of the life of the spirit.
> (*Crisis*, 298–9; Hua VI 347)

Husserl here sees phenomenology as putting the study of culture or 'spirit'
(German: *Geist*), the spiritual life, on a proper scientific footing. It does so
by understanding how spirit is grounded in the life-world.

The life-world

The first formulation of what later became the notion of 'life-world'
(*Lebenswelt*) made its first appearance in *Ideas* I under the title of 'world of
experience' (*Erfahrungswelt*) where it means our ordinary natural concept of
the world as the correlate of all our possible experiences. In the mid-1920s
and especially in the lectures on *Phenomenological Psychology* from 1925 to
1928, Husserl gave the term a more technical meaning, but he did not make
it the main focus of examination until the *Crisis*. The concept of world was
arrived at by Husserl through his application of the reduction. The life-
world is a world as phenomenon, as correlative of our intentional experiences. Especially in his researches around *Ideas* II, Husserl gradually began
to see the life-world as a layer to be inserted between the world of nature and
the world of culture (or spirit). The life-world is the world of pre-theoretical
experience which is also that which allows us to interact with nature and to
develop our own cultural forms. Though, in the *Phenomenology of
Perception*, Merleau-Ponty presented the life-world as a turning in Husserl's
thought away from transcendental idealism, it is more accurate to view the
layer of life-world as one more constituted layer of meaning uncovered by
Husserlian reduction and itself constituted by the anonymous transcendental ego (see *Crisis* § 36, 138ff.; Hua VI 140ff.). In fact, Husserl (*Crisis* § 43)
claims that the reduction can be approached from a new standpoint,
different from the usual so-called 'Cartesian way' of *Ideas* I, *Cartesian
Meditations*, and elsewhere. The new reduction wants to start with the life-
world and ask about the "how of the world's pregivenness" (*dem Wie der
Vorgegebenheit der Welt, Crisis* § 43, 154; Hua VI 157). This new reduction
does not move to an ego empty of content, as in the Cartesian way, but to an
ego which is already intimately tied to the world in many ways.

In the *Crisis* Husserl saw the life-world as the universal framework of
human endeavour – including our scientific endeavours. It is the ultimate

horizon of all human achievement. As conscious beings we always inhabit the life-world; it is pregiven in advance and experienced as a unity. The life-world is the general structure which allows objectivity and thinghood to emerge in the different ways in which they do emerge in different cultures. Although different societies have different outlooks and different ways of understanding nature, Husserl believed that a more basic interrogation of these cultural differences revealed the invariant structure of the life-world. In fact, in Husserl's more generative investigations, it is clear that there is not one single life-world for Husserl, but a set of intersecting or overlapping worlds, beginning from the world which is the 'home world' (*Heimwelt*), and extending to other worlds which are farther away, 'foreign' or 'alien worlds', the worlds of other cultures etc. Husserl's researches on the life-world interested many sociologists and anthropologists, indeed all those interested in relating human culture to the natural world. Husserl himself thought that the investigation of the life-world could form the basis of a new science, a science of opinion, of the much disparaged world of *doxa* (*Crisis* § 44, 155; Hua VI 158).

Husserl's interest in the life-world dates from the period of writing *Ideas* I around 1913, and the unpublished *Ideas* II contains strong reference to the 'environment' or 'surrounding world' (*Umwelt*), as well as to the life of culture and spirit (*Geist*), but it did not become a major theme in his writing until the 1920s and it featured predominantly in the 1930s. Although 'world' and 'being-in-the-world' played a central role in Heidegger's *Being and Time* (1927), Husserl explicitly denied that his notion of the life-world came from Heidegger. Indeed, Husserl had operated with several conceptions of 'world' in his own philosophy.[19] In fact, Husserl's account of *Umwelt* in *Ideas* II had a significant role in shaping Heidegger's own concept of *In-der-Welt-sein*. Husserl himself had been pursuing an interest in the social, cultural, and historical worlds in his phenomenology as a kind of radicalisation of the project of anthropology, what he himself called "intentional anthropology". Indeed Husserl was an admirer of the French anthropologist Lucien Lévy-Bruhl.[20]

In the *Crisis* Husserl was particularly interested in one important aspect of the life-world, namely the way in which scientific consciousness with its guiding norm of rationality emerges out of ordinary non-theoretical forms of everyday lived consciousness and its practices. Heidegger too would make this a central focus of his discussion of human experience of tools and other objects in *Being and Time*. Initially, Husserl does not contrast the scientific and the natural attitudes, rather he emphasises that the scientific world 'belongs' (*gehört*) to the life-world (*Crisis*, Appendix VII, 380; Hua VI Beilage XVII 460). Nevertheless, our failure to make the life-world a subject of investigation may put us in danger of neglecting distortions in our cultural formation including our scientific outlook. In particular, the success of modern science since Galileo has displaced our immediate forms of lived experience with the forms of objects as dictated by science. As early as *Philosophy as a Rigorous Science* (1911), Husserl had identified Galileo, who replaced vague everyday concepts with exact concepts, as the founder of the specifically modern approach to nature which was now universally present in the natural sciences (PRS 100; Hua XXV 24). Husserl always admired the extraordinary achievement of the sciences but he was very interested in how this theoretical outlook was achieved and on what it was grounded. As he will argue the scientific outlook emerges from a purely intellectual 'play' devoid of practical interests. In an unpublished note from the early 1930s Husserl makes this clear as part of his dispute with Heidegger. The following translation is mine:

> Special motives are required in order to make the theoretical atti-
> tude possible, and, against Heidegger, it does appear to me, that an
> original motive lies, for science as for art, in the necessity of the
> game (*Spiel*) and especially in the motivation for a playful
> "intellectual curiosity", one that is not springing from any necessity
> of life, or from calling, or from the context of the goal of self-
> preservation, a curiosity which looks at things, and wants to know
> things, with which it has nothing to do. And no "deficient" praxis is
> at stake here.[21]

Science comes from a special theoretical attitude, one of detached playful-ness and curiosity. However, if the objects produced in this play are then uncritically asserted to be the real objects of our experience in the life-world, then serious problems will arise. This is what has happened in modernity; the scientific world-view has predominated.

Furthermore, this crisis in the sciences is mirrored by a crisis in our social world. Thus in his 1935 Vienna lecture, later appended to the *Crisis*, Husserl says: "The European nations are sick; Europe, it is said, is in crisis" (*Crisis*, 270; Hua VI 315). This crisis is not something arbitrarily thrown up by history, nor is it an "obscure fate, an impenetrable destiny" (*Crisis*, 299; Hua VI 347), rather it is the inevitable consequence of the manner in which European civilisation has interpreted and implemented the goal of universal rationality, the manner in which this teleology has been implemented. As Husserl says:

> In order to be able to comprehend the disarray of the present
> "crisis", we had to work out the *concept of Europe as the historical
> teleology of the infinite goals of reason*; we had to show how the
> European "world" was born out of ideas of reason, i.e., out of the
> spirit of philosophy. The crisis could then become distinguishable
> as the *apparent failure of rationalism*. The reason for the failure of
> a rational culture, however, as we said, lies not in the essence of

rationalism itself, but solely in its being rendered superficial, in its entanglement in "naturalism" and "objectivism".

(*Crisis*, 299; Hua VI 347)

The crisis is in part due to a misguided rationalism (*Crisis*, 290; Hua VI 337). Husserl equated European rationalism with the fate of the West. For him, the term 'Europe' refers not geographically to a continent but to the "unity of a spiritual life, activity, creation" (*die Einheit eines geistigen Lebens, Wirkens, Schaffens*, *Crisis*, 273; Hua VI 319). 'Europe', then, is Husserl's shorthand term for the dream of a universal science, a new theoretical attitude, which has its actual origins in ancient Greece (replacing various kinds of mythological and poetic speculation) and was articulated by Plato in response to the threat of scepticism. Tellingly, Husserl explicitly excludes 'gypsies' (*die Zigeuner*), who wander through Europe, from his account of the European intellectual and spiritual life (*Crisis*, 273; Hua VI 319). Thus, for him, only those contributing to the rise of Western rationalism would count as Europeans, and he undoubtedly saw gypsies and others as relics of pre-historical forms of life. Husserl's exclusion of gypsies exemplified the value judgement of an old European intellectual, but a coarsened version of this prejudice spurred on the Nazis to seek to purge Europe of the very people Husserl had mentally excluded from the European way of life. Indeed, in the period immediately following Husserl's death, from 1939 to 1945, huge numbers of gypsies would be exterminated along with Jews in the Nazi concentration camps. Husserl's own ability to avoid presuppositions is shown here to be limited. Remarks such as "according to the old familiar definition, man is the rational animal, and in this broad sense even the Papuan is a man and not a beast" (*Crisis*, 290; Hua VI 337) seem patronising at best, with an offensive, racist overtone. It is clear that Husserl himself placed a higher value on what he took to be civilisations exclusively devoted to the pursuit of universal rationality.

Husserl's spiritual Europe is "a culture of ideas knowing infinite tasks" (*Crisis*, 279; Hua VI 324), imbued with "a spirit of free critique and norm-giving (*Normierung*) aimed at infinite tasks" (*Crisis*, 289; Hua VI 336), whereas pre-scientific cultures are wrapped in finitude and in the 'mythical–religious attitude' (*Crisis*, 283; Hua VI 330). Husserl is specifically interested in the historical moment when a people – or individuals – raise themselves above the world or context of their own culture and ask about a truth-for-all, a transcendent universal truth (note the similarity to his earliest question as to how the universal truth of mathematics can arise in an individual subjective consciousness) – "truth-in-itself" to borrow Bolzano's formulations.

Husserl's Europe owes to the ancient Greeks the awakening of the quite specific attitude of intellectual contemplation, *theoria*.[22] Husserl describes how, in the natural attitude, humans are directed to the world in a

184

straightforward way; thus it takes a special impetus of the spirit to seek beyond to the good of the society, or more generally to take a theoretical attitude, but the highest attitude is one which takes a universal critical view, 'the universal critique of all life and all life-goals' aiming at "an absolute self-responsibility on the basis of absolute theoretical insights" (*Crisis*, 283; Hua VI 329). This is the guiding idea of universal knowledge and of knowledge gained by pursuance of a method. In *Ideas* II Husserl gives a careful account of the nature of the "doxic-theoretical" attitude of the scientist and how it emerges out of a freely chosen switch in perspective from the normal evaluating consciousness. He points out that the scientist may see a blue sky as beautiful and in the normal attitude this living in the beauty of the sky would be his primary intention; but the scientific mentality somehow freely switches perspective and though still perhaps incidentally appreciating the blue sky, comes to a view of the sky as possessing certain qualities distinct from the experience of beauty which the scientist is nonetheless undergoing. Husserl is fascinated how this "doxic-theoretical" attitude is able to distinguish between properties it attributes to the object and experiences which it attributes to the viewing subject and sees the truly scientific as belonging to the former domain. Husserl comments:

> what is most essential to the theoretical attitude of philosophical man is the peculiar universality of his critical stance, his resolve not to accept unquestioningly any pregiven opinion or tradition so that he can inquire, in respect to the whole traditionally pregiven universe, after what is true in itself, an ideality.
>
> (*Crisis*, 286; Hua VI 333)

Husserl sees this new theoretical stance as guided by a norm of ideal truth, and this behaving towards an ideal actually has a practical effect in transforming culture, leading to a 'universally transformed praxis' (*universal gewandelte Praxis, Crisis*, 287; Hua VI 334). The existing pre-philosophical culture is transformed. As an example of this Husserl cites the case of God which in philosophical culture is logicised – that is, is identified with the *logos*. (It is precisely this analysis which influences Derrida to develop his account of logo-centrism in Western culture.)

In the Vienna lecture Husserl continues his critique of naturalism. It is not enough to oppose naturalism by developing some kind of separate 'science of the spirit' because human and animal life is embodied through and through:

> For animal spirituality, that of human and animal "souls", to which all other spirituality must be traced back, is individually, causally founded in corporeity.
>
> (*Crisis*, 271; Hua VI 316)

185

Human life is moving towards a goal, and as this becomes a matter for consciousness, the goals can be willed. Husserl here is very Hegelian, even in so far as to claim he is not developing a speculation but engaged in a presentiment (*Vorahnung*) which comes through "unprejudiced reflection" (*in vorurteilsloser Besinnung, Crisis*, 275; Hua VI 321). Husserl's claim is that science is the production of the ideal, of what is identically the same in different acts of meaning, what is recognisably the same between people. But beyond the theoretical and the natural attitudes lies a new radical attitude – one which takes seriously the critique of all values – 'the universal critique of all life and all life-goals' aiming at transforming us into a 'new humanity' capable of "absolute self-responsibility on the basis of absolute theoretical insights" (*Crisis*, 283; Hua VI 329). It is clear that Husserl retains his faith in absolutely secure first knowledge, knowledge which is based on evidence. True rationality is still construed as true insight (*wirkliche Einsicht, Crisis*, 296; Hua VI 343).

We need then to relate the scientific understanding back to the structures of the life-world. Understood phenomenologically, we shall see how spirit relates to nature when we understand the manner in which human meaning – including all the accomplishments of culture (which Husserl, following Hegel and Dilthey, calls 'spirit') – are constituted in acts of consciousness. This is only properly understood by transcendental phenomenology.

The origin of geometry

As part of Husserl's *Crisis* there appeared a short text, *On the Origin of Geometry*, which came to have something of an independent life because it was published by Fink in France in 1939, and was commented on by Merleau-Ponty and Derrida among others. This text offers a revision of Husserl's account of the constitution of ideal mathematical objectivities. He is now offering a genetic account. Geometry arose in land surveying, but with increasing demand for exactitude, and with the intellectual spirit of play, it was transformed into an eidetic science of pure shape. Crucial to this move is that the geometrical insights were written down, and thus became accessible to ever new generations of researchers who have to re-enact the basic achievements of insight based on the written marks. Derrida notes that this is one of Husserl's few acknowledgements of the role of writing in his project of achieving knowledge. We will have a much closer look at this text in our chapter on Derrida.

Husserl's achievement

Edmund Husserl's entire life project, as he himself emphasised over and over, was to live the philosophical life, understood in the Socratic sense as a life of self-critical understanding and rational self-responsibility. He saw his duty as identifying the truly rational life and then living it. Furthermore, Husserl identified with the central thrust of modern philosophy, expressed in Descartes's and Kant's desire to make life more rational by carrying out a thorough-going critique of reason and of all knowledge claims, to set knowledge on a secure, rational, foundation. For Husserl, as for Descartes and Kant, the key to this task was the reappropriation of the domain of subjectivity in a more radical manner, attempting to grasp the very essence of subjectivity as the source of all meaning and being. This path led Husserl first to an account of the origins of arithmetic, then to a critique of logic and psychology, and finally to a general phenomenological philosophy expressed as a full transcendental idealism, which saw all truth and meaning grounded in transcendental subjectivity.

Husserl's project of grasping the very essence of subjectivity can be criticised from many angles. In his early writings Husserl is cavalier in his treatment of the notions of objectivity and reality (anything temporal is real according to the Second Investigation). He is equally weak in his treatment of the source of subjectivity in the human person, which though a necessary category he treated in a Humean fashion as a collection of acts. It was not until later that Husserl came to recognise the nature and strength of the Cartesian *cogito* as providing an insight into subjectivity as such, beyond the domain of the particular ego. His later extremely complex reflections on the constitution of this ego in its many layers and in its relation to other egos represent a vast sphere of research which has yet to be fully absorbed and criticised in the current philosophical debate.

In all phases of his career, Husserl assumed that the best way to approach knowledge is to focus on the meaning-constituting acts of consciousness, and, secondly, that these acts and their contents are best approached by concentrating on what is given in immediate intuition (intuition albeit reduced of everything empirical and accidental). Phenomenology always begins with the appearance of the phenomenon to consciousness. However, perhaps the majority of philosophers in the twentieth century, ranging from Ludwig Wittgenstein to Gilbert Ryle and Daniel Dennett, on the one hand, as well as followers of Freud and structuralism on the other hand, are of the strong conviction that much of the data of subjective awareness may be too illusory and unreliable to afford a solid framework upon which to ground a science of consciousness. Thus Dennett, for example, argues that objective description of human behaviour, what he calls 'heterophenomenology', will yield much more than Husserlian 'auto-phenomenology'.[23] Dennett maintains that the much supposed inner observation of conscious states is actually a kind of "gullible theorizing". Of course, defenders of the Husserlian approach can make the counter argument that one can only attempt to understand another person by employing categories by which one understands oneself and hence that one has not escaped auto-phenomenology at all.[24]

Husserl's critics believe his discoveries are too heavily dependent on others 'seeing' things just in the manner Husserl does, because he lays such a heavy stress on essential intuition (*Wesensschau*) rather than on theory formation, hypothesis testing, or even deductive argumentation. If someone disputes Husserl's phenomenological discoveries he can only argue that they have got it wrong; they haven't seen what he has in the phenomenon. His response would be to try again, to undertake more careful scrutiny. Husserl is perhaps his own worst enemy in this regard. He was early on criticised by the Neo-Kantians for adopting a Platonic account of the highest forms of intellectual knowledge: true knowledge involves seeing things as they are, grasping them through a kind of direct insight. Not many philosophers have wanted to follow Husserl's claim that intuition with evidence is an apodictic form of knowing which ultimately validates all other kinds of knowing. This is open to the argument that we can in fact be deeply wrong about what we think is immediately evident to us, and furthermore, it is hard to distinguish Husserl's notion of evidence from the simple psychological feeling of being certain (even though Husserl sought to keep these notions far apart). Husserl himself would counter with the argument that most scientific knowing in fact involves symbolisation, and what is known is not grasped intuitively and with evidence, but, nevertheless, at the very basis of any claim to knowledge is the idea of grasping something as true and this occurs as a normal intuitive experience for us when we understand that two lengths equal to a third are equal to one another, and so on. Husserl in fact shares with Aristotle, Euclid, and Descartes the belief that knowledge is founded on insights which themselves cannot be demonstrated but are grasped intuitively as true. More than these theorists, however, Husserl greatly expanded the domain of the intuitive. Husserl may be defended, however, as really wanting a notion of self-evidence akin to mathematical insight. There is nothing woolly, fuzzy, or purely subjective about a mathematician having insight that $12 \times 12 = 144$. Husserl simply thought similar self-evident truths could be found in all areas of meaning. Husserl's endeavour to achieve essential insight eventually became distorted into Heidegger's gnomic way of letting meanings appear. Thus Heidegger, in thinking of the essence of language, will sum up the insight as 'language speaks'. This inevitably leads to the worry that phenomenology may in the end yield quite trivial insights.

Furthermore, though Husserl excelled in close description, he did not clarify the manner in which language remains hostage to the very intellectual set of assumptions he was trying to bracket. Husserl generally postponed discussion of the role of language in our experience of our own conscious thoughts and intentional experiences. The enabling and distorting role of language will come to the fore in the philosophy of Heidegger and of Wittgenstein, both emphasising that our intuition of our acts of awareness are in a sense secondary to our involvement in the public use of language.

Husserl's 'methodological solipsism' (as Fodor calls it, following Carnap) is not considered to be a reliable method of scientific discovery. Husserl's account of the reduction has been seen to be much ado about nothing. Too much attention is paid to stripping everything empirical from our intuitions as if what remained was the core of cognition itself. Many philosophers have rejected in principle the very possibility of separating the empirical from the a priori sides of our knowledge.

Husserl's claims to be founding a new science have not been borne out by subsequent developments in philosophy. Though his account of intentionality has been revived in recent discussion in the philosophy of mind, there is a strong sense that Husserl did not in fact give a theory of intentionality at all. That is, he has no positive account of the intentional relation. Furthermore, Husserl's science of pure description very quickly ran aground on the problem of interpretation. Description on its own is seen to be highly prejudiced, culturally and historically biased, and so on, and description as such must be carefully interrogated (perhaps with a 'hermeneutics of suspicion' to invoke Paul Ricoeur's phrase). Even Husserl eventually had to concede that his attempts to found an absolutely presuppositionless first philosophy – phenomenology – had ended in failure. Towards the end of his life, in 1935, Husserl bitterly acknowledged, given the current tendencies in philosophy, including the activities of his former students, the impossibility of achieving the ideal of philosophy as a science, when he proclaimed: "Philosophy as science, as serious, rigorous, indeed apodictically rigorous science – *the dream is over*" (*der Traum ist ausgeträumt, Crisis*, 389; Hua VI 508). Notice here that Husserl is not renouncing the ideal itself; he is simply acknowledging the bitter truth that philosophers have not understood this ideal and have been tempted away into irrational substitutes for scientific philosophy. It is not Husserl who has ended the dream but those supposed followers who have been seduced by historicism.

Husserl's greatest contribution lay in his careful mapping out of difficult terrain: the structure of intentional acts, the nature of meaning-intending and meaning-fulfilling, the structural role of the perception of time in the formation of conscious experiences in general, the complex layerings in the self-constitution of the ego and the social and life-world. Furthermore, his critique of naivety in the natural sciences, and even in logic and psychology, is exemplary. He was also an exceptionally honest thinker, haunted by the feeling he was failing to illuminate the domain he so clearly perceived in himself.

Among analytic philosophers, Husserl is now appreciated primarily for his *Logical Investigations* and for his theory of the *noema* as expounded in *Ideas* I. Husserl's critique of psychologism, his defence of logic as a pure science of a priori truth, his account of signs and signification in the *Logical Investigations*, together with what is seen as his generalisation of Frege's doctrine of *sense* (*Sinn*), all these achievements are highly appreciated by analytic commentators such as Dagfinn Føllesdal, Michael Dummett,

Kevin Mulligan, and David Bell. Hilary Putnam is appreciative of Husserl's critique of naturalism and naive objectivism and has invoked the account of European science in the *Crisis* in his own accounts of what is wrong with the contemporary scientific–materialist outlook.

In assessing Husserl's influence, many commentators wish to separate the contribution of his descriptive phenomenology from his later suspect move towards transcendental idealism, but Husserl himself resisted this interpretation. For him phenomenology itself was the proof of transcendental idealism:

> Only someone who misunderstands either the deepest sense of intentional method, or that of transcendental reduction, or perhaps both, can attempt to separate phenomenology from transcendental idealism.
>
> (CM § 41, 86; Hua I 119)

Husserl was a deeply rationalistic philosopher who believed all experience was capable of being studied from the phenomenological standpoint, reduced, robbed of everything empirical, and given in direct intuition. Gradually he came to believe that the source of all acts of meaning is transcendental subjectivity and sought to discover the a priori essential structures of this mysterious entity – far removed from our ordinary empirical consciousness. Husserl's central insight in his later years, especially from the mid-1920s onwards, was that the essential turn to subjectivity could be carried out in two ways – one deficient and one exemplary. One could either psychologise the turn to subjectivity and produce a transcendental psychology or transcendental anthropology, or make the true breakthrough into the transcendental domain which he himself proposed to do. Few of Husserl's followers were able to follow him in that direction. Few could understand the supposed exact "parallelism" which held between the psychological and the transcendental domains.

In general, on the continent of Europe, a number of Husserl's assistants – especially Eugen Fink and Ludwig Landgrebe, carried on Husserl's work in a relatively unchanged manner, developing description within the framework of the reductions. But Husserl's most famous assistant, Martin Heidegger, as we shall see, utterly transformed Husserl's phenomenology by fusing it with principles of interpretation, hermeneutics, and thus radically historicising phenomenology. Although Heidegger had been Husserl's assistant for many years, Heidegger had never accepted Husserl's invocation of transcendental subjectivity and the peculiar kind of solipsism it seemed to entail (despite Husserl's protestations to the contrary). As we shall see in subsequent chapters, Heidegger criticised Husserl for abandoning his own essential discovery of the phenomenological method and for regressing into transcendental idealism. Whereas Husserl had (in *Philosophy as a Rigorous Science*, 1911) vigorously opposed Dilthey's invocation of historicity and dismissed it as a form of relativism, Heidegger, on the other hand, was drawn towards Dilthey's philosophy of life and embraced the notion of the *historicity* of human being in the world. Heidegger's *Being and Time*, published in 1927, gave a detailed account of the finite and historical state of human being in the world. When Husserl read it, he regarded it as a major betrayal of his transcendental turn. Husserl thought Heidegger was merely providing a thorough-going description of the natural attitude instead of an attempt to suspend it as Husserlian phenomenology recommended. For Husserl, *Being and Time* was an exercise in phenomenological anthropology, an exploration of being-in-the-world in the natural attitude, of what is given in the moods of everydayness (anxiety, boredom, anonymity, and so on). As anthropology, Husserl saw *Being and Time* as falling back into the very naivety which the radical transcendental critique of the natural attitude was employed to overcome. Furthermore, Husserl was deeply disappointed in Heidegger's move towards the philosophy of life, the *Lebensphilosophie* of Dilthey and Scheler in particular. True phenomenology, for Husserl, cannot be founded in any science of human being (*Trans. Phen.*, pp. 485–486; Hua XXVII 164).

In the chapters which follow we shall trace the evolution and transformation of Husserl's legacy.

6

MARTIN HEIDEGGER'S TRANSFORMATION OF PHENOMENOLOGY

The enigma of Heidegger

Martin Heidegger is undoubtedly one of the great philosophers of the twentieth century, whose major work, *Sein und Zeit* (*Being and Time*, 1927),[1] though dense and difficult, is without question an enduring philosophical masterpiece on a par with Kant's *Critique of Pure Reason* and Hegel's *Phenomenology of Spirit*.[2] Heidegger himself was a complex and compelling figure. On the one hand, his exceptional gifts as a thinker and teacher attracted brilliant students, such as Hannah Arendt, Hans-Georg Gadamer, Emmanuel Levinas, Herbert Marcuse, Karl Löwith, and Ernst Tugendhat, among many others. For Hannah Arendt he was a "passionate thinker"[3] who brought thinking to life; his steadfast commitment to radical questioning attracted Gadamer and Derrida. On the other hand, Heidegger's conception of philosophy as a kind of solitary thinking,[4] and his opaque style of writing, full of neologisms and wordplay, have led to his work being disparaged. Heidegger's bombastic mode of expression, whereby he sought to express insights in a manner which escaped the distorting effects of traditional philosophical terminology, has been ridiculed by philosophers who advocate clarity and exactness, for example Rudolf Carnap and A. J. Ayer. Even Gilbert Ryle, who appreciated aspects of Heidegger's account of the self, thought that his phenomenology would end up in a "self-ruinous subjectivism", or in a "windy mysticism".[5] Yet, when he wanted to, Heidegger himself could write with astonishing clarity and simplicity and with penetrating insight.

Heidegger also provokes public controversy over his espousal of the National Socialist cause in the 1930s, and his complete silence on issues connected with the horrors of National Socialism, and especially the Holocaust, in the years after the war. Early on, Sartre and Arendt saw Heidegger's political failure to break with the Nazis as revealing an essential weakness of character, while Karl Jaspers portrayed his manner of thinking as "in its essence unfree, dictatorial, and uncommunicative".[6] Moreover, Heidegger's espousal of the Nazis has been linked with his fondness for a certain kind of language which expresses homeliness and belonging to the soil. Thus, Theodor Adorno has analysed the "philosophical banality" of Heidegger's employment of a "jargon" of authenticity which exploited some of the worst aspects of German romanticism, religious enthusiasm for the 'authentic', and popular folk nationalism.[7] More recently, the German historian Klemens von Klemperer has summed up this widespread antipathy to Heidegger:

> I must admit I found him [Heidegger] an unappealing person, how-ever self-possessed and dedicated to his task – humorless, unfaithful to his friends such as Karl Jaspers or Karl Löwith and like all too many Germans during the Nazi era utterly devoid of *Zivilcourage*. I should add that I am unimpressed by his beady eyes and mous-tache, suspicious of his dress – a cross between a Black Forest peasant's jacket and a military blouse complete with swastika, to-gether with the breeches of a cross-country skier – and last but not least, I am impatient with his metalanguage.[8]

Undoubtedly, there are aspects of Heidegger's character and philosophical outlook, not to speak of his political involvements, which are deeply unattractive, but it would be entirely wrong to assess his entire philosophical contribution in this light.

Any fair assessment of Heidegger's contribution must recognise that it changed the shape of twentieth-century philosophy. He rejected the prevailing idealism (whether Neo-Kantian or Husserlian) through his radical anti-subjectivist and anti-anthropological account of human existence or 'being-there' (Dasein). *Being and Time* is appreciated as one of the strongest anti-Cartesian, anti-subjectivist, anti-dualist, and anti-intellectualist explorations of what it is to be human, and how it is that humans encounter the world in concernful dealing which are bound up in situations yet project forward from those situations. He transformed philosophy with his radical articulation of the notion of being-in-the-world, as well as through his deliberately provocative 'destructive' readings of the history of philosophy, where he has given original and challenging readings of Nietzsche, Kant, Aristotle, and the Pre-Socratics. Heidegger has also made challenging and original contributions in other areas of philosophy: for example, his anti-representationalist and ontological account of the nature of truth; his anti-subjectivist and anti-aesthetic appreciation of the ontological nature of the art work; and his meditative studies on the nature of certain kinds of linguistic saying and poeticising (*Dichtung*). Of course, Heidegger has played a huge role in overcoming the Neo-Kantian preoccu-pation with epistemology which links him with contemporary pragmatism and externalism. Heidegger also played a role in reviving ontology and reflection on the question of the meaning of Being which led to a new interest in Aristotle and in the metaphysical tradition generally. Among the most influential aspects of his later work is his complex, but deeply insightful, analysis of the encompassing nature of the global technological framework (*das Gestell*) which now threatens to engulf genuinely human modes of existence.

All of Heidegger's philosophical contribution deserves detailed study and critique, but, for the purposes of this study, we must restrict ourselves to Heidegger's engagement with and contribution to phenomenology. Heidegger was an original phenomenologist of the highest rank, who attempted, in his own unique way, to carry out Husserl's project of getting back to the 'things themselves'. He spent ten years actively engaging with Husserl's philosophy before his own *Being and Time* appeared, which at once claimed phenomenology to be much older than Husserl, as an essentially Greek way of thinking, and also, at the same time, pushed phenomenology *beyond* Husserl, in that it replaced the study of the intentional structures of consciousness with the more fundamental study of the relation between Dasein and Being itself. Heidegger's return to Freiburg after the First World War in 1919 coincided with the beginnings of the decline of Husserl's influence in Germany (although not of Husserl's own intellectual development which was entering a particularly rich period of reflection and, of course, Husserl was beginning to have an influence in France, the USA, and Asia at this time). It was Heidegger much more than Husserl who gained a reputation for his teaching which seemed actually to be bringing matters to light, as Gadamer and others reported. Understanding the subsequent course of phenomenology, then, requires thinking both of Husserl and Heidegger and of their complex relations with one another.

Despite, or perhaps because of, his professed orientation towards the question of Being, Heidegger's thought is deeply phenomenological. *Being and Time* is explicitly an essay in phenomenological ontology, and, particularly in his later years, Heidegger continued to portray himself as a phenomenologist, in the sense that he attended to the appearing or disclosure of things, to the nature of manifestation. This commitment to phenomenology, however, in later years was more a general orientation in thinking rather than an exclusive method. In a late, autobiographical essay, "My Way to Phenomenology", Heidegger claimed that what he gained from phenomenology was the practice of "phenomenological seeing".[9] Indeed, both in his explicitly phenomenological decade (1917–1927) and in his later writings after 1960, Heidegger explicates his philosophy in terms of *phenomenology*, often opposing genuine phenomenological seeing to various concepts of phenomenology which he takes to be superficial, which lay claim to 'essential insight' without justification. Thus, in his letter to Richardson (1962), which is a typical statement of his later outlook, Heidegger portrays himself as a phenomenologist, and confirms that his immediate experience of phenomenology came through his dialogues with Husserl.[10] In a letter to Eugen Fink, on the occasion of the latter's 60th birthday in 1966, Heidegger more or less repeats the view that phenomenology

> does not refer to a particular direction of philosophy. It names a possibility that continues to exist today, i.e., making it possible for thinking to attain the "things themselves", or to put it more clearly, to attain the matter of thinking.[11]

The real appeal of phenomenology for Heidegger is that it is disclosive of the essential *possibilities* of situations. As Heidegger said in the Introduction to *Being and Time*:

> The following investigation would not have been possible if the ground had not been prepared by Edmund Husserl, with whose *Logical Investigations* phenomenology first emerged. Our comments on the preliminary conception of phenomenology have shown that what is essential in it does not lie in its actuality as a philosophical movement. Higher than actuality stands possibility. We can understand phenomenology only by seizing upon it as a possibility.
>
> (BT 62–3; 38)

The question of being

Heidegger was of the view that a philosopher has only a single deep thought, which he or she constantly struggles to express. As he put it in a poem:

> To think is to confine yourself to a
> single thought that one day stands
> still like a star in the world's sky.[12]

In his own case, his whole life's work was a single-minded attempt to re-examine the *question of Being*, a question he saw as inaugurated in ancient Greek philosophy, but which had rigidified into an arid metaphysics, generally neglected in his time. If one is to believe Heidegger's own account of his intellectual formation, it was the inspiration of both Brentano and Aristotle which very early led him to rethink the question of Being. Thus, in *Being and Time* (1927) Heidegger announces that he proposes to investigate "the question of Being" (*die Seinsfrage*, BT 20; 2),[13] that is the "question of the meaning of Being" (*die Frage nach dem Sinn von Sein*, BT 19; 1).

Furthermore, Heidegger proposes to approach this question precisely through the phenomenon of the 'forgetting of Being' (*Seinsvergessenheit*) in contemporary thought. This is a deeply phenomenological move; the subject matter is pursued through the manner in which it appears (or is hidden) in contemporary experience. Even forgetfulness is actually a positive phenomenon, a mode of relating, which reveals Being and brings it to presence in its own special way.[14] In other words, the very fact that Being is no longer a pressing problem in philosophy itself demands a thorough investigation, which will lead Heidegger into a rethinking of the nature of the philosophical tradition in general. In the background, of course, is the broadly Hegelian assumption that the philosophical interests of a culture are an expression of that culture and mirror its health or sickness. A second basic assumption of Heidegger's philosophy is that the origin of a tradition is a radical event which determines from the outset the manner in which that tradition will develop. Philosophy in large part is the work of tracing back to the original emergence of the insights which determine the course of subsequent cultural development.

Reviving the real underlying significance of the question of Being will require coming to terms with the history of traditional metaphysics. The traditional ways of asking the question are actually impediments to a solution. Heidegger saw himself as involved in a radicalisation of ontology which involved connecting it with the nature of historical occurrence. Quite early on – around 1919 – Heidegger began to conceive of the way forward in philosophy as requiring a kind of 'destruction' (*Destruktion*) or 'dismantling' (*Abbau*) of the tradition.[15] Heidegger may have found this notion of 'destruction' (*destructio*) in Luther (who wished to destroy the Aristotelianism in the Christian heritage), but it was certainly also present in Husserl who spoke of *Abbau* in several key texts. In *Being and Time* Heidegger's "destruction of the history of philosophy" included a stripping away of Kantian and Cartesian elements to recover the original existential (and Greek) ways of conceiving of phenomena of human existence, for example to recover the real meaning of Aristotle's conception of human *praxis*. In *Being and Time* § 6 Heidegger says:

> If the question of Being is to have its own history made transparent, then this hardened tradition must be loosened up, and the concealments which it has brought about must be dissolved. We understand this task as one in which by taking the question of Being as our clue, we are to destroy the traditional content of ancient ontology until we arrive at those primordial experiences in which we achieved our first ways of determining the nature of Being – the ways which have guided us ever since.
>
> (BT § 6, 44)

Heidegger rejected traditional metaphysical approaches to the question of Being as having misunderstood the nature of beings by understanding them as 'things', as what is simply there, as occurrent, as 'reality', as present at hand. Traditional metaphysics, which thought it was simply describing things as they are, does not realise that it is constructed on the basis of a certain assumed attitude towards the world, which in fact is not fundamental, but belongs to a distorted way of experiencing due to the way humans are drawn down into everyday existing. Metaphysics has elevated a particular approach to things into the science of beings as such. Heidegger's central insight is that traditional metaphysical understanding is actually a sedimentation of a kind of everyday set of assumptions about reality, and this set of assumptions needs to be shown to be just that, through a deeper exploration of all the ways in which humans relate to the world. In particular the prioritisation of the theoretical, of *theoria* in the Greek sense, of the contemplative outlook so admired by Husserl, is shown to be a particular effect of tradition and not a fundamental feature of Dasein itself. This leads Heidegger to a radical questioning of the traditional metaphysical definition of human beings as *rational animals* as well as the traditional scriptural assumptions about human beings being made in the *image and likeness* of God (BT § 10). Rather human existence must be thought radically in its own terms. There are two sides to this: one is an attempt at an existential analytic of Dasein; the other is an attempt to retrieve the essential meanings of key words expressing existence from beneath the weight of encrusted tradition. To highlight and expose this one-sided partiality of traditional metaphysical accounts (including the medieval Scholastic, the Cartesian, Rationalist, and Kantian approaches), Heidegger favours a new 'fundamental ontology' (BT 61; 37), an enquiry into the manner in which the structures of Being are revealed through the structures of human existence, an enquiry, furthermore, which could only be carried out through *phenomenology*, now transformed into *hermeneutical* phenomenology, since the phenomena of existence always require interpretation, and hermeneutics is the art of interpretation.

Human existence is not an entity which is simply there in the world, accessible from different points of view. Rather human existence is some specific person's existence; it has the character of 'specificity' (*Jeweiligkeit*) or 'mineness' (*Jemeinigkeit*). So too an interpretation of human existence cannot be neutral, dispassionate, theoretical contemplation, but must take into account the *involvement* of the enquirer him- or herself in the undertaking. Human beings are involved with their existence in such a way that hermeneutics must be able to accomplish this movement backwards and forwards between the existence to be examined and the nature of the examining enquirer. Heidegger's fundamental ontology, in *Being and Time*, will try to map out the transcendental conditions which made human existence (Dasein) possible, while recognising that humans are individual existing beings whose Being is an issue for them. Heidegger's analysis of Dasein, of that particular entity or 'being' (*das Seiende*) which is uniquely concerned about its mode of Being, and whose Being is an issue for it, uncovers broadly existential structures of living (which show the influence of Kierkegaard, Jaspers, and Dilthey), but more than any of these philosophers, Heidegger has raised to an ontological level the essential role of humans as *questioning* beings. It is this fundamental questioning concern with Being which marks out human existence as such. Questioning is prioritised over all other forms of interacting. Understanding what it is to be a questioner reveals the purely human mode of 'being-in-the-world' (*In-der-Welt-Sein*) as a kind of projective caring and involvement in the world.

But, in *Being and Time*, Heidegger does not want merely to give an existential analysis of human being. His ultimate aim is to understand the meaning of Being and its relation to *time*. Heidegger rightly sees that traditional metaphysics and theology had an orientation towards thinking of true Being as timeless, eternal, unchanging. In the metaphysical tradition stemming from Plato and Aristotle, Being has been understood as *presence* (*Anwesenheit*, which contains the word '*Wesen*' which means 'essence', the Greek *ousia*) as that which has some kind of static occurrence. Heidegger, on the other hand, sees human existence as essentially taking place in time, spread out between past and future and radically limited by death and so essentially incomplete. Being must be understood radically in terms of time. Unfortunately, the concepts of time available from the philosophical and scientific tradition are inadequate to the task. Heidegger thus proposes in the second half of *Being and Time* to run through various fundamental human experiences in terms of their temporal character to try to develop an authentic sense of temporality as a first step towards approaching the problem of time itself and its relation to Being. For this purpose, Heidegger draws heavily on the German historical tradition of Hegel, Ranke, Dilthey, and Count Yorck, and even invokes Nietzsche, to articulate the historical and social nature of Dasein. At the end of the book, Heidegger recognises that his basic distinction, namely the difference between the Being of Dasein and the Being of other entities, is at best only a provisional distinction which itself must be submitted to a more radical interrogation (BT 487; 436–437). While Heidegger has described the manner in which Dasein relates to entities in the world and the kind of structures which regulate it, he still needs to consider how this disclosing of Being is at all possible for Dasein (BT 488; 437), and hence he is already looking towards the problem of analysing the nature of Being's self-disclosure, which will take him far from his earlier analyses of Dasein and towards his later meditations of truth and on the nature of the event (*Ereignis*).

Some time after the publication of *Being and Time*, and probably around 1930, though exactly when is a matter of much debate, Heidegger's thought underwent a change of orientation, which he himself characterised in his *Letter on Humanism* as a 'turning' (*Kehre, Pathmarks*, p. 250; GA 9, p. 328; see also the note added to the essay, "On The Essence of Truth", *Pathmarks*, p. 154; GA 9, p. 201), whereby he rejected the strait-jacket of transcendental philosophy and sought to explore the meaning of Being

(*Sein*, often in later texts written in the archaic form, *Seyn*)[16] through a meditative, if consciously wilful, even idiosyncratic, examination of poetry, art, architecture, and some significant revelatory moments in the history of philosophy. Heidegger abandoned the project of *Being and Time*, because of a failure of the "language of metaphysics" in the "saying of this turning" (*Pathmarks*, p. 250; GA 9, p. 328). As he later put it to Richardson, his move was really *through* phenomenology to the "thinking of Being" (*das Denken des Seins*, Richardson, pp. xvi–xvii). While Heidegger abandoned the procedure of *Being and Time* he wanted to remain true to the overall question, the general problematic of his 1927 work, namely the problematic of the relation of Being *to* time, but to rid himself entirely of any subjectivist or anthropological bias. For the later Heidegger, it is not that Dasein posits, constitutes, or illuminates Being but that Being itself draws near to Dasein (Richardson, pp. xviii–xix). Human being and Being are caught in an ontological revealing and concealing dynamic which is at the very heart of what it means to be, to come to presence, to appear in time. But Heidegger's later thinking of this revealing/concealing is so distant from any anthropological characterisation that it can at best be expressed in terms of the working of poetry or of language itself.

Heidegger for a long time was of the view that the Greek experience, at least in its very inception, somehow had an experience of this event of appearing/concealing, and that the Greek word *aletheia* expressed this insight, even if the Greeks themselves never came to a full articulated understanding of this revelatory insight. More and more, in later years, Heidegger seems to have come to the view that not even the Greeks had this revelation, that it is something which is an essentially futural promise. All through his life Heidegger had spoken of this dynamic of revealing and concealing, as a sending, or mission, or destiny of Being. Being 'gives itself' (*es gibt*), or conceals itself, and in this giving and withholding is cradled the very history of the world. Heidegger's language tended to take on the rhetoric of epoch, destiny, fate, and it even takes on an apocalyptic tone in some of the late writings. Thus, Heidegger plays with the meaning of 'epoch' to suggest that when Being sends historical epochs, it is at the same time involved in a withdrawing or withholding (*epoché*). At times, Heidegger sounds like a prophet announcing the end of time or the return of the gods, lamenting the world's night and heralding a new dawn and a new relation to Being. In his less extravagant moments, his later concern with the notions of historical destiny takes the form of a questioning of the manner in which Western thought, originally a revealing and manifesting of Being, has been transformed into a global technological instrumental reason, against which have been raised only the voices of a few poeticising thinkers (including Hölderlin, Nietzsche, and Trakl). The later Heidegger thinks of Being apart from beings, trying to think both the disclosing and the concealing nature of Being, to think this fundamental relation between the hidden and the manifest. Heidegger saw certain kinds of poetry as naming this essential revealing/concealing nature of Being far better than could traditional philosophy. However, Heidegger's critics believe he veered off into a private mysticism at this point and, in this chapter, we shall not attempt to discuss Heidegger's later thinking of Being.

Heidegger: life and writings (1889–1976)

Of modest village origins, Heidegger was for a time a Catholic seminarian, then a brilliant but academically ambitious lecturer. Later he became an enthusiastic supporter of National Socialism, and, after the war, his behaviour was self-serving at best, duplicitous at worst. But, even while suspended from teaching, he seems to have been able to isolate himself from all criticism by his single-minded pursuit of his own philosophical mission, perhaps best symbolised by his preference for the small wooden mountain hut he built for himself in Todtnauberg outside Freiburg, where, looking to his idols Hölderlin and Nietzsche, he cultivated the mystique of the solitary thinker.

The early years

Martin Heidegger (1889–1976) was born of lower middle-class Catholic parents in Messkirch in the Baden-Württemburg region of Germany on 26 September 1889. He never severed his connections with Messkirch, and often returned to the nearby Benedictine monastery in Beuron. His father, a cooper by trade, served as sexton in the local Catholic church of St Martin, and Martin attended the local primary school there for eight years, before becoming a boarding student at the state-run Gymnasium in Constance from 1903 to 1906, residing in the Jesuit house for theological students (the 'Conradihaus'). This early education was designed to prepare him for the priesthood. In 1906 he transferred to the prestigious Berthold-Gymnasium in Freiburg where, until 1909, he received a traditional education in the classics. This transfer enabled him to apply for a Catholic Church grant to attend the University of Freiburg.

In the summer of 1907, Fr Conrad Grüber, native of Messkirch and headmaster of the Conradihaus (soon to be the local vicar in Constance and much later Archbishop of Freiburg), presented the young Gymnasium student, Martin Heidegger, with a copy of Brentano's 1862 study, *On the Several Senses of Being in Aristotle*. This book became Heidegger's "rod and staff" (OTB 74), stimulating him to read further in philosophy, specifically Aristotle. A year later, in 1908, he would borrow the original Greek texts of Aristotle's *Metaphysics* from the school library.[17] Brentano's book outlined the different senses of being in Aristotle (being as property, being in the sense of the categories, being in the sense of possibility and actuality, being in the sense of being true), but Heidegger was drawn to the question of what unites these different senses – what determines 'Being' (*Sein*) as such and not just 'beings' (*Seienden*)? As Heidegger later put it in an account of his life presented to the Heidelberg Academy of the Sciences, he was originally preoccupied with the "question of the singleness of the multiplicity in Being" (*Frage nach dem Einfachen des Mannifachen im Sein*, Ott, p. 51).[18] This remained the central focus of his life's work. In his 1962 letter to William Richardson, Heidegger confirms that he puzzled again and again over the multiple meanings of Being as laid out in Brentano's treatise on Aristotle seeking to understand what unified these different determinations of being. But he was also driven to another deeper question: "whence does Being as such (not merely beings as beings) receive its determination?" (*Woher empfängt das Sein als solches (nicht nur das Seiende als Seiendes) seine Bestimmung?*, Richardson, pp. x–xi).

On 30 September 1909, he entered the Jesuit novitiate in Feldkirch, Austria, but was forced to leave after only a few weeks on grounds of ill-health, probably a heart condition which recurred sporadically through his life (Ott, p. 56). He transferred to the diocesan seminary in Freiburg and, as was customary for seminarians, at the same time registered in the Theology Faculty of Freiburg University, where he studied for four semesters from 1909 to 1911. As he later recalled, the two volumes of Husserl's *Logical Investigations* borrowed from the library, and seemingly not requested by other readers, "lay on my desk in the theological seminary ever since my first semester there" (OTB 74). Heidegger thought Husserl, as a student of Brentano, could shed light on the problem of the unity of being. In fact, what he learned from Husserl's book was a strong defence of the ideal self-identity of logical and mathematical truths over and against the psycholo-gistic tendency to reduce them to mental contents. Heidegger was drawn to Husserl's endorsement of the objectivity of truth since it seemed to him to be compatible with Aristotelian and Neo-Thomist realism. But he was also drawn to Husserl's discussion of categorial intuition and the nature of truth in the Sixth Logical Investigation.

One of his theology lecturers, the anti-modernist follower of German speculative theology, Carl Braig (1853–1923), was responsible for deepening his understanding of the problem of Being. Braig's book, *On Being* (1896)[19] contained many etymological explanations of Greek metaphysical terms[20] as well as lengthy extracts from Aristotle, Thomas, and Suarez. It even contained the phrase 'the Being of beings' central to Heidegger's formula-tion of his problematic. Braig also introduced the young Heidegger to the thought of Schelling and Hegel, and to the critique of modernism as a kind of self-certain subjectivity.

It was during these early theological studies also that Heidegger first encountered hermeneutics through Schleiermacher – at a time when Heidegger was concerned with "the relation between the word of Holy

Scripture and theological-speculative thinking".[21] In these early years, furthermore, he began to read the German romantic poets Friedrich Hölderlin, Georg Trakl, Rainer Maria Rilke, as well as Kierkegaard and Nietzsche. Early in 1911, ill-health forced Heidegger to leave the novitiate, and having been granted leave of absence for the whole summer semester of 1911 he returned home to Messkirch, where he wrote poetry and planned his future. He was now burdened with financial concerns should he choose to continue his studies unsupported by the Church.

When Heidegger returned to Freiburg he registered in the Faculty of Mathematics and Natural Science to read mathematics. He became especially interested in mathematical logic. He also took philosophy lectures with the Neo-Kantian Heinrich Rickert, with whom he re-read Husserl's *Logical Investigations* as well as Emil Lask's related work on evidence and truth.[22] For a while, Heidegger deliberated between specialising in philosophy and mathematics, but eventually he did not sit for the state examination in mathematics and opted for philosophy. In 1912, he published his first philosophical essays including "Das Realitätsproblem in der modernen Philosophie" ("The Problem of Reality in Modern Philosophy"),[23] which treated the problem of realism as a sterile, modern problem, arising only with Descartes and Berkeley when thinking gets separated from being. In the course of this essay, he criticised Kant and Hegel's 'extravagant idealism', and opts for a version of critical realism. In the same year, Heidegger also published "Neuere Forschungen über Logik" ("New Investigations in Logic", *Frühe Schriften*, GA 1, pp. 17–43) a survey of logic in three parts mainly concerned with the implications of Husserl's critique of psychologism, published in the *Literarische Rundschau*, a Catholic journal run by the Freiburg Professor, Sauer. Heidegger's orientation was still religious and, between 1910 and 1913, he published, in a Catholic student periodical, *Der Akademiker*, a number of essays critical of the modernist movement (these early writings have been omitted from the *Gesamtausgabe* edition) arguing that the Church was right to strive against individualism and the "destructive forces of modernism" (Ott, pp. 59–63).

In 1912 Heidegger received a grant from a Catholic foundation which stipulated that the holder dedicate himself to furthering the philosophy of Thomas Aquinas. This grant enabled Heidegger, in 1913, to complete his doctoral thesis entitled *Die Lehre vom Urteil in Psychologismus* (*The Doctrine of Judgement in Psychologism*),[24] written under Professor Arthur Schneider, who then held the Chair of Christian Philosophy in Freiburg. This thesis is an analysis of the nature of judgement in which he criticised both Rickert and Lask, but one of the questions he asks in the course of this thesis is: "What is the meaning of meaning?" (*Was ist der Sinn des Sinnes?*) In order to answer this question, he says, we must already in a way know what meaning is. He would later employ the same argumentative strategy concerning our pre-understanding of the meaning of Being in *Being and*

Time. At the end of this thesis Heidegger also expresses the need to "articulate the whole region of Being in its various modes of reality" thus signalling his interest in the question of Being (GA I 186).

With the outbreak of the First World War in August 1914, Heidegger was called up for military service but was soon discharged, on 9 October, on health grounds. Instead, he was required to work as a censor in the post office in Freiburg from 1915 to 1917 (Ott, p. 78). Meanwhile, in 1915, he completed his *Habilitationsschrift*, entitled *Die Kategorien- und Bedeutungslehre des Duns Scotus* (*The Categories and the Doctrine of Meaning in Duns Scotus*, reprinted GA I 189–412), under Heinrich Rickert. This work, published in 1916, was a study of the *grammatica speculativa* of Thomas of Erfurt (at the time wrongly attributed to Duns Scotus) which focuses on the relation between judgement and truth, but clearly shows Neo-Kantian traits in its emphasis on finding the right method for tackling problems. But already in this work, Heidegger, with his assertion that philosophy is closely associated with life, displays an interest in *Lebensphilosophie* then popular in Germany. Heidegger was also becoming interested in problems concerning history generally, and specifically in the work of Wilhelm Dilthey. His lecture, "Der Zeitbegriff in der Geschichtswissenschaften" ("The Concept of Time in Historical Studies", reprinted GA I 413–433), delivered on 27 July 1915 as part of his *Habilitation* proceedings, marks his first entrance into a topic which would later be a central concern. Years later, in his 1973 Preface to *Frühe Schriften*, the collected edition of his early writings, Heidegger recalls that the two questions which interested him in his early writings were (i) "the question of Being" (*die Seinsfrage*), which he then understood as the problem of the categories, and (ii) "the question of language" (*die Frage nach der Sprache*), then understood by him as "the theory of meaning" (*in der Form der Bedeutungslehre*, GA I 55). At that time, he also later claimed, he did not see the relation between these two questions.

In 1915–1916 Heidegger began as an unsalaried lecturer (*Privatdozent*) at Freiburg, lecturing on "the principles of ancient and scholastic philosophy" as well as on Kant and German idealism. Up to 1916 his contact with phenomenology had been minimal, other than that he had espoused the anti-psychologism of Husserl's *Logical Investigations*, an outlook shared also by Neo-Kantians, such as Rickert and Lask. Furthermore, in order to extend his 1912 Catholic foundation grant for a further year to complete his *Habilitationsschrift* on medieval philosophy, Heidegger had expressly promised the foundation that he would devote himself to the study of Christian philosophy (Ott, p. 77). For this reason, he was widely perceived in Freiburg as a Catholic Scholastic philosopher and indeed promoted himself as such. In June 1916, however, he was disappointed not to get the Chair of Christian Philosophy at Freiburg, which had been vacant since the departure of Schneider for Strasbourg in 1913. Heidegger was being groomed for this chair by some Catholic supporters, especially by the

Professor of History, Heinrich Finke, who in fact had pointed Heidegger in the direction of Duns Scotus. Indeed, Heidegger's friend from the Theology Faculty, Fr Krebs, had been temporarily filling this chair and was being assisted in the preparation of his lectures on medieval philosophy by the young Heidegger. But Heidegger was already looking beyond medieval philosophy.

With Husserl in Freiburg 1916–1923

Edmund Husserl assumed the Chair of Philosophy in Freiburg on 1 April 1916, and soon afterwards, on 27 May 1916 (*Briefwechsel* IV 127), he wrote to Heidegger requesting a copy of his *Habilitation* thesis. Subsequently, they met several times over the summer, with Husserl assisting Heidegger in finding a publisher for his thesis. When a lecturing post became available in Marburg in 1917, Paul Natorp wrote to Husserl seeking information about Heidegger as a possible candidate, and Husserl's reply was circumspect: he had not yet formed a solid opinion of him; his *Habilitation* thesis was a "beginner's book" (*Erstlingsbuch*).[25] Furthermore, he suspected that Heidegger was "confessionally bound" (i.e. to Catholicism) and might not be suitable for Protestant Marburg. Needless to say, Heidegger did not get the job. Meanwhile, Heidegger married another Freiburg student, Elfride Petri, a Lutheran, in 1917 in a Catholic ceremony in Freiburg Cathedral.

On 17 January 1918, Heidegger was again called up, this time to serve in the meteorological service, and in August was sent to the Western front (where his work involved preparations for chemical gas attacks; Ott, p. 105). Husserl and Heidegger began corresponding in earnest at this time, with Husserl full of admiration for Heidegger's youth and earnest philosophical dedication. In one letter towards the end of 1918, Husserl tells Heidegger that he too has a copy of Hölderlin's poems by his bedside (*Briefwechsel* IV 136).

On 9 January 1919, immediately after his return from the war, Heidegger wrote a letter to his friend Fr Krebs rejecting Catholicism as a *system* but still expressing high appreciation for the values and religious outlook of the Catholic Middle Ages.[26] In this letter, he also states that he is carrying out research in the phenomenology of religion. At this time, Heidegger was beginning to plan a project of applying phenomenology to the existential phenomena of actual life, hitherto the exclusive preserve of religious and theological modes of thinking. By this time Heidegger had moved decisively outside the framework of Catholicism, and Husserl, now convinced that Heidegger was no longer confessionally bound, sent a more positive assessment of Heidegger to Natorp on 11 February 1920, when another vacancy came up in Marburg (*Briefwechsel* V 139).

In January 1919, Heidegger became Husserl's assistant, replacing Edith Stein. He immediately began lecturing as *Privatdozent* during the special

"War Emergency Semester" (*Kriegnotsemester*) at Freiburg, which ran from the end of January to April 1919, on "The Idea of Philosophy and the Problem of World View". In these lectures, Heidegger criticised both Husserl's conception of philosophy as a rigorous science and Dilthey's and Jaspers' conception of philosophy as the construction of a world-view, *Weltanschauung*. In particular, he criticised Husserl's prioritisation of the realm of the theoretical over the engaged, lived moment in experience with its connection with the world. He also criticised Husserl's flight from historical 'factical' existence into transcendental idealism. For Heidegger, "the world worlds" (*die Welt weltet*), and in this event, there is nothing of the ego.

Heidegger rapidly developed a reputation as an extraordinary teacher, whose seminars and lectures made the topics come alive. Transcripts of his lecture courses began to circulate privately and, as his Marburg student Hannah Arendt later recalled, his name travelled all over Germany "like the rumor of the hidden king".[27] To the post-war generation of students he seemed to be defining and confronting the intellectual crisis which they were experiencing in their own lives, making frequent references to Spengler's *The Decline of the West*, hugely influential in Germany at the time (see, for example, FCM 69–71; GA 103–107) and generally invoking existential questions. As Arendt put it, Heidegger's thought seemed to attract those who saw breakdown and dark times ahead.

The Marburg years 1923–1928

Heidegger had failed to get a post in Marburg in 1917 and again in 1920, but, finally, in the autumn of 1923, he moved to Marburg as Professor Extraordinarius. Since Heidegger had published nothing in the seven years since his *Habilitation* thesis in 1916, he sent to Natorp, as part of his job application in 1922, a hastily written transcript drawn from his lectures, and specifically from his Aristotle interpretations. Heidegger had taught a course on the phenomenological interpretation of Aristotle from 1921 to 1923, interpreting Aristotle's *Nicomachean Ethics* as an examination of concrete life, offering a radically different Aristotle to the one he had encountered during his scholastic training. Aristotle's understanding of change, *kinesis*, for instance, is understood by Heidegger as relating to the temporality of existence.

Heidegger's lectures at Marburg from 1923 to 1928 developed in two directions at once: there is the existential interpretation of Aristotle and the Greeks, on the one hand; and the rethinking of phenomenology as a radical rekindling of the essential motives of philosophy, on the other. *Being and Time* (1927), which Heidegger began writing in his tiny hut at Todtnauberg in the winter of 1923–1924, is the fruit of these reflections. At Marburg Heidegger met Nicolai Hartmann, who had succeeded Natorp to the Chair, and whose interest in Aristotle's ontology helped Heidegger move beyond the Neo-Kantian preoccupation with epistemology. Heidegger was also deeply influenced by Rudolf Bultmann and attended his seminars on St Paul. Around this time also, he began to read the recently published edition of the letters of Count Yorck to Dilthey on the nature of historical experience. During this period, Heidegger was also reading deeply in Dilthey's *Complete Works*, as his student Gadamer recalled. On 25 July 1924, Heidegger gave a lecture, "Der Begriff der Zeit" ("The Concept of Time"),[28] to the Marburg theologians which contrasted the scientific notion of time with the notion of lived time in the historical and social sciences. Heidegger argues that instead of taking a determination of time from eternity (as Augustine and theology in general has done), the philosopher must try to think of time in terms of time. This means grasping the temporal character of human existence (Dasein), in terms of its 'specificity' (*Jeweiligkeit*). The lecture ends by raising the more far-reaching question as to whether Dasein itself may be said to be time.

Though Heidegger was now renowned among students as a powerful and illuminating lecturer, he still had not managed to publish anything since 1916. Thus, when in 1925 he was nominated by the Philosophy Faculty for the Chair at Marburg, recently vacated by Nicolai Hartmann, his nomination was turned down by the Education Ministry because of insufficient publications. To remedy this gap, in 1926 he was pressurised by the Dean of the Marburg Faculty to rush the uncompleted manuscript of *Being and Time* into print. Heidegger promised to have the typescript to Niemeyer by 1 April 1926. Over the spring vacation from February to April 1926 Heidegger retired to Todtnauberg and brought together some 240 pages of *Being and Time* which he arranged – with Husserl's help – to have printed. Husserl himself even visited Todtnauberg that spring to assist Heidegger with the proof-reading. However, in December 1926, the Education Minister in Berlin declared the publication inadequate, and the Chair in Marburg was not offered to Heidegger. Heidegger went on to publish the full text of *Being and Time, Part I* in spring 1927 both as a separate book and as part of Husserl's *Jahrbuch*.[29]

Being and Time Part I consisted of two divisions dealing with the existential analytic of Dasein and the relation of Dasein and temporality. According to the design of the book outlined in BT § 8, Heidegger promised a further division to Part I which would recapitulate the analytic of human nature from the standpoint of time, as well as a detailed account of his proposed 'destruction' (*Destruktion*) of the history of philosophy – chiefly through analyses of Kant, Descartes, and Aristotle in Part II. Neither the third division of Part I nor Part II would ever be published, though much of what Heidegger intended to say there can be reconstructed on the basis of his lecture notes and subsequent writings (especially his 1929 book on Kant and his 1935 lectures on the *Introduction to Metaphysics*).

Being and Time was dedicated to Edmund Husserl, although, on 26 December 1926, Heidegger had written to Jaspers to say that if the book was directed *against* anyone it was Husserl.[30] Soon after the publication of *Being and Time*, moreover, relations between the two cooled as their philosophical differences became obvious. In retirement Husserl finally sat down to read Heidegger's *Being and Time* and the *Kantbuch* in 1929 and wrote on his copy of *Being and Time* the famous words which are attributed to Aristotle in his break with Plato: *amicus Plato, magis amica veritas* (Plato is a friend but truth is a greater friend).[31] Husserl felt that Heidegger was doing philosophical anthropology and had completely misunderstood the crucial step of the transcendental reduction. Furthermore, in his account of Dasein as transcendence, he had trivialised the essential meaning of intentionality (*Trans. Phen.*, p. 310). The two colleagues no longer communicated, and when the Fifth Edition of *Being and Time* appeared in 1941 Heidegger had removed the dedication to Husserl which was not restored until the Seventh Edition.

The return to Freiburg and the turning

In October 1927, the Berlin ministry approved Heidegger's promotion to the Chair at Marburg, but, a year later, in October 1928, he was appointed to succeed Husserl at Freiburg, gaining the post ahead of Pfänder and Cassirer. Heidegger seemed to have had in mind the implementation of the programme of the destruction of the history of philosophy outlined in *Being and Time* beginning with a rethinking of Kant. He offered a lecture course on Kant's *Critique of Pure Reason* in Freiburg in 1927–1928, where he highlighted the problem of time in Kant's schematism of the categories. He lectured on Kant in Riga in 1928, and, from 17 March to 6 April 1929, he took part in a philosophy convention held at the International University Course in Davos, Switzerland, where both Heidegger and the German Neo-Kantian philosopher Ernst Cassirer delivered lectures and engaged in a debate over the meaning of Neo-Kantian transcendental philosophy. For Heidegger, Neo-Kantianism seemed only to theorise about science, whereas he wanted to think about ontological questions. Some months later, Heidegger published the results of this interpretation of Kant as *Kant und das Problem der Metaphysik* (*Kant and the Problem of Metaphysics*).[32] As he earlier had been doing with Aristotle, Heidegger's Kant interpretation sets out to do "violence" to the text in order to set free its deep philosophical core. As Heidegger maintained, in the Preface to the Second Edition published in 1950, the thoughtful confrontation between thinkers need not be bound by the methods of historical philology (KPM xviii).

On 24 July 1929, Heidegger delivered his inaugural lecture at Freiburg entitled "Was ist Metaphysik?" ("What is Metaphysics?"),[33] which sets out to consider the nature of metaphysical questioning in an age given over to the positive sciences: "What is happening to us, essentially, in the grounds of our existence, when science has become our passion?" (*Pathmarks*, p. 82; 103). What subject matter is left for metaphysics? For Heidegger, nothing is left over from the enquiries of the special sciences, but, and here is his radical move, he goes on to claim that the true subject of metaphysical thought is precisely this 'nothing' which escapes the attention of all the other sciences. It was this lecture, with its portentous claim that philosophy studies 'nothing' over and above the special sciences but that this nothing is most important, since indeed "nothing nothings" (*Das Nichts selbst nichtet, Pathmarks*, p. 90; GA 9, p. 114) which attracted the criticism of the Vienna Circle. Rudolf Carnap, who was in the audience, was incensed by what he regarded as a mystification of philosophy and wrote a strong attack on Heidegger attempting to show that Heidegger's claims were non-sensical pseudo-statements.[34] It is also likely that Carnap was provoked by Heidegger's increasingly right-wing political stance, but his critique equated Heidegger to traditional Hegelian metaphysics as a decadent tradition to be overcome.

Another important text from this period is Heidegger's essay *Vom Wesen des Grundes* ("On the Essence of Ground"), his contribution to the *Festschrift* for Husserl, which was published as a supplementary volume to the *Jahrbuch für Philosophie und phänomenologische Forschung* in 1929.[35] Here Heidegger argues that propositional truth is derivative and secondary to the fundamental revelation of beings and this is made possible by a kind of unveiling of Being. In this lecture Heidegger offers his first published account of the "ontological difference" between Being and beings, though it had already been treated explicitly in his 1927 lecture course on *The Basic Problems of Phenomenology* (cf. BPP § 22).

In these writings from the late 1920s Heidegger sees his fundamental ontology as an attempt at laying a foundation and circumscribing in advance "the inner possibility of metaphysics, that is, the concrete determination of its essence" (KPM 2). But Heidegger gradually began to realise that his project for a systematic, transcendental philosophy was impossible. In particular, he saw that the transcendental move which requires objects to live up to a prior conception of them was nothing but a secularisation of the theistic approach to the world which sees it as created and thus as measured against the divine thought. Transcendental philosophy masked the nature of truth as appearing.

Sometime around 1930 Heidegger's thought underwent what he himself styled in his *Letter on Humanism* as a 'turning' (*die Kehre*).[36] He now claimed that he had placed too much emphasis on the relation of Dasein to Being, and that in reality Being itself without Dasein must be at the centre of thinking. Ontology was no longer the right way of approaching this Being; indeed the very term 'Being' needed to be elided, put in quotation marks, crossed out, a practice he announced in his 1955 essay "Zur Seinsfrage" ("On The Question of Being", *Pathmarks*, p. 291; GA 9, p. 385). Heidegger began to explore Nietzsche, Hölderlin, and other poetic thinkers whose 'saying' (*die Sage*) of Being lay outside technical philosophical discourse.

In later years Heidegger wrote some extraordinary essays on the nature of language, whereby he sees things coming to appearance in language (e.g. PLT 146). More and more Heidegger saw in poetic saying (*Dichtung*) a revelation of the truth of Being which is obscured and distorted by the metaphysical tradition of the West which had culminated in a kind of global nihilism. The essence of this nihilism was such that there was no longer even the promise of a new age or the memory of a more authentic experience of Being. Friedrich Nietzsche, Friedrich Hölderlin, and Ernst Jünger were Heidegger's guides to this 'dark time'. In fact, many of Heidegger's later accounts of technological society were based on his reading of the popular German author, and Nazi supporter, Ernst Jünger, especially his novel *The Worker* (*Der Arbeiter*). In the 1930s, Heidegger seemed to have been struck by the theme of the *deus absconditus*, the absent God, and to begin to consider seriously the nature of a world from which the gods had fled. This led him to think seriously about the nature of the Greek gods, inspired by Walter Otto's studies and by Hölderlin's poetry. Heidegger gradually moved away from his concerns with fundamental ontology and existential analytics and into a quasi-mythopoeic reflection on the nature of the fundamental elements which go to make up the human world. Heidegger's thinking now talked of 'mortals' and 'gods' and spoke of a 'fourfold' (*das Geviert*) of earth, sky, mortals, and gods, especially in the essay "Bauen, Wohnen, Denken" ("Building, Dwelling, Thinking"), originally given as a lecture in 1951.[37] Some see Heidegger here as fully shedding his earlier attempts to think through the inheritance of Christianity and embracing a new paganism. Others see Heidegger as attempting, like Hölderlin and Nietzsche, to think through the nature of a world from which both the Christian God and the Greek gods have withdrawn. Indeed, Heidegger writes of a time of darkness when the gods have withdrawn. He is very much echoing Nietzsche's enigmatic exclamation – "2000 years and not a new God!" Through the 1930s Heidegger embarked on his major interpretation of Nietzsche's philosophy, but he also developed something of a sense of historical destiny which led to his dabbling in the dangerous politics of the Third Reich. But Heidegger's meditations on the failure of the divine to reveal itself, and the advent of nihilism, gradually gave way to a kind of resignation before the withdrawal of Being itself. However, before Heidegger moved to this resignation, he struggled to assert his will over this withdrawal, to set out the possibility of a genuine act of creation, a reinvigorated *poeisis*.

Heidegger's political years 1933–1945

While Heidegger had always been academically ambitious, in the late 1920s he began to harbour political ambitions. He strongly sympathised with the emerging National Socialist programme for a renewal and reconstruction of Germany. He wrote approvingly of the Nazis in correspondence with Bultmann from 1928 to 1932. Hannah Arendt commented, much later, that only someone who had never read *Mein Kampf* could equate Nazism with a struggle against technological mass society, but others have argued that Heidegger had in fact read *Mein Kampf* as early as 1928 at the behest of his wife Elfride who was an ardent supporter of Nazism. Indeed, on 26 May 1933 Heidegger had invoked the notion of the hero taken from *Mein Kampf* in his public speech in praise of the former Conradihaus graduate and Freiburg student Albert Leo Schlageter (1894–1923) on the tenth anniversary of his death.[38] Schlageter, who had been shot by the French in May 1923 for participating in acts of sabotage against the French occupying forces in the Ruhr after the First World War, had been made into a Nazi hero, and Heidegger wrote a tribute to him in the Freiburg Student Newspaper stating that Schlageter had placed "before his soul an image of the future awakening of the people to honor and greatness so that he could die believing in this future".[39] Heidegger also co-operated with the Nazi philosopher Ernst Krieck.

Heidegger wrote several articles calling for a revolution in the universities to match the National Socialist revolution. Here he criticises the old liberal view of the university, attacks academic freedom and research for its own sake, and instead recommends that universities rise to the challenge of producing leaders of the new revolution by requiring studies to serve the will of the people. Heidegger supported the concept of students performing labour service as well as studying. He organised youth camps which were quite militarist and was among the first in Freiburg University to introduce the Nazi greeting. Heidegger gave a number of Nazi propaganda talks in this period, urging people to choose Hitler as the only salvation for the Germans. It is true, however, that Heidegger never approved of the Nazi preoccupation with pseudo-sciences based on race, and, indeed, in 1934 the Nazi philosopher Krieck attacked Heidegger in a Nazi journal as a nihilist with no thought for nation or race. In fact, in his lectures Heidegger frequently mocked so-called biologism and the pseudo-science of race. Heidegger was, however, anti-Semitic in the usual casual way – continuing to believe after the war that the world's media were dominated by Jews and, according to his friend Petzet, being a country man was unaccustomed to Jewish cosmopolitan culture.[40] Heidegger not only made no defence when Husserl was stripped of his official title by Freiburg University but actually signed the official letter requiring that non-Aryans be retired from the University.[41] He did not attend Husserl's funeral in Freiburg in 1938, later claiming he was ill at the time. He did, however, refuse to dismiss some Jewish lecturers in Freiburg, but, possibly, more out of fear of international repercussion than from any moral principle.[42] Heidegger was judged by the Nazi leaders to be operating with a "private" notion of National Socialism and was no longer trusted after the mid-1930s. In fact, he was even under investigation by the authorities.

Heidegger's political ambitions were fuelled when he was elected Rektor of Freiburg University on 22 April 1933, chosen by his colleagues in part because they thought he could guide the University through troubling times. In his infamous Rectoral Address (*Rektoratsrede*), "The Self-Assertion of the German University", he pledged the University's allegiance to Hitler and to the cause of National Socialism.[43] Heidegger was effectively endorsing the Nazi programme of *Gleichschaltung*, which was seeking to reorganise university studies to mirror National Socialist doctrine, with its burning of Jewish texts and organised witch-hunts of left-wing lecturers and students.

On 1 May 1933 Heidegger voluntarily and very publicly joined the Nazi Party, and immediately became deeply involved in the Nazification of the University, including introducing the *Führerprinzip* whereby future rectors of the University would be appointed directly by Berlin (a move which the former Rektor, Sauer, saw as the end of the University).[44] On 20 May 1933 Heidegger sent Hitler a telegram announcing the "alignment" (*Gleichschaltung*) of the University with the National Socialist Party.[45] Similarly, as Rector, he wrote several articles and made several addresses to appeal to the German people to support the plebiscite to ratify *ex post facto* Hitler's withdrawal of Germany from the League of Nations.[46]

In his Rectoral Address, Heidegger pours scorn on the traditional liberal notion of academic freedom, and reinterprets freedom as placing oneself under a duty to further the spiritual mission of the German people through 'labour service' (*Arbeitsdienst*), 'armed service' (*Wehrdienst*), and the 'service of knowledge' (*Wissensdienst*). The background assumption is that Europe is in a state of nihilism. As Nietzsche had claimed, God is dead. The Germans must again – like the ancient Greeks – recover their essence. Karl Jaspers wrote to Heidegger in August 1933 praising the talk as the only real document testifying to the "present-day academic will".[47] Nevertheless, Heidegger stopped visiting Jaspers after 1933 and after 1938 stopped acknowledging Jaspers' letters. After 1933 Jaspers was excluded from proper participation in his university, in 1937 he was dismissed from his professorship, and in 1938 banned from publishing.[48] In his 1936 lectures on Nietzsche Heidegger dismissed Jaspers as no longer asking philosophical questions (Ott, p. 32).

Though Heidegger later, in self-exculpatory notes, claimed to have attempted to prevent the worst excesses of Nazism from taking hold in Freiburg University, nevertheless, as Rector, he presided over some scandalous events. He refused to direct the dissertations of Jewish students and tried to force changes in the academic organisation of departments in the University. His defence (that things would have been worse had he not stayed in control and that he had been prevailed on to take the Rectorship to protect the University) is disingenuous. His almost pathological hatred of anything American was manifest in his denunciation of a philosophy lecturer, Eduard Baumgarten, who was interested in American pragmatism and had spent time in the USA.[49] Heidegger interfered in the University in many ways, and not just in the period when he was Rector. He denounced other professors to the Gestapo, including the Professor of Chemistry, Hermann Staudinger, and prevented Max Müller from being appointed to a lectureship in Freiburg in 1938, because of his political antipathy to the Nazi regime. Nevertheless, Heidegger resigned the Rectorship after nine months in April 1934 out of frustration due to the opposition he was experiencing to his plans to revolutionise the University, though later he would claim it was due to his difficulties with the Nazis. He continued to lecture in philosophy until the end of the war and continued his membership of the Nazi Party. In his post-war defence, Heidegger claimed he had not worn Nazi uniform but, when he visited a former student, the exiled Jewish philosopher Karl Löwith, in Rome in 1936, where he gave his famous lecture on "Hölderlin and the Essence of Poetry", he wore the Nazi insignia.[50] In 1930 and again in 1933 Heidegger was invited to take up a chair of philosophy in Berlin but each time he refused and published his reasons in a popular article "Why we remain in the Provinces" (*Warum bleiben wir in der Provinz*), published in *Der Alemanne* on 7 March 1934, which extolled the virtues of peasant life over life in the big city.

In 1935 Heidegger gave a course, *Introduction to Metaphysics*,[51] where he developed his thinking about the nature of being through a reflection on the basic Greek concepts – *ousia, physis*, and so on. Heidegger always presents the present age as being in a crisis with regard to its levelled-out diminished understanding of these fundamental Greek concepts. Heidegger, through a kind of etymological unpacking of the key words of Greek philosophy, introduces a new way of thinking about Being. The Greek word for Being is now *physis* understood as "self-blossoming emergence". The translation of these Greek words into Latin loses their original revelatory power and "marks the first stage in the process by which we cut ourselves off and alienated ourselves from the original essence of Greek philosophy" (IM, p. 11; 10–11). Heidegger's focus is now on the nature of the disclosure of Being. Here Heidegger is already exploring his later view that the revelation of Being takes place in (and also can be concealed by) language: "It is in words and language that things first come into being and are" (IM, p. 11; 11).

Towards the end of the lecture course Heidegger equated the threats from the Stalinist Soviet Union and from the USA as two great levellers of genuine civilisation and saw National Socialism and Germany's mission to become a new force saving the cultural heritage of Europe against these twin threats. Heidegger's remarks about the "inner truth and greatness" (*innere Wahrkeit und Größe*) of the National Socialist movement as consisting in "the encounter between global technology and modern man" (*mit der Begegnung der planetarisch bestimmten Technik und des neuzeitlichen Menschen*, IM,

p. 166; 152) were left unchanged when the lectures were published in 1953. When the 24-year-old Jürgen Habermas reviewed this book in the *Frankfurter Allgemeine Zeitung* on 25 July 1953, he found Heidegger's remarks on National Socialism, published on the fiftieth anniversary of Hitler's accession to power, to be deeply disturbing, all the more so because of a lack of accompanying apology or explanation.[52] Heidegger defended himself in a letter to *Die Zeit* on 24 September 1953, saying that he wanted to respect the original text of his lectures: "the sentence historically belongs to the lecture".[53] It is certainly true that in this period Heidegger, like many Germans, saw Nazism as a bulwark against the Soviet Union and the USA, both forms of nihilism in Heidegger's view. Thus, in 1936 in his lecture course on Schelling, Heidegger portrayed Hitler and Mussolini as opponents of nihilism. In his 1942 lectures on Hölderlin's Hymn "Der Ister" he portrays the USA as the very essence of levelling, nihilism, and ahistoricality whose entry into the war after Pearl Harbor was "the ultimate American act of American ahistoricality and self-devastation" and indeed the USA sought nothing less than the destruction of Europe.[54] Heidegger seems gradually to have shifted in his analysis of nihilism. Jürgen Habermas is undoubtedly correct when he diagnoses Heidegger's reaction to his own disillusionment with the Nazi revolution as an attempt to shift the focus onto world history and to see fascism as part of the global technologisation of the planet.[55] But, on the other hand, Heidegger seems to have gone beyond the decisionism of *Being and Time* by the time he was giving the "On the Essence of Truth" lecture in 1930. Here and elsewhere, though Heidegger characterises truth as possible through human freedom, he interprets human freedom radically as a 'letting be' (*Seinlassen*, *Pathmarks*, p. 144; GA 9, p. 188). It is, therefore, difficult to offer an unambiguous interpretation of the philosophical reasons for Heidegger's dalliance with the Nazis.

During the Second World War, Heidegger published just three short essays: an essay "Plato's Doctrine of Truth" in 1942;[56] a pamphlet on Hölderlin's poem, "When on a feast day...", in 1941; and the very powerful essay "On the Essence of Truth" (originally delivered as a lecture to the monks of Beuron Abbey in 1930) in 1943.[57] Meanwhile, his lectures concentrated on Nietzsche whom he saw as the philosopher who most understood and exemplified the nihilism which currently beset the world. In some of these lectures Heidegger now portrays fascism and world war as just another symptom of the world-wide "will to will" which had overtaken Western history. Thus he comments (possibly on Hitler's proclamation of a thousand-year Reich):

> It is one thing when empires endure for millennia because of their continuing stability. It is something else when world dominions are knowingly planned to last millennia and the assurance of their existence is undertaken by that will whose essential goal is the greatest

possible duration of the greatest possible order of the largest possible masses.[58]

Heidegger now saw Germany itself as exemplifying the total domination of technology which he had previously attributed to the Soviet Union and the USA. He began to conceive of the whole age as dominated by technology and hence as characterised by a 'retreat' of Being.

In October 1944 Heidegger was conscripted into the *Volksturm* (Civil Defence) – as was Gadamer – but again was allowed to return to Freiburg to rescue his manuscripts "for the future of the German people". Towards the end of the war he and the rest of the Philosophy Faculty were evacuated from Freiburg and went to live in the Upper Danube valley near Wildenstein Castle where they continued to hold classes until June 1945 when Heidegger delivered a last lecture on Hölderlin and the Greeks (Ott, p. 305). As Germany yielded to the Allied advance, Freiburg was occupied by French forces, who began a de-Nazification process. Heidegger was charged with being a Nazi and engaging in Nazi propaganda, accused of introducing the *Führerprinzip*, and inciting students against professors not favourable to the regime. Heidegger wrote a self-exculpating account of his life during the Nazi years claiming that he had been investigated by the Nazis and prohibited from travelling abroad. This, of course, was not true, as he had been to Rome in 1936. He also claimed he never wore the Nazi insignia nor commenced his lectures with the Nazi salute, both of which are demonstrably false.[59] The Denazification Committee of Freiburg University found Heidegger guilty of having "consciously placed the full weight of his academic reputation and the distinctive art of his oratory in the service of the National Socialist revolution, and thereby did a great deal to justify this revolution in the eyes of educated Germans" (Ott, p. 327). Heidegger's Nazi associations led him to being forbidden to teach (stripped of his *venia legenda*), and banned from the University for five years, but he was spared any real disciplining because of the support of Jaspers who wrote a letter critical of him, stating that Heidegger "became an anti-Semite, at least in certain contexts" and that he had, as an academic, helped to advance National Socialism as did Alfred Baümler and Carl Schmitt. On the other hand, Jaspers acknowledged Heidegger's greatness as a philosopher, though here too he sees Heidegger as sometimes combining "the seriousness of nihilism with the mystagogy of a magician".[60] Jaspers' recommendation, which seemed to have influenced the Denazification Committee, was that Heidegger be permitted to continue philosophical research but not to resume his Chair or his teaching duties.

The turn towards art as the revealing of truth

Shortly after his Rectoral debacle, Heidegger was back lecturing and at the very height of his powers. Heidegger's new orientation was very well expressed in the lectures he gave in 1935 and 1936 on *The Origin of the Work of Art*. These lectures caused a controversy at the time in Switzerland with some critics noting their closeness to the Nazi rhetoric of "blood and soil" (*Blut und Boden*) and the linking of art to the historical destiny of a people.[61] A distilled version of these lectures was the essay *The Origin of the Work of Art*, first published in 1950 in *Holzwege*.[62] This essay sets out Heidegger's interests in a number of striking ways. In one sense, the essay takes the form of a critique of Kantian aesthetics, by emphasising the ontological character of the art work. Heidegger, in examining the special ontological status of art works, is also rethinking Aristotle's approach to things in terms of the form–matter composition, or as a subject (*hypokeimenon, subjectum*) with accidents, as well as the Neo-Kantian conception of the thing as grasped by sensations in sensibility, combined with the transcendental objectifying structures of subjectivity. Heidegger claims that traditional philosophical approaches have obscured and distorted our understanding of things, levelling down what is pre-conceptually grasped when we encounter a thing, a piece of equipment, or work:

> Thus it comes about that prevailing thing-concepts obstruct the way towards the thingly character of the thing as well as toward the equipmental character of equipment, and all the more towards the workly character of the work.
>
> (PLT 31)

A radical rethinking of the nature of a *thing* (*pragma, res, Ding*) is required. The traditional ontology which thinks of things in terms of form and matter itself springs from human familiarity with equipment, but the nature of equipment itself is manifest not through equipment but through the art work. Thus Van Gogh's painting of a pair of peasant shoes reveals the equipment both as belonging to the *earth* and as "protected in the *world* of the peasant woman" (PLT 34). Works of art are privileged things, things which *work* on us, setting truth to work, disclosing the truth of things, disclosing the *world* in which things manifest themselves and the *earth* which draws them back into itself. Heidegger here talks of works of art in terms of the notions of *world* and *earth*, giving a glimpse of his later use of the notion of a four-fold framework (*das Geviert*) of earth, sky, gods, mortals, terms which in quasi-mythological terms call attention to fundamental features of human 'dwelling' (*wohnen*) where humans live in a tension between mortality and immortality, revelation and withdrawal. For Heidegger, with reference to Van Gogh's painting, "the art work lets us know what shoes are in truth" (PLT 35). For Heidegger, in a work of art, truth has set itself to work. But truth here cannot be thought in terms of some kind of *adequatio* between the art work and the thing it represents; rather in art there is an original happening of truth. This allows Heidegger to understand true art in terms of its *act of creative founding*, what the Greeks called *poeisis*.

A Greek temple or sculpture, a poem, even the founding of a *polis* or state, release truth into the world and in doing so set forth a world and set it forth on an earth which always resists and withdraws. Genuine art founds world, for Heidegger. Art here no longer carries a purely aesthetic meaning but can be used for any original action including the political act of founding a state. Heidegger is thinking of the foundation of the Greek *polis* and possibly also of the new German Reich, as a poetic event, a setting into work of truth. Truth here is an event of Being, *Ereignis*.

Heidegger's later philosophy

Most of Heidegger's later philosophy is an attempt to express the complex revealing–concealing nature of this *Ereignis*. Thus, from 1936 to 1938, Heidegger composed a set of private reflections, published posthumously in 1989 as *Beiträge zur Philosophie* (*Contributions to Philosophy*, GA 65) which some commentators, notably Otto Pöggeler, have claimed as Heidegger's most important work after *Being and Time*. These obscure reflections on the nature of Being (now written with the old German spelling, *Seyn*) attempt to characterise the nature of its withdrawing and appearing, and the nature of the 'event' (*Ereignis*), and also include discussions on the nature of time and of the gods, especially the nature of 'the last god' (*der letzte Gott*), a figure drawn from Nietzsche. This book, though important for under-standing Heidegger's later thinking, is too complex to be considered here.

While Heidegger remained under a cloud in Germany through the late 1940s and 1950s, his thought was beginning to have an impact in France. Heidegger felt that he was appreciated in France even as his own country-men were turning against him (Ott, p. 17). In 1947 Heidegger wrote his famous *Letter on Humanism*, in the form of a letter replying to Jean Beaufret.[63] This essay is more or less a direct reply to Sartre's 1945 essay "Existentialism is a humanism", and as a result became hugely influential in France. Heidegger's critique of humanism as a metaphysical concept and his displacement of man in favour of Being played a significant role in the emergence of anti-humanism in recent French thought (e.g. in Foucault, Lacan, and Derrida, among others). In this letter Heidegger repudiates various traditional forms of humanism (Roman, Marxist, etc.) as not grasping the highest nature of human being. Humanisms remain metaphysi-cal concepts whereas Heidegger wants a thinking which is a thinking of Being. Being appears through humankind, humankind is "the shepherd of Being" and "language is the house of Being" (*Die Sprache is das Haus des Seins*; *Pathmarks*, p. 239; GA 9, p. 313). Human existence is really an 'ek-sistence' which Heidegger explicates as standing in the "clearing of Being" (*Pathmarks*, p. 247; GA 9, pp. 323–324). In this essay, Heidegger speaks of the need for an "other thinking which abandons subjectivity" in order to think Being (*Pathmarks*, p. 249; GA 9, p. 327).

Meanwhile, between 1945 and 1950, Heidegger found audiences by delivering occasional lectures to a businessmen's club in Bremen organised by his friend, the wealthy businessman Heinrich Petzet, as well as lecturing to the Bavarian Academy of Fine Arts in Munich and to the Hölderlin Society. In 1950 the University of Freiburg restored his right to teach and he returned to hold seminars there, but he was never restored to his Chair which went to Werner Marx who had returned from the USA. Later his former student and friend Hans-Georg Gadamer was responsible for having Heidegger elected to the Heidelberg Academy.

Heidegger published an important collection of essays *Holzwege* in 1950. *Holzwege* are woodcutters' paths, paths which go into a forest and dead-end there. The term is suggestive of the Greek term *aporiai*, blockages. But frequently, these paths end in a clearing, and Heidegger constantly speaks of the lighting or clearing of Being. In this and in his later collections of essays, *Vorträge und Aufsätze* (Lectures and Essays), *Erläuterungen zur Hölderlins Dichtung*, *On the Way to Language* (*Unterwegs zur Sprache*), and *Pathmarks* (*Wegmarken*), Heidegger became more and more preoccupied with the future of Western and world culture which had been dominated by technology and to which the only opposition appears to be a kind of poetic speaking.

Heidegger had already began to meditate on the nature of this technologisation of nature in his 1937 essay "The Age of the World-Picture" (*Zeit des Weltbildes*). His 1953 lecture to the Bavarian Academy, *Die Frage nach der Technik* (*The Question Concerning Technology*), is perhaps the apex of his assessment of the new technological, global culture and this essay has been hugely influential in the philosophy of technology and in the development of eco-philosophy. Heidegger's obsession with the 'framework' (*die Stelle, das Gestell*) of technological society was such that, in a lecture on *Das Gestell* that he delivered in Bremen in 1949, an earlier version of *The Question Concerning Technology*, he notoriously claimed that the organisation of concentration camps was not different in kind to the mechanisation of agricultural production:

> Agriculture is now a motorised food-industry – in essence the same as the manufacturing of corpses in gas chambers and extermination camps, the same as the blockading and starving of nations, the same as the manufacture of hydrogen bombs.[64]

Heidegger's moral equation of the genocide against the Jews with mass production farming techniques outraged those who had hoped that Heidegger – who had remained silent about the fate of the Jews – had actually repented of his earlier allegiance to Nazism.[65] In fact, Heidegger remained oblivious to the lack of comparability between the Holocaust and

217

other horrific events, other than to acknowledge privately a certain 'stupidity' (*Dummheit*) on his part. Thus, when in 1947 Herbert Marcuse visited Heidegger in Todtnauberg seeking some words to explain why Heidegger had chosen to remain silent on the Jews, Heidegger replied by comparing their fate with that of the East Germans under the occupying Allied forces. Heidegger had dreamed of becoming the philosopher of the New Reich and was even invited to Berlin by Hitler, but he became disillusioned with public life and retreated to his mountain hut in Todtnauberg. Heidegger had sought the approval of tyrants, which Hannah Arendt later compared with Plato's journey to Syracuse to assist the tyrant Dion.[66]

Heidegger's later work concentrated on the nature of poetic 'saying' (*die Sage*), the task of announcing Being, or even showing up the withdrawal of Being, which gets covered up in ordinary and technical forms of speaking. Much of this later saying is almost tautological. His meditation on the nature of language shows that "language speaks" (*die Sprache spricht*), the essence of a thing is 'to thing' (*Das ding dingt*), nothing nothings, the world worlds, and so on. In part, this 'tautological' approach to the essential insights is deeply phenomenological. After all the aim of phenomenology is to let something show itself as it is. But it is deeply frustrating, as we are rarely allowed to pass beyond the essential concepts, to attempt to express their meaning in other ways. Rather, later Heideggerian thinking operates in a repetitive, incantatory way; like a bell tolling, it echoes the same sound over again but with a deepening effect.

Heidegger continued to philosophise through meditations on the German romantic poets, especially Hölderlin but also on Trakl. These poets are seen as somehow expressive of the nature of poetry itself. Hölderlin is the poet of poetry, of the essence of poetry. The essence of poetry is understood as *naming*, bringing something to revelation in language. In 1955 he gave a talk on 'letting be', invoking the German mystic Meister Eckhart's notion of *Gelassenheit* ('letting be' or 'releasement'). Heidegger had a deep interest in Eckhart from his youth, and more and more came to understand the relation to Being as a kind of passive 'letting be'. Letting be involves a kind of detachment and 'releasement' which allows the essence of Being to shine through.

Heidegger's later contributions took the form of occasional pieces. In 1955 he paid his first visit to France to deliver the lecture "What is Philosophy?" in Cérisy. In 1949 Heidegger began holding seminars with psychoanalysts in Zurich at the invitation of his friend, the psychoanalyst Medard Boss. In 1962 Heidegger gave a radio talk, *On Time and Being*, which attempted to complete the work announced in *Being and Time* by reversing the emphasis. As Heidegger said: "We want to say something about the attempt to think Being without regard to its being grounded in terms of beings" (OTB 2). In 1966 Heidegger gave an interview to the German news magazine *Der Spiegel*, with the stipulation that it not be published until after his death. Heidegger died on 26 May 1976 and *Der Spiegel* published the interview five days later.[67] This interview reopened many of the issues surrounding Heidegger's involvement with the Nazis and analysts of the interview have demonstrated that Heidegger is somewhat economical with the truth regarding this involvement. In the course of the interview, Heidegger also talked about the threat of mass technological society and expressed the view that "only a god can save us now" (*nur noch ein Gott kann uns retten*), giving rise to much discussion about the religious nature of Heidegger's later thought. Heidegger was given a Christian burial in Messkirch and the oration at the graveside was given by his friend, Fr Bernhard Welte.

Heidegger's complete works, *Gesamtausgabe*, are currently being produced in over eighty projected volumes, but the manner in which they are being edited, and the many factual errors of dating, and so on, have led to considerable criticism from scholars.[68] Heidegger claimed his writings were 'not works but paths' (*Wege nicht Werke*), invoking his favourite metaphor of forest paths. It is claimed that Heidegger wanted the works to be published as they left his own hand (*Ausgabe letster Hand*), a way which does not meet with the standards of a critical edition, but even this claim is disputed by some Heidegger experts who state that he left no such instruction. Nevertheless, these works, containing the texts of his lecture courses over a lifetime, often compiled with cross-references to his students' lecture notes, though flawed, help to shed enormous light on Heidegger's intellectual journey – especially during the years leading up to *Being and Time* and throughout the 1930s when his thought was in crisis.

The political implications of Heidegger's philosophy

The argument over Heidegger's involvement with the Nazis has spawned an enormous literature. The tension between the *ontological* analysis and the emphasis on engaging with *history* in order to make for an authentic life had already been noticed by earlier reviewers of *Being and Time*, notably Helmut Plessner and Georg Misch. Karl Löwith, Hannah Arendt, and Herbert Marcuse had been early diagnosticians of the dangers in Heidegger's political thinking. The controversy was given a new impetus in Germany and France (and later in the USA) with the publication of Victor Farias's *Heidegger et le nazisme* in 1987[69] which has led to an enormous commentary, from Derrida and Lyotard to Levinas and to German philosophers and historians, including Gadamer and Ott, all seeking to put Heidegger's political acts in perspective and in particular questioning the effect of his political decisions on his philosophy. Farias was not bringing out new material; the essential German documents had been published by Schneeberger as early as 1962.[70] But Farias's book offered a strong interpretation of the connection between Heidegger's cultural outlook and his involvement with Nazism and brought this to the attention of a philosophical public (especially in France), which had previously clearly sought to ignore Heidegger's Nazi past. Farias's thesis is that Heidegger's involvement with the Nazis, far from being a short dalliance, was actually the culmination of his intellectual and cultural upbringing, with its conservatism and anti-Semitism. According to Farias:

> Heidegger's decision to join the NSDAP was in no way the result of unexpected opportunism or tactical considerations. The decision was clearly linked with his having already acted in a way consonant with National Socialism prior to becoming rector of the University of Freiburg and with his actual political practices as rector and member of the party.
>
> (Farias, p. 4)

It is not enough to simply say that Heidegger as a man was flawed and that his philosophy should be treated on its own merits. The relationship between Heidegger's philosophy of human engagement in *Being and Time* and his later political stance needs to be reassessed. Heidegger's philosophical path set out to be deliberately engaged with the concrete decisions involved in our day-to-day existence, seeking to raise our existence up to a more authentic level, to 'seize the time', as it were. While it is true that Levinas, Marcuse, and others in 1928 read *Being and Time* with no inkling of the political engagement of Heidegger's later thought in the 1930s, on the other hand, close inspection of the political implications of the account of human existence in *Being and Time* makes clear that its empty decisionism is totally open to being interpreted in the National Socialist cause.

While the political implications of the analysis of human existence (Dasein) in *Being and Time* are quite relevant for the assessment of Heidegger's subsequent engagement with Nazism, it would be a mistake to dismiss his philosophical contribution to ontology, phenomenology, and so on, on the grounds of his personal, shameful activities. Heidegger himself emphasised the importance of the *work* and not the individual in his own readings of the philosophers of the past. Thus, for instance, Frege's anti-Semitism should not distract us from his real contributions to logic.[71] What is challenging in Heidegger's case is to read critically his account of human destiny, of fate, of choosing a hero in *Being and Time*, and also to align his penetrating critique of global technologisation with his silence regarding the Holocaust. Though Heidegger may have been rather mean-spirited as a person and, at the very least, did not resist the terrible things that were happening under the Nazis, in this latter respect he is no different from many others in Germany at that time. In terms of the political philosophy implicit in *Being and Time*, it is by no means a blueprint for Nazism but it does encourage people to 'choose a hero', to engage in 'struggle' (*Kampf*), and to commit themselves to loyal following (Heidegger's model here is a kind of secularised Christianity); and these could indeed serve as vehicles for a submission to following the German Führer as Heidegger himself advocated in his Rectoral Address of 1933. There is no doubt that Heidegger for a time fancied himself as the intellectual voice of the National Socialist revolution, and as the diagnostician of the fate of the West. His entirely unrealistic conception of his own role as a leader, or even as a prophet, in matters political means that much of his rhetoric about destiny and fate cannot be taken seriously.

Putting to one side Heidegger's association with the Nazis, we shall now turn to a closer analysis of *Being and Time* and specifically its contribution to phenomenology.

7

HEIDEGGER'S *BEING AND TIME*

Introduction: the road to *Being and Time*

Being and Time is a radical attempt to rethink traditional philosophical approaches to human beings, to Being, to time and history, and, of course, to the history of philosophy itself. The book aims to be both an a priori transcendental phenomenological description of the essential structure of human existence, Dasein, and an appreciation of the temporal, cultural, and the dispersed nature of human historicality. Somehow, Heidegger saw all of these problems as capable of being clarified through a phenomenological approach, although, now, an approach which he had to some extent forged by himself. For, by the time of writing *Being and Time*, he had come to view Husserlian phenomenology as yet another project of idealist philosophy which had got lost from the essential historicity of human nature. As he says in his 1962 letter to William Richardson:

> Meanwhile "phenomenology" in Husserl's sense was elaborated into a distinctive philosophical position according to a pattern set by Descartes, Kant and Fichte. The historicity of thought remained completely foreign to such a position...The Being-question, unfolded in *Being and Time*, parted company with this philosophical position, and that on the basis of what to this day I still consider a more faithful adherence (*sachgerechteren Festhaltens*) to the principle of phenomenology.
>
> (Richardson, pp. xiv–xv)

The complex nature of Heidegger's *Being and Time* has confused many readers. In this chapter we shall attempt to sketch some of its main preoccupations and trace these discussions to their origins in phenomenology. Heidegger's whole architectonic in the book has obscured the mode of its development. However, in recent years, with the publication of Heidegger's massive writings, and a number of exegetical studies, we have come to a better understanding of the development of *Being and Time*. In terms of the evolution of Heidegger's problematic, I shall simply point here to three stages along the way. First is Heidegger's engagement with *Lebensphilosophie* which comes to a head in his critique of Jaspers' philosophy. Second is Heidegger's engagement with Aristotle; and third, Heidegger's engagement with Husserl. I shall discuss each of these stages in the following sections.

The review of Karl Jaspers' *Psychology of World Views* (*c.* 1921)

An important text indicating Heidegger's early concerns is his unpublished review of Karl Jaspers' book *The Psychology of World Views*, written some time before 1921.[1] Around 1919 Heidegger had become friendly with Karl Jaspers, a psychiatrist turned existentialist and one of the foremost figures in German philosophy.

In his review of Jaspers, Heidegger rejects as pointless the criticism of philosophical standpoints which have rigidified into a degenerate tradition, and instead appeals for a rethinking of the original motivational experiences which gave rise to philosophy in the first place (*Pathmarks*, p. 3; GA 9, p. 3). He criticises *Lebensphilosophie* for its shallow approach to the spontaneity of life, and for not possessing the concepts it needs to interrogate properly the phenomenon of life. In this review, furthermore, Heidegger claims to be adopting a phenomenological account, but one whose claim to "presuppositionlessness" really meant that all intuition must be "enacted in the context of a definite orientation and an anticipatory preconception" of the particular region of experience (*Pathmarks*, p. 4; GA 9, pp. 4–5). He speaks of a radical "destruction" (*Destruktion, Abbau*) and "reconstruction" (*Rückbau*) in trying to get to the things themselves while acknowledging their embeddedness in history. This involves taking up one's past historically and projecting ahead in a concernful manner; it is the "how" (*Wie*) of human existence (*Dasein*). Human existence cannot be approached directly; indeed the phenomenon is even distorted when we attempt to reflect on it. The concept of what 'is' is usually taken from the theoretical standpoint, but in my 'factical' existence I have experiences which appear to me in my own way. Heidegger had borrowed the term 'factical' (*faktisch*) and 'facticity' (*die Faktizität*) from the Neo-Kantians to express the particular, concrete, inescapably contingent, yet worldly, involved aspect of human existence in contrast to the 'factual' nature of inanimate existence (see BT § 12, 82; 56). My sense of existence comes from the acts about which I have "anxious concern" (*Bekümmerung, Pathmarks*, p. 28; GA 9, p. 32). In acts of conscience and self-appropriation I renew my self-concern. Furthermore, reflection on experience means grasping its essential temporality, and the past and future cannot be understood if they are thought of as mere appendages around the present moment (*Pathmarks*, p. 27; GA 9, p. 32). My self-understanding requires a hermeneutical, historical mode of approach which cannot be universalised. The challenge for phenomenology is to avoid becoming a sterile dogmatism and to grasp the 'how' of our "factical, historically enacted life" (*Pathmarks*, pp. 30–31; GA 9, p. 36).

One can see from this early review that Heidegger had already sketched his main framework for the existential analysis of Dasein. Furthermore, Heidegger is not only criticising Jaspers' life philosophy, but also critical of the way phenomenology had developed. Thus, he wrote to Karl Löwith in 1923, stating in blunt terms that he was now convinced that Husserl had never been a philosopher and that he, Heidegger, was now "wringing his neck".[2] Similarly he wrote to Jaspers that Husserl had fallen apart and that no one now knew what phenomenology was supposed to be (*Briefwechsel* V 42).

Heidegger's goal at this stage, early in the 1920s, is what he calls a 'hermeneutics of factical life', a self-interpretation of the irreducible structures of life. His approach to phenomenology now sees it as a way of rethinking the basic motivation and nature of early Christian religion; thus, in his analysis of factical life he draws on the writings of St Paul, Augustine, Luther, and Kierkegaard. He chooses the term "factical life" to emphasise the contingent nature of human existence, but also its concreteness, its factuality, its singularity, and indeed its opacity. In Neo-Kantian thought, facticity was usually contrasted with validity, *Geltung*. Human existence is preoccupied with meaning, as is shown by the fundamental structures of human 'concern' and 'care'.[3] Furthermore, human existence involves special ways of relating to time. He singles out the attitude to time in early Christian thought, especially the Pauline notion of the transformation of time (*Zeit, chronos*) into the *kairos* (*Augenblick*, transfiguring moment). According to Paul, the day of the Lord will come like a thief in the night and at that moment (*kairos*) there is the need for Christians to be awake (Paul, I Thesallonians 5: 1–2).

Heidegger's 1920–1921 lecture course, entitled "Introduction to the Phenomenology of Religion", concentrated on uncovering the existential structures of "the factical life-experience" (*die faktische Lebenserfahrung*) focusing especially on Paul's *Epistle to the Galatians* and his two *Epistles to the Thessalonians*, the two oldest Christian documents.[4] Philosophy itself is grounded in these life structures, which the Western tradition of philosophy since Socrates has forgotten, and so it remained unthematised. To gain proper access to life, a "transformation of philosophy" (*Umwandlung der Philosophie*) is needed, a return to what is primarily historical. We must uncover the manner in which living experience interacts with the 'environment' (*Umwelt*). The challenge of philosophy is to gain access to concrete factical life and to remain in the concrete. Heidegger is at this stage struggling to find concepts which appropriately articulate both the concrete particularity of living and its fluid, temporal, one could say 'narrative', nature. Heidegger's key terms are 'concern' (*Bekümmerung*) and 'self-concern' (*Sich-Bekümmerung*), which he takes to be the intrinsic meaning of Aristotle's notion of *phronesis*. In these lectures Heidegger is reinterpreting religious categories as fundamental existential structures. Heidegger conceives of God as given to the early Christians in the form of temporality and especially in a kind of eschatological presentness (*parousia*). Humans have to recover their essence by coming towards what they already are, embracing their finitude, being in a state of 'resolve' (*Entschlossenheit*) concerning their own deaths.

Heidegger's Aristotle interpretation (1922)

As we have seen Heidegger sent a draft of his Aristotle interpretation to Natorp as part of his application for the position in Marburg. Natorp eventually gave this text to Gadamer but it was destroyed in the bombing of Leipzig. However, another copy of this text has since been recovered.[5] This programmatic text, originally intended for publication in Husserl's *Jahrbuch*, is helpful for understanding Heidegger's intellectual progress, since it reads like a basic summary of *Being and Time*. According to this text, the chief problem of philosophy is the problem of gaining access to and interpreting the being of factical life. Philosophy is to be "principal ontology" (*prinzipielle Ontologie*), pursued through a "phenomenological hermeneutics of facticity". This enquiry is phenomenological in the sense of the breakthrough of the *Logical Investigations* (Aristotle text, p. 369); that is, it is not a matter of providing a phenomenological clarification of concepts which are then used in building up a separate science, rather the clarification of the concepts involves the revelation of the philosophical outlook as such. The fundamental philosophical concepts have been worn down and debased in the tradition, but they still retain a certain character of origin, which preserves their primordial meaning. Phenomenology must loosen up this encrusted tradition of concepts, carrying out a kind of "dismantling return" (*abbauende Rückgang*), a "destruction" (*Destruktion*) of these concepts. Philosophy is required to confront its tradition and carry out a "radical logic of origins". Something of the original authentic outlook, namely the Greek–Christian outlook, is still preserved in our basic concepts although hidden under this distorting tradition. In other words, Heidegger is proposing that we read our desire for authenticity guided by the original models for authenticity at the heart of what Heidegger runs together as "the Greek-Christian interpretation of life" (Aristotle text, p. 372). The focus of this exploration must be the being of human life and Aristotle's struggle to articulate this in the *Physics*, *Metaphysics*, and *Nicomachean Ethics*.

According to Heidegger's analysis, the basic structure of factical life is 'caring' (*Sorge, curare*) which involves 'circumspection' (*Umsicht*). Mostly humans are caught up in concern and in these dealings with the world are drawn into the world in a way which Heidegger characterises as "falling" (*Verfallen*). Life is such that it is difficult to bear and so it has an inbuilt tendency to make things easy for itself. In falling, humans live their concrete lives as 'one' ('*das Man*') lives, "bogged down in inauthentic tradition and habituation" (Aristotle text, p. 365):

> On account of its inclination towards falling, factical life lives for the most part in what is inauthentic, i.e. in what is handed down, in what is reported to it, in that which it appropriates in its aver-ageness.
>
> (Aristotle text, p. 369)

Death, for instance, is a feature of factical life, but one which gets covered up in our everyday "world-laden concerns". Nevertheless, death is also the phenomenon which makes the *temporality* (*Zeitlichkeit*) of our human existence manifest to us. As a current against this tendency to falling, there is the concern with *Existenz* which arises in humans from time to time, a questioning of life, a desire for authenticity, for making one's individual life fully one's own. It is clear that in this early text Heidegger is already mapping out the programme which first became public in *Being and Time*.

Heidegger's critical appropriation of Husserl

As we have seen, Heidegger's early formation was in theology, in scholastic philosophy, and in Neo-Kantianism, but he had also been reading Husserl from the beginning of his studies in Freiburg, though they did not meet until 1917, when Heidegger was already a young lecturer. Heidegger's *Habilitationschrift* on Thomas of Erfurt showed little trace of phenomenology, beyond some references to the phenomenological reduction, and a claim that the medievals had some phenomenological insights, though with no consciousness of method. Rather Heidegger seems to be primarily interested in medieval philosophy, and promises to write a book on Eckhart. However, when he returned to Freiburg to begin teaching in the spring of 1919, he had come to see himself primarily as a phenomenologist. Nevertheless, from the very beginning he forged his own path in phenomenology.

Heidegger, in common with many of Husserl's students, including Roman Ingarden, rejected Husserl's Cartesianism and transcendental idealism. In his own application of phenomenology, Heidegger profoundly altered Husserl's. He took his orientation from Husserl's *Logical Investigations*, even after the publication of *Ideas* I in 1913, though it is clear that he had access to the manuscript of *Ideas* II, and that many conceptions in his own work originate from that unpublished work of Husserl, especially the concepts of 'world' and 'environment' (*Umwelt*). Heidegger was especially interested in the Fifth and Sixth Logical Investigation, linking Husserl's enquiries in categorical intuition and his discussion of the recognition of truth with the problem of Being as explored by Brentano and Aristotle. Husserl's notion of categorial intuition was, for Heidegger, an attempt to think through Brentano's notion of the manifold meaning of Being. In fact, Heidegger frequently pressed Husserl to republish the Sixth Investigation, which he eventually did in 1922. In the Sixth Investigation Husserl had discussed categorial intuition, whereby we intuit directly the being or existence of a thing, though in a non-sensory manner. To use Husserl's example, when I see that "this paper is white" I have a sensuous intuition of the whiteness of the paper but I also grasp immediately in a non-sensuous intuition that the paper *is* white. This is, for Heidegger, the grasp of Being (*Sein*) which is given only because there are beings (*Seienden*). Nevertheless, grasping the elusive nature of Being is the primary task of philosophy.

For Heidegger, phenomenology is the attempt to make manifest the matters (*die Sachen selbst*) as they manifest themselves. As a radical allegiance to the things themselves, phenomenology can never be a single method. Thus, in his 1927 lecture course, *Basic Problems of Phenomenology*, Heidegger denies that phenomenology is a method in any specialised sense:

> There is no such thing as *the one* phenomenology, and if there could be such a thing it would never become anything like a philosophical technique. For implicit in the essential nature of all genuine method as a path towards the disclosure of objects is the tendency to order itself always toward that which it itself discloses.
> (BPP, § 22, p. 328; GA 24, p. 467)

From the beginning of his lecturing career in Freiburg, Heidegger resisted the Neo-Kantian and Husserlian view that philosophy was a rigorous science, and indeed he inclined more towards the views of Scheler, Bergson, and Jaspers that concrete human existence is not best approached in scientific terms. Concern with certainty was only an indication of one kind of concern. The basic state of Dasein's concern itself needed to be understood.

In *Being and Time* Heidegger drops all Husserl's central concepts: he no longer talks of consciousness, objectivity, directedness, the *noema*, *noesis*, the transcendental ego. He does not refer to the natural attitude, to the *epoché* and reduction, to the notion of constitution. Instead Heidegger wanted to employ phenomenology as the proper mode of access to the phenomena of concrete human life, factical life, as he had initially called it in his early lecture courses, a way of thinking about human nature that remained faithful to the *historical, lived,* practical nature of human experience. Here Heidegger invoked Bergson's, Scheler's and Dilthey's accounts of human life to overcome Husserl's predominantly *cognitive* approach to human being (see BT § 10). Whereas Husserl made cognition (*Erkenntnis*) the main connection between humans and the world, Heidegger, influenced by Augustine and also by Scheler, saw that humans are primarily caught up in living their lives, wrapped up in moods and emotional commitments, in cares and worries, falling into temptation, projecting themselves into possibilities, seeking to make themselves whole. Cognition and intellectual activity emerged out of the engaged structures of everyday life where we are on top of things, we are 'up for it', able to cope. Intellection and cognition are founded modes, knowing is a derivative mode of the being-in of Dasein, ontologically founded on Being-in-the-world (HCT § 20, 161; GA 20, p. 217).

Phenomenology, for Heidegger, leads to a new way of seeing rather than to a set of philosophical propositions. Heidegger claimed that what Husserl had given him was eyes with which to see. For Heidegger this 'seeing' meant doing away with all philosophical theories, whether idealist or realist, and cultivating a "pure naïveté" (HCT § 5, 39; GA 20, p. 51). When Heidegger read Husserl's 1911 essay "Philosophy as a Rigorous Science" he found the claim in Husserl: "The impulse to research must proceed not from philosophies but from things (*Sachen*) and from the problems connected with them" (PRS 146), and Heidegger commented in the margin: "we take Husserl at his word" (*wir nehmen Husserl beim Wort*);[6] that is, avoid philosophical systems and concentrate on the matters themselves. As Heidegger explains in the Introduction to *Being and Time*, phenomenology is "opposed to all free-floating constructions and accidental findings" and to all "pseudo-problems", rather it relates to a certain kind of "self-evidence" (BT § 7, 50; 28).[7] Heidegger always identifies with Husserl's slogan "Back to the things themselves". But, in his early Freiburg lectures, he had claimed that the slogan of phenomenology should really be "*Freigabe des Daseins!*" ('set Dasein free!'). Phenomenology must be able to understand Dasein from within the concrete particularity of a lived life.

Rather pointedly, in *Being and Time*, Heidegger avoids referring to Husserl to articulate phenomenology; instead he calls attention to the original meanings of the Greek terms embedded in the word 'phenomenology'. Phenomenology, for Heidegger, stems from Aristotle not Husserl! Phenomenology was to be understood in terms of the Greek understanding of *phenomenon* and *logos*, letting what is to be seen show itself in the manner in which it shows itself. Heidegger argued that the true meaning of phenomenology was already understood more radically by the ancient Greeks, in their realisation of how speaking manifests truth. Heidegger later claimed:

What occurs for the phenomenology of the acts of consciousness as the self-manifestation of phenomena is thought more originally by Aristotle and in all Greek thinking and existence as *aletheia*, as the unconcealedness of what is present, its being revealed, its showing itself.

(OTB 79)

Similarly, in 1959, he wrote that, in *Being and Time*: "I was trying to think the nature of phenomenology in a more originary manner".[8] As Heidegger explains in *Being and Time*, the term 'phenomenology' is made up of two Greek terms *'phainomenon'* and *'logos'*. The Greek word *phainomenon* derives from the Greek verb for 'to show oneself' (*phainesthai*). Thus for Heidegger, *phainomenon* means "that which shows itself in itself, the manifest" (*das Offenbare*, BT § 7, 51; 28). Phenomenology has to do with self-manifestation. Things show themselves in many ways, depending on the modes of access we have to them; indeed sometimes things shows themselves as what they are not, in cases of dissembling, seeming, illusion, and other such phenomena. Heidegger gives a careful analysis of these different senses of appearing and strongly emphasises that dissemblance, mere appearance, semblance, and illusion are all secondary senses dependent on the primary meaning of 'phenomenon' as that which shows itself in itself. Here Heidegger wants clearly to distinguish phenomenology as an account of the truth of a thing's appearance from all phenomenalism, from all accounts, including the Kantian account whereby we only grasp the appearances of things and not their real being. Since things don't always show themselves as they are, phenomenology cannot be simply description, it does not depend on the fulfilling intuition as Husserl thought; rather phenomenology is seeking after a meaning which is perhaps hidden by the entity's mode of appearing. In that case, the proper model for seeking meaning is the interpretation of a text and for this reason Heidegger links phenomenology with hermeneutics. How things appear or are covered up must be explicitly studied. The things themselves always present themselves in a manner which is at the same time self-concealing.

In order to emphasise the link between phenomenology and truth, between appearing and the revelation of truth, Heidegger turns to the second Greek term in phenomenology: *'logos'*. The Greek word *logos* normally means 'word', 'concept', 'thought', but Heidegger translates it as 'discourse' (*Rede*). Heidegger also goes back to its etymology which means 'to bind together' (BT § 7, 56; 32), 'to gather up' into a unity or synthesis, and 'to let something be seen'. Discourse brings the matter out into the open, lets it be seen, makes it manifest, although it is always driven by human needs and human interests (as Habermas also emphasises). This, for Heidegger, is also the central notion involved in the concept of truth. Traditionally truth has been understood in terms of a conformity between our judgements and the facts in the world, but Heidegger claims this traditional understanding of truth is derivative from a more fundamental understanding of truth as self-manifestation, revelation, disclosure (BT § 44). Here Heidegger interprets the Greek term for truth, *aletheia*, as having the etymological sense of 'dis-closing', 'un-covering', 'dis-covering', 'revealing', that is: making manifest that which in some sense lies hidden (BT § 7, 56–57; 33). For Heidegger, the primordial meaning of *logos* is assertion, in the Greek sense of *apophansis*, 'letting an entity be seen from itself' (BT § 33, 196; 154). By disclosure, Heidegger means that when I say, "the hammer is heavy", the nature of the hammer is revealed in some way. It is not that I have a thought which simply represents a reality outside my thought, I grasp the truth of the matter directly.

Heidegger notes that anything involved in speech or assertion can get 'passed along' to others, owing to the very nature of discourse, in such a manner that the original power of revelation of the utterance gets covered up or distorted and congeals into an everyday sense which loses its urgency and its power to stimulate:

> That which is put forward in the assertion is something which can be passed along for "further retelling"...what has been pointed out may become veiled again in this further retelling, although even the kind of knowing which arises in such hearsay...always has the entity itself in view and does not "give assent" to some "valid meaning" which has been passed along. Even hearsay is a Being-in-the-world, and a Being towards what is heard.
>
> (BT § 33, 197–198; 155)

Heidegger's recognition that original existential discoveries and disclosure can get covered up in the tradition of discourse led him to realise that descriptive phenomenology has to be aware of the nature of tradition and history. Tradition, as Husserl also knew, involves a constant process of sedimentation whereby original discoveries become absorbed into the general consensus. Understanding operates largely in terms of this common consensus, the kind of public knowledge which is expressed by Heidegger's concepts of 'publicity' (*Öffentlichkeit*) and the inauthentic kind of awareness of '*das Man*'. But, for Heidegger, it is simply not the case that one can live in the truth all the time, that one can bask in the light of disclosure. Our ordinary life constantly draws us back down into forms of complacency and everydayness. This is a structural feature of Dasein; its everydayness is characterised by 'falling' (*Verfallen*, BT § 38, 219; 175), which Heidegger stresses is not meant to have any negative connotation but simply expresses the manner in which human beings live, to borrow a phrase from Arendt, in the midst of the world. Humans become absorbed and lost in the anonymous public self.

Heidegger's critique of Husserl's concept of intentionality

Being and Time first appeared to be a radical deviation from Husserl's phenomenology, but the publication of the drafts of Heidegger's lecture courses from 1917 to 1927 shows Heidegger working his way *through* phenomenology, employing a close reading of Husserl's texts, and situating his own problematic as emerging from them. In his lectures of the early 1920s Heidegger had criticised Husserl's account of intuition as not sufficiently recognising that our original understanding is not theoretical, but grounded in our practical engagements (comportment, *Verhalten*) with the world. Our understanding is *interpretative* from the very start and that interpretative involvement with things need not be at a level of intellection or cognition, but more usually comes in concernful, practical dealings. In *Being and Time*, Husserl's notion of intentionality is replaced by a phenomenological account of Dasein's practical comportments within the world of practical relations with things (*Zuhandensein*). This leads Heidegger to revise Husserl's conception of intentionality and finally to drop it altogether in favour of the conception of Dasein's transcendence.

An indication of how far Heidegger was moving away from Husserl's understanding of phenomenology is the fact that *Being and Time* contains almost no references to intentionality. There is a brief mention of Scheler's view that treating intentional acts as 'psychic acts' robs them of their connectedness with the person as performer of the acts (BT § 10, 73; 48), but the only other mention of intentionality occurs in a note where Heidegger promises to show how intentionality is grounded in the ec-static nature of Dasein, that is, the manner in which human existence always runs ahead of itself in expectation and lingers behind in memory (BT § 69, 498n. xxxiii; 363). This promised section, of course, was never published.

It is in Heidegger's Marburg lecture courses, as we have seen, that Heidegger's evolving critique of Husserlian intentionality can be found. The 1925 course on the *History of the Concept of Time* is a particularly good discussion of Brentano and Husserl on intentionality. Here Heidegger interprets intentionality as 'directedness' and specifically as 'self-directedness', the manner in which we direct ourselves towards things. Of course, one must be careful not to take lecture presentations as the author's last word on the subject, but Heidegger is careful both to unfold his view of Brentano and Husserl and to elaborate on his own view of intentionality in connection with language and the nature of truth. In these lectures Heidegger is developing the nature of our experience with things which will be the central focus of the chapter on "The Worldhood of the World" in *Being and Time*, where the notions of *zuhanden* and *vorhanden* come to prominence (BT §§ 15–17).

Heidegger acknowledges Brentano as having revived the concept of intentionality, but criticises him for having left unexplained the character of the psychical as such, and for remaining within a Cartesian standpoint, which sharply distinguished between the physical world and the psychical realm, still caught up in "metaphysical dogmas" (HCT § 5, 32; GA 20, p. 41). He also criticises Brentano for failing to recognise the true nature of the *content* of the act, what Husserl developed as the notion of the *noema*. For Heidegger, Brentano did not properly distinguish between the object intended and the content through which it was apprehended. Brentano did not properly distinguish between seeing the perceived "thing in its being" (*das Seiende selbst in seinem Sein*) and "*how* it is intended" (*wie Intendiertseins*, HCT § 6, 46; GA 20, pp. 61–62), the manner of its presentation. In other words, Brentano failed to distinguish the thing intended from the mode of presentation, a distinction central to Husserl's account of intentionality, as we have seen. With this fundamental omission, Heidegger claims that Brentano misses the structural totality of intentionality.

Heidegger argued also that Husserlian phenomenology had not completely overcome this problem of how to account for the mode of being of the intentional object. Husserl still sees intentionality primarily as a structure of *consciousness*. Heidegger says we must go beyond this position and question how a *being* is related to its *being intended*; indeed we must question whether we can properly approach the topic in that way at all. But this can be done only by a more radical phenomenology. Heidegger concentrates on the manner in which the Being of the thing intended is present in our comportment towards the thing. He will argue that intentionality can only be understood in terms of the fundamental transcendence of Dasein, whereby Dasein is already in the world.

In the 1925 lectures, Heidegger agrees with Husserl that intentionality is a defining characteristic of all lived experiences (*Erlebnisse*), but, against Husserl, he emphasises the practical, embodied nature of these experiences. Our lived experiences are practical bodily encounters with things in our environment: for example, in moving around a room I am in an encounter with a 'thing in the environment' (*Umweltding*, HCT § 5, 38; GA 20, p. 49), a chair, *not* chair-sensations. Hence I can genuinely say "the chair *is* uncomfortable" and grasp the mode of being of the chair for me, for my living. The chair's being is one of discomfort for me. Abstracting from these practical engagements with the thing makes it an object of theoretical study. At this point, the chair becomes for me a "natural thing" (*Naturding*) and different epithets apply, for example the chair is made of wood, has such and such a weight, occupies space, and so on. By way of illustration, Heidegger says that the botanist studies plants (natural things) not flowers (environmental things), but flowers, not plants, are given as gifts. In "ordinary speech" (*in der natürlichen Rede*) I say "I am giving roses", or "I am giving flowers", but not "I am giving plants" (HCT § 5, 38; GA 20, p. 50). To make Heidegger's point in a different way, we would never say that we gave a 'weed' as a present, even though a weed is a plant, indeed often a flower. Or, to put it in Husserlian language, flowers and weeds occupy different spaces in the life-world. This distinction between environmental things, or useful things, and things which are the objects of neutral detached vision or contemplation appears in a revised form in Heidegger's analysis of the way in which we encounter things in his chapter on the worldhood of the world in *Being and Time*.

Readiness to hand (*Zuhandenheit*) and presence at hand (*Vorhandenheit*)

Dasein is not an entity that stands on its own, like a stone or a chair; it is always caught up in a world. Only Dasein can really be said to have a world; Heidegger thought natural things strictly speaking had no world, and animals were at best "world poor" (*Weltarm*).[9] The fundamental nature of Dasein is always to be in a world. World here means a context, an environment, a set of references and assignments within which any meaning is located (BT § 17). Human being is 'Being-in-the-world'. Furthermore, it is not as if Dasein is somehow sitting side by side with the world. Dasein is world-involved, and as Heidegger will later argue, world-disclosing. Being-in-the-world is such a basic state of Being that it is through it that all the other 'existentialia' (Dasein's equivalent of the categories which apply to inanimate things) of Dasein get determined (BT § 26, 153; 117).

Heidegger explicates this conception of Being-in-the-world through an account of our basic contacts with things in the environment. Traditionally, Heidegger feels, philosophy, including even Aristotle, has prioritised the theoretical encounter with things, things as they are to sight. Sight stands at a distance and seeing does not tamper with the thing seen. Against this traditional metaphysical view, Heidegger emphasises that our initial contact with objects is in terms of their use and availability to us for certain assigned tasks, tasks generated by our interests. We tamper with and manipulate things as determined by our interests and our goals. Things initially present themselves with this kind of available being, what Heidegger calls *Zuhandensein*, 'readiness to hand', or what Hubert Dreyfus renders as 'availability'.[10] Normally we reach for an object to act as a hammer, we see a tree as a source of wood or shelter from the rain, and so on. Heidegger's descriptions give a certain priority to these kinds of 'work-worlds' – the work-world of the carpenter, for instance (BT § 26). Only subsequently, and by a separate act of intention – one which is much more theoretical – do we see the tools as things in themselves, as things standing on their own, available for inspection. This theoretical way of viewing things leads to science, to the pure interest in examining things as they are, bracketed from their connections and engagements with our interests. Things seen in this theoretical mode are *vorhandene* – present at hand, simply there.

Expression (*Aussage*)

For Heidegger here, the nature of our practical encounter with things is encapsulated in our use of language. Husserl's conception of intentionality is not sufficiently tuned in to express our practical engagement with the world. Much more than Husserl, Heidegger is interested in the linguistic dimension of intentionality. Our whole comportment towards things is *expressive*, and this expression can appear as linguistic assertion (*Aussage*). Heidegger reinteprets Husserl's stress on propositional meaning as actually an uncovering of the nature of *expressing* itself. As Heidegger says:

> It is not so much that we see the objects and things but rather that we first talk about them. To put it more precisely: we do not say what we see, but rather the reverse, we see what *one says* about the matter.
>
> (HCT § 6, 56; GA 20, p. 75)

Understanding is not just a matter of having a sensory input, conceptualising it, and reacting to it. The sensory dimension of the experience falls short of what the assertion *says* about it: I *say* the chair is yellow but I do not literally *see* the *being*-yellow of the chair. 'Being', 'this', and so on are not in the subjective reflection, but are correlates of the act. Heidegger develops Husserl's notion of categorial intuition into his account of the experience of being and truth. Heidegger is coming to see that the essential disclosure of things takes place through Dasein's concernful dealing with things in the environment, that it takes place essentially in expression. Relating to things, disclosing them, always relates to our concerns in advance, our relation is primarily interpretative, or *hermeneutical*.

Heidegger's fusion of phenomenology with hermeneutics

Husserl had already acknowledged a certain interpretative component in every intentional act in his discussion of the '*Auffassungssinn*' or 'grasping sense'. When we see something, we always see it *as* something and project a certain set of expectations upon it, expectations which are then fulfilled or exploded in subsequent perceptions. In fact, in *Ideas* II Husserl had already located our relating to things in our bodily activity in the local environment and was in fact anticipating many of the things which Heidegger says in *Being and Time*. But Heidegger gives Husserl's account of practical intentionality an entirely new shape by connecting it with the tradition of hermeneutics.

Heidegger later recalled that he had first encountered hermeneutics as a branch of theological interpretation during his Catholic seminary days. His contact with hermeneutics was greatly stimulated by his reading of Dilthey (who himself was drawing on Schleiermacher). When Heidegger moved to

Marburg in 1923 he encountered there a group of theologians, including Rudolf Bultmann, who saw hermeneutics as central to the task of scriptural interpretation. Thus in *Being and Time* Heidegger explicitly acknowledges Dilthey as the leading stimulus in establishing an existential analytic of concrete human existence, though he criticises Dilthey's extremely limited conceptual apparatus (BT § 10). By 'hermeneutics' Heidegger does not just mean the method specific to the historical and cultural sciences, but the whole manner in which human existence is interpretative, something later developed by Gadamer, as we shall see in the next chapter.

Heidegger locates the judgement, which was the centre of Brentano's and Husserl's account of logic, in the context of speech or 'discourse' (*Rede*), where a certain kind of Being-in-the-world is already presumed. All our assertions and judgements are taken in the context of the background of prejudices (or pre-judgements) we hold, mostly non-theoretical and not explicitly articulated by us. As Heidegger says:

> When as assertion is made, some fore-conception is always implied; but it remains for the most part inconspicuous, because language already hides in itself a developed way of conceiving.
>
> (BT § 33, 199; 157)

All our experience is interpreting and encountering what has already been interpreted by ourselves and by others. *Logos* itself is a kind of *hermeneuein*, a kind of interpreting (BT § 7, 62; 37). Even when we assert something to be the case, we always assert it as something, and this interpreting is not necessarily carried out verbally; rather it is carried out in the way we *relate* to things:

> Interpretation is carried out primordially not in a theoretical statement but in an action of circumspective concern – laying aside the unsuitable tool, or exchanging it, "without wasting words". From the fact that words are absent, it may not be concluded that interpretation is absent.
>
> (BT § 33, 200; 157)

Heidegger calls this way of approaching things the "existential-hermeneutical *as*"; it is a kind of approach which gets pushed into the background when we adopt the more neutral view of a thing as an entity with specific properties. All neutral understanding of things, for example scientific understanding, presupposes our existential encounter with things and our original interpretation of them in the light of our concerns and dealings with the world. If this is forgotten, according to Heidegger, we end up with a theory of truth as judgement instead of an experience of truth as revelation. Heidegger then is seeking to replace the traditional view of knowledge as a kind of intellectual representation with a new view which sees knowing as a sub-species of a kind of concernful dealing with the world. In *Being and Time* Heidegger struggles to develop a new vocabulary to express this kind of relating to the world, using terms like '*Umsicht*' (circumspection) which suggest a connection with '*Umwelt*' (environment).

The hermeneutical structure of the question

Heidegger's philosophy is distinguished by his radical approach to philosophical questioning. From very early in his career Heidegger realised that the performative nature of questioning required quite a different structure from the structure of *assertions* (*Aussagen*), or statements of fact, which traditionally had been analysed by philosophy. Asserting and questioning are both forms of disclosing. The structure of that disclosure is actually more clearly visible in the case of questioning; therefore Heidegger proposes that we pay attention to the nature of questioning itself. Although we are engaged in asking questions all the time, we rarely reflect on what is involved in questioning. Heidegger begins with an examination of the structure of the question (BT § 2). A question seeks for certain information by addressing itself *to* something *about* something *for* some purpose. But in order even to be able to pose a question we must have some initial pre-understanding of what we are asking about. We have a 'fore-conception' (*Vorgriff*) of what is involved, a presupposition or a certain pre-judgement about how things will be. As Heidegger repeatedly emphasises, "every seeking gets guided beforehand by what is sought" (BT § 2, 24; 5). But, furthermore, the kind of answer we get depends on our way of posing the question. So Heidegger claims that both our *pre-understanding* and our *mode of access* (*Zugangsart*) are crucial to the answer which we hear. Our pre-understanding is actually a kind of "vague, average understanding" (BT § 2, 25; 5), perhaps more of a mis-understanding and distortion than a genuine understanding. Heidegger points out that this *average understanding* is shot through with much of the traditional lore and baggage which we have inherited. Our initial standpoint from which we question contains a great deal of what might be called 'folk wisdom' on the subject. As Heidegger is aware, this average understanding is necessary to *enable* the act of questioning to take place in the first instance, but it also can disable the question, prevent it from adequately rendering an answer, because the preconceptions can distort or conceal the answer completely. Heidegger says:

> Further, this vague, average understanding of Being may be so infiltrated with traditional theories and opinions about Being that these remain hidden as sources of the way in which it is prevalently understood.
>
> (BT § 2, 25; 6)

In order to understand how our questioning is distorting the very phenomenon under question, we should carry out a scrutiny of our average understanding in the first instance.

The hermeneutical circle

Heidegger has strongly insisted that all questioning carries certain presumptions which govern the enquiry and even predetermine to a certain extent what can be discovered. We therefore disclose the answer in the light of what we already know. This might appear to be circular – how can we learn anything new if we can only grasp it in terms of what we already know? As Heidegger says:

> Is there not, however, a manifest circularity in such an undertaking? If we must first define an entity *in its Being*, and if we want to formulate the question of Being only on this basis, what is this but going in a circle? In working out the question, have we not "presupposed" something which only the answer can bring?
>
> (BT § 2, 27; 7)

Heidegger's way out of this is to claim that the circle is not closed or 'vicious' as in cases of circular reasoning, but rather it involves a certain "relatedness backward or forward" (*Rück oder Vorbezogenheit*, BT § 2, 28; 8), because our questioning really is a kind of light which casts a certain pattern on the phenomenon, while also filling in our expectation in a way that allows us to formulate further questions, and thus to advance our understanding. Presupposing has the character of "taking a look at it beforehand" (BT § 2, 27; 8). Heidegger is very aware that our understanding grows or decays according to the kind of lives we are leading and the kind of cultural situation we inhabit. So to understand the question of Being we have to be alert to the kind of situation which gives rise to that question or covers it up. In particular, we shall have to be aware of the average understanding of being which our particular culture or mood carries with it. The best place to start is with our everyday, ordinary encounter with things, how things are in their 'average everydayness' (*durchschnittliche Alltäglichkeit*, BT § 5, 38; 16). This is a good starting point, but it will only be a 'provisional' one, because we shall also have to understand the manner we relate to Being at other moments, moments where we are more authentically ourselves and less caught up in the quotidian, perhaps in facing a personal choice or a threat to our everyday situation, perhaps while in states of *anxiety* or *dread* (*Angst*), or contemplating our own death. Heidegger recognises that we have to take account of the mood we are in when examining how we relate to Being.

The nature of Dasein

There has been a great deal of argument over exactly what Heidegger means by Dasein. Does he mean the concrete individual human, something like an essence of human nature in general, or perhaps a set of transcendental conditions which make human existence possible? Heidegger himself made use of the term in his lectures in the 1920s. In *Being and Time* he first introduces Dasein in terms of his discussion of the formal structure of the question of Being:

> Thus, to work out the question of Being adequately, we must make an entity – the inquirer – transparent in his own Being. The very asking of this question is an entity's mode of *Being*; and as such it gets its essential character from what is inquired about – namely, Being. This entity which each of us is himself and which includes inquiring as one of the possibilities of its Being, we shall denote by the term "Dasein".
>
> (BT 27; 7)

Dasein then names human being in so far as it is individualised as myself or someone else and in so far as questioning is its essential mode of relating to Being. Dasein then specifically picks out our individual possession of our existence and the fact that it is a question for us, a question which concerns the nature of Being as such. Introduced in this manner, Dasein refers to the specific mode of Being of humans, emphasising its individuality and its role in the disclosure of Being. Dasein does not just occur factually like rocks and trees; its Being is an *issue* for it. But Heidegger does not think our deepest grasp of ourselves comes in some kind of self-reflection of a Cartesian kind; in fact, he thought that concentration on this kind of self-giving can lead existential analysis astray (BT § 25, 151; 115). Access to Dasein comes through living out a life. Heidegger then is interested in analysing human existence, but since he thinks the terms German life philosophy has used are shallow and ill-considered, he sets out on his own enquiry into the kind of Being of this Dasein, which he calls his fundamental analysis of Dasein. The aim of this analysis is to show up Dasein as having the fundamental structure of Being-in-the-world, being with things and with others in such a way that its whole existence is structured by care (*Sorge*). As Heidegger puts it, the existential meaning of Dasein is care (BT § 41). In examining the manner of Dasein's Being-in-the-world it becomes clear that it is essentially a kind of disclosing of the world. In understanding Dasein as 'care' we seek its structure as falling and facticity.

The human questioner always lives with a certain understanding which also includes a projection of certain possibilities:

> Dasein always understands itself in terms of its existence – in terms of a possibility of itself: to be itself or not itself. Dasein has either chosen these possibilities itself or got itself into them, or grown up in them already.
>
> (BT § 4, 33; 12)

Human beings already inhabit a certain understanding of themselves, although this need not necessarily be 'thematised' or made conscious or explicit. It may not be 'theoretically transparent' to the individual Dasein. We don't necessarily know in what way we already understand ourselves. But our very existentiality is already one of understanding. In part what Heidegger is saying here can easily be grasped: I already understand myself and the world by my approach, by my own situation – as a twentieth-century middle-aged male, as a young girl, as a poor or rich person, as a teacher or as someone who is unemployed, or whatever. My life presents itself in terms of the set of possibilities which I am. Of course, a lot of the way my life presents itself to me is given by the culture I have grown up in, or is simply carried along by a kind of unquestioned horizon of acceptance. But, as Heidegger here indicates, I can choose certain possibilities for myself. This part of Heidegger's analysis was seized on by the existentialists, especially by Sartre, who took from it the view that humans can make themselves who they are by seizing their possibilities, as we shall see in a future chapter. Sartre's account, however, is much more action oriented than that of Heidegger, who is really giving a phenomenological description of how we encounter ourselves in our own lives.

Authenticity and inauthenticity

In terms of the different ways in which these possibilities present themselves to Dasein, Heidegger will distinguish between an *authentic* and *inauthentic* way to be. Again, we have to be careful how we understand Heidegger here. Heidegger will emphasise that the inauthentic is the very *condition* of authenticity. It is absolutely *not* the case that humans can dwell in the authentic all their lives. Most of the time, we are just passing information along, not too caught up in things, not dwelling on the significance of events, but living in the vague average understanding of everydayness. In these experiences, I am no different than others, I am simply experiencing as they do, as one does. There are other moments, however, which bring our personal concerns into sharp relief, so a proper account of our relation to Being must be able to identify and exhibit the essential structures of both our inauthentic and our authentic modes of being.

Heidegger explicates his concept of authenticity in terms of 'ownness' and 'ownership'. My existence is something which is mine; or, put more generally, Dasein has the structure of 'mineness' (*Jemeinigkeit*, BT § 9), that is to say, it is not something which merely occurs in the world, something merely present at hand, but is revealed in a first-person way, though Heidegger acknowledges it is difficult to find the right way of presenting this phenomenon. Now 'mineness' is a structure which itself is capable of being grasped either authentically or inauthentically: "As modes of being, *authenticity* and *inauthenticity* (these terms have been chosen terminologically in a strict sense) are both grounded in the fact that any Dasein whatsoever is characterized by mineness" (BT § 9, 68; 43). Authenticity and inauthenticity can only arise as modes of Dasein's being, because Dasein is always mine or yours, always individualised into the life of an individual. These are a priori features of Dasein. One relates to one's existence either authentically or inauthentically, or else in some kind of undifferentiated state between these two (BT § 12, 78; 53). *Authentic* moments are those in which we are most at home with ourselves, at one with ourselves. I may initiate or take up possibilities as my own; I have a deep, concrete experience of 'mineness' of 'togetherness'. However, in our more usual, normal, everyday, moments, we do not treat things as affecting us deeply in our 'ownmost' being. Heidegger thinks we live in an inauthentic way most of the time. For example, we read about a tragic death in the newspapers but don't necessarily absorb the event into our own selves or experience it personally; we don't take it personally. We are experiencing these kinds of moments *inauthentically*, experiencing them as one does, as anyone does. Being authentic is a kind of potential-to-be-whole: humans have the urge to get their lives together, to collect themselves, to gather themselves into wholeness. When one tries to gather one's life together, one wants to make it whole, to unify it. In later works Heidegger will make the connection between being 'whole' and being 'healthy' where the German word for 'healthy' (*heil*) has an etymological connection with wholeness (as in the English word 'hale'). This desire to be authentic is expressed in the phenomenon of 'conscience' (BT § 45, 277; 234). But the problem for becoming whole is that Dasein is essentially always unfinished, its Being is Being-towards-death (*Sein-zum-Tode*). It is the fact that we are all destined to die, to not finish, to remain *unfinished* that challenges this project of wholeness.

Anxiety and being-towards-death

Human nature is radically finite. It ends in death. Each of us is directed towards death, as the annihilation of all our projects, as that which casts a shadow over all our projects and engagements. Influenced by Kierkegaard, Heidegger recognises the centrality of being-towards-death (*Sein-zum-Tode*) in humans. Moreover, death can only be authentically experienced by us if we become totally secure with our first-person experience of dying – our genuine anticipation of death. We cannot experience other people's deaths in the same authentic manner (BT § 47, 282; 238).

Heidegger's account of anxiety also is a secularisation of Kierkegaard's account. Anxiety leads us to drop the mask of our everyday familiarity with the world. Anxiety makes everything of such little significance that even our own sense of self is lost. Anxiety is the recognition of a certain nothingness, a groundlessness in our existence. As Sartre will later describe it, anxiety leads us into a kind of vertigo where we literally have no ground beneath our feet. For Heidegger, this is not properly understood as a subjective psychological phenomenon, but a structural possibility of our existence which brings us face to face with the problematic nature of our lives and the meaning we attach to living. Anxiety is distinctive in its world-disclosing possibilities. In this sense, following Kierkegaard, Heidegger sharply distinguishes fear (*Furcht*) from anxiety (*Angst*). Fear is always fear of *something*, and for the sake of something, for example, one fears *for* one's life (BT § 30, 180; 141), or one fears about some possibility. Anxiety, on the other hand, is a rather shapeless mood which does not have a precise object. In fact, anxiety is precisely anxiety over *nothing*, that is no object, other than our very Being-in-the-world itself: "Being-anxious discloses, primordially and directly, the world as world" (BT § 40, 232; 187). Anxiety shows up precisely the way in which we are free to choose and take hold of ourselves.

> Anxiety makes manifest in Dasein its *Being towards* it ownmost po-
> tentiality-for-Being – that is, its *Being-free for* the freedom of
> choosing itself and taking hold of itself.
>
> (BT § 40, 232; 188)

Anxiety reveals to us a certain homelessness – we are not at home in the world, the world faces us as something weird, or 'uncanny' (the German for 'uncanny' is '*unheimlich*', which carries the meaning of something being un-familiar, un-homely). Our only way of understanding this is to turn away from it; hence its disclosive, enlightening power for us must always get covered up after the moment of insight has passed. But anxiety thus serves to reveal that we are caught up in a structure of care about the world; that is, it is not a matter of indifference for us. Heidegger's account of care and of human experiences such as anxiety and facing death would interest and influence the existentialists, especially Sartre, but Heidegger himself wants to emphasise how these experiences offer us a peculiar disclosure of the nature of time, and he hoped later in *Being and Time* to go back over these experiences and to analyse their relation to time and temporality.

Mood and state of mind (*Befindlichkeit*)

One of Heidegger's most original contributions in *Being and Time* is his analysis of mood (*Stimmung*), not as a psychological subjective state, but as a way the world itself appears. Heidegger thinks of 'mood' as a way of being

241

tuned in to the world, attuned. *Being and Time* acknowledges that most of our lives are lived in 'everydayness', a mood which is so neutral as not even to be acknowledged as a mood. But it is a fundamental mood and has a fundamental way of relating to the world. In our ordinary everydayness we simply pass information along, not getting wrapped up in it, and our speech is merely 'idle talk' (*Gerede*) – like commenting on the latest disaster on the news without really taking the time to experience the event authentically. In this everyday mood, we are not really ourselves at all, we are simply the same as everyone else; we are in the state of '*das Man*' or 'the one', 'anyone'. This is for Heidegger an inauthentic state but we have to be careful how we understand this. Being inauthentic does not mean being morally bad (as Sartre would later interpret it). Indeed in order to be authentic we must first of all be inauthentic. These are necessary modes of Dasein according to Heidegger. In our everyday mood we are absorbed in the world, caught up in our tasks; we don't reflect on who we are, we are 'thrown' (*Geworfen*). We are also peculiarly constructed so that we actually run away from facing up to aspects of our existence. This structural feature of running away Heidegger calls 'falling'. Falling means getting caught up in the public self, so that we no longer have proper access to our authentic sense of our lives.

Mitsein

It is not true to say that Heidegger ignores the experience of the other or that he privileges the solitary Dasein in his existential analytic in *Being and Time*. For him, it is part of our most primordial experience of being-in-the-world that we experience it as a world shared with others: "the world of Dasein is a *with-world*" (*Mitwelt*, BT § 26, 155; 118), where we relate to others. Even when we encounter things in our practical concerns, we encounter them in a world already 'humanised'. The hammer is encountered according to a set of concerns which I share with others, which take their meaning from relations with others. Others are encountered as belonging to the environment. Heidegger points out that we should not immediately assume that when we talk of others we are opposing everyone else to myself. There are lots of occasions when I too am included in this 'they' (BT § 26, 154; 118). Furthermore, the claim is not simply the factual claim that there are other human beings besides me, for Heidegger 'being-with-others' is an a priori existential category of Dasein even if no others exist at all (BT § 26, 156; 120). In that case, others are experienced as missing. The manner of our relation to others is best understood under the notion of 'care' (*Sorge*). Heidegger wants to identify the basic category of being-with-others in the world and then see how this is actually filled out in different situations, such as in caring for others in a charity situation, for instance. There is a kind of being-with where we will fill in or leap in for the other.

However, it is true that Heidegger's account of our connection with others in *Being and Time* largely stresses that we encounter them in the domain of the public, in idle talk. Thus Heidegger says that "Idle talk is the kind of Being that belongs to Being-with-one-another itself" (BT § 38, 221; 177). There is a tendency is his analysis to oppose the authenticity and wholeness of the individual to the manner in which we fall into the public and into the common. Heidegger's communal vision, however, is developed in the second half of the published part of *Being and Time*. Here he talks about the manner in which humans live in communities and that there is a need in individuals to pattern their lives by 'choosing a hero' (BT § 74, 437; 385) and following the path opened up by the hero. This account of communal life has come under scrutiny recently as to whether it is a blueprint for political quietism at the very least or perhaps even worse, in that it provided a model of political life which left Heidegger open – even enthusiastic – about the heroic, people-leading qualities of Hitler and the Nazis.

At the heart of Heidegger's analysis in *Being and Time* is the temporal dimensions of human living. Dasein is primarily historical (BT § 73, 433; 381). We are thrown into history and can experience this as a kind of fateful acceptance, repeating what is handed down in the tradition, or we can try to achieve a moment of resoluteness, projecting ourselves into possibilities. Heidegger ends the book with some rather scattered meditations on the way in which various philosophical conceptions of time, including those found in Aristotle, St Augustine, and Hegel, all develop from partial insights into human historicality and temporality in its fundamental sense. Unfortunately, Heidegger's fascinating reflections on the nature of history and the meaning of time are beyond the scope of this discussion.

Transcendental homelessness

After 1929 Heidegger continued to see his work as phenomenological in the new radical sense he conceived, but he rarely refers either to phenomenology or to himself as a phenomenologist. At this time he was beginning to realise that the language of academic philosophy was too restricting for the essential insights he wanted to convey about the "ontological difference", that is the distinction between Being and beings. He came to recognise that the Kantian transcendental language which he had inherited from Husserl and which he employed in *Being and Time* did not serve adequately to bring the phenomena under investigation to light. Heidegger, as he put it, wanted to "liberate language from grammar" (*Pathmarks*, p. 240; GA 9, p. 314), and to move into the more creative medium of poetic speaking. Thus Heidegger's later philosophy may be seen as a stretching of language to the limits in a search for an adequate way of communicating his thought on the nature of the 'event of Being' (*das Ereignis*). This involved thinking of phenomenology in terms of the

Greek philosophical enlightenment and also in terms of the 'essential saying' of German romantic poetry (and specifically Hölderlin). Heidegger developed the peculiar view that Greek and German were the only languages to be capable of expressing the nature of Being. He also began to see himself as forecasting the inevitable loss of direction of the German people if they succumbed to technology and to democratisation and Westernisation. For Heidegger the great threat to human existence is that thinking has become a kind of technical information processing. This leads to a fundamental homelessness and rootlessness. Thus in his *Letter on Humanism* he says: "Homelessness is coming to be the destiny of the world" (*Die Heimatlosigkeit wird ein Weltschicksal, Pathmarks*, p. 258; GA 9, p. 339), an insight which Arendt will develop in detail in *The Human Condition*. Against this homelessness, only a kind of poetic thinking expresses itself.

Against this account of transcendental homelessness, for Heidegger, stands genuine philosophy as a kind of home-coming, a thinking back from our current displaced sense back to finding our place and preserving what we have found. In a way this can be understood as a secularisation of the religious notion of the Fall and return. Thus when Heidegger in the *Letter on Humanism* says that "language is the house of Being. In its home human beings dwell" (*Die Sprache ist das Haus des Seins. In ihrer Behausung wohnt der Mensch, Pathmarks*, p. 239; GA 9, p. 313), he immediately goes on to add that: "Those who think and those who create with words are the guardians of this home" (ibid.). Thinking philosophically and poeticising are both ways of guarding the essential nature of the human relation with Being.

Heidegger's later writings develop his thinking on the nature of genuine dwelling and the global homeless of humanity. His account of the techno-logical framework bounding the modern world expands to such a degree that even the early Greeks are seen as having cast the metaphysical fate of the West to be technological in their earliest thinking about *techne* and *episteme*, skill and knowledge. Against this all-engulfing technological framework, philosophy and poetry can fight at best a rearguard action, or engage in a kind of resistance to this totalisation. Technology is not merely a means to accomplish projects. Heidegger sees technology as a way of disclosing and revealing Being. Technology is a form of revealing (*Entbergung*).[11] However, it is a form of revealing which also uses up the material which it is setting forth. It turns nature into a mere stockpile of resources – coal, iron, uranium, water, and so on. The nature of this technological revealing is such that it obscures and does not reveal its own essence. Furthermore, it transforms the humans who are involved in technology. Human beings have been caught up in and claimed by this mode of revealing. Humans, as much as nature, are gathered up in this framing *Gestell*.

Heidegger's influence

The influence of Heidegger on twentieth-century philosophy has been so enormous that it is almost impossible to measure it. Even Ludwig Wittgenstein acknowledged that he could easily understand what Heidegger meant by Being and by anxiety or dread (*Angst*). As Wittgenstein says:

> I can readily understand what Heidegger means by Being and Dread. Man has the impulse to run up against the limits of language. Think for example of the astonishment that anything exists.[12]

Similarly Charles Taylor has said that Heidegger's importance lies in the fact that he is one of the few contemporary philosophers who have helped to free us from the grip of rationalism.[13]

Heidegger first had an extraordinary influence on his students through his meticulous lectures and illuminating seminars, which played exceptionally close attention to reading the text and dwelling with its fundamental problem. Among Heidegger's own students were Hans-Georg Gadamer, who studied with Heidegger from 1923 to 1929, Herbert Marcuse, who studied with Heidegger from 1928 to 1932, Hannah Arendt, who studied with Heidegger in Marburg from 1924 to 1925, Karl Löwith, and Ernst Tugendhat. Apart from his direct influence on his own students, Heidegger's writings had an enormous influence on the development of philosophy in Germany and also in France. In Germany, he influenced the theology of Rudolf Bultmann. The Frankfurt School of Social Criticism, which was reinstituted after the war with Adorno and Habermas, developed largely in reaction to Heidegger, often juxtaposing the young Marx's view of human alienation and domination by ideology against Heidegger's account of man and the domination of technicity. Herbert Marcuse, in particular, sought to link the analysis of man in Marx's early 1844 writings with Heidegger's analysis of Dasein and saw Heidegger's analysis as an account of how bourgeois social life deconstructs from within. As Marcuse said, he saw in Heidegger "a new beginning, the first radical attempt to put philosophy on really concrete foundations – philosophy concerned with human existence, the human condition, and not merely with abstract conditions and principles".[14] Furthermore, for Marcuse, Heidegger had articulated the principles of human historicity, a necessary part of the Marxist attempt to explain man with reference to historical movement. Theodor Adorno met Heidegger once in 1931 but in the 1960s wrote a number of books, including *Jargon of Authenticity* and *Negative Dialectics*, that were deeply critical of Heidegger's project and his language. In 1953 Jürgen Habermas was one of the first to criticise Heidegger's failure to renounce or withdraw statements in support of Nazism which he made in his 1935 *Introduction to Metaphysics* lectures which were published in 1953. In *The Philosophical Discourse of*

Modernity Habermas is highly critical of Heidegger's inability to separate the enlightenment conception of modern reason from self-assertive elements of racism and nationalism, but acknowledges the originality of Heidegger's invocation of the concept of world in order to criticise the philosophy of consciousness. Habermas sees Heidegger's existential analysis as a kind of heroic nihilism in the face of finitude, and concludes that Heidegger remains trapped within "the enchanted circle of the philosophy of the subject".[15]

Heidegger had less success among the followers of positivism. The Vienna Circle in particular targeted Heidegger as a woolly and inflated thinker whose propositions were devoid of substantial meaning. Thus Rudolf Carnap explicitly took issue with the account of nothingness in *What is Metaphysics?*. The influence of Ayer, Russell, and Ryle meant that Heidegger's thought did not gain prominence in Britain until recently.[16] However, there is now considerable interest in Heidegger in analytic circles where his holism is often compared with that of Donald Davidson. In the USA, Heidegger has had an important influence on philosophers such as Richard Rorty and Hubert Dreyfus. Rorty reads the Heidegger of *Being and Time* as essentially a pragmatist in the tradition of Dewey.[17] Rorty also believes that Heidegger's mission in philosophy is basically a 'world-disclosing' one rather than an a problem-solving approach, such as one encounters in Aristotle or Russell. Dreyfus believes, on the other hand, that Heidegger's anti-subjectivist stance can offer a new model for understanding consciousness which escapes the problems of representationalism which has dogged philosophy of mind since Descartes.

In France Heidegger's influence came chiefly through the mediation of Emmanuel Levinas, who had studied with Heidegger at Freiburg in 1928, and after the war through Jean Beaufret and Jean-Paul Sartre. Heidegger's philosophy was enthusiastically absorbed in French existentialism and later reinterpreted in Derrida's deconstruction and Foucault's anti-humanism. Foucault has said: "For me Heidegger has always been the essential philosopher...My entire philosophical development was determined by my reading of Heidegger".[18]

Heidegger will continue to be valued as an original thinker who laid enormous stress on the importance of thoughtful questioning over and against the construction of philosophical systems. Heidegger himself emphasised the role of the thinker as seeking 'what is unthought' (*das Ungedachte*) in that which is announced. Heidegger is always looking for the thought behind our thoughts. Though this seeking after depth can easily be caricatured and satirised (as Adorno, for example, has done), Heidegger inspired a new and radical way of reading philosophical texts. Heidegger's violent destructions of classical texts is the source of Derrida's deconstruction and continues to offer a model of a reading of texts which is tied neither to authorship and authority, nor to the social and historical context, but to the text as embodying the matter (*die Sache*) for thought.

Heidegger's later attention to the nature of poetic speaking can be seen as a kind of mysticism which many see to be the abandonment of the Greek ideal of philosophy as rational dialogue. Heidegger proclaims that questioning is the piety of thinking, but often his later thought seemed more concerned to be a kind of poetic response to a Being whose movements only Heidegger seemed able to hear. Despite his claim to be in dialogue with the great thinkers, Heidegger's dialogue consists of one-sided pronouncements on the state of Being, or the withdrawal from Being, which can seem to be groundless. Heidegger will undoubtedly always be seen as one of the most important and controversial thinkers of the twentieth century. Among those he influenced directly were Hans-Georg Gadamer and Hannah Arendt to whose encounters with phenomenology we shall now turn.

8

HANS-GEORG GADAMER
Philosophical hermeneutics

Introduction: an overview of Gadamer's philosophy

Summarising his lengthy philosophical career, Hans-Georg Gadamer (b. 1900) has claimed that "hermeneutics and Greek philosophy remain the two main foci of my work".[1] Both interests were stimulated by his encounter with Martin Heidegger. Gadamer's manner of engaging with *texts*, and his fascination with the binding character of *tradition*, owe a deep debt to Heidegger's conception of hermeneutics, and more than any other follower of Heidegger, Gadamer has made hermeneutics central to the practice of philosophy itself.

Gadamer's understanding of philosophy as a living, participative activity contrasted strongly with the ahistorical Neo-Kantian tradition, which dominated the philosophical scene in Germany in the early years of this century. Rebelling against this tradition, the young Gadamer was captivated both by the phenomenological approach of Husserl and Heidegger and, at the same time, by the studies of Wilhelm Dilthey on the history of hermeneutics, specifically Dilthey's reconstruction of the earlier hermeneutics of Schleiermacher. Gadamer saw an essential connection between phenomenology and hermeneutics: both were concerned with describing the process by which meaning emerges. Furthermore, Heidegger's emphasis on facticity strongly impressed on Gadamer the manner in which understanding is constantly challenged by historical and cultural distance. Genuine understanding operates across distances, so to speak.

Hermeneutics is the art of interpretation or understanding, and, for Gadamer, always signifies an ongoing, never completable process of understanding, rooted in human finitude and human 'linguisticality' (*Sprachlichkeit*). Gadamer follows Heidegger's *Being and Time* in seeing understanding as *the* central manner of human being-in-the-world. Humans are essentially involved in the historically situated and finite task of understanding the world, a world encountered and inhabited in and through language (BT §§ 32–34, especially). As Gadamer puts it in *Truth and Method*, "language is the medium of the hermeneutic experience", that is language is the medium in which understanding is realised.[2] Furthermore, for Gadamer, language has its true being in 'speech' (*Sprache*), the kind of speech which occurs in the context of a 'conversation' (*ein Gespräch*, TM 446; 422). Philosophy, then, is a conversation leading towards mutual understanding, a conversation, furthermore, where this very understanding comes as something genuinely *experienced*. Moreover, the practice of phenomenology is the best way to access properly and describe the *experience of understanding* itself. Thus Gadamer understands the function of philosophy as the revealing or making manifest (*darstellen*) of 'the matters themselves' (*die Sache selbst*), shedding light on the essence of matters, 'essence illumination' (*Wesenserhellung*). These 'matters' are what are revealed in language. For Gadamer, shared understanding is a genuine 'event' which brings something real into being, something which arises "over and above our wanting and doing". Indeed Gadamer goes further and claims that the 'things themselves' reveal themselves only in and through language: "In truth, however, the illusion that things precede their manifestation in language conceals the fundamentally linguistic character of our experience of the world".[3]

It is true that Gadamer, like his mentor Heidegger, tends to be somewhat vague and elusive about the exact nature of these 'matters themselves' which are experienced and come to light. Gadamer defends himself, however, by arguing that it is in the nature of genuine conversation to allow these matters to emerge in the mind of the participants, rather than being revealed by the speaker him- or herself. The dialogical character of his philosophy is such that Gadamer always interprets the matters themselves as the events which occur 'between' people and their tradition – the common understandings which emerge in a dialogue and which go beyond the intentions of the speakers. A genuine dialogue makes truth manifest beyond the subject: "a genuine conversation is never the one we wanted to conduct" (TM 383; 361).

Gadamer, following Heidegger, is emphasising the essentially anti-subjectivist view of understanding. According to Gadamer, the German word, *Verstehen*, can mean literally to stand in for someone, or to hold a brief for someone, for example a lawyer speaking on behalf of a client. The very notion of understanding, then, carries with it an openness to the other person, an openness encapsulated in the notion of dialogue. As he frequently puts it: "dialectic has to be retrieved in hermeneutics". Our relation to texts in a tradition has to be understood in terms of our model of a dialogue with others.

Like Heidegger, he also thinks this anti-subjectivism accurately captures the outlook of the ancient Greeks. For Gadamer, the ancient Greeks understood *the matters themselves* as coming to light in speech (TM 474; 450). Moreover, Gadamer endorses Heidegger's claim that the Greeks had no word for language in general; what they understood was speech, 'discourse' (*Rede*, BT § 34). For Plato, philosophical discourse was understood as dialectic, which meant "the art of leading a conversation".[4] In this kind of conversation, the understanding reached is "neither mine nor yours and thus exceeds the subjective beliefs of the partners in discussion" (TM 368; 350).

Gadamer was initially attracted to Heidegger's reading of Greek philosophy as a phenomenological attempt to understand concrete, factical life. *Being and Time* is, for him, an essay in human *self-understanding*. Human self-understanding is also the project of hermeneutics. Gadamer continued to maintain his interest in Heidegger after his famous 'turning' (*die Kehre*) of the early 1930s, which involved him reversing the emphasis of *Being and Time* and seeking for the truth of Being apart from beings. Gadamer is attracted to the emphasis in Heidegger's later philosophy on truth as an event of being, a coming into being of something new, akin to the kind of revelation in art. Heidegger's later descriptions of the manner in which humans dwell within the world opened up by language – the way in which, as Heidegger puts it, language 'speaks' man – are in deep agreement with Gadamer's outlook. In a sense, then, Gadamer may be seen as putting into practice Heidegger's theoretical understanding of human cultural formation.

Gadamer's philosophy, then, is a kind of phenomenology of the act of understanding, the central act by which humans engage with the world. It is phenomenological in that it attempts to do justice to the event of understanding and does not reduce it to a subjectivist or epistemological framework. But, as a phenomenological account, Gadamer is also producing a kind of transcendental description of the conditions which make understanding possible, and thus he is not as far removed from his Neo-Kantian and Husserlian heritage as he often claims.

The classical legacy

Gadamer himself was primarily trained in classical philosophy and philology, and his hermeneutics involves an ongoing interpretation of the meaning of the classical philosophical tradition. Thus Jürgen Habermas has justly characterised Gadamer's fundamental motivation as "the drive to clarify for himself and others what the encounter with eminent texts means, what the binding character of the classical is all about".[5] To understand the nature of the classical legacy, Gadamer begins with the interpretation of history within philosophy itself, and specifically within German romanticism. Thus Gadamer explicitly links the philosophical projects of Plato and Aristotle with the reflection on classical life in Hegel and the German idealist tradition. Furthermore, he sees the main way of understanding the classical as coming through an interpretation of their key experiences, chiefly their experience of art. Following Hegel and Heidegger, Gadamer's paradigm of genuine cultural understanding is always the experience of art.

Gadamer, however, while deeply influenced by the German idealist tradition and the romantic movement, believes they have distorted the original experience of history and of art. His project, then, involves a recovery of the true meaning of both. Whereas Schleiermacher had wanted to recover the original psychological experiences of past life, and Hegel had wanted to reintegrate the past into the present, Gadamer emphasises the need to respect and reflect on the very nature of the distances which open up *between* us and the world of a classical text, "the true locus of hermeneutics is in this in-between (*in diesem Zwischen*)" (TM 295; 279).

This leads Gadamer to reflect on the nature of historical and cultural understanding in general. Here Gadamer is influenced by the historical–cultural approach of Wilhelm Dilthey and draws heavily on Dilthey's historical account of the development of hermeneutics, but his own approach distinguishes itself from this tradition. In particular, Gadamer repudiates Dilthey's notion of hermeneutics as characterising the distinctive method of the social and human sciences (*Geisteswissenschaften*). Gadamer opposes the view of hermeneutics as a 'technique' or 'art' (*Kunstlehre*) of achieving understanding of cultural entities, chiefly texts. This view of hermeneutics tends to assume that our everyday encounter with the world is not intrinsically hermeneutical, whereas Gadamer holds, with Heidegger, that hermeneutics is a basic structure constituent of human understanding itself. Hermeneutics is everywhere, in all aspects of human life; hermeneutics is "*a universal aspect of philosophy*" (TM 476; 451). It is also a mistake to contrast cultural *understanding* (*Verstehen*) with scientific *explanation* (*Erklärung*), as Dilthey does, because this contrast usually assumes that scientific explanation is the basic model of reason with which *Verstehen* is then compared and to which, of course, it inevitably fails to measure up. Rather, hermeneutics recognises that understanding is a prerequisite of human life as such, and is carried on within human life with its own structure and paradigms. The model of scientific understanding has always assumed the possibility of a timeless knowledge, such as is possessed by an infinite intellect, whereas in fact all understanding, including scientific explanation, is historically conditioned, is partial, and always comes from a point of view. Understanding takes place within the finite boundaries of essentially limited and historically conditioned human living, as both Hegel and Marx knew well, and as Heidegger concretely described in *Being and Time*. Understanding only takes place in the context of an existing tradition (*Überlieferung*). In this sense, we already presuppose a huge amount in every act of understanding – we take on trust our own presumptions or prejudices.

A condition of genuine understanding is that we also have to accept the good intentions of the other person whom we are seeking to understand. Gadamer, then, seeks a form of encounter with others which is at once wholly open to new possibilities, and, indeed, to the truth of the other's position, while, at the same time, remaining deeply respectful of one's own starting point, one's inherited outlook and presuppositions. Whether this double stance of indebtedness and critique is possible at all is the real question concerning Gadamer's contribution, and a question which has been raised explicitly by Jürgen Habermas in his critique of Gadamer.

The tradition of understanding

Understanding understanding requires coming to self-understanding, shedding light on assumptions which otherwise work "behind our backs" (*Phil. Herm.*, p. 38). For Gadamer, all understanding is determined by 'pre-judgement' (*Vorurteil*) and our pre-judgements are formed by what Gadamer calls "effective history" (*Wirkungsgeschichte*, the "history of effect", TM 300; 284), the historical working out of the effects of actions in which we are inevitably involved. Our consciousness of being affected by history belongs to the manner in which we understand everything, including the nature of history itself. When we understand an object, we do not grasp the object as it is in itself, but rather we grasp it through the accumulations of its historical effectiveness, what it has evolved into being for us, its *Wirkungsgeschichte* or 'effective history', the 'history of the influence' of the object on human communities. This should not be thought of as something extrinsic to the thing, but rather as an essential part of it. It is "more being than consciousness", Gadamer says. Thus when we respond to the statue of a god in a museum, even though it no longer is situated in its original context of the temple, it still has a claim on us and we respond to it by a kind of total self-involvement whereby the world of the object and the world of the subject merge. As Gadamer says, to understand a work of art is to gather it into "the totality of one's self-understanding" (TM xxx; xvi).

Our understanding is essentially enabled and conditioned by our pre-judgements. But it is also limited by the overall 'horizons' of our outlook. Gadamer like Husserl sees all understanding as taking place within a certain horizon. What he wants to oppose is the view that these horizons are mutually exclusive or that our world-views are hermetically sealed. Gadamer wants to emphasise that in fact our horizons are open to other horizons, that they can overlap and indeed *are* overlapping. Against the scepticism of Richard Rorty, for example, Gadamer is emphatic that we can and do reach mutual understanding. This is a process of the interpenetration of our horizons, or what Gadamer calls 'fusion of horizons' (*Horizontsverschmelzung*, TM 306; 290), here taking over Husserl's notion of 'horizon' (*Horizont*), the inner and outer horizons in an act of perception. The attempt to understand the other must begin with the recognition that we are separated by different horizons of understanding, and that mutual understanding comes through overlapping consensus, merging of horizons, rather than through the abandonment by one of the interlocutors of his or her initial horizon.

Gadamer's model for this mutual understanding is the shared enquiry of the Platonic dialogues where the interlocutors embark on a joint journey of discovery and discussion rather than a Sophistic debate which seeks the domination of one outlook by the other. In this kind of dialogue, the presuppositions are brought to light and explored but the context is one of overall acceptance and trust. Thus, in opposition to Michel Foucault and Jacques Derrida, Gadamer rejects any Nietzschean suspicion that all understanding is really an attempt at mastery and will-to-power. Or to put it another way, employing Paul Ricoeur's terms, Gadamer practises a *hermeneutics of trust* rather than of *suspicion*. His approach, however, may be criticised as perhaps too tolerant of the 'given' of tradition, and in this sense he has often been criticised as a 'traditionalist'. He ought, according to some commentators, to give more room to a general suspicion about what presents itself as 'tradition' and 'culture'. Thus, his hermeneutics has been criticised by Jürgen Habermas as lacking a certain emancipatory dimension which would free itself from the distorting aspects of tradition.

Philosophy as dialogue

Gadamer's personal style and commitment to living dialogue has meant that, in general, he does not write systematic treatises and indeed he did not publish any full-length book during most of his teaching career, between 1931 and 1960. He confessed to having trouble writing, always feeling that Heidegger was looking over his shoulder. As a consequence, most of his writings have been in the form of essays, many of which originated as lectures. Even his greatest work, *Wahrheit und Methode* (*Truth and Method*, 1960), takes the form of a loosely related series of essays on central concepts of the classical tradition while arguing for the general point that we can talk of the truth of art and of cultural products in a genuine sense – that not all truth is encapsulated in scientific method.

On the other hand, Gadamer practises what he preaches, namely philosophy as conversation. Thus he has taken part in debates with Derrida, Habermas, Ricoeur, Apel, and others. Jürgen Habermas (b. 1929) has been one of his most persistent critics, beginning with his *Logic of the Social Sciences* and including his contribution to the *Festschrift* for Gadamer's 70th birthday.[6] Gadamer has replied to Habermas on a number of occasions.[7] In 1981 Gadamer took part in a debate with Jacques Derrida in Paris, where he outlined the nature of hermeneutics and his relationship to Heidegger, defending his interpretation of Heidegger against Derrida whom he claimed had been seduced by Nietzsche. This interaction gave rise to four texts, two by Gadamer and two by Derrida. Gadamer begins by discussing Nietzsche, criticising his wilful subjectivism in interpretation, as a way into Derrida's philosophy.[8] Derrida, for his part, avoided dialogue and direct engagement with Gadamer and instead offered a number of questions and made a number of points which seemed quite tangential to the discussion. In particular, Derrida accused Gadamer of being under the shadow of Kant's assumption of the good will, to which Gadamer replied that his assumptions about good will in conversation were taken from Plato's notion of *eumeneis elenchoi* and had nothing to do with Kant. The general feeling was that Gadamer had come off rather better from the encounter.

Hans-Georg Gadamer (1900–): life and writings

Hans-Georg Gadamer is the grand old man of German letters; his life spans the whole of the twentieth century, which gives him an unrivalled position as both participant in and witness to the unfolding of contemporary philosophy in Europe. He attended Husserl's lectures in Freiburg and Heidegger's and Bultmann's seminars in Marburg. He was a contemporary of Hannah Arendt, Herbert Marcuse, Theodor Adorno, Max Horkheimer, and Karl Löwith as well as engaging with what, to him, must seem the younger generation of European philosophers, namely Jürgen Habermas, Rudiger Bübner, Jacques Derrida, and Karl-Otto Apel. Gadamer has written a fascinating account of his encounters with the great philosophers of the twentieth century in his *Philosophische Lehrjahre* (*Philosophical Apprenticeships*).[9] His works are peppered with these cameo portraits, which are recalled with remarkable consistency, given that he is remembering events which occurred up to seventy years earlier. This seems to be the nature of Gadamer's memory – something he claims to be phenomenological – namely, his ability to seize on small singular details and distil from them the essence of the person or of the situation. There is, however, something rather studied, conventional, even formulaic, in these portraits which suggest that they may be masking the events as much as revealing them.

Born in Marburg in 1900, he spent his childhood in Breslau in Silesia, where he attended the Holy Spirit Gymnasium. His father, a research chemist, tried to steer him towards the natural sciences but his own inclinations tended more in the direction of literature and the arts. The First World War cast a long and dark shadow on his secondary schooling, with more and more of the senior boys being called up for military duty, only later to have their names recorded as dead in the class rolls. Gadamer's youth, however, exempted him from military service in the war, and in 1918 he enrolled in Breslau's Higher Education Institute to study the human sciences. He began to read in philosophy, beginning with Kant and Cassirer, and later also discovering Kierkegaard, Lessing, and Hegel.

Gadamer then transferred to Marburg University to read philosophy and classical philology. Here the philosophical atmosphere was thoroughly Neo-Kantian. Marburg's most prominent philosopher, Hermann Cohen, had passed away in 1918 but the Neo-Kantian tradition continued with Ernst

Cassirer, Paul Natorp, and Nicolai Hartmann. There was also a burgeoning theological school forming under the direction of Rudolf Bultmann, who had come to Marburg in 1921. Gadamer immersed himself in this rich world of learning, participating in the theological circle around Rudolph Bultmann, which included Rudolf Otto, and the literary circle around the poet Stefan George which sought a spiritual renewal for Germany. Other friends at Marburg included the left-wing art historian Richard Hamann and the medieval historian E. R. Curtius. Here, Gadamer read Nietzsche, Kierkegaard, Thomas Mann, Hölderlin, and Oswald Spengler. In 1922, he completed his doctorate, *Das Wesen der Lust in den platonischen Dialogen* ("The Essence of Desire in the Platonic Dialogues"), under the supervision of Paul Natorp and Nicolai Hartmann. While he regarded Hartmann as trapped in a naive realism, he considered Paul Natorp (1854–1924) to be an "avant-gardist within the Marburg school",[10] who read Plato as a Kantian transcendental idealist interested in the foundations of scientific method. Natorp, however, was weaving an immensely complicated a priori system, which even sought to show a priori that space must have three dimensions, an approach Gadamer regarded as outmoded.[11] From Hartmann, Natorp, and later Paul Friedländer, who approached Plato's dialogues in both a philological and a literary manner, Gadamer learned a new way of reading Plato, a Plato, moreover, not opposed to Aristotle. Gadamer's later fusion of phenomenology, hermeneutics, and classical philosophy had its foundations in his early Marburg years.

Marburg Neo-Kantianism

Neo-Kantianism was a movement which sought to protect philosophy against the encroachment of the positive sciences, by defining the function of philosophy as providing a transcendental foundation for the natural sciences.[12] The Neo-Kantian solution to the challenge concerning what subject matter was left to philosophy was to make philosophy into a transcendental critique of the nature of the scientific enterprise itself. Whereas the positive sciences are concerned with the sphere of *fact*, philosophy is concerned with *normativity*, with the criteria for genuine knowledge. Heidegger, in his debate with Cassirer in Davos in 1929, outlined the origins of the Neo-Kantian problematic as follows:

> The genesis [of neo-Kantianism] lies in the predicament of philoso-
> phy concerning the question of what properly remains of it in the
> whole of knowledge. Since about 1850 it has been the case that
> both the human and the natural sciences have taken possession of
> the totality of what is knowable, so that the question arises: what
> still remains of Philosophy if the totality of beings has been divided
> up under the sciences? It remains just knowledge of science, not of

beings. And it is from this perspective that the retrogression to Kant is then determined. Consequently, Kant was seen as a theoretician of the mathematico-physical theory of knowledge. Theory of knowledge is the aspect according to which Kant came to be seen. In a certain sense, Husserl himself fell into the clutches of neo-Kantianism between 1900 and 1910.

(Heidegger, KPM 171–172)

In general, Neo-Kantianism regarded the mathematical sciences as providing the paradigm for all knowledge, and this it to adopt an ahistorical, systematic approach, concerned with the stratification of the sciences and the specification of correct method. Natorp even viewed classical philosophers such as Plato and Aristotle as defining the conditions under which genuine scientific knowledge, *episteme*, is possible.

The main opposition to Neo-Kantianism in Germany came from the loosely affiliated followers of *Lebensphilosophie*, associated with the writings of Nietzsche, Simmel, Dilthey, Bergson, Jaspers, and Scheler, which sought to reconnect abstract philosophising with concrete existence and which emphasised the particular finitude and interest-driven nature of the particular enquirer. Gadamer was more favourably disposed towards this philosophy of existence than to the more abstract Neo-Kantian philosophy. For Gadamer, as for many students in the post-war years, the collapse of Germany after the Great War was mirrored in the collapse of Neo-Kantianism as a credible philosophical system.[13] The devastation and demoralisation which followed Germany's defeat in the First World War also removed any lingering patriotism or self-sacrificing idealism from a whole generation of students. In so far as Neo-Kantianism had subscribed to this general mood of progress through science, it was now open to radical questioning. As Gadamer wrote:

It is obvious that the profound cultural crisis that came over the whole European culture at that time would have to express itself philosophically, and it was just as obvious that this would be especially pronounced in Germany, whose radical transformation and collapse was the most visible and catastrophic expression of the general absurdity. The critique of this reigning educational idealism, which was supported primarily by the continuing presence of Kantian philosophy in academia, pervaded during these years and stripped academic philosophy as a whole of its credibility. A consciousness of this complete lack of orientation filled the spiritual situation of 1918, into which I myself had begun to peer.[14]

A number of figures began to offer ways of interpreting Germany's crisis: Stefan George, Oswald Spengler's popular *Decline of the West*, and Paul

Ernst's *The Collapse of German Idealism* (1920–1922).[15] In keeping with an overall mood of pessimism, students, including Gadamer, turned to philosophers of expressing an inward-looking view on life, namely Søren Kierkegaard (in the German translation of Diederichs) and Friedrich Nietzsche. It was, however, the arrival at Marburg of a new and exciting young philosophy lecturer which really awoke Gadamer to a new way of doing philosophy.

The encounter with Heidegger

Gadamer was already somewhat familiar with Husserl's phenomenology from his earliest days in university, not just through Natorp's generally favourable review of Husserl's *Ideas*, which had appeared in *Logos* in 1917, but also from the seminars of Richard Hamann. Furthermore, in 1920, Max Scheler, then considered the second leading light of phenomenology after Husserl, had visited Marburg and had discussed Rudolf Otto's *Idea of the Holy* with the young Gadamer (*Phil. App.*, p. 15). Gadamer first encountered the magic of Heidegger's writings in 1922 when Natorp gave him some forty pages of Heidegger's introduction to his unpublished manuscript on Aristotle,[16] an essay which read Aristotle as a phenomenologist and treated him in connection with Luther, Gabriel Biel, Augustine, and St Paul. Gadamer records that Heidegger's unusual approach "struck him like an electric shock". As soon as he had finished his doctorate in 1922, Gadamer had wanted to visit Heidegger in Freiburg, but he had been struck down with polio, a disease which left him with a permanent limp. However, in the spring of 1923, Gadamer decided to study for a semester in Freiburg and, armed with letters of introduction from Paul Natorp to the Kantians at Freiburg, Gadamer went to see Heidegger. He attended Heidegger's seminar on the *Nicomachean Ethics* where Heidegger concentrated on Aristotle's criticism of Plato's idea of the Good (*to agathon*) and offered a phenomenological interpretation of Aristotle's notion of practical wisdom (*phronesis*). While in Freiburg, Gadamer also met Husserl and attended his lectures, but formed the impression that Husserl was caught up in refining the details of a programme which by this stage had grown stale. Husserl was clinging to his transcendental idealism which no longer held the attention of students. Gadamer recalls that Husserl would invite a question and then would answer it uninterruptedly for the whole lecture period, whereas Heidegger proceeded by allowing the students to come to their own understanding of the texts through questioning. In his later work, Gadamer sought to emulate Heidegger's seminar style rather than Husserl's monologues.

In contrast with the remote Husserl, Martin Heidegger was inspirational, rescuing Aristotle from the Neo-Scholastic dogmatic tradition and making the text come to life, reading Aristotle as someone engaging with the phenomena of practical living. As Gadamer later recalled:

At that time I was strongly influenced by Heidegger's interpretation of Aristotle, the real intention of which was still not completely evident, namely its critique of ontology, and which in essence repeated Aristotle's critique of Plato in the form of an existential, situation-oriented philosophical critique of the idealist tradition.[17]

Heidegger grasped that both Plato and Aristotle were seeking the essential nature of things. Gadamer was immediately drawn to Heidegger as a philosophical visionary, as "one who sees", a kind of seeing which Gadamer connected with Husserl's emphasis on the importance of direct seeing in phenomenology. Gadamer understood the essential motive of Husserl's phenomenology as a bringing us into contact with things through their being perceived in their fleshly presence (*Leibhaftigkeit*):

The fundamental teaching of Husserl's phenomenology was that knowledge is first and foremost a viewing or intuition; that is, it is achieved when a thing is seen comprehensively with one beholding. Sense perception, which places the object before the eye in its incarnate givenness, is the model according to which all conceptual knowledge is to be thought.[18]

But, for the young Gadamer, it was Heidegger – not Husserl – who was actually practising essential seeing: "When Heidegger lectured, one could see the things in front of one, as if they were physically graspable".[19]

While still in Freiburg, in the autumn of 1923, the young Gadamer was among the students invited by Heidegger up to his mountain hut in Todtnauberg for a get-together before Heidegger left for Marburg. On this occasion Heidegger delivered an inspiring talk about the Greeks around a camp fire (*Phil. App.*, pp. 47–48). He was also on hand to greet Heidegger when he arrived at Marburg later in 1923 to take up his professorship. Gadamer attended Heidegger's early morning seminars at Marburg, seminars followed by long discussions on Aristotle in the cafés. Heidegger was lecturing on the 'hermeneutics of facticity' through his radical reading of Aristotle, laying the basis for his account of Dasein in *Being and Time* which he had just begun to write at that time. Heidegger's central message was that understanding is not essentially theoretical cognition but rather is a basic existential category of human existence itself. As Gadamer later acknowledged in *Truth and Method*:

Heidegger's temporal analytics of Dasein has, I think, shown convincingly that understanding is not just one of the various possible behaviors of the subject but the mode of Being of Dasein itself (*die Seinsweise des Daseins selber*).

(TM xxx; xvi)

As Gadamer later claimed, "Heidegger's arrival in Marburg cannot be overdramatized". [20]

Indeed, Gadamer offers independent confirmation for Hannah Arendt's assertion that rumours about Heidegger had been circulating among the students at Marburg for some time, rumours which emanated especially from students who had been in Freiburg and had been impressed by Heidegger's lecturing style and his novel way of using language, and had thus been "Heideggerianised" (*Phil. App.*, p. 46). Gadamer recalls:

> When my decisive encounter with Heidegger occurred, I was a young man and had just completed my doctorate in philosophy with Paul Natorp of the "Marburg School". For the entire time of my study with Natorp and with Nicolai Hartmann, the feeling had accompanied me that something was missing, a feeling whose ultimate sources very likely lay in my own nature and what I had experienced in my intellectual and cultural development, a feeling about which I was somehow reassured when I met Heidegger. All at once I knew. That was what I had missed and what I had been seeking, namely the insight that philosophical thought should not consider history and the historicity of our existence as a constraint, but rather that it should raise this, our very ownmost impulse in our lives, up into thinking.[21]

Gadamer was now in a position to contrast the problem-oriented, anti-historical Marburg Neo-Kantianism with Heidegger's interest in human temporality and historicity, and his emphasis on human finitude as rendering impossible a completely objective science. Natorp had brought Heidegger to Marburg to introduce phenomenology and medieval philosophy into the curriculum there, and Heidegger easily adapted to the role of harbinger of Husserlian phenomenology. Heidegger offered lectures on both phenomenology and classical philosophy. His readings of the Greek philosophers, Aristotle and Plato, were radically challenging and refreshing. Heidegger, moreover, impressed Gadamer because he was interested in Dilthey's and Count Yorck's reflections on the nature of history, whereas Husserl had famously rejected Dilthey's historicism as a self-refuting relativism in his 1911 essay *Philosophy as a Rigorous Science*.

Heidegger and Dilthey awoke Gadamer to the possibility of philosophy as an ongoing attempt to understand the unique and unrepeatable in history and culture. However, whereas Dilthey clung to the notion of scientific objectivity and simply tried to claim that the method for achieving objectivity in the human sciences was different from the normal method of the natural sciences, both Gadamer and Heidegger rejected the very notion of objectivity as a vestige of the Cartesian approach to knowledge. Gadamer came to see that the nature of *understanding*, in the case of aesthetic

259

experience or of history, was quite different from, but no less valid than, that of the natural sciences.

Gadamer was drawn to Heidegger and Jaspers as the main sources of this critique of the prevailing German philosophical situation. Jaspers himself drew on Kierkegaard and developed a philosophy of existence which emphasised the notion of "limit-situations" (*Grenzsituationen*), whereas Heidegger's focus was on the nature of historical human reality, and especially on rethinking the nature of his own fall from theological conviction through a phenomenology of factical life. For Gadamer, it was Heidegger, more than Bultmann, who awoke him to the possibilities inherent in the hermeneutic tradition.

Plato's Dialectical Ethics *(1931)*

Gadamer completed his State Examination in philology in 1927 and then wrote his *Habilitationsschrift*, a phenomenological interpretation of Plato's *Philebus* under Heidegger's direction. The *Habilitation* proceedings dragged on until late in 1928 after Heidegger had already left Marburg for Freiburg, and the thesis was eventually published as *Plato's Dialectical Ethics* in 1931.[22] In his 1931 Preface Gadamer says that he owes a great deal to Heidegger: "by the whole methodological attitude of my work, which tries to extend what I have learned from Heidegger and above all make it fruitful by practising it in a new way" (PDE, p. xxvi). In a later Preface, written on the occasion of the 1982 reprint, Gadamer writes:

> In the force and radicalism of the questioning which the young Martin Heidegger fascinated his students, there lived on something that was inherited not least of all from phenomenology: an art of description that devoted itself to the phenomena in their concreteness, avoiding both the learned airs of the scientific fraternity and, as much as possible, the traditional technical terminology, thereby bringing it about that the things (the facts of the matter) almost forced themselves upon one.
>
> (PDE, p. xxxii)

The American philosopher of language Donald Davidson, who wrote his own PhD thesis on the *Philebus*, has called Gadamer's book "a stunning essay on the origins of objectivity in communal discussion...a demonstration of what the interpretation of a text can be".[23] Gadamer seeks to locate the *Philebus* within the entire corpus of Platonic dialogues and assumes that the doctrine of the Forms is still at work in the dialogue. Plato's *Philebus* is a complex and awkwardly constructed dialogue which treats of the ethical question whether *pleasure* (*hedone*) or *knowledge* (*episteme*) is the best thing in human life, the highest human good. Philebus, through his spokesman,

Protarchus, defends pleasure, whereas Socrates advocates contemplation and wisdom. In the course of treating this question, Plato goes on to give a long and detailed examination of the notion of dialectic, the method of collection and division which is also treated in the *Sophist*. The dialogue ends with Socrates moving to a middle position accepting a 'mixed' life which blends both wisdom and pleasure, since knowledge and pleasure are not true opposites at all.

In the first chapter of his *Habilitationsschrift*, Gadamer tries to establish the relation between Socratic questioning and Platonic dialectic, a central theme of all his subsequent work. Gadamer focuses on the nature of the aim of knowledge as arriving at agreement through shared conversation and reads the Platonic dialectic in terms of the Aristotelian requirements for demonstrative science (*episteme*). As Gadamer says: "The process of reaching a shared understanding of the matter in question through conversation is aimed at knowledge" (PDE, p. 17).

After his *Habilitation*, Gadamer remained at Marburg as a poorly paid *Privatdozent* alongside fellow colleagues Karl Löwith and Gerhard Krüger. Meanwhile Heidegger had moved back to Freiburg. Gadamer's next important encounter with Heidegger came in 1936 when he travelled to Frankfurt to hear Heidegger's lectures on art, later published as "The Origin of the Work of Art" in *Holzwege* (1950). For Gadamer, the central meaning of these controversial lectures was that art is genuinely connected with a particular community.[24] Gadamer essentially agreed with Heidegger's connection of art with the destiny of a 'people' (*Volk*), regardless of how this insight may have been abused in National Socialist theories of art. In 1960 Gadamer wrote an important introduction to the Reclam edition of *The Origin of the Work of Art*,[25] where he correctly situates Heidegger as returning from Neo-Kantian aesthetics to the Hegelian view of art as disclosing truth: "art is the project by which something new comes forth as true".[26] Gadamer portrays *Being and Time* as a detailed account of finite, historical human existence, whose emphasis on historicality and finitude excluded those moments of existence which are not primarily historical: the nature of numbers, for example, the ever-repeated cycle of nature, and "the miracle of art". For Gadamer, while Heidegger's claim that art founds or sets up a world was important, the real breakthrough was in introducing the concept of the *earth* as that which is self-shielding in every art work. Indeed, all of Gadamer's subsequent art interpretation is influenced by his reading of this Heideggerian essay.

Gadamer and the Nazis

When Hitler and the National Socialist Party came to power in early 1933, Gadamer and his fellow old-world liberals, that is cultural conservatives,[27] were taken entirely by surprise as they had not assumed that this party's extreme views would be taken seriously by the electorate. Gadamer and others had assumed that Hitler would divest himself of his non-sensical rhetoric when in power, especially his anti-Semitism.[28] Gadamer's instinct, however, was to survive in the new state by being as apolitical and as unnoticeable as possible. Externally, he was entirely compliant with the new regime, though he acknowledged he was seen as having no more than a "loose sympathy" with the Nazis (*Phil. App.*, p. 76). Heidegger's famous Rectoral Address in Freiburg had committed the universities to serving Hitler. Gadamer admits to being quite impressed with this speech, which Heidegger had sent him, though he soon came to the view that it was not a good idea to get involved in such a national uprising.[29] In fact, in general the Nazis received strong support from sections of the universities, including the poorly paid *Privatdozenten* whom the Nazis organised effectively. The rise of the Nazis even provided Gadamer with his first properly paid teaching post.

As Gadamer records in his autobiography, he went to Kiel in 1934–1935 to teach as replacement for the philosopher Richard Kroner, who, as a Jew, had been suspended from teaching by official decree.[30] Kiel at the time was something of an outpost of the Nazi cultural revolution, strongly active in the *Gleichschaltung*, the 'alignment' of the University to the aims of the Nazi Party, making the University 'toe the line'. Gadamer himself was not anti-Semitic, but he did not have the civic courage to protest about the manner in which his Jewish friends and colleagues were being treated. When his Jewish friends (including Erich Auerbach and Karl Löwith) were forced into exile Gadamer could only comment: "parting was bitter" (*Phil. App.*, p. 77). Nevertheless, Gadamer was comfortable at Kiel; or, as he ironically commented, as comfortable as one can be knowing that it is not one's own goose that is being cooked. Though Gadamer claims never to have been a member of the Nazi Party, and indeed to have been under investigation from time to time, nevertheless, along with many of the other lecturers, in the autumn of 1935 he voluntarily attended a *Wissenschaftslager*, an "academic camp", to undergo a Nazi "rehabilitation" (*Phil. App.*, p. 79), which provided a revised version of his original licence to teach, thus qualifying him to retain his new position at Marburg.

Gadamer delivered an important lecture in January 1934, "Plato and the Poets" (*Plato und die Dichter*), on Plato's famous curb on poets in the *Republic*, an essay which has been read as offering some kind of conservative support to the kind of state renewal that the Nazis were seeking to effect.[31] Gadamer himself portrays the lecture as containing a tiny *frisson* of protest in that it begins by quoting Goethe to the effect that the philosopher is not at one with his times (*Phil. App.*, p. 78).[32] The essay itself ostensibly examines Plato's motivation in banning the poets from the *polis*. Gadamer argues that Plato is a harbinger of a revolutionary *paideia* and is offering a severe criticism of the classical Greek education. Plato recognised the need to jettison poetry in order to bring the new state into being. Indeed, Plato himself, in his 'hour of decision', burnt his own youthful efforts at poetry when he met Socrates. Gadamer draws back from endorsing Plato's move, and so the essay is ambiguous; it could be read as justifying book-burning and a radical shake-up of the educational practice to bring about the new revolutionary state. Nazi ideologues (e.g. Bernhard Rust), writing at the time, had emphasised the connection between the new German state and the *politeia* of Plato, and Gadamer's essay can be read as a typical conservative critique of the weak Weimar state, the *polis* 'fit for pigs' which Plato scorns. Such a view would not be untypical. Other classics professors (including Julius Stenzel, Paul Friedländer, Werner Jaeger) were prominent among those conservative intellectuals who criticised the liberalism, Marxism, and anarchist trends they associated with the doomed Weimar Republic.

In the following years, Gadamer compromised with the regime. He admits that he made use of the Nazi salute (required at the opening of all classes), took part in Nazi conferences, and even attended a rally at which Hitler spoke. Unlike his colleague Karl Löwith, Gadamer did not leave Germany, and his – albeit half-hearted and even reluctant – acquiescence with the Nazi regime represents a less than noble period in his life, though, of course, his survival instinct and lack of civic courage cannot easily be judged, especially by those who have not had to live under tyranny. Gadamer was primarily concerned about his own survival and the protection of his family, and he has written honestly about his deep conformism at the time:

> The younger generation of Germans will also, clearly, not have an easy time imagining how things were for us in those days: the wave of conformism, the pressure, the ideological indoctrination, the unforseeable sanctions, and so on. It can happen today that one is asked: why did you people not cry out? There is a tendency, above all, to underestimate the universally human inclination to conformism, which continually finds new ways and means of self-deception.[33]

Of course, as a result of his acquiescence, or, more properly, lack of threat, to the Nazi regime, and due to some political intercessions made on his behalf by a careerist Nazi, his career in fact prospered. He became Professor Extraordinarius at Marburg on 20 April 1937 and, not long afterwards, in January 1939, he was appointed to a full professorship at the University of Leipzig, where he remained throughout the Second World War.

Whereas the Nazi presence at Marburg had been quite intimidating, they were hardly in evidence at all at Leipzig, according to Gadamer, and indeed Gadamer himself was initially somewhat suspect as someone sent to the University by the Reich. Leipzig encouraged scholarship on its own merits, and in contrast to the war-mongering goings on elsewhere in Germany, Gadamer recalls that in 1939: "The war news was received in Leipzig like a report of death" (*Phil. App.*, p. 95). During the war, Gadamer lectured on the classics, especially on Plato's *Republic*, but in general his stance was completely apolitical. The atmosphere at Leipzig was such that he was even able to lecture on Husserl's *Logical Investigations* without having to mark this course book with a little star, indicating its Jewish origin (*Phil. App.*, p. 98). He did take part in propaganda events organised by the Nazis, including a philosophical conference in 1941 in newly occupied Paris, where he lectured on Herder as a critic of Enlightenment. Again, this lecture has been read as falling into line with Nazi propaganda by asserting the superiority of the Germans over the French Enlightenment. However, Gadamer himself saw it as a purely scholarly talk (*Phil. App.*, p. 99), though he concedes that his audience may have been under some compulsion to attend.

Gadamer claims he came under some political scrutiny for jokes he made in class (the use of the example of universal assertion "all asses are brown" was taken to refer to the Brownshirts), but in general, such was his apolitical nature that the Nazis could not find anyone who would denounce him as a threat to their ideology. One interesting question to ask, however, concerns the nature of Gadamer's relation to Heidegger during this whole period. Gadamer claims to have been somewhat disturbed by Heidegger's stance and to have watched it from a distance with dismay. But what kind of distancing was involved? What were Heidegger's relations with Gadamer between 1933 and 1945? The record is silent. However, as Europe became engulfed in war, Gadamer's own philosophical position developed and he became more critical of Plato (and by extension of the German situation). In 1942 he published an article "Plato's Educational State" (*Platos Staat der Erziehung*), where he argued that the state is only preserved if it instantiates justice and criticises the rule of tyrants. This article can be read as a disguised critique of the Nazi state.

The post-war years

After the war, Gadamer was examined but exonerated by the de-Nazification process run by the Americans and was put in charge of rebuilding Leipzig University, including the drafting of new statutes. However, by the end of 1945, the Americans had withdrawn and the Russians had taken over. Gadamer was elected Rector of Leipzig University under the Russian administration, presumably because he was perceived to be untainted by Nazi associations. In the early days of the Marxist administration in Leipzig, Gadamer was encouraged by the readiness of the students to engage in debate and discussion but gradually he noticed that the atmosphere was giving way to a new dogmatism. In 1947 the opportunity arose to go to the University of Frankfurt to help rebuild the Philosophy Department there. Max Horkheimer and Theodor Adorno had also returned to Frankfurt. So in 1947 he left Leipzig and went, with some difficulty, to Frankfurt. Meanwhile, Ernst Bloch, the Marxist philosopher, became his successor at Leipzig.

In 1949 Gadamer moved to Heidelberg to take the chair formerly held by Karl Jaspers, and he remained there until his retirement in 1968. In 1952, with Helmut Kuhn, he helped to found the journal *Philosophische Rundschau*, still an important philosophical publication in Germany. Gadamer contributed to the *Festschrift* for Heidegger's 80th birthday; he also invited Heidegger to partake in his seminars at Heidelberg, and even helped to get Heidegger elected to membership of the Heidelberg Academy of Sciences, at a time when Heidegger was still under censure for his Nazi activities. Gadamer was a founder member of the Hegel Society and was awarded the Hegel Prize by the city of Stuttgart in 1979. With Joachim Ritter he was active in founding the *Historisches Wörterbuch der Philosophie*, a valuable research tool in philosophy. In 1965 he gave the opening address, "On the Power of Reason", to the International Congress for Philosophy in Vienna.

Between 1931 and 1960 Gadamer had published many articles but no book, and was relatively unknown outside a circle of academic philosophers and classicists. His real prominence both in Germany and abroad came with the publication of *Wahrheit und Methode* (*Truth and Method*) in 1960. Gadamer's most important work, *Truth and Method* was begun around 1950 and finally published in 1960, in Gadamer's 60th year. As Gadamer says in the Foreword to the Second Edition of *Truth and Method*:

> My starting point is that the historic human sciences, as they emerged from German Romanticism and were imbued with the spirit of modern science, maintained a humanistic heritage that distinguishes them from all other kinds of modern research and brings them closer to other, quite different, extrascientific experiences, and especially those peculiar to art.
>
> (TM xxviii–xxix; xiv)

Gadamer follows both Heidegger and the older romantic tradition (e.g. Hölderlin or Coleridge) in holding that art is the site of unique truths not accessible through the normal methodology of the sciences. The concept of truth as such is much broader than the narrower methodical concept of truth with which the exact sciences operate. The title, *Truth and Method*, emerged only when the book was in production, and perhaps the title should have been 'Truth *Against* Method', since Gadamer saw it as "heightening the tension between truth and method" (TM 555). In fact, his question is: "to what extent is method a guarantor of truth?" (*Phil. App.*, p. 179). Gadamer wants to get beyond the preoccupation with 'method' in much of contemporary philosophy (he is, undoubtedly, thinking of the logical positivists and their successors, but also of Husserlian phenomenology) and to recognise that there is an understanding of truth which, as he says, is "beyond the methodological self-consciousness of the human sciences". *Truth and Method* puts forward a theory about how the deepest well-springs of human existence which give rise to truth (such as the experience of art and of historical understanding) proceed in a manner rather different from the 'method' of the natural sciences. This scientific method only arises when humans have in a sense objectified the world, placing thereby a distance between themselves and the world. Thus the modern, mechanistic age feels a certain strangeness or foreignness (*Fremdheit*) in front of the world of nature (TM 65; 61). Gadamer acknowledges that the methods of the natural sciences find application in the world of the human sciences as well. He is not trying to contrast one kind of method with another one more suitable for the human sciences. Rather he is trying to reflect on the kind of conditions which gave rise to the pursuit of method and also to retrieve another tradition which does not emphasise method at all – the tradition of what happens 'beyond our willing and doing'. This is the tradition of history and culture, of the world in which we are absorbed. However, Gadamer insists that he never wanted to suggest a complete opposition between method and truth. His real claim is that scientific truth is not the whole of truth. In agreement with the later Husserl, Gadamer holds that the Copernican discovery of the motion of the earth does not negate the truth-for-us of the rising and setting of the sun: "the truth that science tells us is relative to a specific attitude toward the world and cannot at all claim to be the whole" (TM 449; 425). Truth cannot be limited to what can be gained through the application of scientific method. Gadamer is emphatic that he is not against science; indeed he assumes that science will continue to gain power and control. But he wonders if the preconditions for this scientific control have been fully understood; he wants to understand the hermeneutic situation of the sciences.

Truth and Method immediately generated a lively critical debate in Germany about the nature of the social and historical sciences. Drawing on the tradition of Dilthey, Husserl, and Heidegger (*Phil. App.*, p. 146), as well as the older German historical tradition of Hegel, Schleiermacher, Ranke, and Droysen, *Truth and Method* integrates Gadamer's thinking on the philosophy of history, the history of hermeneutics, and the experience of art into a single sustained argument about the nature of '*Bildung*' which spans a range of meanings including 'education', 'cultural formation', 'acculturation', 'culture', and 'cultivation', the German equivalent of the Greek *paideia*, the Latin *formatio*, and the English term 'formation', as used, for example, by Shaftesbury (TM 11; 8). For Gadamer, the concept of

'*Bildung*' was a genuine innovation of the eighteenth-century Enlightenment, when it was conceived as a universal requirement for humanity as such:

> Now, Bildung is intimately associated with the idea of culture and designates primarily the properly human way of developing one's natural talents and capacities.
>
> (TM 10; 8)

Thus Hegel and Humboldt understood *Bildung* as a task for humanity itself (TM 12; 10). Gadamer wants to appropriate the term '*Bildung*' to stand for the kind of knowledge acquired in the human and moral sciences.

In his *Philosophical Apprenticeships* Gadamer himself describes the impact of *Truth and Method*:

> When the book finally appeared, it was not at all certain to me that it had come at the right time. The "second Romantic age" which had come along with the industrialization, bureaucratization, and rationalization of the world in the first half of our century, manifestly seemed to be coming to an end. A new, third wave of Enlightenment was on the move. Would the word that had been spoken by the great metaphysical tradition of the West and that was still audible throughout the "historical" century, the nineteenth, in the end fall on deaf ears? My hermeneutic attempt, which recalled this tradition, simultaneously sought to go beyond the bourgeoisie's blind faith in education, where this tradition survived, and to bring it back to its original powers.
>
> (*Phil. App.*, pp. 146–147)

While Gadamer was at first worried that *Truth and Method*, with its endorsement of prejudice, would seem "alien to a youthful mode of thinking driven by a critical will to emancipate" (*Phil. App.*, p. 147), in fact the book arrived at the right time. The 1960s saw a renewed interest in the social sciences and the reopening of the debate concerning their nature. *Truth and Method* raises the question of what it means to live in a culture and tradition, to appropriate it, to preserve and transform it, to live within it, and allow it to carry us along.

Gadamer followed the publication of this book with several other collections of hermeneutical essays, including *Kleine Schriften* (1964). After his retirement in 1970, Gadamer lectured at universities in Canada and the USA, including Boston College. At the time of writing (October 1999), Gadamer is still active as Professor Emeritus in Heidelberg and still giving occasional seminars in the University. He has assisted in editing his collected works, *Gesammelte Werke*, ten volumes of which have appeared since 1986.[34]

Gadamer on the Greeks and the Germans

According to Habermas, Gadamer aims to rehabilitate the substance of the philosophies of Hegel and Plato and specifically to question the nature of educational formation, *Bildung*, what the ancient Greeks understood by *paideia*. Thus, Gadamer's encounter with Greek philosophy is an important way of understanding the nature of the intellectual tradition in which we find ourselves. As Gadamer says: "I have been formed more by the Platonic dialogues than by the great thinkers of German Idealism" (*Phil. App.*, p. 184). For Gadamer, then, consideration of German culture leads essentially to a confrontation with classical Greek culture.

Furthermore, Gadamer's hermeneutics is deeply imbued with the ancient Greek – and specifically Socratic – desire to pursue philosophy through *dialogue*. For him, as for Plato and Aristotle, philosophising is a *practice* (*praxis*), a form of activity (*ergon*), a way of life, not a set of propositions or dogmas. Gadamer's approach to classical philosophy also emphasises the continuity between Plato's dialectical method and Aristotle's conception of practical philosophy. Both saw philosophy as engaging in a practice. Insight is achieved along the way and in partnership with others. Only true friends can advise each other in Gadamer's opinion and Gadamer was impressed by the stress Aristotle put on friendship in his *Ethics*. As Gadamer says:

> The Aristotelian program of a practical science seems to me to present the only scholarly model according to which the interpretive sciences can be thought out...Aristotle shows that practical reason and practical insight do not possess the "teachability" of science but rather win their possibility in *praxis* itself, and that means in the inner linkage to ethics.
>
> (*Phil. App.*, p. 183)

Gadamer's essays frequently are careful readings of classical Greek texts, especially the Platonic dialogues. For Gadamer, dialectic is "the art of carrying on a conversation" (*Phil. App.*, p. 186), and his readings take the form of conversations with the voices behind the texts. In a number of studies, Gadamer has compared the Greek concept of dialectic with the notion of dialectic in Hegel. He admires Hegel's readings of Plato and Aristotle which recognise their speculative intention. Gadamer is particularly on the side of Plato whose theoretical assertions are undercut by the literary model of the dialogues. While deeply sympathetic to Hegel's attempt to describe the evolution of experience, Gadamer draws back from Hegel's conception of absolute knowledge as the overcoming of all experience. Gadamer wants to remain within the endless process of establishing meaning which, for Hegel, would remain at the level of the 'bad infinite'.

Gadamer wants to emphasise that practical understanding cannot be completely enumerated in the manner of technical or theoretical understanding. Theoretical understanding, as achieved in the exact sciences, assumes an *intellectus infinitus*, a detached neutral viewpoint which at the same time can see all sides of the matter. However, humans are always finite and situated, and so all that we can aspire to we must be able to achieve within our current practices. Nevertheless, Gadamer is not an *irrationalist*; he does not abandon the traditional quest for knowledge, and indeed he agrees with Plato that the purpose of dialogue is to 'give an account' (*logon tithenai*). This view of philosophy as a kind of *praxis* makes it difficult to summarise the main tenets of Gadamer's philosophy.

In *The Idea of the Good in Platonic-Aristotelian Philosophy* Gadamer describes his need to continue to employ phenomenological means in reading and interpreting Aristotle and Plato:

> The art of phenomenological description, a little of which I was able to learn from Husserl and Heidegger, helped me in my first attempts to master this methodological difficulty. Neither a textual analysis of the dialogues' mimetic form of communication nor of the protocol form of Aristotle's papers can claim the authenticity of a descriptive phenomenological exposition based on the text – a phenomenological exposition of their subject matter itself.[35]

Gadamer, like Heidegger and Husserl, seeks to get to *die Sache selbst* – the matter of thinking, that which is to be thought – which lies beneath the text in many cases as something unsaid.

The importance of language

Gadamer accepts Heidegger's view, expressed in *Being and Time*, that human being in the world is primarily an activity of making sense, of *understanding* (*Verstehen*) as a "thrown projection" (*geworfene Entwurf*, BT § 31, 185; 145) into the world; that is, as already thrown into an interpreted world where the possibilities of action depend on, and are projected onto, that already experienced interpretation. There is in all understanding a kind of circularity, whereby what gets understood is in a way already anticipated in what one expects to be understood. Heidegger, following Schleiermacher, refers to this as a 'hermeneutic circle'. Furthermore, Gadamer accepts that the vehicle of communication and of cultural preservation is *language*. In this sense, Gadamer agrees with the later Heidegger that language in a sense *precedes* and encompasses human experience. Thought is possible only on the basis of language. Invoking a line from the poet Stefan George which is also quoted by Heidegger, "Where the word breaks off, no thing can be" (*Kein Ding sei wo das Wort gebricht*), Gadamer proclaims controversially that "being that can be understood is language" (*Sein, das verstanden werden kann, ist Sprache*, TM 474; 450). This has been understood by critics as a kind of linguistic idealism, a suggestion that there is nothing outside of language. But, for Gadamer, it means that full understanding, which in his view is an *event*, is brought about only because of language and in language. Language is where our understanding, our mode of being in the world, comes to realisation. To put it in Heideggerian terms, language is the site of the disclosure of being, but not all being *is* language *tout court*. For Gadamer, the idea that language is essential to our experience of the world is essentially an ancient Greek view:

> That human experience of the world is linguistic in nature was the thread underlying Greek metaphysics in its thinking about being since "Plato's flight into the logoi".
>
> (TM 456; 432)

Thus Gadamer sees his essential task as one of giving a proper phenomenological description of the essential human activity of understanding as ensouled in language. In this sense Gadamer characterises himself both as a phenomenologist and as an ontologist. Language does not just reflect human being but actually makes humans be, brings about human existence as communal understanding and self-understanding. Thus for him, hermeneutics is neither an art or method of providing accurate interpretations, nor a way of regulating interpretation, but, as Habermas rightly characterises it, a critique which "brings to consciousness in a reflective attitude experiences which we have of language in the exercise of our communicative competence and thus in the course of social interaction with others through language".[36]

Furthermore, language can never be completely neutral, never a simple window on experience. Rather, language is already coloured with the value system of the culture which supports it and which language in turn vivifies. In that sense, we can never see through language or surpass it. This is why he appeals to the artistic experience as paradigmatic. In understanding a literary work of art there is a certain resistance and lack of transparency in the language of the work. In Heideggerian terms, the disclosure of world is always limited by the withdrawal of the *earth*, the other polarity of the art work. It is this very richness of disclosure and withdrawal which the art work celebrates. In reading texts, Gadamer maintains, a truth is gained which cannot be gained in any other way.

For Gadamer every effort to speak or comprehend already carries the baggage of the cultural and educational tradition. However, just because our understanding emerges out of our tradition and its prejudices does not mean that we remain trapped within our own subjective viewpoint. For Gadamer, the desire to seek understanding, or even to speak one's mind, always involves a desire to be understood by the other, and a risking of one's assumptions:

The dialogical character of language, which I tried to work out, leaves behind it any starting point in the subjectivity of the speaker. What we find happening in speaking is not a mere reification of intended meaning, but an endeavor that continually modifies itself, or better: a continually recurring temptation to engage oneself in something or to become involved with someone. Genuinely speaking one's mind has little to do with a mere explication and assertion of our prejudices; rather, it risks our prejudices – it exposes oneself to one's own doubt as well as to the rejoinder of the other.[37]

Gadamer is interested in the deep structures presupposed by the act of conversing, by the act of being involved in a conversation. Gadamer's hermeneutics, as an attempt to open ourselves up to the other, is rather similar to the stress placed on the 'other' in Levinas's philosophy, though Gadamer's inspiration is Platonic dialogue and Schleiermacher's interpretation of tradition as a 'Thou'. In developing the other's point of view and – in the Platonic manner – making one's opponent's argument stronger, in a sense one is bringing the not-yet-fully-understood aspect of the subject matter of the discussion into focus.

The tradition of hermeneutics

In *Truth and Method* (especially TM 173–264; 162–250) and in many of his other essays, Gadamer gives his own, sometimes controversial, account of the emergence of hermeneutics in the modern period. Gadamer's sources are the tradition of Protestant theology from Schleiermacher to Dilthey and the hermeneutical phenomenology of Heidegger.[38] The term 'hermeneutics' itself comes from the Greek verb *hermeneuin* which means to 'interpret', as Heidegger had already explained in *Being and Time* § 7. According to Heidegger: "The phenomenology of Dasein is a hermeneutic in the primordial signification of this word, where it designates the business of interpreting" (BT § 7, 62; 37). In Greek mythology, Hermes was the messenger of the gods, a go-between between gods and humans, who tells lies as well as truths, who misleads as well as leads. Hermes represents the untrustworthy yet necessary link between worlds. Similarly, Aristotle's work *Peri hermeneias* (*On Interpretation*) concerns the ways in which sentences or statements can be understood. Hermeneutics, then, is the traditional name for the art of interpretation.

Biblical hermeneutics

Principles of interpreting were gradually set down in ancient and medieval attempts to interpret sacred texts, for example in the Biblical schools of Alexandria where Judaic and Hellenic learning intertwined. Thus Dilthey,

271

for example, in his 1860 *Preisschrift* cites Philo of Alexandria and Origen as important early practitioners of hermeneutics. Theological hermeneutics has a dogmatic purpose. The text has priority because it is the word of God and hence the hermeneutic requirement is to submit to the will of the text. A particular challenge for early Christian exegetes was to decide how the Old Testament should be read in the light of the New Testament (TM 331; 314). Not everything in the Old Testament simply led up to or prefigured the New. Hermeneutics had the task of differentiation as well as emphasising continuity. Thus, for example, the polygamy of Old Testament figures had to be interpreted in a manner which brought it under the norms of the New Testament. As Gadamer says:

> Tradition, which consists in part in handing down self-evident traditional material, must have become questionable before it can become explicitly conscious that appropriating tradition is a hermeneutic task.
>
> (TM xxxiii; xix)

One of the foundational texts of hermeneutics, and one which had a strong influence on Heidegger in his Marburg years, is St Augustine's *On Christian Doctrine* (*De doctrina christiana*, c. 396–427) which puts forward principles of exegesis for the Bible. Important among these principles were: that the part was always to be understood in the light of the whole, and thus a sentence taken from the Bible must always be read in context (*De. doct. ch.*, Bk III.ii.2); that the interpreter must always seek the intention of the text and not seek to impose his own understanding (*De. doct. ch.*, Bk I.xxxvii.41); and that the interpreter must have sufficient knowledge (e.g. of music or mathematics) to be able to understand a text which employs these concepts (*De. doct. ch.*, Bk II.xvi.25–26). Similarly the principle of consistency will require that seemingly contradictory passages must be read in the most charitable light. For instance, since we know from other passages of the Bible that God is good, we have to take care in interpreting any text which appears to claim that God performs evil deeds. Thus, according to St Augustine's hermeneutics, it is often the case that the true meaning of a text can be the opposite of its literal meaning. Most important of all, the interpreter must read the text in a spirit of humility, not puffed up by his or her own vanity, but allowing him- or herself to be open to the spiritual meaning of the text. Thus, in interpreting the sacred scriptures, Augustine writes:

> We should rather think and believe that which is written is better and more true than anything which we could think by ourselves, even when it is obscure.
>
> (*De. doct. ch.*, Bk II.vii.9)[39]

Hermeneutics in the Middle Ages and Renaissance

During the late Middle Ages, as Gadamer acknowledges, hermeneutics was applied specifically to the interpretation of legal judgments, and in particular to the interpretation of the Justinian code.[40] *Legal hermeneutics* is concerned with the application of general principles as set out in texts to specific situations, often having to relate an old law to a new, modern situation. As in theological hermeneutics, there is a primacy given to the text, to the 'letter of the law'. But this still allows for different possibilities of interpretation. Thus, for example, in interpreting a legal code, attention might be paid to the mind and intentions of the framers of the law. This principle of legal hermeneutics has been revived in the 'originalist' position whereby a principle in the Constitution is taken as meaning just what it meant in the days of the framers. For example, the US Supreme Court Justice Scalia has maintained that capital punishment is not 'cruel and unusual' punishment under the US Constitution because it would not have been considered cruel by the original framers of the document in 1776. Of course, opponents of this hermeneutical approach object that such an insistence on the original meaning of a legal text might equally justify violence against one's wife, or ownership of slaves, on the grounds that that was not considered illegal at the time of writing of the law. The hermeneutic problem thus becomes: how do we know what was in the mind of the original framers of the document?

Besides featuring in theology, and in legal judgments, hermeneutics was revitalised in philology by the efforts of Renaissance humanists to revive classical learning. Owing to their distance from the time and language of the original classical texts, the humanists endeavoured to reconstruct texts on philological principles. But it was the religious Reformation which produced a huge expansion in hermeneutics as both Catholic and Protestant theologians argued over the principles to be employed in interpreting the text of the Bible, with the Protestant reformers emphasising the importance of the individual interpreter reading the text for him- or herself, while the Catholic Church emphasised (reaffirmed in the Council of Trent, 1546) guided reading directed by the authoritative interpretations offered by approved Church scholars. Indeed, Gadamer follows Dilthey in laying great stress on the Protestant Reformation as the beginning of modern hermeneutics. A central Protestant principle may be summed up with the words *sola scriptura*, 'the words alone' (TM xxxiii; xix). But clearly – especially in the case of the project of translating the Bible into vernacular languages – just what those words themselves mean can become contentious. One of the most influential texts of Renaissance hermeneutics was Matthias Flacius Illyricus's *Key to Sacred Scripture* (1567) which became a central text in the development of Protestant hermeneutics. The hermeneutical approach fostered by the Protestant Reformation gradually led to the questioning of the unity of the Bible itself and various attempts were made to discern the hand of the various Biblical authors and their intentions. This approach was in the main resisted by Catholic Biblical scholarship until relatively recently, but no serious theologian now denies that the Bible draws together many different texts written at different times.

Hermeneutics in the Enlightenment and in the romantic era

After the Reformation, it was the task of the Enlightenment to attempt to systematise hermeneutics into some kind of general method of understanding. Thus the great Enlightenment theorist of hermeneutics Johan Martin Chladenius (1710–1759) produced a general primer in hermeneutics in his *Introduction to the Correct Interpretation of Reasonable Discourses and Writings* (1742).[41] Chladenius emphasised the importance of studying a text in terms of its purpose, as indicated by the literary form of the text. One should interpret a text in terms of what it itself sets out to be (e.g. a poem, a manual of instruction, and so on).

In the nineteenth century, hermeneutics emerged, with Friedrich Schleiermacher (1768–1834), as a separate and independent discipline in its own right, as 'general hermeneutics'. Schleiermacher was a German theologian and translator of Plato, inspired by the ideal pioneered by Schlegel and the German romantic movement of returning to the emotional, religious, intellectual sources of our life. Schleiermacher never published a book on this subject but worked out his theory of general hermeneutics in lectures delivered over many years at the University of Berlin, the rather spare and cryptic notes for which have been published.[42] Hermeneutics was a general teachable 'skill' or 'art' (*Kunstlehre*) whose special function was to legitimise the peculiar methodology of the theological sciences. As a theologian, he wanted to rediscover how early Christianity appeared to those receiving the oral Gospel in its original setting and therefore advocated great care in working with the Greek texts of the New Testament, with constant attention to the original Hebraic context. Schleiermacher wanted to discover the intentions of the original authors of the New Testament by peeling back the layers of sedimented tradition encrusted over the original thinking. For example, much of the ritual of Roman Catholicism owes its origins to the Roman Empire and not to Jesus; similarly the language of the King James' Bible reveals the preoccupations and prejudices of the seventeenth-century Puritans. Schleiermacher sought a way of getting behind these prejudices to the original truth, by peeling away the layers of misunderstanding until we arrive at the living intuition which enlivens the text. As Gadamer says:

> Schleiermacher defined hermeneutics as the art of avoiding misunderstanding. To exclude by controlled, methodical consideration whatever is alien and leads to misunderstanding, suggested to us by

274

distance in time, change in linguistic usages, or in meanings of words and modes of thinking – that is certainly far from an absurd description of the hermeneutic endeavor.

("The Universality of the Hermeneutic Problem", *Phil. Herm.*, p. 7)

In order to uncover the original meanings of texts Schleiermacher had to have a theory about the manner in which tradition sediments itself historically, as well as a *psychological* theory concerning the nature of human behaviour and motivation. Schleiermacher thus emphasised that interpretation of a text had to take place along two different axes: *grammatical* and *psychological*. On the one hand we must be familiar with the *language* as it was used at the time the text was written. Thus, for example, in Scripture, we now know the Greek term 'virgin' (*parthenos*) is actually a mistranslation of the Hebrew word '*almah*' which can mean 'maiden' or 'young woman'. But, besides having a sense of linguistic accuracy, we also must be able to get inside the 'mind-set' of the author. A great part of Schleiermacher's technique involved putting oneself in the mind of the other, sympathetically trying to get inside the original lived experience. These requirements of empathy and psychological *nearness* with the author are criticised by Gadamer, who wants to argue that under-standing actually involves an irremovable *distance*. Distance is a necessary precondition for understanding, not something to be overcome; what is completely assimilated does not come into focus for understanding.

Gadamer interprets Schleiermacher's attempt at sympathetic under-standing as a process of psychological empathy, but other commentators believe that, by so doing, he overemphasises the subjective psychological side of Schleiermacher's approach. Schleiermacher, of course, assumed that the text *did* have an original meaning, and the author an original intention, and it is precisely this assumption which has been undermined by Derridian deconstruction. Gadamer, less radically than Derrida, also disagrees with Schleiermacher's central assumption that we can recover the past as it originally happened, seeing this as a residual romantic assumption that hermeneutics is a kind of reproduction of the original production (TM 296; 280). In fact, however, for Gadamer, the past is foreign, and historical understanding is not so much a recovery of the past as a mediation between our sense of ourselves and our sense of this past. We are involved in a process of bringing different horizons, familiar and remote, into line. Furthermore, Gadamer feels that Schleiermacher, with his emphasis on hermeneutics as the avoidance of misunderstanding, ignored the manner in which misunderstanding is also a fruitful act – indeed one which presup-poses a "deep common accord" (*Phil. Herm.*, p. 7). Misunderstanding, *contra* Schleiermacher, can have a creative cultural function.

Gadamer uses Hegel's notion of dialectical mediation to criticise Schleier-macher's romantic attempt to get at the immediate experiences underlying the text. Gadamer, then, is essentially Hegelian in his understanding of hermeneutics, but criticises Hegel's attempts to reintegrate the experience of the past into the present. For Gadamer, the correct exercise of hermeneutics recognises both historical distance and the relation of meaning between ourselves and the past. This recognition of the historicality of the understanding is itself a product of the Enlightenment, whereas, he believes, neither the Renaissance philologists nor the Reformation reformers had a sense of history as such. It was indeed the Enlightenment which made it possible for hermeneutics to recognise its radically historical nature.

Hermeneutics in Dilthey and Heidegger

Wilhelm Dilthey (1833–1911) developed Schleiermacher's account of general hermeneutics with the aim of making it the method of all social sciences in general (the German term *Geisteswissenschaften* covers all the sciences of the human spirit including history, economics, psychology, politics, sociology, philosophy, and so on), in contrast to the empirical method of the natural sciences (*Naturwissenschaften*). Dilthey's objective was a critique of historical reason. His central unifying concept was the concept of lived experience (*Erlebnis*), the manner in which a life is lived historically. This philosophy of human life, *Lebensphilosophie*, greatly influenced Heidegger, even though Heidegger went on to criticise it as superficial in that it failed to enquire into the Being of Dasein. From Dilthey, both Heidegger and Gadamer take the idea that historically lived life is finite, and hence that cultural understanding can never be absolute science.

Dilthey distinguished between the causal *explanation* (*Erklärung*) common to the natural sciences and hermeneutic *understanding* (*Verstehen*). His outlook, rather like that of an anthropologist, was to attempt to get inside the mind of the other, while still treating the other *as other* and not reducing it to what is within one's own experience. Here Dilthey relied heavily on the notion of 'sympathetic intuition' (*geniale Anschauung*). Gadamer criticises Dilthey, however, for still maintaining that the human and social sciences can achieve objectivity and for claiming that these sciences merely differ methodologically from the natural sciences, whereas Gadamer wants to claim that their aims also differ entirely. *Verstehen* seeks to understand the basic motivation behind particular events rather than to seek universal or general laws.

Heidegger's *Being and Time* fused Dilthey's hermeneutics with Husserl's descriptive phenomenology to produce a new hybrid discipline: hermeneutical phenomenology, the very title of which would have had a heretical ring for Husserl. According to Heidegger, reviving a notion found in Schleiermacher, all understanding and questioning operated within a "hermeneutic circle" (BT § 32, 194–195; 153); that is, in order to pose an intelligent question, something about the nature of the subject matter of the question must *already* be understood. There can be no questions arising from pure ignorance. But the answers to the questions force us to revise the presuppositions with which we began. There is thus a 'circle', but not a vicious circle. Gadamer sees Heidegger as giving the hermeneutical circle an essentially positive determination by locating it ontologically in the temporality of Dasein (TM 266; 251). For Heidegger this circle is not a contingent feature of understanding, but is essential to human being as being-in-the-world:

> The 'circle' in understanding belongs to the structure of meaning, and the latter phenomenon is rooted in the existential constitution of Dasein – that is, in the understanding which interprets. An entity for which, as Being-in-the-world, its Being is itself an issue, has, ontologically, a circular structure.
>
> (BT § 32, 195; 153)

To put it in the Hegelian terms which Heidegger shuns in *Being and Time*, a dialectical process is in operation.

Developing Husserl's analysis of perception by emphasising more strongly the interpretative element, Heidegger claims that we do not first perceive something purely present at hand and then interpret it as a house, or whatever (BT § 32, 190; 150), rather we encounter things as already interpreted in terms of a web of possibilities which we apprehend the thing as possessing: "In every case this interpretation is grounded in something we have in advance – in a fore-having (*Vorhabe*)" (BT 191; 150). We grasp and interpret objects in terms of a fore-having, a 'fore-sight' (*Vorsicht*) and a 'pre-grasp' or 'fore-conception' (*Vorgriff*) of the thing. The relation between these advance expectations and future confirmations and disconfirmations constitutes the essence of understanding as *interpreting* (*Auslegung*). As Gadamer says:

> Working out appropriate projections, anticipatory in nature, to be confirmed "by the things" themselves, is the constant task of understanding.
>
> (TM 267; 252)

Heidegger's interpretation of the essentially hermeneutic nature of human being in the world is crucial for Gadamer. For Heidegger, as we have seen, understanding is an 'existentiale', that is a fundamental structure of Dasein akin to the categories which apply to things. Furthermore, all understanding involves self-understanding. Gadamer agrees with Heidegger that the very structure of Dasein is a structure of *understanding* (*Verstehen*).

277

Hermeneutics and the rehabilitation of prejudice

Gadamer, again in agreement with Heidegger, rejects the Cartesian and Husserlian notions of a pure presuppositionless beginning in philosophy. We can only begin to understand from where we are now, and we can only understand a text by identifying correctly where it is coming from by being open to its tradition: "It is the tyranny of hidden prejudice which makes us deaf to what speaks to us in tradition" (TM 270; 254). In this sense Gadamer is influenced by Hegel's view in the *Phenomenology of Spirit* (1807) that we must make use of the knowing process when we attempt to critique it (compare Otto Neurath's image of mending a boat at sea). Similarly, for Gadamer, we have to engage in dialogue in order to bring out and make transparent to ourselves our own presuppositions and prejudgements. We cannot eliminate prejudice, but we can make it visible and thus make it work for us. As Marx said, we are not able to shed our history the way a snake sheds its skin. We cannot extract ourselves from history in our attempts to understand the process of history; history is always already operative in our understanding. The way a tradition operates is summed up by the term 'prejudice'.

For Gadamer our 'prejudices' do not constitute a wilful blindness which prevents us grasping the truth; rather they are the platform from which we launch our very attempt at understanding. To paraphrase Wittgenstein, understanding is a raft floating on a sea of prejudices. The term 'pre-judice' in English and in German (*Vorurteil*) contains the notion of a 'pre-judgement', of a decision which has already been arrived at and which is carried along. Gadamer rejects the usual pejorative view of *prejudice* which he traces to the Enlightenment ideal of a pure reason unencumbered by native prejudice. For Gadamer, this demand to overcome all prejudice is itself a form of prejudice (TM 276; 260). Gadamer even claims that all understanding arises only in and through our prejudices. Following Heidegger's account of *Vorhabe*, *Vorsicht*, and *Vorgriff*, Gadamer claims we always approach a topic with a certain initial understanding or misunderstanding and it is this set of initial beliefs that allow us to interrogate the topic under consideration. All understanding is on the basis of such prejudgements and Gadamer believes we must overcome the Enlightenment "prejudice against prejudice". As Gadamer says:

> It is not so much our judgments as our prejudices that constitute our being...Prejudices are not necessarily unjustified and errone-ous, so that they inevitably distort truth. In fact, the historicity of our existence entails that prejudices, in the literal sense of the word, constitute the initial directedness of our whole ability to experience. Prejudices are biases of our openness to the world. They are simply conditions whereby we experience something.
> ("The Universality of the Hermeneutic Problem", *Phil. Herm.*, p. 9)

Whereas the Enlightenment opposed tradition to pure reason, Gadamer's sense of human historicality wants to see reason within tradition, reason operating in and through traditions. Traditions, furthermore, are not something other or alien to us but are part of what we are. The challenge is to allow ourselves to be addressed by tradition. The relation of myself to historical tradition is not a relation to an object, not a relation to a text as Dilthey tended to assume, but, following Schleiermacher, a relation to a Thou. In order to understand a text we must enter into the dialectic of familiarity and strangeness set up by our relation to the text itself. The text speaks to us out of a tradition, and if it draws us in by its familiarity, it also challenges us by its distance: hermeneutics is based on "a polarity of familiarity and strangeness" (TM 295; 279). Gadamer, in Hegelian language, portrays the whole challenge of human culture as overcoming strangeness in order to be at home with itself.

Furthermore, hermeneutics is not a matter of a subject struggling to understand an object which somehow exists out there independently from us. The "object" to which we relate is always wrapped around by the history of its significance for us, what Gadamer terms its "effective history" or "history of effect" (*Wirkungsgeschichte*):

> If we are trying to understand a historical phenomenon from the historical distance which is characteristic of our hermeneutic situation, we are always already affected by history.
>
> (TM 300; 284)

This complicates the matter of our relation to the text. It is not just that we, as historical beings situated in our culture, have to recognise our own prejudices which apply to the interpreting of a text from a distant time and tradition, but that the nature of that relation itself is historically conditioned and culturally coloured. There is no neutral standpoint from which we can observe the interaction of interpreter and tradition. We are affected by history even as we try to read the effect of history. This is the consciousness of the hermeneutical situation itself (TM 301; 285), which relativises understanding to the complex interweaving of traditions and prejudices in our ongoing search for understanding.

Gadamer's conception of hermeneutics, then, is a direct development of the German tradition from Hegel and Schleiermacher through Dilthey to Heidegger. However, Gadamer himself recognises that the later Heidegger abandoned hermeneutics after his 'Kehre', and so Gadamer's own work involves a fusing of Heidegger's earlier account of hermeneutics with his later account of the primacy of language.

Gadamer is not aiming to produce a new technique or art of understanding, rather he wants to provide a genuinely philosophical description of the nature and role of human understanding in general. Furthermore, he disagrees with Dilthey's view that hermeneutics belongs exclusively to the human sciences. For Gadamer, the sciences, the arts, history are all attempts at human self-understanding and belong to the one global hermeneutic universe. Hermeneutics is a universal aspect of philosophy (TM 476; 451), since the whole of human experience is encapsulated within language and is essentially in need of interpretation.

In his Preface to the Second Edition of *Truth and Method* Gadamer, in Kantian terms, states that his problematic is: how is understanding possible? Indeed, Habermas criticises Gadamer for remaining too closely tied to a Neo-Kantian transcendental approach to philosophy, although Gadamer's own emphasis on the historicity of human understanding considerably softens this transcendental approach. Understanding belongs to the very core structure of *Dasein*, and therefore understanding the nature of understanding will give us a new orientation in the search for truth. As Gadamer puts it in *Truth and Method*:

> I have therefore retained the term "hermeneutics" (which the early Heidegger used) not in the sense of a methodology but as a theory of the real experience that thinking is. Hence I must emphasize that my analyses of play and of language are intended in a purely phenomenological sense...This fundamental methodical approach avoids implying any metaphysical conclusions.
>
> (TM xxxvi; xxii)

Truth and Method (1960)

Truth and Method takes the form of a series of meandering lectures rather than a well-structured systematic treatise.[43] In part, it is a sustained attempt to retrieve the humanist, normative approach to educational formation (*Bildung*) with its emphasis on rhetoric, common sense, judgement, and taste – concepts which Gadamer believes have been improperly deemed unreliable and subjective and hence abandoned by science in its pursuit of objectivity. For Gadamer, the importance of education lies in the development of maturity of understanding, and, following Dilthey, this kind of understanding comes not in the form of scientific explanation (*Erklärung*) but as cultural understanding (*Verstehen*). The certainty achieved by scientific method is no guarantee of truth (TM 491; 465).

In opposition to the pursuit of the positive sciences Gadamer wants to reawaken an appreciation of this classical humanist tradition which, he feels, had been unjustly neglected, and even suppressed, by the more universalistic, rationalist philosophy of the Enlightenment. There is, in the West, a tradition of common sense, *sensus communis* – exemplified in medieval thought and in the Scottish Enlightenment – which has been generally neglected by more recent philosophy. Gadamer invokes Kant's

Critique of Judgement, where Kant is concerned with the judgements of taste, as one of the rare moments when the rational Enlightenment deliberated on elements of this tradition.

The "discovery" of history in the eighteenth and nineteenth centuries led to a new interest in the notions associated with cultural formation and development. Gadamer recognises the positive contribution of romanticism in giving birth to the historical school; the great achievements of romanticism included the rediscovery of the voices of the past through collecting folk-tales, songs, legends, and world-views foreign to our own (TM 275; 259). The Romantic Age became particularly interested in the role of art in education, exemplified in the writings of Schiller, Schlegel, Hegel, and others. The romantics in general made a strong claim that a special and higher kind of truth was to be found in art. Right from the beginning Gadamer has paid particular attention to the aesthetic experience as a paradigmatic instance of the activity of understanding, something which cannot be explicated by the application of any method. Art is a corrective to the "*hubris* of concepts" (*Phil. App.*, p. 190).

Part One of *Truth and Method* is a historical discussion of the concepts of education, judgement, taste, and common sense, with the aim of rehabilitating them as guiding concepts for the understanding of human cultural formation. Gadamer then moves on to discuss the question of the truth of art in opposition to the subjectivisation of aesthetic experience in Kant's work. Here Gadamer sides with Hegel and Heidegger in seeing art as essentially connected to truth, as opposed to the refinement of sensibility or the production of aesthetic pleasure. Gadamer claims that in our experience of art our consciousness of truth is prior to any focusing on the aesthetic experience. When we have a genuine confrontation with art, we are in the realm of truth, and if we have only an aesthetic experience it is because we have become alienated in some way from the art work. For Gadamer, a genuine art work stands within a particular community and is only fully understood within the context of that community, but even there, there will be blindness. Furthermore, Gadamer accepts Heidegger's account of truth as unconcealment, as a simultaneous revealing and concealing. We have to get away from the idea of truth as manifest self-presence, and realise that truth requires a certain amount that is unspoken in the spoken.

Truth and Method Part Two, which we have already briefly sketched in our sections on the history of hermeneutics, provides a long critical analysis of the emergence of the concept of history in German philosophy and in the historical school of Ranke, Droysen, Dilthey, and Yorck. Their analyses of history are seen as surpassed in the achievement of Heidegger who provides, for Gadamer, a correct account of human historicality and lays down the elements for a theory of hermeneutics. The connection of Part Two with Part One is that the concept of truth in art is now extended to a consideration of the meaning of the concept of truth in history, and this leads to a meditation on the interpretation of the nature of history in different historical approaches. Arising out of the consideration of history comes a general theory of hermeneutic activity itself and this is essentially the core of the book. Gadamer felt that the humanities and social sciences had attempted to conceal their hermeneutical and historical character behind a mask of pseudo-scientific method, and he took it to be his task to restore *historical understanding* to the social sciences. In part, this historicity of understanding belongs to the very nature of our understanding as linguistic. The hermeneutic task is the task of trying to find a common language, of coming to a 'common accord' or 'agreement' (*Einverständnis*), where the German term contains the notion of two minds becoming one, that is being of "one mind" with the other person. Hermeneutics enters the picture when this agreement with the text fails to occur. Such failure does not necessarily result in meaninglessness. Gadamer recognises that misunderstanding can be as potent a force as understanding and agreement in human life.

Language and world

The final part, Part Three, of *Truth and Method* has a more metaphysical orientation, in that it turns to language as the medium in which human culture finds expression. Gadamer even speaks here of a 'hermeneutic ontology', and asserts that "being that can be understood is language" (TM 474; 450). Following Heidegger, language is seen as essentially world-creating. Humans live in a world created through language and the medium of our encounter with this world is also language:

> Our inquiry has been guided by the basic idea that language is a medium (*eine Mitte*) where I and world meet, or rather, manifest their original belonging together.
>
> (TM 474; 449)

His notorious assertion, "that which can be understood is language" (*Was verstanden werden kann, ist Sprache*, TM 475; 450), comes dangerously close to a kind of linguistic idealism. However, Gadamer never says with some Derridian deconstructionists that there exists only language, but rather, in phenomenological terms, that language is the mode of manifestation of being. Things other than language come to be in language.

Again, in this section, Gadamer turns his attention to the manner in which understanding a work of art is paradigmatic for the whole process of attempting to understand the nature of human understanding. Art is a special form of language, as Heidegger had seen. Gadamer connects this Heideggerian account of art as "the play of language" with Wittgenstein's notion of 'language games' (*sprachliche Spiele*, TM 490; 464). Gadamer emphasises the nature of 'play' (*Spiel*) in understanding a work of art. For

Gadamer, the notion of 'play' goes beyond the notion of subject or object. In playing, we have to learn to lose ourselves in order to remain true to the game: "it is the game itself that plays, for it draws the players into itself and thus becomes the actual subjectum of the playing" (TM 490; 464).[44] Understanding and involvement in language games is not playful, in the sense of withholding commitment; rather it is self-involving, but not in a subjectivist manner.[45] We should emphasise here that Gadamer's account of play in language and art is not of the same order as Derrida's vision of language as an endless play of signifiers. Its purpose is to emphasise that understanding must not be understood as something that goes on within the head of the subject, so to speak. Both Gadamer and Wittgenstein see language as a rule-governed activity and hence one that is primarily intersubjective, shared and social. As Gadamer puts it, we come into being through the play of language, we do not get lost in it.

In *Truth and Method* Gadamer is emphatic that he is still a phenomenologist and that he is not attempting to teach a new hermeneutic 'method' or 'practice'. He is carrying out an ontological investigation into the human reality which is understanding. Understanding is "part of the total experience of the world". Gadamer is concerned with the end product of the human enterprise which quite traditionally he characterises as knowledge and truth. Hermeneutics is not the art of discerning intentions but rather examines the question of what happens to us "over and above our wanting and doing" (TM xxxviii; xiv). Gadamer – following Heidegger – emphasises that we are in the grip of concepts not of our own making. Furthermore we do not construct our concepts but inherit them within the context of a living historical tradition. We all live and discover ourselves within traditions. As Gadamer says, "philosophizing does not begin at some zero point but must think and speak with the language we already possess" (*Phil. App.*, p. 181).

But the project of human understanding should not be understood as Hegel, and, Gadamer claims, even Dilthey thought; namely, as a historical progression towards a totality of truth. Gadamer believes we must follow Heidegger in recognising that human understanding is shot through with finitude and historicity. There is no end of interpretation when all of the interpretations have been synthesised together. Interpretation is related to a historical context, and whereas a later interpreter may be able to put the event into a wider context and understand its significance in one way, the observer or participant in the event will have his or her own hermeneutic understanding, one which cannot be surpassed or raised up into a higher level of understanding.

Gadamer's influence

Gadamer has inspired a whole generation of students as a living exemplification of his own commitment to dialogue. He has been responsible for reviving the hermeneutical tradition and, along with Paul Ricoeur, for bringing it centre stage in contemporary European philosophy. He has, however, been criticised by other exponents of hermeneutics, for example E. D. Hirsch and Emilio Betti, for failing to put forward criteria for validating interpretations.[46] How does Gadamer distinguish false from true interpretations? Gadamer's acceptance of Heidegger's concept of truth means that he has little use for truth as correctness, and indeed for the notion of measuring truth against falsity. He is clearly more concerned with the phenomenological description of what takes place in the effort to gain understanding, and in recognising the historical ebb and flow of understanding, than with judging the correctness of any particular interpretation. Thus, he readily acknowledges that misinterpretation has as much to teach us as genuine interpretation. However, it is still not clear *how* he deems an interpretation to be a misinterpretation. Gadamer is reluctant to state in advance the criteria for successful communication and understanding, and indeed seems not to have criteria for distinguishing interpretations at all.

As we have already indicated throughout this chapter, Gadamer has been involved in a long-running debate with Jürgen Habermas.[47] Habermas has criticised Gadamer both for a kind of 'linguistic idealism' (*Sprachidealismus*) which elevates language above human beings, and also for neglecting, in his account of reaching consensus in understanding, the manner in which such a consensus can be ideologically distorted. Dialogue is shared understanding, but it may also be an exercise in power and domination. Authority (as legitimated by tradition) is not the same as genuine knowledge, though Gadamer does not appear to appreciate this point, according to Habermas. Habermas suspects that Gadamer sides too much with the conservatism of tradition, and insists that even a reappropriation of tradition is not sufficient to liberate us from domination, and to achieve a genuinely communicative reason. Gadamer, in response, has defended the ability of hermeneutical reflection to cut through ideological distortion and mistaken self-understanding. Gadamer has himself acknowledged that he can be seen as too optimistic. In the Foreword to the Second Edition of *Truth and Method* he posed himself the question:

> Does not the universality of understanding involve a one-sidedness
> in its contents, since it lacks a critical principle in relation to tradi-
> tion and, as it were, espouses a universal optimism?
>
> (TM xxxvii; xxiii)

Does it not belong to the nature of our relation to tradition that we can break with tradition? Gadamer acknowledges that he has emphasised the moment of assimilation of the tradition over moments of criticism, but his philosophy does not deny the perennial need for vigilance in terms of what is taken over from the tradition. However, there is a sense in which

Gadamer's philosophy supports a very conservative view of tradition, especially in its understanding of prejudice as possessing authority. Gadamer does not seem to have learned the lesson of the Nazi period in which a whole culture was distorted through its desire to accommodate to what was expected of it from its leaders. Similarly, Gadamer has been criticised from a feminist perspective for ignoring the role of gender, and for being blind to the forces of domination which may be obscured by such metaphors as being 'at home' in language.[48]

Commentators (e.g. Karl-Otto Apel) have always recognised similarities between Gadamer's interest in language and 'linguisticality' (*Sprachlichkeit*) and the linguistic turn of twentieth-century analytic philosophy. While Gadamer himself invokes the later Wittgenstein, more recently, Donald Davidson has written an appreciative essay recognising Gadamer's emphasis on meaning holism, and his study of the assumptions of shared understanding.[49] Indeed, Davidson sees himself as having arrived by a different route into "Gadamer's intellectual neighbourhood". For Davidson, Gadamer is concerned with the conditions which make objective thought possible and Gadamer concludes that only in interpersonal communication can there be thought. Only through sharing can there be understanding. Davidson, however, while accepting Gadamer's emphasis on shared communication as the basis of understanding, wants to introduce a third element – the shared object itself – as that which enables the process of "triangulating the world".[50]

In a different vein, the American philosopher Richard Rorty has taken over Gadamer's notion of *Bildung* and, under the term "edification", has conceived it as part of the 'conversation which we are'. But Rorty differs from Gadamer in that he denies that edification has anything to do with truth, rather it is to do with possibilities of coping with the world. For Rorty, edification replaces knowledge as the goal of thinking. Gadamer, on the other hand, wants to emphasise the possibility of forms of knowledge and insight into truth which are removed from the realm of natural science.

Yet, despite the attention of Rorty and Davidson, Gadamer has not had a wide influence in analytic philosophy, perhaps because of his devaluation of the mode of arguing through assertion. In *Truth and Method* he cites Collingwood's view that the practice of English philosophy of discussing 'statements', while sharpening the intellect, completely ignored the historicality of understanding (TM 370; 352). Gadamer in general opposes the 'logic of assertion' to his own more dialectical logic of question and answer. This opposition to assertion contributes to the sense of vagueness evident in his writings, a vagueness he acknowledges is part of his dialogical style, and which he credits with allowing ideas to awaken in the readers. Proponents of exact philosophy are impatient with Gadamer's formulations, for example his constant emphasis on seeking "the things themselves" without specifying what these are. Classicists of a more philological bent are also put off by Gadamer's free-wheeling interpretation of Greek texts, which they see as exercises in uncontrolled whimsicality, leading often to quite vapid interpretations.

Gadamer's approach, with its dialogical search for mutual understanding, is perhaps best seen as a corrective to a view of philosophy as systematic and conceptual. Gadamer's main contribution is the success with which he has integrated Heidegger's analysis of the historicality and hermeneutic character of Dasein with Hegelian conception of the development of culture and tradition. His main flaw is that his stress on human linguisticality can be seen as a kind of linguistic idealism, and his embrace of historical relativism may also be a significant weakness in his philosophy. His conviction that mutual agreement and understanding in themselves amount to knowledge seems, however, thoroughly wrong: for example, a society which has convinced itself that the earth is flat may be a well-regulated harmonious society with full agreement; unfortunately it simply does not have knowledge, a point Habermas has made forcibly against Gadamer.

9

HANNAH ARENDT

The phenomenology of the public sphere

Introduction: Hannah Arendt as philosopher

As a new and radical manner of doing philosophy, the phenomenological movement in its early years attracted a small number of pioneering women philosophers, most notably Hedwig Conrad-Martius (1888–1966),[1] Edith Stein (1891–1942),[2] and Gerda Walther (1897–1977),[3] all of whom studied with Edmund Husserl during the early realist phase of his phenomenology. Indeed, phenomenology was the philosophical movement most welcoming of women students up until the 1960s. Hedwig Martius was chairwoman of the Göttingen Philosophy Society (*Göttinger philosophische Gesellschaft*) which met around Husserl. Edith Stein wrote an important study of *empathy* (*Einfühlung*) and, as Husserl's assistant, transcribed and edited Husserl's manuscripts on time consciousness (later published by Heidegger) and the manuscripts which became *Ideas* II. Her conversion to Catholicism in 1922 meant that her later writings moved away from phenomenology. Gerda Walther began as a phenomenologist of social relations but gradually developed interests in parapsychology. Subsequently, the best-known woman associated with phenomenology is undoubtedly Simone de Beauvoir (1908–1986), who studied philosophy at the Ecole Normale Supérieure, and developed her philosophical outlook in close dialogue with Jean-Paul Sartre. Though de Beauvoir does have interesting things to say about the relation of self and other, she is now primarily known, not as a phenomenologist, but on account of her ground-breaking book, *The Second Sex*, which is a social and economic history of women, and a classic of feminist studies.[4]

Although Hannah Arendt (1906–1975) only occasionally characterised herself as a phenomenologist and indeed is not usually included in textbook treatments of phenomenology, her work can be fruitfully understood as a species of phenomenology, a phenomenology of what in German is referred to as '*die Öffentlichkeit*' ('publicity', 'publicness'), that is the 'public space' (*der öffentliche Raum*), the public realm, *res publica*, the 'space of appearances'.[5] Arendt's conception of this world of appearances is essentially phenomenological: everything which is manifest to humans belongs to the world of appearances, to 'phenomenality'. She regarded philosophy as born out of the experienced discrepancy between this 'world of appearances' in which we live and the medium of words which support 'thinking'.[6] In Arendt's case, understanding the world of appearances means an attempt to uncover the nature of the human living 'in the midst of the world'. Her phenomenological interests consisted in shedding light on the realm of public affairs, trying to capture the intrinsic meaning of public events, such as being born (the phenomenon she labels 'natality'), being always caught up in the 'plurality', being caught up in the world (*amor mundi*), and the experience of the 'between' which is neither you nor me, but something to which we both belong. Indeed, she understood the aim of humanity in the twentieth century to be to belong to the world such that it becomes a home.[7]

Arendt first spoke of the public space in her *The Origins of Totalitarianism*.[8] In another essay, in *Men in Dark Times*, she wrote:

> it is the function of the public realm to throw light on the affairs of men by providing a space of appearances in which they can show in deed and word, for better and worse, who they are and what they can do.[9]

Arendt was also aware how this public space is manipulated by governments, by commercial advertising, by 'spin doctors', and, in general, "by speech that does not disclose what is but sweeps it under the carpet, by exhortations, moral or otherwise, that, under the pretext of upholding old truths, degrade all truth to meaningless triviality" (*Dark Times*, p. viii). Arendt saw herself as describing what Heidegger in *Being and Time* had characterised as *Gerede* ("idle talk") and the sphere of *das Man*. Arendt strongly agreed with Heidegger's view that

> everything that is real or authentic is assaulted by the overwhelming power of "mere talk" that irresistibly arises out of the public realm, determining every aspect of everyday existence, anticipating and annihilating the sense or the nonsense of everything the future may bring.
>
> (*Dark Times*, p. ix)

In particular she agreed with Heidegger's paradoxical statement that "the light of publicity darkens everything" (*die Öffentlichkeit verdunkelt alles*, BT 165; 127). Heidegger's conception of worldhood and being-in-the-world are crucial for her analysis. She saw idle talk as destroying the possibility of genuine futurity. She also criticised Heidegger for the isolation of his Dasein and for the inadequacy of his account of world, especially his neglect of co-operative human activity. For Arendt, as she said in her essay on Lessing, the world lies "between" people (*Dark Times*, p. 12). Similarly, she recognised that Heidegger had only succeeded in differentiating two kinds of human relating to the world: the encountering and manipulating of things (*Zuhandensein*), and theoretical contemplation (*Vorhandensein*). In addition to these, Arendt will propose a new existential category of 'action' which we shall discuss in this chapter.

Arendt was in many respects an old-world intellectual, a product of the German Gymnasium with its emphasis on classical education, on reading only the Greeks and the Germans. Thus she could effortlessly evoke the classics as models of her concepts, and knew by heart a great many German poems. Her understanding of the Greek *polis* and the dramatisation of action in Greek tragedy provided the model for her analysis of the nature of being-in-the-world, and the requirements for a life lived in public. From Heidegger and Jaspers, on the other hand, she took her analysis of modern participation in mass society and the disenchantment of the world. More than Heidegger and Jaspers, her account emphasises love of the world, *amor mundi*, and being *of* the world rather than just *in* the world, with all the recognition of the responsibilities that kind of belonging demands.

Arendt's practice of phenomenology is original and idiosyncratic; she exhibited no particular interest in the phenomenological method and contributed nothing to the theory of phenomenology. Indeed she was suspicious of all methods and systems. She first encountered Husserl's phenomenology in Heidegger's seminars at Marburg, and as a result, she was never attracted to Husserl's conception of phenomenology as first philosophy, or as a rigorous science, though she was sufficiently curious about Heidegger's mentor to attend some of Husserl's lectures in Freiburg. As she later explained, the overall attraction of Husserl's phenomenology "sprang from the anti-historical and anti-metaphysical implications of the slogan '*Zu den Sachen selbst*' " (*Thinking*, p. 9). She never showed any interest in Heidegger's project of a fundamental ontology, though she clearly appropriated and creatively transformed many of his conceptions, including Dasein, and the notions of the 'clearing' or 'lighting' of being, as well as Heidegger's analysis of Dasein's tendency for both authenticity as well as inauthenticity, for individual, creative action, and for obscuring itself in the masses, in the anonymity of '*das Man*'. In her late work, *The Life of the Mind*, she portrays herself as involved in a kind of radical break with tradition, "dismantling metaphysics" (*Thinking*, p. 212), akin to Heidegger's 'destruction' (*Abbau*) of the history of philosophy, a dismantling she thought was only possible because the thread of history was already broken.

Arendt was a strongly individual voice, deeply suspicious of all personality cults, not just of the circles around Husserl, but also, later, of Heidegger's devoted followers. Similarly, she had reservations about rigid interpretations of Marxism and the approach of the Frankfurt school. She had a deep personal antipathy to Theodor Adorno, whom she regarded as self-serving. On the other hand, she had a strong spiritual affinity with Walter Benjamin, whose intuitive, fragmentary way of interpreting the broken thread of history she emulated.[10] In general, partly on account of her temperament, and partly through the circumstances of her life, she had a strong ambivalence towards professional, academic philosophy as such, an ambivalence her mentor Karl Jaspers had detected as early as 1930. Indeed Arendt frequently denied being a 'philosopher' at all (*Thinking*, p. 3). For her, as for the later Heidegger, philosophy had come to an end, the old philosophical questions having lost their plausibility (*Thinking*, p. 10). On the other hand, the end of philosophy and the task of thinking were not for her a matter of withdrawing into a kind of poetic 'saying', as in Heidegger's later work. Arendt's strong commitment to public life in the plurality, the requirement to listen attentively to the discord of many voices, meant that, for her, genuine thinking required a public space, and needed to be carried out under public scrutiny and sustained by public participation, and this meant for her the practice of a kind of intellectual journalism. For her, thinking cannot be left to specialists (*Thinking*, p. 13). Similarly, though Arendt portrayed herself as a "political theorist" or "political thinker" (Young-Bruehl, p. 327), she rejected the term 'political philosophy', in that it suggested the valorisation of 'philosophy' over the political realm, which indeed had been the dominant tradition in political philosophy since Plato. In her opposition to academic philosophy, the only exception she makes is Kant, whose deep suspicion of purely speculative thinking and deep appreciation of the nature of the practical she admired.

Arendt is best known for her writing on the subject of politics, yet her overall rethinking of the nature of political action is not an attempt to provide a systematic account of the nature of the state or a critique of institutions. She has no *theory* of democracy, of fascism, republicanism, or, indeed, communitarianism. What she presents is a set of thoughtful meditations on the experiences which gave rise to totalitarianism, to the forging of bureaucratic amoralists such as Eichmann, to the self-deceptions of statehood, to the decline of public action in modern political life. Her American friend, the writer Mary McCarthy, described her as not being a "system-builder" but as someone whose fine discriminations resisted systematisation.[11] Her best work is in the form of essays and she could produce startling new ways of looking at phenomena which had previously been explored in a more conventional way by scholars, for example her exploration of the notion of "world alienation" as contributing to the success of modern science in *The Human Condition* and, of course, her rehabilitation of the Aristotelian notion of *praxis* in her account of 'action' which was deeply influenced by Heidegger's lectures.[12] She had a strong sense of the facticity and contingency of human affairs, that *events* and not humans make history. As a result she had a deep suspicion of Hegelian and Marxist attempts to explain the overall meaning of the historical as such. As she put it in *The Origins of Totalitarianism*:

> Caution in handling generally accepted opinions that claim to explain whole trends of history is especially important for the historian of modern times, because the last century has produced an abundance of ideologies that pretend to be keys to history but are actually nothing but desperate efforts to escape responsibility.
>
> (OT 9)

No system can explain history, because history is really a succession of surprises: "history is a story which has many beginnings but no end".[13] Arendt's independent spirit meant that she was not attracted to Marxism, which she regarded as an outmoded nineteenth-century ideology. In a late interview in 1970, she remarked that "workers of the world unite" was a thoroughly discredited slogan.[14] Earlier, in reply to Gershom Scholem after his critique of *Eichmann in Jerusalem*, she denied that she had come from the tradition of the German Left and claimed that, in fact, she had come rather late to Marx (Young-Bruehl, p. 104). In general, as she observed, the Left were suspicious of her as a conservative, while the Right thought of her as too left wing, or too much of a maverick.[15] In fact she did not regard the struggle for equal pay, employment, or housing as political issues and instead relegated them to the sphere of the social. Indeed it was part of her criticism of modernity that the sphere of the political had been swallowed up in the social sphere of the economy and public administration.

She was also careful not to be rushed into hasty action and denied she was ever an activist in a political sense. Nevertheless, she wrote controversial essays on many topics, including taking a stance both supportive of civil rights and at the same time opposing the state's attempt at forced integration in Little Rock, Arkansas.[16] Another area in which her writing became particularly controversial was her analysis of the notion of Jewish identity, and her discussion of the issue of national or cultural identity in general. This continues to be a very much discussed part of her philosophical contribution. Her own sense of identity was complex. She disliked characterising herself as either German or Jewish, and even admitted, in a letter to Jaspers, that she had found the Jewish question boring until the late 1920s. In a letter to Heidegger in 1950 she says she never thought of herself as a German woman and, though she was a Jewish woman, she preferred to think of herself as the outsider, the perpetual stranger, "the girl from afar" (*das Mädchen aus der Fremde*).[17] Likewise, writing to Karl Jaspers after the Second World War, she stated that she never felt herself to be a German, and, moreover, only characterised herself as Jewish if pressed politically.[18] She wrote to Gershom Scholem that she regarded her Jewishness "as one of the indisputable factual data of my life, and I have never had the wish to change or disclaim facts of this kind".[19] In later years, she renounced both Germanness and all commitment to official religion (including both Christianity and Judaism). At the same time, Arendt herself recognised the impossibility of the assimilationist position, arguing that one could only assimilate to German culture by becoming an anti-Semite. She had to respond as a Jew when attacked as a Jew (Young-Bruehl, p. 109), although, with typical refinement of analysis, she later noted in *Eichmann in Jerusalem* that the Zionist movement, which emphasised Jewish separateness, actually reinforced the National Socialist campaign to mark out Jews through wearing the yellow star and so on. Arendt had a complex attitude towards identity: she was a defender of the universal aspects of the human condition who recognised rootedness in a tradition, and yet required one to take a critical distance towards it.

In this chapter I shall attempt to show that it is difficult to understand the nature of her approach unless one appreciates its phenomenological nature as a genuine attempt to return to the things themselves, which, for Arendt, means the nature of our belonging as humans to a human world, 'the human condition', a term she always understood in a non-essentialist manner, as the historically conditioned manner in which humans live rather than as some delimitation of a human nature as such. She wished to understand the essential nature of the world of appearances and what it means for humans to belong to that world. She has a certain practice of phenomenological seeing, as a kind of careful attention to the phenomena and the avoidance of conventional characterisations. Indeed Arendt's writings are a fascinating example of the kind of independence and richness phenomenology generated. This chapter will introduce Arendt through her life's work and then concentrate on her account of action in *The Human Condition*.

Arendt: life and writings (1906–1975)

Hannah Arendt was born in October 1906 in Königsberg, then in East Prussia and now a part of Russia, into a well-to-do bourgeois family, liberal and tolerant in outlook. Both her parents were Social Democrats. Her father died of syphilis when she was 7 and, although her mother married again, Arendt never liked her step-father. Her rather dismal views on the confining nature of the life of the household, and her tendency to seek the company of father figures (Jaspers, Heidegger, Blücher), may in part reflect her own early experiences. Her family were of assimilated Jewish background, though, later, she recalled that the word 'Jew' was never mentioned in her home.[20] Nevertheless, her family had instructed her to stand up and protest if anti-Semitic statements were made in her school and then to leave the class, which, of course, was a frequent occurrence given the almost official tolerance of anti-Semitism in German culture of the time, about which she later wrote so forcefully. She was so often at home from school that, as a result, she largely educated herself.

At school she was imbued with the classical learning typical of the era; she could read Greek and Latin with facility. As a young teenager, she elected to carry out independent study at the University of Berlin, where she attended Romano Guardini's lectures on Christian existentialism, which awoke in her an interest in theology.[21] At an early age she had read Kierkegaard, and Kant's *Critique of Pure Reason* and *Religion Within the Limits of Reason Alone*. Königsberg had, of course, been home to Immanuel Kant, whom she read with enormous interest throughout her life. She discussed Kant's formal ethics of duty in *Eichmann in Jerusalem*, though it was not until the end of her life that she began to engage fully and critically with Kant's concept of judgement and the formation of the *sensus communis*. Indeed she later claimed that she wrote with Kant looking over her shoulder.

The encounter with Bultmann, Heidegger, and Jaspers

Arendt entered Marburg University in the autumn of 1924 with the initial intention of studying Protestant theology and philology. She enrolled in the theology courses of Rudolf Bultmann (1884–1976), who himself had come to Marburg in 1921. During the initial interview with Bultmann, Arendt showed her independence by specifying to her lecturer that she would join the seminar on condition that there were to be no anti-Semitic remarks made in class (Young-Bruehl, p. 62). Bultmann had a strong influence on Arendt, but she later came to see his theology as a narrowing down of the nature of Jesus, a downplaying of Jesus's active life in order to focus purely on Jesus's function in the transmission of faith, "the narrowing of Christianity into a radicalized Paulinism" (HAKJ 221). It was her encounter with Heidegger which led her to leave theology for philosophy. In fact, perhaps under the influence of Heidegger, she came to see theology as a positive science which assumes the actual existence of its object 'God', and not at all as a philosophy founded on faith. Furthermore, the nature of this science had been compromised by the emergence of modern experimental science, just as the nature of the Churches had been altered when they became political institutions (HAKJ 222).

Arendt attended the newly arrived Professor Extraordinarius Martin Heidegger's seminar in the winter semester 1924–1925 on "Plato's Sophist".[22] At the end of this, her first semester in Marburg, in February 1925, she became personally acquainted with Heidegger, then 35 years old and married with two children. He would become her mentor and her lover for the years between 1925 and 1929, until Heidegger's wife, Elfride, and the force of circumstances (Arendt's move to Berlin) separated them. Heidegger and Arendt soon embarked on a secret affair, with Heidegger writing rather poetic notes and letters in which he discussed his philosophical reading, and recounted his conversations with Husserl during visits to Freiburg.

In order not to compromise their romance, Arendt transferred, on Heidegger's recommendation, to the University of Heidelberg in the summer semester of 1926 to write her doctorate under the direction of Karl Jaspers. During the winter semester of 1926–1927 she travelled to Freiburg to attend Husserl's lectures, but does not seem to have been particularly impressed. On the other hand, she found in Jaspers the perfect teacher. In fact, Arendt always retained a deep admiration for Jaspers, her *Doktorsvater*, and wrote a number of essays on him, including one portraying Jaspers as a "citizen of the world" (a title suggested by Schilpp, HAKJ 173), one of the few voices in Germany who defended the old virtue of *humanitas*.[23] Arendt completed her doctoral thesis on *Saint Augustine's Concept of Love* which was published in 1929.[24] Jaspers gave the thesis the second-highest grade, *cum laude* (HAKJ 689), because he was not entirely satisfied with her writing. He considered that Arendt had interpreted some of Augustine's concepts too narrowly and repeatedly urged her to take more care in her citations and in her general proof-reading; nevertheless, he did recognise that she had achieved a genuinely philosophical perspective, carrying out "objective philosophizing with historical material" (HAKJ 690).

In choosing to write on St Augustine, Arendt was swept up in the *Zeitgeist*. Arendt read Augustine in an existentialist manner. The writings of Christian existentialists, such as Kierkegaard, Paul, Luther, and Augustine, were very popular in German universities in the 1920s, as a Marburg student of those days, Hans-Georg Gadamer, recalls in his *Philosophical Apprenticeships*. Another classmate from her Marburg days, Hans Jonas (1903–1993), also recalls that Augustine's *Confessions* was considered a pivotal text of that time.[25] Arendt boldly focuses on Augustine's philosophy entirely separately from the theological context, a feature of the book which several reviewers, including Jaspers, noticed, as it went against the grain of current German scholarship. Thus J. Hessen, in his short review in *Kant-Studien* in 1931, criticised her phenomenological account of Augustine's concept of love as 'yearning' or 'desire' (*appetitio*) for not citing the authorities or taking note of existing scholarship. Indeed, Arendt's general anti-historical and anti-contextual reading of Augustine is in line with Husserl's radical phenomenology and Heidegger's engaged reading of Greek classical texts and stands opposed to the pedantry of German academic writing of the time.

Most likely influenced by Bultmann's analysis of Pauline anthropology, Arendt in this thesis defines Augustine's Christianity as Pauline. Indeed, as Augustine himself records in the *Confessions*, it was the texts of Paul which helped him through his spiritual crisis and forced on him the need to make a decision to convert. Humans are defined by their being in a state of lack, of desire. Humans always desire the good, but also fear the loss of the object they desire. Death threatens the possibility of humans achieving earthly satisfaction of their desires, so they shift to make the object of their desire to be eternal. To be happy is to desire what we cannot lose. Arendt recognises that a consequence of this analysis is that humans, for Augustine, can never be at home in the world. As part of this radical world-fleeing nature of Augustine's analysis, Arendt focuses on his emphasis on the relation between love of God and love of neighbour. Genuine love of God actually negates the possibility of genuine love for one's neighbour in the world. We love not the individual distinct person but rather love itself. Arendt's early interest in Augustine is the source of her thinking on the contrast between being at home in the world and fleeing it by one means or another. Indeed, in many ways, Arendt's overall outlook remained Augustinian, for example in her insistence that the fleeting temporal nature of existence places a special burden on humans. Arendt was strongly influenced by Augustine's view of the human will as the origin of spontaneity and creativity. She was fond of quoting Augustine's remark in *De civitate Dei* Bk 12, Ch. 20, "that a beginning be made man was created" (*Initium ut esset homo creatus est*).[26] Augustine also featured strongly in her last book, the *Willing* volume of the *Life of the Mind*, where she discusses Augustine as the first philosopher explicitly to recognise the human will.[27]

In Heidelberg she moved in the company of a collection of young intellectuals, which included Paul O. Kristeller, later a renowned Renaissance specialist in the USA. She stood out among her classmates as somewhat Bohemian and unconventional, fond of smoking a pipe. In 1929, having broken with Heidegger, she married Günther Stern, a philosophy student who had completed his PhD dissertation on indexicals with Edmund Husserl and was seeking to complete his *Habilitationsschrift* at Frankfurt on the philosophy of music.[28] When that did not succeed, he became a journalist for a Berlin newspaper, writing under the name of Günther Anders. Possibly on account of Stern's negative experience of Adorno, combined with what she perceived as Adorno's less than honourable attempts at accommodation with the Nazis in the early 1930s (HAKJ 593, 644), before he too was forced to emigrate, Arendt formed an immense dislike for Adorno which she never lost. Indeed, later in New York, she accused Adorno of holding up publication of the Benjamin *Nachlass*.[29]

One of her first forays into contemporary philosophy was her review of Karl Mannheim's *Ideology and Utopia* for the German journal *Die Gesellschaft* in 1930.[30] This essay is significant in that it sheds light on Arendt's first attempt to grasp the meaning of human being as being-in-the-world, through a comparison of Heidegger's and Jaspers' views on the nature of existence and of human 'fallenness' into the everyday. She would constantly return to this topic. In this first version she presents Jaspers and Heidegger as being in close agreement with one another. She and her husband, Stern, also collaborated in writing a long essay closely analysing Rilke's *Duino Elegies* in 1930.

Around this time, Arendt decided to write a study of the German Jewish writer and *salonnière* (salon convenor) Rahel Varnhagen (1771–1833), possibly as a *Habilitation* thesis. She sought funds from several sources, including the forerunner of the German Research Foundation, *Deutsche Forschungsgemeinschaft*, and Heidegger even wrote a reference on her behalf. She eventually succeeded in securing some funds but the political situation was changing rapidly, with growing German nationalism and anti-Semitism. She eventually was forced to escape Germany before her thesis was completed. Given her awareness of the dangers of the growing Nazi movement, she was somewhat put out that her mentor and friend Karl Jaspers published in 1932 a short book, *Max Weber. Deutsches Wesen im politischen Denken*, in which he celebrated Weber as typifying 'the German essence' (*deutsches Wesen*, HAKJ 16). She commented to Jaspers that she thought of Germany in terms of her "mother tongue, philosophy and literature" and not in terms of extreme militant nationalism. Jaspers replied, somewhat defensively, that he was invoking Weber to point out to the extreme nationalist youth that the German essence could be understood differently from their interpretation, though Jaspers does still emphasise what he calls the "historical-political destiny" of Germany in a future united Europe (HAKJ 18). Indeed Jaspers' position on German nationalism in the early 1930s was not particularly critical; he had even praised Heidegger's *Rektoratsrede* in 1933.

After her marriage, Arendt kept in contact with Heidegger, though in a more distant, sporadic way. Sometime in 1932–1933, she wrote to her former mentor enquiring if he was excluding Jews from his classes, as she had heard. He wrote back denying this allegation, and citing the fact that several Jews wanted to study with him, that he had relations with other Jewish academics, and that he had even arranged a scholarship to Rome for Karl Löwith. However, he clarified that he remained an anti-Semite in the same sense as he had been at Marburg, that is, according to Safranski, that he suspected that the Jews held too many positions in the university.[31] At this point, Arendt broke off correspondence with Heidegger, and did not renew it until many years later in 1950.

Berlin and Paris

Stern and Arendt lived a Bohemian life in Berlin as the turmoil of the political scene in Germany erupted all round them. Left-wingers were being rounded up and Günther Stern was worried about being arrested by the Nazis, on account of his friendship with Berthold Brecht. He left Germany for Paris soon after the Reichstag fire in 1933 (Young-Bruehl, p. 102). Arendt remained in Berlin to assist the Zionists by trying to compile documentation on anti-Jewish activity in Germany, but she was arrested and detained for eight days. On her release, realising that the situation had changed permanently, she and her mother fled Berlin for Prague. She moved to Paris in August 1933, where she found work with a Zionist youth organisation assisting refugees. In Paris she got to know many of the *émigré* intellectuals, including Walter Benjamin and Alexandre Koyré, and she attended Alexandre Kojève's lectures on Hegel. She also formed lasting friendships with Raymond Aron and Jean Wahl, but she was never particularly friendly with Sartre, who was too literary and too ambitious for her taste. She met Sartre again in New York in 1945 but, when she returned to France in the 1950s, she had no interest in looking him up again (Young-Bruehl, p. 117).[32] She thought that Sartre and Merleau-Ponty had simply superimposed Marxism on their existentialist theories to get themselves out of the impasse of nihilism. On the other hand, she admired Albert Camus and saw him as one of the most intellectually honest of French intellectuals (HAKJ 56 and 66).

During her first years in Paris, her relationship with Stern seems to have gradually waned. Early in 1936 in Paris she met a fellow German *émigré* and committed communist activist, Heinrich Blücher, whom she later married and with whom she travelled to the USA. He was working class, self-educated, a member of the German Communist Party, who admired Rosa Luxemburg and had actually participated in the Sparticist uprising in 1919. Arendt soon began living with Blücher; they married in Paris in 1940 and remained partners till she died. In many ways, he, being about ten years older than Arendt, acted both as a fatherly and brotherly figure, solid, supportive, and practical, while remaining in her shadow.

Rahel Varnhagen

It was during her stay in Paris that she finally managed to complete her study of Rahel Varnhagen (1771–1833). The first nine chapters had been written by 1933, as Jaspers later confirmed in letters to the German government, but her flight from Germany disrupted the work. She did not finish the manuscript until 1938, and because of the war, the book was not published until 1957 in English translation, and in German two years later, in 1959.[33] The book is an attempt to describe the coming to self-consciousness of a Jewish woman, and may be viewed as actually more autobiographical than it is biographical.[34] It is clear that Arendt, through her analysis of Varnhagen, was gradually facing up to the ineliminable difference of the Jew in the emerging German Christian state and was thus coming to her own awareness of Jewishness, something which would modify her commitment to the universalism of Kant and the Enlightenment. She had written to Jaspers about this project, and, on 30 March 1930, he replied that he could not understand her attempt to ground Jewish existence employing existential categories since he regarded Jewishness as a mere contingent fact, no more than a *façon de parler* (HAKJ 10). Arendt replied that she wanted to analyse a certain possibility of existence which arises from being Jewish, a characteristic she termed "fatefulness", arising out of the foundationlessness of the Jewish condition. Arendt goes on to describe

Varnhagen in terms of categories of Jewishness as *"pariah"* or *"parvenu"*, categories she had borrowed from the French writer and Dreyfus defender, Bernard Lazare. Later in 1948, while working for Schocken Books, Arendt edited and wrote an introduction to Lazare's book, *Job's Dung Heap* (Young-Bruehl, p. 122).[35]

Rahel Varnhagen is a difficult, abstract book, essentially a phenomenological treatise rather than a biography. Arendt deliberately eschewed psychological interpretation and historical situating of Varnhagen in German romanticism and instead tried to narrate Varnhagen's life from the inside, "as she herself might have told it" as she says in her 1956 Preface. Arendt is deeply critical of Varnhagen's assumption that she could transform her life into a work of art and so escape her destiny through the process of *Bildung* (the very process about which Gadamer is so positive). She is critical of the withdrawal of Varnhagen and her romantic contemporaries into the realm of *Innerlichkeit*, of introspection, which for Arendt dissolves everything into mood (and mood is here understood in the manner of Heidegger). This withdrawal compounds the 'worldlessness' which Varnhagen and others diagnosed and suffered. Varnhagen is not able to participate in the public world.

An émigré in the USA

Soon after the war broke out, all German nationals were detained by the French authorities. She was detained by the French in the notorious sports centre of Vélodrome d'Hiver, and then transported to an internment camp for women at Gurs from which she was finally able to escape by procuring liberation papers from the French underground. Others were not so lucky and many were transported from Gurs to the extermination camps during the German occupation. Indeed Arendt tried to monitor these transportations in her articles written for *Aufbau*, the German language newspaper in New York. Her husband, Blücher, was in a separate camp but he too was lucky to be released. They eventually met by accident on the street and resolved to go to the USA. They obtained visas for the USA, and they travelled to Marseilles to board a ship there. While in Paris, she had become a close friend of Walter Benjamin (1892–1940), and in Marseilles, waiting to go to the USA, she again met Benjamin who was also attempting to leave. She agreed to carry Benjamin's papers to New York while Benjamin set off for the border to Spain. Fearing arrest at the border, Benjamin committed suicide. Meanwhile Arendt and Blücher arrived in New York in May 1941, where Arendt was deeply upset on hearing the news of Benjamin's death. She brought Benjamin's manuscripts to the newly founded Institute for Social Research headed by Adorno. Arendt, however, became impatient when Adorno did not proceed to publish Benjamin's papers immediately, and she suspected they were being suppressed. Eventually, Scholem and Adorno brought out a collection of Benjamin's papers but Benjamin's *Illuminations* did not appear until 1968, edited by Arendt herself.[36]

Officially a stateless person, Arendt found herself impressed by American political liberty and by the citizens' genuine defence of freedom, but, like many old-world European intellectuals, she disliked the social atmosphere and the entirely anti-intellectual climate, including the widespread casual anti-Semitism she encountered (HAKJ 30). She wrote that all intellectuals of necessity belonged to the opposition in the USA and diagnosed the fundamental contradiction of the country as "the coexistence of political freedom and social oppression" (HAKJ 31). From 1941 on she saw herself as a freelance writer, describing herself as "something between a historian and a political journalist" (HAKJ 23). She began writing articles on Jewish issues for *Aufbau*, including articles supporting the idea of a Jewish army to fight Hitler. In 1945 she wrote an important essay, "German Guilt", for a journal, *Jewish Frontier*, which Jaspers praised, as he had written on a similar topic.[37] She also found a job teaching European history part time at Brooklyn College from 1945 to 1947. This was to be the first of many teaching appointments: at Wesleyan University (where she wrote *Eichmann in Jerusalem*), at Chicago as a Visiting Fellow of the Committee of Social Thought, at Princeton, as well as the New School for Social Research. In 1946 she took a job with Schocken Books in New York. She contributed book reviews to *The Nation* and wrote some famous essays for the *New Yorker*.

The Origins of Totalitarianism

More or less as soon as the war ended in 1945 Arendt began research on *The Origins of Totalitarianism* which was completed in 1949, and published in 1951. The book is a major analysis of the emergence of totalitarianism in Nazi Germany and in Stalinist Russia with reflections on the manner totalitarianism made anti-Semitism a central feature. The issues of alienation, homelessness, and isolation of modern humanity are central to her analysis. Arendt's treatment of the global nature of totalitarianism is Heideggerian in manner: totalitarianism aims at "total conquest and total domination" (OT xxx). Totalitarianism is only possible in specifically modern society where everything – including our sense of reality – is managed. People are deracinated and endlessly manipulated. In particular totalitarianism feeds on the isolation of modern humanity and its sense of homelessness:

> What prepares men for totalitarian domination in the non-totalitarian world is the fact that loneliness, once a borderline experience usually suffered in certain marginal social conditions like old

age, has become an everyday experience of the ever growing masses of our century.

(OT 478)

Before totalitarianism takes hold it requires a huge mass of "atomized, isolated individuals" (OT 323); it is therefore possible only under the conditions of modernity. She also offers a historical survey of European anti-Semitism. Like Sartre, Arendt sees anti-Semitism not as an accidental feature of German totalitarianism but as central to it. Furthermore, she characterises the peculiar appeal of National Socialism as its ability to unite for a time the mob and the elite. The mob and the elite found each other because in a sense they had both felt excluded from modern bourgeois society. The mob were not cured by the First World War, but continued to see war as the great leveller, as "the true father of the new world order" (OT 329). The philosophy of terror became "a kind of political expressionism" (OT 332) and the elite delighted in the destruction of bourgeois respectability.

Despite cataloguing in detail the horrors of totalitarian systems, Arendt ends the book on a note of hope. Arendt is always optimistic about the genuinely surprising nature of history and of the human condition, which is always throwing up something new:

> But there remains also the truth that every end in history necessarily contains a new beginning; this beginning is the promise, the only "message" which the end can ever produce. Beginning, before it becomes a historical event, is the supreme capacity of man; politically, it is identical with man's freedom. *Initium ut esset homo creatus est* – "that a beginning be made man was created" said Augustine. This beginning is guaranteed by each new birth; it is indeed every man.
>
> (OT 478–479)

To her surprise, as she was actually quite a private person, she became something of a reluctant celebrity as a result of the publication of this book. Again, Arendt was criticised for not being more scholarly. The *émigré* German political thinker Eric Voegelin criticised Arendt for assuming that human essence can change and for locating the origins of totalitarianism in modernity rather than much earlier. She replied to Voegelin in 1953 in *The Review of Politics*.[38] For Arendt totalitarianism emerged from roots which were subterranean in European society and had no connection with the great tradition of Western political thought.

Coming to terms with Heidegger

It was not until the war had ended that Arendt returned to philosophy with an attempt to assess Heidegger in an essay, "What is *Existenz* philosophy?", published in the *Partisan Review* in 1946.[39] In this important essay, she rejects fundamental ontology as egoism and criticises Heidegger's account of Dasein as an isolated, "atomised" self, capable only of "mechanical reconciliation" with others in an "over-self". In contrast, she defended Jaspers' notions of 'communication' (*Kommunication*) and responsible *Existenz*. Heidegger's politics, she argues in this essay, had been irresponsible, nihilist, and romantic. In a famous footnote she derided Heidegger's attempts to be a serious intellectual and accused him of mistreating Husserl. She was particularly outraged that Heidegger had sent Husserl a letter suspending him from teaching. (Separately, in a letter to Jaspers, she pointed out that Heidegger's defence that he was only countersigning an official circular was lamentable, HAKJ 47). In this essay Arendt claims that she never had "any professional or personal attachment to old Husserl", but felt that Heidegger's letter had the effect of almost killing him, provoking her to label Heidegger "a potential murderer" (HAKJ 48).

Meanwhile Jaspers was sending her information about Heidegger. In his letter of 1 September 1949, Jaspers informs her that he has received letters from Heidegger and fills her in on Heidegger's later philosophy of Being (including his revival of the antiquated spelling, *Seyn*), wondering how an impure soul who distorted so much can live with this guilt. Arendt replies on 29 September agreeing with Jaspers' description of Heidegger, and goes further by painting Heidegger as lacking character to such an extent that he possessed no character at all (HAKJ 142). She did concede, however, that Heidegger's *Letter on Humanism*, though ambiguous and questionable in its philosophical outlook, was up to his former high standard, as opposed to his awful babbling about Nietzsche (HAKJ 142). Both Jaspers and Arendt expressed fears that Heidegger's talk of existence and being, and his attempt to link his researches back to *Being and Time*, would start to distort everything again. On the other hand, it is clear that Heidegger's discussion of the transcendental homelessness of humankind in the *Humanismusbrief* subsequently had definite resonances for Arendt, since homelessness appears as a major theme in her *The Human Condition* (1958).

In the immediate aftermath of the war, Arendt was busy writing essays on Jewish identity and about the need for Jews to have their own state. Nevertheless, she feared for the Palestinian people and was strongly against reproducing the errors of other European states in Palestine. As part of a Commission on European Jewish Cultural Reconstruction seeking the recovery of Judaica stolen by the Nazis, Arendt visited Europe in November 1949 for a visit that would last four months. On this trip she made time to visit Jaspers in Basel, Switzerland. Jaspers showed her Heidegger's recent letters to him, which Arendt judged to be full of the old mixture of genuineness and cowardly deceit.

As part of her work for the Commission, she had to visit Freiburg on business and she used this as an occasion to contact Heidegger for the first time since 1933. On 7 February, on her arrival in Freiburg, she sent a message to Heidegger seeking to meet him. He delivered the answering letter direct to her hotel and they spent the evening talking, speaking together as if for the first time, as Arendt wrote to Blücher (Young-Bruehl, p. 246). They reconciled and continued to correspond on an occasional basis over the following years with some meetings. On her return to the USA, Arendt sent Heidegger food parcels and began to arrange for translations of his books. Arendt did not see Heidegger between 1952 and 1967 when she visited him again. Some time later, Elfride wrote to Arendt enquiring about the possibility of selling the original manuscript of *Being and Time* and Arendt advised concerning the possibility of auctioning it. Despite the fact that Arendt sent her publications to Heidegger, he never displayed any interest in them; indeed he studiously ignored them. In fact, as Arendt quickly realised, Heidegger was actually jealous of her own success (HAKJ 457).

Much later, in her extraordinary essay "Martin Heidegger at Eighty", written in 1969 and published in 1971 in the *New York Review of Books*, Hannah Arendt portrayed Heidegger as a high intellectual, a deep thinker who was not understood by the Nazis nor did he really understand them. Heidegger, for her, was the great teacher of the period from 1919 to 1927, the period which laid the groundwork for *Being and Time* and provided the basis for her own thinking about the worldliness of human beings. As she recalled, in this period of general economic chaos in the 1920s in Germany with its runaway inflation, the study of philosophy was not for "breadwinners", namely those interested in material survival, but was "the study of resolute starvelings",[40] those unconcerned with the wisdom of the world. It was these idealistic students who were attracted to Heidegger's mesmerising lectures. For Arendt and her contemporaries, Heidegger was someone who knew that "the thread of tradition was broken" and who was "discovering the past anew" (Murray, p. 295). Heidegger was someone who practised *thinking*, penetrating deep into the matters themselves and doing so in a manner withdrawn from ordinary human affairs. She saw him, however, as involved in a thinking which had lost connection with practice and invokes Plato's story in the *Theaetetus* about the philosopher Thales who falls in a well while looking at the stars, provoking the peasant girl from Thrace to laugh at him. Arendt is obviously identifying with the peasant girl; the great thinkers have let humanity down by not laughing enough:

> Men have obviously not yet discovered what laughter is good for –
> perhaps because their thinkers, who have always been ill-disposed
> towards laughter, have let them down in this respect, even though a
> few of them have racked their brains over the question of what
> makes us laugh.
> ("Martin Heidegger at Eighty", Murray, p. 301)[41]

Arendt portrays Heidegger as being drawn to the tyrant Hitler, as Plato was to Dion, and the trip to Berlin, as Plato's to Syracuse, should have provoked more laughter than Thales' behaviour ever did. She points out the naivety of Heidegger's Nazism: only someone who had never read *Mein Kampf* could interpret National Socialism as a struggle against technological domination. Heidegger's account in his *Introduction to Metaphysics* of the "inner truth and greatness" of the National Socialist movement as consisting in "the encounter between global technology and modern man" was evidence that Heidegger did not know what he was talking about. Arendt is permanently shocked by those who could dress up Nazi thuggery in the name of ideas such as Hegel, Nietzsche, or Plato, or similarly those who could justify Stalin's mass murdering in the name of industrialisation and rationalisation. Arendt chose to see Heidegger as politically inept. On the other hand, in private, for example in letters to Jaspers and in her own notebooks, she portrays Heidegger as an inveterate liar, incapable of facing his responsibility and hence has retreated to his foxhole in Todtnauberg.

Eichmann in Jerusalem

In the USA, Arendt was very active as a displaced European intellectual, becoming part of the circle which included the novelist Mary McCarthy, the critic Irving Howe, the poet and critic Randall Jarrell, the poet Hermann Broch, and even T. S. Eliot, among others. She was extremely critical of the anti-communist hysteria of the McCarthy era in the 1950s. In illustration of this poisonous atmosphere, she wrote to Jaspers recounting that the American conservative philosopher Sidney Hook had told her it was un-American to quote Plato (HAKJ 213)! In 1961 as a correspondent for *The New Yorker* magazine she attended the trial in Jerusalem of Eichmann, who had been kidnapped from Argentina and brought to Israel in 1960, publishing the series of articles in 1963 which became an important book when separately published as *Eichmann in Jerusalem. A Report on the Banality of Evil.*[42] Her phrase "the banality of evil", coined to describe monstrous deeds which could be perpetrated by weak, anonymous, bureaucratic personalities such as those of the major Nazi functionaries, had immediate impact. According to Arendt's penetrating analysis, Eichmann was no monster, though he was something of a clownish figure, a small-minded career bureaucrat, not at home in the world of ideas, but muddled and capable only of 'official-speak' (*Amtssprache*). Eichmann typified a kind of self-deception Arendt found endemic in German society, where the vast majority of the German people had believed in Hitler (EIJ 98). Her critique of the collapse of German morality is devastating. She understood the German relation to the law as the application of a kind of diluted version of Kantian philosophy which consisted solely of acting as if one is oneself the author of the law. She quotes a Nazi formulation of

Kant's categorical imperative: "act in such a way that the Führer, if he knew your action, would approve it" (EIJ 136).

Many interpreters understood Arendt's portrayal of Eichmann to mean that anyone could become an Eichmann under the appropriate circumstances. But Arendt vigorously repudiated that interpretation. Her claim was in fact the opposite: human beings are not predictable; we are constantly surprised by how people will act. For Arendt, the point is that we have a responsibility to recognise the claim that events have on our thinking and acting. Eichmann was not even aware of such a claim on his thinking. Moreover, she repudiated any grand systematic theory of evil. As she later wrote in *The Life of the Mind. Thinking*, "behind that phrase I held no thesis or doctrine", other than being dimly aware that her notion of evil ran counter to the traditional religious characterisation of evil as demonic in source (*Thinking*, p. 3).

Her book was controversial, particularly her discussion of the manner in which some of the committees of Jewish elders collaborated with the Nazis in the selection of Jews for the camps, often persuading themselves that by so doing they were helping others to escape (EIJ 117–118). Over the following years, she was subjected to quite vicious attacks, including one by her former friend Gershom Scholem and others. The discussions often centred around the meaning of the concept of 'good Jew', and Arendt's views were not often appreciated, as earlier she had found when in 1948–1949 she had advocated a state of Israel which gave equal value to both the Palestinian Arabs and the Jewish settlers. Her views at that time turn out to have accurately predicted the turmoil of Israel for the next forty years. Overall, Arendt argues against the notion of collective guilt but in favour of the notion of collective responsibility, though as she says in her essay on Jaspers, collective responsibility may be too heavy a burden for humankind to bear.

The return to philosophy

Arendt's most important book, *The Human Condition. A Study of the Central Dilemmas Facing Modern Man*, appeared first in English in 1958, published by the University of Chicago. It appeared in German, translated by Arendt herself, under the title *Vita activa* in 1960. Arendt's book originally began as an attempt to supplement *The Origins of Totalitarianism* with a thorough critical study of the Marxist interpretation of labour (HC 79). This, however, became a separate project, "The Totalitarian Elements of Marxism", for which she received a Guggenheim fellowship in 1952 and some of which was finally published in *Between Past and Future*. Her 1953 lectures in Princeton on "Karl Marx and the Tradition of Political Thought" were also an elementary set of reflections on the origin, nature, and fate of the *vita activa*. But she soon realised she needed to explore the nature of work in greater detail, which she did in a series of lectures given in the University of Chicago in 1956, and which provided the basis of the book.

For Arendt, the 1960s were an active political period, during which she wrote about desegregation, the Cuban missile crisis, the Bay of Pigs, the assassination of Kennedy, and other issues. Her 1965 essay *On Revolution* invoked her key distinction between the social and the political, to distinguish between the failure of the French revolution and the success of the American revolution, claiming that the French had failed by concentrating on the social, such as efforts to alter the class structure, whereas the Americans had succeeded in founding something political. For Arendt, it was a mistake to confuse the social with the political. Social goals such as adequate housing, employment, and equal wages are to be sharply distinguished from political goals such as founding a republic and creating space for action. In *On Revolution* Arendt distinguished between power and violence and was very influential among the left-wing campus radicals in Germany and in the USA during the 1960s. For her, violence arises out of impotence and is the opposite of power. Violence could dramatise grievances, but it was essentially "mute", as she put it in *The Human Condition*. She wrote *On Violence* to address this question.[43] Her position is complex. She was not a pacifist and supported the use of violence in certain circumstances. But she always emphasises that as a form of action violence is unpredictable and uncontrollable. It is very different from the kind of action and communication produced through speech.

She also wrote a number of important essays criticising American foreign policy in Vietnam, including a review of the Pentagon papers, "Lying in Politics", where she diagnosed a certain self-deception creeping into the policy makers' own thinking in their efforts to manipulate public opinion.[44] She gave lectures at most of the distinguished American universities: Princeton, Berkeley, Notre Dame, Harvard, Yale, Columbia, at the Committee for Social Thought at the University of Chicago, and, from 1967, at the New School for Social Research. She was awarded the Lessing Prize of the city of Hamburg as well as honorary doctorates from many institutions. Her husband Blücher had died in 1970. He had been a very successful teacher at Bard College but had published nothing. Mary McCarthy describes Arendt as very lonely after the death of Blücher. In her last years Arendt returned to philosophy and commenced a large three-volume study on the mind, planned as a major study of the evolution of the concepts of thinking, willing, and judging. The sections on thinking and willing were based on the Gifford lectures she gave in Aberdeen in 1973–1974. The first set of lectures, on thinking, were delivered in 1973 but the second set in 1974 were abandoned owing to a heart attack Arendt suffered after her first lecture on willing. As soon as she recovered she insisted on a strenuous trip to Germany to see Heidegger.[45] She had just completed the second volume when she died from a second heart attack on 4 December 1975, some months before Heidegger's own death on 26 May 1976. The first two volumes were published posthumously as *The Life of the Mind* in 1978, though the first volume, *Thinking*, appeared initially in the *New Yorker*. In her *Life of the Mind* she again attempted to come to terms with Heidegger's philosophy. Thinking for her is opposed to knowing. Knowing had an object whereas thinking did not. Thinking is a kind of withdrawal from the world, a kind of homelessness (*Thinking*, p. 199); it is always "out of order" (*Thinking*, p. 197). On the other hand, non-thinking can lead to evil. Therefore, to come properly to understand the nature of ethical action, we need an account of what Kant called 'judging'. She left on her typewriter the opening sentence of this third volume, *Judging*, when she died.[46] This part was based on her lectures on Kant given in the New School for Social Research in 1970 and was eventually published as *Lectures on Kant's Political Philosophy* in 1982.[47] She named her friend Mary McCarthy as literary executor. Her papers are deposited in the Library of Congress in Washington where they fill more than ninety containers and constitute about 28,000 items including many draft lectures and notes.

The Human Condition

Arendt's *The Human Condition*, first published in 1958, offers a careful phenomenological account of the nature of human action, situating it in the public realm, drawing heavily on Aristotle and using an idealised model of the Greek city-state or *polis*. *The Human Condition* is an attempt, invoking Aristotle's *Nicomachean Ethics* Book Six, which she had studied with Heidegger in Marburg, to characterise the nature of the sphere of the practical life, the *bios politikos* (Latin: *vita activa*) as opposed to the *bios theoretikos* (Latin: *vita contemplativa*), or the life of the philosopher, which Heidegger had characterised in his Marburg course on Plato's *Sophist*.

Arendt's title reflects an acceptance of a kind of historical and existential understanding of humanity, derived from Jaspers and Heidegger, whereby humanity should not be considered to have a permanent essential nature but only a certain condition: human condition is not the same thing as human nature (HC 9–10). For Arendt, as for Sartre and Heidegger, we are always dealing with individual humans, not with abstract "Humanity". She was equally critical of Marx's appeal to 'species being' (*Gattungswesen*). For her, we should avoid talk about a human essence, and rather we should think primarily of individuals in the concrete. This human condition is through and through contingent and, for her, it is important for thought to be constantly brought back from abstract speculation to recognise this contingency. She regards the notion of a fixed human nature to be a product of philosophical thought and exemplified in the Enlightenment conception of universal human nature. Arendt, on the other hand, thinks that what is permanent about the human condition is that it conditions and is conditioned by everything with which it comes into contact. In this respect, she recognises the dialectical development of human freedom in a manner quite close to Merleau-Ponty, whose account of incarnation she admired in *The Life of the Mind* (*Thinking*, p. 33). Human beings have being in the world. For Arendt, the world is our home and yet the modern experience is one of alienation and homelessness. The book opens with a reflection on the commentary surrounding the 1957 event of the Soviet launch of the first satellite into space. For Arendt, what is extraordinary is that the event is heralded as the beginning of a new era which will free humans of their shackles to the earth:

> The banality of the statement should not make us overlook how extraordinary in fact it was; for although Christians have spoken of the earth as a vale of tears and philosophers have looked upon their body as a prison of mind or soul, nobody in the history of mankind has ever conceived of the earth as a prison for men's bodies or shown such eagerness to go literally from here to the moon.
>
> (HC 2)

Arendt sees the event as marking a new era in human secularisation. Now humans want to be released not only from God but from the life-sustaining earth itself. For Arendt there had been a two-fold alienation: a "flight from the earth into the universe and from the world into the self" (HC 6); and her aim is to trace this alienation back to its roots.

The Human Condition develops its defence of the life of action in terms of a kind of philosophical, anthropological account of the rise of the public sphere in the state or *polis* and the development of the relation between humans and their work, from *animal laborans*, to *homo faber*, to doer of public deeds. Arendt had been actively recovering her Greek in the 1950s and *The Human Condition* relies heavily on a conceptualisation of classic Greek political life. The influence of Hobbes, Weber, and Marx is also readily apparent, and, in particular, Arendt thought of herself as providing a critique of the Marxist account of labour. But, most of all, the account is deeply Heideggerian in its interest in the notion of being-in-the-world. Arendt owes a deep debt to Heidegger's interpretation of Aristotle's concept of *phronesis* (which also influenced Gadamer's own analysis of the commonsense tradition in *Truth and Method*). Some time before she completed the book she wrote to Heidegger in May 1954 telling him she was studying the various basic forms of doing (labour, work, action) inspired in part by both Marx and Hobbes, and that she could not have done this "without what I learned from you in my youth".[48] While deeply influenced by Heidegger, however, the book offers radical revisions of Heideggerian philosophy.

The Human Condition questions the major Western tradition from Plato to Marx which sees humans coming to the full realisation of their potential in the theoretical life. For Arendt this emphasis on the theoretical is a betrayal of the practical, which came to its fullest expression in the otherworldly nature of the Christian religion in the Middle Ages, exemplified by Augustine. Later Arendt admitted that a major flaw of the book was the fact that it did not attempt to analyse the life of the mind, the *vita contemplativa* which she contrasted with the active life. Arendt's approach is to provide a phenomenological account of the different ways in which humans are in the world through their work and action. As with Heidegger, Jaspers, Marcuse, Adorno, and most of the intellectuals of her generation, she is deeply critical of consumer society and the manner in which human life is distorted by the 'world-alienating' effect of modern science and by modern mass communication. Heidegger, for instance, had stated in *Being and Time* that 'publicity' (*Öffentlichkeit*) covers up and obscures everything (BT 165; 127). For Arendt, humans achieve their fulfilment in intersubjective, political *action*, which is only possible if certain conditions prevail and, she believes, the modern state has led to the decline of the possibilities for genuine action.

As Arendt acknowledges, the book was written under the shadow of the threat of global nuclear destruction during the Cold War. This world-destroying power of contemporary humanity is for Arendt a logical outgrowth of the special power of modern natural science. Leaning heavily on her friend Alexandre Koyré's research on the emergence of the seventeenth-century scientific world-view (HC 249 n.1),[49] and providing an analysis that merits comparison with Husserl's account of Galilean science in the *Crisis*, she sees the greatness of modern science lying in its detached symbolic power. The capacity of human subjects to take a standpoint beyond the world while remaining in the world is the source of the success of modern science. Just as one can map a terrain better from an aeroplane, so also the more one distances oneself from the earth the more one is able to comprehend it in thought. Her reflections here are also very close to Heidegger's later reflections on the nature of technology. Indeed Heidegger had sent Arendt his essays on this topic. Thus Arendt sees work as involving both objectification (reification) and also a violation of nature. *Homo faber* wants to become, in the words of Descartes, master and possessor of nature through this violation and destruction of what is given (*Amor Mundi*, p. 35). The book, however, wants to point out that such a race to overcome human dependence on the earth actually involves turning our backs on what is essential to humanity, its very being-in-the-world, its love of the world. Arendt sees in the event of the launch of the sputnik, "a rebellion against human existence as it has been given, a free gift from nowhere (secularly speaking), which he wishes to exchange, as it were, for something he has made himself" (HC 3).

In *The Human Condition* Arendt pays close attention to the factors which gave rise to the modern world and to the loss of world. She acknowledges the usual factors – the discovery of the New World, the Reformation, the new science of Galileo (including his "discovery" of the telescope), the new scepticism of Descartes. However, what is particularly interesting is Arendt's quite original interpretation of the nature of these phenomena. What is important for her is not the loss of religion, or the collapse of transcendence, but the loss of the world itself, the retreat from the earth, 'earth alienation' (HC 264) leading to the domination of science by abstraction and mathematics. Modern science's dependency on mathematics overrules even the testimony of nature itself (HC 267). Humans now can achieve a universal standpoint, a point of view which takes them beyond the world. The nature of Galileo's discovery is such that he shows that the world of the senses is an illusion. Human beings lose their faith in the world and their answer is to attempt to overcome their dependence on this world, through dominating it and through distancing themselves from it. This analysis is an interesting variation of the assessment of the role of modern scientific outlook in the late Husserl of the *Crisis*, in Heidegger's discussion of "the age of the world picture", and Gadamer's discussion of Galileo in *Truth and Method*. Indeed the critique of the effect of the modern natural scientific outlook on human being in the world is one of the major contributions of German phenomenology.

The core of her original analysis is her distinction of three fundamental levels of human activity: "work", "labour", and "action":

> With the term *vita activa*, I propose to designate three fundamental human activities: labor, work and action. They are fundamental because each one corresponds to one of the basic conditions under which life on earth has been given to man.
>
> (HC 7)

Arendt's strategy is to provide a phenomenological account of this distinction in order to correct both the traditional philosophical attitude to the active life and to correct Marx's distorted view of human labour. She delineates these three forms of human activity in the ancient Greek model and then charts their transformations in the development of modernity. Thus the realm of the private in Greek society becomes transformed into the realm of the intimate in modern life, whereas the concept of intimacy was entirely unknown to the Greeks. Similarly, whereas in Greek life, economy was confined to the domain of the household, in modern society the rule of the economic is extended to all society. She sees contemporary society as having reduced medieval hierarchy by reducing everyone to labourers. Even princes and prime ministers see their positions as jobs, and now increasing automation in the workplace is producing a society of labourers without labour. This phenomenon needs to be rethought. As she puts it in the Prologue to *The Human Condition*:

> What I propose in the following is a reconsideration of the human condition from the vantage point of our newest experiences and our most recent fears...What I propose, therefore, is very simple: it is nothing more than to think what we are doing. "What we are doing" is indeed the central theme of this book.
>
> (HC 5)

Her analysis begins with a discussion of the nature of the public and private realm and the nature of what she terms 'labour'.

Labour *(ponos)*

Labour is humankind's "oldest and most natural burden" (HC 4). Labour is our most basic way of relating with the world; as Arendt puts it, "the human condition of labor is life itself" (HC 7). According to Arendt's characterisation, the world of *labour* is the endlessly repetitive and enclosed world of, for example, the peasants labouring in the fields, where the labour once completed must begin all over again. Labour includes the perennial circle of life and death, seeking nourishment, clothing, protection from the elements, and so on. To the extent that labour is cyclical and its products are consumed, it differs from the kind of production of artefacts brought about through *work*. Labour produces products which are consumed and leave no permanent trace in the world (HC 94). Labour implies necessity and the constant struggle for biological survival and is very closely tied to the body for Arendt. Hence, one speaks of labour in the act of giving birth to a child. Labour is the domain of the household and presupposes inequalities and indeed violence. Slavery is a condition of the household, for Arendt, following Aristotle. For Arendt, the whole institution of slavery was created so as to free humans from labour by enforcing it on others. Arendt refers to the fact that labouring peasants are classified with slaves by both Plato and Aristotle (HC 83 n. 9): "To labor meant to be enslaved by necessity, and this enslavement was inherent in the conditions of human life" (HC 83–84). Arendt thinks that both Adam Smith and Marx actually recognised this dimension of labour but treated it under the category of unproductive work.

Work *(ergon, poeisis)*

Having characterised the nature of *labour* Arendt then goes on to distinguish it from *work* (HC 79), contrasting the nature of *homo faber* with *animal laborans*. The labouring animal must earn his or her living by the

310

sweat of his or her brow. Work, on the other hand, is, by contrast, a specifically human enterprise, an essentially creative activity, as Marx had rightly recognised. By 'work' Arendt means the kind of artisan work where the products become independent of the producers and take on a life of their own – creating the human world of the marketplace, the production of "whatever is needed to house the human body" (*Amor Mundi*, p. 29). Work comes to an end with the production of the object, whereas labour ends only to commence again. It involves the production of artefacts which have a quasi-permanence about them. Work reflects "the unnaturalness of human existence" (HC 7). She admits that her distinction between *labour* and *work* was ignored in the philosophical analysis in the past (HC 85). She herself claims to have been inspired by John Locke's distinction between "the labor of our body and the labor of our hands" (HC 79). But, in her view, the contrast between these two modes of life is *pre-philosophical*, rooted in society, and indeed is recognised in the two separate etymological roots for the distinct words for both preserved in many languages (e.g. German: *Arbeit* and *Werk*).

She accepts Marx's account of the extraordinary transformation brought about by the exchange of goods in the marketplace. Work produces objects which last beyond the activity of the maker and the process of reification means that these objects stand over and against humans and make up the world for humans – the houses we live in, the roads we walk on, and so on:

> Viewed as part of the world, the products of work – and not the products of labor – guarantee the permanence and durability without which a world would not be possible at all.
>
> (HC 94)

It is through *work* that humans come to find themselves in a *world*: "the human condition of work is worldliness", "within its borders each individual life is housed" (HC 7). Work creates a human world as opposed to labour which struggles with nature. Objects of work stand over and against humans, thus contributing to what Arendt calls the 'durability' of the world. As Arendt maintains: "Against the subjectivity of men stands the objectivity of the man-made artifice, not the indifference of nature" (*Amor Mundi*, p. 35). Work leads to reification, as Marx saw, and also to the instrumentalisation of the world.

It is hard to know how far Arendt wishes to push the separation between *labour* and *work*, between the cyclical labour of the peasant tied to the vagaries of season and weather, and the free creative life of the artisan. Somehow Arendt's contrast does not seem to be very sharply drawn. For Arendt, consumer goods are produced by *work*. But if the factories are employing slave labour, are these consumer goods not also the product of labour? Arendt complicates the distinction by claiming that goods of consumption like fuel, food, and drink are relatively short-lived and that the only joy produced in the labour to make them comes in the brief period of rest in which they are consumed (an analysis which goes back to Augustine's discussion of the difference between goods which are consumed and those which are abiding). For Arendt, then, farms produce food on the basis of labour. Consumer goods are produced by labour whereas 'use objects' are produced by work. Use objects have a certain durability:

> What distinguishes the most flimsy pair of shoes from mere con-
> sumer goods is that they do not spoil if I don't wear them, they are
> objects and therefore possess a certain "objective" independence of
> their own, however modest. Used or unused they will remain in the
> world for a certain while unless they are wantonly destroyed.
>
> It is this durability which gives the things of the world their rela-
> tive independence from men who produced and use them, their
> "objectivity" that makes them withstand, "stand against" and en-
> dure at least for a time the voracious needs and wants of their living
> users.
>
> (*Amor Mundi*, pp. 34–35)

Arendt is not interested in nature as such. She is interested in the world produced by human work and action. The world is what lies "between man and nature" (*Amor Mundi*, p. 35). Arendt really is seeing *work* and *labour* as two poles in a process which usually involves both.

Action (praxis)

The world of *action* represents the highest sphere of human engagement, especially when it emerges in joint co-operative undertakings and in discussion. It is only in the life of action, as opposed to the life of abstract thought, that humans become fully authentic. Action for Arendt means what it does for Aristotle, namely *political action, praxis*. The realm of action is the realm where it is possible to achieve *arete*, excellence, where individuals seek to immortalise themselves through great deeds. For Arendt the Greek *polis* opened a space where humans could freely interact with one another. To be active means both to be individual and to be in common. The public space is the realm where individual achievements occur in the space made by a life lived with others: "plurality is specifically *the* condition...of all political life" (HC 7). In the past, both the Greek *polis* and the Roman *res publica* preserved public space as a testimony against the futility of a purely individual life. However, this space of great deeds is also a very competitive space, and one gains attention here only in the struggle with others.

For Arendt the conditions which give rise to the public space are complex. A condition of this individual struggle for action is that humans are both equal to one another and also different from one another. Furthermore, action requires language and *speech* and it is only through speech that politics is possible; indeed, a life without speech and action is literally death (HC 176):

> Men in the plural, that is, men in so far as they live and move and act in the world, can experience meaningfulness only because they can talk with and make sense to each other and to themselves.
>
> (HC 4)

Since actions involve risk, not everyone is capable of action; it is rather the preserve of the valiant few. Action, for Arendt, must be original, it must involve initiating something new, providing a new 'beginning' (*initium*). To initiate an action something must be removed or destroyed (*Crises of the Republic*, p. 5). The impulse towards action comes from wanting to make a beginning. Arendt agrees with Heidegger's account of 'origin' (*der Ursprung*) as expressed in *The Origin of the Work of Art*:

> It is of the nature of beginning that something new is started which cannot be expected from whatever may have happened before. This character of startling unexpectedness is inherent in all beginnings and all origins.
>
> (HC 177–178)

Arendt makes special claims about the nature of beginning, about the nature of what she terms 'natality'. *Natality* is the condition of being born and of being able to give birth.[50] Action is the "actualization of the human condition of natality" (HC 178). Arendt introduces the notion of *natality* as her counterpart to Heidegger's notion of *Verfallen*, of "falling". Natality must acknowledge the manner in which being born binds us to the world and at the same time creates our opportunities. Natality can be understood to mean both physical birth and birth into the social and political domains, birth into the life of the mind.

Humans are newcomers and beginners by virtue of birth. Natality means beginning from the beginning, *initium*, which for Arendt enables humans to take initiatives, to begin an action freely. To act is "to take initiative, to begin" (HC 177). *Initium* here refers to the beginning of human action as opposed to the beginning of the world. The new appears "in the guise of a miracle" (HC 178). The fact of natality is the "miracle that saves the world" (HC 247), the birth of new humans giving rise to new possibilities of action. Labour and work are both rooted in natality for Arendt (HC 9). Labour and work are there to ensure the continuity of the world for the incoming strangers. Birth and death presuppose the world. Without human involvement in the world there would only be the endless cycle of nature. Action is the business of creating and preserving (Heidegger too sees political action in this manner but also includes artistic creation). Part of the function of human action is to preserve what is common in the world, while being open to welcoming the new. A correct understanding of the human condition and natality in particular should contribute to the achievement and heightening of *amor mundi*, love of the world into which we are born.

Action is intimately connected with the nature of specifically human time. Action, for Arendt, creates the conditions necessary for remembrance (HC 9), for history. On the other hand, action also creates the conditions for deception and covering up. Because action involves risk and uncertainty, men who act are also men who are tempted, as Arendt says, to want to control the past (*Crises of the Republic*, p. 12). Action involves having to produce a narrative concerning oneself and the past. The most important kind of thinking is a kind of reflectiveness which is tied to action, a reflection which is narrative in nature. As she put it:

> Everyone who tells a story of what happened to him half an hour ago on the street has got to put this story into shape. And this putting the story into shape is a form of thought.
>
> (HAHA 303)

Arendt's own form of historical analysis has been compared with a kind of story-telling. For her, a hero is someone about whom a story can be told. In general, Arendt maintains that action is close to speech since the initiation of human entrance into society is accompanied by the question asked of every newcomer, "who are you?" Part of the function of preserving the world is to provide a basis for the existence of the other. "I wish that you are" (*volo ut sis*). For Arendt, speech is required for an action to have a revelatory force (HC 178). A doer of deeds is possible only if the doer is also a speaker of words. The 'who' of the speaker is disclosed in speech (HC 184). Actions are disclosed by the word and hence actions only reveal themselves to the story-teller (HC 192).

Along with speech, another prerequisite of action is what Arendt calls "plurality". For her, "plurality rules the earth" (HAHA 305). She is very critical of Heidegger's later turn to the "earth" which for her was an attempt to provide a mythological foundation for human belonging together which should instead be provided by an account of human political action. For Arendt actions are communally binding:

> Action, moreover, no matter what its specific content, always establishes relationships and therefore has an inherent tendency to force open all limitations and cut across all boundaries.
>
> (HC 190)

Human action brings about the space of appearances. This space "does not survive the actuality of the moment that brought it into being" (HC 199). For Arendt it was the very fragility and uncertainty of action which led to it being overturned in Plato's philosophy as the highest good for man. The Platonic preference for the contemplative life was then adopted by Christianity so that all forms of human labour, work, and action became subordinated to the contemplative. For Arendt, the evaluation of the life of contemplation over action was situated in this orientation in ancient Greek thought, which Christianity merely replicated. It is one of Arendt's most powerful criticisms of philosophy that philosophers have always overemphasised the nature and role of abstract thought. Thus Plato emphasised knowledge and making over action, an account which has been at the root of all subsequent forms of political domination according to Arendt (HC 225). Arendt, moreover, is not simply reversing the categories. She acknowledged that Aristotle was right to see pure thought as something separate. Indeed, Arendt is deeply suspicious of the philosophical move which simply inverts the categories, for example when Marx turned Hegel on his head. This kind of reversal did little to rethink the scope of the philosophical concepts themselves.

Arising from her distinctions between the realms of labour, work, and action, Arendt offers an important distinction between the *private* and the *public*. She begins with the model of the household, *oikia*, which is controlled by the father, often with force. The household is the sphere of the private, of dark forces. Yet the household also in a certain way protects its members from violation by the state. Arendt has been criticised for her rather narrow conception of the familial, which does not locate the family as the basis of the ethical, as in Hegel. People are struggling to move from mere biological life (*zoe*) to a freely chosen form of human life (*bios*). In political behaviour I am not primarily concerned with my own self (HAHA 311). Societies need to create public spaces in order for the political domain of action to be disclosed. Thus, in the ancient *polis* the marketplace, the *agora*, was the public realm; in the Middle Ages, the cathedral; and in the USA, the town hall. Arendt greatly admired the discourse which takes place in the public arena, whether it be the dispute in a town hall over a local planning issue or the deliberation of a jury during a trial. Some of her critics have argued, however, that it is precisely her inability to distinguish between larger political decisions and local meetings to discuss local issues that tends to trivialise her notion of action. Arendt is not so much concerned to distinguish between different kinds of action as to account for the possibility of it being allowed to take place. She is deeply concerned with the manner in which the space for action is being restricted in contemporary society. Hence, her analysis of the isolation of humans in modernity led her to believe that it had led to a decrease in common sense and an atrophy of the public space. But one unusual area where action is still present, for Arendt, is in the area of forgiveness and promising, even among two people. We keep our identities by binding ourselves in promises. Similarly, forgiving someone establishes a strictly personal relation with that person. Promising and forgiveness are human ways of dealing with the unpredictability and irreversibility of human action:

> The possible redemption from the predicament of irreversibility is the faculty of forgiving, and the remedy for unpredictability is contained in the faculty to make and keep promises. The two remedies belong together: forgiving relates to the past and serves to undo its deeds, while binding oneself through promises serves to set up in the ocean of future uncertainty islands of security without which not even continuity, let alone durability of any kind, would ever be possible in the relations between men.
>
> (*Amor Mundi*, p. 41)

This last example of forgiveness as a kind of action is an important indication of the care which must be taken in reading Arendt. Though she uses terms which seem superficially to repeat traditional analyses, she very quickly draws us into her own world, a world where the common terms are given a new and original meaning. Reading Arendt, then, is always a surprising experience. On the other hand, it is the very flexibility of her terminology and the individuality of her outlook which also are responsible for the difficulty in fitting her into any tradition.

Arendt's contribution

Hannah Arendt, the high-minded, publicly spirited intellectual, critically analysing and commenting on society, epitomises in an astonishing way this very world she inhabits: the twentieth century as characterised by political catastrophes, moral disasters, and yet at the same time by astonishing growth in the arts and sciences, and hence in human originality and opportunity. Arendt sees the way in which the modern technological world both alienates humans and gives their lives a radically new kind of shape. She is a critic of modernity in the spirit of Heidegger and Jaspers, of Marx and the Frankfurt school, but also of Hans Blumenberg. Thus *The Human Condition* had an influence on the account of modernity in Hans Blumenberg's *The Legitimacy of the Modern Age* first published in 1976.[51] Arendt describes this world as a world of "dark times" – a phrase she said she took from Bertholt Brecht's poem "To Posterity". For Arendt, dark times are not just times of human suffering and misery but specifically those times in which the public sphere of action has been darkened and diminished. According to Arendt's analysis, it is precisely because of dark times that humans are forced together into "fraternities" or other groups to protect their humanity which can no longer be exercised in the public realm. Thus she traces the modern emphasis on freedom to eighteenth-century secret societies. Against all attempts to eliminate difference in the world, she opposes the value of 'plurality'.

Arendt had a gift for friendship and, like Aristotle, she extolled the virtues of friendship: "For the Greeks the essence of friendship consisted in discourse" (*Dark Times*, p. 24). She admired Rosa Luxemburg, Brecht, Benjamin, and many of the left-wing German Jewish intellectuals, but her own background was more academic, steeped in classical and German philosophy. Her intellectual friendship with Jaspers had a lasting effect on her manner on enquiry.

Arendt has been recognised as one of the most powerful political thinkers of the twentieth century, particularly with her analysis of the nature of totalitarianism. She was a political thinker and yet not a political activist, since she thought she understood the realm of politics all the better by being an outsider in it. She claimed she had *acted* (in her sense) only a few times in her life, and then only because circumstances had forced her. Her aim, she claimed, was always to *understand* (HAHA 303–304). She was, however, an accomplished political theorist and philosopher of the social, two dimensions she carefully distinguished, ranking the political above the social. Jürgen Habermas, for example, has praised her for her renewal of the Aristotelian concept of *praxis*.[52] In many ways her concept of political action, as opposed to instrumental action, can be seen as agreeing with Habermas's critique of instrumental thought. Indeed, Habermas himself attributes his own notion of communicative action to the influence of Arendt. Others see her as defending a kind of communitarianism and the importance of the tradition of moral judgement, the *sensus communis* (HC 280–282). She was, like Habermas, also a forceful critic of the prevailing mood of positivism in American political science. Like many German philosophers, she was a strong opponent of liberalism within the political tradition exemplified by Locke as too atomistic. She was also a critic of behaviourism in the human sciences, and argued against biological determinism in various explanations of violence or other forms of human behaviour.

Though Arendt has been recognised for her philosophical reflections on the nature of identity and specifically of Jewish identity, she has never contributed much to the analysis of gender. In her work she tended to see the role of childbearing etc. as belonging to the sphere of labour, and family life as belonging to the private arena. For this reason, she has never been fully accepted by feminist critics.[53] Thus Adrienne Rich criticised *The Human Condition* as "a lofty and crippled book". According to Rich, Arendt withheld women from participating in the realm of the *vita activa*. Rich sees Arendt as embodying "the tragedy of a female mind nourished on male ideology".[54] Seyla Benhabib too notes Arendt's almost total silence on the question of women. In 1932, in a review of a book entitled *The Problem of Women in the Present Day*, Arendt did list factual evidence of the ongoing discrimination against women, but then went on to criticise the book for its individualist orientation.[55] In fact, Arendt's stance on this issue, as in others, is subtle and complex. Though she sees motherhood as part of the bonds which tie humans to the cycle of labour and hence as potentially enslaving, her concept of natality and of the new beginning represented by each birth raises her concept of motherhood to a participation in freedom. On the other hand, Arendt had absolutely no time for superficial ideologies which wanted to claim a certain kind of thinking as male and another kind as female. For her, thinking as such was genderless.

Because of her fascination with things Greek, Arendt has also been criticised as a nostalgic thinker, hopelessly longing for the restoration of the public space of the Greek *polis*. Thus, she frequently speaks in *The Human Condition* of the 'lost' distinction between public and private and of seeking to 'restore' it. In this respect she has been accused of accepting wholesale the anti-modernism of Heidegger, and she certainly did share many aspects of Heidegger's and Jaspers' antipathy to mass society. But the more telling criticism is that her account of action is purely formal. Though action is crucial to creating a fully human space, she never specifies exactly what deeds constitute actions in her sense. Thus the 'political' sphere is, for her, not necessarily related to social goals such as equality of opportunity or alleviation of poverty. Arendt takes a high-minded 'republican' view of the political where it is a discussion of 'ends' not of means; political action is divorced from all instrumental means. As such her account of political action has been interpreted as a kind of meta-discourse about the possibility of politics itself. Her conception of action is so formal, it has been dismissed as entirely empty. Arguing over parking issues in a local residence meeting could count as action in Arendt's sense, as long as the argument was over principle! But, in fact, action is neither empty talking nor theoretical reflection, for Arendt, rather it is the opening up of public space, the making possible of a specifically human world, closely modelled on the role of the art work in Heidegger's philosophy. Action founds world.

In contrast to Arendt's influence on Habermas and in political philosophy, her influence on analytic moral philosophy has been almost negligible. Isaiah Berlin[56] believes her work has been overpraised, and that there is something unprofessional and amateur about much of her efforts – thumbnail sketches rather than carefully researched, closely argued treatises. Similarly Stuart Hampshire thought her inaccurate in argument and parading learned allusion rather than careful study of texts.[57] Berlin is correct that Arendt scarcely ever argues; rather she is involved in phenomenological intuiting. But phenomenological intuition can often be seen as mere assertion, a subjective, impressionistic view of things. Arendt is always interesting, full of illuminating insights, and never relapsing into stock characterisations, but, on the other hand, she rarely fleshes out her analysis with close detail. She has been criticised for making distinctions which are entirely her own and for inventing concepts which she then named with words drawn from a different context – for example, work, action, power, force.[58] Arendt's defence is that as a phenomenologist she was more interested in the things themselves which the words disclose. She claimed she was more interested in the disclosive power of words than in their communicative value. Arendt's popularity is such today that there is an inevitable tendency to exaggerate her importance as a philosopher. In large measure, her overall framework is heavily dependent on the philosophies of Heidegger and Jaspers and their concerns for human existence and being-in-the-world. Arendt's distinctive contribution to this framework is her account of action as an individual achievement, her unique moral voice among the voices of the tradition,[59] and her phenomenological account of the conditions necessary for the creation and maintenance of the public space which makes possible the performance of action.

10

EMMANUEL LEVINAS
The phenomenology of alterity

Introduction: ethics as first philosophy

Emmanuel Levinas (1906–1995) has contributed to the development of phenomenology in a number of decisive ways. First, in the early 1930s, he played a crucial role in introducing phenomenology to France through his translation of Husserl's *Cartesian Meditations*,[1] and through his book on Husserl's theory of intuition.[2] In subsequent decades he wrote a number of exegetical studies of the phenomenologies of Husserl and Heidegger. But his reputation as an independent and original philosopher came in 1961 with the publication of his major work, *Totalité et infini* (*Totality and Infinity*), in which he gave phenomenology a radically *ethical* orientation, an orientation it has lacked since the death of Scheler.[3] In this chapter, we shall try to understand Levinas's phenomenological attempts to think through the nature and meaning of the ethical relation, his 'phenomenology of alterity' (*alterité* – from the Latin *alter* meaning the 'other', as in 'alternative' or 'alter ego'), since he puts concern for the other at the centre of ethics.

Against Heidegger, who explicitly excluded ethics from fundamental ontology, Levinas's original contribution is his claim that ethics *precedes* metaphysics, that ethics is the true *prote philosophia*, or 'first philosophy'; that what he calls 'metaphysics' (a broad term which includes epistemology) must be subordinated to ethics and the sphere of justice. However, it must be made clear at the outset that Levinas has nothing to say about ethics as traditionally practised in Western philosophy, since he thinks this tradition has either ignored ethics or made it secondary and provisional. Indeed, he explicitly repudiates the traditional understanding of ethics as a discipline within philosophy which examines different ways of motivating and justifying certain forms of behaviour. He deliberately avoids such topics as the nature of ethical justification, the various forms of ethical theory (e.g. utilitarianism, deontology), or the meta-ethical analysis of ethical discourse; rather he is interested in reminding Western philosophy of the manner in which the other person and 'otherness' in general intervenes in and subverts all our attempts to provide global and totalising explanations. Levinas sees all traditional ethics and philosophy as grounded in *egoism*, which understands my relation to myself as the primary relation (e.g. as in the work of Hobbes, Locke, or even Freud's account of auto-eroticism). Against this egoism, he wants to argue that my *responsibility to the other* is the fundamental structure upon which all other social structures rest (TI 79; 51). The term 'ethics', then, for Levinas, has a special and unique meaning. For him, ethics is never an egocentric mode of behaving, nor the construction of theories, but involves the effort to constrain one's freedom and spontaneity in order to be open to the other person, or more precisely to allow oneself to be constrained by the other. The first question of philosophy is not the ontological question of Leibniz and Heidegger, 'why is there something rather than nothing?', but rather the ethical question: 'How does my being justify itself?' Since, for Levinas, all social interaction is already in some sense taking place within the sphere of the other, the demand for ethics is always present, and as such it is an inescapable aspect of being human. He therefore wants to argue that the "ethical is the spiritual itself, and there is nothing that overcomes the ethical".[4] His philosophy, then, may be characterised as a kind of humanism. It is, to invoke the title of one of his books, a "humanism of the other man", a humanism which wants to speak of the other, not objectively in the third person, but addressing the other directly, in the vocative case, invoking his or her 'proper name'.

Levinas claims to be describing the meaning of ethical relations, and, specifically, attending to the moment of the advent of the ethical into a situation: "My task does not consist in constructing ethics; I only try to find its meaning (*le sens*)".[5] Levinas's dense, ambiguous, poetic descriptions of the ethical experience seem, however, to have a *prescriptive* element, to incorporate a demand about how humans *should* behave, rather than merely describing how they *do* behave. The ethical dimension is a dimension where the descriptive and prescriptive meet, or where they are originally inseparable. It is this deliberate ambiguity which makes Levinas's ethics difficult to classify; it is never clear when he is moving from the 'is' to the 'ought', or how he justifies this move.

A further difficulty in reading Levinas is that much of Levinas's writing, though broadly phenomenological in orientation, strays into mysticism. Indeed he has published several volumes of Talmudic writings, and has often written of an eschatology which is beyond the 'totality' (*totalité*) of history.[6] Though Levinas claims to keep his philosophy separate from his religious and mystical interests, it is not easy to read him with this distinction in mind as the mystical intrudes into the phenomenological description. The result is that Levinas is an exceptionally difficult philosopher to read, even judged in relation to the demanding, complex prose of authors such as Husserl, Heidegger, and Derrida. Indeed he is perhaps the most deliberately opaque of contemporary European philosophers. His style is to make assertions, followed by further assertions, without any attempt to justify them, other than through some kind of appeal to deeply human, perhaps even mystical, intuitions, or alternatively, to phenomenological insight, though such notions are never systematically explicated by him. Furthermore, his writing is infuriatingly sloppy. At times he capitalises key words and at other times does not. He introduces distinctions which later on are forgotten or transgressed. But most of all he produces extraordinary metaphorical assertions which are difficult to unpack and hence to grasp critically, for example "ethics is an optics" (*l'éthique est un optique*, TI 23; xii), the feminine is the wholly other, and so on. Before we have unpacked the first metaphor he has moved on to another. For this reason, he is largely ignored in the analytic tradition, which, of course, he too ignores entirely.

Emmanuel Levinas: life and writings (1906–1995)

Levinas was born in Kaunas, Lithuania, on 12 January 1906, making him a year younger than Sartre and two years older than Merleau-Ponty. He was born into an orthodox Jewish family which spoke Yiddish as well as Lithuanian. During his childhood, Levinas read the Bible in Hebrew, but at this stage knew nothing of the Talmud, which he did not discover until he went to France. His secondary schooling was conducted in the Russian language, but he also studied German. His father owned a bookshop, and the young Levinas immersed himself in Russian literature, especially the writings of Pushkin, Gogol, Dostoyevsky, and Tolstoy. He also read Shakespeare and other classics of world literature (EI 22; 16–17). Owing to the disruptions of the First World War, his family moved to Charkow in the Ukraine in 1916. While living in the Ukraine he witnessed the Russian revolutions of February and October 1917. In 1920 his family returned to Lithuania, but in 1923 he went to Strasbourg University in France, where he gained his *licence* in philosophy. However, he continued to return to Lithuania every summer and has even published an article in Lithuanian.[7]

At Strasbourg, following a year of Latin, he studied psychology, sociology, and philosophy in preparation for the *licence*.[8] One of his mentors was the French philosopher Charles Blondel (1876–1939). In Strasbourg he was introduced to Durkheim and Bergson, whose concepts of lived temporality and of 'concrete duration' (*la durée concrète*) he saw as liberating philosophy from the scientific model of time (EI 27; 22).[9] Levinas later, in his first book, explicated Husserl's phenomenology in terms of Bergson's theory of intuition, and thus played a role in smoothing the path for the acceptance of Husserl in France. At this time also, he became friends with the literary critic and philosopher Maurice Blanchot, with whom he remained friends, despite Blanchot's monarchist leanings and questionable association with anti-Semitic journals.[10] Under the influence of Gabrielle Peiffer, Levinas began to study Husserl's *Logical Investigations* and *Ideas* I. He also studied phenomenology with one of Husserl's early students at Göttingen, Jean Héring (1890–1966).[11] He was drawn to phenomenology as a form of

322

radical thinking, which brought one close to things, but, at that time, Heidegger was unknown to him.[12] In 1928 he registered at the University of Freiburg for two semesters, where, as luck would have it, he was able to attend Husserl's last seminars on phenomenological psychology and intersubjectivity, as well as Heidegger's first seminars as Husserl's successor, in the autumn of 1928.

While Levinas greatly appreciated the time which Husserl generously afforded him (EI 32; 28), he was nevertheless captivated by Heidegger's lecturing style. In his own assessment of phenomenology, Levinas sided with many of Heidegger's criticisms of Husserl, with Heidegger's existential account of being-in-the-world against Husserl's transcendental idealism. Levinas was drawn to Heidegger's concrete application of the phenomenological method, his descriptions of 'anxiety' (*Angst*), 'being-towards-death' (*Sein zum Tode*), 'being with others' (*Mitsein*), and his emphasis on both the finitude and transcendence of Dasein. Interestingly, the particular lecture series of Heidegger which he attended in Freiburg was the series "Introduction to Philosophy", where Heidegger rejected Husserl's understanding of philosophy as a rigorous science, and saw philosophy as a way of understanding human transcendence. Human being-in-the-world *is* transcendence, a theme which reverberates in Levinas's own writings. Levinas was perhaps most taken with Heidegger's analysis of 'state of mind' (*Befindlichkeit*) and his account of moods as attunements to Being. As he himself later put it, he admired the way Heidegger was able to "educate our ears to hear Being in its verbal resonances" (*grâce à Heidegger notre oreille s'éduqua à entendre l'être dans sa résonance verbale*).[13] Levinas even attended the famous debate between Heidegger and Cassirer at Davos, Switzerland, in 1929.

Levinas's first publication was a review of Husserl's *Ideas* I for the French journal *Revue Philosophique de la France et de l'Etranger* which offered a careful exposition of the text. The review concludes by pointing out that the analysis of genuine objectivity requires, not a quasi-solipsistic egological reduction but rather, here developing a hint in Husserl's text, a phenomenology of the intersubjective realm which constitutes world and nature itself.[14] Subsequently, Levinas will constantly insist on this *intersubjective* dimension in genuine phenomenology. In 1929 he was awarded his doctorate by the University of Strasbourg for his prize-winning thesis on the meaning of intuition in the philosophy of Husserl, published in 1930 as *The Theory of Intuition in Husserl's Phenomenology*. Being an admirer of the French Republic, Levinas became a naturalised French citizen and got married in the same year.

Having completed his military service, Levinas got a job as an administrator with the *Alliance Israélite Universelle* in Paris, an organisation which assisted Jews from Eastern European countries by providing them with access to education. It was at this time that he began to study the Talmud. Along with Sartre and Merleau-Ponty, Levinas attended the lectures of the idealist Léon Brunschvicg (1869–1944) at the Sorbonne, as well as Alexandre Kojève's (1902–1968) famous lectures on Hegel's *Phenomenology of Spirit*. During the 1930s Levinas was also a regular visitor at the Saturday *soirées* organised by the French Christian existentialist Gabriel Marcel (1889–1973). In *Totality and Infinity* (TI 68; 40), Levinas paid tribute to Gabriel Marcel's emphasis on the irreducibility of the other, as revealed in his *Metaphysical Journal* (1927), a work which also influenced Merleau-Ponty. Marcel also drew attention to the lack of self-sufficiency (*autarkhia*) of the self.[15] Levinas was also a close friend of the Jewish philosopher and poet Jean Wahl (1888–1974), who contributed enormously to the revival of Hegel studies in France with his 1929 study *The Unhappy Consciousness in Hegel's Philosophy*, which also influenced Sartre.[16] Levinas later paid tribute to Wahl in an essay published in *Outside the Subject*.[17] Wahl's influence on Levinas was enormous. Wahl provided him with a genuine conception of the Absolute as that which surpasses and escapes from totality.[18]

In the early 1930s Levinas had planned to write a book on Heidegger, and even published an article, "Martin Heidegger and Ontology", one of the first French studies on Heidegger, in 1932.[19] Initially Levinas saw Heidegger's concern with Being (*Sein*) as an attempt to overcome Husserl's subjectivism, but gradually he began to see that, rather than overturning traditional Western ontology in his 'destruction' of the history of philosophy, Heidegger was in fact in direct continuity with this tradition. Levinas had initially supported Heidegger's development of phenomenology beyond Husserl. Heidegger's account of *Angst*, care and being-towards-death represented for Levinas "a sovereign exercise of phenomenology" (EI 39; 36). But, when enlightened by Alexandre Koyré (1882–1964), then an *émigré* in Paris, about Heidegger's adherence to National Socialism in 1933, Levinas was horrified.[20] Levinas now began to understand Heidegger's emphasis on authenticity to be a self-centred weakness which was open to exploitation in the Nazi system. In 1934 Levinas published a revealing, but much neglected, article, "Some Reflections on the Philosophy of Hitlerism", published in the Catholic intellectual journal *Esprit* (reprinted in 1994 in *Les Imprévus de l'histoire*).[21] This essay is an early assessment of the irrationalism of the Nazi movement, treated as a manifestation of an elemental evil in being which is concerned with itself, an evil which traditional philosophy has been unable to address. Levinas later regretted that he had dignified Hitler's view with the title 'philosophy'. In this obscurely written essay, Levinas attempts to trace Hitlerism back to a problem at the heart of civilisation itself. He speaks of a stage in Western thought which ties spirit to the body. Nazism interpreted this chain to the body in a strong way in its commitment to biologism and the supposed purity of race. Levinas contrasts genuine freedom, as expressed in Christianity, with this enslavement in the body. "Man's essence no longer resides in freedom, but in a kind of bondage" (*Hitlerism*, p. 69). But the main concern of the essay is that a philosophy which finds the meaning of being in being itself, as he understood Heidegger's philosophy to do, ends up excluding the very possibilities of freedom and transcendence which belong to humanity, and usher in a world where being itself is evil, a theme to which he will return in *De l'existence à l'existant* (*Existence and Existents*).

In 1935 Levinas published an important essay, "De l'évasion" (*On Evasion*), in the avant-garde journal *Recherches Philosophiques*, edited by Jean Wahl, Alexandre Koyré, Gaston Bachelard, and others. This essay, recently reprinted in book form,[22] argued against the imprisonment in brute being (*l'être*) which all humans face and urges the need for an evasive action, for an 'excendence' (*excendance*, Levinas's own neologism, *Evasion*, p. 74), a non-willed escape from being, which is not the same thing as transcendence. As Levinas will explain it in his 1947 work *De l'existence à l'existant*, it is not transcendence understood in theological terms, but a 'departure from being' and from the categories which describe it.

At the outbreak of the Second World War in September 1939, Levinas was called up to serve in the French Army as an interpreter, because of his fluency in German and Russian. In 1940, he became a prisoner of war and spent the remainder of the war in a prison camp for officers in Germany, shielded, as a French officer, from the annihilation of Jews going on around him, but required, as a Jew, to do forced labour. Both his parents, his brothers, and many of his relatives were murdered in the Nazi-inspired genocide in the Ukraine. During his imprisonment he continued to read Hegel, Proust, Rousseau, and others, but, in general, he experienced this period of captivity as frozen in time, a hiatus which interrupted life. In some of his writings he echoes the guilt frequently experienced among survivors of the Holocaust. Thus later he wrote: "Soon death will no doubt cancel the unjustified privilege of having survived 6,000,000 deaths" (*Proper Names* 120; 142). After the war, he was appointed to the Ecole Normale Israélite Orientale and was active in developing its programme of Jewish studies. In 1947 Levinas published a short essay, *De l'existence à l'existant* (translated as *Existence and Existents*),[23] which returned to the theme of the brutal inescapability of existence, a theme initially broached in *On Evasion*.

After the war, Levinas published articles in the journal *Les Temps modernes* edited by Merleau-Ponty and Sartre, including some essays on existentialism, but his main focus in the late 1940s and 1950s was on matters concerned with Jewish tradition. He did not hold a full-time lecturing post but, in 1946–1947, he was invited by Jean Wahl to give four lectures at the *Collège de philosophie*, a non-academic institute which Wahl had set up. These lectures, first published in 1948, and reprinted in book form in 1979 under the title *Temps et l'autre* (*Time and the Other*),[24] focus on themes connected with existentialism: time, death, solitude, materiality, relations with others, joy, sexuality, and parenthood, repeating much of the analysis of *Existence and Existents*.

Levinas spent most of his life working without a proper academic position in the French university system. This would change in 1961 with the publication of *Totality and Infinity. An Essay on Exteriority*, which was the main thesis for his *Doctorat d'Etat* and quickly became his most important book. Dedicated to Jean Wahl, the book relies heavily on Wahl's conception of transcendence.[25] According to the subtitle, *Totality and Infinity* is 'an essay in exteriority', though Levinas is by no means clear in his use of the term. In general he means by 'exteriority' the manner in which the human person is outside the *totality*. 'Exteriority' is Levinas's name for whatever escapes the acquisitive, totalising aspect of knowledge, that is *being* in so far as it exceeds *thought*.

Following the publication of *Totality and Infinity*, Levinas was appointed Professor of Philosophy at the University of Poitiers, and, in 1967, moved to the new University of Paris-Nanterre along with Paul Ricoeur and Mikel Dufrenne. In 1973 he took up a position at the Sorbonne (Paris IV). Responding to an explosion of interest in his work stimulated by *Totality and Infinity*, after 1961 Levinas published a great flurry of books, as well as republishing many of his earlier articles. The most notable of these later publications, *Otherwise than Being or Beyond Essence* (1974),[26] may be read in part as a response to the criticisms made by Jacques Derrida in his essay "Violence and Metaphysics" (reprinted in *Writing and Difference*). Here Levinas tried to avoid the ontological language he had utilised in *Totality and Infinity* and to express his notion of the other in a manner which is 'beyond being' with increasingly metaphorical and opaque language, for example 'otherwise than being' (*autrement qu'être*). Thus in the essay "God and philosophy", in *De Dieu qui vient à l'idée* (*Of God Who Comes to Thought*, 1982), Levinas speaks of the "ethical and prophetic cry" to overcome Western ontology.[27] At the same time, Levinas published several collections of Talmudic commentaries, although he always sought to keep his Talmudic writings separate from his philosophy – even using a separate publisher.

Levinas wrote articles on aesthetic and political themes also. He was a lifelong supporter of Zionism (i.e. of the right of the Jewish people to their own state), though he was often critical of the manner politics and Zionistic mysticism led to the denial of ethics. However, despite his sensitivity to the suffering of the other, Levinas was slow to recognise the culpable role of Israel in the Sabra and Chatilla massacres in Lebanon in 1982; indeed, in the radio interview in which he discusses this horrific event with Alain Finkielkraut, he is less than forthright in his condemnation of Israel's role. Levinas in this interview recognises the right of Israel to an army and to take military action, which in the context effectively justified the slaughter. The other can also be an enemy who must be faced in war: "In alterity we can find an enemy".[28] In regard to the actual events, Levinas can say no more than that he would have preferred they had not happened. In his later years Levinas suffered from Alzheimer's disease. He died on 25 December 1995. Jacques Derrida delivered a moving funerary tribute, "Levinas Adieu", subsequently published as an extended essay.[29]

Levinas and phenomenology

Levinas has constantly acknowledged his debt to the phenomenologies of Husserl and Heidegger. In *De Dieu qui vient à l'idée* (1982) he writes: "Despite everything, what I am doing is phenomenology, even if there is no reduction according to the rules set by Husserl, even if the whole Husserlian method is not respected".[30] For Levinas, the phenomenological approach analyses the modes of givenness of things and events, but remains open to the surprises of recognising meanings not deliberately or centrally thematised:

> My method is phenomenological; it consists in restoring that which is given, which bears a name, which is objective, to its background of intention, not only that intention which is directed towards the object, but to everything which calls it to concreteness, to the horizon. I've often said that it is research into the staging [*mise en scène*] of that which is the object; the object, which, left to itself, is clarified, as much as it closes off the gaze – as if the giving was like an eyelid which lowers itself as an object appears, and consequently as if the objective is always abstract. Concreteness is the ensemble of what is lived, of intentionality, which is not entirely heuristic; it includes the axiological and the affective. Consequently meaning is given in this concreteness, and there can be surprises here over the general role of thematization.[31]

For Levinas, the great advance of phenomenology over previous forms of totalising philosophy is that it allows for the possibility of recognising what is distinctly human:

> No one combatted the dehumanization of the Real better than Husserl, the dehumanization which is produced when one extends the categories proper to mathematized matter to the totality of our experience, when one elevates scientism to absolute knowledge…Husserl's phenomenology has furnished the principal intellectual means for substituting a human world for the world as physicomathematical science represents it.
>
> (*Discovering Existence*, p. 131)

Levinas's point of departure is based on his interpretation of the fundamental significance of the Husserlian thesis of intentionality, which, for him, sums up the whole impetus of Western philosophy. Levinas credits Husserl with reawakening philosophy to the possibility of being able to describe concrete, lived human life, without reducing it to a series of inner psychic experiences (as with the Cartesian way of viewing consciousness). Human life always already involves meaningfulness:

> All consciousness is consciousness of something. Consciousness is not only the lived experience of the psychism, of the cogitations assured of their subjective existence: it is meaningfulness, thoughts casting themselves towards something that shows itself in them. For a whole generation of students and readers of the *Logical Investigations*, phenomenology, heralding a new atmosphere in European philosophy, meant mainly thought's access to being, a thought stripped of subjectivist encumbrances, a return to ontology without criticist problems, without relativism's fears – the flowering of the eidetic sciences, the contemplation of essences, the method of the disciplines named regional ontologies.
>
> (*Outside*, p. 153)

Thus Levinas, like Sartre, holds that contemporary phenomenology has overcome the notion of man as an isolated ego and has restored him to the world. Levinas praises the Husserlian reduction for recognising that the meaning of the world can only be understood by a certain standing back from the world. The significance of the reduction lies in the separation it brings about between humans and the world: "It is not by being in the world that we can say what the world is" (EE 42; 64).

For Levinas, Husserl's phenomenology is entirely encompassed by the study of intentionality. Levinas praises Husserl for recognising that thought (French: *pensée*) always involves something thought-of (*pensé*), and thus "an opening of thought onto something present to thought and quite distinct from the lived experience of that thought" (*Outside*, p. 152). However, he criticises the Husserlian account of intentionality for being in thrall to the notion of representation, whereby the question of representing the objective world truly is the fundamental focus of philosophy. This has the effect of bringing the other within the immanence of the same; in intentionality thought "satisfies" itself in being. Too often, for Levinas, phenomenology portrays the notion of intentionality as an "adequation with the object" (*adéquation à l'objet*, TI 27; xv), that is as a kind of measuring up to the objective world, whereas a deep understanding of intentionality would emphasise transcendence and infinity, and these are understood as forms of 'non-adequation' by Levinas. Levinas sees Husserl's understanding of the basic intentional act of giving meaning (*Sinngebung*) as being caught in the paradigm of knowledge as a kind of possession or grasping of its object. Or, in the case of bodily intention, as a kind of reaching out with the hand and grasping.[32] Every act of thinking is a certain overcoming of subjectivity, a certain transition towards the object, so that transitivity is an essential feature of thinking. But focusing on this side of thinking ignores our primary situation of a lived relation with others. Consciousness should be understood not primarily as a disclosing power which seeks to represent the object adequately (Levinas's view of Husserl), but as an overflowing, which can never be fully expressed. "Intentionality, where thought remains an adequation with the object, does not define consciousness at its most fundamental level" (TI 27; xv). Levinas believes that Husserl's emphasis on intentionality is a distortion of human experience; as he puts it, the caress of a lover cannot be captured in any account of intentionality. In a sense then, Levinas wants a phenomenology *beyond* intentionality.

In criticising Husserl, Levinas also aims to subvert many of the traditional assumptions of philosophical rationality, in so far as that rationality becomes an all-consuming force which absorbs everything into itself (what Levinas calls 'totality' characterised by the drive for 'representation'). He is constantly challenging the Husserlian conception of philosophy as a rigorous science, itself the logical outcome of the whole tradition of Western philosophy. In trying to break through the stranglehold of 'totality', Levinas evokes experiences of the unbounded and indeed infinite nature of the 'other'. For Levinas, that which challenges the sphere of totality may be understood as 'transcendence', the 'other', and 'the infinite'; and Levinas may be seen as trying to open up phenomenology to describe this transcendent dimension of human experience.

The role of philosophy

Levinas employs a rather restricted conception of philosophy which, nevertheless, he claims circumscribes the whole Western rational tradition. He invokes Plato, Descartes, Kant, Husserl, Bergson, and Heidegger in his philosophical discussions, citing repeatedly the same key passages: Plato's discussion of the Good as 'beyond being', Descartes's placing of the idea of an infinite God into the heart of the isolated thinking *cogito*, Kant's separation of sensation from understanding in the *Critique of Pure Reason*, Husserl's account of intentionality, and Heidegger's account of being-in-the-world, including being-with-others (*Mitsein*) and being-towards-death (*Sein zum Tode*). Outside of these philosophers Levinas appears to have little familiarity with technical philosophy (apart from occasional references to Spinoza, Leibniz, and others) and certainly no experience of the riches of twentieth-century philosophy outside of phenomenology. Indeed, more often he quotes Shakespeare, Proust, or the Bible rather than a philosophical text. Furthermore, like Derrida, Levinas tends to see all philosophy as accomplished in the Cartesian–Kantian–Hegelian tradition where all truth is made relative to the subject. The whole of Western philosophy is summed up as 'ontology'.

Moreover, as Levinas is essentially a modernist, he believes the purpose of philosophy is to reflect on the present. As he puts it, at no time in our past has history weighed so heavily on our ideas (*Proper Names* 3; 8). In the twentieth century, philosophy has been directly challenged by the reality of global war and the systematic destruction or corruption of culture. As a result, his philosophy is dominated by the metaphors of war and peace. For Levinas European culture is now permanently overshadowed by the Holocaust: "if there is an explicitly Jewish moment in my thought, it is the reference to Auschwitz, where God let the Nazis do what they wanted".[33] Similarly, in his biographical sketch "Signature" (in *Difficult Freedom. Essays on Judaism*, 1976) Levinas claimed that his thought "is dominated by the anticipation and by the memory of the Nazi horror". The enormity of this horror calls for humans to reflect on the totality of their cultural possession. As he has written, employing a Biblical metaphor, the experience of the war had the effect of returning Jews to the desert, experiencing life without possessions "in a universe at war" (*l'universe en guerre, Proper Names* 121; 144). Human capacity for global war seems a direct affront to the claim to civilisation as the appreciation of the other. War reduces morality to something absurd. Yet at the same time ethical obligation too is primary and inescapable. In the stark contemporary situation, philosophy must become a vigilant attempt to "lodge the whole human world in the shelter of conscience" (*Proper Names* 122; 144). In a sense, then, Levinas's philosophy is an act of commemoration, an act of remembrance, confronting the traditional paradigm of Western philosophy as a Greek enterprise with the 'other' of the ethical, which, for him, is also the core of the Jewish tradition.

The religious dimension of Levinas's thought

Indeed, Levinas's distinctive interest and main preoccupation is the clash and rift between the dual sources of Western culture: Greek philosophy and Judaic ethico-religious expression. Derrida, in characterising this aspect of Levinas, has quoted from James Joyce's *Ulysses*, "Jewgreek is greekjew" (WD 153). Or as Levinas himself puts it: "Europe, that's the Bible and the Greeks".[34] Levinas wants to keep the traditions distinct, yet at the same time allow them to measure each other. What the Jewish tradition emphasises above all else is the force of moral claims on us: "the otherness of the other is the beginning of all love".

The notion of God runs through Levinas's work, but independently of the issue of the existence of God. In fact, overall, Levinas follows Heidegger in seeing the traditional concept of God as too infused with the notion of being. He is not interested in the ontological characterisation of God as

330

first being, or pure existence; he is interested in the figure of God as a face with authority. God, for Levinas, is not necessarily a being, but rather the commandment to love. Thus, in *Totality and Infinity*, Levinas appears to reject traditional theology and sees himself as involved in a kind of agnosticism, even a "metaphysical atheism" (TI 77; 49–50) which seeks the "dawn of a humanity without myths", but his later writings seem to be more explicitly religious in outlook. In *Of God Who Comes to Thought* (1982) Levinas denies that we can understand God as first cause of the world, or as a ground of being; rather, he suggests, we experience an 'encounter' with God. Although not appealing to religious revelation, Levinas nevertheless derives his intuition of the nature of the ethical from the Bible. The Bible then offers a certain kind of encounter with God and this is what Levinas likes to express in his Talmudic writings. In general, Levinas resists treating God as the 'Other par excellence' (*l'Autrui par excellence*) or as the first 'other'. Rather God must be seen as 'other than the other', here employing formulations close to those of the Neo-Platonic tradition, for example the German Christian mystic Nicholas of Cusa (1401–1464), who calls God the 'not-other' (*non aliud*). Levinas uses the term 'illeity' (*illeité*) to express the kind of remote otherness of God, deriving from the Latin demonstrative pronoun *ille, illa, illud* which means 'that over there' as opposed to the demonstrative *hic, haec, hoc*, which means 'this here' (e.g. *in illo tempore* means 'in that bygone time'). This is the remote hidden God, the God expressed in the word for 'good-bye' (*à Dieu*). God is never a graspable or comprehensible notion; it is at best the 'trace' of something other which disrupts the present. The notion of 'trace', which Levinas connects with the notion of illeity, became increasingly important in Levinas's writings after *Totality and Infinity*, and has strongly influenced Derrida (there is a parallel notion in Merleau-Ponty).[35] The concept has, of course, as Levinas recognises, its philosophical and theological origins in Neo-Platonism, specifically Plotinus, and in Augustine's *De Trinitate* (*vestigia dei*). In both cases, trace refers to what the One or God leaves behind in the world. Levinas is aware that in the Neo-Platonic meaning at least, the trace does not necessarily come after the original event. Levinas's conception is similar: "A trace is a presence of that which properly speaking has never been there, of what is always past".[36] Levinas could also have found discussion of the notion of the trace in traditional hermeneutics, especially in Schleiermacher, who speaks of the interpretation and critique of "texts and traces". For Levinas, as for Derrida, one should not think of the trace as the imprint of something which was originally present. The trace is not a sign pointing to a signified. No memory could remember this immemorial past which the trace evokes. In *Otherwise Than Being* (1974), the face is understood ('figured') as a trace. Elsewhere Levinas writes that a face is in "the trace of the utterly bygone, the utterly past absent" (CPP 103). He also speaks of a "trace lost in a trace" (OBBE, p. 93). The ethical relation is understood to be a "trace of infinity, the trace of a departure" (OBBE, p. 117). Trace, for Levinas, signifies 'beyond being' (CPP 103). However, beyond reiterating Levinas's own pronouncements, I am afraid I am unable to shed further light on this obscure notion.

Early writings

Levinas's doctoral thesis, *The Theory of Intuition in Husserl's Phenomenology*, was the first full-length study of Husserl in French. It is informed as much by Heidegger as by Husserl, drawing most heavily on *Ideas* I and *Philosophy as a Rigorous Science*, though constantly referring back to the *Logical Investigations* which, however, is read in the light of Husserl's later transcendental idealism. Levinas's account of Husserl is penetrating and intelligent, correctly describing Husserl's philosophy as a philosophy of intuition and giving an accurate account of the manner in which perceptual acts are fulfilled. Levinas portrays Husserl as overcoming the epistemological crisis of the nineteenth century by articulating an *ontology* which is meant to combat naturalism. The critique of psychologism in the *Prolegomena* of 1900 is meant to usher in, not a new logic, but a new *ontology*. Levinas begins with an analysis of Husserl's critique of naturalism. While the physical sciences try to construct an ideal object on the basis of the study of the appearances in which an object manifests itself, naturalism errs in taking the scientific description for the thing itself: "naturalism seems to be a bad interpretation of the meaning of natural science" (THI, p. 9). Naturalism betrays the internal meaning of the perceptual experience (THI, p. 10); it is the rejection of everything "immediate, concrete, and irreducible in direct perception" (THI, p. 16). In opposition to naturalism, Levinas sketches what he takes to be Husserl's true ontology of the physical object and of consciousness. Whereas spatially existent things reveal themselves in profiles and are contingent in their very essence, that is always capable of not being, this is not true of consciousness (THI, p. 33) which, for Husserl, in *Ideas* I, has absolute existence. The world of transcendent things depends on consciousness. Material things are in a necessary relation to consciousness even though they elude consciousness in their totality. Levinas thus defends Husserl's idealism:

> The fundamental intuition of Husserlian philosophy consists of attributing absolute existence to concrete conscious life and transforming the very notion of conscious life.
>
> (THI, p. 25)

Conscious life is a life in the presence of transcendent things, so we are not here in the closed circle of Berkeleyan idealism. Levinas goes on to give an account of Husserl's theory of intentionality, and especially of objectivating acts, understood as an *ontological* account (an interpretation which will hugely influence Sartre). Here Levinas accuses Husserl of intellectualism (THI, p. 63), in so far as Husserl always privileges theory, perception, and judgement, whereas Levinas agrees with Heidegger that being is primarily a field of action and solicitude.

When Levinas returned from Freiburg he brought with him a new understanding of phenomenology. With Gabrielle Peiffer, he published a French translation of Husserl's *Cartesian Meditations*, which not only became a standard text for French students, but was all the more significant for Husserl studies since Husserl never authorised publication of the German text of the *Cartesian Meditations*, which was not finally published until 1950, some twelve years after Husserl's death.

Levinas's next important essay, *On Evasion*, offers an idiosyncratic and non-Heideggerian description of being or existence (he uses the words interchangeably) as overwhelming, all encompassing, indeed as brutal, as trapping the human spirit. Against this enveloping being, the human spirit, which for Levinas is close to Bergson's *élan vital*, can do little more than seek to evade: "Evasion is the need to go out of oneself" (*le besoin de sortir de soi-même*, *Evasion*, p. 73). Furthermore, according to Levinas, when one confronts this absolute enclosing nature of existence, one is struck down with 'nausea' (*la nausée*), here offering an account of nausea strikingly similar to Sartre's as found in his novel *Nausea*, published some years later in 1938. Though Sartre never acknowledged Levinas as a source, it is possible that he had read Levinas's article when it appeared in *Recherches Philosophiques*. Sartre published his "Transcendence of the Ego" in the same journal a year later. Levinas claims that, when nausea overwhelms us, it is "the experience of pure being" (*l'expérience de l'être pur*, *Evasion*, p. 90), it discovers the 'nudity' of being as pure existence, and recognises its inability to escape from this sheer presence. In this study Levinas praises idealism for its attempts to go beyond sheer being, and regards any culture which remains committed to being as deserving the name of 'barbarism' (*Evasion*, p. 98). In this early essay, then, Levinas is already beginning to formulate his critique of ontology for its denial of transcendence and hence of ethics.

Levinas's next book, *Existence and Existents*, partly written during his time in detention, drew on his wartime experiences of insomnia, fatigue, hunger, horror, and indolence, as phenomena which are revelatory of the nature of existence. The title is an attempt to distinguish in French between Heidegger's terms '*Sein*' (*l'existence*, *l'être*) and '*Seiendes*' (*l'existent*). Levinas begins with the Heideggerian ontological difference but argues that this philosophical distinction is easily overlooked if we examine the "emptiness of the verb to exist" (*le vide du verbe 'exister'*, EE 17; 15) which seems to make our thought dizzy. It is easier to think of beings. The notion of being itself seems impersonal. But, though Levinas employed Heidegger's terms, he was already invoking the necessity of leaving behind "the climate" of Heidegger's philosophy, though, he emphasises, not by a retreat to the "pre-Heideggerian" (EE 19; 19).

Existence and Existents claims to be a preparatory study of the relation between the problem of the Good, time, and the relation with the other (EE 15; 9). Levinas endorses the Platonic formula in *The Republic* which places the Good 'beyond being' (*epekeina tes ousias*). To achieve the Good one must achieve not transcendence but 'departure', 'excendence', a flight from being:

> It affirms that what is essential in human spirituality does not lie in our relationship with the things which make up the world, but is determined by a relationship, effected in our very existence, with the pure fact that there is Being, the nakedness (*la nudité*) of this bare fact. This relationship, far from covering over nothing but a tautology, constitutes an event, whose reality and somehow surprising character manifest themselves in the disquietude in which the relationship is enacted. The evil in Being, the evil of matter in idealist philosophy, becomes the Evil of Being (*le mal de l'être*).
>
> (EE 19; 18–19)

Against Heidegger, then, Levinas will locate evil in the nature of being itself. Horror of being is as primal as anxiety in the face of death (EE 20; 20). The phrase '*il y a*', or 'there is', Levinas's translation of Heidegger's '*es gibt*' (BT § 43, 255; 212), expresses the impersonal nature of being, which always breaks through the circle of subjectivity. The *il y a* is not the happening or event of being (as it is in Heidegger), but the brute given which encircles us, the 'impersonal, non-substantive event', an experience of darkness, of night (EE 63; 102). In the *Letter on Humanism* Heidegger identifies the '*es gibt*' as the essence of Being, as that which gives and confers truth. In contrast, Levinas's conception of *il y a* has none of the donational, gift-like or grace-like character of Heidegger's *es gibt* as Levinas put it: "None of the generosity which the German term '*es gibt*' is said to contain revealed itself between 1933 and 1945".[37] For Levinas, this experience of being is so all encompassing that it cannot be negated. The *il y a* is "beyond contradiction; it embraces and dominates its contradictory" (EE 64; 105). In experiencing being, we feel glued to existence, just as reality is always there when we open our eyes (EE 22; 27). Being has no outlets, it embraces everything. Reacting to the strangeness of being is what provokes the question of being, but "there is no answer to Being" (EE 22; 28), "Being is essentially alien and strikes against us", "there is a pain of Being"; it has a "suffocating embrace, like the night" (EE 23; 28).

In *Existence and Existents* also, Levinas criticises Sartre's ethics for its atheism and self-centredness. Paraphrasing Sartre, Levinas writes that we are condemned to being. Levinas later admitted that he had given Sartre's

Being and Nothingness only a cursory reading when he had come home after the war. Statements like "to be weary is to be weary of being" (*se fatiguer, c'est ce fatiguer d'être*, EE 35; 50), emphasising the weight and burden of existence, sound typically Sartrean. For example, Levinas writes:

> There exists a weariness which is a weariness of everything and eve-ryone, and above all a weariness of oneself. What wearies then is not a particular form of our life – our surroundings, because they are dull and ordinary, our circle of friends, because they are vulgar and cruel; but the weariness concerns existence itself.
>
> (EE 24; 31)

Unlike Heidegger's Dasein, which seizes on the possibility of existence and makes itself authentic thereby, Levinas emphasises that existence is there prior to our entry to the world: "Existence is not synonymous with the relationship with a world; it is antecedent to the world" (EE 21; 26). There is no free act, such as is spoken of by the existentialists whereby one appropriates or takes over one's own existence. On the other hand, humans *can* take a stance towards existence even if they can never outrun it completely. Levinas gives an account of human consciousness as attempting to tear away from the bruteness of being, whereas Sartre claims that consciousness is actually a kind of non-being which always seeks to become being. For Levinas: "to be conscious is to be torn away from the *il y a*" (EE 60; 98). Levinas also criticises Heidegger's account of Dasein in *Being and Time*. Concern (*le souci*) is not an act on the brink of nothingness but an act of possession of being (EE 27; 36). Levinas thinks Heidegger has misunder-stood the nature of being-in-the-world as care; Heidegger has not given sufficient attention to the kind of sincerity attached to originary human living, eating, sleeping, and so on. Levinas emphasises the desire to sidestep the suffocation of being; alongside Heidegger's anxiety before death there is the phenomenon of *horror* before the burden of being itself. Horror is a participation in existence: "In horror a subject is stripped of his subjectivity, of his power to have private existence" (EE 61; 100). To understand the nature of being we must avoid reflection and focus on the phenomena which are more revelatory of the pre-reflective nature of existence – phenomena such as fatigue and indolence. Weariness is a kind of pre-reflective refusal of the world; indolence is a kind of aversion to effort, an impossibility of beginning. In insomnia, for example, we lie awake experiencing the weight of the world. But as Levinas says: "Wakefulness is anonymous. It is not that there is *my* vigilance in the night; in insomnia it is the night itself that watches" (EE 66; 111).

Although Levinas wants to analyse those moments that are in flight from being, he wants also to give proper acknowledgement to those moments where we feel at home in being. Living in the world is not meaningless or

335

absurd. In analysing the extent to which we are pervaded by existence, Levinas wants to recognise that there are aspects of human life which respond genuinely to this experience of being overwhelmed by being. Certain items are required to live in the world, they are things we 'live from' (*vivre de*), such as food, shelter, clothing. These belong to the sphere of 'need' (*le besoin*) and are part of the 'sincerity' of human life. As Levinas remarks, anticipating his view in *Totality and Infinity*: "Life is a sincerity" (*Vivre est une sincerité*, EE 44; 67). It is wrong to characterise as 'everyday' certain events which bring us to completion, events such as eating. Whereas, for Heidegger, hunger would belong to the everyday and hence the inauthentic, for Levinas it is a natural expression of sincere living and of enjoyment. As Levinas says, "Heidegger's Dasein is never hungry". On the other hand, Levinas says we eat and drink for the sake of eating and drinking. As he repeats in *Totality and Infinity*, "what we live from does not enslave us; we enjoy it" (TI 114; 86–87). However, given his typical ambiguity, it is difficult to see what role this sincerity has *vis-à-vis* the desire for excendance, non-willed escape from being.

In contrast to hunger and need, Levinas posits another category, 'desire', which seeks that which can never be achieved or consummated. Levinas claims that the experience of the other and the experience of desire break with the cycle of being. *Desire* (in Levinas's capitalised form: *le Désir*) is an indication of our being as a kind of privation, and points beyond itself towards the unlimited or infinite. Food puts us in a different relation to desire and its satisfaction. When we eat we fulfil a need. Items like food, clothing, warmth, and shelter belong to the domain of need. They are enjoyed in being consumed but their status is not well understood if they are seen as mere tools (as in Heidegger's analysis in *Being and Time*) or as raw material to be consumed. Eating is an absorption or coming into identity with the object. On the other hand, when we relate to a friend we express or inhabit a desire which can never be met. In *Totality and Infinity*, Levinas develops this distinction between the satisfaction of a need (*besoin*) and the expression of a desire. Thus he writes:

> Let us again note the difference between need and Desire: in need I can sink my teeth into the real and satisfy myself in assimilating the other; in Desire there is no sinking one's teeth into being, no satiety, but an uncharted future before me.
>
> (TI 117; 89)

Needs constitute me as the Same and not as dependent on the Other, as Levinas puts it (TI 116; 89). Levinas does not want to downgrade need and the sphere of sameness, but at the same time he wants to call attention to those few moments which break with the cycle of need. These are the moments when we experience the other as other.

The same and the other

After *Existence and Existents*, Levinas's entire focus turned towards elucidating the irreducible priority of the 'other', a priority which he feels has been ignored by the entire tradition of Western philosophy, from Plato to Hegel and Husserl, understood as the domain of 'ontology', which has prioritised 'the Same' (*le Même*), the self-identical, over the diffuse and wholly other. Levinas wants to disrupt the philosophy of the Same in order to leave room for the other. He employs two different words for speaking of the other: *l'Autre* (the 'other' in general, the non-personal other, e.g. language, culture, institutions, rendered in the English translation as 'other', lower case) and *l'Autrui* (the other person, rendered in the English translation as the 'Other', with upper case, TI 24n.). In the French text, sometimes these terms are capitalised, sometimes not. As Levinas puts it in typically ambiguous manner: "The other qua other is the Other" (*L'Autre en tant que l'autre est Autrui*, TI 71; 42–43). As in all other matters, Levinas is not consistent, sometimes capitalising '*l'Autre*' without clearly signalling what he means. His main point is that the 'other' is not another me, nor is it something defined by its relationship with me, but rather something or someone completely other and unique. The other is *incommensurate* with me. Moreover, the other, as that which calls to me, calls for a *response* from me, is the very source of all language and culture, and hence is a source of instruction: "the absolutely foreign alone can instruct us" (*L'Absolument étranger seul peut nous instruire*, TI 73; 46). The other is also what challenges the dominance of the present, of presence, and as such, as Levinas says, the other may be either past or future.

Though Levinas castigates the Western philosophical tradition for emphasising the same at the expense of the other, he also recognises and draws on the tradition of discussion of the other within Western thought. The terminology of 'same' and 'other' is, of course, found in Plato, especially in the *Sophist* and *Parmenides*, and is a central feature of Neo-Platonic thought, for example Plotinus and Proclus, from whom it entered into Western philosophy. One of the key medieval texts on the nature of otherness is Nicholas of Cusa's *De li non aliud*, on the not-other, which struggles to find an appropriate language to express the transcendence and immanence of God, the infinity of the divine nature. God is 'other than the other', or 'not other' (*non aliud*). Through Nicholas of Cusa and Jacob Boehme the concept of the other was taken up in the dialectic of Hegel, who is Levinas's proximate source. But Levinas's chief target in his discussion of the other is Husserl's Fifth Cartesian Meditation. Levinas is critical of Husserl's account of the other, because, for Levinas, Husserl reduces the alterity of the other to the sameness of myself, that is to say I experience the other as similar to myself. I understand the other's facial gestures because of the meaning they already have for me, as I live them. Levinas criticises Husserl here because he thinks the other can never be represented by me.

For Levinas, the other must always be understood as transcendence. (It could be argued that Husserl too always acknowledges the foreignness of the other.) The problem of the other is directly addressed in Levinas's 1948 lectures, *Time and the Other*.

Time and the Other

The lectures published as *Time and the Other* (1948) analyse the usual existential themes of temporal existence, solitude, death, and so on, as found in Heidegger and Sartre, but Levinas finds in these phenomena an openness to the other which existentialism had misunderstood. Thus, in examining the nature of time, Levinas wants to show that time is not a solitary experience of an individual, but a way of relating to others (TO 39; 17), a 'dia-chrony'. Time is not a horizon of being but a mode of going beyond being, opening up to otherness. In a similar manner, Levinas interrogates the ontological root of solitude in order to see how solitude may be exceeded (TO 41; 19). Solitude, for Levinas, is linked to the primal state of existing itself. Levinas takes issue with Heidegger's account of authenticity as grasping one's own being towards death. Again Levinas thinks Heidegger has misdescribed the meaning of the phenomenon. Heidegger's account of facing one's death in a freely chosen act is related to ancient accounts of heroism, it is an act of "supreme lucidity and supreme virility" and indeed of 'mastery', whereas Levinas believes that the phenomena of suffering and of facing death are more a giving up of one's 'mastery' and accepting that the possible is no longer possible for one. In suffering, the subject reaches the "limit of the possible" (TO 70; 57–58). What fascinates him about the experience of dying is our *passivity* in the face of death. The anticipation of death does not leave us any room for initiative, for seizing a chance. *Time and the Other* also makes direct criticisms of Sartre's account of humans as fundamentally free and unable to communicate with the other. Levinas recognises the paradox of positing humans as free and alone and immediately giving them over to a responsibility, a paradox which is also at the heart of Sartre's ethics. For Levinas, however, the other is not founded in freedom, but the essence of alterity comes first (TO 87–88; 80).

Besides offering a reinterpretation of familiar existential phenomena, in these lectures Levinas also introduce new themes, especially his controversial analysis of 'the alterity of the feminine' and of concepts such as 'fecundity' (*la fécondité*), which he introduces as part of his investigation of traces of the other in civilised life (TO 84; 77), and which for him provide examples of the relation to the other which are not circumscribed within the typically existentialist vision of one freedom engaging with another. Thus, fecundity, for Levinas, is a way of expressing the alterity of the other without domination. Furthermore, phenomena such as fecundity express experiences which are not illuminated by light but rather are somehow shrouded in darkness. Fecundity expresses a phenomenon in which I can be related to the other without being either annihilated (as in death) or absorbed completely by the other. Fecundity is, for Levinas, a kind of exteriority of the self. His example is the relation between parent and child, *filialité*, a relation not reducible to 'ownership', 'having', 'causing', and so on (TO 91; 85). The child is not an alter ego, but is entirely different from the parents, yet, in some strange way the parent is the child, though, of course, precisely in what way is never made explicit. Fecundity is again taken up in *Totality and Infinity* (TI 267–269; 244–247) where, again, it is elucidated in terms of parenthood, the parent's relation to the child, and understood in terms of a future of myself and of the other: "fecundity encloses a duality of the identical" (TI 268; 245). In *Time and the Other* Levinas had already recognised that phenomena such as paternity, sexuality, and death express an irreducible duality in human existence: "Existing itself becomes double. The Eleatic notion of being is overcome" (TO 92; 88). Levinas's strategy seems to be to find moments in human existence which point to the fracturing of this totality of englobing existence or being. But Levinas's own sense of where he is going is quite confused. In these lectures, he claims to be exploring ontology in a dialectical manner, and indeed, in his analysis of forms of relation to the ego, he says: "I have not proceeded in a phenomenological way" (TO 92; 87). Yet, in his analysis of eros, he says he is providing a "phenomenology of voluptuousness" (TO 88; 82). The difficulty of locating Levinas's discussion is clearly a difficulty for Levinas also. Levinas seems unsure how to describe his approach – in part an existential corrective to Sartrean and Heideggerian existentialism, in part a Hegelian 'dialectical' analysis of the way modes of selfhood are already open to the other (inspired by the master–slave dialectic), in part an attempt to do ontology and to go beyond ontology. Indeed, it is not surprising that these lectures went largely unnoticed until Levinas reiterated many of the same themes in greater depth in *Totality and Infinity*.

The lectures went largely unnoticed with one major exception. Simone de Beauvoir criticised Levinas's language as sexist, thus beginning a considerable debate in recent French feminism regarding the nature of the feminine, a debate which continues today. In *The Second Sex* (1949) de Beauvoir criticises Levinas's identification of the feminine with the wholly other, as having been made from the man's point of view: "When he writes that woman is a mystery, he implies that she is a mystery for man. Thus his description, which is intended to be objective, is in fact an assertion of masculine privilege."[38] In *Time and the Other*, as we have seen, Levinas is looking for a positive experience of the other. In his section on 'eros' he claims to find a situation in which alterity appears in its purest from, not as the opposite of identity but as pure otherness: this is the encounter with the 'feminine' (*le féminin*), characterised as the "absolutely contrary contrary" (*le contraire absolument contraire*, TO 85; 77), a contrariety whose otherness is not affected by entering into relation with the self. As we have come to expect from Levinas, this claim is introduced bluntly. It is simply asserted. Furthermore, Levinas, while dissociating his claim of the absolute mystery of the feminine from all romantic literary distortions of the phenomenon, nevertheless thinks these very literary distortions testify to the phenomenon. Levinas does not see himself as being anti-feminist in this account, since he takes feminism to be the claim that women must share equally with men in all the fruits of civilisation (TO 86; 79). Rather he thinks none of these distinctions come close to articulating the absolute 'mystery' of the feminine, as a mode of being which is "slippage away from the light...flight before light" (*une fuite devant la lumière*, TO 87; 79). The feminine withdrawal is the very opposite of the movement of consciousness outwards towards its object, a transcendence towards the light, rather the feminine is withdrawal, occlusion, hiding; it is the essence of *modesty* (*la pudeur*, TO 88; 81).

Even a careful, nuanced reading of this strange text cannot eliminate its identification of the project of selfhood and reason with the male and obscurity, mystery, and modesty with the essence of the feminine. While it may provide fascinating material for a psychoanalyst seeking to understand Levinas himself, it can hardly provide the basis for the phenomenological account of positive experiences of alterity. However, in *Totality and Infinity*, Levinas returns to the theme of the phenomenology of eros, now somewhat revising his account of the feminine other, speaking not just of the feminine but of woman (*la femme*). This account generated more controversy by characterising femininity as 'frailty' (*faiblesse*, TI 257; 235), locating it in the sphere of the home (TI 155; 128; cf. Hannah Arendt's characterisation of the sphere of the household and domestic labour, and its exclusion from the sphere of action, in *The Human Condition*), the ambiguous, the voluptuous, and the virginal: "The feminine presents a face that goes beyond the face...In the feminine face the purity of expression is already troubled by the equivocation of voluptuousness" (TI 260; 238). Woman is ambiguous; her speech is silence, her presence is absence, she is both temptress and mother. Furthermore, Levinas, while recognising the connection between love and voluptuousness, seems to think love finds fullest expression in childbearing. He understands love to be a relation between two people which does not unite them but keeps them separate so that they engender a child (TI 266; 244). When Levinas announces these themes, it always seems we are on the brink of deep existential analysis; but, unfortunately, Levinas always introduces too many variables at once with little extended discussion, and then veers off in another direction, almost as soon as the topic is broached. Concepts such as fecundity, the feminine, the voluptuous, desire, all appear together and are jumbled together with no concrete examples. To this extent, in describing human phenomena such as love and desire, Sartre stays much closer to the phenomena themselves than does Levinas.

A defence of subjectivity

As we have seen, Levinas sees the history of Western metaphysics as a grand project of totalisation, of reducing everything to the sphere of the ego, the self, and thereby eliding the difference between *being* and *thought*. Following Parmenides and the Eleatic tradition, philosophy has identified being with thought, wherein being is reduced to whatever is thought-of, or represented in thought. This absorption of being into thought concludes with the highest kind of being: being understood as self-consciousness. Philosophy is a carrying out of the edict "Know Thyself". This project of self-knowledge has led Western culture, which identifies knowledge with control, to master itself through the mastery of the universe. The entire project of Western science, the struggle for knowledge, for *episteme*, is then, for Levinas, an attempt at total control, at the enclosing of everything within a system. The ontology of sameness reaches its apotheosis in Hegel's philosophy which asserts the 'identity of identity and difference'. This sameness and self-identity is also typified, for Levinas, in the nature of the 'I' (*le Moi*). Clearly, the sphere of the same, in Levinas's sense, is primarily the sphere of Cartesian subjectivity and by implication Husserl's sphere of the I, the *Originärsphär*. This is the sphere of the I which is 'at home' with itself (*chez soi*, TI 37; 7), which exists on its own, *autochthonous* in its being. For Levinas the sphere of the 'same' is also the sphere of 'the Said' (*le Dit*): that is, that which gets asserted in anonymous fashion, as in the objective knowledge of the sciences (or possibly Heidegger's 'idle talk', *Gerede*). For Levinas, philosophy must always be an attempt to defend the priority of the other and resist its reduction to the sphere of sameness. Against the sphere of 'the Said' Levinas wants to oppose the sphere of the 'Saying' (*le Dire*), authentic speech, again a notion close to Heidegger's *Rede*.

For Levinas, all knowledge involves objectification and in a certain sense a violation of the object:

> Knowledge seizes hold of its object. It possesses it. Possession denies the independence of being, without destroying that being – it denies and maintains.
>
> (*Difficult Freedom*, p. 8)

Knowledge then is intrinsically connected with violence in Levinas's conception:

> The violent man does not move out of himself. He takes, he possesses. Possession denies independent existence. To have is to refuse to be...To know is to perceive, to seize an object – be it a man or a group of men – to *seize* a thing.
>
> (*Difficult Freedom*, p. 9)

The 'other' (*l'Autre*), on the other hand, is everything which resists such totalisation, and hence resists violence. The other means that which cannot be objectified, the sphere of subjectivity, although not understood in the spirit of mastery, but rather as founded on openness to the other. Levinas claims that our first experience is not of isolated subjectivity, but of a subjectivity already shot through with the experience of others. Subjectivity, then, is an ambiguous phenomenon, but it has a deeper sense as the opposite of totality. Levinas is committed to the primacy of subjectivity in this sense; thus he characterises his major work, *Totality and Infinity* (1961), as a 'defence of subjectivity' (TI 26; 11). Levinas's phenomenology aims to restore a true sense of subjectivity, and criticises Husserl's accounts of intentionality and representation as too restrictive in their approach to the subjective life. The first systematic expression of this new phenomenology of subjectivity was Levinas's *Totality and Infinity*.

Totality and Infinity *(1961)*

Totality and Infinity is a difficult book, with no clear structure, highly repetitive in style, replete with turgid prose, idiosyncratic use of philosophical terms, and contradictory assertions – more an impressionistic collage of ideas than a philosophical treatise. It is meant to provide an account of the richness of human being-in-the-world as a corrective to Husserl and Heidegger, while at the same time exploring various ways of escaping the world, forms of 'exteriority'. It contains phenomenological descriptions of all kinds of human experiences – the state of being at war, domesticity, enjoyment, nourishment, dwelling, love, separation, and the experiences of the feminine and of fecundity. But the book is best known for its conception of ethics and of the face-to-face relation. Much of the analysis in *Totality and Infinity* is anticipated in earlier essays, specifically, "Philosophy and the Idea of Infinity" (1957) and the essay commemorating Husserl, "The Ruin of Representation" (1959).[39] The global experience of *totality* prevents the experience of genuine transcendence and otherness, concepts which cannot be completely appropriated by us and which Levinas designates by the name 'infinity' (a term he takes from Franz Rosenzweig). The infinite, for Levinas, is everything which transcends our grasp. Levinas opposes *infinity* to *totality*. "What remains ever exterior to thought is thought in the idea of infinity" (TI 25; xiii). According to Levinas infinity cannot be thought in terms of representation, because it cannot be represented: "the relation with infinity will have to be stated in terms other than those of objective experience" (TI 25; xiii). We cannot have a representation of infinity, but we do have an 'idea' (TI 27; xv) of infinity, as is evident from Descartes's uncovering of the idea of an infinite God at the very heart of the self. Subjectivity is the key to this infinity. Subjectivity, for Levinas, is not the subjectivity of Descartes, Kant, Husserl, or even Kierkegaard; it is not any form of egoism, or self-reflexive subjectivity, nor a kind of authentic subjectivity focused on death (as in Heidegger):

> This book then does present itself as a defense of subjectivity, but it will apprehend the subjectivity not at the level of its purely egoist protestation against infinity, nor in its anguish before death, but as founded in the idea of infinity.
>
> (TI 26; xiv)

Elsewhere, Levinas will interpret the meaning of 'subjectivity' as 'subjection to the other'; the subject is not 'for itself' but 'for another' (*pour un autre,* EI 96; 103).

While Levinas always wants to restore the priority of the 'inner life' (*la vie intérieure, Proper Names* 122; 144), he rejects both traditional Enlightenment humanism and the kind of triumphant interiority expressed by Kierkegaard, which he believes is redolent of a certain kind of violence. Thus, in a conference on Kierkegaard held in 1964 in Paris, Levinas criticised Kierkegaard's "exhibitionistic immodest subjectivism" and "violence" in doing philosophy, which Levinas sees as an anticipation of the verbal violence of National Socialism.[40] Kierkegaard distorts the notion of subjectivity by holding it entirely separate from ethics.

Totality and Infinity opens with the worry that, perhaps after all, morality 'dupes' us. How can there be morality in a world at war? The state of war, moreover, is connected with the totalisation of reason in Western thought. Levinas holds that Heraclitus was right to identify the nature of reality with *polemos,* 'war' or 'strife': being reveals itself as war. The nature of war is such that it forces us out of the normal pathways of our lives, it disrupts the normal relations of identity which we have, destroying our self-identity:

> But violence does not consist so much in injuring and annihilating persons as in interrupting their continuity, making them play roles in which they no longer recognize themselves, making them betray not only commitments but their own substance, making them carry out actions that will destroy every possibility for action.
>
> (TI 21; ix)

War and violence "destroy the identity of the same". In his discussion of war and the attempt to gain 'mastery' over others, Levinas is utilising much of the language and concepts of Hegel's account of the master–slave dialectic in the *Phenomenology of Spirit.* Initially each seeks the death of the other. Individuals are drawn into this violent upheaval and no longer remain individuals but are absorbed into the huge complex structure of war. Elsewhere, Levinas interprets this original violence as something like a Darwinian struggle for survival (*Provocation of Levinas,* p. 172). As he sees it, the essential nature of animals is to struggle for life, and the self-preoccupation of an animal or a human being is really an expression of the state of nature which puts our own survival first. This struggle to exist is well expressed in Spinoza's notion of the *conatus essendi*. Levinas understands this as a struggle to remain in being; it is a primal persistence of beings in being. This struggle for being is the struggle to maintain identity. Existence *is* identity for Levinas. However, he believes true human existence has modalities of life which offer a break from this bleak vision. Levinas sees this desire to escape expressed in the metaphysical desire to journey beyond this world to what is other, seeking somewhere which will never be a homeland. *Totality and Infinity* then is a kind of phenomenological odyssey, an exploration of ways in which humans desire what is beyond, and embark on a voyage which will never settle down again in the world of the same. As such, it offers an alternative to Hegel's *Phenomenology of Spirit* which encloses everything in the life of absolute spirit. Levinas reads the spirit, not as coming to completion in absolute self-knowledge, but rather in the sense of the Biblical theme of exile, as undergoing *separation*, a separation from what he calls 'history' (TI 55; 26). Against Hegel, the movement of spirit is achieved not in history but in its moving away from the pull of history.

The only voice which speaks against war, for Levinas, and which remained unabsorbed by the totality, is the eschatological voice, for example the voices of the Old Testament prophets, who oppose peace to war and who speak of a 'beyond' which transcends the totality, a messianic peace beyond all war:

> The eschatological vision breaks with the totality of wars and empires in which one does not speak. It does not envisage the end of history within being understood as a totality, but institutes a relation with the infinity of being which exceeds the totality.
>
> (TI 23; xi)

And Levinas continues: "we oppose to the objectivism of war a subjectivity born from the eschatological vision" (TI 25; xiv). Thus the notion of subjectivity in Levinas is very much a religiously inspired vision of the subject, a subject who is born out of its relations to the other, a subject whose nature is connected with the notion of infinity. Furthermore, subjectivity, for Levinas, is not hostility to the other, as in Hobbes or Sartre, but rather is *welcoming* of the other: "This book will present subjectivity as welcoming the Other, as hospitality; in it the idea of infinity is consummated" (TI 27; xv). Levinas wants to focus – like Ernst Bloch – on moments of intimacy in human life, the experience of *hospitality*, of *welcoming*, love, the experience of hope, and so on, phenomena that have been neglected in traditional ethical discussion. Indeed, *Totality and Infinity* has been characterised by

344

Derrida as a "vast treatise *of hospitality*".[41] The challenge to totality comes in the experience of the other:

> Without substituting eschatology for philosophy, without philosophically "demonstrating" eschatological "truths", we can proceed from the experience of totality back to a situation where totality breaks up, a situation that conditions the totality itself. Such a situation is the gleam of exteriority or of transcendence in the face of the Other (*le visage d'autrui*).
>
> (TI 24; xiii)

To characterise this domain of 'totality', Levinas turns to Husserl, characterised as the philosopher of 'representation' and 'intentionality', themes which Levinas believes stand for the whole thrust of Western philosophy since the Greeks. Levinas wants to criticise both intellectualist and activist forms of philosophy as having misunderstood the basic nature of human existence. All philosophical accounts of practical life have been inadequate; they have missed the notion of the *enjoyment* in life, enjoyment which sweeps away other distinctions. Against Sartre, Levinas denies that we find ourselves in an absurd world in which we are thrown (TI 140; 114). Against Heidegger, Levinas says we do not encounter the world primarily as tools. We encounter things (such as food) as objects of enjoyment:

> Moreover furnishings, the home, food, clothing are not *Zeuge* [tools] in the proper sense of the term: clothing serves to protect the body or to adorn it, the home to shelter it, food to restore it, but we enjoy them or suffer from them, they are ends.
>
> (TI 133; 106)

As Levinas insists, to enjoy "gratuitously, without referring to anything else, in pure expenditure – this is the human" (TI 133; 107): "In enjoyment I am absolutely for myself. Egoist without reference to the Other, I am alone without solitude, innocently egoist and alone" (TI 134; 107). In recognising human adaptation to the totality, Levinas wants carefully to characterise this sphere of the same, where the ego is at home in eating, in enjoyment, in fulfilling bodily activities. However, besides this natural sphere of living and enjoyment, there is also the domain of objectifying intentionality which seeks to represent everything, whose assumption is that knowledge is power. Intentionality understood as representation is the beginning of a 'separation' from which human existence never recovers. In intentionality, there is of course recognition of transcendence, but this relation to the transcendent is usually distorted. Levinas understands 'representation' in terms of Husserl's philosophy of constitution; *representation* always involves a "transcendental constitution" (TI 38; 8) and hence representation always means bringing the other under the power of the same. *Representation*, for Levinas, belongs to the sphere of the Same.

In *Totality and Infinity*, Levinas seeks to chart the origin of our break with totality. Levinas contrasts the experience of the 'face' with the way in which humans relate to things in the world, the manner in which objects are 'represented' in our intentional acts (Husserl), and the way tools are used for certain purposes (Heidegger). Against this region of utilisation and representation, Levinas wants to invoke the manner in which others appear to us, presenting us with an ineliminable ethical demand. The other breaks through and threatens my being-at-home with myself. It is only because the other calls forth a response from me that I hear what the other says as a language, as a demand for a response. The relation to the other is irreducible to 'objective knowledge' (TI 68; 40).

Levinas claims that the self–other relation is not reciprocal, but rather that there is a priority of the other over the self. This is what he calls the *'asymmetry'* of the relation between self and other. One example of this *asymmetry* is that I can demand things of myself which I cannot demand of the other. This lack of reciprocity is precisely what Levinas thinks is missing from Hegel's analysis of the relation with others. At the same time, I must be able to place myself in the shoes of the other, to experience as he or she experiences, to stand in for the other, and this is what Levinas calls *substitution* in an essay of that name in *Otherwise than Being* (pp. 117–118). In part, Levinas thinks such an irruption of the other at the heart of the self is inevitable. The distinctness of the ego in its own sphere is what Levinas calls 'separation': the *cogito* is a model for this separation (TI 54; 24). Humans are at their most separate in experiences of isolation, and also paradoxically in self-sufficient happiness (TI 117; 90), which is purely 'for itself'. However, the I cannot remain separate: "the I is not unique like the Eiffel Tower or the Mona Lisa" (TI 117; 90). The sense of self-identical separateness, its 'ipseity' (*l'ipséité*), actually also holds the key to the breaking up of totality.

To elucidate this claim, Levinas frequently invokes the experience of Descartes, who at the heart of his *Meditations*, as a solitary meditating *cogito*, discovers God right at the centre of his own most subjective thought (in Meditation Three). For Levinas, this illustrates the truth that the very idea of a self or subject carries within it the notion of transcendence. The true character of the other, for Levinas, does not present itself with the sense of self-identity which one experiences in the ego. The appearance of the other is an epiphany which breaks with the world:

> The Other (*Autrui*) remains infinitely transcendent, infinitely foreign; his face in which his epiphany is produced and which appeals to me breaks with the world that can be common to us, whose vir-

tualities are inscribed in our *nature* and developed by our existence. Speech (*la parole*) proceeds from absolute difference.

(TI 194; 168)

Language is the means by which the other communicates him- or herself to me but by so doing his or her 'otherness' is not brought down to the sphere of the same, rather the other still transcends me. The ethical relation puts the 'I' in question, Levinas says. He quotes Pascal's assertion that "the I is hateful". But only through language can I attest my face. This presentation of the face is the essence of non-violence and peace, the peaceful welcoming of the other is paradigmatic for Levinas (TI 203; 177–178). My welcoming of the other is the "ultimate fact" (*le fait ultime*, TI 77; 49).

The face to face

Emmanuel Levinas's moral phenomenology, his 'phenomenology of sociality', starts from the experience of 'the face' (*le visage*) of the other person, from the other's 'proximity'. No term in Levinas's strange moral vocabulary has been subject to more analysis or given rise to more confusion. Levinas uses the term 'face' to refer to the real concrete presence of another person, as for example when we 'confront' someone 'face to face', but in his writing the term also blossoms into a metaphor for all those aspects of human personhood and culture which escape objectification, which cannot be treated in the manner in which we treat objects in the world, which cannot be the object of an intentional act: "A face confounds the intentionality that aims at it" (CPP 97). He even claims that the face is not a concrete entity, but something 'abstract' (CPP 96); it is 'signification' itself. Levinas does not mean that ethics takes on a special personal significance when we look at the other directly in the face. Looking at the face in that sense is a kind of reification for Levinas. In fact, the 'face' in Levinas's sense escapes phenomenality altogether. He repeatedly emphasises that the face escapes sight: "It cannot be comprehended, that is encompassed (*englobé*)" (TI 194; 168). In contrast to the dominating factor present in all forms of knowledge, Levinas considers that in the conversational speech between humans, the 'face' addresses the 'face', and this leads to mutual respectful non-dominating recognition. Indeed Levinas claims that the presence of the face of the other is not an *experience* at all – rather it is a moving out of oneself.[42] Yet, in true Levinasian fashion, he elsewhere contradicts himself in claiming that: "The fundamental experience which objective experience itself presupposes is the experience of the Other. It is experience *par excellence*" ("Signature", *Difficult Freedom*, p. 293). Levinas writes at great length of the manner in which we are confronted by the face in our everyday experience, an experience which cuts through our selfish enjoyment of being at home in the world, it stands in opposition to the will

347

to be and to live, against the *conatus essendi*, and the will to power. For Levinas, the face can never be fully characterised, never fully represented. It is the 'infinite' or indeterminate element, which breaks up the unity of my world. It is that which calls for conversation, for turning of one's face towards the other, the 'face to face' (*le face à face*, TI 79; 52). "The face resists possession, resists my powers" (TI 197; 172).

Employing his ambiguous and unrestrained metaphorical rhetoric, Levinas claims that the face of the other is the origin of language and meaning. The other is the source of all signification; the presence of the other is heard as language (TI 297; 273). Levinas is drawing here on Heidegger's account of language as that which 'speaks' man and Husserl's analysis of the importance of the communicative function of the sign in the First Logical Investigation, an account which also motivates Derrida's philosophy. As we have seen, Husserl maintained that spoken sounds or written marks have a communicative function in that they announce that the speaker has a certain intention to say something. All signs, including signs functioning as expressions, have that *communicative* or *intimating* side. Communication is always communication with another consciousness, as Husserl maintained. Therefore, there is a sense in which Husserl supports Levinas's claim that the other is the basis of signification. As we have seen, Husserl did not consider the communicative or 'intimating function' (*kundgebende Funktion*) of signs to be required for signification as such; *Kundgabe* is not required, for instance, when a solitary I is thinking or talking to him- or herself. Levinas, in a sense, turns this analysis of communication around. Speech and the desire to communicate emerge because we find ourselves *addressed* by the other. It is because someone faces us and addresses us that we are called to speak. This addressing to us from the other is the condition of the possibility of language. Levinas places huge importance on the way in which the other emerges in and through language and speaking. Knowledge represents the domain of what is said, the domain of the assertion, which is part of 'totality', whereas the act of speaking attests to the presence of the other, and is never fully capable of being captured in thought or represented in knowledge.

According to Levinas, the other presents him- or herself to me by speaking: "Here I am!" (*me voici*, EI 97; 104; Levinas is here referring to the Bible, I *Samuel* 3: 4; *Genesis* 22: 1, 7, and 11, and elsewhere). I am called on to respond to that claim. The other presenting him- or herself to me opens up the demand for justice. According to Levinas: "Prior to any act, I am concerned with the Other, and I can never be absolved from this responsibility".[43] For Levinas "to see a face is already to hear 'Thou Shalt Not Kill' ".[44] Speech is already part of the moral domain. The other is not always a threat to my self-image as is the case in Sartre's phenomenological descriptions of shame. The presence of the other is what enables me to be myself and to recognise myself for the first time. I experience an "I" which is not myself.

The speech of the other provokes a response from me and my *response* is at the same time my *responsibility*; Levinas never tires of emphasising the close connection between these two terms. Responsibility is accountability. As Levinas says: "to recognise the Other is to give" (*Reconnaître Autrui – c'est donner*, TI 75; 48). My response may be to ignore, but I am defined by my response:

> I can recognize the gaze of the stranger, the widow, and the orphan only in giving and refusing; I am free to give or to refuse, but my recognition passes necessarily through the interposition of things. Things are not, as in Heidegger, the foundation of the site, the quintessence of all the relations that constitute our presence on the earth...The relation between the same and the other, the welcoming of the other, is the ultimate fact, and in it the things figure not as what one builds but as what one gives.
>
> (TI 77; 49)

For Levinas, it is impossible to give a phenomenological description of the face-to-face relation, because for him the face is a primitive notion, 'a fundamental event'.[45] Certain things go beyond phenomenology as the description of what is manifest: "The welcoming of the face and the work of justice – which condition the birth of truth itself – are not interpretable in terms of disclosure" (TI 28; xvi). The face is neither a thing, something which can be understood in knowledge, nor is it something we meet in everyday practices. The face escapes Heidegger's categories of the present-at-hand and the ready-to-hand. For Levinas the face is "a demand not a question. The face is a hand in search of recompense, an open hand".[46] The face of the other is an 'enigma'. One does not actually have to see someone to face the ethical demand of their 'face'. I *discover* my ethical responsibility in the starving face of a child or in the outstretched hand of a beggar. Moreover, the notion of the face is always ambiguous – the face which confronts me may be peaceful or threatening violence and extinction. Hence, Levinas thinks that the appearance of the face may call for a legitimately violent response, the requirement to protect myself against the other (as we have seen, Levinas thinks a state has a right or even an obligation to defend itself against its enemies). The other can be an enemy. Levinas is not saying, despite all the rhetoric about hospitality and welcoming, that the face of the other demands only one kind of response. The nature of the ethical is to provide the *appropriate* response, whatever that may be. However, how this appropriateness is to be regulated is never discussed by Levinas, and yet one would have thought that the moral regulation of the encounter with the other is what constitutes ethics in the first place. Ethics for Levinas is the recognition that there must be a response not a specification of the kind of response.

Levinas maintains that our experience/non-experience of the human face is primordial and inexhaustible. The appeal of the face is pre-reflective, not the result of my entertaining Kantian ethical commands, but rather a kind of lived, felt presence, an experience which I feel in my body. I am always already 'beholden' to the other. Levinas speaks of my "pre-logical subjection to the other" (CPP 135–136). He does not want to treat the face-to-face relation as a relation built upon two already-existing beings. This would be to make the ethical relation into a kind of ontological relation. Rather for him it is a kind of moral a priori, a condition for the possibility of ethics, but as we have just seen, it does not seem to be a very illuminating condition.

Attributing a face to something is a condition for it having a call on us. Thus we only understand the notion of God having a face because of our human experience of the face. Levinas agrees that we cannot actually refuse to acknowledge the faces of animals; nevertheless, at the same time, he has no adequate discussion concerning the attribution of faces, no criterion for 'facehood' as it were. Does a fish have a face, or an amoeba? Does a human embryo in the womb have a face? Levinas admits he is not able to give an account or set limits to the ascription of face: "I cannot say at what moment you have the right to be called 'face' ".[47] But surely this is an extraordinarily serious admission. For Levinas, morality is a response to the face. If I don't see something as having a face, it has no call on me and I have no responsibility towards it. Then, surely, how one accords face is crucial. If there is no account of this, it is hardly a philosophy of the face at all.

Levinas's influence

As we have seen, up until the publication of *Totality and Infinity* Levinas was known to philosophers largely for his careful, sympathetic, yet critical studies on the phenomenology of Husserl and Heidegger, which had a huge influence in France, on Sartre, Merleau-Ponty, Derrida, and Ricoeur, all of whom have been captivated by Levinas's account of the complexity of signification and of presence. Though Levinas had been writing about the 'other' since the 1940s, he emerged publicly as a phenomenologist of alterity only with *Totality and Infinity*. Levinas's emphasis on the concrete ethical relation and the richness of the experience of the other stand in stark contrast to Sartre's ethics of self-projection and his critique of the experience of the other in 'the look'. Levinas's account of the face-to-face relation has revived Continental ethics, to such an extent that writers like Derrida are now preoccupied with the notions of ethics and justice as understood in Levinasian fashion. Levinas has also been influential in psychotherapy in his discussion of the role of the face-to-face relation and in his analysis of notions like 'mastery' and the 'name of the father' (*le nom du père*). Levinas's account of 'the other' has also, somewhat paradoxically, considering his treatment of woman as other is not without sexist assumptions, had a strong influence on European feminist thought, specifically in the writings of Simone de Beauvoir, Julia Kristeva, and Luce Irigaray. As we have seen, de Beauvoir criticised Levinas for his adoption of an exclusively male point of view and treating the woman as the other. Similarly, more recent French philosophers such as Luce Irigaray and Hélène Cixous have all critically, if somewhat obscurely, discussed this aspect of Levinas.[48]

Levinas's philosophy continues to have significance as a counterweight to much of the subjectivist basis of contemporary philosophising. However, its opaque, metaphorical, inexact style of writing inevitably means that there can never be an authoritative interpretation of his philosophy. It is impossible to 'master' it. Perhaps this is Levinas's intention. The exact status of his discourse is never clear. At times he seems to recognise that his language is metaphorical; thus he repeatedly employs the phrase 'as if', for example it is *as if* I am responsible for the other's death or the other's protection. If this 'as if' is genuine then it significantly weakens Levinas's discussion. If, in my existence, it is only 'as if' I am responsible for the other, it is hard to see how true ethical responsibility can be grounded on this 'as if' relation. Levinas never discusses this 'as if' in terms of Kant's hypothetical imperatives.

There is also a sense that in simply reorienting the focus away from egoism to alterity, Levinas is creating a new dogmatism, centred now around the other rather than the self or ego. Though Levinas claims to be doing ethics, his ambiguous account of the role of the other (my enemy, my friend, to whom I show love, against whom I must fight) is of no assistance in resolving conflicting moral claims which, for instance, often force us to choose *between* others, rather than between self and other, as Levinas portrays it. Thus, for Levinas, the presence of the other's face is both a temptation to kill and a command not to kill. This may be a first condition for the possibility of ethics but it tells us nothing about what regulates right conduct.

What is the status of Levinas's claims about the primacy of the other? Are they phenomenological discoveries, uncovering neglected phenomena of our social life, falsifiable empirical claims? Or are they idealisations, a fantasy picture of what ethical relations with others ought to be? What sense can we make of claims like "since the Other looks at me I am responsible for him" (EI 96; 102)? What force does the connective "since" have here? In what sense does my obligation follow from the presence of the other?

Furthermore, Levinas is too quickly dismissive of the whole tradition of Western philosophy as one large movement of representation and of rationalisation, of knowledge as grasping (*greifen*), terminating in the concept (*Begriff*). His too-ready identification of reason with violence will not attract philosophers who believe that the very essence of philosophy is reasoned argument and refutation of counter-claim. Levinas rarely offers arguments; he simply presents his analysis as if it were the way it must be for everyone, not a position, to paraphrase Levinas himself, open to the views of others. We are, in Levinas's own terms, sucked into the sphere of the same. Levinas seems always to assume that the reader will see exactly what he is saying and will be convinced. This makes it difficult, if not impossible, to argue against him, other than to say that one sees things differently.

Levinas's supporters do not seem to be put off by the deep unclarity at the heart of his work. They seem untroubled by his many contradictory assertions and metaphorical exuberance. But surely a more dispassionate, even if still sympathetic, critical gaze cannot ignore the blatant contradictions in Levinas's account of the experience or non-experience of the face, for example. Levinas does not open a space for questioning; indeed, for him, the other presents itself as a demand, not a question. However, even if we know what he means by 'face', many of the pressing problems in modern ethics, for example the issue of abortion, self-defence, treatment of animals, and so on, all turn on the fact that we do not have clear criteria for what counts as a face. The animal rights movement claims that all animals are worthy of respect just as humans are. They extend the notion of 'face' to animals. On the other hand, Levinas claims the notion of face comes primarily from the human domain. The problem is to set down criteria for counting something as a 'face' and for negotiating what happens when there is a direct clash between competing 'faces', for example when a choice has to be made to favour one of two equally valuable, indeed infinitely valuable, human beings. It is pointless piling up quote after quote from Levinas on the nature of the face, as indeed I have tried to do above. The sum total of these entirely unsupported, not to say downright contradictory, claims about the nature of this so-called non-disclosive encounter with the face is not going to add up to a coherent picture. Of course, Levinas would concur, the face resists totalisation. On the other hand, it is not a case of 'either you see it or you don't', because the face is not a phenomenon, not something which can be seen. It is entirely unclear how this phenomenology of alterity can be a phenomenology at all.

Because of its dense style and apparent abandonment of rational argument and justification in favour of repetitive, dogmatic assertions which have the character of prophetic incantations and quasi-religious absolutist pronouncements, Levinas's work is largely ignored among analytic philosophers. One is tempted to say that, rather than revealing things in the phenomenological sense, Levinas's thought appears to levitate above them, completely preoccupied with its own self-referential system. Nevertheless, his concentration on the manner in which aspects of human beings escape or transcend all objective classification is an important development of phenomenology even if it goes against the very essence of Husserl's conception of philosophy as rational self-responsibility.

11

JEAN-PAUL SARTRE

Passionate description

Introduction: the *engagé* intellectual

Jean-Paul Sartre (1905–1980) is known far beyond philosophy as a brilliant *littérateur*, an accomplished novelist and playwright, as a Bohemian intellectual who popularised existentialism in post-war Europe, and as a radical political activist who was a relentless critic of the pretensions of the bourgeoisie (*les salauds*, 'the swine') and of colonial exploitation in all its forms. As a writer in Paris in the 1930s and 1940s he mixed with the intellectual and artistic elite of that city, including, to name but a few, Pablo Picasso, André Malraux, Jacques Lacan, and Michel Leiris. His brilliance as a writer was recognised with the award of the Nobel Prize for Literature in 1964, which, however, he declined to accept for political reasons. Sartre more than anyone else exemplified the figure of the French philosopher as a kind of public intellectual, a denizen of Parisian cafés, a talk-show guest always willing to make pronouncements on public matters, someone who was always interesting and could write well about almost anything.

Whereas Sartre's literary interests emerged early, he was not originally political in outlook, but his life was profoundly altered by the Second World War, which, according to his own testimony, forced him to move "beyond traditional philosophical thinking to thinking in which philosophy and action are connected".[1] After the war, partly through the influence of his friend Maurice Merleau-Ponty, he became a supporter of the French Communist Party, and, in essays, defended the Stalinist USSR, even for a time offering justifications for Stalin's labour camps and his regime of terror. After the Hungarian uprising of 1956, Sartre broke with the communists and adopted a more independent, but always engaged, political stance. A much travelled public figure, Sartre met with revolutionary leaders across the world, including Tito, Castro, and Che Guevara. In his later years, he protested on behalf of various left-wing causes, including travelling to Germany accompanied by Daniel Cohn-Bendit to visit jailed members of the Baader-Meinhof Group. He associated himself publicly with many radical causes, including the Maoists and the French anarchist group *Action Directe*. At the end of his life, however, he had broken with Marxism and was defending a kind of "libertarian socialism" (Schilpp, p. 21).

Sartre saw himself primarily as a writer, and even his philosophical efforts were for him part of his exploration of the literary outlook. Indeed, from an early age, he believed himself destined for literary genius. Sartre never completed a doctorate, never held a university teaching post, and was not enamoured of academic life generally. Most of the philosophical works for which he became famous were completed by the time the Second World War ended in 1945, and, indeed, as soon as he had a chance, he gave up teaching to live fully from his writing. Besides producing novels, drama, and short stories, Sartre wrote, with a restless brilliance, on literary theory, biography, psychoanalysis, and politics, all dashed off at a breathless, frenetic pace. He rarely regarded any of his projects as finished. Thus, at the end of his masterpiece, *L'Être et le néant* (*Being and Nothingness*, 1943), he promised an ethics which he sketched in outline in his notebooks.[2] Similarly, his *Critique de la raison dialectique* (*Critique of Dialectical Reason*, 1960) was only the first part of a projected larger work, and when the second unfinished part was published posthumously, it amounted to more than 700 pages.[3]

From his student days at the Ecole Normale Supérieure, Sartre had a long relationship, both intellectual and passionate, with Simone de Beauvoir (1908–1986), an unconventional relationship which challenged bourgeois convention in many ways. De Beauvoir had trained in philosophy with Sartre and, although her own writing career developed somewhat later than his, there is considerable evidence that, besides promoting and defending his philosophy, de Beauvoir strongly influenced the formation of Sartre's philosophical outlook, especially his theory of the other. De Beauvoir continued to influence and comment on almost everything Sartre wrote, and, indeed, Sartre himself always acknowledged that her philosophical sense was sharper than his own.

Given the extraordinary breadth of his political interests and the range of his literary production, it would be impossible to do justice to Sartre's thought in a single chapter. Our intention here is to focus specifically on Sartre's contribution to phenomenology, especially in his earlier writings up to the publication of *Being and Nothingness* in 1943. Sartre's philosophical interests manifest themselves in the form of an undisciplined eclecticism. Nevertheless, he undoubtedly did influence the development of phenomenology. Sartre enlarged the scope of phenomenological reflection, not so much through his critical readings of Husserl and Heidegger, or through his development of the phenomenological method, but through his finely observed description of human action and interaction, where one's sense of oneself is at stake. His specific contribution is to show both the desire for and fear of freedom at work in the dynamics of human relationships, to show that freedom is a value at stake in many more occasions of human encounter than classical philosophy and psychology had recognised. Though his *Critique of Dialectical Reason* (1960) offers an important modification of his earlier position on freedom by situating individual freedom in the context of social and political relations, the analysis moves into the area of Marxist political philosophy and as such is, unfortunately, outside the compass of this book.

Sartre's philosophical outlook

In general, Sartre's outlook is something of a hodge-podge of different ideas, hammered somewhat idiosyncratically into a system, which never received the refinements to which an academic career would have exposed his thought. Indeed, Sartre himself always seemed to hanker after a traditional philosophical system of a rationalist variety. He was a distinguished student at the Ecole Normale Supérieure and an avid reader of traditional philosophy. An atheist from the age of 12, his ontology begins with the explicit recognition that the removal of a deity from the world leaves us with the sheer fact of the existence of things, sheer *contingency*. Contingency may be said to be Sartre's first and greatest philosophical illumination, discovered while he was still at the Ecole Normale, reputedly while watching a film. Contingency is the concept that the world exists but does not have to be there. For Sartre, contingency means that there is no rationale, no overall plan, no intrinsic meaning in events. There is no necessity governing the fact of existence. Being just is, but as such it is 'superfluous', *de trop* (BN xlii; 33). More than any other philosopher, Sartre explores the psychological, moral, and human consequences of facing up to the radical contingency of the world, its sheer lack of sense, 'absurdity'. Sartre opposes the fallacy he labels 'creationism' (BN xl; 31), the assumption that if being is understood as created then somehow it is explained. Sartre held that nineteenth-century rationalism and humanism had wanted to acknowledge the death of God, and yet had thought it could conduct business as usual, assuming a groundplan of rationality, whereas Sartre maintains that without a divine plan the world is literally meaningless, absurd (Sartre tends to use the term 'absurd' where Husserl would use '*sinnloss*' rather than '*widersinn*').

In a sense, Sartre subscribes in part to a Parmenidean vision of this being: being is; non-being is not. Moreover, being is undifferentiated, pure self-identity, *être en-soi*. He differs from Parmenides in not seeing a relation between being and reason, and in not seeing being as necessary. Being is opaque to itself, brute, inert, neither active nor passive, meaningless, resistent to consciousness, pure 'immanence' (BN xli; 32). In this sense, Sartre's concept of *être en-soi* is not unlike Levinas's description of being and existence in *De l'évasion* and *De l'existence à l'existant*, where existence is all encompassing, beyond both affirmation and denial. Sartre too claims,

356

for instance, in agreement with Levinas, that "being is equally beyond negation as beyond affirmation" (BN xli; 32). The world is full of brute, inert matter; for Sartre, it is pure 'being in-itself' (*être en-soi*). This terminology of *en-soi* and *pour-soi* is found in German philosophy from Hegel on (including Husserl and Heidegger). In Sartre's case, Hegel was mediated through the writings of his classmate at the Ecole Normale, Jean Hyppolyte, as well as through the lectures of Alexandre Kojève, and Jean Wahl's influential study *Vers le concret* (*Towards the Concrete*). Indeed, Sartre later credited Wahl with challenging the absolute idealism of Sartre's teachers (e.g. Brunschvicg) by emphasising the paradoxes, ambiguities, and unresolved issues in this philosophy of total knowledge.[4] Being does not require the for-itself. The for-itself is as contingent as the in-itself. The world as such is meaningless, absurd. Furthermore, even the self-identity of being, whereby every being is what it is, is simply a contingent fact. Against Husserl, Sartre maintains a naturalistic view that the principle of identity (A = A) is not a purely a priori logical truth, but is actually based on the simple, contingent fact that being is (BN xli–xlii; 33).

Opposed to this monolithic and undifferentiated being in-itself is being 'for-itself' (*pour-soi*), or consciousness, which, in Hegelian terms, is always seeking to develop itself and come into identity with itself. The *en-soi* is a condition of the *pour-soi*. The *pour-soi* is not its own foundation (though Sartre sometimes talks as if it were self-founding), rather it depends utterly on the in-itself. Consciousness is always described, in a manner which suggests the influence of Heidegger, as an irruption into being, or as a fissure in being. Yet, as will be discussed further in this chapter, Sartre constantly claims that there is no relation possible between in-itself and for-itself – these two regions do not communicate. Sartre wants to give primacy to being in-itself, and, in his later writings especially, he is more explicitly materialist, yet he curiously denies that consciousness is produced from matter in a causal manner.[5] Sartre, then, denies that he is an ontological dualist, because for him the for-itself is not a being, but rather is a gap or disruption of being, which allows being to reveal itself. It is this focus on consciousness as the revelation of being which binds Sartre to the phenomenological tradition.

Being in-itself is contingent, but it seems not to be temporal. Temporality is a feature of the for-itself. Being in-itself then is not present as such (something both Levinas and Derrida will also claim), as most being is made present through consciousness. What meaning there is comes entirely from human meaning-giving, Husserlian *Sinngebung*. But, more radically than Husserl, Sartre insists that the meaning-giving function is a completely free act of consciousness. Humans give meaning to things by wrapping them up in their projects. In short, there is, for Sartre, only being in-itself on the one hand, and human projects on the other. These projects are attempts of consciousness to achieve being in-itself while still remaining conscious. Thus the for-itself has an ultimate, fundamental project: to be both being and knowing, in short to be what it never can be, namely God.

Sartre's Cartesianism

Sartre's philosophical starting point is always Cartesianism, a Cartesianism mediated through the idealist outlook of his teachers, especially Léon Brunschvicg (1869–1944). As a philosopher, Sartre wanted clear concepts. Against the vague, fuzzy, optimistic formulations of the idealists, Sartre opposed and sought to emulate what he took to be the sharp edge of Cartesian thought:

> Descartes by refusing intermediaries between thought and extension, displays a catastrophic and revolutionary cast of mind: he cuts and slashes, leaving to others the task of re-stitching. We cut and slashed in his wake.[6]

Sartre also thought of philosophy primarily in terms of ontology (Schilpp, p. 14), an ontology which he elaborated at length in *Being and Nothingness*. He was attracted to Descartes precisely because of the latter's strict metaphysics of two incommunicable realms – extension and consciousness. Descartes's error, however, was to understand the existence of consciousness in terms of substance (what Sartre calls the "substantialist illusion"). In many ways, Sartre offers an a priori metaphysics of 'being in-itself' (*être en-soi*) and 'being for-itself' (*être pour-soi*). Some commentators, notably Gregory McCulloch, have argued that Sartre is providing a *phenomenological* ontology, that is speaking of *ways* or *modes* of being, rather than of ontological kinds in the strict sense, and is really asserting only the single entity – being-in-the-world.[7] But this interpretation goes against Sartre's own claims to be providing an ontology in the traditional sense. As Sartre put it: "I wanted my thought to make sense in relation to being. I think that I had the idea of ontology in mind because of my philosophical training. Philosophy is an inquiry concerning being and beings" (Schilpp, p. 14). Furthermore, Sartre explicitly rejected phenomenological attempts to bring together his two incommunicable regions of in-itself and for-itself, and singled out both Merleau-Ponty's 'interworld' and Heidegger's musings on Being as mystifications on an essentially clear ontology. Sartre, then, is a Cartesian at heart, though he differs from Descartes in making the for-itself into a non-thing, to be essentially the *desire* for thinghood.

Sartre's conception of freedom, often thought to be highly original, also derives ultimately from Descartes. Freedom is absolute, not a matter of degree, and to that extent human freedom is the same as divine freedom. Furthermore, freedom resides in a decision of the intellect, in autonomous thinking, rather than arising in action. One can be free and yet unable to act. Freedom is a stance of consciousness, in fact the fundamental stance. For Sartre, Descartes had claimed that no one can do my thinking for me: "In the end we must say yes or no and decide alone, for the entire universe, on what is true".[8] Sartre agrees with Descartes's optimistic view that humans make themselves through their use of what they have been given, and that most humans possess more or less the same abilities.

Even Sartre's attraction to Husserlian phenomenology came through Descartes. Though he must have encountered some phenomenology in the Ecole Normale, he was most interested in Descartes, Spinoza, and Bergson, and, under the influence of his teachers, saw himself involved in a quest for the Absolute (though he later claimed not to have read any Hegel at this time). For Sartre, Husserl was the great Cartesian of the twentieth century,[9] who radicalised the Cartesian *cogito*.

From Descartes to Husserl

Sartre himself records that he was first introduced to phenomenology through Raymond Aron, who was studying Husserl in Berlin in 1932. This meeting prompted Sartre to read Emmanuel Levinas's book, *The Theory of Intuition in Husserl's Phenomenology*, from which he gained the impression that Husserl was promoting a kind of realism. He was sufficiently excited by what he heard about phenomenology, understood as the effort to draw meaning from even the most insignificant aspects of life, that he arranged a study trip to Berlin from 1933 to 1934, where he read more deeply in phenomenology and drafted his first philosophical essays.

Sartre brought his own particular and original focus to bear on Husserl's phenomenology, rejecting much of Husserl's methodological apparatus, including the *epoché*, the reduction, Husserl's account of the *noema* and the intentional object, and his account of the appearance of the ego in consciousness. Sartre claims that all reduction is imperfect, that it is impossible to carry out a complete reduction, because we can never simply return to objects as they are given to consciousness, as the object will always escape the grasp of the *pour-soi*. In fact, Sartre rejects just about the whole of Husserl and yet continues to regard himself – at least until 1940 – as a Husserlian. At first, Sartre considered Husserl a realist, but later came to realise that his position was closer to Kant and hence was a "bad realism" (Schilpp, p. 13). Sartre's early grasp of Husserl as a realist is evident in his 1939 short essay "Intentionality: A Fundamental Idea of Husserl's Phenomenology", where he declares that Husserl's phenomenology puts us in direct contact with the world: "Husserl has restored to things their horror and their charm...if we love a woman, it is because she is lovable." [10] By the time of *Being and Nothingness*, however, Sartre considered Husserl to be a phenomenalist who thought of the object as the sum of its appearances, and who tended towards Kantian idealism (BN 73; 111). Influenced by Levinas, Sartre interpreted Husserl's thesis of intentionality as an ontological thesis. The structure of intentionality uncovers a fairly simplistic ontology of being in-itself and a parasitic consciousness, a consciousness which is never 'in-itself' but always striving beyond itself 'for-itself', transcending itself to cling to being. Husserl, for Sartre, is a Cartesian committed to the *cogito*, to thinking the relation between *cogitatio* and *cogitatum*, whereby the absolute freedom of consciousness meets directly the transcendent nature of the intentional object. Consciousness is a 'nothingness', a 'lack', a "hole of being at the heart of being" (*un trou d'être au sein de l'Etre*, BN 617; 681); in contrast, the intentional object is pure being, and yet consciousness is somehow in direct contact with being and is nothing other than this grasp of being.

In his first published article, *La Transcendance de l'égo* (*The Transcendence of the Ego*, 1936), Sartre accepts Husserl's view of phenomenology as the search for essences, as eidetic analysis, but he never separated these essences from the world of facts, and, in that sense, was already leading phenomenology in an existential direction:

> Phenomenology is a scientific, not a critical study of consciousness. Its essential way of proceeding is by intuition. Intuition, according to Husserl, puts us in the presence of *the thing* (*la chose*). We must recognize, therefore, that phenomenology is a science of *fact*, and that the problems it poses are problems *of fact*, which can be seen, moreover, from Husserl's designation of phenomenology as a *descriptive* science.[11]

In agreement with Husserl, Sartre accepts the view that phenomenology is simply the faithful recording of what is given in immediate intuition, though Sartre's notion of intuition differs from Husserl's in several ways. Thus, in *Being and Nothingness*, Sartre asserts:

> There is only intuitive knowledge. Deduction and discursive argument, incorrectly called examples of knowing, are only instruments which lead to intuition. When intuition is reached, methods utilized to attain it are effaced before it...If someone asks for a definition of intuition, Husserl will reply, in agreement with the majority of philosophers, that it is the presence of the thing (*Sache*) "in person" to consciousness...But we have established that the in-itself can never by itself be *presence*. Being-present, in fact, is an ekstatic mode of being of the for-itself. We are then compelled to reverse the terms of our definition: intuition is the presence of consciousness to the thing (*l'intuition est la présence de la conscience à la chose*).
>
> (BN 172; 212–213)

Sartre is here stressing, following Heidegger, that presence is a mode of human being rather than a mode of being of the in-itself.

In his brief 1939 essay on intentionality, Sartre claims Husserl has freed philosophy from the epistemological paradigm, which sees knowledge as a kind of digestion of the object, in the way a spider traps things and reduces them to its own substance. Knowledge is "nutrition, assimilation". Husserl, Sartre claims, "persistently affirmed that one cannot dissolve things in consciousness...[A thing] could not enter consciousness, for it is not of the same nature as consciousness" (*Intentionality* 4; 30). Sartre reads Husserl as claiming that consciousness and the world are essentially correlative and that being is not consciousness. Consciousness is a 'bursting out' (*éclater vers*) towards the world (Levinas has the same phrase). Likewise Sartre rejects all representationalist and immanentist accounts of consciousness as a kind of reflection of the world: "Consciousness has no inside" (*la conscience n'a pas de "dedans"*, *Intentionality* 5; 30). Furthermore, consciousness relates to the world in more ways than solely in terms of knowledge. Hating someone is a way of bursting out towards them. But the key point in all relations between consciousness and being is that consciousness is congenitally oriented towards a being which it is not (*la conscience naît portée sur un être qui n'est past elle*, BN xxxvii; 28).

The influence of Heidegger

Besides Descartes and Husserl, Sartre's other great philosophical source is Heidegger, though Sartre was always aware of, and despised, Heidegger's compromises with the Nazi movement. Sartre's first contact with Heidegger originally came through the essay *What is Metaphysics?*, which had been translated into French by Henri Corbin and appeared in the same issue of the journal *Bifur*, edited by Paul Nizan, in which Sartre himself had a speculative essay, "The Legend of Truth".[12] *What is Metaphysics?*, Heidegger's *Antrittsrede* at Freiburg, contains an account of 'nothingness' (*das Nichts, le néant*) close to that which Sartre employed in *Being and Nothingness*, whereby negation depends on a prior nothingness rather than vice versa. But Sartre does not appear to have made much of Heidegger through the 1930s. He began to study *Being and Time* in some depth first during his days as a prisoner of war in 1940, and Heidegger's influence was such that Sartre reconceived phenomenology as the 'phenomenological ontology' of *Being and Nothingness* (1943). It was not until 1952 that Sartre visited Heidegger in Freiburg. As we have seen, when Heidegger first received Sartre's book he had displayed little interest in it. According to Gadamer's recollection, Heidegger read about forty pages at the beginning (the remaining pages were uncut) before passing it on to a student. However, on 28 October 1945, Heidegger, seeking to ameliorate his position with the French occupation forces in Freiburg, wrote to Sartre praising the book.[13]

Eventually in 1947 Heidegger wrote his own *Letter on Humanism* largely as a response to Sartre's existentialism. Sartre, on the other hand, always admired Heidegger's early philosophy, and was able to appreciate it, while decrying Heidegger's personal weakness in his association with the Nazis.

Sartre read *Being and Time* largely as an essay in existential anthropology, offering an account of human existence as both free and situated, thrown into the world and yet always able to project itself into various futural projects. Heidegger's claim that the essence of Dasein is its 'to be' is reinterpreted by Sartre to mean that human nature has no nature, that it is pure freedom. Whereas Heidegger portrays Dasein as 'thrown projection' (*geworfene Entwurf*), Sartre takes the view that although humans are always limited by their *facticity* (their sex, height, economic position in society, and so on) and always uniquely 'situated' in space and time, they nevertheless make themselves through their 'projects' (*projets*). Freedom always operates in relation to this facticity and situatedness. As Sartre says in his *War Diaries* (p. 109): "Facticity is nothing other than the fact that there's a human reality in the world at every moment." He adds that it is thanks to facticity that he is thrown into the war. Sartre then does not make a precise distinction between facticity and situatedness. On Sartre's interpretation, Heidegger is revealing the fundamental existential condition of finite, being-unto-death, and meaningless freedom, thus leading to the assimilation of phenomenology into existentialism. Sartre does not think Heidegger's claim that no one can experience another's death is particularly significant. He believes it to be merely a particular expression of a more general Cartesian truth – no one can immediately experience another person's consciousness.

Anxiety and authenticity

By the mid-1940s Sartre was describing his position as existentialism, and was paying special attention to moments of vertigo, anxiety, and nausea, and other experiences usually neglected by philosophers, but which, for Sartre, are revelatory of the nature of human existence. Sartre's existentialism maintained that there was no blueprint for human existence, no framework which could be adopted to make life meaningful. Rather we must face up to the dizzying formlessness and groundlessness of our existence, an experience which provokes anxiety. Of course, anxiety was also a theme in Kierkegaard and Heidegger. Nevertheless, although Sartre's philosophy endorsed existentialism, in the sense that the only possible meaning a life has is that given by living it, and therefore the challenge to live authentically is the highest human challenge, in his own life Sartre denied he ever experienced existential crises or *Angst*, or that he ever struggled to live authentically. He denied that he ever personally suffered from anxiety or nausea in this existential sense. Despite his genius for vivid existential description of such authentic and inauthentic choices, Sartre portrays himself as a cold, dispassionate, even scheming, intellectual. He had a very clear sense of his own capacities and the following passage from his *War Diaries* is extremely revealing:

> It's true. I'm not authentic. With everything that I feel, before actually feeling it I know that I'm feeling it. And then, bound up as I am with defining and thinking it, I no longer more than half-feel it. My greatest passions are mere nervous impulses. The rest of the time I feel hurriedly, then elaborate in words, press a little here, force a little there, and lo and behold an exemplary feeling has been constructed, good enough to put in any bound volume. All that men feel, I can guess at, explain, put down in black and white. But not feel. I fool people: I look like a sensitive person but I'm barren. Yet when I consider my destiny, it doesn't seem to me so contemptible: it seems to me I have before me a host of promised lands that I shall never enter. I haven't felt Nausea, I'm not authentic, I have halted on the threshhold of the promised lands. But at least I point the way to them and others can go there. I'm a guide, that's my role. It seems to me that, at this moment, I am grasping myself in my most essential structure.
>
> (*War Diaries*, pp. 61–62)

This entry is extraordinarily revealing in that it shows Sartre as primarily a *writer*, one who can imaginatively envision and describe, rather than as someone who lives through existential commitment. He is exploring moments as a creative writer does, not necessarily drawing on lived experience. The enduring philosophical merit of his writings lies, then, less in his systematic theorising, and certainly not in his ontology, which is superficial and confused, and more in what de Beauvoir called his "psychological penetration". Sartre is the great psychologist, especially of those moments of personal betrayal, of self-recognition in the dynamics of one's engagement with others (catching someone acting as *voyeur*, encountering others in public, deciding whether to become a Resistance fighter or stay at home to mind one's mother, and so on). In so far as these descriptions may be termed phenomenological in a loose sense, Sartre has greatly expanded the field of phenomenology, while at the same time, he is certainly guilty of emptying out the phenomenological method until it is no more than a form of creative intuition, or artistic insight into the world.

Jean-Paul Sartre: life and writings (1905–1980)

Sartre was born in Thiviers in the Dordogne on 21 June 1905. His father, Jean-Baptiste, a marine officer, died less than a year later, and the resultant sudden impoverishment in family circumstances forced Sartre's young mother to move with her infant son to live with her parents, the Schweitzers, in Meudon, near Paris. In his autobiography of his early years, *Words*, Sartre interpreted the premature death of his father as a fortunate event which gave him his freedom: "Jean-Baptiste's death was the great event of my life: it returned my mother to her chains and it gave me my freedom".[14] In 1911 he moved back to Paris with his grandparents where his grandfather had set up an Institute of Modern Languages to help support the family. His grandfather's study with its huge collection of books became the young Sartre's playground, where he first began to dream of becoming a great writer. In the autumn of 1913 he began attending the Lycée Montaigne. Soon after, his grandfather died, and following a period in a communal school and in private tuition, in 1915 he moved to the prestigious Lycée Henri IV (where Paul Nizan was a classmate).

In 1916 his mother married again and Sartre initially remained with his grandmother. When, however, his mother and stepfather moved to La Rochelle in 1917, they took the young Sartre with them, and enrolled him in the local school, which was an unhappy experience for the boy. To his great relief, in 1920 he returned to Paris to the Lycée Henri IV, where in 1922 he gained his Baccalauréat with distinction. He then attended, along with Paul Nizan, the Lycée Louis-Le-Grand (which Derrida would also attend some years later) for two years of *hypokhâgne* and *khâgne*, in preparation for the extremely competitive entrance examination to the prestigious Ecole Normale Supérieure, one of France's most elite educational institutions or *grands écoles*, which was situated only a short distance from the *lycée*. At an early stage in his schooling, the young Sartre had already been writing stories, but he first seriously became interested in philosophy in the year of *khâgne*, although at this stage philosophy was to be a kind of 'raw material' for his writing (Schilpp, p. 6). The first philosophical author he read was Bergson, and though he was never a Bergsonian as such, he was drawn to the manner in which Bergson attempted a detailed study of consciousness as it is experienced (Schilpp, p. 7).

Discovering philosophy at the Ecole Normale

Having succeeded in the entrance examination, Sartre attended the Ecole Normale Supérieure from 1924 to 1928 as a boarding student; fellow students included Paul Nizan, Raymond Aron, Henri de Gandillac, and Maurice Merleau-Ponty. Sartre took courses in philosophy and psychology, and was known as a voracious reader, a prankster, a composer of bawdy lyrics, and as something of a boxer. He was small and ugly but exceptionally strong. At the Ecole he wrote his first novel, *Une défaite* (*A Defeat*) in 1927, based loosely on the relation between the composer Richard Wagner, his wife Cosima, and Friedrich Nietzsche, though he failed to get it published.

He took courses with Brunschvicg but was not drawn to his idealism. In 1927 he wrote his *diplôme* thesis on the imagination, "L'Image dans la vie psychologique: rôle et nature", which refers to Piaget, Freud, Jaspers, and even Husserl, in the course of a study of the role of the image in perception and conception. This thesis would form the basis of his first two books on the imagination, yet he managed to fail the written examination for the *agrégation* (licence to teach) in 1928 coming fiftieth in the class of fifty. Sartre later claimed that he failed because he sought to be too original. According to his classmate, Raymond Aron, who had taken first place in the same examination, Sartre had outlined his newly discovered insights on the contingent nature of existence in the examination. Sartre was forced to repeat the examination as an external student, and in the following year of 1929, he took first place in the class.

It was while preparing for this second examination that he met Simone de Beauvoir, who was only 21 at the time, and the two became friendly and studied together for the examination. De Beauvoir in fact took second place in the same examination in 1929 and Jean Wahl, who was one of the examiners, later recalled that it was difficult to decide whether Sartre or de Beauvoir should get the first place (Cohen-Solal, p. 74). From then on, for the rest of their lives the two had an extraordinarily intense, amorous, and open relationship, which did not rule out taking other lovers and having affairs which they often discussed in detail with each other. In 1929 de Beauvoir and Sartre famously made a pact of 'necessary love' (*amour nécessaire*), a commitment to be absolutely truthful with one another while not excluding other 'contingent loves' (*amours contingentes*).[15]

Though Sartre planned to travel, he was required to undergo military service and, from 1929 to 1931, he completed his eighteen months of military service at St-Cyr in the Meteorological Corps, sending up weather balloons, a position he acquired thanks to the efforts on his behalf of Raymond Aron who was also stationed there. In 1931 Sartre began teaching philosophy in a *lycée* in Le Havre, while de Beauvoir got a teaching job at the other end of the country in Marseilles. Sartre made a strong impression as an engaging, informal teacher, who never wore a tie to class. Though undisciplined and anarchic in his teaching methods, he nevertheless managed to achieve great results with the students in their examinations. However, he found the stratified, bourgeois atmosphere of Le Havre suffocating, and he applied his energies to carousing and to composing the first draft of a so-called 'memo on contingency' (*factum sur la contingence*), which eventually was published as the novel *La Nausée* (*Nausea*), in 1938.

Encountering phenomenology

Sometime in 1932, on one of his breaks from Le Havre, Sartre had his famous conversation with Raymond Aron and Simone de Beauvoir in a

Paris café about phenomenology. Aron was on holiday from Berlin where he was studying Husserlian phenomenology at the French Institute. Sartre had been talking about his study of contingency when Aron mentioned Husserlian phenomenology as a way of getting to concrete things themselves. According to de Beauvoir's recollections, Aron explained to Sartre that, as a phenomenologist, one could talk about the very glass on the table. According to de Beauvoir, Sartre almost turned pale with emotion.[16] Sartre was so excited, he dragged de Beauvoir around the Paris bookshops to find something on Husserl and found Levinas's study which he devoured, and from which he discovered that Husserl knew of contingency, the concept Sartre himself was exploring. According to Levinas, Husserl recognised the contingency of all physical objects but not the contingency of consciousness, which is absolute being. Sartre immediately embraced phenomenology as a way of overcoming the idealism and indirect realism – the view that reality is apprehended only indirectly through mental representations of ideas – of his teachers. There was now a way to discuss the manner in which consciousness was immediately in the presence of things.

Sartre decided to follow Aron to Berlin and he obtained a grant to study at La Maison Académique Française, the French Institute in Berlin, in 1933–1934. Sartre thus arrived in Berlin after Hitler's accession to power. All around him, Nazi Germany was coming into being, but Sartre appears to have remained detached from it, not noticing the intimidation of Jews on the streets, or the military build-up. Instead, he rediscovered "the irresponsibility of youth" (*War Diaries*, p. 77), visiting cafés and enjoying the rich Berlin nightlife. He read phenomenology (notably Husserl's *Ideas* I) in the mornings, and worked on his 'factum on contingency' in the evenings. It was in Berlin in 1934 that Sartre wrote the first of his phenomenological studies, *The Transcendence of the Ego*, published in 1936–1937 in the short-lived, avant-garde philosophical journal *Recherches philosophiques*. *The Transcendence of the Ego* (to which we shall return later in this chapter) remains an interesting phenomenological study which shows that Sartre could get to grips with key conceptions of Husserl, while at the same time offering original criticisms of his concept of the pure ego.

In October 1934 Sartre returned to his teaching position in Le Havre, which Aron had occupied in his absence. On return to France he fell into a depression, perhaps compounded by the fact that his 'factum on contingency', now entitled, *Melancholia*, was rejected by the publishers, Gallimard, in 1936. Meanwhile, after a short stint teaching in Laon, in 1937 Sartre returned to Paris to teach at the Lycée Pasteur at Neuilly, where he enthralled students with his lectures on madness, anger, despair.

Sartre recovered from his depression and threw himself into both philosophical and literary works. In 1936 he published *L'Imagination*,[17] commissioned by one of Sartre's former professors at the Ecole Normale. This book was essentially a critical survey of existing theories of imagination, but towards the end he raises questions for further study. In 1937 he wrote a collection of short stories, *Le Mur* (*The Wall*), eventually published in 1939. After entreaties from his friend Paul Nizan, now a successful novelist, and from Pierre Bost, Jean Paulhan, on behalf of the publishers Gallimard, finally accepted his philosophical novel. Gallimard requested a change of title and it was published in April 1938 as *La Nausée* (*Nausea*),[18] dedicated to 'Castor'. Simone de Beauvoir's nickname was 'Castor', the French word for 'Beaver', a name given her by her friend René Maheu because it echoed her name, and because of her industriousness.[19] The publication of his collection of short stories and his novel so close together meant that Sartre attracted the attention of the critics and soon he was being acclaimed as a new writer on the Parisian scene. Sartre's novel attracted distinguished admirers such as André Gide, and was nominated for the Prix Goncourt. Paul Nizan, in his review, compared Sartre to Kafka. The young Albert Camus also reviewed it in *Alger républicain*, praising it, as did Gaston Bachelard who, in his review, admired its account of imagination.[20]

Nausea

Nausea purports to be the diary of a failed historian, Antoine Roquentin, living in a fictitious town of Bouville (modelled on Le Havre). The book has a thinly disguised autobiographical flavour. As Sartre later wrote:

> I was Roquentin; in him I exposed, without self-satisfaction, the web of my life; at the same time I was myself, the elect, the chronicler of hells.
>
> (*Words*, p. 156)

Nausea offers a powerful critique of bourgeois life as well as a description of a disintegrating psyche. Some psychedelic passages in the novel were possibly influenced by Sartre's depression of 1935, during which he had allowed himself to be injected with mescaline by his friend Daniel Lagache, then an intern in psychiatry in a nearby hospital.[21] For months afterwards, Sartre suffered flash-backs, in particular the hallucination that he was being followed by a lobster. In the novel, Roquentin has a growing experience of alienation from objects, which seem to touch him as if they were alive. His own face in the mirror appears to him to be an alien thing. He sees a hand not as part of a human body, but as a kind of fat slug resting on the table. He experiences bouts of nausea and vertigo brought on by the sheer contingent senseless facts of existence, the feeling that everything is 'superfluous', *de trop* (*Nausea*, p. 184). The climax of the novel is an existential experience of pure existence: "existence is being there" (*Existence, c'est être là, Nausea*, p. 188). Staring at a tree root in a park, the narrator has a 'horrible ecstasy' (*une extase horrible*), an experience of existence itself:

It had lost its harmless appearance as an abstract category: it was the very stuff of things, that root was steeped in existence. Or rather the root, the park gates, the bench, the sparse grass on the lawn, all that had vanished; the diversity of things, their individuality, was only an appearance, a veneer. This veneer had melted, leaving soft, monstrous masses, in disorder – naked, with a frightening obscene nakedness.

(Nausea, p. 183)

In fact, Sartre had earliler written to de Beauvoir, in a letter dated 9 October 1931, about a possibly similar experience of contemplating a tree in Le Havre for some twenty minutes, trying to discover the essence of the tree.[22] Having exhausted every attempt to make the tree into something else, he came to realise that, in the very resistance and refusal of the tree to come into his consciousness, he had in fact intuited the essence of the tree. Elsewhere, in his *War Diaries*, Sartre writes about those philosophical moments where something is grasped and understood. These moments are conceptually impoverished, yet, on the other hand, they are truly metaphysical:

For many students, their first contact with philosophy had expressed itself as a kind of amazement – which was genuinely existential and authentic, though pretty silly for all that – at death, time, the existence of other consciousnesses. The Beaver, precisely, didn't escape this, because she's more naturally authentic than me. At the age of eighteen, she was sitting on an iron chair in the Luxembourg Gardens, leaning back against the Museum wall and thinking: "I'm here, time is flowing by and this instant will never return", and this caused her to fall into a state of stupefaction resembling sleep. But this philosophical poverty is, in reality, very authentic philosophy: it's the moment at which the question transforms the questioner.

(War Diaries, p. 85)

In the novel *Nausea*, the encounter with the tree reveals the pure, alien, contingent, sheer facticity of things, something which is experienced as dizzying. This experience of nausea at the very fact of existence provides an illumination to the narrator: life is absurd.

The essential thing is contingency. I mean that by definition, existence is not necessity. To exist is simply to be there; what exists appears, lets itself be encountered, but you can never deduce it. There are people, I believe, who have understood that. Only they have tried to overcome this contingency by inventing a necessary, causal being. But no necessary being can explain existence: contingency is not an illusion, an appearance which can be dissipated; it is absolute, and consequently perfectly gratuitous.

(*Nausea*, p. 188)

Passages such as these introduce the notion of pure existence as something completely contingent, absurd, and yet everywhere. "Existence is a plenum which man cannot leave", Sartre says, very much echoing Levinas's description of existence in *De l'evasion*, published some three years earlier in 1935. Sartre is describing the encounter with *être en-soi*, being in-itself.

The success of his literary efforts stimulated Sartre to plunge himself into an extraordinary amount of diverse projects. He planned a major work of phenomenological psychology, *La Psyché* (*The Soul*), but after writing 400 pages, he abandoned it, only publishing a small fragment as *Esquisse d'une théorie des émotions* (*Sketch for a Theory of the Emotions*)[23] in December 1939, where Sartre argues that emotions act by incantation to create a magical world. When our reason fails, our emotions act to effect a kind of magical attainment of what we have failed to get rationally. Sartre begins with a critique of William James who maintained that emotions are our reactions to physiological processes going on in us. Our emotions are not blind processes caused in us, nor are the emotions themselves the object of our intentions. They are stances adopted by us towards things and events in the world. A hatred towards Paul is not a feeling, but a certain orientation towards Paul, a way of relating to him: "the emotional consciousness is primarily consciousness *of* the world" (*Sketch*, p. 56). Furthermore, it is a way of relating to the world which effects a transformation of that world. Sartre also sketches here his critique of the psychoanalytic account of the unconscious and affirms his view that there is a pre-reflective *cogito* implicit in all conscious experiences. The following year, in 1940, he published his second study of imagination, *L'imaginaire*, translated as *The Psychology of Imagination*,[24] a follow-up to his 1936 study. *L'imaginaire* is a deliberately phenomenological study, as the subtitle, "A Phenomenological Psychology of the Imagination", suggests. We shall discuss this work in detail later in this chapter.

The war years

Sartre's bourgeoning literary and philosophical career was suddenly interrupted by the outbreak of war; and indeed he would later write that the war divided his life in two (Cohen-Solal, p. 131). On 1 September 1939 Germany invaded Poland, and, on the same day, the French government issued orders for general mobilisation. Sartre was conscripted into the French Army, as a private in the meteorological service attached to an artillery division stationed near Strasbourg. The almost surreal experience of official disorganisation and incompetence left Sartre bemused and detached. In particular, he found himself forced to share his living quarters with ordinary people, a new experience for a man who mostly lived in hotels. During the "phony war" of 1939–1940, Sartre found himself with little to do, so he began a diary, the surviving parts of which were published posthumously as *Carnets de la drôle de guerre* (*War Diaries. Notebooks of a Phony War*). He also started work on the first book, *Les Chemins de la liberté* (*Roads to Freedom*), of what eventually would become his trilogy of novels, *The Age of Reason. The War Diaries*, a neglected masterpiece, shows that Sartre was already well advanced in sketching out the ideas which would eventually be published in *Being and Nothingness* (1943). Sartre has long discussions on contingency, facticity, on the experience of freedom, on the nature of the in-itself and for-itself, on consciousness as negativity, and on the nature of anxiety as an existential category rather than a psychological state. Many of Sartre's more famous formulations in *Being and Nothingness* are already to be found in the *War Diaries*, for example "consciousness is defined as being what it is not and not being what it is" (*War Diaries*, p. 178). Indeed, in many ways, the *War Diaries* is a clearer and more accessible version of *Being and Nothingness* which shows Sartre's thought evolving. These diaries are also important in that they explicitly situate Sartre's thinking on being and nothingness in relation to Descartes's distinction between extension and consciousness.

The phony war ended with the German advance and the French armistice signed by Marshal Pétain. Sartre was made prisoner of war on his birthday, 21 June 1940, his surrender coinciding both with the announcement of the terms of the armistice and with his first glimpse of the German Army! He was detained in a number of camps, first at Baccarat, then, in August 1940, he was moved to Stalag XIID at Trier, where he began to hold philosophy discussions with a number of priests. From one of the priests Sartre received a copy of Heidegger's *Sein und Zeit*, smuggled into the camp from the nearby Benedictine Abbey. Sartre had gradually been shifting his allegiances from Husserl to Heidegger. He remarks in his diary on 23 April 1940: "My novel is clearly Husserlian, which I find rather distressing considering that I am now a partisan of Heidegger" (Cohen-Solal, p. 141). The new interest in Heidegger was mainly due to Sartre's awakening interest in historicity and his realisation that we find ourselves in a world of irrationality. He began writing *Being and Nothingness* in the Stalag camp in the autumn of 1940. There, Sartre also wrote and produced a Christmas play, *Bariona ou le fils de thonnerre* (*Bariona or the Son of Thunder*) set in Bethlehem. This play, with the Roman soldiers symbolising the German occupation, was something of a protest against the German occupation, but nevertheless was not censored by the camp authorities.

At the end of March 1941 he was released from the camp, though the circumstances of his release are unclear. According to Sartre's biographer, Annie Cohen-Solal, Sartre was released owing to a fake medical certificate which testified that he had a form of partial blindness (Cohen-Solal, p. 159). Another account has it that he was released in a case of mistaken identity. Either way, he did not make a heroic escape, as is sometimes claimed. He was in fact put on a train to Paris where he was given an official release, which allowed him to resume his job teaching at the Lycée Pasteur, where he was reinstated only days after his rearrival in Paris (which could scarcely have happened if he were a fugitive). One of his students from that time, Jean-Bertrand Portalis, recalls that Sartre had changed, being more reserved and distant, and mute about current affairs. De Beauvoir also noticed the change in Sartre. He resented the German presence in Paris, and was initially shocked by some of the compromises de Beauvoir has been forced to make (she had signed a testimonial confirming that she was not a Jew to keep her job in the Lycée Henri IV). At the same time, as he later wrote, the Occupation suited him well. They had never been so free as under the Germans (Cohen-Solal, p. 218). He was never active in any form of serious opposition to the German occupation. In the summer of 1941, Sartre did attempt to found a short-lived group, *Socialisme et Liberté* with Merleau-Ponty and other intellectuals. The results were risible, as nobody could decide what to do, and a lot of time was spent talking in a room and drawing up impossible plans. One such plan was to enlist Gide as one of its members, which involved Sartre and de Beauvoir going off on a bicycle holiday in the south of France, ostensibly to find Gide. Gide did not join and Sartre's interest in resistance waned, and he turned to other matters including passing his time at the Café Flore and La Coupole, which had the advantage of being heated cafés, where he could write in comfort (the presence of German officers did not appear to be a difficulty).

Later in 1941 Sartre moved to the Lycée Condorcet, continuing to teach philosophy to an increasingly receptive student audience. In June 1943 his major study *Being and Nothingness* was published having been passed by the German censor. Initially its publication was hardly noticed in France and it received only a few reviews before 1945. For its immediate post-war audience, it proclaimed the end of the traditional philosophical and rationalist claim that human nature had a definite essence. As Sartre says of his efforts in *Being and Nothingness*, "I cheerfully demonstrated that man is impossible" (*Words*, p. 156).

Sartre, as we have seen, was a resolute atheist, but now he had a disproof of the existence of God. God defined as the 'in-itself-for-itself' (*En-Soi-Pour-Soi*, BN 623; 686–687) was in fact an impossible union of the two contrasted modes of being, *en-soi* and *pour-soi*. God was an ontological impossibility, a contradiction in terms. Having rejected the notion of a divined plan for humanity, he also rejected the very idea of a complete human nature, or of genuine order in the universe. The world is absurd. All meaning comes from human projection of meaning. Moreover, the error of traditional humanism is that it assumed we could go on working with the concept of a fixed human nature even in the absence of God. But a complete nature is not given to us from the outset, and therefore it is our task to make our own nature, to choose our own 'project' and not allow ourselves to be separated from it by some demand to be conventional, to act as one ought to act, and so on. Sartre takes over from Heidegger's *Being and Time* the notion of a 'project'. Man's project is to be God. However, no project will actually provide the self-completion we aspire to, and therefore, as Sartre concludes at the end of the book, "man is a useless passion" (*l'homme est une passion inutile*, BN 615; 678).

The war had changed things for ever. Paul Nizan had been killed in action, and Raymond Aron, who was Jewish, had fled to England. Meanwhile, Sartre passed through the war as an intellectual living relatively free under the German occupation, surviving as everyone else did. As Merleau-Ponty would later write, war compromises everyone. Sartre's most serious compromise with the Vichy regime came when he agreed to write an article on Melville's *Moby Dick* for a collaborationist weekly newpaper, *Comoedia*. This led to him being distrusted by members of the Resistance. In any event, Sartre was too well known and too talkative to be a useful member of the Resistance, so they left him alone. However, in 1943, Sartre did join the *Comité National des Écrivains*, an intellectual group which included Gide and others, and did contribute articles to their underground publications. Among the plays he wrote at this time was *Les Mouches* (*The Flies*, 1942),[25] for which Merleau-Ponty actually arranged the financial backing. It was during a dress rehearsal of his play that Sartre met Camus for the first time. The play, though set in ancient Greece, and based on the idea of Zeus as god of flies and death, was seen as a protest against the German occupation. *The Flies* also proclaims that humans are free and that "human life begins on the far side of despair" (*Flies*, p. 311). In 1944 he wrote in a matter of two weeks a new play, *Huis Clos* (*No Exit*), which premiered on 27 May 1944, and which contains the famous claim "hell is other people" (*l'enfer, c'est les autres*). During the days leading up to Liberation, Sartre wrote wonderfully evocative pieces about the fighting and the general situation in Paris for Albert Camus's journal *Combat*.

Les Temps modernes

In 1944 with the Liberation, Sartre founded a journal published by Gallimard, *Les Temps modernes* (the title is a deliberate reference to Charlie Chaplin's film, *Modern Times*), with Merleau-Ponty, Simone de Beauvoir, Raymond Aron, and others, on the Editorial Board. *Les Temps modernes* quickly developed into the leading intellectual journal of the period, publishing Samuel Beckett, Francis Ponge, Maurice Blanchot, Jean Genet, Nathalie Sarraute, among others. Sartre and de Beauvoir, who also had published several novels as well as several philosophical essays, were now both very well-known literary figures. From January to May 1945, at the instigation of Camus, and funded by the US State Department, Sartre visited the USA in the company of other journalists as a correspondent for *Combat* and for *Le Figaro*. During the visit they met with President Roosevelt at the White House. In the USA he also met *émigré* French intellectuals, including Claude Lévi-Strauss. Later in the year he returned to the USA to give lectures there, and this time he would meet Hannah Arendt, who, however, was not particularly impressed with him. Back in France, on 24 October 1945, Sartre gave his famous lecture "Existentialism is a Humanism", defending existentialism against the attacks of communist critics, who denounced it as a bourgeois philosophy, and against Catholic critics, who saw it as ignoble and a base portrayal of human life. The lecture was advertised in *Le Monde* and took place before a huge audience at the Club Maintenant. When it was published in 1946,[26] this essay, more than anything else, made Sartre an instant success in that it argued that existentialism was the only moral choice open to honest humans who recognised, with Dostoyevski, that if God is dead everything is permitted. Sartre argued that this recognition did not lead to amorality and nihilism, but rather that it brought the freedom back to individuals to make of their lives what they wanted. Sartre's only moral prescription is a version of the Kantian universalisability principle that one must act to promote one's own freedom and also the freedom of others. Soon after the original lecture was delivered, French philosophers, including Jean Wahl and Emmanuel Levinas, were debating the origins of existentialism. Levinas speculated that existentialism had its origins in the difference between *to be* and *being* found in Heidegger's work, and, indeed, Sartre's essay begins with a bowdlerised version of Heidegger's conception of Dasein, translated as '*la réalité humaine*', human reality. For Sartre, man makes himself what he is, and therefore his existence precedes his essence, unlike other entities such as pocket-knives whose essences are first conceived and then they are produced. There is no human nature because there is no God to make it, and hence man simply is.

Sartre spent the years from 1945 to 1947 working on the book on ethics promised at the end of *Being and Nothingness*. The uncompleted manuscript was finally published after his death.[27] However, in 1948, Simone de Beauvoir published her *The Ethics of Ambiguity* which was intended to be the ethical complement to Sartre's book.[28] Sartre also wrote essays on Camus and an important study of the issue of anti-Semitism, *Anti-Semite and Jew*, which he had completed as early as 1943, but which was not published until 1946.[29] Here he argued that an anti-Semitic attitude is not a merely accidental feature of a personality but is a 'passion' which is

> a free and total choice of oneself, a comprehensive attitude that one adopts not only towards Jews but towards men in general, towards

history and society; it is at one and the same time a passion and a conception of the world.

(Anti-Semite, p. 17)

One chooses such a passion in order to provide density and impenetrability to one's being, out of fear of facing up to one's own terrifying freedom. The anti-Semite chooses to be thus; he "chooses the permanence and impenetrability of stone" (*Anti-Semite*, p. 53). In 1947 he brought out his study of Baudelaire,[30] and an important series of essays on the philosophy of literature, translated as *What is Literature?*.[31] Here Sartre offers a vison of engaged literature (*littérature engagée*), arguing that to write is to reveal and that writers' words change things. Therefore, writers must be aware of their involvement (*embarquement*) in the world, in order to raise it to the level of a self-conscious commitment (*engagement*).

Post-war politics

Immediately after the war, Sartre had been critical of the French communists, proposing instead a revolutionary humanism, but he gradually came to the view that only a genuinely communist system could provide a salvation from the problems which afflicted society. In 1949 he travelled to Gautemala, Panama, and Cuba and in the same year Simone de Beauvoir published her long study, *The Second Sex*, which has become a classic of feminist theory. In 1950–1951 Sartre began to re-read Marx and in 1952 he published his major study of the French criminal dramatist and anti-hero Jean Genet, ironically entitled *Saint Genet*.[32] Sartre had met Genet in 1944 and had been championing him since the end of the war. In 1952 Sartre publicly broke with Camus. His relations with Camus had always been mercurial; he had not liked Camus's *The Rebel* (1951) and had initially refused to carry a review of it in *Les Temps modernes* and then carried a negative review written by Francis Jeanson.[33] When Camus protested, Sartre wrote a farewell to their friendship. Between 1952 and 1954 Sartre published in *Les Temps modernes* his rapprochement with Soviet communism, *The Communists and Peace*. In 1956, however, he condemned the Soviet invasion of Hungary and later in 1968 condemned the crushing of the Czech revolution. He broke completely with Soviet Marxism and its French counterpart, the French Communist Party, and began to adopt a more independent critique of colonialism in the developing world. It was not until 1977 that he finally renounced Marxism as a political philosophy.

Sartre had always been interested in but critical of Freud. In 1958 the film director John Huston commissioned Sartre to write a screenplay on the life of the founder of psychoanalysis. Sartre wrote a draft and briefly travelled to Ireland to discuss it with Huston in 1959.[34] It appears that John Huston, something of a country squire with a passion for horse-riding, was somewhat taken aback by the dishevelled Sartre who talked incessantly. Sartre agreed to rewrite the script but ended up enlarging it so much that it would have emerged as a film seven hours long! In the end the film appeared having been reworked by other writers.

In 1957 Sartre turned again to philosophy, and specifically discovered the nature of dialectic in the writings of Hegel and Marx. He began writing his second major opus, *Critique of Dialectical Reason*, which was not published until 1960, though he published a long preface, *Questions de méthode* (*Questions of Method*), in 1957 in *Les Temps modernes*.[35] This proclaimed the possibility of situating existentialism within the historical analysis of human nature offered by Marxism. Sartre now had drawn away from existentialism as an outdated fashion, and instead proposed to use a 'regressive–progressive method' to examine the totalisation of knowledge and the historical forces at work in this totalisation. Whereas *Being and Nothingness* is about the individual in a universal way, the *Critique* is about the social and concrete.[36] Sartre, who once accepted that historical materialism was the only valid approach to history, now rejects the "Scholasticism of the totality" found in recent Marxism (*Search for a Method*, p. 28).

Throughout the 1960s Sartre was the very symbol of public protest. In 1960 he again visited Cuba with de Beauvoir and met Castro and Che Guevara. He became active in the Algerian controversy in France, writing many articles condemning the French government's refusal to recognise Algerian independence. There was even a bomb attack on his flat at this time. In July 1966 he joined Bertrand Russell's Tribunal investigating war crimes in Vietnam. He sided with the students and workers during the events of May 1968 and participated in public debates at the Sorbonne with Daniel Cohn-Bendit. He gradually moved from Soviet communism to supporting the Maoists (without actually becoming a Maoist), and in 1970 became editor of their paper, *La Cause du peuple*. In 1974 he protested against the mistreatment of members of the Baader-Meinhof Group in German jails. He visited Andreas Baader in prison and interviewed him. Meanwhile he also found time to write a huge study of Flaubert, *The Idiot of the Family*, published in three volumes between 1971 and 1972.[37] Like his other biographies, they tell us more about Sartre than about their subjects, but Sartre here sets out to explore Flaubert by exploring everything around him – his history, his society, and so on. In the early 1970s, after a number of heart attacks, his eyesight began to fail. Nevertheless he participated in a three-hour film on himself, *Sartre par lui-même*, made in 1976 and continued to give interviews. He died on 15 April 1980 after increasingly debilitating illnesses and incontinence, later chronicled by Simone de Beauvoir. His funeral procession to the cemetery of Montparnasse on 19 April was attended by a huge crowd of some 50,000 people and was televised nationally. A second incomplete section of *Critique of Dialectical*

Reason was published in French in 1985 and, most recently, the unfinished *Notebooks for an Ethics*. A number of manuscripts remain to be edited.

Despite his commitment to various causes, Sartre retained to the end an independent and Bohemian streak. He was, as his own biographical portrait attests, always utterly self-obsessed, convinced that he was a genius. He also could be quite an opportunist when it came to seeking publicity for himself and his ideas. However, he was always a fascinating companion, generous with the money he earned, and entirely uninterested in material possessions, living in his mother's small flat and in hotels for much of his life.[38] Sartre had become rich on the basis of his prodigious literary output, but he always lived in Bohemian style and generously supported a large entourage of hangers-on, members of Sartre and de Beauvoir's extended 'family'. He consumed large quantities of alcohol and drugs, especially amphetamines (Schilpp, p. 11), and was an inveterate tobacco smoker to the end. In many ways, Sartre's policy of engagement and of active intervention in current affairs means that much of his work seems dated. His adventures into Marxist theory were never very successful. Though he claimed to be closely following a materialist dialectic, one instead gets the impression that Sartre was erecting yet another massive metaphysical system. Nevertheless, Sartre's prose style and the mere force of his personality continue to attract readers. Sartre is extremely original in his manner of reading or interpreting the ideas of others. In this respect, Sartre anticipated many of the claims of later French authors, especially Derrida, who tended, however, to neglect Sartre. We shall now turn to an examination of some of Sartre's key works in so far as they shed light on his understanding of phenomenology.

The Transcendence of the Ego (1936)

Sartre's first published work was a study of the ego which seeks to repudiate the traditional view that the ego is an inhabitant of consciousness, whether as an element to be found 'materially' in consciousness (as some psychologists maintain), or, as the Kantians hold, as a formal organisational aspect of consciousness. Rather the ego is outside consciousness altogether, "a being of the world, like the ego of the other" (*un être du monde, comme l'Ego d'autrui*, TE 31; 85). I never encounter myself in active, engaged consciousness, and, at best, I have a pre-reflective awareness of myself at this stage. However, this stage can be reflected on. The essay, probably influenced by Aron Gurwitsch's interpretation of Husserl's concept of consciousness, is an exceptionally clearly written piece, with many remarks which prefigure much of Sartre's later ontology. In fact, Sartre always retained this analysis of the ego (see Schilpp, p. 10). Overall, however, much of the argumentation is quite weak, as is quite to be expected in a first published essay, and it relies on an idealistic language, particularly in its notion of a consciousness which limits itself.

Sartre begins with Kant's celebrated remark that the "I think must be able to accompany all our representations", and acknowledges that Kant himself treated the unity of consciousness as a purely formal requirement, a set of conditions for the possibility of an empirical consciousness, and not a thing, but he explicitly criticises the Neo-Kantians for having reified the transcendental ego (TE 33; 86). Against the Neo-Kantians and the empiricists, Sartre turns instead to Husserlian phenomenology, which, through the *epoché*, allows us access to self-consciousness in its concrete reality, and allows us to understand the I as a concrete existent thing. Sartre, however, criticises Husserl for positing a pure ego behind consciousness, whereas in fact the self is a projection from consciousness and lies outside it like an object. Sartre accepts Husserl's account of a constituting transcendental consciousness, but he rejects the idea that we need to make this into an ego:

> Like Husserl, we are persuaded that our psychic and psycho-physical *me* (*notre moi psychique et psycho-physique*) is a transcendent object which must fall before the *epoche*. But we raise the following question: is not this psychic and psycho-physical *me* enough? Need one double it with a transcendental I (*un Je transcendantal*), a structure of absolute consciousness?

(TE 36; 87–88)

There is therefore no transcendental *ego* for Sartre. It is a doubling up of consciousness, 'superfluous', indeed the "death of consciousness" (*la mort de la conscience*, TE 40; 90). Instead, Sartre proposes a distinction between the empirical ego which is an object of consciousness and what he calls the 'transcendental field' (*le Champ transcendantale*, TE 93; 117) which is pre-personal, a non-I, a 'nothing' (*un rien*). This field of consciousness is a nothing precisely because it is the consciousness of all things. Sartre, then, accepts a version of Husserl's account in the *Logical Investigations* of the empirical ego as a "synthetic and transcendent production of consciousness", but he believes Husserl's account of the individual and personal transcendental ego in *Ideas* I is wrongheaded (TE 37; 88). Instead Sartre argues for a pre-personal upsurge of consciousness towards the world, and a pre-reflective '*cogito*' quite distinct from the Cartesian reflective *cogito*. It is not that I have consciousness of a chair but *there is* consciousness of the chair. In *Transcendence of the Ego* Sartre further argues that 'non-positional' consciousness of self is the necessary and sufficient condition of consciousness of objects. Sartre argues that if consciousness were not self-consciousness it would not be consciousness at all:

> Indeed the existence of consciousness is an absolute because consciousness is consciousness of self.

(TE 40; 90)

Consciousness is aware of itself because it is aware of objects. This is essentially an endorsement of the Cartesian position whereby all consciousness must be at least in principle capable of self-consciousness. My own consciousness of myself is not 'positional' (*positionelle*, TE 41; 90), because I grasp myself in the act of positing some object other than myself. In ordinary consciousness the 'I' never appears; it appears only on the basis of a reflective act, the reflexive *cogito*. There is no 'I' in the unreflected consciousness. There is only consciousness of the streetcar-having-to-be-overtaken, when I am chasing a streetcar (TE 49; 94). But there is also no 'I' in the reflecting consciousness: "there is an unreflected act of reflection (*un acte irréfléchi de réflexion*), without an I, which is directed on a reflected consciousness" (TE 53; 96). Those who want to maintain that all our acts are motivated by egoism, and hence that the ego resides materially in consciousness, have also misunderstood the matter. In particular they have confused the structures of unreflected acts and reflective acts. Sartre analyses a situation in which I pity Peter and go to help him. Unreflectively, there is only the object 'Peter-to-be-helped'. Though psychologists want to place a second layer in the act, whereby I help Peter in order to bring about an end to some disagreeable state in me, this confuses the unreflected with the reflected act. In both cases, the object transcends the act. The unreflected has ontological priority over the reflected and not the other way round. Sartre eventually claims that the distinction between the I and the me is simply functional. The 'I' is a centre of actions whereas the 'me' (*le Moi*) is a centre of states and qualities (TE 60; 99).

In this first essay, Sartre offers his interpretation of Husserl's notion of intentionality. Intentionality, for Sartre, is the doctrine of the self-transcendence of consciousness. Consciousness "unifies itself by escaping from itself" (*elle s'unifie en s'échappant*, TE 38; 88). It is the transcendent object which founds the unity of consciousness; there is no need to posit a unifying agent of consciousness on the part of the subject. Consciousness makes possible the unity of the 'I' and therefore there is no need for phenomenology to posit a transcendental ego prior to consciousness. Sartre points out that Husserl, in his analyses of internal time consciousness, admits the need for syntheses linking consciousness of present and past, but points out that this can be done without introducing the I as this synthetic power (TE 39; 89). In this sense Sartre holds that consciousness limits itself. This is unsatisfactory. Consciousness is supposed to be purely a negating power which latches on to the in-itself. How can it possess this self-limiting power? Sartre is unable to answer this question.

In this essay, moreover, Sartre is already operating with the dualistic ontology which surfaces in *Being and Nothingness*. Everything which is not consciousness is the *en-soi*, so any ego is not something in or behind consciousness but rather something external to and transcending consciousness. According to Sartre:

All is therefore clear and lucid in consciousness: the object with its
characteristic opacity is before consciousness, but consciousness is
purely and simply consciousness of being consciousness of that object.

(TE 40; 90)

The object is already characterised as heavy, opaque, impenetrable, 'passive'
(TE 79; 109). In this text, Sartre makes good criticisms of Husserl's concept
of the ego as a 'subject pole' and gives a good account of the essential
passivity of conscious experience as well as of the nature of constitution.
But it is clear that he sees Husserl as having announced a new ontology –
the ontology of objects and the consciousness which are correlative to them.

L'Imaginaire (1940): the phenomenology of imagining

Sartre followed up his essay on Husserl with two books devoted to a
psychological and phenomenological study of imagination. The earlier 1936
study, L'imagination, contained more of Sartre's criticisms of previous
theories, including those of Berkeley, Hume, and Bergson, as well as the
psychologists Bühler, Titchener, Köhler, Wertheimer, Koffka, and other
experimental psychologists. Sartre's second study, L'Imaginaire, in 1940,
offers his own positive, *descriptive* account, a phenomenological study of
the nature and role of imaginative consciousness, an account which eschews
philosophical theories. The French term '*imaginaire*' is a difficult concept,
usually translated as the 'imaginary'. It suggests both the function of
imagining and the kind of world which this imagining generates. For Sartre,
this connotes the noematic correlate of acts of imaginative or fictive
consciousness. In Cartesian fashion, the first part of the essay is entitled
'The Certain', and the second section 'The Probable', referring to what can
be grasped with certainty from the self-aware nature of conscious acts.
Again Sartre gives his Cartesian account of consciousness. Alongside the
various modes of thetic positing, consciousness always possesses a non-
thetic, non-positional self-awareness:

It is necessary to repeat at this point what has been known since
Descartes: that a reflective consciousness gives us knowledge of absolute certainty; that he who becomes aware of "having an image"
by an act of reflection cannot deceive himself.

(PI 1; 13)

The latter half of the book deals with the imaginary in thinking, in emotion,
and in life generally. The book is a fascinating extension of Husserl's
account of imagining, with insightful analyses of various kinds of imagining
and depicting, as well as a more speculative theorising about the nature of

consciousness in general. It is, like all Sartre's works, written in a vivacious if repetitive style, full of sound psychological observations, but also quite speculative in an unconstrained way. It argues strongly against all traditional representationalist theories of imagination and instead sees imagining as a mode of being in the world. However, Sartre cannot avoid reimporting a certain representationalism into his own account, as we shall see. Sartre also points out that imagining, like emotion, promises more than it delivers. There is an essential failure of imagination to accomplish what it promises to do.

Sartre begins from, but takes issue with, Husserl's account of imagining as a kind of consciousness which depends on perception. Rather, imagination is an independent type of consciousness, not derivative from or reducible to perception, one whose acts generate *sui generis* objects (PI 107; 183). Against Descartes, who, in the Sixth Meditation, sees sensing and imagining as products of the combination of pure consciousness with an extended physical body, and hence extraneous to pure consciousness, Sartre argues that imagining is a central feature of consciousness; imagining plays the crucial role of *constituting* the world as such. Furthermore, for Sartre, imagination is unthinkable without freedom; it is because humans possess the ability to think of things *as they are not* that they are able to exercise freedom. Especially in the concluding chapter of this work Sartre's analysis of imagination anticipates his account of human freedom as a nihilating power in *Being and Nothingness* (1943).

Imagining is a form of consciousness, and since consciousness is intrinsically intentional, so imagining is a kind of consciousness of an *object*. Drawing on Husserl's emphasis on the intentionality of consciousness, Sartre argues that imagining is a form of intending an object:

All consciousness is consciousness *of* something. Non-reflective consciousness is directed towards objects different in kind from consciousness: for example, the imaginative consciousness of a tree is directed towards a tree, that is, a body which is by nature external to consciousness; consciousness rises out of itself, it transcends itself.

(PI 10; 28)

Rejecting immanentist and representational theories of imagining, Sartre claims that in ordinary life we are misled about what is given in imagination, misled by a prevalent illusion, which he names '*the illusion of immanence*' (*illusion d'immanence*, PI 2; 16), whereby we think that imagined pictorial images are actually little pictures or events *within* consciousness and not in the world. But, for Sartre, these images are not in consciousness at all; they are, rather, modes of appearing of the object imagined. Images are not to be thought of as entities like pictures, they are purely relational, a *relation* between consciousness and the object: "an image is nothing else than a relationship" (*une image n'est rien autre qu'un rapport*, PI 5; 20), an orientation towards the object. We are not conscious of an image of an object, but have an imaginative consciousness of the object. Sartre continued to endorse this view to the end of his life (Schilpp, p. 15). Similar to the manner in which Sartre, in *Sketch for a Theory of the Emotions* (1939), had already characterised our emotional life, the act of imagining is here treated as a kind of magical possession of its object. Imagining, Sartre says, is a magical act:

> We have seen that the act of imagination is a magical one. It is an incantation destined to produce the object of one's thought, the thing of one's desires, in such a way that one can take possession of it. In that act there is always something of the imperious and the infantile, a refusal to take distance or difficulties into account. Just so does the very young child act upon the world from his bed by orders and entreaties. The objects obey these orders of consciousness.
>
> (PI 141; 239)

Imagining, then, is, as Husserl had already discussed in some detail, a special way of making objects present.

At the outset, Sartre distinguishes a number of specific features of imagining: it is a form of consciousness which is 'quasi-observational', meaning that it projects beyond what is actually given in perception, since outer awareness gives only a partial one-sided glance at the object, in which the object is given in a series of profiles or *Abschattungen* (PI 7; 22). The objects of imagining are, as it were, tainted by a kind of nothingness, and imagining is characterised by .a deep *spontaneity* that causes images to spring up in our minds, and acts of will whereby we deliberately set about constructing or contemplating an image. He also claims that whereas in perception we grasp objects serially and in profiles, in conception we grasp objects directly and as a whole. However, perception and imagination are radically different processes. They are both forms of thetic awareness, and both carry non-thetic awareness of themselves, but whereas perception posits its object as actually existing and the perception as a kind of passivity before the object; imagination posits it as absent, or elsewhere or as non-existing, or else it suspends judgement about whether it exists or not. According to Sartre, perception posits the object as existing, whereas the object of imagining either does not exist and is not posited as existing or it is not posited (*posé*) at all (PI 13; 32). There is in imagining an object the "immediate awareness of its nothingness" (*la conscience immédiate de son néant*, PI 13; 33). For Sartre, we can never completely deceive ourselves into believing that the imagined object really exists. Adapting Husserl's notion of the bodily givenness (*Leibhaftigkeit*) of the object in perception, Sartre claims that the 'flesh' (*la chair*), the intimate texture, of the object is not the same in imagination as in perception. "By flesh I understand the intimate texture" (*Par 'chair' j'entends la contexture intime*, PI 15; 37). Whereas the perceived object has an indefinitely rich set of shadings and possible perspectives (a rich horizon), an infinity implicit in every actual perception, the imagined object is rather limited, never fully itself, possessing an 'essential poverty' (PI 151; 255). Sartre is here expanding on Husserl's claim that imagining, in contrast to perception where the object is present *in propria persona*, recognises the absence of the object.

Sartre makes the strong claim that focusing on the image given in imagination can never be a source of knowledge. This "essential poverty" (PI 8; 24) in the image means that we find in the image only what we have put there. If I imagine the Parthenon, I gain no knowledge from counting the columns given in the image. Images are not faded versions of original impressions, they are not quasi-objects, they are not objects at all, they don't meet the requirements to be existing objects of any kind. Interestingly, in this analysis, Sartre is implicitly rejecting a central plank of Husserl's methodology, namely that, through imaginative variation, we can arrive at new essential truths about an object. Sartre denies that we gain any new knowledge from imagination, and goes against Husserl in denying that mathematicians have gained new knowledge from the contemplation of shapes in consciousness:

> If I amuse myself by turning over in my mind the image of a cube, if I pretend I see its different sides, I shall be no further ahead at the close of the process than I was at the beginning: I have learned nothing.
>
> (PI 7; 23)

According to Sartre, although I grasp the image in an act of quasi-observation, I can learn nothing from it:[39]

> Our attitude is, indeed, one of observation, but it is an observation which teaches nothing. If I produce an image of a page of a book, I am assuming the attitude of a reader, I *look* at the printed pages. But I am not *reading*. And actually I am not even *looking*, since I already *know* what is written there.
>
> (PI 9; 26)

Clearly, Sartre does not think that the kind of imaginary exploration or reconstruction of an event can ever yield new knowledge. But this seems to be an exaggeration. Surely a vivid recall of the image of a man could yield new information, for example the colour of his hair might be recognised on the basis of a studied recall.

For Sartre, as for Husserl, imagining involves a 'projective synthesis' that aims at Peter, the actual man. For Sartre, consciousness is "through and through a synthesis", relying on retention and protention. In this 1940 text, as in his earlier essay, Sartre has a view of consciousness as a 'synthetic unity'. Moreover, he denies that consciousnesses have causal relations between them. Rather the only relation is that of protention and retention at the heart of the consciousness itself; there are only "internal assimilations" and motivations (PI 27; 56). Sartre describes Husserl's concept of retention not as the possession of an image from the present, but that there is possession, as part of the knowledge of the now, of the realisation that the now is already an *after* (PI 84; 150). Protention presents this same sensation as also a *before*. Sartre offers a good phenomenological description of what occurs when I trace a figure of eight in the air with my index finger. I see the loops in the air as a completed figure and it remains there 'luminously' for moments after my finger has completed its trajectory (PI 84; 149).

Sartre gives a rather detailed phenomenological description of imagining, sharply distinguishing it from perceiving. This account is an elegant elaboration of Husserl's distinction between the kind of 'presentation' (*Gegenwärtigung*) which takes place in perception, as opposed to the re-presentation of calling to mind (*Vergegenwärtigung*), and empty signification. Recall involves a kind of bodily presentation but not one which is actually present. As Sartre explains, somewhat more clearly than Husserl, when I think of Peter I think of him bodily, "the Peter I can see, touch and hear", but, at this moment in recall, I know that I cannot touch him. On the other hand, according to Sartre, consciousness of a sign involves a directing of attention without positing anything as existent. To read the sign on the door, "Office of the Assistant Manager", draws our attention to something without positing (PI 24; 51). Sartre rejects the notion that the sign operates by resemblance to the thing signified. He shifts attention to art works, cartoons, and so on, noting the whole context of human intentions presupposed in perceiving these works.

> When I look at a drawing I posit in that very glance a world of human intentions of which that drawing is a product.
>
> (PI 39; 53)

Let us recall Peter from a photograph and from a sketch. This leads him to distinguish between empty intending such as we relate to signs, and a kind of recall that brings the person Peter present for us: "The picture thus delivers Peter, though Peter is not here" (PI 25; 53). Peter is presented as absent. For Sartre, the nature of a sign is completely different, it does not present the object, Peter, at all. In a sketch or schematic drawing or caricature, the image is stripped to a few poor signs. For Sartre what happens is that there is a shift from a perception to an act of imagining: I *see* a set of lines and I *imagine* them as a face (PI 34; 68). Sartre gives some detailed suggestions as to how this linking of the sign to the object takes place. In part the function of drawing is connected to the nature of the eye. The lines of certain kinds of drawing are not static but operate by giving certain rules of movement to the eye (PI 37; 72). Sartre is conscious of the manner my eye moves along the line (from left to right or bottom to top) in part dictated by the contour and inclination of the line itself. In his discussion of the manner we observe lines, Sartre cites the Müller–Lyer illusion (PI 36; 71) some five years before Merleau-Ponty's discussion of it in his *Phenomenology of Perception* (1945). According to Sartre, our judgement about the length of the lines is determined by our eye traversing the line and running up against a closed angle as opposed to an open one.

Although closely following Husserl's analysis of perception, Sartre disagrees with Husserl about the nature of the image and its relation to the intending consciousness. For Husserl there is a 'fulfilment' (*Erfüllung*) of meaning in an image; that is, we can have an empty intention which is then filled by the image. For example, I can hear the word 'sparrow' and merely understand that it refers to a bird, or I can have an intuitive presentation of a sparrow, an image which then provides a kind of intuitive fulfilment for the act of intending. Sartre, on the other hand, cannot admit that first there is empty consciousness and then consciousness "filled in" with an image. Sartre believes Husserl himself fell prey in this regard to the *illusion of immanence* (PI 65; 118). However, ultimately, Sartre's attempt to account for imagination without positing an internal image runs aground in that he is forced to posit some kind of 'analogon' in the act which serves to recall or signify the imagined object. His account of imagining, though an interesting attempt to get beyond representationalism, ends up endorsing what it sets out to reject.

The *Psychology of Imagination* does have other interesting things to say – about dreams, hallucinations, and so on. For example, Sartre discusses the case of imaginative disgust, nausea, and vomiting, brought on by imagining a repugnant object. He does not want to say that the image *causes* the behaviour, as the unreal object is an effect and never a cause. On the other hand, he also wants to deny that the appearance of the image is a mere epiphenomenon which makes no difference to the event (PI 159; 267). Sartre wants to claim that the disgust is disgust of itself rather than being brought on by an object as in the case of disgust caused by a perception. Similarly, at the end of the book, Sartre raises the metaphysical question of what the nature of a consciousness capable of imagining must be. For Sartre, this question can only be approached phenomenologically, from within the transcendental reduction. The very essence of consciousness is that it is *constitutive of a world*, and in order to be such it must be able to free itself from the world:

For consciousness to be able to imagine, it must be able to escape the world by its very nature; it must be able by its own efforts to withdraw from the world. In a word it must be free.

(PI 213; 353–354)

Sartre focuses on the free, negating power of consciousness with regard to the real world; consciousness is a power of withdrawal. This theme will be fully developed in Sartre's next book, *Being and Nothingness*. Already in 1940, as we have seen, Sartre refers to the negating power of consciousness (*la fonction néantisatrice propre à la conscience*), invoking Heidegger, as '*dépassement*' (PI 217; 358). Sartre is already describing human being as "crushed in the world, run through by the real" and freedom as a "lack, an empty space" (*un manque, un vide*, PI 217; 360). Consciousness has a power of "annihilating" (*anéantissant*) the world (PI 210; 348) but at the same time it is totally caught up in being in the world. Sartre concludes then that imagination is not an additional or contingent aspect of consciousness but "it is the whole of consciousness as it realizes its freedom" (PI 216; 358).

Being and Nothingness (1943): phenomenological ontology

The sub-title of Sartre's *Being and Nothingness* is "Essay on Phenomenological Ontology", which suggests the influence of Heidegger's *Being and Time*, which Sartre had begun reading in 1940. However, as we have seen, *Being and Nothingness* is more accurately understood as offering a purely speculative metaphysics of a very traditional kind, the very kind repudiated by Husserl, Heidegger, and the phenomenological tradition generally. Thus, Sartre presents an ontological proof of the world at the beginning of the book. It begins from the assumption of intentionality: that all consciousness is consciousness of something. It then moves on to say what consciousness is aware of is not consciousness. Therefore what consciousness is aware of is being. Of course, the argument assumes what it sets out to prove, namely that the object of consciousness is a being beyond consciousness.

Sartre begins *Being and Nothingness* by arguing that modern philosophy is characterised by a rejection of the distinction between being and appearance (he is perhaps thinking of the phenomenalisms of Comte or Mach) and also by the distinction between thing in-itself and appearance. Sartre, on the other hand, wants only to recognise the distinction between the appearing and the whole series of appearances. The nature of the appearing is now all important and here Sartre endorses the phenomenological approach which recognises both the relativity of the phenomenon relative to a subject viewing it, and also the absoluteness of the phenomenon, since there is no assumption of a Kantian thing in-itself behind the phenomenon (BN xxii). Everything appears, so even the essence, which is the principle of the series of appearances, also appears, and this is why it can be grasped in what Husserl calls *Wesensschau*. However, with the realisation that every appearance of something is a one-sided *Abschattung*, there comes also the realisation that there are infinitely many possible ways of viewing the phenomenon; there is thus a certain transcendence of the object in our experience, the infinite in the finite (BN xxiii). The new problem becomes not the being behind appearance but the very being of appearances themselves. But since the 'being of appearances' must itself appear, there must be a *phenomenon of being* which itself announces itself. Sartre makes a sudden leap in reasoning to claim:

> Being will be disclosed to us by some kind of immediate access – boredom, nausea, etc., and ontology will be the description of the phenomenon of being as it manifests itself; that is, without inter-mediary.
>
> (BN xxiv; 14)

Sartre assumes that being is a phenomenon which is revealed in certain psychological states, a position which coincides with his descriptions in *Nausea*. However, he does not want to claim that all being reduces simply to the phenomenon of being. Sartre criticises Husserl for returning to a Berkeleyan *esse est percipi*. For Sartre, being cannot be reduced to the knowledge we have of it, since we would then have to have some kind of guarantee about the *being* of that knowledge. In fact, Sartre is arguing for a certain 'transphenomenality' in the phenomenon of being. Furthermore, idealism concerning being cannot be correct because it misunderstands the intentional nature of consciousness which is parasitic on being, and 'exhausts itself' in its positing of being (BN xxvii; 18). Sartre invokes Husserl's account of intentionality but now gives it a thoroughly original and non-Husserlian spin. Contrary to Husserl, who carefully distinguished the content and the object of intentional acts, Sartre claims that "there is no consciousness which is not a positing of a transcendent object, or if you prefer, that consciousness has no 'content' " (BN xxvii; 17). The first procedure of a philosophy is to expel everything out of consciousness, in order to establish the true connection of consciousness with the world (BN xxvii; 18). Sartre never seems to have accepted Husserl's account of the intentional object and the *noema*. He does not understand Husserl's intention to reduce everything to its manifestation for consciousness. For Sartre, all consciousness is grasping at the reality of being in-itself.

Sartre goes on to propose a simple dualism of two kinds of thing: beings and consciousness. Being is "divided into two regions without communica-tion" (*scindé en deux régions incommunicables*, BN xxxix; 30). Being in-itself is uncreated, neither active nor passive. Being is not necessary, since necessity is a feature of propositions and ideal meanings, not of beings (BN xlii; 33). Being in itself is contingent, superfluous, '*de trop*' (BN xlii; 33), again invoking a term for Being already employed in *Nausea*. Being for-itself, on the other hand, is never in complete identity with itself; it is a 'decompression of being' (*une décompression d'être*, BN 74; 112). While we cannot speak of the in-itself as being self-identical, since it does not have a 'self' or reflective level, we can speak of it as utterly coinciding. On the other hand, the for-itself is always fissured or fractured. Consciousness, the for-itself, even in its direct presence to self, never completely coincides with itself. Presence to self always implies a certain absence and distance (BN 77; 115–116). Self-conscious *pour soi* is pure 'translucency'. Sartre claims that consciousness is a 'non-thing', that it is a nothingness; everything belongs to being in-itself except consciousness which is pure for itself. For Sartre, consciousness is always oriented to and supported by what is not itself, namely being in-itself. Whereas, in his *War Diaries*, he was claiming that consciousness is its own foundation (*War Diaries*, p. 109), he now claims that the for-itself cannot found itself. Consciousness is a kind of 'nothingness' or 'gratuitousness' in the world. Consciousness arises as a "No!", as a rejection of what is. Following Heidegger, Sartre claims that nothingness is not an abstract noun formed on the basis of the possibility of the act of negation, rather it is the other way round: nothingness enables us to make negation. Sartre understands negation to be of two kinds. There is a form of negation, for example when I say 'a cat is not a dog', where the negation has no effect on either of the objects. There is another kind of negation which affects the object internally, as it were.

As Sartre has already argued in his earlier studies, every consciousness is already implicitly a self-consciousness. Self-consciousness is an "immediate, non-cognitive relation of self to itself" (BN xxix; 19). Every positional consciousness is at the same time a non-positional consciousness of self (BN xxix; 19). This self-consciousness is the only mode of existence possible for consciousness. The being of consciousness is the opposite of what traditional philosophy thought it to be. Consciousness is such that "in rising to the centre of being, it creates and supports its essence" (BN xxxi; 21), which is a set of possibilities. Consciousness is self-positing: "The existence of consciousness comes from consciousness itself" (*la conscience existe par soi*, BN xxxi; 22). Sartre has a peculiar and entirely unexplained view of a self-creating consciousness emerging at the heart of a brute being. He dismisses the possibility that consciousness emerges from the unconscious or from the physiological. This whole account in fact contradicts Sartre's equally strongly held view that consciousness is not its own foundation. There is not much point in trawling through Sartre's works for a more nuanced resolution of this contradiction. All one will succeed in doing is multiplying the assertions – one will not discover an argument.

The real merit of *Being and Nothingness* is, however, not this rather simplistic and unsustainable ontology, but the manner in which it provides close descriptions of various human situations which are rich in phenomenological and philosophical insight. Chief among these descriptions are accounts of what it is to be in 'bad faith' (*la mauvaise foi*), to adopt a 'persona' which is at odds with one's Protean shifting amorphous existence. Later Sartre himself would claim that *Being and Nothingness* presented an "eidetic analysis of self-deception (*mauvaise foi*)".[40] In bad faith, a person is denying their true choice. Thus in a situation where a woman meets a man on a first date, she may allow her hand to be casually held by her partner:

> We know what happens next; the young woman leaves her hand there, but she *does not notice* that she is leaving it. She does not notice because it happens by chance that she is at this moment all intellect.
>
> (BN 55–56; 91)

In other words, the woman has effected a divorce between her body and her mind, her desire and her decision. This for Sartre is 'bad faith'. Human consciousness is truly free, truly Protean. It can be anything, it is pure possibility. Yet, on the other hand, at every instant we are embedded in the historical situation, *situé*. Human nature is caught up in facticity, in what Sartre calls 'the situation'. Authenticity is how we respond to the situation in a manner which acknowledges and preserves our freedom. Husserl had characterised the situation known as 'mineness' (*Jemeinigkeit*), which Heidegger had analysed in *Being and Time* and made the basis of the possibility that one may appropriate one's life either in an 'authentic' (*eigentlich*) or in an 'inauthentic' (*uneigentlich*) manner. In a way, Sartre's *Being and Nothingness* is an extended meditation on these notions. To be authentic is to grasp one's freedom and recognise it. Being inauthentic means being in flight from one's freedom, attempting to cover it by clinging to a persona. In 'bad faith', I am merely mimicking myself. A man is playing at being a waiter and deliberately imitates the mechanical movements he associates with perfect serving.

Bad faith is a kind of self-deception. Sartre criticises Freud for the paradox involved in the notion of an unconscious which has repressed items it did not want to face. It must know of these items in order to repress them. Similarly in order to deceive ourselves we must be aware of what it is we want to keep from our selves: I must know in my capacity as deceiver the truth which is hidden from me in my capacity as the one deceived. Sartre argues that we cannot understand self-deception modelled on the structural feature of *Mitsein*, namely lying to others. According to Sartre lying is a characteristic feature of being-with-others. For Sartre, our encounter with others is a challenge. We wish to dominate them and they us. There is therefore struggle, along the lines discussed by Hegel in *The Phenomenology of Spirit*. Sartre's most interesting discussions concern the manner by which we come to consciousness of ourselves in the light of how others see us. Not only do we give ourselves projects, we also have ourselves as we are viewed by others, our being-for-others (*être-pour-autrui*). This is a 'third-person' perspective on ourselves.[41]

Sartre on the body

Being and Nothingness includes a long chapter on the body which was extremely influential for Merleau-Ponty's formulation of the concept of one's own body (*le corps propre*) in his *Phenomenology of Perception*. Though never fully developed, Sartre's account provides some interesting contrasts with Merleau-Ponty. First of all, Sartre has spoken on the for-itself solely in terms of consciousness; nevertheless, it is not disembodied consciousness. The for-itself in humans always resides in and expresses itself through a body. Furthermore, Sartre claims, following Gabriel Marcel, that I *am* my body, not that I *have* a body. However, Sartre has difficulties connecting this consciousness with the physical body. My body is not 'for me' like any other physical object. I do not apprehend my body in the way that I apprehend objects in the world. I have a first-person experience of my body as the basis of my action, as my centre of reference and orientation. It is part of my facticity that I always see things from a point of view (which of course could be another point of view, BN 308; 356). In a way, my body is for me something that I transcend and surpass in my intentions which are directed towards the world. I see other things as useful, or as having properties (the hammer is heavy), because my body mediates this information. As I write I use my pen to form the letters, but my hand is not an instrument in the same way: "I am my hand" (BN 323; 371). In a sense then, my body is everywhere in the world. If I do see my body (in X-rays and so on), then I do not see it as *my* body, but simply as a bit of the world: "I see my hand only in the way that I see this inkwell" (BN 304; 351). I see it as I see an external object, or as it is seen by another. What I do learn from my body, as seen externally, is my 'being-for-others' (*être-pour-autrui*, BN 305; 352). My body is what I see of myself and what others see of me. Like Merleau-Ponty, Sartre recognises the spatiality of the body, that things are presented as to the left or right of me. Unlike Merleau-Ponty, Sartre does not give any special significance to the phenomenon of 'double sensation', that is when one hand can touch another, and one has a sensation both of touch and of being touched. When I touch my leg to put a bandage on it, I surpass my leg as such and am now intending curing my leg. There is really, therefore, no such phenomenon as the double sensation. In later interviews with Simone de Beauvoir Sartre admitted always to feeling fearful of the possible failure of his body in skiing or swimming.[42] In the end, he is unable to integrate fully his account of self-creating consciousness and location in a body.

Sartre's influence

Sartre's philosophy is philosophy understood as a kind of brilliant literature. However, not all his writing ascends to the level of literary elegance. *Being and Nothingness* is excessively long, tediously repetitive, lacking any real structure, and replete with rhetorical flourishes, full of paradoxes and straightforward contradictions (not to mention inconsistencies in capitalisation and hyphenation, e.g. '*Pour-Soi*', '*pour soi*'). Part of the problem is that Sartre was obsessed with creating monuments to his genius. Even though he engaged in debates and interviews, these are always manifestations of himself. Sartre never seems to have had the patience to revise anything he wrote, and his lack of interest in academic life meant that he was never subject to scholarly constraints. Everything pours out in a breathless torrent of words. Sartre's ontology is so crude that philosophers such as Daniel Dennett have wondered how anyone could take it seriously. Sartre himself does not seem to know how to develop it. It seems to have arrived as an intuition, and to have been elaborated repetitively rather than justified. Nevertheless, there are wonderful psychological observations floating in this torrent. Sartre is at his best in showing in detail that there are many situations in which people are more free than they realise, that many of what they take to be their in-born psychological traits are in fact affectations, reactions to the situation.

In general, Sartre is today the most neglected of recent French philosophers. Derrida barely refers to him, yet Sartre's account of the non-presence of self to self is an important forerunner of Derrida's conception of *différance*. Similarly, in his *Notebooks for an Ethics*, Sartre discusses the ethical relation in terms of gift, which has become prominent in the work of Levinas and Derrida. There is some evidence of a new attention being paid to Sartre's work within analytic philosophy, especially the philosophy of mind, for example the studies of Gregory McCulloch and Kathleen Wider.[43] Sartre's greatest contributions to phenomenology are his very clear defence of a non-egological conception of consciousness, his careful discussion of different kinds of imaginative consciousness, and his wonderfully vivid accounts of the dynamics of intersubjective life.

12

MAURICE MERLEAU-PONTY
The phenomenology of perception

Introduction: a philosophy of embodiment

Maurice Merleau-Ponty (1908–1961) has made the most original and enduring contribution to post-Husserlian phenomenology in France, through his attempts to offer a radical description of the primary experiences of embodied human existence. In opposition to all forms of dualism, in his major work, *Phenomenology of Perception* (1945),[1] he offers a phenomenological account of our 'being-in-the-world' (*être au monde*) as a corrective to the distorted accounts of experience found, on the one hand, in rationalism, idealism, and what he calls 'intellectualism', and, on the other hand, in empiricism, behaviourism, and experimental science. If he had not died so early in his career, there is no doubt that he would have been regarded as the most brilliant of contemporary French philosophers, offering a very challenging and complex account of what he sees as the 'mysterious', 'paradoxical', 'ambiguous' nature of our embodiment in a world which seems pre-ordained to meet and fulfil our meaning-intending acts.

Maurice Merleau-Ponty: life and writings (1908–1961)

Maurice Merleau-Ponty was born in Rochefort-sur-Mer on the west coast of France on 14 March 1908. According to Sartre, Merleau-Ponty confessed to him that he had "never recovered from an incomparable childhood", where he had known, in Sartre's words, that "private world of happiness from which only age drives us" (*Situations*, p. 157). In fact, Sartre provides a rich insight into Merleau-Ponty's motivation for his lifelong attempts to develop a philosophy of the "beginnings of the beginning" by returning to the pre-reflective world of experience. Sartre sees this as Merleau-Ponty's attempt to recapture the immediacy of his happy childhood. Merleau-Ponty remained, for Sartre, like a child "surprised by everything" (*Situations*, p. 222).

When his father died in 1913, his family moved to Paris, and he was educated in the French *lycée* system, first at Janson-de-Sailly and then at

Louis-le-Grand, where, subsequently, Derrida too would study. In later interviews, Merleau-Ponty stated that he had always wanted to become a philosopher and, in 1926, he passed the rigorous entrance test to become a day student at the Ecole Normale Supérieure. There he first became acquainted with the young Jean-Paul Sartre, who had been a boarding student there since 1924. They first became acquainted when Sartre intervened in a dispute between some students and Merleau-Ponty who had been hissing at them for singing traditional songs.[2] Sartre's intervention diffused the matter, but the two men did not become closer friends at that time. Another student, Simone de Beauvoir, recalled Merleau-Ponty as a quiet, serious student, possessed of a "purely cerebral inquietude".[3] Moreover, in contrast to the atheist Sartre, the young Merleau-Ponty was still a committed believer at that time.

At the Ecole Normale Supérieure Merleau-Ponty took courses with the Neo-Kantian idealist Léon Brunschvicg (1869–1944), the most important philosopher in France active at the time (Bergson had retired from teaching), who emphasised the discovery of the transcendental ego and of philosophising as a kind of Cartesian reflection on the subject.[4] Brunschvicg's course treated various attempts and failures to gain knowledge of the Absolute.[5] Following Kant, Brunschvicg held that the thing-in-itself is unknown to us and that the world is the world created by knowledge, a view Merleau-Ponty in part espoused. In the *Phenomenology of Perception*, for instance, he rejected the possibility of a thing-in-itself which is not also known to us. Brunschvicg also accorded special primacy to the *cogito* and hence to the transcendental ego. From Brunschvicg, Merleau-Ponty took the notion that scientific knowledge "cannot be closed in on itself, that it is always an approximate knowledge, and that it consists in clarifying a pre-scientific world the analysis of which will never be finished" (*Primacy,* p. 20; see also PP 57; 69). Merleau-Ponty's earliest philosophical endeavours, however, were of a more traditional kind, and he wrote his diploma thesis on Plotinus, supervised by the classical scholar Emile Bréhier.[6] In 1930, a year after Sartre's graduation from the same institution, Merleau-Ponty achieved second place in the *agrégation de philosophie*.

Having completed his military service, Merleau-Ponty taught first at the Lycée de Beauvais (1931–1933) and then got a fellowship to do research from the Caisse Nationale de la Recherche Scientifique. From 1934 to 1935 he taught at the Lycée de Chartres, before returning to Paris in 1935 to become a tutor and doctoral student at the Ecole Normale. During these years, Merleau-Ponty's overall outlook was that of a Christian socialist. He was associated with left-wing Catholic intellectual journals such as *Sept* and *Esprit*, edited by the Christian philosopher Emmanuel Mounier. His first publications were reviews, in the French journal *La Vie Intellectuelle*, of books by two philosophers who combined existentialism with Catholicism:

the French translation of Max Scheler's *Ressentiment in der Moral* and Gabriel Marcel's *Être et avoir* (*Being and Having*, 1935).[7] Merleau-Ponty, however, was deeply shocked by the role of the Catholic Church in supporting action by Dollfus against the workers in Austria. Similarly, the Church's support for violent dictators alienated Merleau-Ponty and precipitated a religious crisis which led him in the 1930s in the direction of Marxism. Merleau-Ponty began to attend the lectures which the Russian *émigré* philosopher, Alexandre Kojève (1902–1968), gave on Hegel's *Phenomenology of Spirit* at the Ecole Pratique des Hautes Etudes from 1933 to 1939. These lectures attracted many Parisian intellectuals, including Raymond Queneau, Raymond Aron, Georges Bataille, Jacques Lacan, Jean-Paul Sartre, and, indeed, for a time, Hannah Arendt.[8] Around this period also, Merleau-Ponty began to read Marx's 1844 *Economic and Philosophical Manuscripts*, which had been translated into French in 1937. For Merleau-Ponty, Hegel and the young Marx were phenomenologists of concrete social life, not purveyors of closed and arid intellectual systems.

From 1935 to 1938, at the Ecole Normale Supérieure, Merleau-Ponty conducted postgraduate research on the topics of "the nature of perception" and "the problem of perception in phenomenology and Gestalt psychology".[9] His preliminary thesis, or *thèse complémentaire*, entitled *La structure du comportement* (*The Structure of Behaviour*), was submitted in 1938, but not published until 1942.[10] In this thesis Merleau-Ponty offers a description of 'behaviour' (*comportement*) which not only criticises the physiological psychology of the time, notably the behaviourism of John B. Watson (1878–1958) and the studies of reflex of I. P. Pavlov (1849–1936), which treat behaviour as a kind of thing (SB 129), but also criticises Bergson's *vitalist* account of human action. Against behaviourism, Merleau-Ponty maintained that complex human behaviour cannot be explained in terms of rigid mechanical responses to stimuli except where a kind of pathological dissociation from our body takes place (SB 45). Merleau-Ponty's criticism of behaviourism here is an early version of the 'feigned anaesthesia' criticism, namely that to be a true behaviourist one must pretend that the subject feels nothing. Moreover, the body cannot be understood in terms of the mere sum of its parts. In order to offer an alternative account of human activity, Merleau-Ponty drew on the more holistic tradition of German Gestalt psychology, including Wolfgang Köhler, Kurt Koffka, A. Gelb, and K. Goldstein. *Gestalt* means 'form' or 'structure' and the Gestalt school argued that structure or form was an irreducible part of the experience of anything. We always experience things against a background or structure, and psychology is wrongheaded if it attempts explanation by breaking down every experience into its supposed component elements. Stimuli are always perceived and interpreted in a rich and complex environment.

The interaction between individual and 'environment' (*Umwelt*) operates as a kind of 'circular causation'. The stimuli themselves are not neutral but are made *for* the specific organism, in a certain sense. The interaction between the living subject and the environment is much more of a seamless web and, in Merleau-Ponty's terms, a 'dialectics' of freedom and nature than either the behaviourists or the empiricists have acknowledged. As Merleau-Ponty later puts it, "matter is 'pregnant' with form, which is to say that in the final analysis every perception takes place within a certain horizon and ultimately in the 'world' " (*Primacy*, p. 12). In claiming, in the *Structure of Behaviour*, that every living organism must be understood in terms of its world, Merleau-Ponty is recognising the important links between the Gestalt approach and the phenomenological understanding of being-in-the-world which he also invokes at the end of the book.

The war years

The outbreak of the Second World War disrupted Merleau-Ponty's researches. In August 1939, he was called up for military duty, serving as an officer – a second lieutenant in an infantry division (Sartre served as a private). He was detained by the Germans and seemingly tortured. However, in September 1940, following the French armistice, he was discharged from the army and resumed teaching. Subsequently, in 1945, in the first issue of *Les Temps modernes*, the journal he helped to found with Sartre, he published an important reflection on the nature of the war, "The War Has Taken Place" (SNS 139–152; 245–270). This essay already contains explicit criticisms of the Sartrean position that humans are ineluctably free. Merleau-Ponty argues that the concept of freedom is itself historically conditioned, and that the supposedly normal state of peace and freedom enjoyed in France prior to 1939, far from being a natural condition, was itself a unique product of contingent historical forces. Moreover, Merleau-Ponty argues, war changes all values. In war, everyone is compromised: "We are in the world, mingled with it, compromised with it" (SNS 147; 259). Freedom exists only "in contact with the world not outside it" (SNS 148; 261). Even our relation to the other is not absolute, but hedged around by the limits of the situation. In 1946, in debate with his former teacher Emile Bréhier, recalling his military service, Merleau-Ponty pointed out that when he was required to call in an air-strike on an enemy position, he was forced to think of the other in a different way:

> M. Bréhier asked me just now, "Do you posit the other as an absolute value?" I answered, "Yes, in so far as any man can do so."
> But when I was in the army, I had to call for an artillery barrage or an air attack, and at that moment I was not recognising an absolute value in the enemy soldiers who were the objects of these attacks. I can in such a case promise to hold generous feelings towards the

enemy; I cannot promise not to harm him...Perception anticipates, goes ahead of itself.

(*Primacy*, pp. 35–36)

On demobilisation, Merleau-Ponty was appointed to a post in the Lycée Carnot, where he taught from 1940 until 1944, before moving to the Lycée Condorcet, taking over from Sartre who had been teaching there, but had resigned to promote his writing career. In 1936 Merleau-Ponty had reviewed Sartre's *Psychology of the Imagination* for a psychology journal, but, beyond that, they had had no contact until 1941, when he encountered Sartre again as members of a short-lived Socialist Resistance group called 'Socialism and Liberty'. Although the group itself was a failure, Merleau-Ponty and Sartre emerged from it as firm allies in their pursuit of phenomenology and existentialism, although they disagreed in their interpretation of Husserl. As Sartre recalled in his moving obituary for Merleau-Ponty:

> Born of enthusiasm, our little group caught a fever and died a year later, of not knowing what to do...As for the two of us, in spite of our failure, "Socialism and Liberty" had at least brought us into contact with one another...The key words were spoken: phenomenology, existence. We discovered our real concern. Too individualist to ever pool our research, we became reciprocal while remaining separate. Alone, each of us was too easily persuaded of having understood the idea of phenomenology. Together, we were, for each other, the incarnation of its ambiguity.

(Sartre, *Situations*, p. 159)

As Sartre put it, their bond and their division was the subject of Husserl and phenomenology. From 1942 the two began to co-operate closely. Merleau-Ponty even assisted Sartre by raising funds for the production of his play, *Les Mouches* (*The Flies*) in 1943. During the period from 1942 to 1945 Merleau-Ponty worked on his major doctoral thesis which was eventually published as *Phenomenology of Perception* in 1945. Meanwhile, Sartre's *Being and Nothingness* had already appeared in 1943.

Sartre and Merleau-Ponty were immediately seen by post-war French intellectuals as offering rival versions of existential phenomenology. Indeed, in *Phenomenology of Perception*, Merleau-Ponty explicitly portrays phenomenology as in essence existential philosophy: "the phenomenological reduction is that of existential philosophy" (PP xiv, translation altered; ix). Despite the powerful influence of Sartre's *Being and Nothingness* on his own ontology, Merleau-Ponty criticised the stark antithetical dualism of Sartre's account of the clash of *pour-soi* and *en-soi*, whereby consciousness never achieves thinghood and remained always an empty project, and similarly that the object never possesses consciousness. In contrast, Merleau-Ponty wants always to emphasise the *dialectical* relation between subject and object. As he wrote of Sartre's *Being and Nothingness* in his 1945 essay "The Battle Over Existentialism":

> In our opinion the book remains too exclusively antithetic: the antithesis of my view of myself and another's view of me and the antithesis of the *for itself* and the *in itself* often seem to be alternatives instead of being described as the living bond and communication between one term and the other.
>
> (SNS 72; 125)

Indeed Sartre, as we have seen, explicitly claimed there was no communication between *en-soi* and *pour-soi*. Sartre and Merleau-Ponty disagreed, furthermore, about the nature of human existence and consciousness. *Contra* Sartre, Merleau-Ponty did not see the possession of consciousness as an all-or-nothing affair, since his interest in psychology and biology led him to recognise complex shadings of perceptual awareness (e.g. in animals) whereas Sartre took a more Cartesian view about the nature of consciousness. Merleau-Ponty agrees with Sartre that consciousness can never turn itself into a thing, never be purely *en-soi*, and is through and through imbued with freedom. But Merleau-Ponty is critical of Sartre's radical claims for human freedom. Merleau-Ponty denies Sartre's claim that to refuse is to exercise choice and to be free. Consciousness which thinks itself radically free has ignored the circumstances of its birth (PP 453; 517). There is no such thing as an original choice. Merleau-Ponty asserts that "To be born is both to be born of the world and to be born into the world" (PP 453; 517).[11] Merleau-Ponty was deeply critical of Sartre's isolated account of the self, an account which viewed social interaction (e.g. in the 'look') as inevitably hostile, negative, and restricting. Nevertheless, he defended Sartre's necessary focus on the ugly and the imperfect in human existence in a 1947 essay in *Figaro littéraire*, "A Scandalous Author" (SNS 41–47; 73–84). He also offered an interesting defence of Sartre's claim that hell is other people:

> To say "Hell is other people" does not mean "Heaven is for me." If other people are the instrument of our torture, it is first and foremost because they are indispensable to our salvation. We are so intermingled with them that we must make what order we can out of this chaos. Sartre put Garcin in Hell not for being a coward but for having made his wife suffer.
>
> (SNS 41; 74)

Sartre and Merleau-Ponty co-operated so closely on political issues in the immediate post-war years that Sartre initially appears not to have noticed the differences between their philosophical positions. Sartre acknowledged that Merleau-Ponty had helped to shape his own political formation from being a "throw-back to anarchy" (*Situations*, p. 176) to formulating a committed Marxism. However, in Sartre's opinion, Merleau-Ponty was never a dogmatic historical materialist (indeed Merleau-Ponty could never accept any absolute philosophical system) and was rather a Marxist simply "*faute de mieux*" (Sartre, *Situations*, p. 164), engaged more in a critique of Cold War politics than in the attempt to foment class revolution.

Meanwhile, Merleau-Ponty's academic career was taking shape. He was appointed as lecturer (*Maître de conférences*) in the University of Lyons in 1945 and in 1948 was elevated to a professorship. He also began giving lecture courses at the Sorbonne. In November 1946 he delivered a key lecture, later published as "The Primacy of Perception" (*Primacy*, pp. 12–42), to the *Société française de philosophie* outlining the topic of his recently published *Phenomenology of Perception*. His interests were also gradually broadening from philosophy and psychology to ethics, politics, and aesthetics. Though a highly skilled academic philosopher, Merleau-Ponty was also of revolutionary bent, and he engaged actively in critical commentary on culture and politics, both national and international.

The political years 1945–1955

After the appearance of *Phenomenology of Perception*, and with France emerging from the Second World War, Merleau-Ponty turned his interests primarily to political commentary and analysis.[12] In 1945, spurred by the conviction that philosophy had to become engaged in the real world, Merleau-Ponty and Sartre founded the left-wing journal *Les Temps modernes*. Sartre recalls: "We had dreamed of this review since 1943...We would be hunters of meaning, we would speak the truth about the world and about our own lives" (*Situations*, p. 168). Although Merleau-Ponty was overall editor for several years as well as being especially responsible for the journal's attitude towards politics, he rarely allowed his name to appear on the editorial page (Sartre himself admitted he never knew Merleau-Ponty's reason for this reticence). In political terms, Merleau-Ponty saw his mission of reconciling dialectical materialism with freedom. In his Marxism he was strongly influenced by Leon Trotsky as well as by the Hungarian philosopher Georg Lukács. An early indication of this abiding interest in Marxism is the long footnote on historical materialism in *Phenomenology of Perception* (PP 171–173; 199–202) where he argues that its account of history should not be understood in reductionist *causal* terms but rather in terms of *motivations* whereby external conditions are internalised.

When the French Communist Party entered into a coalition government in France after the war, Merleau-Ponty wrote in *Les Temps modernes* committing himself to their ideology: "in short we must carry out the policy of the Communist Party". Merleau-Ponty resolutely refused to condemn the Soviet Union, lest his condemnation give succour to the imperialist enemies of the international workers' movement. He even defended the show trials in the Soviet Union in a review of Arthur Koestler's *The Yogi and the Commissar*, collected in *Humanism and Terror* published in 1947. This book contains Merleau-Ponty's reflection on history. While he criticises the Stalinist regime from the standpoint of what he regarded as a more genuine Marxism, he also vigorously criticises bourgeois liberal denunciations of Stalinist terror, arguing that all regimes use force. *Humanism and Terror* caused a scandal not only among the Left but among the Right, as Sartre recalled. Camus bitterly recriminated with Merleau-Ponty for defending the trials, but Merleau-Ponty felt that to attack the Soviet Union was somehow to absolve the West of political culpability.

In 1950 the news broke of the existence of the Russian labour camps, and though Merleau-Ponty was particularly upset with this grim news, he still argued that the camps existed as a stepping stone to socialism and not for the sake of death, as in the case of the Nazi concentration camps. As Sartre recalled, Merleau-Ponty refused to be distracted by the news of the Soviet camps from carrying on his anti-colonial campaign:

> At the same moment as Europe discovered the camps, Merleau finally came upon the class struggle unmasked: strikes and repression, the massacres in Madagascar, the war in Vietnam, McCarthyism and the American Terror, the reawakening of Nazism, the Church in power everywhere, sanctimoniously protecting the rebirth of Fascism under her cloak. How could we not smell the stench of the bourgeois cadaver? And how could we publicly condemn slavery in the East without abandoning, on our side, the exploited to their exploitation?
>
> (*Situations*, p. 185)

While Sartre and Merleau-Ponty defended Stalin's camps, they disagreed over the nature of the Korean War. The French Communist Party interpreted the Korean War as part of the communist struggle against imperialist aggression whereas it was clear to Merleau-Ponty that North Korea had been the aggressor, and that Soviet communism was actually another form of imperialism. Initially, Merleau-Ponty decided to keep silent about all political matters as he feared that the Korean War would escalate into a global war where force, not reason, would prevail. In 1952 he finally resigned from the editorial board of *Les Temps modernes* and publicly disagreed with Sartre over the latter's uncritical support of the Soviet Union's role in the Korean War. He later recorded his disaffection with Soviet-style communism and his support for a new liberalism in *Adventures of the Dialectic* published in 1955, which also included his critique of Sartre, "Sartre and Ultrabolshevism", to which Simone de Beauvoir vigorously responded, defending Sartre and accusing Merleau-Ponty of having invented a strawman, a non-existent philosophy she labels "pseudo-Sartreanism".[13] By Sartre's 'ultrabolshevism', Merleau-Ponty signified Sartre's placid acceptance of all the doings of the Soviet Communist Party in the name of solidarity.

Merleau-Ponty had gradually separated his theoretical Marxism from the doctrinaire outlook of the Soviet Communist Party. He saw that where the Marxists came to power (e.g. in Russia) they had abandoned global revolution and returned to the familiar methods of governing, that is through "hierarchy, obedience, myth, inequality, diplomacy and police" (SNS 4; 10). Immediately after the Second World War he had naively hoped the American masses would rise up and embrace Marxism but gradually he acknowledged the failure of this analysis. Though he abandoned Marxism in the early 1950s, he remained a committed radical intellectual throughout his life, always attempting to find a middle way between totalitarianism and abstract liberalism. He was strongly anti-colonial in his attitudes and was outraged, for example, when the French Catholic intellectual and novelist François Mauriac defended French colonial interference in Indo-China (Vietnam) as an example of bringing civilisation to the local inhabitants.

Sartre and Merleau-Ponty did not reconcile after 1955 and remained aloof when they met each other at conferences, neither did they dispute with one another, publicly or otherwise. Both were in agreement in opposing the French government's stance during the Algerian War of Independence.

Merleau-Ponty was grievously affected by the death of his mother in 1952. According to Sartre's extraordinary reminiscence of Merleau-Ponty published in 1961, Merleau-Ponty had a deep attachment to his mother, an attachment which enveloped him (*Situations*, pp. 208–209). The adult Merleau-Ponty's desire to discover the sources of this sense of being absorbed in and enveloped by the world and all his attempts to find community, first in Christianity and then with the Communist Party, were, for Sartre, attempts to rediscover this original happiness. Sartre is perhaps finding psychological reasons for his own break with Merleau-Ponty which happened at that time. Whether or not Sartre's psychological analysis is entirely accurate, Merleau-Ponty became more withdrawn and after 1956 he became a recluse, only leaving his home to go to the Collège de France. However, Sartre and Merleau-Ponty reconciled to a degree when they both met at a conference in Geneva in 1956. Though they were no longer co-operating philosophically, Merleau-Ponty never ceased referring to Sartre's work. Sartre, on the other hand, confessed that *Phenomenology of Perception* was a mystery to him.

The metaphysical turn

Alongside his political activism as editor of *Les Temps modernes*, Merleau-Ponty continued his interests in the phenomenological description of experience. Indeed, his retreat from doctrinaire Marxism and Soviet Communist Party politics coincided with a new interest in metaphysics and in reshaping the account of perception of his earlier books to expand it to take account of intersubjective relations and the formation of the cultural world. From 1948 to 1949 he spent a year's leave of absence from Lyons in Mexico and from 1949 until 1952 he held a chair of child psychology at the Sorbonne, the chair which would later be held by Jean Piaget. Merleau-Ponty was strongly influenced by, though critical of, Piaget's studies and had an abiding interest in the child's perception of the world as is evident from his last lecture series, "The Child's Relation to Others" (*Primacy*, pp. 96–155). Here, criticising classical psychology, he argues that the child's encounter with others is not secondary and subordinate but that the encounter with the other and the encounter with language are the very basis of the child's developing sense of self.

In 1952 he was appointed to the Chair of Philosophy in the Collège de France, a most prestigious chair which had been held by Henri Bergson, Louis Lavelle, and immediately prior to Merleau-Ponty, by Étienne Gilson. In his inaugural lecture, "In Praise of Philosophy", delivered on the 15 January 1953, Merleau-Ponty paid tribute to his predecessors (studiously ignoring Gilson) and characterised the philosopher as marked by both a taste for evidence and a feeling for ambiguity.[14] He published several sets of essays including *Sens et non-sens* (*Sense and Non-Sense*) in 1948 and *Signes* (*Signs*) in 1960. He continued to lecture at the Collège de France until his death in 1961, where he numbered among his friends and colleagues the anthropologist Claude Lévi-Strauss, with whom he discussed the emerging structuralist movement.[15] During the late 1940s, Merleau-Ponty even became a qualified supporter of structuralism, acknowledging that there must be close links between the linguistic, economic, and social structures we inhabit ("From Mauss to Claude Lévi-Strauss", *Signs*, p. 118; 148). In 1949 Merleau-Ponty began to lecture on Saussure and was generally attracted to structuralist forms of explanation, particularly to the manner in which structuralist explanation bypassed the boundaries between sociological, economic, and psychological explanation to see the deep common structures underlying these different human levels.

Merleau-Ponty's last published work was the essay "Eye and Mind", published in *Art de France* in January 1961, and intended to be part of *The Visible and Invisible*.[16] Merleau-Ponty begins this essay by stating that "science manipulates things and gives up living in them" (*Primacy*, p. 159). Following Husserl, he sees science as making models of things which it can then manipulate. Science makes everything appear as an 'object in general'. However, he believed classical science still had a hope of rejoining the concrete world and had a respect for the opacity of the world, whereas contemporary science sees itself as free floating, constructivist, working with 'blind operations':

> Thinking "operationally" has become a sort of absolute artificialism, such as we see in the ideology of cybernetics, where human creations are derived from a natural information process, itself conceived on the model of human machines.
>
> (*Primacy*, p. 160)

To avoid the consequences of such a deracination of human beings, science must be called back to examine its relation with the world and look more closely at the site or soil of the opened world we experience. In fact attention to this rootedness in the world is precisely how art operates. Merleau-Ponty contrasts the manipulative nature of science which knows, as he says, neither truth nor falsity, with the kind of truth that emerges in painting. In this essay he discusses Paul Klee, Cézanne, and Matisse, as painters who abandon a stylised formal representation of the world and rediscover the lived immediacy of vision and truly capture the vibrant reflective surfaces of things. Only art has the capacity of innocent looking without trying to form an opinion. The painter is involved in a giving birth to the visible rather than attempting to produce a representation of the world.

Merleau-Ponty, the philosopher of radical contingency, died of a stroke on 3 May 1961 at the age of 53. His passing was mourned by Sartre, Ricoeur, Levinas, Lévi-Strauss, and Lacan, among others. He left behind a number of unfinished manuscripts, notably the essays contained in *Prose of the World*[17] and six chapters of *The Visible and Invisible*,[18] which had been envisaged as a major rewriting of *Phenomenology of Perception* and where he put forward the view of *flesh* (*la chair*) as the 'prototype of being', and *thought* as a 'sublimation of flesh' (*une sublimation de la chair*, VI 145; 191). He saw himself as evolving towards a new philosophical position which totally abandoned traditional philosophical dualisms of subject and object, soul and body, and was especially interested in the problem of the relations with others, the problem of *intersubjectivity*.

A phenomenology of origins

Merleau-Ponty's overall aim was to uncover 'the roots of rationality' using the methods of Husserlian phenomenology. He saw the function of philosophy as the reawakening of an understanding of the original acts whereby humans come to awareness in the world: "true philosophy consists in relearning to look at the world" (PP xx; xvi). Philosophy will shed light on the "birth of being for us" (*la genèse de l'être pour nous*, PP 154; 180). Moreover, philosophy as such is identical with phenomenology.

Phenomenology aims at "disclosure of the world" (*révélation du monde*); its task is "to reveal the mystery of the world and of reason" (PP xx–xxi; xvi). Merleau-Ponty's understanding of phenomenology derives from his original reading of Husserl, transforming the latter's difficult, unfinished phenomenological studies into beautifully written, almost poetic, accounts of lived human experience. In particular, Merleau-Ponty draws on Husserl's accounts of the life-world in the *Crisis,* and in particular develops the notion of 'prepredicative awareness' found in *Experience and Judgement.* Against the notion of intentionality as a voluntary, primarily cognitive act, Merleau-Ponty lays great emphasis on Husserl's notion of 'functioning' or 'operative intentionality' (*fungierende Intentionalität*) as "that which produces the natural and antepredicative unity of the world and of our life" (PP xviii; xiii). Our bodily intentions already lead us into a world constituted for us before we conceptually encounter it in cognition. Furthermore, Merleau-Ponty extended Husserlian phenomenology in an existential direction, to take cognisance of our corporeal and historical situatedness.

Merleau-Ponty's 'phenomenology of origins' aims to teach us to view our experience in a new light, not relying on the fully formed categories of our reflective experience, but developing a method and a language adequate to articulate our pre-reflective experience, specifically the world of perception. Phenomenology's slogan of returning to the things themselves means

> to return to that world which precedes knowledge, of which knowledge always *speaks*, and in relation to which all every scientific schematization is an abstract and derivative sign-language, as is geography in relation to the countryside in which we have learned beforehand what a forest, a prairie or a river is.
>
> (PP ix; iii)

Moreover, this description of our pre-conceptual experience aims to correct the distortions of 'objective thought' prevalent in modern science and psychology. Objective thought too often has ignored the complex ambiguous '*milieu*' in which human meaning comes to expression, "objective thought is unaware of the subject of perception" (PP 207; 240), and instead presents the world as already made. Philosophy, then, must counter objective thought by reawakening our immediate contact with the world.

Merleau-Ponty aims at a special kind of reduction – a return to the perceptual pre-conceptual experience of the child. As he puts it in a late essay, "La métaphysique dans l'homme" ("The Metaphysical in Man"), the aim of his philosophy is "to rediscover, along with structure and the understanding of structure, a dimension of being and a type of knowledge which man forgets in his natural attitude" (SNS 92; 162). But Merleau-Ponty's reduction avoids the idealist slant of Husserl, by recognising the irreducibility of the real world: "The real is to be described not constructed or constituted" (PP x, my translation; iv). Phenomenological description can play a vital role in reminding us of what our pre-reflective experience is like against various philosophical and scientific distortions. We need to understand how it is that we normally experience with complete confidence that the world is there. Furthermore, my perception is not simply a Kantian synthesis of representations (PP x; iv–v). Rather I experience a world as real 'in one blow'. Merleau-Ponty's emphasis is on the inseparability of self and world. Although, normally, I can distinguish my perceptions from dreams, yet I am also able to 'dream around things', projecting imagination into the world in a seamless way which shows the real world is a 'closely woven fabric' (*un tissu solide*, PP x; v) not constructed out of a series of syntheses performed in my inner self. It is this whole weave of myself with the world which I must come to understand. Our insertion into the world is through the body with its motor and perceptual acts. The incarnate domain of relations between body and world is an 'interworld' (*l'intermonde*). The world confronts our bodies as flesh meeting with flesh. Merleau-Ponty, in his last unfinished work, *The Visible and Invisible*, even speaks of the fabric of the visible and sensory world as "the flesh of the world" (*la chair du monde*, VI 248; 302). Having offered an analysis of perception as the bedrock of human experience, Merleau-Ponty's later philosophy moved to reflect on the nature of linguistic and social communication in general. As he put it in the early 1950s in an account of his work offered to Martial Gueroult as part of his candidature for a professorship at the Collège de France:

> My first two books sought to restore the world of perception. My works in preparation aim to show how communication with others, and thought, take up and go beyond the realm of perception which initiated us into truth.
>
> (*Primcacy*, p. 3)

Merleau-Ponty expresses the intimate relation of body and world as follows: "Our own body (*Le corps propre*) is in the world as the heart is in the organism; it keeps the visible spectacle constantly alive, it breathes life into it and sustains it inwardly, and with it forms a system" (PP 203; 235). In general terms, Merleau-Ponty's philosophical outlook may be characterised as a kind of *dialectical naturalism*, though he himself does not employ the word 'naturalism' which he associates with various forms of biological reductionism and scientism. Nevertheless, Merleau-Ponty's outlook is *naturalistic* in that it sees human beings as integrated into the natural order, as fundamentally belonging to the world, though not merely as objects in the world as their presence generates the social world of culture: "Man and society are not exactly outside of nature and the biological; they distinguish themselves from them by bringing nature's 'stakes' together and risking them together."[19] Merleau-Ponty's naturalism may be described as *dialectical* in that he sees the relations between humans and the world as so intertwined as if by a kind of 'pre-established harmony'. The world's colours proclaim themselves to our visual systems; space reveals itself through our bodily gestures and our desire to traverse distances. Traditional science and philosophy have not adequately managed to describe the nature of this interaction or 'intertwining' (*l'interlacs*) between body and world, between vision and movement (*Primacy*, p. 160). This emphasis on the interwoven tapestry of the world and the body (a conception itself derived from Husserl who frequently speaks of the 'interweaving', *Verflechtung*, of self and world) leads Merleau-Ponty to be a constant critic of any form of Cartesianism which radically divorces consciousness from the world. Indeed, Merleau-Ponty sought to rescue Husserl's phenomenology from its apparent commitment to Cartesianism, as evident in the *Cartesian Meditations* and elsewhere, which emphasised the sense of the world as a product of a disembodied transcendental ego. In place of the traditional Cartesian picture of body as *res extensa*, having parts outside parts with no interior, and of mind as *res cogitans*, wholly present to itself without distance, Merleau-Ponty wants to present a more complicated picture based on the more ambiguous way of existing of our own body (PP 198; 231). For Merleau-Ponty, Descartes, while he acknowledged the union of body and soul, had no proper means of thinking about that union and preferred to consider the concepts of 'body' and 'mind' as separate from one another and hence as clear and distinct. However, it is precisely because our lived bodily insertion in the flesh and in the world is not clear and distinct that philosophy must respond by a radical reflection on this very ambiguity and complexity. Against both Cartesianism and Kantian or Husserlian transcendental idealism, the ego is not an absolute source of truth separate from the world, but rather a 'subject destined for or pledged to the world' (*un sujet voué au monde*, PP xi, translation modified; v).

Following Hegel, Bergson, Husserl, and Heidegger, who all emphasise the temporality and historicality of human existence, Merleau-Ponty's commitment to the phenomenology of concrete lived experience and embodiment also required him to rethink the meaning of human historicality and temporality: "one cannot get beyond history and time" (SNS 147; 260); "time and thought are mutually entangled" (*Signs*, p. 15; 21). For Merleau-Ponty thought is tied to time in a unique way: time is the 'other side' of our thought. Future and past are disclosed because of the nature of thought itself. This emphasis on our radical temporality and historicality leads Merleau-Ponty to reject any kind of absolute system of knowledge which would be a timeless overview of this world of change. History can never be understood as a single stream of meanings; there is no perspective from which we can view the course of history from the outside, anymore than we can achieve a perceptual view of a house as 'seen from nowhere' (*vue de nulle part*, PP 67; 81). All thought, like all perception, is situated and perspectival. This insight led Merleau-Ponty to develop a critique both of

Hegel's conception of absolute knowledge and also, in political terms, of the Marxist and French communist approach to history, which tended to explain the living course of history in static and a priori terms.

Inspired by the late Husserl of the *Crisis* and the *Origin of Geometry* and also influenced by the social anthropology of Claude Lévi-Strauss and Mauss, Merleau-Ponty sees the tendency towards disregarding historicality and temporality as in part due to the manner in which thought comes to expression in language. The congealing of temporal thinking into language and concepts acts to fix meanings, to give the appearance of absoluteness. Furthermore, through language and signs the constituted human social world is brought about, and constitutes a 'system'. Indeed, this focus on the nature of language and social institutions as expressing a deep structure brought Merleau-Ponty into close contact with structuralism. Merleau-Ponty lectured on Férdinand de Saussure's *System of General Linguistics* during the late 1940s, and was a close friend of Lévi-Strauss. Indeed, Merleau-Ponty welcomed structuralism's attempt to go beyond the "subject–object correlation" (*Signs*, p. 123; 155), though he was also quick to criticise the overuse of the term 'structure' in contemporary writings. However, Merleau-Ponty does not view language as an anonymous system as the structuralists did. Though Merleau-Ponty is in agreement with Heidegger that "language speaks man", he nevertheless always interprets language as grounded in perception. Our employment of language is like our use of a new sense organ, which itself retreats from view and presents us only with the world. As in the visual field, what is seen shades off into a blur, so also in language there is an indefinite boundary to our linguistic domain, where language shades off into silence (see, for example, Merleau-Ponty's essay, "Indirect Language and the Voices of Silence", *Signs*, pp. 39–83; 49–104).

Besides his contributions to phenomenology and structuralism, Merleau-Ponty had a lifelong interest in literature and in art, especially painting. He was a particular admirer of Cézanne's paintings but also wrote on Paul Klée and others. His essays on art have been justly regarded as among the best philosophical commentaries on contemporary painting which the twentieth century has produced. He saw painting as providing evidence of the primordial connection between body and world which could not be expressed in philosophical terms. A painting explores the manner our vision seizes on objects in the world in a more subtle way than any philosophy or psychology. Merleau-Ponty frequently quotes Cézanne: "colour is the place where our brain and the universe meet" (*Primacy*, p. 180). The perception of colour is connected with our experience of the world as having depth. Painting allows us to "possess the voluminosity of the world" (*Primacy*, p. 166). In his essay "Cézanne's Doubt", in *Sense and Non-Sense*, Merleau-Ponty portrays Cézanne as a phenomenologist of the primordial, visible world, a painter who reveals how the human world is installed within 'inhuman nature' (for more on the nature of the human world, see also PP

405

23–24; 31–32). According to Merleau-Ponty, Cézanne discovered lived perspective – not geometrical perspective – "by remaining faithful to the phenomena" (SNS 14; 23). In this sense, Cézanne is a genuine phenomenologist for Merleau-Ponty. Philosophy ought to be creative in the manner of art. Philosophy assists at the birth of the world of human experience; it aims to be present at the dawning of truth: "Philosophy is not the reflection of a pre-existing truth, but, like art, the act of bringing truth into being" (PP xx; xv). Though this sounds like Heidegger's views on art and truth, it is more likely that Merleau-Ponty is here thinking of Marx and Feuerbach's view of the role of philosophy to bring about the new world rather than merely to understand it. Similarly, Merleau-Ponty clearly sees the radical phenomenological reduction and the break with the natural attitude as a kind of revolutionary act, and refers to the act of rediscovery of the original world of perception as 'an act of violence' (*un acte violent*, PP xx; xvi).

Merleau-Ponty's intellectual background

The intellectual background to Merleau-Ponty's philosophy, as for Levinas, Sartre, and Derrida, as we shall see, assumes a certain conception of modern philosophy as configured by Hegel, Husserl, and Heidegger. As a student, Merleau-Ponty reacted against the rather arid academic philosophy taught in France during the 1920s, rejecting both Neo-Kantianism and various forms of idealism. Instead he was drawn to the philosophy of the concrete, living experience as emphasised by Henri Bergson (1859–1941) and by the Christian existentialist Gabriel Marcel (1889–1973). Merleau-Ponty was particularly influenced by Marcel's *Metaphysical Journal* (1927) which discussed themes such as incarnation and 'being in the world' (*être au monde*) which Merleau-Ponty incorporated into his own thought. Merleau-Ponty refers in particular to Marcel's claim (independently stated by Sartre in *Being and Nothingness*) that I do not so much *have* a body as that 'I *am* my body' (*je suis mon corps*).[20] Merleau-Ponty also takes over Marcel's definition of a 'mystery' as a problem in which I myself am involved as opposed to an objective puzzle which simply can be solved.

The influence of Bergson

Although Merleau-Ponty did not recognise Bergson as a major influence in his early years at the Ecole Normale (since Bergson had retired from teaching), he later acknowledged the importance of Bergson in his 1953 lecture, *In Praise of Philosophy*, in his essay "Bergson in the Making" (*Signs*) and in his 1947–1948 lectures on Bergson.[21] For Merleau-Ponty, as for Levinas, Bergson was preparing the way for phenomenology by emphasising the living vitality of concrete intuition in philosophy. Bergson's book *Matter and Memory* (1896), with its account of perception and memory, contains discussion of many themes later taken up by Merleau-Ponty.[22] In particular, Bergson's opposition to both materialism and idealism, his critique of various representational accounts of perception, his notion of the embodied subject as a centre of action, and his emphasis on the living flux of our experience all find echoes in Merleau-Ponty, though he criticised Bergson for treating the body as an objective body and consciousness as primarily cognitive (PP 78n.; 93n.).

Merleau-Ponty first encountered Husserl in the lectures of Léon Brunschvicg at the Ecole Normale, where Husserl was presented in the context of Neo-Kantian idealism. He took further lectures on Husserl and Heidegger from Georges Gurvitch (1894–1965) at the Sorbonne from 1928–1930.[23] According to Maurice de Gandillac, Merleau-Ponty was in attendance for Husserl's own lectures in Paris delivered on 23 and 25 February 1929, though Husserl lectured in German and Merleau-Ponty's grasp of that language was quite poor at that time. According to Sartre's version, both he and Merleau-Ponty discovered German phenomenology quite independently of each other around the same time in the mid-1930s. For Merleau-Ponty, as for Sartre and Aron, phenomenology suggested the possibility of a serious, rigorously scientific philosophy, which at the same time was not abstracted or divorced from concrete, lived experience. An important event in Merleau-Ponty's understanding of Husserl was the special commemorative issue on Husserl of the *Revue Internationale de Philosophie* which appeared in 1939, and contained an important essay by Eugen Fink, as well as Fink's edition of Husserl's late text, *The Origin of Geometry*, a text which would also play a decisive role in Derrida's development. This encounter with Husserl's later philosophy prompted Merleau-Ponty to travel to the newly opened Husserl Archives in Louvain in April 1939, where he spent six days examining some of Husserl's unpublished papers, especially the typescripts of the full *Crisis* and of *Ideas* II (not published until 1952). In these texts Husserl makes the distinction, crucial for Merleau-Ponty, between the body as physical object (*Körper*) and the body as animate being (*Leib*). Through the Second World War, Merleau-Ponty remained in contact with the director of the Archives, Fr Van Breda, had a copy of Van Breda's thesis on the later Husserl, and even sought to establish a second Husserl Archive in France. Merleau-Ponty's knowledge of Husserl deepened through this contact, and he continued to engage with Husserl throughout his life, for example his essay "The Philosopher and his Shadow" (*Signs*, pp. 159–181; 201–228), and his late lecture on "Husserl at the Limits of Phenomenology" at the Collège de France in 1959 and published in 1960, shortly before his death.[24]

The influence of Husserl

Merleau-Ponty had a strong sense of the presence of Husserl in his own, constantly evolving, thought. He saw the importance of reduction even if he reinterpreted it. He recognised that Husserl saw the reduction as the beginning of all genuine enquiry; the reduction "never ceased to be an enigmatic possibility for Husserl, and one he always came back to" (*Signs*, p. 161; 203). Similarly in the Preface to *Phenomenology of Perception* he wrote:

> There is probably no question over which Husserl has spent more time – or to which he has more often returned, since the "problematic of reduction" occupies an important place in his unpublished work. For a long time, and even in recent texts, the reduction is presented as the return to a transcendental consciousness before which the world is spread out and completely transparent, quickened through and through by a series of apperceptions which it is the philosopher's task to reconstitute on the basis of their outcome.
>
> (PP xi; v)

Merleau-Ponty highlights the rich ambiguity in Husserl's understanding of the reduction. On the one hand, Husserl emphasised the *unnaturalness* of the reduction and the difficulty of overcoming our normal absorption in the world in the natural attitude. On the other hand, Husserl also emphasised the centrality of the natural attitude itself in giving us a rich, concrete, immediate form of knowledge about the world. Merleau-Ponty agrees with Husserl that phenomenology proceeds by suspending the natural attitude in a special form of reflection. But he disagrees with Husserl that this suspension leads us back to a transparent transcendental consciousness. Rather, overcoming the natural attitude is not a matter of installing us in "a closed, transparent milieu" (*Signs*, p. 162; 205), but of recognising the manner in which thought arises out of its immersion in the natural attitude. Things are not merely pure extended objects in the Cartesian manner but are disclosed in their properties precisely because of the nature of my body and its sensory and motor capacities. The thing is "caught up in the context of my body" (*Signs*, p. 168; 212). Moreover, I do not discover myself as an isolated consciousness, rather "the *Cogito* must reveal me in a situation, and it is on this condition alone that transcendental subjectivity can, as Husserl puts it, *be* an intersubjectivity" (PP xiii; vii). It is interesting to note that Merleau-Ponty frequently quoted from Husserl the claim that transcendental subjectivity is an intersubjectivity, citing the then unpublished *Crisis*. However, this exact claim is not to be found in Husserl's *Crisis*, where the nearest remark is the statement that subjectivity is what it is, namely an ego functioning constitutively only within intersubjectivity.[25] In fact, Merleau-Ponty is reversing the order of priority in Husserl's own account. For Husserl the constituting ego only becomes fully itself in intersubjectivity, it is not that there first is intersubjectivity and the ego comes to be from it. Our acts of reflection always return to the unreflective attitude from which we begin and perception is this background from which all acts stand out. The reduction is always provisional and is to be understood as a leading back to the sources of my experience rather than as a transcending of those sources in thought (which is idealism).

In *Phenomenology of Perception*, Merleau-Ponty had already pointed to the complexity of our sense of touch, particularly when we touch ourselves, the phenomenon of 'double sensation' already discussed in classical psychology (see PP 93; 109), in Husserl's *Ideas* II (§ 36, 152; Hua IV 145), and in Sartre's *Being and Nothingness* (BN 304; 351), two texts with which Merleau-Ponty was familiar. When one hand touches another I get a glimpse of the "integument or incarnation" (*l'enveloppe ou l'incarnation*, PP 93; 109) of that other hand. Whereas Sartre had not attached any special significance to this phenomenon, Merleau-Ponty thinks it revelatory of our complex relations to our bodies, and as a paradigm case for understanding the nature of our self-reflection. We cannot experience touching and being touched at the same time, rather we pass from one role to the other. Our activity and passivity are different moments and this leads us to pass over the activity of our bodies in perception. Similarly, when reflecting on our actions, "the body catches itself from the outside engaged in a cognitive process" (PP 93; 109). Merleau-Ponty wants to overcome the subject–object duality by emphasising the manner in which the visible and the body meet as 'flesh applied to flesh' (*chair appliquée à une chair*, VI 138; 182). The body and the visible are both intimately connected and separated by a gulf. They are intertwined with one another. Years later, in the chapter on "The Intertwining – the Chiasm" (*L'Entrelacs – le chiasme*) in the unfinished draft of *The Visible and Invisible*, Merleau-Ponty again took up the notion of the intertwining of body and world, of subject and object: for example, when one hand shakes the other, the left hand touches the right and the right hand also feels touched and this situation is reversible (VI 143; 188). To touch is at the same time to be touched, and yet these are distinctly different sensations. It is a specific feature of our human experience that our eyes are in such a position that we can see our own bodies (at least in part). This special intertwining, chiasmic relation between the act of seeing and the visible became the central focus of Merleau-Ponty's last writings, but the general preoccupation with the manner in which perception is already an insertion into the world prior to reflective thought had been a theme of Merleau-Ponty's writings from the beginning.

The influence of Hegel

The notion of a *philosophy of the concrete* had currency in France at that time, owing to the work of Bergson and Jean Wahl, who read Hegel as mapping the contours of concrete human historical consciousness in terms of a dialectic which is exemplified by the master–slave dialectic at the core of

Hegel's *Phenomenology of Spirit*.[26] Merleau-Ponty's version of Hegel came through Wahl, as well as through Alexandre Kojève's lectures and the writings of Jean Hyppolite, who had been a contemporary at the Ecole Normale. These French interpreters read Hegel as an existentialist and an historically aware social thinker. They emphasised the growth of human social awareness through various historical forms, a kind of Hegelianism which Merleau-Ponty also found present in Husserl's *Crisis*. Merleau-Ponty in fact effected something of a synthesis of the views of Hegel, Bergson, and the later Husserl. For him, dialectic and intuition were compatible, indeed converged:

> Through Bergsonism as through Husserl's career we can follow the laborious process which gradually sets intuition in motion, changes the positive notation of "immediate data" ("*données immédiates*") into a dialectic of time and the intuition of essences into a "phenomenology of genesis," and links together in a living unity the contrasting dimensions of a time which is ultimately coextensive with being.
>
> (*Signs*, p. 156; 197)

Furthermore, Hegel, not Kierkegaard, was the first existentialist, for Merleau-Ponty (see his 1946 essay, "Hegel's Existentialism", published in *Les Temps modernes*).[27] According to Merleau-Ponty:

> Hegel's thought is existentialist in that it views man not as being from the start a consciousness in full possession of its own clear thoughts, but as a life which is its own responsibility and which tries to understand itself.
>
> (SNS 65; 113)

In this essay he portrays Hegel as the source of all the important philosophical ideas of the previous hundred years – including the work of Marx, Nietzsche, phenomenology, existentialism, and psychoanalysis. Here also, Merleau-Ponty acknowledged his debt to Jean Hyppolite's reading of Hegel, and argued that Kierkegaard's opposition to the late Hegel should not obscure the rich account of personal existence to be found in Hegel's early *Phenomenology of Spirit* (1807). In this work, Hegel attempts to "recapture a total sense of history, describing the inner workings of the body social" until one arrives at an absolute knowledge "wherein consciousness at last becomes equal to its spontaneous life and regains its self-possession", and this stage is, for Merleau-Ponty, not so much a philosophy as a way of life (SNS 64; 112). From Hegel, the young Merleau-Ponty adopted the notion of a living, concrete dialectic operating in history, in social life, and in the relations between the human beings and their environment. Merleau-Ponty was particularly interested in Hegel's account of the emergence and transformation of the structures of consciousness and self-awareness in his *Phenomenology of Spirit*, in particular the region Hegel called 'objective spirit' (*objektiver Geist*), the institutionalised social world of roads, houses, governments, and objectified cultural forms such as food, money, and talk. For Merleau-Ponty, Hegel was the philosopher "who started the attempt to explore the irrational and integrate it into an expanded reason, which remains the task of our century" (SNS 63; 109). Hegel is essentially a phenomenologist, describing conscious experience as it occurs and yet discovering in it a certain order and logic (*Primacy*, p. 52), though in the end the later Hegel becomes more interested in the logic of the system rather than in describing the unfolding experiences themselves. But Merleau-Ponty departed from Hegel in refusing to absorb the contingent nature of our existence into some kind of global rational plan and was utterly disinterested in Hegel's attempts to develop a system of absolute knowledge. Merleau-Ponty, in agreement with Sartre, always wants to emphasise the central irreducible brute fact of contingency (*la contingence*). As he put it in his 1947 essay, "The Metaphysical in Man":

> The contingency (*La contingence*) of all that exists and all that has value is not a little truth for which we have somehow or other to make room in some nook and cranny of the system: it is the condition of a metaphysical view of the world.
>
> (SNS 96; 168)

The influence of psychology

In common with Husserl, Bergson, and Sartre, Merleau-Ponty combined an interest in philosophy with an interest in scientific, experimental psychology. Through the 1930s especially, Merleau-Ponty informed himself about developments in twentieth-century scientific psychology in its various strands, including behaviourism, positivism, and German Gestalt psychology. In part his knowledge of Gestalt psychology was mediated through the work of Husserl's student Aron Gurwitsch (1901–1973), a Lithuanian Jew who had left Nazi Germany for Paris in the 1930s and whose lectures at the Sorbonne were attended by Merleau-Ponty.[28] As a result of the influence of Gurwitsch, Merleau-Ponty combined his Hegelian–Husserlian concrete phenomenology of social experience with the holistic psychological approach of the German Gestalt psychologist Adhemar Gelb (1887–1936) and the psychiatrist Kurt Goldstein (1878–1965) who studied war veterans with brain damage. Indeed, much of what readers consider original in Merleau-Ponty, notably his detailed discussions of individual cases of brain dysfunction, is drawn directly from Gelb and Goldstein, as mediated through Gurwitsch, and through Ernst Cassirer's *Philosophy of Symbolic Forms*, Book Three (1923), an important but neglected influence on

411

Merleau-Ponty.[29] Cassirer discusses cases of aphasia and pathological disruptions of action in a manner which comes very close to many of Merleau-Ponty's formulations in *Phenomenology of Perception*. Merleau-Ponty's particular originality comes from the way he is able to effect a synthesis between these diverse influences and weave them into a seamless web in his own thinking.

The influence of Heidegger

The early Merleau-Ponty of *The Structure of Behaviour* cites Hegel, Husserl, and Bergson, but not Heidegger. Heidegger only gradually came to be influential and indeed Merleau-Ponty is still quite dismissive of Heidegger in 1945 (PP vii; i). Sartre's assessment is correct that, though Merleau-Ponty's affirmation that humans seemed to exist in order to reveal the nature of being sounded like Heidegger, Merleau-Ponty was not in fact influenced by Heidegger at that time. As Sartre puts it: "Their paths crossed, that was all".[30] Initially, Merleau-Ponty saw Heidegger as merely extending Husserl's analysis of the natural attitude of being-in-the-world; it was not until Merleau-Ponty began to think deeply of language and art that he would come to appreciate Heidegger's importance.

While Heidegger was interested in Being as such, Merleau-Ponty remained primarily interested in human being. In fact, Merleau-Ponty read Heidegger more as Husserl's student who was developing Husserl's account of the *Lebenswelt* than as a radically original philosopher in his own right. Thus in the Preface to *Phenomenology of Perception* Merleau-Ponty writes:

> the whole of *Sein und Zeit* springs from an indication given by Husserl and amounts to no more than an explicit account of the "*natürlicher Weltbegriff*" or the "*Lebenswelt*" which Husserl, towards the end of his life, identified as the central theme of phenomenology.
>
> (PP vii; i)

In other words, Merleau-Ponty saw Heidegger's *Being and Time* in much the same way as Husserl himself did – as a developed account of the natural mode of being-in-the-world. Merleau-Ponty did not follow Heidegger's invocation of ontology in *Being and Time*. Indeed he felt that Heidegger neglected to engage with contemporary science (unlike Husserl and Bergson) and had no account of perception or the role of the body.

The critique of reductionism in *The Structure of Behaviour* (1942)

Merleau-Ponty's starting point, his critique of current scientific accounts of human experience, is found in his first published book, *The Structure of*

Behaviour (1942). Here he argues that the accounts of animal and human behaviour (*comportement*) found in certain forms of empiricism (e.g. Mill), reflex physiology (Pavlov), and behaviourism (Watson) are all reductionist and give a false account of these experiences. He draws on Gestalt psychology and, in the last chapter, on Husserlian phenomenology, to emphasise that human experience in particular is not reducible to a sum of atomistic parts each of which conforms to a simple stimulus–response pattern. Rather human experience is an immensely complex weave of consciousness, body, and environment, best approached in terms of a holistic philosophy. Merleau-Ponty seeks to strike a balance: it is not sufficient to criticise reductionism and oppose to it a form of idealistic description. While the flaws in the reductionist causal explanation must be exposed, nevertheless the strong emphasis on the physiological and sociological must be positively embraced (SB 176). Merleau-Ponty's own positive account employs the notion of 'form' (*Gestalt*) as understood by the German Gestalt psychologists. The notion of form overcomes the opposition "between materialism and mentalism" (SB 131); in the internal working of a system each local effect depends on the functioning of the whole "upon its value and its significance with respect to the structure which the system is tending to realize" (SB 131). True behaviour is a *structure*, neither a thing nor a consciousness (SB 127), and surpasses both *pour-soi* and *en-soi* (SB 126).

Merleau-Ponty's starting point in *The Structure of Behaviour* is Cartesianism. According to the traditional Cartesian account, physical things are extended outside each other – they have 'parts outside parts' (*partes extra partes*) – whereas the mental, in this traditional account, is not extended and is known all at once (SB 40). At the outset of *The Structure of Behaviour*, Merleau-Ponty states that his overall aim was to understand the relation between the realm of nature (governed by fixed laws) and the realm of human culture:

> Our goal is to understand the relations of consciousness and na-
> ture: organic, psychological or even social. By nature we under-
> stand here a multiplicity of events external to each other and bound
> together by relations of causality.

> (SB 3)

Merleau-Ponty's definition of nature here is fairly traditional – nature is the sphere of events which obey strict causal laws. (He will later criticise this as an outlook of 'objective thought'.) Merleau-Ponty understands natural events as taking place in the external spatial world. In this first book he wants to 'start from below' and study human behaviour in a way which is neutral with respect to the classical distinctions between the mental and the physical (SB 4). He attacks Watson's behaviourism for systematically

413

excluding consciousness and for reducing human behaviour to a system of reflexes responding to stimuli. The notion of the reflex is a notion drawn from the laboratory and inappropriate to describe the living, vital reactions of an animal:

> The reflex as it is defined in the classical conception does not represent the normal activity of the animal, but the reaction obtained from an organism when it is subjected to working as it were by means of detached parts, to responding not to complex *situations* but to isolated *stimuli*. Which is to say that it corresponds to the behavior of a sick organism…and to "laboratory behavior" where the animal is placed in an anthropomorphic situation since, instead of having to deal with those natural unities which events or baits are, it is restricted to certain discriminations, it must react to certain physical and chemical agents which have a separate existence only in human science.
>
> (SB 43–44)

Instead of viewing the animal as a set of conditioned responses to stimuli, as a set of reflexes, rather the animal should be seen as a system of forces which are dynamic and flexible, and interact with the environment. The relations of an organism to its milieu are not "mechanical but dialectical" (SB 160). Elsewhere he says "the reactions of an organism are not edifices constructed from the elementary movements, but gestures gifted with an internal unity" and a proper account of behaviour would see it as "a kinetic melody gifted with a meaning" (SB 130). According to Merleau-Ponty, understanding an organism in its interaction with its environment rules out treating it as a thing with *partes extra partes* (parts outside parts), rather its behaviour should be understood as part of an 'embodied dialectic' radiating over its milieu (SB 161).

According to Merleau-Ponty, the distinction between the subjective and objective domains has been badly made by physiological psychology (SB 10). In criticising these forms of naturalism, Merleau-Ponty does not want to retreat either to a Kantian transcendental philosophy or to a kind of idealism. He criticises Kantianism for treating the relation between cognition and speech as merely accidental rather than essential and primitive, 'indecomposable' (SB 171). In particular, he attacks the notion of consciousness as reducible to representation:

> the possession of a representation or the exercise of a judgment is not coextensive with the life of consciousness. Rather consciousness is a network of significative intentions which are sometimes clear to themselves and sometimes, on the contrary, lived rather than known.
>
> (SB 173)

Consciousness is not pure transparency and self-presence, as both Descartes and Sartre tended to emphasise; rather consciousness is lived in the body in a more complex and intimate way than previous philosophy, including Sartre, had understood. Later, Merleau-Ponty will develop the critique of the notion of self-consciousness as self-presence in *Phenomenology of Perception*, a critique which anticipates Derrida's similar conception of the self.

Already in the *Structure of Behaviour* Merleau-Ponty was focusing on the nature of perception, which he was trying to define in an organic manner. In particular, Merleau-Ponty attacked what he called the 'hypothesis of sensations' (SB 166), the empiricist claim that all knowledge is composed out of a bedrock of simple sensations, for example Hume's impressions. This is simply mistaken: for Merleau-Ponty there are no isolated sensations; all sensations are already drawn up into a world of particular significance for us. The new-born infant is oriented immediately towards his or her mother's face, not towards a bundle of sensations or towards objects in the world (SB 166).[31] The first 'objects' infants see are smiles. Similarly, one can recognise a face without being explicitly aware of particular details of the face, the colour of the eyes or of the hair, for example:

> The human signification is given before the alleged sensible signs.
> A face is a center of human expression, the transparent envelope of
> the attitudes and desires of others, the place of manifestation, the
> barely material support for a multitude of intentions. This is why it
> seems impossible for us to treat a face or a body, even a dead body,
> like a thing. They are sacred entities, not the "givens of sight".
>
> (SB 167)

Human beings do not as infants see objects and then relate them as similar, they learn to pick them out by learning the words for them, and it is through the use of the same word that they come to observe diverse objects as similar (SB 169; see also PP 177–178; 207). Indeed Merleau-Ponty's position is now the generally accepted view in contemporary psychology.

Already in the *Structure of Behaviour* Merleau-Ponty gives evidence of his special interest in visual perception in relation to the fine arts and especially painting. He cites both Cézanne and El Greco's way of rendering the human form. For Merleau-Ponty, Cézanne has taught us to see faces as objects (SB 167). He also discusses El Greco's physiological problem, widely thought to be an astigmatism, in terms of the manner it acted to transform his whole way of perceiving the world. Merleau-Ponty rejects a reductionistic explanation of El Greco's resultant work solely in terms of a purely physiological defect:

> If one supposes an anomaly of vision in El Greco, as has sometimes
> been done, it does not follow that the form of the body in his

415

paintings, and consequently the style of the attitudes, admits of a "physiological explanation". When irremedial bodily peculiarities are integrated with the whole of our experience, they cease to have the dignity of a cause in us. A visual anomaly can receive a universal signification by the mediation of the artist and become for him the occasion of perceiving one of the "profiles" of human experience. The accidents of our bodily constitution can always play this revealing role on the condition that they become a means of extending our knowledge by the consciousness which we have of them, instead of being submitted as pure facts which dominate us. Ultimately, El Greco's supposed visual disorder was conquered by him and so profoundly integrated into his manner of thinking and being that it appears finally as the necessary expression of his being much more than as a peculiarity imposed from outside.

(SB 203)

El Greco's physical defect or peculiarity is taken up and integrated into the form of life of the artist as a whole. He transformed his astigmatism and absorbed it, integrating his peculiarities into his overall 'style'. Deterministic mechanical explanations, explanation in terms of the "pure facts that dominate us", do not capture the full truth of the way in which someone takes up and lives through their physical defects. Merleau-Ponty is equally against explanations which invoke conceptions of free-floating rationality and free choice. Humans live between necessity and freedom. Our peculiar life experience is formed out of physical contingency and the manner in which we inhabit this contingent realm and make it our own. Merleau-Ponty returned to give a fuller analysis of freedom in *Phenomenology of Perception*.

Behaviourist psychology not only oversimplified sensory experience, but also misconstrued the nature of rationality. Rationality has more than one form for Merleau-Ponty, and we should think more of a gradual continuum of different kinds of embodied rationality rather than of one standard type, against which all candidates for rationality are measured. Thus he stated in an essay, "The Metaphysical in Man", that he realised that Köhler's work on the intelligence of monkeys set new standards for our understanding of the world:

Koehler's work shows indisputably that, in addition to our own perceptual universe, we have to reconstruct the animal's universe in all its originality, with its "irrational" connections, its short-circuits, and its lacunae, and any success we have will come from taking our human experience of the animal as our starting point, describing the curve of its conduct as it appears to us...one cannot attach the same meaning to intelligence when referring to animals as when referring to people.

(SNS 83–84; 146–147)

But, though Merleau-Ponty drew on the findings of Gestalt psychology, he also criticised the Gestalt psychologists for trying to squeeze all their findings to fit into the laws of physics and thus still assuming that physical laws were sufficient to explain all behaviour, falling back into a 'scientistic or positivistic ontology' (*Primacy*, pp. 23–24). Against this kind of physicalism, Merleau-Ponty wants to oppose Gestalt findings concerning the manner in which conscious beings inhabit the material world by 'reliving' it. Gestalt psychology demands concepts borrowed from human experience, and hence requires an irreducibly human element. This means, of course, that Merleau-Ponty did not believe in an overall science of psychology which explained all behaviour, animal and human, just as later on, in his writings on language, he rejected the Husserlian dream of a universal grammar. Merleau-Ponty wants always to emphasise the particularities of the relations to the world of different kinds of organisms, their specific kinds of embodiment, and their different environments, from which all talk of stimulus and response simply abstracts.

Phenomenology of Perception (1945)

Merlau-Ponty's *Phenomenology of Perception* is a very long, complex book, written in Merleau-Ponty's difficult dialectical style, produced in a typically French way without scholarly apparatus such as an index, and laid out in byzantine fashion in an almost unintelligible set of divisions and chapter headings. In the tradition of Sartre's *Being and Nothingness*, Merlau-Ponty has attempted another large, rambling, overambitious book. The aim of *Phenomenology of Perception* is "to restore the world of perception" through phenomenological description. But Merleau-Ponty also discusses the origins of our experience of community, our experience of the other, and the nature of time. In fact, the range of the book is astonishing: remarks about dialectical materialism jostle with analyses of empirical psychology experiments. Furthermore, Merleau-Ponty provides few clues to the reader as to his own position; it is not always easy to tell when Merleau-Ponty is expounding or summarising a position he will then criticise, or making the criticism within the exposition.

Merleau-Ponty's aim was to carry on the project of *The Structure of Behaviour* but now to concentrate specifically on the formation of the human awareness of the world. Whereas the *Structure of Behaviour* had focused on animal behaviour generally, with only the last chapter devoted to humans, *Phenomenology of Perception* treats solely of humans. Merleau-Ponty aims to get close to the "present and living reality" of perception as a basis for studying complex issues such as the relation of humans to each other in language, culture, and society (*The Primacy of Perception*, p. 25). As he wrote in a piece which was published in 1962, a year after his death:

> We never cease living in the world of perception, but we go beyond it in critical thought – almost to the point of forgetting the contribution of perception to our idea of truth…The perceiving mind is an incarnate mind. I have tried, first of all, to re-establish the roots of the mind in its body and in its world, going against doctrines which treat perception as a simple result of the action of external things on our body as well as against those which insist on the autonomy of consciousness.
>
> (*Primacy*, pp. 3–4)

In his 1946 lecture, the *Primacy of Perception*, Merleau-Ponty explains himself further:

> By these words, "the primacy of perception", we mean that the experience of perception is our presence at the moment when things, truths, values are constituted for us; that perception is a nascent *logos*; that it teaches us, outside all dogmatism, the true conditions of objectivity itself; that it summons us to the tasks of knowledge and action. It is not a question of reducing human knowledge to sensation, but of assisting at the birth of this knowledge, to make it as sensible as the sensible, to recover the consciousness of rationality. This experience of rationality is lost when we take it for granted as self-evident, but is, on the contrary, rediscovered when it is made to appear against the background of non-human nature.
>
> (*Primacy*, p. 25)

Most philosophy concentrates on the processes of sophisticated, well-formed, rational thought, on our use of concepts and of language. What is ignored here is what Merleau-Ponty aptly calls "the *experience* of rationality", the manner in which thought and conceptual ability arise out of a more primordial, less articulated form of experience which he calls, following Husserl "the pre-predicative life of consciousness" (*la vie antéprédicative de la conscience*, PP xv; x), that is experience not yet articulated in propositional form (i.e. subject/predicate form). This pre-predicative experience is always the experience of a being with a body caught up in a finite and limited situation but nevertheless with the experience of possibilities within that situation. Every human situation is both finite and ambiguous. The finitude comes from our embodied and temporally incarnated manner of living. Our bodies and the specific formation of the sense organs reveal the world for us in a very special way. Merleau-Ponty invites us to consider what our notion of the world or of external objects would be like if we had eyes on either side of our heads rather than mounted so they both see the same things. Our whole understanding of the world is grounded in our corporeal nature.

This pre-reflective awareness cannot be caught in transcendental reflection as Husserl thought, but rather by examining breakdowns in the bodily circuit which bring to light routines and procedures which are hidden and assumed in our normal conscious state. One of Merleau-Ponty's most useful methods was to examine cases where our normal, assumed relation to the world breaks down. It is failures of the system which reveal most clearly how the system works. These systems, these matrices of habitual action through which we approach the world (PP 104; 121), are not transparent to consciousness and can never be uncovered simply by reflection. We need to study people with malfunctioning systems in order to make manifest the nature of the system, which, when working properly, is invisible. Nowhere is Merleau-Ponty's analysis more successful than in the chapter on the spatiality of one's body and the nature of our motor intentionality. Here, Merleau-Ponty significantly expanded the scope of the phenomenological method and removed it entirely from the domain of introspection, with which it has often been confused. He reinterpreted Husserlian reduction as a leading back to the pre-predicative and incarnate well-springs of our experience back to the *Lebenswelt*.

In order "to see the world and grasp it as paradoxical, we must break (*il faut rompre*) with our familiar acceptance of it and, also...from this break we can learn nothing but the unmotivated upsurge of the world" (*le jaillissement immotivé du monde*, PP xiv; viii). Thus, Merleau-Ponty drew on empirical studies of brain-damaged people, most notably a First World War veteran called Schneider, studied by Gelb and Goldstein. Schneider, whose brain had been damaged by shrapnel, exhibits a number of curious symptoms.[32] Though his motor ability is functioning, he is unable to perform bodily movements in the normal flowing human manner; rather he is mechanical, his whole body becomes an expression of a single movement. Similarly, though he can see shapes and outlines, he has to infer the nature of the objects in question by a process of reasoning. Part of the problem with Schneider as Merleau-Ponty analyses the diagnosis is that he is unable to step back mentally from the actual moment and explore the movement virtually before actually performing it. Merleau-Ponty points to the flexibility and plasticity of the normal human relation to the world of sensory experience and movement. We have as it were a 'virtual body' or phenomenal body wherein we can explore movements before actually performing them, and this 'virtual body' is correlated to a 'virtual space'. We do not have to locate our hands in space before moving them. When we see scissors they already mobilise certain potentialities of movement in us. It is our 'phenomenal body' (*le corps phénoménal*) and not the 'objective body' (*le corps objectif*) which is moved when we reach for the scissors (PP 106; 123).

In *Phenomenology of Perception* Merleau-Ponty continues the theme, prominent in his earlier *Structure of Behaviour*, of the inadequacy of contemporary empiricist and scientist accounts of human experience. The sciences have objectified human behaviour, separated the senses from one another, and have failed to grasp the subject in a holistic manner. Moreover, the inductive method and causal thinking generally have to be challenged (PP 115–116; 134). Merleau-Ponty claims that cause-and-effect explanation, suitable for physics, is not suitable in psychology. What we need to look for are not causes but *reasons* motivating the behaviour of the patient (PP 120; 140). We need to understand the way that patients attempt to construe the situation in which they find themselves in their impaired physical state. We have to treat the human subject as "an irresolvable consciousness which is wholly present in every one of its manifestations" (PP 120; 140). As part of this approach, Merleau-Ponty emphasises the necessity to take human freedom into account. But our freedom is constituted by the way we live in and adapt to a world of meanings where the significance of those meanings has already been chosen for us in a certain way. Whereas Sartre had emphasised the absolute nature of human freedom in his famous slogan "we are condemned to be free", Merleau-Ponty prefers a somewhat modified version of this slogan: "we are condemned to meaning" (PP xix; xiv). Furthermore, though Merleau-Ponty was seen as an atheistic existentialist like Sartre, he never agreed with Sartre's pessimistic account of intersubjective interaction. Against Sartre, who famously claimed that "hell is other people", Merleau-Ponty's motto had a more Hegelian ring: "history is other people" (*Primacy*, p. 25).

The role of sensation in perception

Phenomenology of Perception returns to a central preoccupation of the philosophies of Brentano, Stumpf, Meinong, and the early Husserl, namely an exact description of the nature of sensory perception. Merleau-Ponty, however, is drawing on Gestalt psychology, itself, through Ehrenfels, an outgrowth of the school of Brentano. Curiously, beyond appropriating Husserl's conception of 'profiles' (*Abschattungen*) and of perception's grasping its object bodily in the flesh (*leibhaftig*),[33] Merleau-Ponty does not discuss Husserl's account of perception in any great detail. He does not talk about the nature of perceptual fulfilments as distinct from those of memory or expectation. Instead Merleau-Ponty shifts more towards Husserl's critique of objective thought for assuming it grasps the thing beyond the perspectives through which it approaches them in perception. Our concept of a house more or less compresses our different perceptual *Abschattungen* into a single conceptual grasp, the house seen from nowhere, an invisible house. Merleau-Ponty does recognise that my vision of the house posits it as something beyond and independent of my vision, as having unseen aspects that are enclosed in various horizons of my perception (PP 69; 83). But, for Merleau-Ponty, the seen object is not the sum of the series of profiles or adumbrations. Rather it is seen directly and grasped in a special manner which Merleau-Ponty cannot fully articulate.[34] I don't form a mental concept of an object on the basis of sensuous experiences, rather it is "constituted in the hold which my body takes on it; it is not first of all a meaning for the understanding, but a structure accessible to inspection by the body" (PP 320; 369). To perceive something is to live it, Merleau-Ponty says cryptically.

In adapting Husserl's account of perception, Merleau-Ponty does take up Husserl's direct epistemological realism and also his critique of the role of sensory *hyle* in traditional representationalist accounts of perception. For Merleau-Ponty, traditional philosophy from Aristotle to Hume had misunderstood the role of perception in the formation of experience and awareness. We do not perceive sensations, though sensations are part of the make-up of the sensory process. In order to develop his account of the formation of our perceptual experience, Merleau-Ponty begins by taking issue with standard empiricist accounts of experience that begin by postulating sensory experience as a field of atomic sensations, the *sensation* as the assumed 'unit of experience'. He sees this as a traditional prejudice which must be overcome if we are truly to return to the things themselves. He rejects the view which treated sensory items (this patch of red) as primary givens which are then combined to produce our concepts of objects. As Merleau-Ponty says, in his later essay "The Metaphysical in Man", our awareness is not of colour patches or sounds but of real objects in the world:

> When I am aware or sensing, I am not, on the one hand, conscious of my state, and, on the other, of a certain sensuous quality such as red or blue – but blue or red are nothing other than my different ways of running my eyes over what is offered to me and of responding to its solicitation.
>
> (SNS 93; 164)

There are no pure sensations for Merleau-Ponty. The perceived thing (be it a patch of colour) is always perceived as having a certain figure or form against a background. This is what Merleau-Ponty took from Gestalt psychology, but he developed it further by describing phenomenologically just how we experience the world visually. Thus, although the "greyness which, when I close my eyes, surrounds me, leaving no distance between me and it" (PP 3; 9) may be considered to be the closest thing in our experience to a pure sensation, it is already laden with meaning. What we see is not just 'red' colour on the carpet but a specific 'woolly red' ('*rouge laineux*', PP 5;

10) which belongs specifically to this kind of textured material. In his later writings, Merleau-Ponty persisted in criticising the fragmented, dissociated approach to sensations found in empiricism. As he put it in his last unfinished text, *The Visible and the Invisible*, the thing that I see is not a "wandering troop of sensations" (*un troupeau errant de sensations*, VI 123; 164), and he saw his task as showing that sensation is neither a matter of an opaque sensible *quale*, nor a matter of penetrating through to the universal essence, but of grasping the nature of "sensory matter", the "sensible for itself" (*sensible pour soi*), the world which is made up of the same stuff that I am. I experience "a segment of the durable flesh of the world" (VI 123; 164).

Assuming that experience is made up of sensations is a prejudice which must be removed before we can do true phenomenological description of perception. Similarly we also have to rid ourselves (as Husserl also argues in the *Crisis*) of the seventeenth-century assumption that an object is made up of a set of properties some of which are genuinely in the object and others of which are just assumed to be in the object by the perceiving subject (the primary–secondary quality distinction). Merleau-Ponty was well aware that we frequently assume that aspects of the object are also properties of our experience of the object. We are not able to separate clearly the world from our experience of the world. The one is always invading the other: "We are involved in the world (*Nous sommes pris dans le monde*) and we do not succeed in extricating ourselves from it in order to achieve consciousness of the world" (PP 5; 11). It is not that the world is quite determinate and that our experience is somehow fuzzy and vague; rather we inhabit a world which is indeterminate in a strong sense and this indeterminacy must be made the subject of philosophical scrutiny. Merleau-Ponty wants to explore this 'pre-objective realm' (*ce domain préobjectif*, PP 12; 19) of our lived experience but to do so properly we must abandon a distorting traditional epistemology and concentrate on describing the manner in which objects genuinely confront us in the world. Grasping the unity of objects as I walk around them, it is clear that "I could not grasp the unity of the object without the mediation of bodily experience" (PP 203; 235). This is an important modification of the Kantian claim that I cannot have an experience of objectivity without already having a concept of the unity of the self. For Merleau-Ponty, I grasp the unity of objects through having a prior pre-cognitive grasp of the unity of my bodily experience. The different sensory paths are all experienced as part of the one body, and I have no experience of the senses working separately; rather the senses overlap and 'transgress' each other's boundaries. I *see* a wall as climbable, scissors as graspable, an apple as edible.

Alongside his critique of sensory experience and false epistemological theories about the nature of the object, Merleau-Ponty wants us to rethink our traditional dualism of soul and body, mind and body, consciousness and body. Here, too, Merleau-Ponty wants to move between empiricism and idealism. He is particularly opposed to the view that reason sits on top of a physical, sensory experience. Rationality itself is imbued with sensibility and vice versa. Just as he attacked empiricism, he also attacked intellectualist and idealist Cartesian psychology (including Sartre's account) which sees consciousness as transparent and given all at once. For Merleau-Ponty, this is to ignore the many ways in which humans are incarnated, to ignore disease, madness, and other aspects of the human condition. Merleau-Ponty focused on precisely those phenomena that indicate the close relation of mind and body, the phenomenon of going to sleep, of moving one's limbs, the nature of memory, and the world-views of people with brain damage. Thus in discussing the way in which we prepare our bodies for sleep by lying down, relaxing, curling up, or whatever, we 'invite' sleep which comes to us not by an explicit conscious willing on our part but not entirely without our participation either. The ambiguity of our attitude in the case of sleep is indicative of the whole complex nature of our embodiment.

One's own body (*Le corps propre*)

In *Phenomenology of Perception*, Merleau-Ponty argues that our physical body is not experienced by us as an object among other objects in space. Merleau-Ponty utilised Husserl's distinction between the inanimate physical body (*Körper*) and the living animate body (*Leib*) to argue that humans are indeed inserted into the world in a very specific, organic way, determined by the nature of our sensory and motor capacities to perceive the world in a specific way. Merleau-Ponty's notion of one's own or proper body (*le corps propre*) has some anticipations in Bergson's discussion of the body in the opening chapter of *Matter and Memory*, in Marcel's discussion in his *Metaphysical Journal* of the manner in which I am my body as opposed to having a body (PP 174n.; 203n.), and seems especially to be a critical meditation on Sartre's chapter on the body in *Being and Nothingness* (BN 303–359) where Sartre uses the verb 'to exist' in a transitive manner to form such novel expressions as "I exist my body" (BN 329; 378), "I live my body" (BN 325; 373), to show that there is no separation between my existence and my embodiment. Like Merleau-Ponty, Sartre claims that I cannot perceive my body, except as an external object like any other. Unlike Merleau-Ponty, Sartre sees no special significance in our ability to touch ourselves, to touch and to be touched at the same time. However, he draws heavily on Sartre's account of how my body is somehow 'everywhere' (*partout*) in my experience of the world. As Sartre says:

> That is why my body always extends across the tool which it utilizes: it is at the end of the cane on which I lean and against the earth, it is at the end of the telescope which shows me the stars; it is

on the chair, in the whole house, for it is my adaptation to these tools.

(BN 325; 373)

We don't just take up space, we *inhabit* it, we relate to it, in Merleau-Ponty's judicious image, "like a hand to an instrument" (*Primacy*, p. 5). The relations between consciousness and body are by no means straightforward. Perception for Merleau-Ponty, developing Husserl's concept of 'lived experience' (*Erlebnis, expérience vécue*), is a manner in which we, as embodied beings, are projected into the world. We discover ourselves in a world, as a part of the world, but not as simple spatial objects in a spatial world. For Merleau-Ponty, it also seemed as if the world is also made to be discovered by, and to respond to, our sense organs. It is this mutuality and interrelatedness of the relation between self and world which fascinated Merleau-Ponty. Husserl in *Ideas* II had discussed the relation between the world of culture and of nature, and Merleau-Ponty saw these two worlds as united together in the experience of the sensory, in perception, in the ambiguous world of the flesh. As Merleau-Ponty says that when in touching one hand with the other, I touch myself touching, then, in fact,

> my body does not perceive, but it is as if it were built around the perception that dawns through it; through its whole internal arrangement, its sensory motor circuits, the return ways that control and release movements, it is, as it were, prepared for a self-perception, even though it is never itself that is perceived or itself that perceives.

(VI 9; 24)

For Merleau-Ponty, the body brings me into a spatial world in a special way. I discover things as left and right, tall and small, etc., all on the basis of my orientation wherein my body occupies the 'zero point', as Husserl had already described in *Ideas* II. My body also brings me into the world of sexuality depending on the kind of sexual orientation which my body unfolds for me. My concrete existence is always 'sexual being' (*l'être sexué*); perception has an erotic structure. Again, Merleau-Ponty uses the case of Schneider, whose sexual dysfunction shows up the normally sexed manner of our bodily awareness and sensations. The breakdown of sexual reaction in Schneider occurs, not at the level of an automatic physiological reaction nor on the level of conscious representation, but in a 'vital zone' where Eros "breathes life into an original world" (PP 156; 182). Merleau-Ponty thinks that the real significance of Freud is not his claim that human behaviour is explained by its sexual substructure, but rather a discovery that sexuality itself possesses "relations and attitudes which had previously

424

been held to reside in consciousness" (PP 158; 184). In our sexuality is projected our manner of being in the world; our sexual life has its own intentional and meaning-giving powers, though some feminist critics have accused Merleau-Ponty of assuming that the lived body is implicitly or explicitly male in his descriptions of the sexuality of our being-in-the-world.

The notion of the body-subject cannot be reached through the sciences, it is more like a specific characterisation of what Heidegger more generally calls Dasein. The body, for Merleau-Ponty, has its own set of motivations, for example the manner in which the colours in our visual field remain relatively constant for us despite changes in the quality of the light and so on (the phenomenon known as 'colour constancy'). The body discloses the world for us in a certain way. It is the transcendental condition for the possibility of experiencing objects at all, our means of communication with the world (PP 92; 109).

The body as expression

Speech is also an expression of my body and Merleau-Ponty devotes separate chapters of *Phenomenology of Perception* to describing the spatial, sexual, and linguistic aspects of embodiment. Again, the nature of speech is examined from the cases of breakdown of the circuit, in this case, Goldstein's analysis of aphasia and anarthria (breakdown of articulate speech). Merleau-Ponty's account of language is close to that of the later Heidegger, and indeed the later Wittgenstein of the *Philosophical Investigations* (with which Merleau-Ponty appears to have been unfamiliar, though he was acquainted with the *Tractatus*). Our possession of language is a matter of how we *use* words not our possession of the stock of words. Going further than Husserl, Merleau-Ponty maintains there can be no thought without language. For Merleau-Ponty, thought requires articulation in speech if it is to achieve anything like a determinate form:

> A thought limited to existing for itself (*pour soi*), independently of the constraints of speech and communication, would no sooner appear than it would sink into the unconscious, which means that it would not exist even for itself.
>
> (PP 177; 206)

Thought is incarnated in speech in the same manner that the mind is incarnated in the body. Speech is not the articulation of a completed thought but rather the accomplishment of the thought itself (PP 178; 207):

> The orator does not think before speaking, nor even while speaking; his speech is his thought.
>
> (PP 180; 209)

425

Speech is a new sense organ for Merleau-Ponty which brings into focus meanings which would never otherwise arise. In speaking we take up a position in the world. However, besides emphasising the manner we inhabit a world of language as an institution, Merleau-Ponty points out that there must also be an original learning of speaking:

> Our view of man will remain superficial so long as we fail to go back to that origin, so long as we fail to find, beneath the chatter of words, the primordial silence, and as long as we do not describe the action that breaks the silence. The spoken word is a gesture, and its meaning a world.
>
> (PP 184; 214)

Moreover, for Merleau-Ponty, it is the body which points out and which speaks.

Other chapters in *Phenomenology of Perception* deal with our relations to others, with temporality, and with our insertion into history. Our relationship with others is the basis of history. Against Husserl, Merleau-Ponty dismisses the view that we construct the other on the basis of an analogy with our own subjectivity. Rather we are already in a world of others, *Mitsein*. The infant can react to me opening my mouth by opening his or her mouth; the infant already experiences my mouth as a mouth like his or hers, even if our teeth and so on are very different. The pages on the nature of time are more unsatisfactory, and even contradictory, in that Merleau-Ponty appears to be propounding an ontological thesis about time itself as well as a phenomenological account of our experience or consciousness of time. Whereas Merleau-Ponty had earlier talked about a natural and objective time, he now talks of time as self-constituting and as something produced by the relation between self and world.[35] The world in itself, in terms which echo Sartre, appears as a kind of Parmenidean indivisible and changeless one (PP 411; 470), too much of a 'plenum' to contain time. Merleau-Ponty goes on, "[t]ime is not a real process...It arises from *my* relation to things" (PP 412; 471). Time disrupts the plenitude of being, a conception which may derive from Plotinus, the subject of Merleau-Ponty's earliest thesis. Merleau-Ponty follows Augustine, Hegel, Marx, Bergson, Husserl, and Heidegger in seeing time and temporality as essentially constituted in human consciousness. But, Merleau-Ponty rejected any ability of thought to pierce through time, to transcend it to a world of timeless meanings, which he took to be a flaw in Husserl's earlier logicist programme. According to Merleau-Ponty, "thought does not bore through time" (*Signs*, p. 14; 21). In a certain sense, our entire reality is temporal to the extent that we somehow bring about time, constitute it, and yet Merleau-Ponty, following the late Husserl, takes consciousness itself to be a kind of presence outside of time (PP 422; 483). We must get over the view that, in thinking, our thoughts connect only with each other; rather they are rooted in the historical event (*Primacy*, p. 48). Events have their particular nature only because of our standpoints and interests; events are sliced out of the whole. Unfortunately, as is often the case with Merleau-Ponty, these pages on time are imaginative, suggestive, well informed concerning various traditional approaches, but entirely unclear as to their final outlook on the puzzling nature of time and temporality.

Merleau-Ponty's later philosophy

In his overall metaphysical outlook, as in his view of time and history, Merleau-Ponty is a philosopher who emphasises contingency, finitude, situatedness through incarnation, embodiment in just this structure of sensibility. In a lecture delivered in Geneva he described the tasks facing philosophers as follows: "Incarnation and the other are the *labyrinth* of reflection and of sensibility for our contemporaries" (quoted by Sartre, *Situations*, p. 213). Merleau-Ponty acknowledged that Christianity with its emphasis on the mystery of the Incarnation had got hold of a central mystery of the human condition even though it misunderstood it and shifted the focus to the relation between God and human embodiment. The real mystery is human embodiment itself which Cartesian, Humean, and Kantian philosophy have all misunderstood and undervalued. In traditional philosophy the body was at most an object among objects, subject to the same physical laws as other things. In the twentieth century several philosophers and psychologists – including Bergson, Marcel, Freud, Dewey, Whitehead, and Sartre – reacted against the Cartesian inheritance by emphasising that the world is revealed to us through our body. We understand the nature of spatiality through the way our body inhabits and moves through space. We also are incarnated in a specific manner with a specific gender and with a sexual outlook which colours our relations to everything in the world. The body – through the speech organs – also is what gives rise to the possibility of thought in us. We are incarnate through and through.

Merleau-Ponty's later philosophy was particularly concerned with studying how the other is experienced by us – both in our visual seeing of other bodies and in our encounter with others in language. For Merleau-Ponty, here developing a theme of Hegel and coming close to the views on language expressed by the later Heidegger, the other is already within us when we use language. Merleau-Ponty is now analysing the nature of communication beyond the realm of perception. He is now interested in the manner in which signs and symbols take us far beyond the world of immediate perception. However, this does not lead Merleau-Ponty beyond Husserl, as indeed one of Husserl's central themes was how symbolic thought was possible. The nature of this new world of communication is summed up in Merleau-Ponty's phrase 'the prose of the world', the title of a planned book which derives from Hegel's statement that the Roman state was the prose of the world (*Prose*, p. ix). In the 170 pages of typescript and working notes which survive of this project, Merleau-Ponty sets out to understand the manner in which the intersubjective world is brought about through language understood as expression and gesture. As always he is trying to retrace the links between the bodily perceptual world and the world of culture and signification:

> We are certainly not denying...the originality of the order of knowledge vis-à-vis the perceptual order. We are trying only to loose the intentional web which ties them to one another, to rediscover the paths of the sublimation which preserves and transforms the perceived world into the spoken world.
>
> (*Prose*, pp. 123–124; 173)

In charting the relation between the perceived world and the world of speech and expression, Merleau-Ponty conceives of the relation between the domains traditionally described as 'spirit' and 'matter' as actually a closer relation, the relation between a painter and his or her style, for example. The *style* of the painter inhabits the hand of the painter. In fact, Merleau-Ponty attributes to Husserl the introduction of the term 'style' to translate our original relation to the world (*Prose*, p. 56; 79). This style is characterised by a spontaneity over which we have no conscious control (see Husserl's Fourth Cartesian Meditation). Merleau-Ponty had discussed the notion of 'style' in *Phenomenology of Perception* but it comes to the fore in his later writing on art.

However, Merleau-Ponty abandoned the *Prose of the World* project in the mid-1950s and turned to another project, which had various working titles, including *The Visible and Invisible* and *The Origin of Truth* (VI 165; 219). Merleau-Ponty now wants to rework *Phenomenology of Perception* but from the perspective of ontology (VI 168; 222), which he sometimes calls an 'indirect ontology'. The project of *Phenomenology of Perception* has become impossible because he had still assumed a consciousness–object relation (VI 200; 253), whereas he really needs to do justice to the ontological state of 'brute or wild being' (*l'Être brut ou sauvage*), from which perception and consciousness emerge as a kind of 'rupture'. This later thought seeks a kind of ontology or metaphysics not as a system, but rather as a way of sketching more accurately our encounter with the world which is accounted for in a distorted way by science. The world of perception is now referred to as the domain of the 'visible' interwoven with the 'invisible'. The whole world of the visible is spread out like a field of possibilities. As he says in "Eye and Mind", my body is visible and mobile, and a thing among things. It is not, however, just a "chunk of space" but an "intertwining of vision and movement" (*Primacy*, p. 162). For Merleau-Ponty, the fact that the body is both perceiver and perceived is expressed by our experience of flesh. Things are encrusted in the flesh of the body, just as the body is part of the fabric of the world (*Primacy*, p. 163). The term 'flesh' is to indicate a certain experience of a surface which has an inside and yet where the inside and outside meet, Merleau-Ponty's way of overcoming the traditional subject–object dichotomy. We belong to a 'system of exchanges'. Colours, sounds, and things are "the focal points and radiance of being" (*Signs*, p. 15; 22). Furthermore, he rejected the superficial distinction between outer and inner world which even Husserl had continued to promulgate. In later texts, Merleau-Ponty emphasised our conviction of living in a common world, of there being only one world for us, a world whose visible skin is especially made for our bodies to see. The deepest faith we have is faith in the perceived world. "And it is this unjustifiable certitude of a sensible world common to us that is the seat of truth within us" (VI 11; 27). A child perceives before it can think or talk, and the sensible world is there for us before any thought. Thought emerges out of sensory immersion in the world. Merleau-Ponty termed this realm of immersed sensory thought "wild thought" (*pensée sauvage*), no doubt directly alluding to Lévi-Strauss's term for the mytho-poeic thought of primitive peoples.[36] Our scientific reflective thought is removed from this thought, so it is necessary for us to undergo a special form of reflection to get back to this primitive contact with the world. This is the meaning which Merleau-Ponty took from Husserl's suspension of the natural attitude; on the one hand, we have to put aside our reflective categories, but, on the other hand, we discover the natural hooks that connect us to the world. That is why for Merleau-Ponty the reduction can never be complete, it leads us back to the realm of "wild being" (*l'être sauvage*) of pre-reflective thought. As he says in his essay "Everywhere and Nowhere", a concrete philosophy must be empirical but it must not limit itself to the empirical, but rather "restore to each experience the ontological cipher which marks it internally" (*Signs*, p. 157; 198). In attempting to sketch out this new ontology, Merleau-Ponty depended heavily on a rethinking of the basic terms of *en-soi* and *pour-soi* of Sartre's ontology. The characterisation of the world as 'brute being' seems to echo Sartre's conception of the opacity of the *être en-soi*. But contrary to the strong dichotomy which Sartre has between the two domains, Merleau-Ponty always maintains that the in-itself is already for-us. It has been argued that Merleau-Ponty's attempts to create this new ontology were unsuccessful because he was unable to articulate successfully this "intra ontology" (VI 227) which he was seeking. He employed terms like 'chiasm' which suggest a kind of crossing over and intertwining, but his working notes are so cryptic that it is really impossible to construct a workable ontology from them.

The metaphysics of contingency

Merleau-Ponty was strongly opposed to all attempts to posit an absolute completely distinct from human experience and remained agnostic in religious terms. As he wrote in 1947: "metaphysical and moral conscious-ness dies upon contact with the absolute" (SNS 95; 167). Contingency is not a fact that we simply acknowledge and then proceed in constructing abstract systems of thought, rather contingency is the very condition of a metaphysical view of the world (SNS 96; 168). Merleau-Ponty, like Sartre, rejected the possibility of an absolute point of view from which the totality of the world could be viewed. His philosophy is always a philosophy of immersion in the world, of incarnation. Merleau-Ponty, however, did write some interesting essays on the one feature of Christian theology which interested him – the mystery of the Incarnation. Indeed, he saw himself as developing a secular version of that all-too-human mystery. He claimed to be not denying the absolute but rather bringing it down to earth. As he put it in his lecture, "The Primacy of Perception": "To tell the truth, Christian-ity consists in replacing the separated absolute by the absolute in men" (*Primacy*, p. 27). In his last writings, he planned a discussion of Catholicism, though he noted that he must present himself without any compromise towards theology. The whole division of the world into God–man–creatures had becomes unthinkable for him (VI 274; 328).

We should mention, finally, that Merleau-Ponty's thought, with its emphasis on the impossibility of transcending history, tends towards a kind of *relativism*. Indeed his critics accused him of reviving the relativism of the ancient Greek philosopher Protagoras. We can never grasp the world in its totality but we grasp it according to the mode in which we inhabit it. Humans can only understand the world as it is revealed and uncovered to humans with our specific forms of being-in-the-world. There is no doubt that Merleau-Ponty was convinced that our experience of objective things in the world was deeply conditioned by the kind of perceptual apparatus we have. If we were creatures with eyes on either side of our heads, there is little doubt but that we would propose very different ontologies. The kind of relativism Merleau-Ponty endorses involves a denial of any absolute truth about the world. It is a relativism of the relation between being and human being: being is everything but would not be what it is without us, as he says in *In Praise of Philosophy* (*Praise*, p. 5). There is always only what is 'absolute for us'.

Merleau-Ponty's influence on contemporary philosophy

Maurice Merleau-Ponty was one of the most exciting and brilliant thinkers of the twentieth century, yet his work has never been given the public attention accorded to Sartre, Levinas, or Derrida. Perhaps in part, Merleau-Ponty's comparative obscurity is due to his own retiring personality. He was an austere intellectual, too individualistic, as Sartre acknowledged, to collaborate in research with anyone. Indeed, his influence in France came mainly through his political writings in *Les Temps modernes*. In philosophy he had many admirers but, apart from his editor, Claude Lefort, few followers. Some of the difficulties following Merleau-Ponty lie in his flowing, literary, metaphorical mode of expression. His philosophical attempts to be 'present at the birth of meaning' and to 'sing the world' mean that literary language often appears at the very moment the reader seeks conceptual precision. Merleau-Ponty himself felt that philosophy lacked the power of visual art to convey the meanings he sought. As he put it, "philosophy limps".

As we have seen, Merleau-Ponty was an important influence on Sartre's political outlook. In addition, Merleau-Ponty himself always drew on Sartre's philosophy, for example Sartre's studies of the imagination are discussed in his Sorbonne lectures (*Primacy*, pp. 59–60) and, of course, Merleau-Ponty helped himself liberally to Sartre's analyses of the body and to his general ontology. Merleau-Ponty's use of the terms 'for-itself' and 'in-itself', though superficially Sartrean, also has a close debt to their use in the writings of Hegel as conveyed by Kojève. Sartre and Merleau-Ponty both agree in seeing human consciousness as a kind of fissure in the world; quoting the poet Paul Valéry, perception is the 'flaw in the great diamond' (*le 'défaut' de ce grand 'diamant'*, PP 207; 240).

Levinas in *Totality and Infinity* (TI 205–207; 180–182), published in 1961, acknowledges Merleau-Ponty but without discussing him in any great detail. But, in other essays, Levinas showed himself to be deeply impressed by Merleau-Ponty's lucid interpretation of Husserl's unpublished writings. Levinas was particularly interested in Merleau-Ponty's account of intersubjectivity and incarnation. Furthermore, for Levinas, Merleau-Ponty showed the manner in which the body is already a field of intentions: "thought operates in the 'I can' of the body" (TI 206; 181), echoing Merleau-Ponty's statement that "consciousness is in the first place not a matter of 'I think' but of 'I can' " (PP 137; 160), which itself is derived from Husserl. Regarding 'carnal subjectivity' Levinas says:

> It is difficult for me to find terms adequate to express my admiration for the subtle beauty of the analyses in Merleau-Ponty's work of that original incarnation of mind in which Nature reveals its meaning in movements of the human body that are essentially signifying, i.e. expressive, i.e. cultural...the French philosopher's own quest doubtless permitted him to say the non-said (of at least the non-published) of Husserl's thought.[37]

Anticipating Levinas's writings, Merleau-Ponty was particularly preoccupied with phenomenologically describing the experience of the other in appropriate terms. In particular, he rejected Cartesian and Husserlian attempts to construct the other out of my own conception of him or her. The other is not "an offspring of my spirit", Merleau-Ponty says, but "my twin or flesh of my flesh" (*mes jumeaux ou la chair de ma chair, Signs*, p. 15; 22). The other's body is "an unexpected response I get from elsewhere" (*Prose*, p. 134; 186). The other and myself are like two nearly concentric circles, but the other's dwelling elsewhere "deprives me of my central location" (*Prose*, p. 135; 187). However, against Levinas, Merleau-Ponty sees the mystery of the other as really nothing more than the mystery of my relation to myself, my own ability to adopt perspectives other than mine. The following passage suggests Merleau-Ponty's possible response to Levinas:

> The experience of the other is always that of a replica of myself, of a response to myself. The solution must be sought in the direction of that strange filiation which makes the other forever my second, even when I refer him to myself and sacrifice myself to him. It is in the very depths of myself that this strange articulation with the other is fashioned. The mystery of the other is nothing but the mystery of myself. A second spectator on the world can be born from me.
>
> (*Prose*, p. 135; 188)

From his earliest book, *La Structure du comportement* (1942), Merleau-Ponty was interested in interpreting the world in terms of the importance of structures and absorbed both Marxist and linguistic structuralism as is evident from the frequent references in his writing. Although Merleau-Ponty lectured on de Saussure and through his close friendship of Claude Lévi-Strauss was strongly connected to the structuralist movement, nevertheless Merleau-Ponty is rarely included in studies of structuralism.[38] Both Gilles Deleuze and Michel Foucault in fact interpreted Merleau-Ponty, with his appeal to lost origins, as a foundationalist and defender of a humanism which structuralism was seeking to overcome.[39]

With regard to post-structuralism, Merleau-Ponty's influence has until recently been almost completely ignored, eclipsed by Derrida and Levinas, though there have been efforts, especially in the USA, to make Merleau-Ponty the father of postmodernism by emphasising his discussions of the body, sexuality, and otherness.

Though they never met, Derrida acknowledges the brilliance of Merleau-Ponty, with whom he corresponded briefly with regard to arranging a French translation of Husserl's *Crisis*. Nevertheless, the true importance of Merleau-Ponty as pioneer of many of the concepts which Derrida later writes about has yet to be fully documented. Paul Ricoeur, on the other hand, has always recognised the importance of Merleau-Ponty. The French psychoanalyst Jacques Lacan also saw in Merleau-Ponty the philosophical

432

account he needed to express his own insights into the unconscious (e.g. like Lacan, Merleau-Ponty was interested in the 'mirror stage' of the child's development, and both agreed that the unconscious is structured like a language).

There is, however, the beginnings of a revival of interest in Merleau-Ponty, especially among those interested in phenomenology's answers to questions currently being posed in analytic philosophy of mind. Merleau-Ponty is a consistent naturalist, who treats the human as inserted into nature in an organic manner, and who rejects all dualism of mind and body. His view of the embodied subject still has something to contribute to the philosophy of spatial perception and somatic awareness. In the USA Merleau-Ponty has had a major influence on phenomenological and psycho-therapeutic approaches to the body. Merleau-Ponty is an enormous influence in the work on place and space in Edward Casey and on the existential psychiatrist and author Oliver Sacks's studies of human perception of the world as revealed when some part of the system is malfunctioning, for example *The Man Who Mistook His Wife for a Hat*.[40] Merleau-Ponty's relativism and his emphasis on the relation of human being to the environment are also themes which have become current in recent philosophy. However, Merleau-Ponty's very ambiguities in attempting to lay the groundwork for a new ontology in his later writings have themselves inhibited any definite structure being built on his thought.

Merleau-Ponty had little contact with Anglo-American philosophy during his life (besides participating in a conference with Gilbert Ryle and discussing philosophy with A. J. Ayer).[41] Notwithstanding, Merleau-Ponty's stature is growing in contemporary analytic philosophy – especially as his attempt to describe the incarnate body-subject, drawing on up-to-date empirical research in psychology, is emulated by some philosophers of mind. Merleau-Ponty's claim, in late notes written in June 1960, that we have no idea of the mind without somehow employing the image of the body (VI 259; 312) is close to the claim of Wittgenstein that the best image of the soul is the body. In his critique of stimulus–response explanation and behaviourist reductionism, he anticipates Noam Chomsky's criticisms of Skinner. Merleau-Ponty's account of the spatial orientation of the body and his discussions of sense perception have influenced Christopher Peacocke's notion of non-conceptual awareness. As I have suggested here, Merleau-Ponty may be read profitably as espousing *naturalism* – in his attempt to read consciousness as a specific feature of human and animal embodiment drawing on biology and psychology – but he distances himself from naturalism in so far as it becomes a reductive scientism. Nevertheless, Merleau-Ponty's emphasis on embodiment and finitude, and his careful discrimination between reasons and causes in his discussion of the nature of explanation in the human sciences, find many contemporary echoes, though, unfortunately, usually without reference to Merleau-Ponty. But he has undoubtedly produced the most detailed example of the manner in which phenomenology can interact with the sciences and the arts to provide a descriptive account of the nature of human bodily being-in-the-world.

13

JACQUES DERRIDA

From phenomenology to deconstruction

Introduction – neither philosophy nor literature

Jacques Derrida (b. 1930) is an exciting, challenging, but highly controversial, philosopher, best known for spawning the intellectual movement (fashionable in some intellectual circles, particularly in the USA, during the 1970s and early 1980s) known as 'deconstruction'. In his many publications Derrida has offered deconstructive readings of texts drawn from such diverse areas as phenomenology, structuralism, psychoanalysis, literature, painting, and, more recently, texts on political, legal, and even religious, matters. Derrida, however, is difficult to categorise, as he denies that he is doing philosophy or developing a new philosophical 'method'. Nor is he composing literature or claiming that philosophy reduces to literature. He prefers to situate his work at the *limits* or borderlines between disciplines, exploring what he calls the 'turbulence' of the relation between philosophy and literature. His strategy is to call attention to the *contexts* of texts and to show how their meanings are transformed when recontextualised, that is through being inserted into different narratives, compared with other texts, and so on. This has led him deliberately to challenge many of the typical categorical distinctions in Western thought, for example the distinctions between literature and philosophy, speech and writing, sensibility and intellect, the literal and the metaphorical. His writing is always difficult, complex, and allusive; he obsessively seizes on seemingly insignificant marginal details to overturn the supposed central message of the text. To explore the complexity of language and reference, Derrida, drawing on the French symbolist and surrealist tradition, has also often resorted to producing various kinds of experimental texts, where he engages in a kind of *playfulness*, experimenting with typographies and graphic representations, writing under pseudonyms, and so on.

Derrida's general claims about language and meaning, and his complex style of writing, have provoked a diversity of passionate responses, ranging from uncritical adulation and emulation to denunciation, even derision. Such is the contested nature of his work that, in 1992, the decision of Cambridge University to award him an honorary doctorate brought protests, and even the accusation by a number of philosophers that his work does not meet acceptable standards of academic rigour.[1] However, he also has his defenders among the philosophical community (including John Sallis, John D. Caputo, Simon Critchley, and others). Many of his deconstructive readings emerge from his seminars, and his teaching is widely acknowledged as charismatic. Derrida is infamous for his highly stylised, self-reflexive, at times even self-indulgent, lecturing performances, during which he may speak without notes for many hours at a time, exhibiting a powerful memory, as he traces and retraces his own attempts and failures ('aporias', i.e. blockages, dead-ends) to get to grips with a certain text or train of thought. One such talk given over two days and lasting six hours has been published as *Aporias*.[2] However, Derrida can expound his views clearly and cogently, and has done so in many interviews. Part of the problem of Derrida exegesis, then, becomes the attempt to bring his rather clear assertions and repudiations of positions, as given in his interviews, into consistency with his more complex, indeed richly ambiguous, written texts. This, of course, itself raises a theme which Derrida himself has treated at great length, namely the relation between speech and writing.

Unfortunately, in this chapter, we cannot here assess Derrida's work as a whole, but shall concentrate mainly on his writings up to 1972, paying particular attention to his key 1968 lecture, "*la différance*". Derrida's earlier writings lay the framework for his later interpretations. His more recent writings, published at an increasingly frenetic pace, are simply too voluminous to be covered here. We shall, therefore, leave to one side much of Derrida's recent essays on ethical and political matters, in order to focus on his central philosophical claims regarding meaning, especially in so far as these claims emerge from his engagement with phenomenology.

Since Derrida portrays himself as having gone beyond both phenomenology and philosophy, it might be argued that his *oeuvre* ought not to be treated under the rubric of phenomenology or even philosophy at all. But Derrida's path *beyond* philosophy is essentially a route which went *through* phenomenology. He began his philosophical career rather conventionally as a student of Husserlian phenomenology, writing a number of close, critical studies of both the *Logical Investigations* and *The Origin of Geometry*. In these essays, Derrida sought to expose the hidden metaphysical presuppositions of traditional Husserlian phenomenology, which, in his view, far from being a presuppositionless science, actually belonged to the history of metaphysics. Indeed, Husserlian phenomenology, with its commitment to self-identical ideal truths, remains, for Derrida, trapped in "the metaphysics of presence in the form of ideality".[3] Derrida's critique, however, does not constitute a complete abandonment of the phenomenological mode of enquiry, rather he wants to liberate phenomenology from its attachment to the very metaphysical standpoint it claims to have overcome, seeking to get beyond phenomenology's addiction to the intuition of presence. In effect,

Derrida is 'deconstructing' phenomenology. Indeed, Derrida's central conceptions, for example 'presence', 'repetition', 'trace', *différance, écriture*, etc., and his advocacy of deconstruction both as a textual strategy, even as a kind of moral duty, and as something like an inevitable process in the history of philosophy, are best understood in terms of his critique of Husserl's phenomenology of signification as logocentric and his radicalisation of the problematic of language in a manner which is deeply Heideggerian.

Jacques Derrida: life and writings (1930–)

Derrida has often drawn attention to the complexities involved in relating an author's biography to his or her written work. Yet, autobiographical references are interwoven in his own texts. It is worth, therefore, attending to the circumstances of his life and writings. Of Sephardic Jewish extraction, Jacques Derrida was born in Algeria, on 15 July 1930, in the El-Biar suburb of the capital, Algiers. He began attending the local *lycée* there in 1941, but his family life and school studies were disrupted by the Second World War, and especially by the restrictions imposed on Jews by the local regime, even in the absence of the Germans, as he has bitterly remarked. He failed his *baccalauréat* on the first attempt in 1947, but passed it in 1948. He then enrolled in an *école préparatoire*, a school which prepared students for university education, and, at that time, began reading Camus, Bergson, Sartre, Nietzsche, and Gide, while also publishing some poetry. In 1949 he moved to France to attend the prestigious Lycée Louis-le-Grand (where Sartre had earlier studied), to prepare for the competitive entrance examinations to the exclusive French institutes of higher learning. He was now becoming increasingly interested in philosophy. At first he failed the difficult entrance test for the Ecole Normale Supérieure, but eventually passed it in 1952 and was admitted to study philosophy at the institute from which Sartre, Aron, de Beauvoir, Hyppolite, and Merleau-Ponty had all graduated a generation earlier.

On his first day at the Ecole Normale he encountered Louis Althusser who became a close friend. He also began attending the lectures of Michel Foucault and Jean Hyppolite. Initially he focused on Husserlian phenomenology and in 1953–1954 he prepared his *Diplôme d'études supérieures*, under the direction of Jean Hyppolite and Maurice de Gandillac, entitled *The Problem of Genesis in Husserl's Philosophy*, a 'panoramic' study of Husserl's development from the *Philosophy of Arithmetic* through the *Crisis*. While preparing this thesis, Derrida consulted the Husserl Archives in Louvain. Though Hyppolite urged the young Derrida to publish the work, it did not appear in print until 1990.[4] In this early work, Derrida shows himself to be well grounded in Husserl's texts, and also to have been strongly influenced by the French philosopher Jean Cavaillès, and the

Vietnamese phenomenologist and Marxist Tran-Duc-Thao. In his Preface, Derrida examines Husserl's oppositions (e.g. eidetic/empirical; transcendental/worldly; original/derived; pure/impure; genetic/constitutive) arguing that Husserl ignored the manner in which these oppositions in fact enter in some kind of 'dialectic', and, as Derrida says, 'contaminate' each another.[5]

On completing his *diplôme*, Derrida embarked on a doctoral thesis on "The Ideality of the Literary Object", but eventually abandoned the project, in part because of the death of his thesis director, Jean Hyppolite. However, many years later, in 1980, he was awarded the *Doctorat d'Etat* (state doctorate), on the basis of his published work (*'sur travaux'*). His thesis defence has been translated as "The Time of a Thesis: Punctuations".[6] In 1956–1957 he visited Harvard on a scholarship, with the pretext of studying some manuscripts of Husserl but actually read James Joyce's *Ulysses* in earnest (allusions to Joyce's attempts to escape history turn up in Derrida's introduction to Husserl's *Origin of Geometry*). Indeed, Derrida's later embrace of the double affirmative ('yes, yes') is a conscious reference to Molly Bloom's speech at the end of *Ulysses*, and Derrida has even called Joyce's work "a great landmark in the history of deconstruction".[7] From 1957 to 1959, Derrida underwent military service in the French Army, stationed in a school in Algiers. In 1959 he began to teach, first at a *lycée* in Le Mans, then at the Sorbonne (1960–1964), where he assisted Paul Ricoeur and Jean Wahl. In 1959 he gave a paper on the concepts of genesis and structure as applied to the work of Husserl at a colloquium at Cérisy-La-Salle, where he introduced his concept of '*différance*'. Derrida published his earliest essays in *Critique* and in the left-wing French journal *Tel Quel*, edited by Philippe Sollers, and to which Roland Barthes, Julia Kristeva, and other French intellectuals contributed. Derrida, however, eventually broke with this journal in 1972 in disagreement with its hard-line communist stance.

In 1962 Derrida translated Husserl's short text *The Origin of Geometry*, which had originally been published in France in the 1939 special issue of *Revue internationale de philosophie*, and later included in the 1954 Husserliana edition of *Crisis of European Sciences*.[8] This text had already had a considerable influence on Merleau-Ponty. Derrida's accompanying commentary displays thorough familiarity with both Husserl's original texts and Husserlian scholarship of that time, citing Eugen Fink, Emmanuel Levinas, Paul Ricoeur, Gaston Berger, among others. When Derrida was preparing this text for publication, Merleau-Ponty, then general editor of the project to translate Husserl's works into French, wrote to Derrida asking whether he would be interested in translating Husserl's entire *Crisis*. This led to an exchange of letters between Derrida and Merleau-Ponty, but the project never came to fruition, as Merleau-Ponty died soon after.[9]

In 1964 Derrida was invited by Hyppolite and Althusser to lecture at the Ecole Normale Supérieure. In that year also, he published the first of his essays on Levinas, "Violence and Metaphysics", in the *Revue de Métaphysique et de Morale* (reprinted in 1967 in *Writing and Difference*). This important essay, a major review of Levinas's publications, played a role in highlighting Levinas's work. Derrida criticises Levinas's interpretation of Heidegger's concept of Being but is drawn to Levinas's notions of eschatological history, and his conception of ontology as inescapably wedded to violence and war.

In 1966 Derrida visited the USA to attend a seminar at Johns Hopkins University, where he delivered a critique of the structuralism of Claude Lévi-Strauss, setting down his own relation to structuralism. Structuralism had come to dominate the French intellectual scene in the 1960s, and, indeed, Derrida frequently locates his own notion of *déconstruction* as a deliberate reaction against French structuralism, directing himself against Claude Lévi-Strauss in particular. Although he always acknowledges his deep debt to the structuralist problematisation of language (WD 3), Derrida's position can be characterised as an 'anti-structuralism',[10] rather than as 'post-structuralism' (a term he always rejects). Derrida attacks structuralism's basic assumption that a finite system of oppositions can be identified which is generative of the whole network of a culture. Furthermore, as part of his general strategy of claiming that opposites contaminate each other, he rejects the structuralist opposition between the genetic and the structural, between the *diachronic* and the *synchronic*. Indeed the whole point of his introduction of the notion of *différance* is to show that the two cannot be separated (WD 293). Paradoxically, but typically, Derrida is both critical of structuralism and deeply indebted to it, especially to its manner of approaching a subject matter in terms of binary oppositions (e.g. Lévi-Strauss's classification of the 'raw' and the 'cooked'). In his 1972 interview with Julia Kristeva in *Positions*, Derrida explains why the concept of *structure* cannot be simply dropped or replaced:

> Doubtless it is more necessary, from within semiology, to transform concepts, to displace them, to reinscribe them in other chains, and little by little to modify the terrain of our work and thereby produce new configurations; I do not believe in decisive ruptures, in an unequivocal "epistemological break", as it is called today. Breaks are always, and fatally, reinscribed in an old cloth that must continually, interminably be undone.[11]

At the Johns Hopkins conference, Derrida drew attention to Lévi-Strauss's difficulties with the nature/culture dichotomy and with the status of his treatments of myth. Myths cannot be analysed logically into their component parts, nor can their origin be located or a fixed meaning attributed. They are marked by the absence of a subject, the absence of a centre. Derrida sees Lévi-Strauss caught between a traditional desire to explain, to classify, and to put in order, and a second recognition that the nature of myth puts everything into play. Rather than choosing one or the other way, Derrida feels Lévi-Strauss must live in the very tension between these attitudes. Here *différance* is seen as emerging from problems within Lévi-Strauss's interpretation of structuralist anthropology as a social science. Derrida developed his critique of Lévi-Strauss in an essay, "The Violence of the Letter: From Lévi-Strauss to Rousseau", published in *On Grammatology*, an essay ostensibly about the violence produced by the introduction of writing into a pre-literate society. Lévi-Strauss writes about pre-literate societies, societies which have no writing, and Derrida shows up the paradoxes of such a position. Derrida is opposed to structuralism's explanation of phenomena in terms of a static structure of oppositions. In a sense, Derrida continues the work of identifying oppositions and assumed hierarchies in different areas of discourse, but he likes to show the movement and play of these oppositions. It is a matter not just of identifying or even overturning hierarchies but of studying their transformation by seeing them at work in different contexts, destabilising them, and making them provisional.

Though Derrida had published a number of influential articles in philosophy throughout the 1960s, he really came to prominence in France with the publication of three books in 1967. Remarkably, he published a further three books in 1972, and has subsequently managed to publish at least a book a year. The full significance and originality of the six books was only grasped when they appeared together: they all aim to 'deconstruct' the history of philosophy as metaphysics and to show the process of '*différance*' at work. The 1967 books were *La Voix et le phénomène* (*Speech and Phenomena*), an essay which explores critically Husserl's 'phenomenology of signification', and offers a critique of his phonocentrism; *De la grammatologie* (*On Grammatology*), which focuses mainly on Rousseau's and other Enlightenment texts on writing and language, as well as Ferdinand de Saussure and Claude Lévi-Strauss, all presented as essays in 'grammatology'; and *L'Écriture et la différence* (*Writing and Difference*), which included essays on Hegel, Foucault, Freud, Bataille and Levinas. His 1972 books were: *La Dissémination* (*Dissemination*,[12] which includes essays on Mallarmé, Sollers, and an essay on the nature of writing in Plato's *Phaedrus*, which teases out his ambiguous use of the term *pharmakon* as signifying both 'poison' and 'cure'); *Marges de la philosophie* (*Margins of Philosophy*, which includes the important essay '*Différance*', as well as essays on Hegel and Heidegger);[13] and a collection of three early interviews, *Positions* (including one with Julia Kristeva).

Since 1972 Derrida has maintained an impressive output of critical studies and also more imaginative literary writings (including essays on Mallarmé, Joyce, Kafka, and so on) – some very ingenious, all of them labyrinthine, ironic, and playful (in a manner similar to Kierkegaard's adoption of different styles and pseudonyms).[14] Between 1974 and the mid-1980s Derrida's publications (e.g. *Glas, Spurs, Truth in Painting, The Postcard*) became increasingly, indeed obsessively, self-reflexive and stylistically self-conscious, playing outrageously with academic norms, and even with the form of the book itself as medium. Derrida has been deliberately seeking to overcome the conventional divide between philosophy and literature, and thereby seeking to place his form of discourse outside philosophy. Thus in *The Postcard* (*La Carte postale*) Derrida writes a diary (covering 1977 to 1979) which includes a series of fictitious postcards, missives (*envois*) to his family, friends, and to famous philosophers, referring to his relations with Plato, Socrates, Heidegger, Freud, and even Oxford philosophers, offering reflections of a deeply personal and psychoanalytic kind including some rather odd fantasies (e.g. fantasising Plato having an erection against Socrates' back) and as usual playing with words (e.g. '*Carte*', 'card', and '*écarte*', division or 'interval').[15]

In *Glas*,[16] Derrida set out, in parallel columns (a technique already used in *Margins*), texts from Hegel and Jean Genet (the French criminal turned writer), with commentaries, in an attempt to have the texts disrupt each other, thereby seeking to challenge the notion of the self-contained nature of any genre, whether philosophical or literary. The title '*Glas*' is said in the work to be an echoing sound which announces the end of signification (*Glas*, p. 31; 39). This work also questions the notion of 'signature', the apparently simple act of appending one's name to a text which, for Derrida, in fact involves many complicated assumptions concerning authorship, authority, consent, and self-identity, and the relation between inside and outside. Derrida had first raised the problem of the nature of signature in an 1971 essay, "Signature, Event, Context", originally delivered in Montreal, and reprinted in *Margins*. This essay became the focus of a critique by John R. Searle, published in 1977 in *Glyph*.[17] In his original essay, Derrida, commenting on Condillac, had argued that written language, since it functions in the absence of the addressee, is independent of the intention of the author. Derrida used this as testimony against the view that writing is the communication of intended meaning.

This led Derrida to criticise aspects of John Austin's account of speech acts, including his naive assumption of sincerity. John Searle in turn criticised Derrida for, among other things, having confused the relative permanence of literary texts with the essential iterability of linguistic signs. Searle's essay itself provoked an ironic and deflective reply by Derrida (published as *Limited Inc*), which included Derrida rather ungraciously punning on Searle's name (Sarl = '*Société à responsabilité limitée*', 'limited liability company'). This exchange has subsequently attracted the attention of many commentators, including Richard Rorty, Stanley Cavell, and others.[18] Though Searle dismisses Derrida's reading of Austin as simply mistaken and as not being a serious confrontation between two traditions, nevertheless Derrida's conflict with Searle is widely seen as typifying the rift between the so-called 'Continental' and 'analytic' traditions of philosophy. Derrida himself has represented his dispute as a clash occurring "midway between California and Europe".[19] In the course of this exchange, Searle invoked Michel Foucault's private communication to Searle characterising Derrida's method as involving an *"obscurantisme terroriste"*, whereby an author writes in an obscure style and then criticises his opponent for his inevitable failure to understand.[20] Derrida, incensed that such gossip should appear in print, retorted that he would not report what other students said of Searle's teaching!

In keeping with the French tradition that the intellectual must be *engagé* (i.e. committed socially and politically), Derrida has been active politically, usually espousing typical liberal and broadly left-wing popular causes, while keeping a distance from institutional forms of political practice, such as communism. Originally associated with the French left-wing intellectual tradition, during the 1980s in particular, Derrida has written on the nature of the law and justice, and on the unity of Europe, and has lent his name to a number of political and human rights causes, for example campaigns against apartheid, racism, nationalism, and in favour of human rights, and also for improving the status of refugees.[21] Since 1975 he has been active with GREPH (Le Groupe de Recherche sur l'Enseignement Philosophique), a group interested in developing the manner in which philosophy is taught in French schools and universities.[22] In 1981, while visiting dissidents in Prague, he was arrested on a trumped-up charge of drug smuggling and expelled from Czechoslovakia. In 1983 he was active in founding the Collège Internationale de Philosophie in Paris, and served as its first director. These political interventions Derrida justifies as being part of his new thinking concerning the meaning of his earlier claim that "there is no outside-text". For Derrida, this means that one cannot separate texts from their social and political contexts. Indeed, the lack of an 'outside' for the text allows for forms of political action to be read as belonging to the text.

Derrida is currently attached to the Ecole des Hautes Etudes en Sciences Sociales in Paris and, since 1987, has been a visiting professor at the University of California at Irvine and at the State University of New York in Buffalo. He has received honorary doctorates from Leuven, Essex, and Columbia Universities as well as the controversial award from the University of Cambridge. His current focus is on the nature of religion and prophecy.

Deconstruction and morality

Derrida's deconstruction seems so wedded to singularity and lack of closure, so characterised by *undecidability*, that many critics (e.g. Simon Critchley, Peter Dews, Richard Kearney, among others) have worried about the possibility of taking any moral or political stance while remaining a deconstructionist. Deconstruction often appears as a kind of moral *scepticism*, which finds equally strong arguments for opposing moral positions, or a moral *relativism* which denies all absolute values and fixed meanings, and ends up in a moral paralysis, or in a Nietzschean 'do what thou wilt' attitude to moral norms, or, perhaps, finally, in *nihilism*. Unsurprisingly, the allegation has been made that deconstruction has dispensed with morality, and has made the taking of any definite moral stance either arbitrary or actually impossible. Against this commonly repeated charge, Derrida has struggled to connect his deconstructive strategies, which resist coagulating into fixed positions, with the many practical ethical and political stances which he has taken. Engagement with ethical and political matters is justified, Derrida argues, because deconstruction never proposed an endless deferral of meaning, rather it is precisely because a decision cannot wait that the issues appear to us as undecidable. Undecidability, for Derrida, does not mean that nothing can be done, but rather that something *must* be done and that we cannot be certain what to do. Morality entails *risk*, and the very notion of responsibility is predicated on the idea that the right action has not been clearly signalled in advance. Derrida therefore believes that deconstruction is ethical in its very core; it is in its very essence responsibility (i.e. if one can speak of deconstruction having an essence). Furthermore, he denies that the turn to ethics and politics is recent; indeed, he claims that a concern with ethics has been present in his writing since the beginning. Derrida's earlier ethical resonances apparently went unnoticed because of his more evasive textual strategies. In so far as there is anything vaguely ethical or political in Derrida's thought, it comes in the form of a kind of critical discussion of some key terms drawn from the social and communal world, terms such as: friendship,[23] otherness, the gift, donation.

Influenced by Marcel Mauss, by Lévi-Strauss (and possibly by Sartre and Merleau-Ponty, both of whom discussed the nature of the 'gift'), Derrida has attempted some critical studies of the anthropological notion of the exchange of gifts in primitive societies and associated notions such as charity and hospitality, where the cycle of exchange is broken and something new enters, as the basis of his understanding of the nature of the ethical and the political. In particular, Derrida has proposed to rethink the nature of the ethical and the political by meditating on the nature of friendship, drawing on Aristotle's *philia*, Cicero's *amicitia*, Enlightenment *fraternité*, Levinas's notion of hospitality, Nietzsche, and on the distinction between 'friend' (*Freund*) and 'enemy' (*Fiend*) as found in an unlikely source, namely the thought of the German political philosopher and Nazi theorist, Carl Schmitt.[24]

As part of this turn towards the political, since the late 1980s, and especially in response to the publication of Victor Farias's book on Heidegger,

Derrida has also attempted to understand and evaluate Heidegger's political commitment to National Socialism. In *De l'esprit* (*Of Spirit*) Derrida approaches Heidegger's politics indirectly through an examination of the ambiguous role of the term *Geist* ('spirit') in Heidegger's writings of the 1930s, arguing that Heidegger's fatal connection with Nazism came through his commitment to metaphysics and voluntarism.[25] Whereas Heidegger was initially cautious in his employment of the term 'spirit' in *Being and Time*, he later adopts the term in his *Rektoratsrede* of the 1930s in an uncritical and dangerous way.

Soon after his discussion of Heidegger's involvement with Nazism, Derrida became involved in a dispute concerning the anti-Semitic nature of some early writings of his friend, the Belgian literary critic, Paul de Man (1919–1983).[26] Derrida had already published a careful critical appreciation, *Memoires for Paul de Man*, acknowledging de Man as an important source of American deconstruction.[27] De Man's anti-Semitic essays had originally appeared in a pro-Nazi Belgian paper during the war years, but were only discovered after de Man's death. Indeed, de Man's own post-war silence about these writings led to questions as to whether 'deconstruction', which de Man espoused, in fact masked an anti-liberalism which could easily accommodate fascism or totalitarianism. Derrida angrily questions why there appears to be a public mood to link deconstruction to forms of totalitarianism, whereas for him deconstruction is of its very essence an exercise in responsible critique which ought to take nothing for granted.

Following the spectacular collapse of the Soviet Union in the late 1980s, Derrida returned to a rethinking of Marx. On his own admission, Derrida has something of an emotional attachment to Marx and sees in his work a possibility of justice, something which cannot be deconstructed. In *Specters of Marx* he offers a re-reading of Marx, exploring the manner Marx still haunts Western political thought (in this essay, Derrida coins the awful pun, 'hauntology').[28]

Derrida and the end of philosophy

To understand Derrida it is necessary to understand his rather restricted conception of the nature of philosophy. Derrida belongs to the second generation of French phenomenologists, a phenomenology which had already been transformed into a French philosophical outlook by Emmanuel Levinas, Paul Ricoeur, Gaston Berger, Maurice Merleau-Ponty, and others. Derrida himself emerged on the French philosophical scene at a time when the structuralist movement, and especially Lévi-Strauss, Louis Althusser, and Michel Foucault were in the ascendant, and the elderly Sartre and existentialism were already *passé*. Influenced by the rather special sense of philosophy dominant in France in the 1950s and 1960s, Derrida understands philosophy primarily in terms of the contributions of Hegel,

Nietzsche, Husserl, Heidegger, Levinas, and contemporary French theorists (Lacan, Bataille, Foucault). Philosophy as such can be summarised by the triad Hegel–Husserl–Heidegger. As Derrida has remarked: "My philosophical formation owes much to the thought of Hegel, Husserl and Heidegger".[29] Probably because of the influence of Jean Hyppolite, Derrida thinks of philosophy as exemplified in Hegel's system of absolute knowledge. To interrogate the meaning of philosophy, therefore, is to confront Hegel. Hegel is an ambiguous presence, both encapsulating the essence of modern philosophy and also going beyond it: the philosopher of totalisation and yet also "the thinker of irreducible difference" (*le penseur de la différence irréductible*, *Gramm.*, p. 26; 41); "the last philosopher of the book and the first thinker of writing" (*Gramm.*, p. 26; 41). Furthermore, with Hegel, philosophy has reached its completion (*Vollendung*), and Derrida accepts Heidegger's claims about 'the end of philosophy', a theme emphasised, for example, in his essay on Levinas (WD 79). Hegel represents, for Derrida, the very self-consciousness of philosophy, a dream of absolute knowledge which is now over:

> We will never be finished with the reading or rereading of Hegel and, in a certain way, I do nothing other than attempt to explain myself on this point. In effect, I believe that Hegel's text is necessarily fissured; that it is something more and other than the circular closure of its representation. It is not reduced to a content of philosophemes, it also necessarily produces a powerful writing operation, a remainder of writing, whose strange relationship to the philosophical content of Hegel's text must be re-examined, that is, the movement by means of which his text exceeds its meaning, permits itself to be turned away from, to return to, and to repeat itself outside its self-identity.
>
> (*Pos.*, pp. 77–78)

Indeed Husserl's demand for a science of universal rationality remains totally Hegelian, according to Derrida. This view broadly endorses Heidegger's account of the increasing rigidification, even 'closure' (*clôture*), of Western metaphysics, so that other paths, other ways of thinking, must now be developed. Derrida wants to diagnose the nature of the 'closure' of this entire project of metaphysics. He wants to find a 'non-site' from which to question the whole enterprise of Western philosophy and rationality. For Derrida, inspired by his readings of Heidegger, Freud, Nietzsche, and Marx (the latter three authors being what Ricoeur calls 'the masters of suspicion'), the very project of philosophy is somehow inhibited and compromised from the beginning. Indeed, Derrida's suspicion of global rationality, of metaphysics as an overarching explanation of everything, of all totality and closure, is well understood as a reaction to Hegelian systematisation. Of course, Habermas has rightly queried why Derrida is pitting himself against a system which has not been at the centre of philosophy for more than a century and a half. But Derrida believes he is really attacking the whole tradition which sees philosophy as a separate, self-sufficient, and self-reflexive practice.

Derrida, then, unites his suspicion of Hegelian totalising rationalism with a Heidegger-inspired view of the entire history of metaphysics (expanded by Derrida to include Husserl and even Heidegger himself) as the history of *presence* (WD 279). Derrida accepts outright Heidegger's characterisation of Western metaphysics as the "history of a determination of being as presence" (*Gramm.*, p. 97; 145). Breaking through into a more radical form of thinking requires rethinking this commitment to presence, especially through a critique of the self-presence of consciousness, which characterises modern philosophy from Descartes to Husserl. Derrida refers to this apotheosis of self-consciousness as *"la métaphysique du propre"*, the metaphysics of the proper, of what belongs to oneself (*Gramm.*, p. 26; 41).

The critique of Husserl's *The Origin of Geometry*

Derrida's first works on Husserl already reveal his particular view about the history of philosophy. Derrida's commentary on *The Origin of Geometry* takes the form of an immanent critique of Husserl, concentrating on an account of signs and writing, and on his assumptions concerning the nature of historicity. Specifically, Derrida highlights ambiguities and difficulties latent in Husserl's notions of transcendental phenomenology, his notions of ideal history and ideal origins, his concept of an 'historical a priori', and so on. While Husserl had believed the very essence of the historical could be understood through imaginative variation and essential insight, Derrida argues that phenomenological imagination is never rich enough to reconstruct the intellectual lives of people of radically different cultures. Husserl is forced to admit "an irreducible, enriching, and always renascent equivocity into pure historicity" (OG 103). Derrida also criticises Husserl's view of an absolute emerging in history, claiming instead that "the absolute is present only in being *différant*" (OG 153), here utilising the conception of *différance* introduced in 1959. In his Introduction to *The Origin of Geometry*, furthermore, Derrida refers to Kurt Gödel's notion of 'undecidable propositions' (OG 53), which he later (e.g. in *La Dissémination*) adapted for his own purposes, applying to other fields as well, giving rise to talk of a general 'logic of undecidability'.[30] Most recently, for example, Derrida has invoked the notion of 'undecidability' to express the nature of ethical decision.

Husserl's *The Origin of Geometry* recapitulates the philosophical problematic of the *Philosophie der Arithmetik*, namely the manner in which objective mathematical (in this case, geometrical) knowledge is produced by temporally bound, individual acts of thinking. Husserl's approach in this late text, however, is explicitly 'regressive' (OG 158), 'genetic', and 'historical' (OG 172–173): how do timeless, objective, invariant truths (e.g. the Pythagorean theorem) get constituted in the living, historical context of changing human culture? As Husserl says:

> Our problem now concerns precisely the ideal objects which are thematic in geometry: how does geometrical ideality (just like that of all sciences) proceed from its primary intrapersonal origin, where it is a structure within the conscious space of the first inventor's soul, to its ideal objectivity?
>
> (OG 161)

The regressive–historical method requires a thoughtful reconstruction of the human practices and mental acts which gave birth to geometry, which originally emerged from the practice of land surveying and, through a set of idealisations and transformations, solidified into a pure eidetic science. Removed from the intuitions of the original geometers, geometrical discoveries become objectified in written forms. In writing down symbols, the addressee is removed, and what is written down becomes a 'sedimentation' which can be reactivated by new acts of understanding (OG 164). Husserl, whose constant theme is the importance of symbolic thought for science, here recognises the need for written language to underpin the ideality of meaning. The objectivity of geometry is made possible, for Husserl, through the 'body of language' (*Sprachleib*, OG 161). As Derrida puts it elsewhere, Husserl is the first philosopher to recognise that writing is "the condition of the possibility of ideal objects and therefore of objectivity" (*Gramm.*, p. 27; 42–43), and in *Writing and Difference* he remarks:

> Meaning must await being said or written in order to inhabit itself, and in order to become, by differing from itself, what it is: meaning. This is what Husserl teaches us to think in *The Origin of Geometry*.[31]
>
> (WD 11)

Husserl's emphasis on the role of written language in preserving scientific insights provided the main inspiration for Derrida's claim that Western culture has, since Plato's *Phaedrus*, prioritised *full* speech over *derivative* writing, a trait Derrida labels '*phonocentrism*' or '*logocentrism*'. In subsequent publications, especially *Of Grammatology*, Derrida proposed a new, general science of writing, grammatology (*Gramm.*, p. 4; 13). Grammatology is meant to be, not just one science among others, but the true science of science, directly contradicting Bolzano and the early Husserl who saw logic as the exemplary for science as such. Derrida argues that the inscription of meaning in sound is only one form of inscription or writing in

447

general. Furthermore, the whole area of the relation of signification itself must be put under scrutiny. Derrida will argue that traditional philosophy, and especially Husserlian phenomenology, located the origin of meaning in subjectivity, whereas he sees it as produced in a play of 'difference' and of 'trace', key concepts of his own grammatology.

Logocentrism

Derrida sums up the essence of philosophy in the West in a single word, *logocentrism*. *Logocentrism* refers to the manner in which the traditional prioritisation of reason in philosophy has led to everything deemed 'irrational' to be swept aside, treated as marginal and insignificant. Derrida claims the Western philosophical tradition is obsessed with being understood as presence (ontotheology), and with the universal nature of logic and rationality (logocentrism). Logocentrism, for Derrida, is tied to the assumption of a fixed, foundational principle which can be uniquely named (see WD 278–279), whether it be 'being' or 'God'. The Greek word *logos* can mean reason, account, word, or justification, and Derrida is playing with all of these significations. The term 'logocentrism' implies the assumption of the centrality of the *logos*, of rationality, of logic, of the spoken word. The whole history of Western philosophy since the ancient Greeks has been circumscribed in "the epoch of the *logos*" (*L'époque du logos*, *Gramm.*, p. 12; 24), perhaps best exemplified in the Christian doctrine of creation. Derrida defines *logocentrism* as "the metaphysics of phonetic writing" (*Gramm.*, p. 3; 11), or 'phonologism', and often couples it with phallocentrism, or *phallogocentrism*, the structure of traditional patriarchal culture, conceived in loosely Freudian terms as the privilege of the phallus as signifier. Western culture is dominated by the phallus, which means, by linear direct thinking. Derrida couples these notions together, to give a picture of Western rationality as a kind of calculative thinking (as Heidegger calls it), involving deductive reasoning from premises to conclusion and excluding everything which cannot be enclosed in this chain of reasons.

Both logocentrism and phallocentrism are attempts to dominate and master the whole field of being and meaning and to force it under the narrow confining framework of logic, and, indeed, the imperative of law ('his master's voice'). The domination of reason is, as Nietzsche and Foucault have seen, driven by the will to power, which has traditionally also been the will to male power, to patriarchy. Logocentrism, with its concern for linear logic, in Derrida's view, betrays the true movement of meaning as *dissemination*, that is a constant scattering which is not unified by a single principle. Logocentrism, for Derrida, is based on a profound misunderstanding of the relation between signifier and signified, namely the belief that a sign adequately represents its signified meaning, that language is a transparent window on reality. Such a view automatically privileges speech over writing, and full presence over absence. Logocentrism is "the privilege of the *phonè*" (*Gramm.*, p. 7; 17). Aristotle, for instance, is guilty of phonocentrism in *De Intepretatione*, I, 16a, when he takes a written word to be a sign of a spoken word which itself is a sign of an inner mental experience (*pathema tes psyches*). Contrary to the common assumption, Derrida wants to claim that there is no linguistic sign before writing (*Gramm.*, p. 14; 26).

Derrida, like Freud and Foucault, is suspicious of any kind of repression of the marginal and irrational. Derrida, however, denies that his diagnosis of logocentrism is a form of psychoanalysis: "Despite appearances, the deconstruction of logocentrism is not a psychoanalysis of philosophy" ("Freud and the Scene of Writing", WD 196). Rather, the repression involved in logocentrism makes Freudian repression *possible*. (Here Derrida typically makes a transcendental move, dealing with the conditions of the possibility of the phenomenon.) Derridian deconstruction emerges as an internal struggle with this dominant image of rational philosophy. This usually leads to a kind of hyper self-conscious, principled hesitation regarding the employment of traditional philosophical vocabulary, invoking Husserl's concept of 'cancellation' (*Durchstreichen*) and Heidegger's practice of crossing terms out, putting them, in Derrida's terms, '*sous rature*' (*Gramm.*, p. 60; 89). All metaphysical terms can be allowed to operate only under cancellation, but they must be used as we have no other (WD 280).

There is a tendency among some of Derrida's followers to diagnose all Western thought as logocentric, and then to reject all oppositions (temporal/eternal, darkness/light, matter/form, falsity/truth) as belonging to this logocentrism. This has led Richard Rorty to comment with exasperation that he finds "the knee-jerk suspicion of all binary oppositions among deconstructionists baffling".[32] Derrida himself, however, does not attempt to overturn all oppositions, since this would be simply to put in place another order of signs with their own hegemony. He wants rather to force us to question why we valorise them as we do. On the other hand, Derrida's position has also given rise to the charge that, in rejecting logocentrism, he is also rejecting the law of non-contradiction, the fundamental logical principle of all reasoning. If this law is revoked no assertion can be contradicted and indeed no assertion can even be made. Though Derrida indeed often talks as if he is denying traditional logic and replacing it by his 'logic of undecidability', in fact he denies having contested the principle of non-contradiction. He claims that, like Heidegger, he is concerned to analyse and deconstruct Leibniz's principle of sufficient reason, but he does not attack logic itself. His concept of logical assertion and the limits of assertion, however, remains unclear.

For Derrida, then, broadly speaking, the function of philosophy after Hegel is *critique*. As for most contemporary philosophy, this critique calls for close attention to the manner in which language wraps up our world and both manifests and obscures our concerns. But Derrida does not turn to Wittgenstein or ordinary language philosophy, except briefly in his consideration of John Austin. In his attention to language, Derrida's distinctive view draws heavily on Heidegger's deep questioning of the metaphysical heritage and especially his later probings into the essence of language and of saying, which he combines with a certain reading of the theory of the sign as found in the linguistics of Ferdinand de Saussure (1857–1913). Thus although he tends to agree with Heidegger that the contemporary science of linguistics can offer no insight into the working of language in the sense uncovered by Heidegger, Derrida does turn frequently to examine the various views of language found in the philosophical tradition, for example in Plato, Rousseau, Condillac, and others. As we shall see, Derrida is also impressed by the way in which Saussure absorbed linguistics into semiology (the general theory of signs, or semiotics), thereby paving the way for grammatology.

Deconstruction: 'more than one language'

Derrida's 'strategy' for overcoming 'logocentrism' and the 'metaphysics of presence' is called *deconstruction*. Derrida began to use this term in the mid-1960s and claims to have been surprised at the way this single word (originally coupled with other terms – trace, supplement, difference) became a watchword for his approach as a whole. Derrida, of course, does not accept that *deconstruction* names an essence or a procedure, much less a system of thinking. What then is deconstruction?

Derrida never tires of asserting that deconstruction is not to be understood as a philosophical 'method' (*Dialogues*, p. 124); it is not a set of tools or procedures to be added to the philosophers toolkit; it does not carve out a particular genre. Nor is it the name of an era or an epoch. As with the notion of *différance* which we shall shortly address, *deconstruction* is not an action, nor a process, though, indeed, he often talks as if it were something like an anonymous process which is always already at work in the world, prior to our conceptualisations, as the very transcendental source of our conceptuality. Indeed, Derrida emphasises from the beginning that deconstruction is 'inescapable' and 'necessary'. But, paradoxically, as with the 'concept' or 'non-concept' of *différance*, Derrida believes deconstruction cannot be truly named or signified.

In Derrida's hands, 'deconstruction' involves the process of tracking the unravelling of meaning, which is going on anyway, similar to the way in which the system of language is always changing outside of the control of the individual speakers of that language. Deconstruction involves taking apart the text to show that its supposed argument or thesis actually turns against itself owing to the impossibility of meanings being present in their essence. Every speech act contains, as it were, the seed of its own negation.

This is an essentially Hegelian insight which Derrida interprets in a new manner.

Derrida claims he first encountered the term 'destruction' (*Abbau, Destruktion, Zerstörung*) in Heidegger. In Heidegger's 1927 lecture course, the *Basic Problems of Phenomenology*, 'deconstruction' (*Destruktion*) is contrasted with 'construction' (*Konstruktion*, BPP § 5). In *Being and Time* Heidegger saw 'destruction' as a hermeneutic tool to recover the originary experiences which gave rise to philosophy. As a way of listening to the heritage of philosophy and reappropriating it, destruction has, for Heidegger, a positive meaning. Derrida found the term '*déconstruction*' in the French dictionary *Littré*, when seeking to translate Heidegger's *Destruktion*. As Derrida says, Heidegger's destruction signified "an operation bearing on the structure or traditional architecture of the fundamental concepts of ontology or of Western metaphysics".[33] There are also elements in his thinking of deconstruction which owe a debt to Nietzsche's 'overcoming' or 'reversal' or traditional values, including his critique of metaphysics (WD 278–279).

Besides the obvious Heideggerian and Nietzschean echoes, the term 'deconstruction' emerged in Derrida's writings in the mid-1960s as an anti-structuralist stance, most especially in his 1966 lecture "Structure, Sign, and Play in the Discourse of the Human Sciences", at Johns Hopkins University where he criticises the notion of a structure as constructed around a central plank, *arche*, or *telos*. Here he used the term 'deconstruction' to talk about the manner in which a text harbours within itself the history of assumptions that generated it. Deconstruction, like Lévi-Strauss's structuralism, proceeds by identifying opposing structures at work in the text: the oppositions of preface and text, of signifier and signified, of sensible and intelligible, male and female, body and soul, etc. But structuralism tends to keep these opposing terms separate, whereas deconstruction shows how they complicate each other. Indeed, a recurrent tactic of Derrida's writing, derived from the structuralist approach, is to set up typical oppositions that operate as the two extreme poles of our thinking in a particular area, and to show that our assumption that these poles must be kept apart is groundless and that eventually the two poles 'contaminate' each other ('contamination' being a favourite Derridian term). Derrida's mission is to demonstrate the contaminations rather than purities at work in meaning. He sees decon-struction as a set of *active interventions* in the weave of textuality that forms our culture: "effective or active...interventions, in particular political and institutional interventions that transform contexts without limiting themselves to theoretical or constative utterances even though they must also produce such utterances".[34] Derrida's interrogative interventions take the form of a certain disruptive reading of the text, putting philosophical texts in juxtaposition with other forms of writing, for example literature, to show up the ambiguities surrounding the notion of the limits of philosophy.

He wants to disrupt the 'mastery' of philosophy to question its command of its territory by a questioning itself sited on the 'borders' of metaphysics (*Margins*, p. xix).

Derrida rejects any philosophical analysis which proceeds in terms of what he considers to be static or reified concepts. For Derrida, concepts, including the concept of sign itself, can be understood only within *texts* and then with reference to specific *contexts*. He therefore rejects what he considers to be the static Enlightenment conceptions of reason, human nature, freedom, and so on. Paying close attention to the relations between concepts and their contexts often produces more complications than clarifications and the consequent breaking down of rigidification in thinking Derrida calls 'deconstruction'. Derrida claims "the movements of deconstruction do not destroy (*sollicitent*) structures from the outside" (*Gramm.*, p. 24; 39), but rather *inhabit* those structures, *subverting* them from the inside. In effect, Derrida is questioning the priority of the assertion and the logic of the assertion (to which Husserl gave so much credit) by complicating the nature of reference, not denying reference as such.

Deconstruction then is related to texts and their relation with their contexts. Often this problematic is united with the problem of translation, and the multiplicity of languages. In his "Letter to a Japanese Friend" Derrida claims that the question of deconstruction is above all the question of *translation*. In his *Memoires for Paul de Man* Derrida says that if he has to characterise 'deconstruction' he will offer the phrase '*plus d'une langue*', more than one language and no more of a language (*Memoires*, p. 15). Deconstruction calls attention to the plurality of voices and forces at work in texts. But, most frequently, deconstruction is to be understood as a *strategy*. As Derrida says, every attempt to get at *différance* involves strategy and risk: "In the delineation of *différance* everything is strategic and adventurous" (*Margins*, p. 7; 7). The same can be said of deconstruction. However, Derrida, in contradiction to his view that deconstruction is a strategy or a set of active interventions in texts, also often claims that deconstruction names the processes of meaning and the unravelling of meanings *already* going on within texts. Thus in the *Memoires for Paul de Man* he says: "there is always already deconstruction, at work in works, especially in literary works. Deconstruction cannot be applied, after the fact and from the outside, as a technical instrument of modernity. Texts deconstruct *themselves* by themselves" (*Memoires*, p. 123).

Derrida downplays any suggestion that deconstruction is the general name for an intellectual practice or technique. He claims not to be venturing self-standing universal claims, but to be standing on the side of the individual, and the *singular*, against the general, the universal, the ideal. He wants all his interpretations to be woven into the fabric of a specific event, a specific text, a singular situation. In the end, Derrida even claims he has little to say, and that deconstruction lacks content, that it offers nothing, and indeed is, in that sense, a 'poor thing'.[35] Despite the claims not to have a set doctrine nor to make assertions, it is possible to distinguish a definite number of moves or patterns, a set of *strategies*, which are significantly repeated in his various writings, and indeed a number of distinctive claims, for example that '*différance*' pervades all meaning. These assertions and strategies, taken together, may be held to constitute Derrida's philosophical position, and may be criticised as such, despite his protests. Derrida, for instance, has claimed that deconstruction as such cannot be criticised: "a critique of what I do is indeed impossible".[36] But Derrida's frequent attempts to dictate the stance from which any criticism of his work must come, must be, to consider the matter solely on his own terms, contrary to the deconstruction of meaning going on in his own texts.

The world as text: "there is no outside-text"

Following Heidegger's conception of the art 'work' (*Werk*) as a working process, as well as from the structuralist conception of texts as being set up through a play of oppositions, Derrida generalises to claim that all forms of organised social intercourse, including political institutions, actions, and so on, may be profitably viewed as *texts*, and hence as conforming to the laws which govern the process of manufacturing meanings which is the main work of texts. Texts are not just books or pieces of writing in the usual sense, but complexes of interrelated meanings which relate to other such complexes. Thus, even *events* (e.g. the French revolution, apartheid in South Africa, etc.) may be treated as texts and their manner of being constructed may be examined by the kind of reverse engineering which Derrida calls 'deconstruction'. The initial process of manufacturing and setting up meaning is what Derrida refers to as 'structuring' or 'structurality' (*structuralité*, WD 280). One of Derrida's central intuitions is that texts of all kinds work in a certain way in close connection with their contexts to produce the illusion or fiction of attaining to or disclosing a central meaning, whereas closer analysis of this working shows that this proposed meaning is in fact never attained, and may even be subverted by other meanings clustering in the text. Deconstruction can then be understood as unmasking the very manner in which texts set up their system of pretence, or 'pretext'. Each text is always an unfulfilled promise, leading Derrida to be suspicious of all assertions or conclusions of a generalised form regarding the final meaning of a text. He therefore opposes a traditional understanding of *structure* which sees it as assembled or built around a central core or root, that is an *arché*. Indeed the nature of language is such that it is a system of *play* (*jeu*, WD 289). He seems, however, to see texts as at least purporting to embody a definitive *intent*, whether authorial intent, or some other suggestion of fixed meaning. Derrida's main technique is to show that all such promises of meaning are disrupted from within the texts themselves.

453

Thus, a text may ostensibly purport to be about one topic whereas the actual meanings at work in the text itself suggest a very different set of intentions. The main point is that texts make these pretences but dissimulate their manner of so doing. The pretext of the text is 'effaced', as Derrida says. As Derrida has explained in Freudian terms:

> To deconstruct a text is to disclose how it functions as desire, as a search for presence and fulfilment which is interminably deferred.
>
> (*Dialogues*, p. 128)

In Husserlian terms, a text is a set of meaning-intentions which aim for a certain kind of fulfilment and even have the illusion of providing that fulfilment. The task of reading is to interrogate and undermine that process at work in the text. Furthermore, texts always overflow their supposed intentions and contexts; they *exceed* their contexts in certain ways.

Both Derrida and the structuralists prioritise the notion of the 'text' and 'textuality' – where texts can be any set of codes, from written books to gestures, to political acts. Furthermore, Derrida insists that all texts are embedded in contexts, and *contextualising*, that is putting the text into its social, historical, political context, is a large part of the deconstructive strategy. Texts and contexts must be thought together. Derrida originally made this claim in the form of the now notorious pronouncement in his essay on Rousseau: "*il n'y a pas de hors-texte*", "there is no outside-text" (*Gramm.*, p. 158; 227). This assertion has often been interpreted as promoting a kind of linguistic idealism, as claiming that there is no reality outside of texts (a similar accusation has, as we have seen, been made against Gadamer's view of *die Sprache*). As always Derrida repudiates such an interpretation, yet there is no doubt that he has made pronouncements to that effect. In fact, a little further on in the same essay, Derrida explicitly says that the axial proposition (*le propos axiale*) of the essay is that "there is nothing outside the text" (*il n'y a rien hors du texte*, *Gramm.*, p. 163; 233). When pressed, Derrida always opts for the more modest interpretation of the claims as meaning that the text has no outside, in other words we make a mistake when we separate texts and things as two distinct kinds of entity. Texts are always already outside themselves and encompass the world in such a way that it can be said that there is no perimeter or outside to a text; a text is always open to future interpretations, future insertions into the world. Signs always refer to signs; there is a play or circulation of signs which makes self-presence and closure impossible. On this interpretation, Derrida's claim is that there is "nothing outside the context". As Richard Rorty has commented, Derrida does not appear to be subscribing to anything other than the Wittgensteinian thesis that "meaning is a function of context, and that there is no theoretical barrier to an endless sequence of recontextualizations".[37] Derrida in fact supports Rorty's reading (though naturally he repudiates it publicly as he does all attempts to interpret his work as *just* saying this or that):

> It is totally false to suggest that deconstruction is a suspension of reference. Deconstruction is always deeply concerned with the "other" of language. I never cease to be surprised by critics who see my work as a declaration that there is nothing beyond language, that we are imprisoned by language; it is, in fact, saying the exact opposite.
>
> (*Dialogues*, p. 123)

Furthermore in his *Limited Inc* Derrida says:

> The phrase, which for some has become a sort of slogan, in general so badly understood, of deconstruction ("there is nothing outside the text"), means nothing else: there is nothing outside context.
>
> (*Limited Inc*, p. 136)

Against the supposed finitude and closure of textual claims, Derrida believes philosophical reading must be pursued only by the kind of openings and reversals of meaning made possible by certain contexts. Our claims can never outrun these contexts, and we can never be entirely sure if we have correctly identified the appropriate context.

More recently Derrida has proffered yet another interpretation of the slogan: there is nothing *beyond* the text, meaning thereby that text should not be thought of as excluding actions and interventions. One should not make simplistic assumptions about what lies within and without the purview of the text. Hence, as we have seen, even political action is not outside the text, but belongs to it.[38] Furthermore, as he says in *La Dissémination*, there is no separation between text and pre-text, because everything is a sign.

Derrida recognises the challenge to distinguish his own kind of radical textual interrogation from traditional philosophical questioning, as well as traditional literary analysis. Deeply influenced by Heidegger's meditation on the question, Derrida is also deeply suspicious of traditional metaphysical questions of the form "what is x?". Derrida thinks that, along with the priority of assertion, the role of questioning itself needs to be interrogated and resituated. He therefore wants to 'question the question', that is question the priority of questioning in the traditional philosophical practice. Derrida is unsure about the nature of what is revealed in such a practice of questioning and in some of his writing evokes Nietzschean yes-saying as an alternative to critical questioning. This leads his thought into many paradoxes. Thus in the essay "*Différance*", Derrida claims there can be no running away from or effacing *différance*; rather it must be affirmed "in the sense in which Nietzsche puts affirmation into play, in a certain laughter

455

and a certain step of the dance" (*Margins*, p. 27; 29). Derrida is left with Nietzschean affirmation, *Ja-sagen*, or the 'double yes' of Joyce, which means affirming contradictions, leaving a sense that nothing at all is being said. Perhaps, rather than following Derrida in these Dadaist and surrealist celebrations, as his more enthusiastic followers are wont to do, it is more fruitful to sketch Derrida's concepts as they emerge in his readings of Husserl, Heidegger, and the structuralists.

Derrida's engagement with Husserlian phenomenology

As we have seen, Derrida began rather conventionally as a critic of Husserl. Derrida claims to have taken over Husserl's conception of philosophy as open-ended, radical enquiry. Furthermore, he was especially influenced by Husserl's employment of *epoché*:

> It is true that for me Husserl's work, and precisely the notion of *epoché*, has been and still is a major indispensable gesture. In everything I try to say and write the *epoché* is implied. I would say that I constantly try to practice that whenever I am speaking or writing.[39]

Derrida is particularly influenced by the *anti-metaphysical*, presupposition-less thrust of Husserl's phenomenology with its emphasis on philosophy as a rigorous descriptive science, and thus his unmasking of Husserl's dependence on metaphysical assumptions is meant to point to the inability of phenomenology to be the radical science it wants to be, the inability of philosophy 'to think its other' (*penser son autre*, *Margins*, p. xii; 1). To think the nature of this other, one must learn to operate the *epoché* as a kind of "self-interruption".[40]

In *Speech and Phenomena* (1967) Derrida seeks to evaluate Husserl's entire project through a "patient reading" (*lecture patiente*, SP 3; 1) of the *Logical Investigations*. Derrida interprets Husserl as holding a set of principles which are in tension with the public philosophy he is trying to develop. This identification of inner tension, the unmasking of repressed tendencies, epitomises deconstruction in operation. The main claim of *Speech and Phenomena* is that Husserl, who proposes a phenomenology of signification in the First Logical Investigation, never fully appreciates the manner in which signification is constituted, and hence he remains trapped in a metaphysics of presence and a logocentrism which privileges the spoken act of meaning over all other forms of inscription. Phenomenology has clung to the link between *logos* and *phonè* (SP 15; 14), whereas Derrida wants to emphasise the priority of *writing* (*écriture*), the set of signs which function in the absence of the subject who utters or expresses them (SP 93; 104).

Derrida is critical of Husserl's assumption of the presence of meaning in fulfilled intuition, and he is especially critical of Husserl's retention of

Platonic, essentialist elements, and especially his positing of self-identical ideal meanings and other kinds of general objects. In agreement with Heidegger, and against Husserl, Derrida criticises the presumption that the present is the totally real moment which gives itself to us in our intuitions. Husserl thought of the paradigmatic case of perceptual intuition as one in which what is meant or intended is fully present in our intuition, as when I perceive something in front of me; the thing is given with what Husserl called 'bodily presence' (*Leibhaftigkeit*). As we have seen, Husserl's foundational principle of phenomenology, his 'principle of all principles', assumed a core of self-giving, presenting intuitions, intuitions which, in a quasi-Cartesian manner, guaranteed their own validity. Or as Derrida puts it:

> For in fact what is signified by phenomenology's "principle of principles"? What does the value of primordial presence to intuition as source of sense and evidence, as the a priori of a prioris, signify? First of all it signifies the certainty, itself ideal and absolute, that the universal form of all experience (*Erlebnis*), and therefore of all life, has always been and will always be the present (*le présent*). The present alone always is and ever will be. Being is presence or the modification of presence.
>
> (SP 53; 59–60)

More generally, Derrida is critical of Husserl's apparent avoidance or postponement of the question of the role of language and signification in phenomenology. As Derrida says, for Husserl, "the unity of ordinary language (or the language of traditional metaphysics) and the language of phenomenology is never broken" (SP 8; 6). Derrida believes Husserl assumed that logic is at the essence of language, and hence ignored the crucial role of the act of signification itself. He accuses Husserl of misunderstanding the nature of the sign, and, therefore, of never questioning metaphysical assumptions that suggested it mediated between the sensible and the intelligible. Instead of recognising, with Saussure and the semiotic tradition, the primordiality of the sign, Husserl wants to make signification depend on prior presence. The signifying act presents something as already a sign, and, hence, as a *trace* of something which has never been present. Derrida maintains that language itself is in part responsible for appearance of presence as well as for the endless deferral of determinate meaning. "Language preserves the difference that preserves language" (SP 14; 13). There is, in Derrida's terms, no transcendental signified.

For Husserl, a sign was understood very generally as anything which can stand 'for something' (*für etwas*, LI I § 1), but, according to Derrida, Husserl never interrogated precisely how signs do this work of *standing for* (*à place de*, SP 88; 98). Husserl distinguished between two functions of a sign: *expression* and *indication*, but, although Derrida acknowledges that

Husserl sees these as different functions, he claims Husserl does not fully recognise how these two functions of the sign 'contaminate' each other. For Derrida, signs work through repetition and reiterability, and every sign has a structure which Derrida calls 'primordial substitution', whereby it always stands 'for something' other than itself. Derrida interprets the nature of the sign as a kind of 'supplementarity' (*supplément* is a technical term for Derrida), whereby the sign actually *supplies* the very thing it is supposed to be simply *supplementing* (WD 289). According to Derrida's use of the term, 'supplement' refers to something additional which supplies something essential (think of dietary supplements which are added to our diet in order to supply something essential). On the other hand, the Western semiotic tradition, exemplified by Husserl, has always treated signs as somehow added on to or tacked on to the things they announce; their status is thus secondary and derivative. Hence Husserl demoted reflection on the sign as he was interested only in logic as the essence of rationality. But in fact signs bring about what they announce. As Derrida says:

> The strange structure of the supplement appears here: by delayed re-action, a possibility produces that to which it is said to be added on.
> (SP 89; 99)

For Derrida, phenomenology, though supposed presuppositionless, and hence anti-metaphysical, ironically turns out to be metaphysics "restored to its original purity" (SP 5; 3). Husserl's phenomenological principle in fact harbours, for Derrida, an unanalysed *metaphysical* presupposition (SP 4; 3). Husserl continued to assume "the self-presence of transcendental life" (SP 6; 5). In other words, Husserl assumed that all meaning is constituted by the transcendental ego, but he never adequately explained how the transcendental ego itself gets constituted. It is as if one can empty out one's own experience of everything contingent, factual, and singular, and still be left with pure presence to oneself, or temporal self-presence. Indeed, Husserl sometimes seems to be maintaining that a kind of formal, empty self-presence can survive even death. For Derrida, drawing here on Levinas and Heidegger, Husserl is thereby in denial of the death of the self. Phenomenology claims to be *Lebensphilosophie*, a philosophy of life, of living experiences, but in so doing it neglects the possibility of death (SP 10; 9), and instead affirms an endless life of meanings.

As part of his critique of self-presence, Derrida criticises Husserl's claim in the First Investigation that the solitary thinking consciousness has no need for signs to indicate or point to things. Since meanings are directly present to the self, Husserl argues, we have a conception of a speech which hears itself "in the absence of the world" (SP 16; 15–16). In the First Logical Investigation Husserl had assumed that in the interiority of self-consciousness no indicative signs would be needed, as strictly speaking there is no communication involved, since we do not have to signal our inner mental states to ourselves. Consciousness would thus have immediate self-presence, a 'for-itself' (*für-sich*) unmediated by signs. Derrida attacks this claim, pointing out that the self is actually a process of *différance*. He criticises Husserl's assertion that in pre-linguistic subjective thought, there can be no signification; rather there is the direct experience of one's mental life, which nevertheless may be represented as a kind of inner monologue. Derrida questions what 'representation' (*Vorstellung*) means here for Husserl (SP 49; 54), and points out that Husserl has assumed that representation is somehow not essential to self-communication. If, however, one considers linguistic communication, Derrida believes it is simply impossible to separate reality from representation. As Derrida puts it, Western philosophy has always considered that "the sign is from its origin and to the core of its sense marked by this will to derivation or effacement" (SP 51; 57). Derrida wants to argue that the sign is more basic than the meaning which is present, that the notion of presence itself depends on the notion of representation. Representation is older than presence, as Derrida says.

Derrida recognises that Husserl was troubled by the problem of how, in repeated yet *different* acts of thinking, each a unique, unrepeatable, occurrent psychological episode, we can intend the *same* meaning and succeed in referring again and again to the *same* object. How can the *sameness* of the intended meaning be guaranteed in the midst of the *different* acts of thinking? In the *Prolegomena* (1900) and elsewhere, Husserl's answer is to posit, besides the object of the act, an *ideal* domain of multiply accessible 'senses' or 'meanings' (*Bedeutungen*) which are instantiated within the act of thinking, but which nevertheless, because ideal, can sustain approaches from different paths at different times. In Husserl's later work the ideal is constituted by acts of repetition or 'repeatability' (Husserl uses the German term *Wiederholbarkeit*, repeatability, in *The Origin of Geometry*). As Derrida explains:

> According to Husserl the structure of speech (*discours*) can only be described in terms of ideality. There is the ideality of the sensible form of the signifier (for example the word), which must remain *the same* and can do so only as an ideality. There is, moreover, the ideality of the signified (of the *Bedeutung*) or intended sense, which is not to be confused with the act of intending or with the object, for the latter two need not necessarily be ideal. Finally, in certain cases, there is the ideality of the object itself, which then assures the ideal transparency and perfect univocity of language, this is what happens in the exact sciences. But this ideality, which is but another name for the permanence of the same and the possibility of its repetition, *does not exist* in the world, and it does not come from another world; it depends entirely on the possibility of acts of

repetition. It is constituted by this possibility. Its "being" is propor-
tionate to the power of repetition; absolute ideality is the correlate
of a possibility of indefinite repetition. It could be said therefore
that being is determined by Husserl as ideality, that is, as repetition.

(SP 52; 58)

Derrida is claiming that, within Husserl's account of self-understanding,
there is an assumption of the presence of ideal meaning which runs counter
to Husserl's own analysis of ideality depending on representation and
repetition. Husserl has effaced the key concept at the very heart of
signification: the endless differentiation of meanings, difference without
sameness. Derrida is claiming that in fact the notion of representation is tied
in with the notions of difference and repetition and that Husserl is unaware
of the operation of this system of concepts.

Moreover, for Derrida, *repetition* is not a repeating of an original givenness, but rather it is *through* repetitions that the illusion of simple presence
and self-identity is composed. In Derrida's paradoxical formulation,
repetition itself is what is original. Thus Husserl, in spite of himself, arrived
at Derrida's own position, namely that "the presence-of-the-present is
derived from repetition and not the reverse" (SP 52; 58). For Derrida,
Husserl's identification of being with ideality is itself a valuation, "an
ethico-theoretical act that revives the decision that founded philosophy in
its Platonic form" (SP 53; 59). Husserl, the great presuppositionless
philosophiser, turns out to be committed to a Platonic outlook in philosophy. Derrida recognises that Husserl's Platonism consists in the normative
valuation of the ideal over the sensuous (SP 53; 59), and thereby, in
Derrida's view, Husserl's philosophy has recourse to what it originally
excluded from itself.

Derrida's interpretation of Husserl has been praised as a rigorous reading
of the text, but it has also been criticised for grossly distorting Husserl's
central claims.[41] Derrida is essentially correct in seeing the *Logical Investigations* as paradigmatic for Husserl's work as a whole, as the conception of
science and rationality in that work is never later repudiated. Derrida also
raises legitimate questions over Husserl's commitment to the ideality of
meaning. It is indeed true, as Husserl himself recognised, that his account of
signification in the First Investigation falls short of a full treatment of the
topic, and that he underestimated the importance of signification as such.
Nevertheless, Derrida is exaggerating and clearly distorting Husserl when he
claims that Husserl thought of expression primarily in terms of spoken
speech. For Husserl, expression is associated with language but not
necessarily speech. Furthermore, Husserl's recognition that in private mental
awareness one does not have to intimate to oneself that one is expressing
meanings is surely correct against the Derridian view that expression,
indication, and intimating cannot be disentangled.

Derrida's debt to Heidegger

Derrida's relation to phenomenology is based not only on his detailed studies of Husserl but also on his complex relation to Heidegger. Thus in *Positions* Derrida states:

> What I have attempted to do would not have been possible without the opening of Heidegger's questions...would not have been possible without the attention to what Heidegger calls the difference between Being and beings, the ontico-ontological difference such as, in a way, it remains unthought by philosophy.
>
> *(Pos.,* p. 9)

In Heidegger, especially, Derrida discovered the nature of *radical questioning*, the manner in which questions always carry their own presuppositions and open up a space which is limited by the nature of the question itself. Heidegger's repeated attempts to name the 'ontological difference' between Being (*Sein*) and beings (*Seienden*), which, according to Heidegger, remains unthought in the philosophical tradition, his critique of 'ontotheology' (the reification of Being as a unique substance – God), his project of overcoming the metaphysics of presence, and his attempt to uncover the 'unthought' (*das Ungedachte*) in all thinking, as well as his attempted 'destruction of the history of philosophy', are all taken up in their own way in Derrida's work. Yet Derrida also sees in Heidegger some remainder of the traditional metaphysics of presence, a kind of 'nostalgia' for presence, evident, for instance, in Heidegger's discussions of early Greek philosophy. Though Heidegger is a thinker of difference, he does not grasp the full force of *différance* as Derrida finds it. Derrida then wants to make Heidegger more radical, to release Heidegger's texts of a certain commitment to presence and to metaphysics.

Heidegger's deep interrogation of the question of the meaning of Being itself disrupts our confidence in the logocentric tradition which assumes an identity of being and meaning; as Derrida writes, "destroying the securities of ontotheology, such a meditation contributes...to the dislocation of the unity of the sense of being" (*Gramm.,* p. 22; 35–36). In common with the later Heidegger he believes in the power of language to shape and misshape thought, and also agrees with Heidegger in holding that 'language speaks man'. In other words, humans are not the creators of meaning but rather inhabit a world created by the impersonal forces of language. Furthermore, Derrida connects this Heideggerian view with Saussure's similar claim that "language...is not a function of the speaking subject" (*Margins,* p. 15; 16).

The influence of structuralism: de Saussure and Lévi-Strauss

The role played by Heidegger on Derrida's thought is almost matched by the influence of Saussure. As a student, as we have seen, Derrida was deeply

461

influenced by the *linguistics* pioneered by the Swiss linguist Ferdinand de Saussure in his lecture courses published posthumously in 1916 as *Course in General Linguistics*.[42] In France during the 1950s, structuralist theories of language based on Saussure were being promulgated by Merleau-Ponty, Lévi-Strauss, Althusser, Roland Barthes, and, to an extent, by Michel Foucault. Indeed, Paul Ricoeur had already drawn attention to the relation between Husserl's theory of signs and structuralist linguistics, and had called Husserl's early phenomenology of the *Logical Investigations* 'the phenomenology of signification' in his 1967 study.[43]

Derrida's view of Saussure is complex; he sees Saussure as being trapped in phonocentrism and yet also credits him with laying the groundwork for grammatology, locating linguistics within grammatology. Saussure's official position is indeed *phonocentric*, in so far as he explicitly privileges the spoken sign over and against the written, and asserts a 'natural bond' (*lien naturel*) between a sound and its sense (*Gramm.*, p. 35; 53). Indeed Saussure thinks of language and writing as different systems of signs and begins by excluding the written signs from consideration. Writing is deemed to be something secondary, representative, and derivative. The empty symbolism of the written notation distances us from the true phenomenon of language (*Gramm.*, p. 40; 60). Furthermore, Saussure claimed the very essence of language to be totally unrelated to the phonic character of the linguistic sign. Saussure thereby opened the field for grammatology by proclaiming the arbitrary nature of the sign (*Gramm.*, pp. 43–44; 65–66).

Derrida focuses on two significant features of language which Saussure highlighted: the *differential* character and *arbitrary* nature of linguistic signs. The first feature concerns the human ability to pick out the same phoneme as uttered by speakers with different voices, accents, intonations, and so on, or to recognise letters written in different ways but which stood for the same alphabetical letter. Saussure concluded that phonemes are not identified by having a particular unique sound attached to them, but rather are always differentiated by their distance and distinction from other phonemes. Saussure sums this up with the notorious claim: "in language there are only differences without positive terms". In other words, the phonemes are marked out not by a set of essential sounds but by a set of differences from one another. This is what Derrida frequently refers to as "the differential character of the sign".

The second significant feature of language for Saussure is the purely *arbitrary* nature of linguistic signs: for example, it is purely arbitrary that the sounds 'dog', '*chien*', or '*Hund*' in their respective languages all pick out animals of the canine variety. As Derrida explains: "There can be arbitrariness only because the system of signs is constituted by the differences in terms and not by their plenitude" (*Margins*, p. 10; 11). For Derrida and for Saussure, these two features are related: the arbitrariness of the sign is made possible only because of the differential character of language. Derrida thus quotes Saussure with approval: "Arbitrary and differential are two correlative characteristics".

Saussure gives Derrida the basis for his generalised account of meaning. Derrida believes this is the key to understanding the general notion of the deferral of meaning which he believes is operative in all texts. Saussure's view of language and meaning is *holistic*, that is the meaning of any term is related to the other terms in the language. This is fairly easy to see: the differences between 'sofa', 'settee', and 'couch', for instance, may best be expressed by comparing each term with the other. As Wittgenstein would say, there is a family resemblance between these notions, rather than there being a set of fixed essences with essential characteristics. In Derrida's way of putting it, each concept is inscribed in a chain of concepts and they refer to each other by means of a play of differences. One can imagine going in to buy a particular shade of paint from a hardware store. Usually these shops produce charts where different colours and shades are laid out side by side. We can say: "I'd like that green but with a bit more yellow in it, or else shading a little more towards an earthy brown, or else a green with a slight hint of blue". Each shade is distinguished by differences which are themselves not identifiable in positive terms. Of course, as Searle has shown, the claim that there are only differences and no positive characteristics is profoundly wrong, and that the system of differences between phonemes is not a question of presence or absence but of their relative distinction from one another.[44]

As part of his overall claim that opposites contaminate each other, Derrida objects to the traditional linguistic opposition between 'sign' (*signifiant*) and 'signified' (*signifié*). Indeed he prefers to complicate the relation between signs. From Saussure Derrida borrowed the notion of the inseparability of the signifier/signified relation (where they are like two sides of the same coin, *Pos.*, p. 18). There is no signified outside the concourse of signifiers, and so Derrida concludes there is no 'transcendental signified', by which he means there is no pure meaning outside of the play of signifiers; every signified is also in the position of signifier (*Pos.*, p. 20). Derrida is dismissive of a kind of Platonism which treats the signifier as sensible and the signified as something intelligible, that is a meaning. From Saussure also, Derrida takes the view that 'the play of difference' is essential to every sign. This leads us to a discussion of another central notion of Derrida – his notion of *différance*.

The nature of '*différance*'

Derrida's influential essay "*la différance*" was originally a lecture delivered to the *Société Française de Philosophie* at the Sorbonne on 27 January 1968, and first published in the *Bulletin de la société française de philosophie* (July–September, 1968) and reprinted (with slight amendments referring chiefly to Lacan) in *Margins* (1972), which translation we shall cite here.

Derrida's overall aim in the essay is to invoke and broaden Saussure's account of the differential character of signs as a means of interrogating Husserl's and Heidegger's assumptions concerning the nature of presence and the ontological difference. The essay is a programmatic statement of the necessity for deconstruction, and as we shall see *différance* and *déconstruction* are linked terms. The essay proposes a 'non-concept'[45] of *différance*, a term Derrida had been invoking since 1959, as we have seen. Derrida proposes to expand Saussure's account of the linguistic sign to signs in general:

> we will designate as *différance* the movement according to which language, or any code, any system of reference in general, is constituted "historically" as a weave of differences (*comme tissu de différences*).
>
> (*Margins*, p. 12; 12–13)

Derrida claims *différance* is "neither a word nor a concept" (*Margins*, p. 7; 7) but actually "the possibility of conceptuality" (*Margins*, p. 11; 11).

Derrida, however, does not want to be read as proposing a new single philosophical principle in the manner of traditional metaphysics (e.g. Descartes's *cogito ergo sum*). For Derrida, *différance* is not a principle or origin from which all things flow in the Neo-Platonic manner. It is not a present being and does not rule or exercise authority over anything (*Margins*, pp. 21–2; 22), rather it is a non-originary, non-principle. It differentiates itself from any principle having that foundational and archetypal force, and hence *différance* is not an *arche*: Yet, despite this rejection of *différance* as a metaphysical first principle, Derrida allows himself to say that in the traditional language of metaphysics *différance* could "be said to designate a constitutive, productive, and originary causality, the process of scission and division which would produce or constitute different things or differences" (*Margins*, p. 9; 9). Derrida is thus showing how one who tries to subvert traditional metaphysical argument and thinking still ends up making metaphysical statements. He wants to posit a differentiating process ('*différance*') at the origin of meaning and history but he is well aware that such a positing will hypostasise it, giving it the status of a principle or origin. Thus, "to say that *différance* is originary is simultaneously to erase the myth of a present origin" (WD 203; see also *Gramm.*, p. 23; 38).

But, though Derrida insists that *différance* is non-foundational and irreducibly polysemic, he also claims it is omnipresent. Even though it is not a metaphysical principle in many ways it behaves just like a metaphysical first principle. Again, Derrida's technique is to allow the various contexts in which he has used the concept of *différance* to resonate against one another. In this essay he seeks to "reassemble in a sheaf" (*rassembler en faisceau*) the different senses of the term (*Margins*, p. 3; 3). Rather in the manner of the structuralists, Derrida says he does not just want to list these contexts, or provide a history of his uses of the new term, rather he wants to explicate "the general system of this economy" as something that has the structure of a "weaving" or an "interlacing" (*Margins*, p. 3; 4). Similarly, when Derrida introduces the notion of *différance* in *Of Grammatology*, he refers to it as "an economic concept designating the production of differing/deferring" (*Gramm.*, p. 23; 38).

Derrida begins the essay by introducing his usual theme of the contrast between *speech* and *writing* with the paradoxical statement: "I shall speak, then, of a letter" (*Je parlerai, donc, d'une lettre*, *Margins*, p. 3; 3). Derrida goes on to comment on two French words, '*différant*' and '*différent*', whose difference in meaning cannot be heard, but which can be seen in their written forms where the presence or absence of an 'a' distinguishes one from the other. Derrida is making the point that certain distinctions of meaning require *writing* and cannot be easily communicated in *speech* alone: "It is read or it is written, but it cannot be heard" (*Margins*, p. 3; 4). Derrida will exploit this ambiguity in meaning through a "discreet graphic intervention" (i.e. by inserting the letter 'a' into the French word '*différence*') he will aggravate its intrusive character, and encourage "a kind of insistent intensification of its play"; that is, he will allow the different meanings to be heard together in the discussion that follows. Derrida makes much of the effect of introducing a silent letter 'a', which he says has the function of signifying beyond itself. He goes on to say that the letter stands in "pyramidal silence", "it is a tomb...that is not far from signalling the death of the tyrant", "a mute mark...a tacit monument" (*Margins*, p. 4; 4). In Derrida's inflated rhetoric, the letter stands in the word in the manner the Egyptian pyramids stand as a cypher. Here Derrida is making an allusion to Hegel, but no doubt he is also referring to the shape of the letter 'a' itself – at least in its capitalised form 'A' which has the triangular, pyramidic shape. Part of his point in referring to a silent letter which makes a difference in meaning is to demonstrate that there is "no purely and rigorously phonetic writing" (*Margins*, p. 5; 5), that is a writing which simply marks out or copies the sounds of our speech. All writing contains non-phonetic signs such as inverted commas, spaces, and so on.

Encountering this typically Derridian chain of free association, the reader might be forgiven for thinking that Derrida has lost the run of himself. Surely Derrida is going too far in claiming not only that this *différance* cannot be heard but that it is beyond the order of understanding, and "exceeds the order of truth" (*Margins*, p. 6; 6)? What is at stake, however, is rather simple. The French verb '*différer*' has two meanings. In French the word '*différence*' can mean to '*differ*' or to '*defer*' whereas English, from the same Latin root, has developed two words: 'differ' and 'defer'. Similarly, French has not developed nouns such as 'deferral' to indicate the process of temporal spacing and distantiation. Thus, in a way, all Derrida is doing, despite his inflated rhetoric, is coining a French word to express the double meanings of *differentiation* and *deferral!* Actually Derrida claims that the term *différance* is not just ambiguous between these two sets of meaning but rather is "immediately and irreducibly polysemic" (*Margins,* p. 8; 8). According to Derrida, *différance* has a whole set of meanings which can never simply be sketched out or traced in writing. *Différance* means non-identity, otherness, alterity, being discernible, distinct, and, secondly, it can connote some kind of temporal and/or spatial separation, interval, distance, spacing, distantiation, which may include temporal distancing, deferring, "the action of putting off until later...a detour, a delay, a relay, a reserve, a representation" (*Margins,* p. 8; 8). This double kind of differing/deferring will be Derrida's key term for explicating the movement of signs in general and of linguistic meaning in particular.

Derrida proceeds by utilising what he has provisionally designated as "the word or concept of *différance*", but is really "neither a word nor a concept", to explore aspects of the problem of signs and writing. All signs, by pointing away from themselves, involve a deferral of meaning, while at the same time creating the illusion that the meaning is present. The sign stands for the absent and represents the presence in its absence. According to classical semiology: "The sign, in this sense, is deferred presence" (*présence différrée, Margins,* p. 9; 9). This feature of language is what Derrida calls '*différance*'.

Derrida is opposed to the interpretation of a sign as something sensible which points beyond itself to something intelligible. To say that the difference between the 'a' and the 'e' cannot be heard and therefore is not a sensible difference, is not thereby to say that the difference must belong to the understanding, to the domain of intelligibility. Rather, according to Derrida, we are going beyond or outside philosophy's usual distinction between the sensible and the intelligible, between what is accessible to sensation or to intellection. The order of *différance* is prior to that distinction and sustains it. This makes *différance* sound very like a transcendental condition for the possibility of language and meaning. But Derrida will resist that move also, even though he is clearly exploiting the resources of transcendental philosophy. Derrida suspects this kind of transcendental move and resists interpreting these differentiations in language and in other systems as some kind of force which is there *before* the differences. We should not suppose that differentiation has a unique origin; *différance* is for Derrida prior to any origin. To think of origin is to think of unity not differentiation:

> *Différance* is the non-full, non-simple, structured and differentiat-
> ing origin of differences. Thus the name "origin" no longer suits it.
> (*Margins,* p. 11; 12)

Derrida is thus denying all attempts to locate the origin of the process of differentiation, seeking its cause or its governing principle. He is rejecting any 'originality' in *différance*. In other words, we are always already caught up in the processes of differentiation and there is no single logic to that process. In fact Derrida even resists using the term 'process' for what is going on.

Différance is, according to Derrida, neither active nor passive, but is undecided between active and passive, and hence comparable with the middle-voiced form (*la voix moyenne*) which speaks of "an operation which is not an operation" (*Margins*, p. 9; 9). The middle-voiced form occurs in Indo-European languages, such as classical Greek. Normally, we think of the *active* or *passive* voice of the verb – 'I hit the dog', 'I was hit by the stick' – or the reflexive form – 'I dress myself'. The middle-voiced form, however, indicates a kind of passive whereby something is done *which has a personal interest to me*; for example, in the Greek present middle-voiced form, *paideuomai* means 'I am involved in self-education', and this meaning is close but not entirely identical to the reflexive form, 'I educate myself' (*emauton paideuo*). The middle-voiced form differs from the reflexive in that the subject is not the actor but is nevertheless involved in the outcome of the action. This is what Derrida means by saying that it is 'an operation which is not an operation'. It does not consider action as starting either from the doer and completing in the deed (active form), or, conversely, from the deed back to the doer (passive). The middle-voiced form is 'intransitive' in that it does not take an object in the usual sense. So in emphasising the supposed middle-voiced nature of deconstruction, Derrida really means that it is an action in which I am involved but of which I am not the agent. Heidegger had made similar comments about the importance of the middle-voiced form in ancient Greek for expressing the workings of Being. Derrida goes on, however, to make the hyperbolic claim that philosophy has been involved in repressing the middle-voiced form. Thus, for Derrida, we cannot ask the question 'who or what differs?', because this would be to draw *différance* back under the sway of being-present. We would in effect be claiming that *différance* could be mastered (*Margins*, p. 15; 15).

Derrida concludes the essay by denying that *différance* 'is' at all. It is not a source, it is not written with a capital letter, it represents not a new principle but a kind of subversion. The history of Being indeed is only one aspect of this *diapherein* of this differentiating.

Sketch of a history of *différance*

Despite being a non-concept, Derrida claims *différance* has a philosophical history. Indeed he frequently makes the transcendental claim that 'différance' makes history possible. As part of his elaborate textual weaving around the term *différance*, Derrida invokes comparable notions in

Saussure, Hegel, Husserl, Heidegger, Freud, Nietzsche, Levinas, and even in Bataille. Actually Derrida holds that *différance* is 'older' than any ontological differences, but nevertheless he gives a brief history of its occurrence in Western thought. The notion of difference is, of course, firmly established in Hegel's philosophy; it appears in the very title of Hegel's 1801 essay, *The Difference Between Fichte's and Schelling's Systems of Philosophy*. Furthermore, this text opens with the claim that "division (*Entzweiung*) is the source of the need for philosophy". Hegel sees both reality and thought as proceeding by dialectic, understood as a process of differentiation and overcoming of differences through their transformation and 'sublation' (French, *la relève*; German, *die Aufhebung*) into higher unities. Derrida relates *différance* to the Hegelian notion of *Aufhebung*, that is the manner in which concepts are transformed in different contexts which mark the progress of history. In fact the whole of Hegel's dialectic moves by *Aufhebung* which means taking a concept, displacing it, and then reutilising it. As Derrida says: "the *Aufhebung* is constrained into writing itself otherwise" (*Margins*, p. 19; 21). Hegel's notion of *Aufhebung*, then, is already a kind of trace of Derrida's *différance*.

Hegel's invocation of difference was already closely scrutinised by Heidegger in his 1957 essay *Identity and Difference*, and much of what Derrida has to say is close to Heidegger's account in that essay,[46] though in his '*différance*' essay Derrida refers to a passage in the Jena *Logic* where Hegel speaks of a 'different relation' (*differente Beziehung*) employing the rare Latin form rather than the more usual German adjective '*verschieden*'. Hegel wants in that passage to draw attention to a difference within the present moment itself. Derrida neither wants to break with Hegel nor endorse Hegel's terms. Rather, he wants to achieve a certain displacement of the Hegelian notion of difference.

Heidegger, too, in his *Letter on Humanism* has his own version of difference: the *ontological difference* between Being and beings. Derrida admits that his notion is in 'communication' with this Heideggerian discussion, even if the two are not necessarily linked. Derrida claims, however, that the questioning of presence in Heidegger had already been thought in various ways by both Freud and Nietzsche: "both of them as is well known, and sometimes in very similar fashion, put consciousness into question in its assured certainty of itself" (*Margins*, p. 17; 18). Indeed, Derrida points out, Nietzsche's main critique of philosophy concerns its "active indifference to difference". In Freud, something repressed is delayed, but also undergoes a deviation. The Freudian unconscious should not be seen as a kind of hidden presence, but as a kind of differing from oneself whereby a kind of permanent process of substitution is taking place: "[the unconscious] sends out delegates, representatives, proxies; but without any chance that the giver of proxies might 'exist', might be present, be 'itself' somewhere, and with even less chance that it might become conscious" (*Margins*, p. 21; 21).

Différance and the trace

As Derrida built his account of the manner in which meaning operates in his essays in the 1960s, he introduced other technical terms and neologisms. While struggling to articulate how *différance* can be responsible for the production of differences, and yet not a cause in the classic sense (because it has no being in itself, no fullness, no presence), Derrida introduces the notion of the 'trace'. The term 'trace' has its remote origins in Neo-Platonic thought, for example in Augustine's discussion of traces of the divine (*vestigia Dei*) left behind in created things. The concept of 'trace' (German, *die Spur*) can also be found in Freud. For Freud, the effect of a psychological trauma does not have to be fully present initially but can defer itself (WD 203). Discussion of 'trace' also occurs in Heidegger, especially in his *Anaximander* essay, which Derrida quotes. Heidegger sees the forgetting of Being as belonging to Being itself and so the effacement of the trace also belongs to the trace. As we have seen, the concept of 'trace' appears in both Merleau-Ponty and Levinas. From Levinas in particular, Derrida takes the notion of '*trace*' as a mark of something absent that has never actually been present. Thus, for example, our nostalgia for an Arcadia or Garden of Eden is a *trace* of something that has never existed. As Derrida comments, following Levinas, a 'trace' is not an effect since it does not actually have a cause. All signs are in effect traces. Indeed, the act of signifying itself can only be understood as a trace. Derrida talks of language as a 'play of traces' (*un jeu de traces*, *Margins*, p. 15; 16), which is a kind of *archi-writing*, the manner in which the play of signs precedes writing, the writing before the opposition between speech and writing. In Derrida's use of the term *trace*, it applies as much to the future as to the past, and indeed constitutes the present by its very relation to what is absent.

Derrida and religion

In his essay on *différance*, Derrida acknowledges that what he has produced is an account which is very much like a *metaphysics of différance*, but at the same time he rejects the possibility of such a metaphysics. Similarly, he denies that *différance* should be seen as a theological concept, or that he is postulating something like a God as the unnameable source of all differentiation. He is not engaged in a "theological" thematic (*Margins*, p. 7; 7). Derrida states that *différance* is not something behind language in the manner in which the transcendent God is behind negative theology. Rather it does not belong to being either present, or absent, though much of the language of negative theology does actually apply to it. Derrida's *différance* is the surpassing of onto-theology and of philosophy itself. It is clear, therefore, that Derrida was conscious of the theological meanings of *différance* from early in his career, and that this is not a recent preoccupation, as some critics believe. For instance, Habermas has commented:

469

> Derrida does not want to think theologically; as an orthodox Hei-
> deggerian, he [Derrida] is forbidden any thought about a supreme
> entity...As he assures us at the start of his essay on *"différance"*, he
> does not want to do any theology, not even negative theology.[47]

From his earliest writings on *différance*, as in his essays on Levinas, Derrida himself has acknowledged some kind of correlation between his work and religious discourse, especially negative theology and even prophecy. Some of Derrida's formulations of deconstruction explicitly acknowledge a connection with the 'sacred', and with what he calls 'the messianic'. Thus in 1984 Derrida had said: "it is possible to see deconstruction as being produced in a space where the prophets are not far away" (*Dialogues*, p. 119). Increasingly, and while still keeping a distance from organised, institutionalised religions as such, Derrida has been paying more attention to aspects of religious mysticism and, in particular, exploring the manner in which Nicholas of Cusa and others kept a dialectic of saying and non-saying at work in order to signify the realm of the completely transcendent. In his *Specters of Marx* he invoked the possibility of a 'messianic future' – an absolutely undetermined future which breaks through the horizon of all given possibilities and yet remains purely futural. With this paradoxical "messianic without messianism", Derrida seeks to preserve a sense of a longed-for future state while distancing himself from institutional religions. He is even attracted to the very unfulfillability of the promise of liberation involved in the notion of the 'messianic'. Derrida is here acknowledging the need to posit a structure of hope in human beings, but, as ever, his assertions are fenced around with many hesitations and qualifications. Indeed, if Derrida's thought does leave room for the transcendent, an openness to some kind of call, it is in its recognition of the *unsayable* in philosophy, something which has drawn Derrida closer to Levinas. Thus, in his funeral address on the occasion of the death of Emmanuel Levinas in December 1995, Derrida acknowledges the powerful influence of Levinas's evocation of the other, and his exploration of the demand of the other on us. Derrida agreed with Levinas that once a third person (Levinas's *illeity*) intervenes in the relation between myself and the other, then the sphere of justice (and of religion) also appears. In these discussions of religious hope, Derrida appears to be giving a kind of transcendental account of the *conditions for the possibility of religion* while abstaining from the possibility of affirming any particular future to come. This turn to the messianic is fuel to those critics who feel that deconstruction is all too often presented as a kind of religion, a religion without doctrinal content, even a cult. Indeed, Derrida's portentous, apocalyptic style of announcing philosophical crises and 'epochs', while playfully undercutting these portents with irony, has infuriated some of his critics, but there is no sign of Derrida tempering his rhetoric. Indeed, his work now seems to be finding its natural home in theology departments, having once flourished in Comparative Literature.

Derrida's contribution to twentieth-century philosophy

As we have seen, Derrida claims that meaning has no original source, no *arché*; that meanings endlessly divide and differ, and there can never be a total or complete meaning, except as an ideal or indeed a fiction. He also, of course, claims not to be making such claims – he is certainly not putting them forward as theses or propositions – rather he claims to be reacting to certain specific textual occasions and contexts. Derrida's claim that deconstruction is nothing in itself and that he is making no global pro-nouncements makes it difficult to form any overview of his philosophy without being accused of distorting his intentions. The main problem is that it is always difficult to get from Derrida a clear, unambiguous statement of his claim (Derrida himself objects to this 'tyranny' of clarity and to the claims that he is making claims!). In claiming that meaning differs, or defers, it is not entirely clear whether he is insisting that our grasp of a particular meaning is *incomplete*, or necessarily *distorted*, or both. He would agree that our grasp of the meaning of a sentence is *incomplete*, provisional, but he denies that this provisional meaning is to be measured against the impossi-ble ideal of the complete meaning of the sentence. Rather the meaning of the sentence will always involve some 'slippage' (*glissage*), so that we will never actually master the meaning of any sentence. He appears to think also that all understanding involves ineliminable distortion (like a radio receiving the signal with some interference) and, furthermore, subsequent attempts at correction of distortion lead only to further distortion.

Because of this vagueness it is hard to assess Derrida's originality. For instance, the loose manner in which he has formulated his own maxim that 'there is no outside-text' has given rise to multiple interpretations which he can hardly disown, as they are not only valid inferences from his statements, but sometimes even found expressed by Derrida himself. Similarly, when Derrida says there are no fixed meanings, Richard Rorty is undoubtedly right to read Derrida as saying little more than that the meaning of a sentence is always a function of its context, and recontextualisations cannot be controlled or predicted in advance. Furthermore, Derrida vigorously denies that he ever said that meanings are endlessly deferred, or that texts can mean anything at all. According to Derrida, contexts are usually quite specific and uniquely determined. He denies that he holds the thesis of the indeterminacy of meaning (whereas Hilary Putnam, for instance, claims that Derrida and Quine arrive at the same conclusion here by different routes). Rather for Derrida the words in a sentence are always precisely determined; indeed the problem is that the determination is so precise that we usually avoid confronting it with the full rigour of close reading. It is not that texts

471

can mean anything, but that readers usually decide what they mean much too soon.

Derrida does insist that the multiple meanings of words are *irreducible*. Thus, as we have seen, *différer* has an irreducible double meaning, just as the Greek word *pharmakon* means both 'cure' and 'poison'. Derrida, then, suggests that this irreducibility sets up a barrier preventing any mastery of meanings. But this in fact does not follow. Derrida has shown that meanings are multiple, but *not* that they carry an indefinite or infinite range of meanings. It is true that words can always gain new meanings by insertion into new contexts, but our inability to predict these new contexts does not prevent us from having a reasonably secure grasp of the quite finite range of meanings our words have in their present contexts.

For these reasons, Derrida's work is controversial among professional philosophers of both the analytic or Continental European traditions. Habermas, for instance, has complained that Derrida does not proceed by advancing arguments.[48] The truth is that he does not engage in argument with others, other than to claim that they have misunderstood him. Furthermore, although Derrida draws attention to the ambiguities of meaning, circumscribing all his assertions with brackets, warnings, and denials, often this caution gives way to utterances of an overblown, exaggerated, and apocalyptic variety. Derrida too often adopts an inflated apocalyptic tone: treating the announcement of *différance* as an event of being, talking as if the destiny of Europe is at stake, and so on. Derrida has himself ironically commented on his own use of a portentous tone in his essay, "On the Apocalyptic Tone Recently Adopted in Philosophy", where he tries to show that the so-called neutral, dispassionate tone of conventional academic writing is also suspect.[49] Many find Derrida's tone somewhat risible and his rhetoric bombastic, repetitive, and obscurantist.

On the other hand, it is undeniable that Derrida has been a major influence in contemporary literary theory and cultural criticism (particularly art criticism, but deconstruction has even influenced architecture). In the USA in particular he has had a significant following among literary theorists (notably Paul de Man and Geoffrey Hartman),[50] though the overly dogmatic approach of 'American deconstruction' has prompted Derrida to distance himself from some of his more ardent American followers. His claims for deconstruction, moreover, are seen as part of a more general anti-foundationalist tendency in philosophy since Wittgenstein, but his version of Saussure has not been followed up by serious work in syntactics or semantics. Philosophers of language in the analytic tradition tend not to be interested in Derrida's work.

One example of Derrida's exaggerated rhetoric is to be found in his discussion of decision and the experience of future possibilities. Derrida clearly exaggerates the sense of the risk involved in thinking of the future: "the future can only be anticipated in the form of an absolute danger"

(*Gramm.*, p. 5; 14). Decisions are made in fear and trembling, as it were, since the future is absolute novelty and surprise. This seems to be radically distorting of our usual approach to the future. Derrida's overdramatised and distorted account does not seem to fit the phenomenology of decision making. If I promise to do something tomorrow, I am not necessarily casting myself into a world of indeterminacy and risk. In general, our being in the world is marked by continuity, the sun rising again tomorrow, and so on. Derrida thinks genuine decisions exist only in the form of blind leaps into the abyss.

Perhaps it is a mistake to take Derrida so seriously. Rorty has suggested that Derrida should be considered an *ironist*, close in spirit to Kierkegaard, or Nietzsche, or the French surrealist movement (e.g. André Breton). Rorty argues that Derrida is not producing philosophy in the traditional sense, but is doing the valuable work of alerting readers to the often undisclosed possibilities in certain texts. Derrida, needless to say, does not accept Rorty's assessment, protesting that his work, though not philosophical, is not merely literary either. But Derrida does seem happy with the notion that what he is doing is a kind of play of the kind he describes in his *différance* essay:

> The concept of play keeps itself beyond this opposition (of theology to empirical science); on the eve of philosophy and beyond it, the unity of chance and necessity in calculations without end.
>
> (*Margins*, p. 7; 7)

The difficulty with attempting to interpret Derrida is that, since he is not really making straightforward assertions or universal claims, then denials and refutations do not trouble him. Indeed, Derrida's elusiveness has infuriated many philosophers, rather in the manner in which the slipperiness of the Sophists infuriated the Platonic Socrates. Indeed, Derrida's philosophical outlook exhibits many traits in common with ancient *scepticism*. The accusation of scepticism has frequently recurred during Derrida's career. Of course, Derrida resists being called a sceptic because he does not wish to be drawn back to occupying a position clearly delineated within the history of metaphysics and because of the self-refuting character of scepticism, but nevertheless Derrida recognises how scepticism promotes difference.[51] Nevertheless there are clear affinities between Derrida's reluctance to make assertions and the sceptic recommendation of suspension of judgement before theses of equal weight (we saw earlier the impact of scepticism in Husserl's understanding of the *epoché*).

Derrida's own claims can, of course, be turned against him, and there does seem to be a straightforward problem of self-reference in his work. On the one hand, he draws attention to the endless play and unravelling of meaning, and, on the other hand, wants to assert firmly (and without ambiguity) that he is not a relativist, that he has never said there are only texts, that he has never said that all meanings endlessly differentiate, and so on. If there is no univocity in language, there is no univocal assertion which he is making, and hence there is no single philosophical thesis which can be attributed to Derrida (an assertion which he himself paradoxically makes). Derrida's pronouncements actually come as insights derived from practising many traditional philosophical skills: careful attention to meanings, awareness of the philosophical tradition in which the text is inserted, recognition of presuppositions, and so on. In fact, precisely how to involve deconstruction in the general programme of philosophical critique remains obscure. But it is clear that his rejection of the metaphysics of presence and of the belief in meanings as ideal unities leads him to move beyond the tradition of Husserlian phenomenology.

NOTES

INTRODUCTION

1 Edmund Husserl, *Logische Untersuchungen*, erster Band, *Prolegomena zur reinen Logik*, text der 1. und der 2. Auflage, hrsg. E. Holenstein, Husserliana XVIII (The Hague: Nijhoff, 1975), and *Logische Untersuchungen*, zweiter Band, *Untersuchungen zur Phänomenologie und Theorie der Erkenntnis*, in zwei Bänden, hrsg. Ursula Panzer, Husserliana XIX (Dordrecht: Kluwer, 1984), p. 6, trans. J. N. Findlay, *Logical Investigations*, 2 vols (New York: Humanities Press, 1970), Vol. 1, p. 249. Hereafter LI followed by section number, page number of English translation, followed by German pagination of Husserliana edition. Henceforth Husserliana will be abbreviated to Hua and volume number. Thus the reference would read LI, Intro. § 1, p. 249; Hua XIX/1 6.

2 E. Husserl, *Cartesianische Meditationen und Pariser Vorträge*, hrsg. Stephan Strasser, Hua I (Dordrecht: Kluwer, 1991), § 10, 63, trans. D. Cairns, *Cartesian Meditations* (The Hague: Nijhoff, 1967), p. 24. Hereafter CM and section number, English page number, and page number of German original, for example CM § 10, 24; Hua I 63.

3 P. Ricoeur, *A l'école de la phénoménologie* (Paris: Vrin, 1987), p. 9: "Si bien que la phénoménologie au sens large est la somme de l'oeuvre husserlienne et des hérésies issues de Husserl".

4 M. Heidegger, *Grundprobleme der Phänomenologie* (Frankfurt: Klostermann, 1975), trans. A. Hofstadter, *The Basic Problems of Phenomenology*, (Bloomington, IN: Indiana University Press, 1982), p. 328; GA 24, 467. (*Gesamtausgabe* = GA.)

5 Those who wish to study the earlier phase of the phenomenological movement are recommended to read Herbert Spiegelberg's monumental *The Phenomenological Movement. A Historical Introduction*, 3rd revised and enlarged edition, with the collaboration of Karl Schuhmann (Dordrecht: Kluwer, 1994).

6 Simone de Beauvoir, *The Prime of Life*, trans. P. Green (Harmondsworth: Penguin, 1965), p. 135.

7 E. Husserl, *Formale und transzendentale Logik. Versuch einer Kritik der logischen Vernunft. Mit ergänzenden Texten*, hrsg. Paul Janssen, Hua XVII (The Hague: Nijhoff, 1974), trans. D. Cairns, *Formal and Transcendental Logic* (The Hague: Nijhoff, 1969), § 94, p. 233–234; Hua XVII 239–240.

8 See the entry "Phänomenologie", in *Historisches Wörterbuch der Philosophie*, hrsg. J. Ritter, ed. (Darmstadt: Wissenschaftliche Buchgesellschaft, 1974), Vol. 7, cols 488–505.

9 H. Spiegelberg, *The Phenomenological Movement. A Historical Introduction,* op.

cit., p. 11. See also Michael Inwood, "Phenomenology", in *A Hegel Dictionary* (Oxford: Blackwell, 1992), pp. 214–216.

10 G. W. F. Hegel, *Enzyklopädie der philosophischen Wissenschaften* III. *Die Philosophie des Geistes* (Frankfurt: Suhrkamp, 1970), § 415, trans. William Wallace and A. V. Miller, *Hegel's Philosophy of Mind* (Oxford: Clarendon, 1971), p. 156.

11 See J. Hoffmeister's introduction to his edition of Hegel's *Phänomenologies des Geistes* (Hamburg: Meiner, 1952).

12 Georg Wilhelm Friedrich Hegel, *Phänomenologie des Geistes* (Frankfurt: Suhrkamp, 1973), trans. A. V. Miller, *Hegel's Phenomenology of Spirit* (Oxford: Oxford University Press, 1977).

13 For Mach, see H. Spiegelberg, *The Phenomenological Movement*, op. cit., p. 8 and p. 23 n. 11. For Husserl's reference to Mach in the Amsterdam lectures, see "The Amsterdam Lectures on Phenomenological Psychology", in T. Sheehan and R. Palmer, eds, Edmund Husserl, *Psychological and Transcendental Phenomenology and the Confrontation with Heidegger (1927–31)*, Collected Works VI (Dordrecht: Kluwer, 1997), hereafter *Trans. Phen.*, p. 213; Hua IX 302.

14 Franz Brentano, *Psychologie vom empirischen Standpunkt* (Hamburg: Meiner, 1973), 3 vols, trans. A. C. Rancurello, D. B. Terrell, and L. L. McAlister, *Psychology from an Empirical Standpoint,* 2nd edition, with new introduction by Peter Simons (London: Routledge, 1995).

15 Franz Brentano, *Deskriptive Psychologie*, ed. R. Chisholm and W. Baumgartner (Hamburg: Meiner, 1982), trans. B. Müller, *Descriptive Psychology* (London: Routledge, 1995), hereafter DP.

16 See Sartre, *Being and Nothingness. An Essay on Phenomenological Ontology*, trans. Hazel Barnes (London: Routledge, 1995), p. 53ff., and John R. Searle, *The Rediscovery of the Mind* (Cambridge, MA: MIT Press, 1992), pp. 151–173.

17 H. Bergson, *An Introduction to Metaphysics*, trans. T. E. Hulme (London, 1913), pp. 6–7.

18 E. Husserl, *Ideas pertaining to a Pure Phenomenology and to a Phenomenological Philosophy, First Book*, trans. F. Kersten (Dordrecht: Kluwer, 1983) § 24, p. 44; Hua III/1 44. Hereafter *Ideas* I followed by section number, page number of the English translation, and page number of German text.

19 M. Heidegger, *Grundprobleme der Phänomenologie (1919–1920)*, hrsg. Hans-Helmuth Gander (Frankfurt: Klostermann, 1992), GA 58, 5.

20 Husserl, Erfahrung und Urteil. Untersuchungen zur Genealogie der Logik. Redigiert und hrsg. von L. Landgrebe (Hamburg: Felix Meiner Verlag, 1999), p. 21, trans. J. Churchill and K. Ameriks as *Experience and Judgment. Investigations in a Genealogy of Logic* (Evanston, IL: Northwestern University Press, 1973), § 6, p. 27. Hereafter EJ followed by section number and page number of English translation, and German original.

21 M. Merleau-Ponty, *Phénoménologie de la perception* (Paris: Gallimard, 1945), p. ii, trans. Colin Smith, *The Phenomenology of Perception* (London: Routledge & Kegan Paul, 1962), p. viii. Hereafter PP followed by English and then French pagination.

22 Owen Flanagan, for example, in *Consciousness Reconsidered* (Cambridge, MA: MIT Press, 1992), speaks of getting the phenomenology right with regard to our mental life, pp. 153–175.

23 Colin McGinn, *The Problem of Consciousness* (Oxford: Blackwell, 1991).

24 See Daniel C. Dennett, *Consciousness Explained* (London: Penguin, 1993).

25 Gregory McCulloch, "The Very Idea of the Phenomenological", *Proceedings of the Aristotelian Society*, New Series, Vol. XCIII (1993), pp. 39–58. David Armstrong is the main exponent of the idea that sensory experiences have no phe-

nomenological content and are transparent in this sense; see D. Armstrong, "The Causal Theory of the Mind", in B. Lycan, ed., *The Nature of Mind and Other Essays* (Ithaca, NY: Cornell University Press, 1990).

26 T. Nagel, "What is it like to be a Bat?", *Philosophical Review* 83 (1974), reprinted in William Lyons, ed., *Modern Philosophy of Mind* (London: Everyman, 1995), pp. 159–174.

27 T. Adorno, *Die Transzendenz des Dinglichen und Noematischen in Husserls Phänomenologie*, in *Philosophische Frühschriften, Gesammelte Schriften* Band I (Frankfurt: Suhrkamp, 1973), pp. 7–77.

28 See the excellent study of Bernhard Waldenfels, *Phänomenologie in Frankreich* (Frankfurt: Suhrkamp, 1983).

29 Max Scheler, *Der Formalismus in der Ethik und die materiale Wertethik* (1913, 3rd edition 1926, Gesammelte Werke 7), trans. M. S. Frings and R. L. Funk, *Formalism in Ethics and Non-Formal Ethics of Values* (Evanston, IL: Northwestern University Press, 1973).

30 M. Heidegger, "Preface/Vorwort", in William Richardson, *Through Phenomenology to Thought* (The Hague: Nijhoff, 1963), pp. xiv, xv.

31 Max Horkheimer, "Traditional and Critical Theory", in Paul Connerton, ed., *Critical Sociology. Selected Readings* (London: Penguin, 1976), pp. 207–208.

32 T. Adorno, *Negative Dialektik* (Frankfurt: Suhrkamp, 1966), trans. E. B. Ashton, *Negative Dialectics* (London: Routledge & Kegan Paul, 1973).

1 FRANZ BRENTANO: DESCRIPTIVE PSYCHOLOGY AND INTENTIONALITY

1 Brentano, *Aristoteles und seine Weltanschauung* (Leipzig, 1911, reprinted Hamburg: Meiner, 1977), trans. Rolf George and Roderick Chisholm as *Aristotle and His World View* (Berkeley, CA: University of California Press, 1978).

2 See *The Vienna Manifesto*, quoted in Liliana Albertazzi, Massimo Libardi, and Roberto Poli, eds, *The School of Franz Brentano* (Dordrecht: Kluwer, 1996), p. 7. In fact, the public organisation founded by several members of the Vienna Circle was called the 'Ernst Mach Verein'.

3 For Brentano's assessment of Nietzsche, see, for example, his essay "Nietzsche", in *Geschichte der Philosophie der Neuzeit* (Hamburg: Meiner, 1987), pp. 297–298.

4 See L. Albertazzi *et al.*, eds, *The School of Franz Brentano*, op. cit., and Robin Rollinger, *Husserl's Position in the School of Brentano* (Utrecht: Utrecht University Dept of Philosophy, 1996).

5 See Josef Novák, "Masaryk and the Brentano School", in Josef Novák, ed., *On Masaryk* (Amsterdam: Rodopi, 1988), pp. 27–38.

6 See Wolfgang Stegmüller, *Main Currents in Contemporary German, British, and American Philosophy* (Dordrecht: Reidel, 1969), pp. 24–62.

7 On 'reism', see Jan Wolenski, "Reism in the Brentanist Tradition", in L. Albertazzi *et al.*, eds, *The School of Franz Brentano*, op. cit., pp. 357–375. The term 'reism' itself was coined by Tadeusz Kotarabinski (1886–1981) in 1929 but Kotarabinski differs from Brentano in maintaining a 'pansomatism', the doctrine that all individuals are physical entities, whereas Brentano believed in the existence of disembodied souls. On Kotarabinski, see *The Routledge Encyclopedia of Philosophy* (London: Routledge, 1998), Vol. 5, pp. 293–296.

8 F. Brentano, *Aenigmatias. Rätzel* (1878, reprinted Berne: Francke Verlag, 1962).

9 His father, Christian, wrote Catholic pamphlets; his uncle and godfather was the Romantic poet Clemens Brentano (1778–1842); his aunt was Bettina von

Arnim (1785–1857); his brother, Lujo, became a distinguished economist; a nephew, Georg Von Hertling, became President of Bavaria.

10 For an account of his life, see W. Baumgartner and F.-P. Burkard, "Franz Brentano: Eine Skizze seines Lebens und seiner Werke", *International Bibliography of Austrian Philosophy* (Amsterdam: Rodopi, 1990), pp. 16–53. See also Massimo Libardi, "Franz Brentano", in L. Albertazzi *et al.*, eds, *The School of Franz Brentano*, pp. 25–79. Also useful are the article by Dieter Münch, "Franz Brentano", in Lester Embree, ed., *The Encyclopedia of Phenomenology* (Kluwer: Dordrecht, 1997), pp. 71–75 and R. M. Chisholm and P. M. Simons, "Brentano, Franz Clemens", in *The Routledge Encyclopedia of Philosophy*, op. cit., Vol. 2, pp. 12–17.

11 O. Kraus, "Biographical Sketch of Franz Brentano", in L. McAlister, ed., *The Philosophy of Franz Brentano* (London: Duckworth, 1976), pp. 1–9.

12 Franz Brentano, *Von der mannigfachen Bedeutung des Seienden nach Aristoteles* (Freiburg, 1862), trans. Rolf George as *On the Several Senses of Being in Aristotle* (Berkeley, CA: University of California Press, 1975). Hereafter OSS.

13 See Martin Heidegger, "My Way to Phenomenology", in *On Time and Being*, trans. Joan Stambaugh (New York: Harper and Row, 1972), p. 74.

14 Adolf Trendelenburg, *Geschichte der Kategorienlehre* (Berlin, 1846, reprinted Hildesheim: Olms, 1963).

15 These essays are collected by Alfred Kastil and published as Brentano's *Kategorienlehre* (Leipzig: Meiner, 1933), trans. R. M. Chisholm and N. Guterman as *The Theory of the Categories* (The Hague: Nijhoff, 1981).

16 Brentano, *Die Psychologie des Aristoteles insbesondere seine Lehre vom Nous Poietikos* (Mainz, 1867, reprinted Darmstadt: Wissenschaftliche Buchgesellschaft, 1967), trans. Rolf George, *The Psychology of Aristotle, In Particular His Doctrine of the Active Intellect* (Berkeley, CA: University of California Press, 1977).

17 Brentano's theses are reprinted in F. Brentano, *Über die Zukunft der Philosophie* (Hamburg: Meiner, 1968), p. 136. Among the theses Brentano defended was one claiming that a conclusion can be drawn from a single premiss (in opposition to classical syllogistic logic). According to Brentano's notes for the defence of this thesis, he argued that from a proposition such as "There is no devil" one can draw the conclusion "There is no red devil".

18 See Eliam Campos, *Die Kantkritik Brentanos* (Bonn: Bouvier Verlag Herbert Grundmann, 1979).

19 F. Brentano, *Auguste Comte und die positive Philosophie* (1869), reprinted in *Die vier Phasen der Philosophie* (Hamburg: Meiner, 1968), pp. 99–135. See also his 1868 lecture course "Auguste Comte und die positive Philosophie", in F. Brentano, *Geschichte der Philosophie der Neuzeit*, ed. Klaus Hedwig (Hamburg: Meiner, 1987), pp. 246–294.

20 Carl Stumpf, "Reminiscences of Franz Brentano", in L. MacAlister, ed., *The Philosophy of Franz Brentano*, op. cit., pp. 10–46, esp. p. 23. Stumpf began as a student of jurisprudence but was attracted to philosophy and theology by Brentano. Stumpf recalls Brentano insisting on rigorous logical proof in his philosophical discussions with students. Stumpf wished to follow Brentano into the priesthood but changed his mind when Brentano himself had his spiritual crises. Instead Stumpf wrote a *Habilitation* thesis on the mathematical axioms and became *Privatdozent* in Göttingen under Lotze.

21 See Stumpf, "Reminiscences of Franz Brentano", in McAlister, ed., *The Philosophy of Franz Brentano*, op. cit., p. 37.

22 Brentano, *Psychologie vom empirischen Standpunkt* (Hamburg: Meiner, 1973), 2 vols, trans. Antos C. Rancurello, D. B. Terrell, and Linda McAlister as

Psychology from an Empirical Standpoint (London: Routledge & Kegan Paul, 1973, reprinted with a new preface by Peter Simons, London: Routledge, 1995), hereafter PES and page number of the English translation.

23 W. Wundt, *Principles of Physiological Psychology*, trans. from the 5th edition by E. B. Titchener (London: Sonnenshein, 1902).

24 *Psychologie vom empirischen Standpunkt*, p. 8; PES 5. See Heidegger's explanation, *Prolegomena zur Geschichte des Zeitbegriffs*, HCT § 4, pp. 20–21; GA 20, p. 25.

25 J.-P. Sartre in *Being and Nothingness*, trans. Hazel Barnes (London: Routledge, 1995), p. xxi (hereafter BN and page number of English translation), applauds the modern move to replace the object by the sum of its appearances. In this respect, Brentano is obviously one included among Sartre's 'moderns'.

26 The first edition of *Psychology from an Empirical Standpoint*, published in Leipzig in 1874, was divided into two books, with three further books promised, and indeed even a sixth book on "the relationship between mind and body", according to the Foreword to the 1874 Edition (PES xv). Brentano republished the second book with some additional essays in 1911. In 1924 a second edition of the whole of PES was produced by Oskar Kraus with additional essays and notes.

27 F. Brentano, *Deskriptive Psychologie*, ed. R. M. Chisholm and W. Baumgartner (Hamburg; Meiner, 1982), trans. Benito Müller as *Descriptive Psychology* (London: Routledge, 1995). Hereafter cited as DP followed by page number of the English translation.

28 F. Brentano, *Vom Ursprung sittlicher Erkenntnis* (Leipzig, 1889, reprinted Hamburg: Meiner, 1969), trans. Roderick Chisholm and Elizabeth Schneewind as *The Origin of Our Knowledge of Right and Wrong* (London: Routledge & Kegan Paul, 1969). Hereafter RW and page number of the English translation. This book influenced both G. E. Moore and Max Scheler in their conceptions of ethics. See R. M. Chisholm, *Brentano and Intrinsic Value* (Cambridge: Cambridge University Press, 1986).

29 F. Brentano, *Wahrheit und Evidenz*, ed. Oskar Kraus (Leipzig: Meiner, 1930), trans. R. M. Chisholm *et al.*, *The True and the Evident* (London: Routledge & Kegan Paul, 1966), pp. 3–25. Hereafter *The True* and page number.

30 For an excellent discussion of the complexities of Brentano's theory of truth and evidence, see Roberto Poli, "Truth Theories", in L. Albertazzi *et al.*, eds, *The School of Franz Brentano,* pp. 344–349.

31 F. Brentano, *Meine letzten Wünsche für Österreich* (Vienna, 1894).

32 F. Brentano, *Untersuchungen zur Sinnespsychologie*, ed. R. M. Chisholm and R. Fabian (Hamburg: Meiner, 1979).

33 F. Brentano, *On the Existence of God*, trans. S. Krantz (Dordrecht: Nijhoff, 1987).

34 See F. Brentano, *Philosophical Investigations of Time, Space and the Continuum*, trans. Barry Smith (New York: Croom Helm, 1988).

35 L. Albertazzi *et al.*, eds, *The School of Franz Brentano*, op. cit., p. 5.

36 For a description of the *Nachlass*, see J. C. M. Brentano, "The Manuscripts of Franz Brentano", *Revue Internationale de Philosophie* 20 (1966), pp. 477–82.

37 F. Brentano, *Die vier Phasen der Philosophie und ihr augenblicklicher Status* (first published 1895, then Leipzig: Meiner, 1926, reprinted Hamburg: Meiner, 1968), trans. Stephen Satris, "The Four Phases of Philosophy and its Present Condition", *Philosophy Today* 43(1/4) (Spring 1999), pp. 14–28.

38 F. Brentano, *Die vier Phasen der Philosophie*, op. cit., p. 9.

39 F. Brentano, *Die vier Phasen der Philosophie*, op. cit., p. 58.

40 See Brentano, *Philosophical Investigations of Time, Space and the Continuum*, op. cit., p. 59.

41 See L. Albertazzi, "Kant in the Brentanian Tradition", in L. Albertazzi, M. Libardi, and R. Poli, eds, *The School of Franz Brentano*, op. cit., pp. 423–464.

42 Husserl, *Studien zur Arithmetik und Geometrie. Texte aus dem Nachlaß (1886–1901)*, ed. I. Strohmeyer, Hua XXI 220.

43 Brentano even corresponded with Mill on the issue of Mill's acceptance of subject–predicate form in logic. Mill's letters to Brentano are published in J. S. Mill, *The Later Letters of John Stuart Mill 1849–1873*, ed. F. E. Mineka and D. N. Lindley, J. S. Mill, Collected Works Vol. XVII (Toronto and London: University of Toronto Press, 1972), see especially pp. 1927–29 and 1934–35.

44 See F. Brentano, "Auguste Comte und die positivistische Philosophie", in *Die vier Phasen der philosophie*, pp. 99ff. See also Dieter Münch, "Brentano and Comte", *Grazer Philosophische Studien* 35 (1989), pp. 33–54.

45 Ernst Mach (1838–1916) was born in Turas, Moravia (now Czech Republic) and studied in Vienna before becoming Professor of Mathematics in Graz in 1864. In 1867 he accepted the Chair of Physics in Prague and in 1895 returned to the Chair of History and Theory of Inductive Science in Vienna. He contributed to several areas of physics, including thermodynamics, optics, and mechanics, as well as to psychology and the study of perception. His attitude was strongly positivistic and anti-metaphysical and for this reason he was greatly admired by the Vienna Circle. See "Mach, Ernst (1838–1916)", in *The Routledge Encyclopedia of Philosophy*, op. cit., Vol. 6, pp. 13–16. Mach was an admirer of Berkeley and Hume and regarded his own sensationalism as a development of the empiricist position. His most important works were a "historical-critical" treatise on mechanics, *Die Mechanik in ihrer Entwicklung historisch-kritisch dargestellt* (Prague, 1883), trans. T. J. McCormack as *The Science of Mechanics* (La Salle, IL: Open Court, 1960) and *Die Analyse der Empfindungen* (1906), trans. C. M. Williams and S. Waterlow as *The Analysis of Sensations* (Chicago, 1914).

46 Brentano in *The True and the Evident* (1889) acknowledges that in PES (1874) he had inclined towards the view that one's degree of conviction was analogous to intensity of pleasure or pain. Also, negative judgements would never be possible on the view that judgement is a presentation with intensity. In fact, Brentano denies that there are degrees of evidence (RW 83). Either something has evidence or it does not. I simply read the evidence off the act but this evidence must be present with a certain *noetic* rather than emotional character. Evidence is not the same as apodicticity for Brentano. One can even have an evident perception that something is mèrely probable; see Jan Srzednicki, *Franz Brentano's Analysis of Truth* (The Hague: Nijhoff, 1965), p. 96.

47 See R. M. Chisholm, "Brentano's Conception of Substance and Accident", in R. M. Chisholm and R. Haller, *Die Philosophie Brentanos* (Amsterdam: Rodopi, 1978), pp. 197–210.

48 See Barry Smith, "Logic and the *Sachverhalt*", in L. Albertazzi, M. Libardi, and R. Poli, eds, *The School of Franz Brentano*, pp. 323–342.

49 Ibid., pp. 327–328.

50 See W. Baumgartner and P. M. Simons, "Brentano's Mereology", *Axiomathes* V(1) (April, 1994), pp. 55–76. Lesniewski constructed four different axiomatisations of his mereology between 1916 and 1921 drawing in part on Russell's paradox concerning classes. See S. Lesniewski, "On the Foundations of Mathematics", *Collected Works* 2 vols (Dordrecht: Kluwer, 1992), Vol. 1, pp. 174–382.

51 Aristotle discussed the notion of a 'part' (*meros*) in *Metaphysics*, 1014a 26ff.; 1023b 12ff.; 1025b 1ff.; 1034b 20ff.; and in *Physics*, 210a 14–24. For Brentano's criticism, see Brentano, *The Theory of the Categories*, op. cit., p. 82.

52 See Peter M. Simons, "Brentano's Reform of Logic", *Topoi* 6 (1987), pp. 25–

38. A compilation of Brentano's lecture notes on logic was published as *Die Lehre vom richtigen Urteil* (Berne: Francke Verlag, 1956). See also Peter M. Simons, "Logic in the Brentano School", in L. Albertazzi *et al.* (eds), *The School of Franz Brentano*, op. cit., pp. 305–321.

53 See Peter M. Simons, "Brentano's Reform of Logic", *Topoi* 6 (1987), pp. 25–38.

54 In classical logic, 'all men are mortal' is a *universal affirmative* judgement (symbolised as 'A'), 'some men are mortal' is *particular affirmative* (I), some men are not mortal is *particular negative* (O), and 'no man is mortal' is *universal negative* (E). See Irving Copi, *Introduction to Logic*, 7th edition (New York: Macmillan, 1986), p. 346.

55 David Bell, *Husserl* (London: Routledge, 1991), p. 13: "no mental act can be properly said to have a content which is of the form: '*that p*' ".

56 See Brentano's 1914 brief remarks, "Der Vorwurf des Psychologismus", in *Versuch über die Erkenntnis* (Hamburg: Meiner, 1970), pp. 194–195.

57 G. T. Fechner, a professor at Leipzig, proposed in his *Elements of Psychophysics* (1860) that an exact and constant quantitative relation could be made between the material stimulus on the one hand and the experienced changes in the intensity of the mental sensation on the other. According to Fechner's 'Fundamental Psychophysical Law', the strength of the experienced mental sensation increases in an arithmetical series relative to the strength of the physical sensation. See PES 67ff. where Brentano challenges the assumption that noticeable changes in mental sensation must increase in equal amounts.

58 For Brentano's discussion of induction, see "Das problem der Induktion", *Versuch über die Erkenntnis*, op. cit., pp. 68–95.

59 Brentano expanded on these matters in his lectures on the theory of correct judgement, *Die Lehre vom richtigen Urteil* (Hamburg: Meiner, 1956).

60 See Brentano's letter to O. Kraus, 24 March 1904, trans. in RW 111–113.

61 On Brentano's rejection of the synthetic a priori, see Brentano, *Versuch über die Erkenntnis*, op. cit., p. 12ff. See also Stephan Körner, "On Brentano's Objections to Kant's Theory of Knowledge", *Topoi* 6 (1987), pp. 11–19.

62 Brentano's (PES 29) terminology is not exactly in line with Wundt, see W. Wundt, "Selbstbeobachtung und innere Wahrnehmung", *Philosophische Studien* 4 (1888), pp. 292–309. See K. Danzinger, "The History of Introspection Reconsidered", *Journal of the History of the Behavioral Sciences* 16 (1980), pp. 241–262.

63 See William Lyons, *The Disappearance of Introspection* (Cambridge, MA: MIT Press, 1986), and the article "Introspection, Epistemology of", in *The Routledge Encyclopedia of Philosophy*, op. cit., Vol. 4, pp. 837–847.

64 See, for example, Daniel C. Dennett, *Consciousness Explained* (London: Penguin, 1993), pp. 66–70, and the critique by David Carr, "Phenomenology and Fiction in Dennett", *International Journal of Philosophical Studies* 6(3) (October, 1998), pp. 331–344.

65 Brentano already explicated this doctrine in his *Habilitationsschrift*, *The Psychology of Aristotle*, op. cit., p. 90.

66 *On the Lorenz-Einstein Question*, 30 January 1915, Appendix to F. Brentano, *The Theory of the Categories*, trans. R. M. Chisholm and N. Guterman (The Hague: Nijhoff, 1981), p. 208.

67 Against Aquinas, Brentano denies inner perception involves a remembering subsequent to the original act (PES 126n.): there is no time lag between the original and the reflexive acts, otherwise the reflexive act would be fallible.

68 Brentano, *The Psychology of Aristotle*, op. cit., p. 58.

69 Brentano, *Versuch über die Erkenntnis*, op. cit., p. 168.

70 Similar to Leibniz's *petites perceptions*. See Leibniz, *Preface to New Essays*, in R. Ariew and D. Garber, eds, *G. W. Leibniz. Philosophical Essays* (Indianapolis: Hackett, 1989), p. 295. Leibniz says one does not hear a mill which runs all day nearby. He also holds that to perceive the sound of the roar of the sea is to perceive the individual sounds of the waves even though they are not distinctly noticed.

71 Compare John R. Searle, *The Rediscovery of the Mind* (Cambridge, MA: MIT Press, 1992), p.148.

72 It is noteworthy that John R. Searle, *Intentionality* (Cambridge: Cambridge University Press, 1983), p. 6, introduces the term 'psychological mode' without reference to Brentano.

73 Brentano argues that a three-fold classification of mental acts had been proposed by Plato but he accepts Aristotle's division as more authoritative and have been followed fairly closely by Descartes (*idea, iudicium, voluntas*). In particular, Brentano rejects the Kantian dualism of sensibility and understanding. See also RW 50–54.

74 Alexius Meinong, *On Assumptions*, trans. James Heanue (Berkeley, CA: University of California Press, 1983).

75 J. N. Findlay, *Meinong's Theory of Objects and Values* (Oxford: Clarendon Press, 1963), pp. 5–6, speaking of Meinong's theory, says:

> The *Vorstellung* is in itself a wholly passive experience, to which we surrender ourselves without endeavouring to make anything out of it; such experiences are, in their pure form, infrequent in adult mental life, but of their occasional occurrence there can be no doubt.

76 Even pains, itches, etc., present, though just what is presented is obscure. Pain, for Brentano, is a complex of a presentation, a judgement, and an emotion of repulsion (PES 83). Pain presents some feeling governed by qualities which he calls 'intensity', 'lightness', and 'saturation', together with a location. The presentation produces an aversion (a feeling of hate). In experiences like pain we tend to confuse the feeling presented and the emotional reaction, whereas, Brentano argues, no one hearing a sound and enjoying it would confuse the hearing with the enjoyment. Similarly a blinding flash of light can be painful, but there is no doubt that we experience a presentation of light as well as feeling of pain and aversion.

77 Brentano, *Sensory and Noetic Consciousness, Psychology from an Empirical Standpoint III*, trans. U. McAlister and M. Scattle (London: Routledge & Kegan Paul, 1981). Hereafter SN.

78 Kraus criticised Husserl for not recognising that Brentano's later doctrine of the temporal modes of consciousness is similar to Husserl's own view in the *Phenomenology of the Consciousness of Internal Time*. See O. Kraus, "Towards a Phenomenognosy of Time Consciousness", in L. McAlister, ed., *The Philosophy of Franz Brentano*, pp. 224–239.

79 See Robin Rollinger, "Husserl and Brentano on Imagination", *Archiv für Geschichte der Philosophie* 75 (1993), pp. 195–210.

80 The technical term '*intentionalitas*' did have currency in the late Middle Ages, and used to refer to the character of the logical distinction between *prima* and *secunda intentio*, but the modern use of the term 'intentionality' owes to Husserl not Brentano.

81 *Psychologie vom empirischen Standpunkt*, Erster Band, Zweites Buch, Erstes Kapitel, § 5 (Hamburg: Meiner, 1973), pp. 124–125.

82 Husserl will later employ the term '*einwohnen*' in the *Logical Investigations*, to

characterise the manner in which the meaning-content of an act belongs to the act.

83 Twardowski, *Zur Lehre vom Inhalt und Gegenstand der Vorstellungen. Eine psychologische Untersuchung* (Vienna, 1894), trans. R. Grossmann, *On the Content and Object of Presentations. A Psychological Investigation* (The Hague: Nijhoff, 1977), p. 22. Hereafter COP and page number of English translation.

84 Brentano had already interpreted Aristotle's theory of the sensory impression in imagination as being 'objectively' in the mind, in his *Habilitationsschrift, The Psychology of Aristotle*, op. cit., p. 67.

85 Alexius Meinong, "The Theory of Objects", trans. R. M. Chisholm in *Realism and the Background of Phenomenology* (Glencoe, IL: The Free Press, 1960), p. 83. See also R. M. Chisholm, "Beyond Being and Nonbeing", in Rudolf Haller, ed., *Jenseits von Sein und Nichtsein* (Graz: Akademische Druck- und Verlagsanstalt, 1972), pp. 25–36.

86 Letter to Oscar Kraus 14 September 1909, quoted by Kraus, PES 385. German text of the letter is found in F. Brentano, *Die Abkehr vom Nichtrealen* (Hamburg: Meiner, 1977), pp. 201–208, see esp. p. 204.

87 Letter to Oscar Kraus 14 September 1909, quoted by Kraus, PES 385; *Die Abkehr vom Nichtrealen*, op. cit., p. 200.

88 Gareth B. Matthews, "Commentary on Caston", in John J. Cleary and W. Wians, eds, *Proceedings of the Boston Area Colloquium in Ancient Philosophy Volume IX (1993)* (New York: University Press of America, 1995), pp. 246–254. See also Barry Smith, "The Substance of Brentano's Ontology", *Topoi* 6 (1987), pp. 39–49.

89 The German text of this passage is found in F. Brentano, *Die Abkehr vom Nichtrealen*, op. cit., pp. 119–120.

90 For a discussion of Marty's account of language, see Kevin Mulligan, "Marty's Philosophical Grammar", in K. Mulligan, ed., *Mind, Meaning and Metaphysics* (Dordrecht: Kluwer, 1990), pp. 11–27.

91 Letter to Kraus 14 September 1909, *Die Abkehr vom Nichtrealen*, op. cit., p. 206.

92 M. Heidegger, *Die Grundprobleme der Phänomenologie*, GA 24 (Frankfurt: Klostermann, 1989), trans. A. Hofstadter, *Basic Problems of Phenomenology* (Bloomington, IN: Indiana University Press, 1982), p. 60. Hereafter BPP and page number of English translation, followed by page number in German edition.

93 See Herman Philipse, "The Concept of Intentionality: Husserl's Development from the Brentano Period to the *Logical Investigations*", *Philosophy Research Archives* XII (March, 1987), pp. 293–328, esp. p. 297.

94 See Dermot Moran, "The Inaugural Address: Brentano's Thesis", *Proceedings of the Aristotelian Society*, Supplementary Vol. LXX (1996), pp. 1–27.

95 Trans. modified. Brentano, however, immediately qualifies this analogy by denying that physical and psychological sciences split the field of science, on the grounds that there are psychological facts which can be studied by the empirical sciences (p. 6). He further acknowledges that physical events can have mental effects and vice versa.

96 Despite being part of an inner psychological episode, Brentano's content can be communicated. When we hear words spoken, we apprehend the content of the speaker's mind. But since Brentano's content remains resolutely that which is psychologically before the mind, his analysis was to say that the mental content of the speaker evinces in the hearer a mental content which gives notice of the speaker's intentions. Twardowski reproduces this account, which conspicuously fails to demonstrate how private mental contents can be turned into common meanings.

97 A. Höfler and A. Meinong, *Philosophische Propädeutik. I. Logik* (Leipzig, 1890), p. 7. Cited in Twardowski, COP 2.

98 Kasimir (or Kazimierz) Twardowski was born in Vienna in 1866 and studied under Brentano at the University of Vienna from 1885 to 1889, overlapping with Husserl, though Twardowski was just beginning his studies in philosophy, whereas Husserl had already graduated with his doctorate, so the two did not know each other well. Following studies in Munich and Leipzig, Twardowski wrote his doctoral thesis on *Descartes' Theory of Ideas* in 1892, and completed his *Habilitation* thesis, *On the Content and Object of Presentations*, in 1894. He became *Privatdozent* in Vienna and subsequently taught in Lvov, Poland, then part of the Austrian Empire. Aside from a few essays he published little in his life, though he had a huge impact on Polish philosophy and sent his student Ingarden to study with Husserl. He died on 11 February 1938. See Jan Wolenski's article, "Twardowski, Kazimierz (1866–1938)", in *The Routledge Encyclopedia of Philosophy*, op. cit., Vol. 9, pp. 507–509.

99 For this correspondence, see J. N. Mohanty, *Husserl and Frege* (Bloomington, IN: Indiana University Press, 1982).

100 See E. Husserl, "Critical Discussion of K. Twardowski", *Zur Lehre vom Inhalt und Gegenstand*", in *Early Writings in the Philosophy of Logic and Mathematics*, trans. Dallas Willard, Collected Works V (Dordrecht: Kluwer, 1994), pp. 388–395; Hua XXII 349–356. Hereafter EW. Husserl's article, "Intentional Objects", is translated EW 345–387 and another draft is translated by Robin Rollinger, *Husserl's Position in the School of Brentano*, op. cit., pp. 195–222.

101 See Jens Cavallin, *Content and Object. Husserl, Twardowski and Psychologism* (Dordrecht: Kluwer, 1997), p. 29.

102 Husserl was very taken aback when one of the founder members of the Vienna Circle, Moritz Schlick, in the first edition of his *Allgemeine Erkenntnislehre* (Berlin, 1918), p. 121, trans. Albert E. Blumberg, *General Theory of Knowledge* (New York: Springer Verlag, 1974), scathingly attacked Husserl for claiming that psychic acts were not a real part of the psychic flow at all, were not actual events in the world, but were ideal acts. Husserl rejects this 'insane' view in his Foreword to his 1920 Second Edition of Book Two Part Two of the *Logical Investigations* (LI 663; Hua XIX/2 535).

103 See J. Cavallin, *Content and Object. Husserl, Twardowski and Psychologism*, op. cit., p. 31.

2 EDMUND HUSSERL: FOUNDER OF PHENOMENOLOGY

1 Husserl, *Ideas pertaining to a Pure Phenomenology and to a Phenomenological Philosophy, First Book*, trans. F. Kersten (Dordrecht: Kluwer, 1983), § 63, p. 148; Hua III/1 121. Hereafter *Ideas* I, followed by section number, page number of English Translation, and German page number.

2 E. Husserl *Briefwechsel*, ed. Karl Schuhmann in collaboration with Elizabeth Schuhmann (Dordrecht: Kluwer, 1994), 10 vols. Hereafter *Briefwechsel*, followed by volume and page number. The reference here is IX 171. See also *Briefwechsel* III 485, where Husserl talks of "a wholly new form of philosophy".

3 Edmund Husserl, *On the Phenomenology of the Consciousness of Internal Time (1893–1917)*, trans. John Barnett Brough, Collected Works IV (Dordrecht: Kluwer, 1991), p. 360; Hua X 349. See also *Cartesian Meditations*, trans. D. Cairns (Dordrecht: Kluwer, 1993), § 20, p. 49; Hua I 86. Hereafter CM.

4 Husserl, *Die Krisis der europäischen Wissenschaften und die transzendentale Phänomenologie*, ed. W. Biemel, Hua VI (The Hague: Nijhoff, 1962), trans.

David Carr, *The Crisis of European Sciences and Transcendental Phenomenology. An Introduction to Phenomenological Philosophy* (Evanston. IL: Northwestern University Press, 1970). Hereafter *Crisis* followed by the English page number and then German page number.

5 See Eugen Fink's 1939 article trans. as, "The Problem of the Phenomenology of Edmund Husserl", in W. McKenna and L. E. Winters, eds, *Apriori and World. European Contributions to Husserlian Phenomenology* (The Hague: Nijhoff, 1981), pp. 21–55.

6 See William McKenna, *Husserl's "Introductions" to Phenomenology. Interpretation and Critique* (Dordrecht: Kluwer, 1982).

7 This world is well characterised by Hans-Georg Gadamer, *Philosophische Lehrjahre*, trans. R. Sullivan, *Philosophical Apprenticeships* (Cambridge, MA: MIT Press, 1990). Hereafter *Phil. App.* and page number of English translation.

8 Karl Jaspers, *Philosophische Autobiographie* (München, 1977), p. 93, recalled that "he seemed to me somewhat petit bourgeois" (*Er schient mir etwas Kleinbürgerliches*).

9 See, for example, Husserl's *Freiburgur Antrittesrede*, Inaugural Address, delivered on 3 May 1917, *Aufsätze und Vorträge (1911–1921)*, ed. T. Nenon and H. R. Sepp, (Dordrecht: Kluwer, 1986), Hua XXV 68–81, trans. in Frederick Elliston and Peter McCormick, *Husserl. Shorter Works* (Notre Dame, IN: University of Notre Dame Press, 1981), pp. 9–17. Hereafter HSW and page number.

10 Karl Schuhmann, *Husserl-Chronik. Denk- und Lebensweg Edmund Husserls.* (The Hague: Nijhoff, 1977), p. 22; hereafter *Chronik* and page number; *Briefwechsel* I 157: "der böse Daïmon der Nervosität". Husserl refers to bouts of depression, in 1906, 1909, 1932, and 1936, in many letters, for example *Briefwechsel* IX 45; III 283; IX 407; III 493; IV 73.

11 See H. L. Van Breda, "Préface", Hua I vii. See also H. L. Van Breda, "Le sauvetage de l'héritage husserlien et la fondation des Archives Husserl", in H. L. Van Breda and J. Taminiaux, eds, *Husserl et la pensée moderne* (The Hague: Nijhoff, 1959), p. 10. See also R. Sokolowski, "The Husserl Archives and the Edition of Husserl's Works", *New Scholasticism* 38 (1964), pp. 473–482. Subsequently, Husserl Archives were set up in Cologne, Freiburg, Paris, and Buffalo, New York. Most nineteenth-century German academics used the Gabelsberger system and it continued to be used in the twentieth century, by Husserl and Gödel for example. As Husserl wrote best in Gabelsberger (see *Briefwechsel* X 2–3), likewise he communicated best with those who could read it, such as Fink and Heidegger.

12 Husserl's marginal remarks in Martin Heidegger, *Being and Time*, have now been newly edited and translated by T. Sheehan and Richard Palmer, in *Psychological and Transcendental Phenomenology and the Confrontation with Heidegger (1927–1931)*, Collected Works VI (Kluwer: Dordrecht, 1997), pp. 264–422. Hereafter *Trans. Phen.* and page number.

13 Husserl, *Ding und Raum. Vorlesungen 1907*, ed. Ulrich Claesges (The Hague: Nijhoff, 1973), Hua XVI, trans. R. Rojcewicz, *Thing and Space: Lectures of 1907*, Collected Works VII (Dordrecht: Kluwer, 1997).

14 Re-edited by Rudolf Boehm, as *Zur Phänomenologie des inneren Zeinbewußtseins (1893–1917)*, Hua X (The Hague: Nijhoff, 1966), trans. John Barnett Brough, *On the Phenomenology of the Consciousness of Internal Time*, Collected Works IV (Dordrecht: Kluwer, 1990).

15 As Hans Rainer Sepp put it, language is the medium of his dialogue (*Das Medium seiner Dialoge ist das Schreiben*), in H. R. Sepp, ed., *Edmund Husserl*

und die phänomenologische Bewegung. Zeugnisse in Text und Bild (Freiburg/ München: Karl Alber Verlag, 1988), p. 160.

16 Helmut Plessner, "Bei Husserl in Göttingen", in H. L. Van Breda and J. Taminiaux, eds, *Edmund Husserl 1859–1959. Recueil commémorative publié à l'occasion du centenaire de la naissance du philosophe* (The Hague: Nijhoff, 1959), p. 33. In an essay in the same volume, "La ruine de la représentation", Emmanuel Levinas describes discussion with Husserl as "almost always a monologue which one dared not interrupt", op. cit., p. 73.

17 H.-G. Gadamer, *Philosophische Lehrjahre*, p. 31, trans. Robert R. Sullivan as *Phil. App.* p. 35.

18 William Ernest Hocking, "From the Early Days to the '*Logische Untersuchungen*' ", in H. L. Van Breda and J. Taminiaux, eds, *Edmund Husserl 1859–1959. Recueil commémorative publié à l'occasion du centenaire de la naissance du philosophe*, p. 3.

19 See Claire Ortiz Hill, *Word and Object in Husserl, Frege and Russell* (Athens, OH: Ohio University Press, 1991).

20 *Briefwechsel* IV 121–123. Hartshorne wrote to Husserl informing him that Peirce, whose *Collected Papers* had just appeared, edited by C. Hartshorne and Paul Weiss (1931–1935) also made use of the term 'phenomenology'. Hartshorne opined that he hoped Peirce had not stolen the term from Husserl. There is no evidence for this, as Peirce had dropped the term 'phenomenology' as early as 1904 in favour of 'phaneroscopy'.

21 On the problems in tracing Husserl's intellectual development, see R. Sokolowski, *The Formation of Husserl's Concept of Constitution* (The Hague: Nijhoff, 1964); Theodor DeBoer, *The Development of Husserl's Thought*. (The Hague: Nijhoff, 1978); Walter Biemel, "The Decisive Phases in the Development of Husserl's Philosophy", in R. O. Elveton, ed., *The Phenomenology of Edmund Husserl. Selected Critical Readings* (Chicago: Quadrangle, 1970), pp. 148–173; and J. N. Mohanty, "The Development of Husserl's Thought", in B. Smith and D. Woodruff Smith, eds, *The Cambridge Companion to Husserl* (Cambridge: Cambridge University Press, 1995), pp. 45–77.

22 For an excellent pictorial account of Husserl's life, see Sepp, ed., *Edmund Husserl und die phänomenologische Bewegung*, op. cit.

23 Sepp, *Edmund Husserl und die phänomenologische Bewegung*, p. 120. See Malvine Husserl, "Skizze eines Lebensbildes von Edmund Husserl", ed. Karl Schuhmann, *Husserl Studies* 5 (1988), pp. 105–125. See also *Chronik*, p. 2–3, and Andrew Osborn, *The Philosophy of Edmund Husserl in its Development from his Mathematical Interests to his First Conception of Phenomenology in the Logical Investigations* (New York: International Press, 1934), p. 10.

24 See K. Schuhmann, "Husserl and Masaryk", in J. Novák, ed., *On Masaryk* (Amsterdam: Rodopi, 1988), pp. 129–156.

25 Dorion Cairns, *Conversations with Husserl and Fink*, Phaenomenologica 66 (The Hague: Nijhoff, 1975), p. 47.

26 *Chronik*, p. 9. Husserl confirmed this in a letter to Mahnke on 4 May 1933, *Briefwechsel* III 500.

27 Letter to Arnold Metzger, 4 September 1919, trans. in HSW 360.

28 For Husserl's relation to religion see Karl and Elizabeth Schuhmann's introduction to the *Briefwechsel* X 35–36.

29 M. Heidegger, *History of the Concept of Time. Prolegomena*, trans. T. Kisiel (Bloomington, IN: Indiana University Press, 1985), p. 23.

30 See, for example, *Logical Investigations*, op. cit. Prolegomena, § 40, p. 158; Hua XVIII 147. For a critique of Husserl's treatment of Hegelian dialectic as soph-

istry, see T. Adorno, *Against Epistemology: A Metacritique*, trans. W. Domingo (Oxford: Blackwell, 1982), pp. 49–50.

31 See E. Husserl, *Vorlesungern über Ethik und Wertlehre (1908–1914)*, ed. U. Melle (Dordrecht: Kluwer, 1988), Hua XXVIII 460.

32 B. Bolzano, *Paradoxes of the Infinite*, trans. Donald A. Steele (London: Routledge & Kegan Paul, 1950). Originally published in 1851. For Bolzano's influence on Husserl, see Husserl, *Introduction to the Logical Investigations*, ed. E. Fink, trans. P. J. Bossert and C. H. Peters (The Hague: Nijhoff, 1975), p. 37; Fink, p. 129.

33 Bernard Bolzano, a contemporary of G. W. F. Hegel, was born in Prague in 1781. He studied at the University of Prague and wrote a thesis on the foundations of mathematics. He was a professor of religion there from 1805 until 1819, when he was dismissed by imperial decree. From 1820 to 1830 he retired to Techobuz where he worked on his main book, *Wissenschaftslehre*, or *Theory of Science*, published in 1837. See B. Bolzano, *Theory of Science*, ed. and trans. Rolf George (Oxford: Blackwell, 1972). After completing this work he went on to work on mathematical problems.

34 Husserl, "Erinnerungen an Franz Brentano", *Aufsätze und Vorträge (1911–1921)*, Hua XXV 304–315, esp, p. 305, trans. R. Hudson and P. McCormick, as "Recollections of Franz Brentano", in P. McCormick and F. Elliston, eds, *Husserl. Shorter Works*, (Notre Dame, IN: University of Notre Dame Press, 1981), pp. 342–348, see p. 342.

35 The phrase "new star" comes from Ehrenfels's letter to Meinong of 26 February 1886; see R. Rollinger, *Husserl's Position in the School of Brentano*, p. 14.

36 See H. Spiegelberg, "On the Significance of the Correspondence Between Franz Brentano and Edmund Husserl", in R. M. Chisholm and R. Haller, eds, *Die Philosophie Franz Brentanos* (Amsterdam: Rodopi, 1978), pp. 95–116.

37 Husserl's letter to Marvin Farber, 18 June 1937, translated in Kah Kyung Cho, "Phenomenology as Cooperative Task: Husserl-Farber Correspondence during 1936–37", *Philosophy and Phenomenological Research* 50, Supplement (Fall, 1990), pp. 36–43.

38 Brentano wrote to Stumpf on 18 October 1886 recommending Husserl as a "mathematician and for some years an enthusiastic student of philosophy" who was working on problems of the continuum; see Rollinger, *Husserl's Position in the School of Brentano*, op. cit., p. 68. The first volume of Stumpf's *Tonpsychologie* had appeared in 1883 and the second was published in 1890 (Leipzig: Hirzel, 1883/1890). Stumpf's *Über den psychologischen Ursprung der Raumvorstellung* had appeared in 1873.

39 See H. Spiegelberg, *The Context of the Phenomenological Movement* (The Hague: Nijhoff, 1981).

40 Husserl, *Über den Begriff der Zahl, Psychologische Analysen*, reprinted in *Philosophie der Arithmetik: Mit ergänzenden Texten (1890–1901)*, ed. Lothar Eley (The Hague: Nijhoff, 1970), Hua XII.

41 Cantor wrote a letter to Husserl on 7 April 1915, *Briefwechsel* VII 51, sympathising with him on hearing of the wounding of his son. On Cantor and Husserl see Claire Ortiz Hill, "Abstraction and Idealization in Edmund Husserl and Georg Cantor Prior to 1895", *Poznan Studies in the Philosophy of the Sciences and the Humanities* XX (1998), pp. 1–27.

42 Reprinted as *Philosophie der Arithmetik: Mit ergänzenden Texten (1890–1901)*, Hua XII. An English translation by Dallas Willard is in preparation as part of the Collected Works series from Kluwer.

43 Husserl's attempts at the second volume are published in Hua XII 340–429 and Hua XXI 3–215; 252–261.

44 Letter to Stumpf, Hua XXI 244–251, trans. EW 12–19.
45 Hubert Dreyfus and Dagfinn Føllesdal accept the view that Frege influenced Husserl. But see J. N. Mohanty's *Husserl and Frege* (Bloomington, IN: Indiana University Press, 1982), which argues that Frege played little or no role in Husserl's change of mind, as the change is already evident from 1891, that is in EW.
46 Bolzano, *Theory of Science*, op. cit., pp. 88–89:

> It is true that most ideas have some, or even infinitely many, referents. Still, there are also ideas that have no referent at all, and thus do not have an extension. The clearest case seems to be that of the concept designated by the word "nothing". It seems absurd to me to say that this concept has an object too, i.e. a something that it represents...The same holds of the ideas "a round square", "green virtue", etc.

47 Rollinger, *Husserl's Position in the School of Brentano*, op. cit., p. 17 n. 1.
48 See Husserl's "Review of M. Palagyi, *Der Streit der Psychologisten und Formalisten in der Modernen Logik*", (The Dispute Between Psychologists and Formalists in Modern Logic), trans. EW 201; Hua XXII 156.
49 Sepp, *Edmund Husserl und die phänomenologische Bewegung*, op. cit., p. 162.
50 William Ernest Hocking, "From the Early Days to the '*Logische Untersuchungen*' ", in H. L. Van Breda and J. Taminiaux, eds, *Edmund Husserl 1859–1959*, op. cit., p. 1, and Wilhelm Schapp's "Erinnerungen", in the same volume, p. 13.
51 See Claire Ortiz Hill, "Husserl and Hilbert on Completeness", in J. Hintikka, ed., *Essays on the Development of the Foundations of Mathematics* (Dordrecht: Kluwer, 1995), pp. 143–163.
52 Husserl refers to T. Lipps at *Logical Investigations*, op. cit. Prolegomena § 17, p. 91; Hua XVIII 64, and in the Foreword to the Second Edition, LI, p. 47; Hua XVIII 12.
53 On Johannes Daubert, see Reinhold Smid, "An Early Interpretation of Husserl's Phenomenology: Johannes Daubert and the *Logical Investigations*", *Husserl Studies* 2 (1985), pp. 267–290. For a more recent development of Daubert's approach, see K. Schuhmann and B. Smith, "Questions: An Essay in Daubertian Phenomenology", *Philosophy and Phenomenological Research* 47 (March, 1987), pp. 353–384.
54 Alexander Pfänder studied mathematics in the Engineering School in Hanover before moving to Munich to study with Lipps with whom he wrote a doctorate and then a *Habilitation* on the nature of willing, published as *The Phenomenology of Willing* in 1900 and thereby anticipating by one year the general use of the term 'phenomenology'. See A. Pfänder, *Phenomenology of Willing and Other Phaenomenologica*, trans. Herbert Spiegelberg (Evanston. IL: Northwestern University Press, 1967). Pfänder sees in the experience of willing a genuinely experienced act which cannot be reduced to presentation, judgement, or feeling. He was a critic of Lipps's psychologism and also of the psychology of William James. He was appointed *Privatdozent* in Munich in 1900 and remained there until he retired in 1935. He was an unsuccessful candidate against Heidegger for Chair of Philosophy at Freiburg, made vacant by Husserl's retirement in 1928.
55 Reinach wrote his *Habilitation* on the theory of judgement with Husserl in Göttingen in 1909 and became *Privatdozent* there, where he was considered a much clearer exponent of phenomenology than Husserl himself. He assisted Husserl in the revising of the *Logical Investigations*; see Husserl's Foreword to the Second Edition, (LI, p. 50; Hua XVIII Bxvii). He wrote a number of important articles, including one on negative judgements for Lipps's *Festschrift*.

Husserl published an *In Memoriam* for Reinach in the *Frankfurter Zeitung* on 6 December 1917 and again in *Kant-Studien* in 1918; see Hua XXV 296–303.

56 See Roman Ingarden, *On the Motives which led Husserl to Transcendental Idealism* (Dordrecht: Kluwer, 1975).

57 Husserl, *Ideas pertaining to a Pure Phenomenology and to a Phenomenological Philosophy, Second Book*, trans. R. Rojcewicz and A. Schuwer (Dordrecht: Kluwer, 1989), p. 374; Hua IV 364.

58 See Jean Héring, "Edmund Husserl. Souvenirs et reflexions", in H. L. Van Breda and J. Taminiaux, eds, *Edmund Husserl 1859–1959*, op. cit., pp. 26–28.

59 When the Nazis gained power, A. Koyré, a Russian emigré, went into exile in Paris where he befriended Hannah Arendt. He later went to the USA where he worked at Princeton.

60 See H. Spiegelberg, *The Phenomenological Movement*, 3rd edition (Dordrecht: Kluwer, 1994), pp. 166–170.

61 See Husserl's letter to Lipps of January 1904, *Briefwechsel* II 124.

62 See, for example, "Husserl's Inaugural Lecture at Freiburg im Breisgau (1917)", HSW 14; Hua XXV 75.

63 Husserl, *Einleitung in die Logik und Erkenntnistheorie. Vorlesungen 1906/07*, Hua XXIV (Dordrecht: Kluwer, 1984), pp. 165ff. and 212.

64 *Die Idee der Phänomenologie. Fünf Vorlesungen*. Not published until 1950, ed. Walter Biemel, now 2nd edition (1973), Hua II, trans. W. P. Alston and G. Nakhnikian, as *The Idea of Phenomenology* (The Hague: Nijhoff, 1964). These lectures were intended as a general introduction to his lectures on the thing, *Dingvorlesung*, now Hua XVI.

65 *"Philosophie als strenge Wissenschaft"*, *Aufsätze und Vorträge (1911–1921)*, Hua XXV 3–62, trans., "Philosophy as a Rigorous Science", in Q. Lauer, *Phenomenology and the Crisis of Philosophy* (New York: Harper and Row, 1965), pp. 71–147. Hereafter PRS. Husserl, at Rickert's invitation, joined the Editorial Board of *Logos* but seems to have had played no further active part in the journal. For Walter Biemel's remarks see his "Einleitung des Herausgebers", Hua IX xvi.

66 See "The Dilthey-Husserl Correspondence", trans. in HSW 203–209.

67 Husserl, *Phänomenologische Psychologie Vorlesungen Sommersemester 1925*, ed. W. Biemel (The Hague: Nijhoff, 1968), Hua IX 6; trans. J. Scanlon, *Phenomenological Psychology. Lectures, Summer Semester 1925* (The Hague: Nijhoff, 1977), § 1, p. 3.

68 See Karl Schuhmann, "Husserl's Yearbook", *Philosophy and Phenomenological Research* L, Supplement (Fall, 1990), pp. 1–25.

69 An edition of these manuscripts is currently being prepared in Leuven by Ullrich Melle for the Husserliana series.

70 A. Schütz, in H. L. Van Breda and J. Taminiaux, eds, *Edmund Husserl 1859–1959*, op. cit., p. 88.

71 In his early writings Husserl had treated the ego as a bundle of acts, and had rigorously bracketed the psychological 'I'; however, he later developed an understanding of the person as an entity with a unity distinct from that of a natural object. Scheler, on the other hand, had made the category of the person central to his phenomenology from an early period.

72 For Husserl's political views, see Karl and Elizabeth Schuhmann, "Einführung in die Ausgabe", Edmund Husserl, *Briefwechsel* X 18–23, and K. Schuhmann, *Husserls Staatsphilosophie* (Freiburg/Munich: Alber, 1988).

73 See Husserl's 1915 letter to the Harvard philosopher Hugo Münsterberg, originally published in Münsterberg's *The Peace and America* (New York: Appleton, 1915), pp. 222–224, where he speaks of his admiration at the manner

in which individuals subordinated themselves to the national will (HSW 352; Hua XXV 293–294).

74 See Husserl, "Fichtes Menschheitsideal. Drei Vorlesungen", *Aufsätze und Vorträge (1911–1921)*, Hua XXV 267–293, and trans. James G. Hart as "Fichte's Ideal of Humanity [Three Lectures]", *Husserl Studies* 12 (1995), pp. 111–133. On Husserl's moral and political vision, see James G. Hart, *The Person and the Common Life. Studies in a Husserlian Social Ethics* (Dordrecht: Kluwer, 1992).

75 For an account of Rickert at Heidelberg, see Karl Jaspers' autobiography. Jaspers originally got on well with Rickert but later had a falling out over the question as to the possibility of scientific philosophy (which Rickert supported and Jaspers attacked).

76 Husserl, "Die reine Phänomenologie, ihr Forschungsgebiet und ihre Methode", first published in German in 1976, in the *Tijdschrift voor Filosofie* 38 (1976), pp. 363–378, reprinted in *Aufsätze und Vorträge (1911–1921)*, Hua XXV 68–81, trans. "Husserl's Inaugural Lecture at Freiburg im Breisgau (1917)", in HSW 9–17.

77 H. Plessner, in H. L. Van Breda and J. Taminiaux, eds, *Edmund Husserl 1859–1959*, op. cit., p. 35.

78 In a letter to Winthrop Bell of 11 August 1920, Husserl characterises the mood at Freiburg and complains of a Kierkegaard movement sweeping Germany, *Briefwechsel* III 15.

79 See H.-G. Gadamer's remembrance in Sepp, *Edmund Husserl und die phänomenologische Bewegung*, op. cit, p. 13. For Husserl's reference to the "decline of the West" as "this latest theory born of faint-hearted philosophical scepticism", see *Aufsätze und Vorträge (1922–1937)*, ed. T. Nenon and H. R. Sepp (Dordrecht: Kluwer, 1989), Hua XXVII 122, trans. as "Shaw and the Vitality of the West", in HSW 356.

80 Sepp, *Edmund Husserl und die phänomenologische Bewegung*, op. cit., p. 270.

81 Reprinted in Husserl, *Aufsätze und Vorträge (1922–1937)*, Hua XXVII. The first Kaizo article, "Renewal: its Problem and Method", has been translated in HSW 326–334. A new translation of the four lectures by Philip Buckley will appear in the Husserl Collected Works series.

82 See H. Spiegelberg, "Husserl in England: Facts and Lessons", *Journal of the British Society for Phenomenology* 1(1) (1970), pp. 4–17. For a synopsis of the lecture topics see Edmund Husserl, "Syllabus of a Course of Four Lectures on 'Phenomenological Method and Phenomenological Philosophy', delivered at University College, London June 6, 8, 9, 12, 1922", *Journal of the British Society for Phenomenology* 1(1) (1970), pp. 18–23. These lectures were a forerunner to the *Cartesian Meditations* lectures later given – appropriately – in the Amphithéatre Descartes in Paris in 1929.

83 *Phänomenologische Psychologie*, Hua IX, trans. J. Scanlon, *Phenomenological Psychology*, op. cit.

84 For a list of Heidegger's lecture course titles see Theodore Kisiel, *The Genesis of Heidegger's Being and Time* (Berkeley, CA: University of California Press, 1993), pp. 469–476; for an account of the development of his phenomenology of religion see, *idem*, pp. 112–219.

85 Heidegger refers, in his 1925 lecture course published as *History of the Concept of Time. Prolegomena*, § 13, p. 121, GA 20, p. 167, to the fact that Husserl was aware of Heidegger's criticisms of him in his lecture courses in Freiburg and later in Marburg.

86 See Herbert Spiegelberg, "On the Misfortunes of Edmund Husserl's *Encyclopaedia Britannica* Article 'Phenomenology' ", in HSW 18–20. For a full

discussion of the affair, see Thomas Sheehan, "The History of the Redaction of the *Encyclopaedia Britannica* Article", in *Trans. Phen.*, pp. 36–59.

87 See Husserl's letter to Alexander Pfänder, 6 January 1931, *Briefwechsel* II 180–184, trans. Burt Hopkins, in *Trans. Phen.*, pp. 479–483.

88 See Richard Palmer, "Husserl's Debate with Heidegger in the Margin of *Kant and the Problem of Metaphysics*", *Man and World* 30 (1997), pp. 5–33. Husserl's comments on Heidegger's *Being and Time* and his *Kantbuch* have now been translated in Edmund Husserl, *Trans. Phen.*

89 Hua IX 302–49; trans. *Trans. Phen.*, pp. 213–253.

90 Emmanuel Levinas, "La ruine de la représentation", in H. L. Van Breda and J. Taminiaux, eds, *Edmund Husserl 1859–1959*, p. 73.

91 Heidegger, "Vom Wesen des Grundes", reprinted in *Wegmarken* GA 9 (Frankfurt: Klostermann, 1976), pp. 123–176, trans. William McNeill, "On the Essence of Ground", *Pathmarks*, ed. William McNeill (Cambridge: Cambridge University Press, 1998), pp. 97–135.

92 Alfred Schütz, "Husserl's Importance for the Social Sciences", in H. L. Van Breda and J. Taminiaux, eds, *Edmund Husserl 1859–1959*, op. cit. p. 86

93 For a copy of this letter see Sepp, *Edmund Husserl und die phänomenologische Bewegung*, op. cit., p. 384. Hermann Heidegger has claimed that Husserl's *Beurlaubung* has already been officially sanctioned by the previous rector, Sauer; see H. Heidegger, "Der Wirtschaftshistoriker und die Wahrheit. Notwendige Bemerkungen zu den Veröffentlichungen Hugo Otts über Martin Heidegger", *Heidegger Studies* 13 (1997), pp. 177–192, esp. p. 186.

94 Arendt, "What is Existenz Philosophy", *Partisan Review* 13 (1946), p. 46.

95 *Hannah Arendt Karl Jaspers Correspondence 1926–1969*, ed. L. Kohler and H. Saner (New York: Harcourt Brace, 1992), p. 43. See Hugo Ott, *Martin Heidegger. A Political Life*, trans. Allen Blunden (London: Harper Collins, 1993), p. 172.

96 These references to Husserl in the Nazi journal, *NS-Frauenwarte* 20 (1937/8), p. 625, are cited in Peter Prechtl, *Husserl. Zur Einführung* (Hamburg: Junius, 1991), p. 14.

97 Schütz, in H. L. Van Breda and J. Taminiaux, eds, *Edmund Husserl 1859–1959*, op. cit., p. 88.

98 See H. L. Van Breda, "Le sauvetage de l'héritage husserlien et la fondation des Archives Husserl", in H. L. Van Breda and J. Taminiaux, eds, *Husserl et la pensée moderne* (The Hague: Nijhoff, 1959), for the exciting story of the smuggling of the manuscripts.

99 Stephen Strasser and Walter and Marly Biemel were early researchers in the Institute; Rudolf Boehm and Sam Ijssling have been recent directors. The current director is Rudolf Bernet.

100 There is some doubt about the fate of Husserl's remains, as they may have been part of his effects which were destroyed in the bombing of Antwerp in 1940. I thank Philip Buckley for this information.

101 Letter to Albrecht, 22 December 1931: "Daß ich mich völlig isoliert, von meiner Schülern völlig abgesondert habe, daß ich zum größten Feind der berümten 'Husserlschen phänomenologische Bewegung' geworden bin", *Briefwechsel* IX 79.

3 HUSSERL'S *LOGICAL INVESTIGATIONS* (1900–1901)

1 David Bell, *Husserl* (London: Routledge, 1991), p. 85.

2 Husserl explains this approach in his 1906–1907 *Lectures on the Logic and Theory of Science*, Hua XXIV § 2, 5–6.

3 Husserl will give a much fuller discussion of *Evidenz* in his *Formal and Transcendental Logic* (§§ 105–107, pp. 277–290; Hua XVII 277–295). For a clear explication of Husserl's concept of evidence, see Dagfinn Føllesdal, "Husserl on Evidence and Justification", in R. Sokolowski, ed., *Edmund Husserl and the Phenomenological Tradition* (Washington, DC: Catholic University of America Press, 1988), pp. 107–129.

4 Husserl, 1906–1907 *Lectures on the Logic and Theory of Science*, Hua XXIV § 3, 8.

5 See Husserl's unpublished essay, *c.* 1893, "Intuition and *Repräsentation*, Intention and Fulfilment", EW 313–344; Hua XXII 269–302).

6 See Kevin Mulligan, "Husserl on States of Affairs in the *Logical Investigations*", *Epistemologia* XII (1989), Special Issue, pp. 207–234.

7 For an excellent discussion of this distinction, see J. N. Mohanty, *Edmund Husserl's Theory of Meaning* (The Hague: Nijhoff, 1976).

8 For a thorough study of the varieties of psychologism, see Martin Kusch, *Psychologism. A Case Study in the Sociology of Philosophical Knowledge* (London: Routledge, 1995). See also Thomas M. Seebohm, "Psychologism Revisited", in Thomas Seebohm, Dagfinn Føllesdal, and J .N. Mohanty, eds, *Phenomenology and the Formal Sciences* (Dordrecht: Kluwer, 1991), pp. 149–182.

9 John Stuart Mill, *A System of Logic, Ratiocinative and Inductive, Being a Connected View of the Principles of Evidence, and the Methods of Scientific Investigation* (London: Parker, 1843) 2 vols, Vol. 1 § 7, p. 13.

10 Paul Natorp reviewed the *Prolegomena* to the *Logical Investigations* in *Kantstudien* VI (1901), pp. 270–283, trans. as in J. N. Mohanty, ed., *Readings on Husserl's Logical Investigations* (The Hague: Nijhoff, 1977), pp. 55–66. Natorp later reviewed *Ideas* I in *Logos* VII (1917–18), pp. 224–246.

11 A. Reinach, "Concerning Phenomenology", trans. Dallas Willard, *The Personalist* 50 (1969), pp. 194–221.

12 In the *Logical Investigations* Husserl used the expressions 'state of affairs' (*Sachverhalt*) and 'situation' (*Sachlage*) more or less interchangeably. Later in *Experience and Judgment* § 59, Husserl will claim that they express different states of affairs based on the same situation (*Sachlage*). Husserl never developed a full account of states of affairs. See Guillermo E. Rosado Haddock, "On Husserl's Distinction Between State of Affairs (*Sachverhalt*) and Situation of Affairs (*Sachlage*)", in T. M. Seebohm, D. Føllesdal, and J. N. Mohanty, eds, *Phenomenology and the Formal Sciences*, op. cit., pp. 35–57.

13 See K. Mulligan and B. Smith, "A Husserlian Theory of Indexicality", *Grazer Philosophische Studien* 28 (1986), pp. 133–163.

4 HUSSERL'S DISCOVERY OF THE REDUCTION AND TRANSCENDENTAL PHENOMENOLOGY

1 Husserl, "Author's Preface to the English Edition", *Ideas. General Introduction to Pure Phenomenology*, trans. W. Boyce Gibson (London: Allen and Unwin, 1931), p. 21. The German version is printed in Hua V 138–162.

2 See the explanation in Husserl's 1909 Göttingen summer semester lectures on "Introduction to the Phenomenology of Knowledge", in Edmund Husserl, *On the Phenomenology of the Consciousness of Internal Time (1893–1917)*, trans. J. Barnett Brough, Collected Works IV (Dordrecht: Kluwer, 1990), p. 348.

3 Hans Jonas, "Philosophy at the End of the Century: A Survey of its Past and Future", *Social Research* 61(4) (Winter, 1994), p. 815.

4 For a list of Husserl's lecture courses in Göttingen, see R. Bernet, I. Kern, and E. Marbach, *An Introduction to Husserlian Phenomenology* (Evanston, IL: Northwestern University Press, 1993), pp. 238–240.

5 Brough, *On the Phenomenology the Consciousness of Internal Time*, p. 350; Hua X 339. See also *Cartesian Meditations* § 11, 25; Hua I 64.

6 Paul Ricoeur, *Husserl. An Analysis of His Phenomenology*, trans. Edward G. Ballard and Lester Embree (Evanston, IL: Northwestern University Press, 1967), p. 26.

7 According to J. N. Mohanty, "The Development of Husserl's Thought", in Barry Smith and David Woodruff Smith, eds, *The Cambridge Companion to Husserl* (Cambridge: Cambridge University Press, 1995), p. 57, Husserl first wrote an account of the reduction in his *Seefelder Blättern* of summer 1905.

8 See Roman Ingarden's letter to Husserl in which he queried Husserl's turn to idealism. This letter is translated as Roman Ingarden, "The Letter to Husserl About the VI Logical Investigation and Idealism", in A.-T. Tymieniecka, ed., *Ingardiana*, Analecta Husserliana IV (Dordrecht: Reidel, 1976), pp. 418–438. Ingarden studied with Husserl at Göttingen from 1912 to 1915.

9 Similarly, Husserl, in *Ideas* I § 62, 142; Hua III/1 118, says Hume almost set foot in phenomenology "but with blinded eyes". Elsewhere Hume is portrayed as actually doing phenomenology though in a naive manner. See *Erste Philosophie*, Erster Teil, Hua VII 157–172.

10 See Husserl's 1924 lecture, which he planned to publish in his *Jahrbuch*, trans. Ted E. Klein and William E. Pohl, as "Kant and the Idea of Transcendental Philosophy", *Southwestern Journal of Philosophy* 5 (Fall, 1974), pp. 9–56; Hua VII 230–287.

11 Husserl, "Kant and the Idea of Transcendental Philosophy", *Southwestern Journal of Philosophy* op. cit., pp. 50–51.

12 *Crisis*, § 30, p. 114; Hua VI 116. Husserl had accused Kant of employing "mythical concepts of understanding" as early as the *Logical Investigations*, *Prol.* § 58.

13 See W. V. Quine, "Epistemology Naturalised", in *Ontological Relativity and Other Essays* (New York: Columbia University Press, 1969).

14 David M. Armstrong, "Naturalism, Materialism, and First Philosophy", in Paul K. Moser and J. D. Trout, eds, *Contemporary Materialism. A Reader* (London: Routledge, 1995), p. 35.

15 Husserl, "Kant and the Idea of Transcendental Philosophy", *Southwestern Journal of Philosophy* op. cit., p. 20; *Erste Philosophie*, Hua VII.

16 Ingarden cites in particular the passage at *Ideas* I § 49, 109; Hua III/1 91. See Roman Ingarden, "The Letter to Husserl About the VI Logical Investigation and Idealism", in A.-T. Tymieniecka, ed., *Ingardiana*, Analecta Husserliana IV op. cit., pp. 422–424.

17 See *Crisis*, § 70, p. 243; Hua VI 246. The reduction first appears in the *Seefelder Blättern* A VII 5. Some critics have argued that the reduction is already implicitly present in the First Edition of the *Logical Investigations*, even before it was officially inserted into the revised Second Edition of 1913.

18 See Iso Kern, "The Three Ways to the Transcendental Phenomenological Reduction in the Philosophy of Edmund Husserl", in F. Elliston and P. McCormick, eds, *Husserl. Expositions and Appraisals* (Notre Dame, IN: University of Notre Dame Press, 1977), pp. 126–149.

19 Husserl, *Encyclopaedia Brittanica* Article draft E, in T. Sheehan and R. E. Palmer, eds, *Trans. Phen.*, p. 188.

20 See Philip J. Bossert, *The Origins and Early Development of Edmund Husserl's Method of Phenomenological Reduction*, PhD thesis, Washington University, St Louis, 1973. Bossert finds in the *Crisis* mention of positivistic reduction (Hua VI 3), phenomenological reduction (VI 80), transcendental (VI 150), phenomenological–psychological (VI 239), transcendental–phenomenological (VI 239), psychological (VI 242), universal (VI 248), and a behaviouristic reduction (VI 251). In Bossert's account, the positivistic, universal, and behaviouristic are not true forms of phenomenological reduction.

21 Iso Kern, "The Three Ways to the Transcendental Phenomenological Reduction in the Philosophy of Edmund Husserl", in F. Elliston and P. McCormick, eds, *Husserl. Expositions and Appraisals*, pp. 126–149. See also Bernet, Kern, and Marbach, *Introduction to Husserlian Phenomenology*, pp. 65–75.

22 Husserl read Raoul Richter's *Der Skeptizismus in der Philosophie*, Vol. I (Leipzig, 1904), and Albert Gödeckemeyer's *Geschichte der grieschen Skeptizismus* (1905). See Guido Küng, "The Phenomenological Reduction as *Epoche* and Explication", in Elliston and McCormick, eds, *Husserl. Expositions and Appraisals*, op. cit., p. 340. See also H. Spiegelberg, with Karl Schuhmann, *Phenomenological Movement*, op. cit., p. 160. Husserl refers to Plato's attempts to refute scepticism in FTL, p. 1; Hua XVII 5.

23 Jonathan Barnes, *The Toils of Scepticism* (Cambridge: Cambridge University Press, 1990), p. 9.

24 Jonathan Barnes, *The Toils of Scepticism*, op. cit., p. 11.

25 Husserl, *Zur Phänomenologie des Intersubjektivität. Texte auf dem Nachlass, Erster Teil; (1905–1920)*, trans. in Bernet, Kern, Marbach, *An Introduction to Husserlian Phenomenology*, op. cit., p. 59; Hua XIII 200.

26 R. Bernet, "Le concept de noème (Husserl)", *La Vie du sujet. Recherches sur l'interprétation de Husserl dans la phénoménologie* (Paris: PUF, 1994), p. 73 n.1.

27 See Robert Sokolowski, "Intentional Analysis and the Noema", *Dialectica* 38(2–3) (1984), pp. 113–129, esp. 127–128.

28 D. Føllesdal, "Husserl's Notion of Noema", *Journal of Philosophy* 66 (1969), pp. 680–687. See also his "Noema and Meaning in Husserl", *Philosophy and Phenomenological Research* L, Supplement (Fall, 1990), pp. 263–271.

29 Husserl, *Ideas* III, trans. T. E. Klein and W. E. Pohl, § 16, 76; Hua V 89. As we have seen in earlier chapters, Husserl does not distinguish, as Frege does, between *Sinn* and *Bedeutung*.

30 D. Føllesdal, "Noema and Meaning in Husserl", *Philosophy and Phenomenological Research* L, Supplement (Fall, 1990), p. 266.

31 For an excellent discussion contrasting the Føllesdal and Gurwitsch approaches, see Robert Solomon, "Husserl's Concept of Noema", in F. Elliston and O. McCormick, eds, *Husserl. Expositions and Appraisals* (Notre Dame, IN: University of Notre Dame Press, 1977), pp. 168–181. Solomon emphasises the different motivations behind each account. For Føllesdal, following Frege, the problem is to account for indirect reference in opaque contexts; for Gurwitsch, it is to achieve reidentification of the same object in different acts. For an excellent survey of the different positions, see B. Smith and D. Woodruff Smith's, "Introduction", *The Cambridge Companion to Husserl*, op. cit., pp. 22–27.

32 David Bell, *Husserl*, p. 180: "noemata include any and every factor capable of determining an act's significance that is not a real (and hence noetic) part of that act. The concept of a noema is a ragbag concept". Similarly, Bell calls 'noesis' a ragbag concept (p. 175).

33 David Bell, *Husserl*, op. cit., p. 162.

5 HUSSERL AND THE CRISIS OF THE EUROPEAN SCIENCES

1 E. Fink, "Operative Concepts in Husserl's Phenomenology", in W. McKenna, R. M. Harlan, and L. E. Winters, eds, *Apriori and World. European Contributions to Husserlian Phenomenology* (The Hague: Nijhoff, 1981), pp. 56–70, esp. p. 67ff.

2 See R. Sokolowski, *The Formation of Husserl's Concept of Constitution* (The Hague: Nijhoff, 1964), p. 196.

3 For an exploration of this form of social construction (in a Husserlian vein) see John R. Searle, *The Construction of Social Reality* (London: Penguin, 1995).

4 See Husserl's remarks in his lectures on "Nature and Spirit" from the Summer Semester of 1927, quoted in Bernet, Kern, and Marbach, *An Introduction to Husserlian Phenomenology*, op. cit., p. 203.

5 R. Sokolowski, *The Formation of Husserl's Concept of Constitution*, op. cit., pp. 200–201: "the immediate present is not constituted in any way; it is the only element in Husserl's entire phenomenology that has this characteristic".

6 See *Edmund Husserl 1859–1959*, op. cit., p. 87.

7 See J. J. Kockelmans, "Husserl and Kant on the Pure Ego", in F. Elliston and P. McCormick, eds, *Husserl. Expositions and Appraisals* (Notre Dame, IN: University of Notre Dame Press, 1977), pp. 269–285. See also E. Marbach, *Das Problem des Ich in der Phänomenologie Husserls* (The Hague: Nijhoff, 1974).

8 James Mensch, "What is a Self?", in Burt C. Hopkins, ed., *Husserl in Contemporary Context* (Dordrecht: Kluwer, 1997), p. 65, cites William James' view, that psychology only needs psychic states, as another influence on Husserl at this time.

9 See A. Gurwitsch, "A Non-egological Conception of Consciousness", in *Studies in Phenomenology and Psychology* (Evanston, IL: Northwestern University Press 1966), pp. 287–299.

10 Husserl, *Fifth Logical Investigation*, § 6, LI, p. 544; Hua XIX/1 368, Husserl adds in the Second Edition that unless we have a conception of the ego as a 'residuum' there can be no real self-evidence attaching to the 'I am', *ego sum*.

11 Elizabeth Ströker, *Husserl's Transcendental Phenomenology* (Stanford, CA: Stanford University Press, 1993), p. 118.

12 For Reinach's discussion of convictions, see B. Smith, "On the Cognition of States of Affairs", in K. Mulligan, ed., *Speech Act and Sachverhalt. Reinach and the Foundations of Realist Phenomenology* (Dordrecht: Nijhoff, 1987), pp. 205–210.

13 Edith Stein, *On the Problem of Empathy*, trans. Waltraut Stein, *Collected Works of Edith Stein*, Vol. 3 (Washington, DC: ICS Publications, 1989).

14 Husserl, "Kant and the Idea of Transcendental Philosophy", *Southwestern Journal of Philosophy* 5 (1974), p. 31.

15 Husserl, *Zur Phänomenologie der Intersubjektivität. Texte aus dem Nachlaß. Zweiter Teil: 1921–1928*, Hua IV 641–642. See also CM § 52, 115; Hua I 145.

16 "Phenomenology and Anthropology", in E. Husserl, *Psychological and Transcendental Phenomenology and the Confrontation with Heidegger (1927–1931)*, trans. and ed. T. Sheehan and R. E. Palmer (Dordrecht: Kluwer, 1997), p. 498; Hua XXVII 178–179.

17 See, for example, *The Amsterdam Lectures* (1928) § 5, trans. in E. Husserl, *Trans. Phen.*, p. 221; Hua IX 311.

18 Similarly, Heidegger saw both communism and American capitalism – the two major cultural forces of the post-war era – as both forms of a technological rationality which was unthought in its essence and in its implications for human cultural life and its relation to Being.

19 See Rudolf Bernet, "Le monde (Husserl)", in *La Vie du sujet. Recherches sur l'interprétation de Husserl dans la phénoménologie* (Paris: PUF, 1994), pp. 93–118.

20 Husserl had read Levi-Bruhl's books and wrote him a letter admiring his enquiry into the nature of ahistorical, primitive societies as a breakthrough into a radical anthropology. See *Briefwechsel* VII 156–159. Merleau-Ponty frequently refers to this letter.

21 Husserl Archiv B 1 32, Nr 17. I thank Dr S. Luft for drawing my attention to this passage. I thank the Husserl-Archiv, Leuven, for permission to quote from this unpublished text. The German reads as follows:

> Es gehören besondere Motive dazu um theoretische Einstellung möglich zu machen, und gegenüber Heidegger will es mir scheinen, daß ein ursprüngliches Motiv liege, für Wissenschaft wie für Kunst, in der Notwendigkeit des Spieles und speziell in der Motivation einer spielerischen, das ist nicht aus Lebensnotdurft, nicht aus Beruf, aus Zweckzusammenhang der Selbsterhaltung entspringenden "theoretischen Neugier", die sich die Dinge ansehen, sie kennenlernen will, Dinge, die sie nichts angehen. Und nicht "defiziente" Praxis soll hier vorliegen.

22 For a strikingly similar account see Hannah Arendt, *The Human Condition* (Chicago: University of Chicago Press, 1958).

23 See Daniel C. Dennett, *Consciousness Explained* (London: Penguin, 1993), pp. 66–98.

24 For a critique of Dennett along these lines, see David Carr, "Phenomenology and Fiction in Dennett", *International Journal of Philosophical Studies* 6(3) (September, 1998), pp. 331–344.

6 MARTIN HEIDEGGER'S TRANSFORMATION OF PHENOMENOLOGY

1 M. Heidegger, *Sein und Zeit*, 17th edition (Tübingen: Max Niemeyer, 1993), trans. John Macquarrie and Edward Robinson, *Being and Time* (Oxford: Basil Blackwell, 1962). Hereafter BT followed by English pagination and German pagination.

2 See J. Habermas, "Martin Heidegger, On the Publication of the Lectures from 1935", in R. Wolin, ed., *The Heidegger Controversy. A Critical Reader* (Cambridge, MA: MIT Press, 1993), p. 191.

3 Michael Murray, ed., *Heidegger and Modern Philosophy* (New Haven: Yale University Press, 1978), p. 297.

4 Heidegger was actually warm and approachable with students, but his conception of the duties of a thinker and the task of philosophy has been described as 'monomaniacal'; see Herman Philipse, *Heidegger's Philosophy of Being* (Princeton, NJ: Princeton University Press, 1998), p. xiv.

5 Gilbert Ryle, "Heidegger's *Sein und Zeit*", in Murray, ed., *Heidegger and Modern Philosophy*, op. cit., p. 64.

6 Karl Jaspers, "Letter to the Freiburg University Denazification Committee", in R. Wolin, ed., *The Heidegger Controversy. A Critical Reader*, op. cit., p. 149, translation modified.

7 See Theodor W. Adorno, *The Jargon of Authenticity*, trans. K. Tarnowski and F. Will (Evanston, IL: Northwestern University Press, 1973).

8 K. von Klemperer, "Martin Heidegger's Life and Times", in K. Harries and C.

Jamme, eds, *Martin Heidegger. Politics, Art and Technology* (New York: Holmes and Meier, 1994), p. 2.

9 M. Heidegger, "My Way to Phenomenology", trans. Joan Stambaugh, *On Time and Being* (New York: Harper and Row, 1972), p. 78, translation altered. Hereafter OTB and page number.

10 M. Heidegger, "Preface/Vorwort", in William J. Richardson, *Heidegger. Through Phenomenology to Thought* (The Hague: Nijhoff, 1963), pp. x–xi. Hereafter Richardson followed by page number.

11 M. Heidegger, "For Eugen Fink on His Sixtieth Birthday", in *The Fundamental Concepts of Metaphysics. World, Finitude, Solitude*, trans. William McNeill and Nicholas Walker (Bloomington, IN: Indiana University Press, 1995), p. 367. Hereafter FCM and page number of English translation.

12 M. Heidegger, "The Thinker as Poet", *Poetry, Language and Thought*, trans. Albert Hofstadter (New York: Harper and Row, 1975), p. 4. Hereafter PLT and page number. The original poem is contained in M. Heidegger, *Auf der Erfahrung des Denkens* (Pfullingen: Neske, 1954).

13 We shall follow the translator's custom of using the word "Being" with a capital 'B' to translate Heidegger's use of the word '*Sein*' which is both the infinitive of the verb 'to be' and also the present participle, 'being'. Heidegger refers to individual beings or entities using the present participle (*seiend*) as a verbal noun, *das Seiende*, which we shall render as 'being' with a lower case 'b'. Right from the beginning of *Being and Time* Heidegger alternates between referring to "the meaning of the question of Being" and the shortened form "the question of Being" (*die Seinsfrage*).

14 M. Heidegger, "On the Essence of Truth", *Pathmarks*, ed. William McNeill (Cambridge: Cambridge University Press, 1998), p. 149; GA 9, p.195. Hereafter *Pathmarks* followed by English pagination and then pagination of German *Gesamtausgabe* edition.

15 See Dermot Moran, "The Destruction of the Destruction: Heidegger's Versions of the History of Philosophy", in K. Harries and C. Jamme, eds, *Martin Heidegger. Politics, Art and Technology*, op. cit., pp. 175–196.

16 Sometimes, for example in his 1938 work *Beiträge zur Philosophie. Vom Ereignis* (Frankfurt: Klostermann 1994) GA 65, Heidegger refers to '*Sein*' using the old German spelling '*Seyn*'. We shall ignore these spelling variations.

17 Hugo Ott, *Martin Heidegger. A Political Life*, trans. Allan Blunden (London: Harper Collins, 1993), p. 51. Hereafter Ott and page number. For Heidegger's biography, see also Rüdiger Safranski, *Martin Heidegger. Between Good and Evil*, trans. Eward Osers (Cambridge, MA: Harvard University Press, 1998).

18 Ott, *Martin Heidegger. A Political Life*, p. 51; German, p. 54.

19 Carl Braig, *Vom Sein. Abriss der Ontologie* (Freiburg: Herder, 1896). For an account of the parallels between this book and Heidegger's thinking, see John D. Caputo, *Heidegger and Aquinas. An Essay on Overcoming Metaphysics* (New York: Fordham University Press, 1982), pp. 45–57.

20 Braig, for instance, offers an etymological explanation of the German word '*Zeit*' back to the Greek word for stretching out (*tanumi*, I stretch out) which is to be found in Heidegger (BT 425; 373), where Dasein is thought of in terms of stretching along (*Erstreckung*) between birth and death.

21 M. Heidegger, "A Dialogue on Language", trans. Peter D. Hertz, *On the Way to Language* (New York: Harper and Row, 1971), pp. 9–10.

22 For Lask's impact on Heidegger, see Theodore Kisiel, "Why Students of Heidegger Will Have to Read Emil Lask", in Deborah G. Chaffin, ed., *Emil Lask and the Search for Concreteness* (Athens, OH: Ohio University Press, 1993). See Heidegger's reference to Lask (BT 493–494 n.34; 218), where

Heidegger credits Lask for recognising that Husserl's positive phenomenological account of truth in the Sixth Investigation differs from his Bolzano-inspired theory in the *Prolegomena*.

23 M. Heidegger, *Frühe Schriften*, GA 1 (Frankfurt: Klostermann, 1978), pp. 1–15.

24 *Die Lehre vom Urteil in Psychologismus. Ein kritisch-positiver Beitrag zur Logik* (Leipzig: Barth, 1914), republished in *Frühe Schriften*, op. cit., GA 1, pp. 59–188.

25 Husserl's letter to Natorp of 8 October 1917 is published in *Briefwechsel* V 131–132. See Thomas Sheehan, "Heidegger's Early Years; Fragments for a Philosophical Biography", *Listening* 12 (1977), p. 8.

26 See Thomas Sheehan, "Reading a Life: Heidegger and Hard Times", in Charles Guignon, ed., *The Cambridge Companion to Heidegger* (Cambridge: Cambridge University Press, 1993), pp. 71–72.

27 Hannah Arendt, "Martin Heidegger at Eighty", in Michael Murray, ed., *Heidegger and Modern Philosophy*, op. cit., p. 294.

28 M. Heidegger, *Der Begriff der Zeit* (Tübingen: Niemeyer, 1989), trans. William McNeill, *The Concept of Time* (Oxford: Blackwell, 1992).

29 In later years Heidegger recalled that *Being and Time* was published in February 1927, whereas T. Kisiel, *The Genesis of Heidegger's Being and Time* (Berkeley, CA: University of California Press, 1993), p. 489, dates it to April 1927. On 8 April 1926, Husserl's birthday, Heidegger had presented Husserl with a hand-written dedication page for the book.

30 Martin Heidegger–Karl Jaspers *Briefwechsel 1920–1926*, hrsg. Walter Biemel and Hans Saner (Frankfurt: Klostermann, 1990), p. 71.

31 See "Husserl's Marginal Remarks in Martin Heidegger's *Being and Time*", trans. Thomas Sheehan, in Edmund Husserl, *Psychological and Transcendental Phenomenology and the Confrontation with Heidegger (1927–1931)* (Dordrecht: Kluwer, 1997), p. 270. Hereafter *Trans. Phen.* and page number.

32 M. Heidegger, *Kant and The Problem of Metaphysics*, trans. Richard Taft, 4th edition (Bloomington, IN: Indiana University Press, 1990). Hereafter KPM and page number of English translation.

33 M. Heidegger, "What is Metaphysics?", *Pathmarks*, op. cit., pp. 82–96; GA 9, pp. 103–122.

34 See R. Carnap, "Überwindung der Metaphysik durch logische Analyse der Sprache", *Erkenntnis* 2 (1931), trans. Arthur Pap, "The Overcoming of Metaphysics through Logical Analysis of Language", in M. Murray, ed., *Heidegger and Modern Philosophy*, op. cit., pp. 23–35. For a discussion of Carnap's critique, see Michael Friedman, "Overcoming Metaphysics: Carnap and Heidegger", in R. Giere and A. Richardson, eds, *The Origins of Logical Empiricism, Minnesota Studies* XVI (1996), pp. 45–79.

35 M. Heidegger, "On the Essence of Ground", trans. William McNeill, *Pathmarks*, op. cit., pp. 97–135; GA 9, pp. 123–175.

36 Heidegger had been using this term for the change in direction of his thinking in his lecture courses since the early 1930s. For an interesting discussion of the place of *die Kehre* in Heidegger's thought, see Laurence Paul Hemming, "Speaking Out of Turn: Heidegger and *die Kehre*", *International Journal of Philosophical Studies* 6(3) (October, 1998), pp. 393–423.

37 M. Heidegger, "Bauen, Wohnen, Denken", *Vorträge und Aufsätze* (Pfullingen: Neske, 1954), pp. 139–56, esp. p. 144, trans. *Poetry, Language and Thought*, op. cit., esp. p. 150.

38 Tom Rockmore, *On Heidegger's Nazism and Philosophy* (London: Harvester Wheatsheaf, 1992), p. 117. See also Victor Farias, *Heidegger and Nazism* (Philadelphia: Temple University Press, 1989), pp. 87–95.

39 Heidegger's Schlageter address was originally published in Guido Schnee-berger, *Nachlese zu Heidegger: Dokumente zu seinem Leben und Denken* (Bern: Suhr, 1962), trans. in R. Wolin, ed., *The Heidegger Controversy*, op. cit., pp. 40–42. See also, K. Löwith, "The Occasional Decisionism of Carl Schmitt", in Karl Löwith, *Martin Heidegger and European Nihilism*, ed. R. Wolin (New York: University of Columbia Press, 1995), p. 161.

40 H.-G. Gadamer, "Interview: The German University and German Politics", in Dieter Misgeld and Graeme Nicholson, eds, *Hans-Georg Gadamer on Education, Poetry and History. Applied Hermeneutics* (Albany, NY: SUNY Press, 1992), p. 11. See Heinrich Petzet's recollections of Heidegger, *Auf einen Stern zugehen* (Frankfurt: Societäts-Verlag, 1983), trans. as *Enounters and Dialogues with Martin Heidegger 1929–1976* (Chicago: University of Chicago Press, 1993).

41 For a copy of this letter see Sepp, *Edmund Husserl und die phänomenologische Bewegung*, op. cit., p. 384. But see Hermann Heidegger, "Der Wirtschaftshistoriker und die Wahrheit. Notwendige Bemerkungen zu den Veröffentlichungen Hugo Otts über Martin Heidegger", *Heidegger Studies* 13 (1997), pp. 177–192, esp. p. 186.

42 Thomas Sheehan's review of Farias, "Heidegger and the Nazis", *New York Review of Books* 16 June 1988, p. 41.

43 Martin Heidegger, *Die Selbstbehauptung der deutschen Universität* (republished, Frankfurt: Klostermann, 1983), trans. Karsten Harries, "The Self-Assertion of the German University Address, Delivered on the Solemn Assumption of the Rectorate of the University, Freiburg", *Review of Metaphysics* 38 (March, 1985), pp. 467–480.

44 Thomas Sheehan's review of Victor Farias, "Heidegger and the Nazis", *New York Review of Books* 16 June 1988, p. 39.

45 *Gleichschaltung* was the preferred National Socialist term for an institution's "toeing the line".

46 The speech is translated in R. Wolin, ed., *The Heidegger Controversy*, pp. 46–52.

47 Martin Heidegger and Karl Jaspers, *Briefwechsel*, ed. Walter Biemel and Erhärt Kastner (Frankfurt, 1990), p. 155.

48 K. Jaspers, "Philosophical Autobiography", in Paul A. Schilpp, ed., *The Philosophy of Karl Jaspers* (New York: Tudor Books, 1957), p. 62.

49 Thomas Sheehan's review of Farias, "Heidegger and the Nazis", *New York Review of Books* 16 June 1988, p. 40. Baumgarten's case was referred to by Jaspers in his letter to the Denazification Committee. Husserl refers to the Baumgarten affair in his letter to Elisabeth Rosenberg 31 May 1931, *Briefwechsel* IX 406.

50 M. Heidegger, "Hölderlin and the Essence of Poetry", trans. Douglas Scott, in Werner Brock, ed., *Existence and Being* (Chicago: Henry Regnery, 1949), pp. 270–291.

51 M. Heidegger, *Einführung in die Metaphysik* (Max Niemeyer Verlag, 1953), trans. Ralph Manheim, *An Introduction to Metaphysics* (New York: Doubleday, 1961). Hereafter IM and page number of English translation, followed by page number of German original.

52 Jürgen Habermas, "Martin Heidegger: On the Publication of the Lectures from 1935", trans. in R. Wolin, ed., *The Heidegger Controversy*, op. cit., pp. 186–197.

53 This defence has been seen as somewhat disingenuous in that other similar sentences have been excised from the Gesamtausgabe editions of Heidegger's lectures.

54 M. Heidegger, *Hölderlin's Hymn "Der Ister"*, trans. W. McNeill and J. Davis (Bloomington, IN: Indiana University Press, 1996), pp. 54–55 and p. 143. See also p. 70 where Heidegger claims that "Bolshevism is only a derivative kind of Americanism".

55 J. Habermas, "Life Forms, Morality and the Task of the Philosopher", in Peter Dews, ed., *Habermas. Autonomy and Solidarity* (London: Verso, 1986), pp. 195–196.

56 M. Heidegger, "Plato's Doctrine of Truth", trans. Thomas Sheehan, *Pathmarks*, pp. 155–182.

57 M. Heidegger, "On the Essence of Truth", *Pathmarks*, pp. 136–154.

58 M. Heidegger, *Basic Concepts*, trans. Gary E. Aylesworth (Bloomington, IN: Indiana University Press, 1993), p. 14. This lecture course was delivered in the winter semester of 1941.

59 There are extant photographs of Heidegger wearing the Nazi pin.

60 Jaspers' letter is translated in Richard Wolin, ed., *The Heidegger Controversy. A Critical Reader*, op. cit., pp. 147–151. Jaspers cites Heidegger's treatment of Eduard Baumgarten who sought a post at Göttingen; Heidegger criticised his politics and said Baumgarten was consorting with "the Jew Fraenkel". On the other hand, Jaspers balances this with his report of Werner Brock, another Jew, being treated well as Heidegger's assistant and indeed Heidegger helped him get settled in England.

61 Gadamer attended these lectures and subsequently commented that Heidegger's insight, though misused by the Nazis, did have truth, namely that art is always tied to a community.

62 M. Heidegger, *Holzwege* (Frankfurt: Klostermann, 1950), reprinted with changes as *Der Ursprung des Kunstwerkes* (Stuttgart: Reclam, 1960), trans. Albert Hofstadter, "The Origin of the Work of Art", *Poetry, Language and Thought* (New York: Harper and Row, 1971), pp. 17–87.

63 Heidegger, "Letter on 'Humanism'", trans. Frank Capuzzi, *Pathmarks*, op. cit., pp. 239–276; GA 9, pp. 313–364.

64 Translated by Thomas Sheehan in his essay, "Heidegger and the Nazis", *New York Review of Books* 16 June 1988, pp. 41–42.

65 See Alan Milchman and Alan Rosenberg, eds, *Martin Heidegger and the Holocaust* (Atlantic Highlands, NJ: Humanities Press, 1997).

66 Murray, ed., *Heidegger and Modern Philosophy*, op. cit., p. 302.

67 "Nur noch ein Gott kann uns retten", Spiegel-Gespräch mit Martin Heidegger am 23 September 1966, *Der Spiegel* 31 May 1976, pp. 193–219, trans. Maria Alter and J. Caputo, "Only a God Can Save Us: *Der Spiegel*'s Interview with Martin Heidegger (1966)", in R. Wolin, ed., *The Heidegger Controversy*, op. cit., pp. 91–116.

68 See, for example, Thomas Sheehan, "Caveat Lector: The New Heidegger", *New York Review of Books* 4 December 1980, pp. 39–41. According to Sheehan, paragraphs are shifted around, summaries of lectures are sometimes merged with the text, sometimes kept separate, and references are added to editions of texts which Heidegger could not have used.

69 Victor Farias, *Heidegger et le nazisme* (Paris: Editions Verdier, 1987), trans. as *Heidegger and Nazism*, ed. Joseph Margolis and Tom Rockmore (Philadelphia: Temple University Press, 1989). Hereafter Farias and page number of the English translation. See also Thomas Sheehan's review of Farias, "Heidegger and the Nazis", *New York Review of Books* 16 June 1988, pp. 28–47.

70 Guido Schneeberger, *Nachlese zu Heidegger*, op. cit.

71 See "Gottlob Frege's Political Diary", trans. Richard L. Mendelson, *Inquiry* 39(3–4) (December, 1996), pp. 303–342. Frege kept this diary from 10 March to 9 May 1924 in his 75th year. Frege was connected with the anti-Semitic philosopher Bruno Bauch whose Deutsche Philosophische Gesellschaft sought to reform philosophy in Germany. See H. Sluga, *Heidegger's Crisis: Philosophy and Politics in Nazi Germany* (Cambridge, MA: Harvard University Press,

1993). Frege's remarks in the diary display an antipathy to social democracy, and a concern for Germany in those turbulent and inflationary years, and an admiration for early Nazi leaders including Erich Ludendorff. But his most offensive remarks concern his complaint that the Germans have let too many Jews into the country and now due to liberal policies impose no restrictions of movement on them unlike in former times.

7 HEIDEGGER'S *BEING AND TIME*

1 M. Heidegger, "Anmerkungen zu Karl Jaspers *Psychologie der Weltanschauungen*", in *Wegmarken* GA 9 (Frankfurt: Klostermann, 1976), pp. 1–44, trans. John Van Buren, "Comments on Karl Jaspers' *Psychology of World Views*" in M. Heidegger, *Pathmarks*, ed. William McNeill (Cambridge: Cambridge University Press, 1998), pp. 1–38. Hereafter *Pathmarks*. See David Farrell Krell, "Towards *Sein und Zeit*", *Journal of the British Society for Phenomenology* 6 (1975), pp. 147–156.

2 See Thomas Sheehan, "General Introduction", to Edmund Husserl, *Psychological and Transcendental Philosophy and the Confrontation with Heidegger (1927–1931)*, ed. T. Sheehan and R. E. Palmer, Collected Works VI (Dordrecht: Kluwer, 1997), p. 17.

3 Heidegger's word here is *Bekümmerung*, which means 'to be troubled by something'; later in *Being and Time*, he will replace it with the word 'care', *Sorge*.

4 See Thomas Sheehan, "Heidegger's Introduction to the Phenomenology of Religion, 1920–21", *The Personalist* LX(3) (1979), pp. 312–324.

5 See M. Heidegger, "Phenomenological Interpretations with Respect to Aristotle", trans. Michael Baur, *Man and World* 25 (1992), pp. 355–393. Hereafter Aristotle text. This copy had been sent to Georg Misch in Göttingen in 1922 as another job opportunity presented itself there. Misch, however, thought Heidegger's language obscure and that Heidegger was twisting Aristotle to suit his own philosophical outlook.

6 Thomas Sheehan, "Heidegger's Early Years; Fragments for a Philosophical Biography", *Listening* 12 (1977), p. 5.

7 Of course, since no philosophy is actually in favour of 'pseudo-problems', this characterisation of phenomenology is hardly informative.

8 *Unterwegs zur Sprache* (Pfullingen: Neske, 1959), trans. Peter D. Hertz, *On the Way to Language* (New York: Harper and Row, 1982), p. 9.

9 See M. Heidegger, *Die Grundbegriffe der Metaphysik. Welt–Endlichkeit–Einsamkeit* GA 29/30 (Frankfurt: Klostermann, 1992), §§ 46–47, pp. 284–294, trans. William McNeill and Nicholas Walker *The Fundamental Concepts of Metaphysics. World, Finitude, Solitude* (Bloomington, IN: Indiana University Press, 1995), pp. 192–200.

10 Hubert L. Dreyfus, *Being-In-The-World. A Commentary on Heidegger's Being and Time, Division I* (Cambridge, MA: MIT Press, 1991), pp. 60–87.

11 Heidegger, "The Question Concerning Technology", in *The Question Concerning Technology and Other Essays*, trans. William Lovitt (New York: Harper and Row, 1977), p. 13.

12 Ludwig Wittgenstein, "On Heidegger on Being and Dread", in Michael Murray, ed., *Heidegger and Modern Philosophy* (New Haven, CT: Yale University Press, 1978), p. 80.

13 Charles Taylor, "Engaged Agency and Background in Heidegger", in Charles B. Guignon, ed., *The Cambridge Companion to Heidegger* (Cambridge: Cambridge University Press, 1993), p. 317.

14 Quoted in Thomas McCarthy, "Heidegger and Critical Theory: The First Encounter", in K. Harries and C. Jamme, eds, *Martin Heidegger. Politics, Art and Technology* (New York: Holmes and Meier, 1994), p. 213.

15 J. Habermas, *The Philosophical Discourse of Modernity*, trans. F. Lawrence (Cambridge: Polity Press, 1987), p. 152.

16 For evidence of this recent interest in Britain, see, for example, Stephen Mulhall, *Heidegger and Being and Time* (London: Routledge, 1996), and Michael Inwood, *Heidegger* (Oxford: Oxford University Press, 1997).

17 Habermas agrees in *The Philosophical Discourse of Modernity*, op. cit., p. 148.

18 Quoted in H. Dreyfus, *Being-In-The-World*, op. cit., p. 9.

8 HANS-GEORG GADAMER: PHILOSOPHICAL HERMENEUTICS

1 H.-G. Gadamer, "Reflections on my Philosophical Journey", in Lewis Edwin Hahn, ed., *The Philosophy of Hans-Georg Gadamer,* Library of the Living Philosophers (La Salle, IL: Open Court, 1997), p. 26.

2 H.-G. Gadamer, *Wahrheit und Methode. Grundzüge einer philosophischen Hermeneutik* (Tübingen: Lohr, 1960; 2nd edition, 1965). The English translation by Joel Weimsheimer and Donald G. Marshall, *Truth and Method*, 2nd revised edition (London: Sheed & Ward, 1989), actually translates the Fourth German Edition. Hereafter TM followed by the page number of the English translation and the pagination of the German Second Edition. Hence this reference is TM 384; 361.

3 Gadamer, "The Nature of Things and the Language of Things", in D. Linge, ed., *Philosophical Hermeneutics* (Berkeley, CA: University of California Press, 1977), pp. 77–78. Hereafter *Phil. Herm.* and page number of the English translation.

4 H.-G. Gadamer, "Gadamer on Gadamer", in Hugh J. Silverman, ed., *Gadamer and Hermeneutics* (London: Routledge, 1991), p. 16.

5 J. Habermas, "Gadamer: Urbanizing the Heideggerian Province", *Philosophical-Political Profiles*, trans. Frederick Lawrence (Cambridge, MA: MIT Press, 1983), p. 192.

6 J. Habermas, "Der Universitätsanspruch der Hermeneutik", trans. as "On Hermeneutics' Claim to Universality", in K. Mueller-Vollmer, *The Hermeneutics Reader* (Oxford: Blackwell, 1986), pp. 294–319.

7 See his essay, "Rhetorik, Hermeneutik, Ideologiekritik", *Kleine Schriften* I (Tübingen: Mohr, 1967), trans. as "Rhetoric, Hermeneutics, and the Critique of Ideology: Metacritical Comments on *Truth and Method*", in K. Mueller-Vollmer, *The Hermeneutics Reader*, op. cit., pp. 274–292.

8 H.-G. Gadamer, *Dialogue and Deconstruction. The Gadamer-Derrida Encounter*, ed. D. P. Michelfelder and R. E. Palmer (Albany, NY: SUNY Press, 1989), p. 55.

9 H.-G. Gadamer, *Philosophical Apprenticeships*, trans. Robert R. Sullivan (Cambridge, MA: MIT Press, 1990). Hereafter *Phil. App.* and page number. For a feminist critique of these reflections, see Robin May Schott, "Gender, Nazism and Hermeneutics", in L. E. Hahn, ed., *The Philosophy of Hans-Georg Gadamer*, op. cit., pp. 499–508.

10 H.-G. Gadamer, *Heidegger's Ways*, trans. J.W. Stanley (Albany, NY: SUNY Press, 1994), p. 30.

11 H.-G. Gadamer, *Reason in the Age of Science*, trans. Frederick G. Lawrence (Cambridge, MA: MIT Press, 1981), p. 11.

12 H.-G. Gadamer, *Heidegger's Ways*, op. cit., p. 30.

13 Gadamer, "Reflections on my Philosophical Journey", in Hahn, ed., *The Philosophy of Hans-Georg Gadamer*, op. cit., p. 4.

14 "Existentialism and the Philosophy of Existence", in Gadamer, *Heidegger's Ways*, op. cit., p. 4.

15 O. Spengler, *Der Untergang des Abendlandes*, 2 vols (Munich: Beck, 1927), trans. C. F. Atkinson, *The Decline of the West*, 2 vols (New York: Knopf, 1947).

16 Gadamer, "The Marburg Theology", *Heidegger's Ways*, op. cit., p. 31; see also "Martin Heidegger – 85 Years", in *Heidegger's Ways*, op. cit., p. 113.

17 Gadamer, *Dialogue and Dialectic. Eight Hermeneutical Studies on Plato*, trans. P. Christopher Smith (New Haven, CT: Yale University Press, 1980), p. 198.

18 Gadamer, "Martin Heidegger – 85 Years", in *Heidegger's Ways*, op. cit., pp. 17–18.

19 Gadamer, "Martin Heidegger – 85 Years", in *Heidegger's Ways*, op. cit., p. 113. See also Gadamer, *Phil. App.*, p. 47.

20 H.-G. Gadamer, "Martin Heidegger – 85 Years", in *Heidegger's Ways*, op. cit., p. 115, and see also J. Habermas, "Gadamer: Urbanizing the Heideggerian Province", *Philosophical-Political Profiles*, op. cit., p. 191.

21 Gadamer, "Martin Heidegger's One Path", in T. Kisiel and J. Van Buren, eds, *Reading Heidegger from the Start* (Albany, NY: SUNY Press, 1994), p. 21.

22 H.-G. Gadamer, *Platos dialektische Ethik. Phänomenologische Interpretationen zum Philebus* (1931), reprinted with further essays as *Platos dialektische Ethik* (Hamburg: Meiner, 1968), trans. Robert Wallace, *Plato's Dialectical Ethics* (New Haven, CT: Yale University Press, 1991). Hereafter PDE and page number of English translation.

23 D. Davidson, "Gadamer and Plato's *Philebus*", in Lewis Edwin Hahn, ed., *The Philosophy of Hans-Georg Gadamer*, op. cit., p. 422.

24 Gadamer, "The Universality of the Hermeneutical Problem", originally in *Kleine Schriften* I, pp. 101–112, trans. *Phil. Herm.*, p. 5.

25 Heidegger, *Der Ursprung des Kunstwerkes* (Stuttgart: Reclam, 1960). Gadamer's introduction has been translated as "Heidegger's Later Philosophy", in David Linge, ed., *Phil. Herm.*, pp. 213–228.

26 Gadamer, "Heidegger's Later Philosophy", *Phil. Herm.*, p. 228.

27 On this old-world liberalism, see the interview in Dieter Misgeld and Graeme Nicholson, eds, *Hans-Georg Gadamer on Education, Poetry and History. Applied Hermeneutics* (Albany, NY: SUNY Press, 1992), p. 140.

28 Gadamer, *Phil. App.*, p. 75. See also H.-G. Gadamer, "Back from Syracuse", trans. J. McCumber, *Critical Inquiry* 15 (Winter, 1989), p. 428.

29 See the 1986 interview in *Hans-Georg Gadamer on Education, Poetry and History*, op. cit., p. 9.

30 *Phil. App.*, p. 76. Jonathan Barnes has pointed to this moral lapse in his review of Gadamer's *Philosophical Apprenticeships*, in the *London Review of Books* 8(19) (6 November 1986).

31 See Teresa Orozco, *Platonische Gewalt. Gadamers politische Hermeneutik der NS-Zeit* (Hamburg: Argument-Verlag, 1995).

32 Gadamer, *Dialogue and Dialectic. Eight Hermeneutical Studies on Plato*, op. cit., p. 39.

33 Gadamer, "Back from Syracuse", *Critical Inquiry*, op. cit., p. 427.

34 H.-G. Gadamer, *Gesammelte Werke*, 10 Bande (Tübingen: Mohr, 1985–1995). This edition by the author himself is self-selected and not a complete gathering of all Gadamer's works.

35 Gadamer, *The Idea of the Good in Platonic-Aristotelian Philosophy* (New Haven, CT: Yale University Press, 1986), pp. 4–5.

36 J. Habermas, "On Hermeneutics' Claim to Universality", in K. Mueller-Vollmer, *The Hermeneutics Reader*, op. cit., p. 294.

37 Gadamer, "Text and Interpretation", in Michelfelder and Palmer, eds, *Dialogue and Deconstruction*, op. cit., p. 26.

38 Wilhelm Dilthey had already made an extensive study of the historical development of hermeneutics in his early prize essay, *Preisschrift*, of 1860, "Schleiermacher's Hermeneutical System in Relation to Early Protestant Hermeneutics", transl. in Dilthey, *Hermeneutics and the Study of History*, Selected Works IV, ed. Rudolf Makkreel and Fritjhof Rodi (Princeton, NJ: Princeton University Press, 1996).

39 St Augustine, *On Christian Doctrine*, trans. D. W. Robertson, Jr (Indianapolis: Bobbs-Merrill, 1958), pp. 38–39. *De doctrina christiana* was also an important text for Heidegger in the 1920s.

40 For Gadamer's account of the tradition of hermeneutics, see his article "Hermeneutik", *Historisches Wörterbuch der Philosophie*, ed. J. Ritter (Darmstadt: Wissenschaftliche Buchgesellschaft, 1973), Vol. 3, cols 1062–1073.

41 See the excerpt from Johan Martin Chladenius, "On the Concept of Interpretation", in Kurt Mueller-Vollmer, ed., *The Hermeneutics Reader*, op. cit., pp. 55–71.

42 F. D. E. Schleiermacher, *Hermeneutics: The Handwritten Manuscripts*, trans. J. Duke and J. Forstman (Atlanta, GA: Scholar's Press, 1977).

43 For an interesting discussion of the composition of the text see Jean Grondin, "On the Sources of *Truth and Method*", *Sources of Hermeneutics* (Albany, NY: SUNY Press, 1995), pp. 83–110.

44 See Hans-Herbert Kögler, *Die Macht des Dialogs. Kritische Hermeneutik nach Gadamer, Foucault, und Rorty* (Stuttgart: Metzler, 1992), p. 40.

45 On the holism of play and the manner in which expertise in a skill is not reducible to the exercising of the steps one uses to learn a skill, see Hubert Dreyfus, "Hermeneutics and Holism", *Review of Metaphysics* 34 (1980), pp. 3–23.

46 See E. D. Hirsch, *Validity in Interpretation* (New Haven, CT: Yale University Press, 1967), and E. Betti, "Hermeneutics as the General Methodology of the *Geisteswissenschaften*", in J. Bleicher, ed., *Contemporary Hermeneutics: Hermeneutics as Method Philosophy and Critique* (London: Routledge & Kegan Paul, 1980), pp. 51–94.

47 See J. Habermas, "A Review of Gadamer's *Truth and Method*", in Brice R. Wachterhauser, *Hermeneutics and Modern Philosophy* (Albany, NY: SUNY Press, 1986), pp. 243–276.

48 See Robin Schott, "Whose Home is it Anyway? A Feminist Response to Gadamer's Hermeneutics", in Silverman, ed., *Gadamer and Hermeneutics*, op. cit., pp. 202–209.

49 D. Davidson, "Gadamer and Plato's *Philebus*", in Lewis Edwin Hahn, ed., *The Philosophy of Hans-Georg Gadamer*, pp. 421–432; for Gadamer's reply see ibid., pp. 433–436.

50 D. Davidson, "Gadamer and Plato's *Philebus*", in Lewis Edwin Hahn, ed., *The Philosophy of Hans-Georg Gadamer*, op. cit., p. 432.

9 HANNAH ARENDT: THE PHENOMENOLOGY OF THE PUBLIC SPHERE

1 Hedwig Martius (1888–1966) was born in Berlin and first enrolled to study literature in the Universities of Rostock and Freiburg before moving to the University of Munich to study psychology with Alexander Pfänder, who recommended that she go to Göttingen to study with Husserl. Her PhD thesis,

"The Epistemological Foundations of Positivism", was completed in Munich in 1912 under Pfänder and in the same year she married another student of Husserl's, Theodor Conrad (1881–1969). Her attempts to gain a *Habilitation* during the 1930s were frustrated by the fact that she had Jewish ancestry. After the war, from 1949, she lectured at the University of Munich and wrote books on a number of ontological and cosmological topics, including books on space and time. She did not follow Husserl into transcendental phenomenology, but remained an admirer of the *Logical Investigations* and a practitioner of essential seeing. In the 1920s, she published some studies on the nature of being (including an essay defending realism, "Realontologie" in 1923) and in 1938 her book, *The Origin and Structure of the Living Cosmos*, appeared. Conrad-Martius was particularly interested in enriching the understanding of the nature of reality (including the domain of plants and animals) through phenomenological description. See Herbert Spiegelberg with Karl Schuhmann, *The Phenomenological Movement. A Historical Introduction*, 3rd edition (Dordrecht: Kluwer, 1994), pp. 212–222.

2 Edith Stein was born in Breslau on 12 October 1891 and studied philosophy there before moving to Göttingen, where, from 1913 to 1916, she studied with Husserl, completing her PhD thesis in 1916, "On the Problem of Empathy". From 1916 to 1918 she worked as Husserl's private assistant in Freiburg. After her conversion to Catholicism in 1922, she taught at a Dominican school in Speyer until 1931, when she moved to teach at an institute of pedagogy in Münster. In 1933 she entered a Carmelite convent in Cologne, and in 1938 transferred to a convent in Holland. In 1942 she was arrested by the Nazis and deported to Auschwitz concentration camp where she perished.

3 Gerda Walther was born in Nordrach in the Black Forest on 18 March 1897 and studied with Pfänder in Munich and with Husserl in Freiburg in 1917–1918. She published "On the Ontology of Social Communities" in Husserl's *Jahrbuch* in 1923, an original study of the nature of social relations which carefully analysed the essential social feeling of mutual belonging (*Zusammengehörigkeitsgefühl*), and also published a book, *Phänomenologie der Mystik* (*Phenomenology of the Mystic*), in the same year. She maintained an interest in religion and parapsychology. Her autobiography, *Zum anderen Ufer*, appeared in 1960.

4 Simone de Beauvoir, *Le Deuxième sexe* (Paris: Gallimard, 1949), trans. H. M. Parshley, *The Second Sex* (London: Picador, 1988). This text is significant for phenomenology for de Beauvoir's important brief, early criticisms of Levinas's conception of the other and the nature of the feminine; see *The Second Sex*, p. 16n.

5 For example, Arendt does not appear at all in H. Spiegelberg's *The Phenomenological Movement*, op. cit., and does not feature in the *Routledge History of Philosophy*, Vol. VIII, *Continental Philosophy in the Twentieth Century*, ed. R. Kearney (London: Routledge, 1994). On the other hand, see the entry, "Hannah Arendt" by John Francis Burke in Lester Embree, ed., *Encyclopedia of Phenomenology*, ed. L. Embree *et al.* (Dordrecht: Kluwer, 1997), pp. 29–34, which claims that Arendt "pursues an existential phenomenology of political experiences" and stresses the primacy of the life-world. Seyla Benhabib has shown that Arendt characterised herself as a phenomenologist and utilised the existential categories of being at home and homelessness found in Heidegger's *Being and Time*. See S. Benhabib, *The Reluctant Modernism of Hannah Arendt* (London: Sage, 1996), p. 49. See also Elizabeth Young-Bruehl, *Hannah Arendt. For Love of the World* (New Haven, CT: Yale University Press, 1982), p. 405. Hereafter Young-Bruehl and page number.

6 H. Arendt, *The Life of the Mind. Thinking* (New York: Harcourt Brace, 1971), p. 8. Hereafter *Thinking* and page number.

7 Arendt, "Understanding and Politics", *Partisan Review* XX/4 (1954), p. 377, reprinted in Hannah Arendt, *Essays in Understanding 1930–1954* (New York: Harcourt Brace, 1994), pp. 307–327, esp. p. 323.

8 H. Arendt, *The Origins of Totalitarianism* (London: Allen and Unwin, revised edition 1967). Hereafter OT and page number.

9 Arendt, *Men in Dark Times* (New York: Harcourt Brace Jovanovich, 1955; reprinted 1968), p. viii. Hereafter *Dark Times* and page number.

10 See Arendt's statement with Note A, appended to Walter Benjamin's "Theses on the Philosophy of History", *Illuminations*, ed. H. Arendt (New York: Schocken Books, 1969).

11 Mary McCarthy, "Saying Good-by to Hannah", *New York Review of Books* 22 January 1976, p. 8.

12 H. Arendt, *The Human Condition* (Chicago: University of Chicago Press, 1958), trans., *Vita activa oder Vom tätigen Leben* (Stuttgart: Kohlhammer, 1960). Hereafter HC and pagination of English language edition.

13 Hannah Arendt, *Essays in Understanding 1930–1954*, op. cit., p. 320.

14 Hannah Arendt, "Thoughts on Politics and Revolution", *Crises of the Republic* (New York: Harcourt Brace Jovanovich, 1972), pp. 210–211. Hereafter *Crises of the Republic* and page number.

15 "Hannah Arendt on Hannah Arendt", *Hannah Arendt: The Recovery of the Public World*, ed. M. Hill (New York: St Martin's Press, 1979), pp. 333–334. Hereafter HAHA and page number.

16 H. Arendt, "Reflections on Little Rock", *Dissent* VI(1) (Winter, 1959), pp. 45–56. Arendt interpreted the demand of blacks to be accepted in white schools as equivalent to the newly arrived social parvenues who seek to be accepted in high society. Her views were attacked by Ralph Ellison in *Who Speak for the Negro?*, ed. R. Penn Warren (New York: Random House, 1965), pp. 342–344.

17 Hannah Arendt/Martin Heidegger, *Briefe 1925 bis 1975 und andere Zeugnisse aus den Nachlässen*, hrsg. Ursula Ludz (Frankfurt: Klostermann, 1998), p. 76. Heidegger's response was to write a poem for her entitled "Das Mädchen aus der Fremde", ibid., pp. 79–80.

18 Hannah Arendt–Karl Jaspers: *Correspondence 1926–1969*, ed. Lotte Köhler and Hans Saner, trans. Robert and Rita Kimber (New York: Harcourt Brace, 1992), p. 70. Hereafter HAKJ and page number of English translation.

19 Hannah Arendt, *The Jew as Pariah*, ed. Ron Feldman (New York: Grove Press, 1978), p. 246.

20 Arendt's 1964 interview with Gunther Gaus, Hannah Arendt, *Essays in Understanding 1930–1954*, op. cit., p. 6.

21 She remained an admirer of Guardini and in 1952 again attended his lectures in Munich; see Young-Bruehl, p. 283.

22 These lectures have now been edited by Ingeborg Schlüssler, published in M. Heidegger, *Platon: Sophistes*, GA 19 (Frankfurt: Klostermann, 1992), and translated by R. Rojewicz and A. Schuwer as M. Heidegger, *Plato's Sophist* (Bloomington, IN: Indiana University Press, 1997).

23 Hannah Arendt, "Jaspers as Citizen of the World", *The Philosophy of Karl Jaspers*, ed. Paul Arthur Schilpp (New York: Tudor Books, 1957), pp. 539–549.

24 Hannah Arendt, *Der Liebesbegriff bei Augustin. Versuch einer philosophischen Interpretation* (Berlin: Springer-Verlag, 1929), trans. as *Love and Saint Augustine*, ed. Joanna V. Scott and Judith C. Stark (Chicago: University of Chicago Press, 1996).

25 Arendt, *Love and St. Augustine*, op. cit., p. xv.

26 See H. Arendt, "Labor, Work, Action", in *Amor Mundi. Explorations in the*

Faith and Thought of Hannah Arendt (The Hague: Nijhoff, 1987), p. 42 (hereafter *Amor Mundi*). See also OT 479.

27 *The Life of the Mind. Willing* (New York: Harcourt Brace, 1978), pp. 84–110.

28 Günther Stern (1902–1992) was born in Breslau and completed his PhD in 1924 with Husserl with a dissertation entitled "The Role of Situation Categories in Logical Sentences". He attended Heidegger's seminar in Marburg in 1925. He published a book on the ontology of knowledge in 1928 but failed in an attempt to find a sponsor for his *Habilitation*. He left Germany for France in 1933, and emigrated to the USA in 1936. In 1950 he returned to Europe and became a freelance writer living in Vienna. He was active in the anti-nuclear movement. He wrote an article critical of Heidegger: "On the Pseudo-Concreteness of Heidegger's Philosophy", *Philosophy and Phenomenological Research* 8(3) (1947–1948), pp. 337–370.

29 It is alleged by his critics that, in the early 1930s, Adorno made some attempt to ingratiate himself with the Nazis. Thus in 1934, in *Die Musik*, Adorno reviewed some contemporary choral compositions, including a composition by Münzel setting to music the poetry of Baldur von Schirach which was dedicated to Hitler. In praising the piece, Adorno invokes Goebbel's concept of "Romantic realism". This review was discovered in 1964 and provoked a public controversy in Germany. See HAKJ 793–794 and Theodor Adorno, *Musikalische Schriften* VI, *Gesammelte Schriften* Band 19 (Frankfurt: Suhrkamp, 1984), p. 332.

30 The review is translated as H. Arendt, "Philosophy and Sociology", in *Essays in Understanding 1930–1954*, op. cit., pp. 28–43.

31 R. Safranski, *Martin Heidegger. Between Good and Evil* (Cambridge, MA: Harvard University Press, 1998), pp. 255–256.

32 Hannah Arendt wrote to Blücher in 1952 regarding Sartre (Young-Bruehl, p. 281).

33 Hannah Arendt, *Rahel Varnhagen. The Life of A Jewish Woman*, trans. Richard and Clara Winston, revised edition (New York: Harcourt Brace Jovanovich, 1974).

34 See S. Benhabib, "The Pariah and Her Shadow: Hannah Arendt's Biography of Rahel Varnhagen", in *The Reluctant Modernism of Hannah Arendt*, op. cit., pp. 1–34.

35 Bernard Lazare, *Job's Dung Heap* (New York: Schocken Books, 1948).

36 Walter Benjamin, *Illuminations*, ed. H. Arendt (New York: Schocken Books, 1969).

37 H. Arendt, "German Guilt", *Jewish Frontier* 12 (1945), reprinted as "Organized Guilt and Universal Responsibility", *Essays in Understanding 1930–1954*, op. cit., pp. 121–132. Jaspers' 1946 essay is *Die Schuldfrage* (Heidelberg, 1946), trans. E. B. Ashton as *The Question of German Guilt* (New York: Dial Press, 1947).

38 H. Arendt, "Rejoinder to Eric Voegelin's Review of *The Origins of Totalitarianism*", *Review of Politics* 15 (January, 1953), pp. 76–85.

39 Arendt, "What is *Existenz* philosophy?", *Partisan Review* (1946), reprinted as "What is Existential Philosophy?" in H. Arendt, *Essays in Understanding 1930–1954*, op.cit., pp. 163–187.

40 Arendt, "Martin Heidegger at Eighty", in M. Murray, ed., *Heidegger and Modern Philosophy* (New Haven, CT: Yale University Press, 1978), p. 294. Hereafter Murray and page number.

41 Arendt repeats this analysis, criticising Plato, in *The Life of the Mind. Thinking*, pp. 82–83. See Jacques Taminiaux, *The Thracian Maid and the Professional Thinker*, trans. Michael Gendre (Albany, NY: SUNY Press, 1997).

42 H. Arendt, *Eichmann in Jerusalem. A Report on the Banality of Evil*, 2nd revised edition (New York: Penguin, 1964). Hereafter EIJ and page number.

43 Hannah Arendt, "On Violence", in *Crises of the Republic*, op. cit., pp. 105–198.
44 H. Arendt, "Lying in Politics", *Crises of the Republic*, op. cit., pp. 1–48.
45 According to Young-Bruehl (p. 460), the visit was not a success as Elfride would not leave Arendt alone with Heidegger.
46 See Mary McCarthy, "Saying Good-by to Hannah", *New York Review of Books*, op. cit., pp. 8–10.
47 H. Arendt, *Lectures on Kant's Political Philosophy*, ed. Ronald Beiner (Chicago: University of Chicago Press, 1982).
48 Hannah Arendt/Martin Heidegger, *Briefe 1925 bis 1975*, op. cit., pp. 145–146.
49 Alexandre Koyré wrote a number of studies of Galileo and his own study, *From the Closed World to the Infinite Universe* (Baltimore, MD: Johns Hopkins University Press, 1957), appeared just before Arendt's *The Human Condition*. She cites this book at HC 258.
50 See Patricia Bowen-Moore, *Hannah Arendt's Philosophy of Natality* (Basingstoke: Macmillan, 1989).
51 Hans Blumenberg, *The Legitimacy of the Modern Age*, trans. Robert M. Wallace (Cambridge, MA: MIT Press, 1985), pp. 8–9.
52 Jürgen Habermas, "Hannah Arendt: On the Concept of Power", *Philosophical-Political Profiles*, trans. Frederick Lawrence (Cambridge, MA: MIT Press, 1983), p. 174.
53 See Elizabeth Young-Bruehl, "Hannah Arendt Among Feminists", in Larry May and Jerome Kohn, eds, *Hannah Arendt. Twenty Years Later* (Cambridge, MA: MIT Press, 1997), pp. 307–324.
54 Adrienne Rich, "Conditions for Work: The Common World of Women", in *On Lies, Secrets and Silence* (New York: Norton, 1979), p. 212.
55 Arendt reviewed Alice Ruehle-Gerstel, *Das Frauenproblem der Gegenwart* (The Problem of Women in the Present Day) for the journal *Die Gesellschaft* 10 (1932), pp. 177–179, transl. as "On the Emancipation of Women", in *Arendt: Essays on Understanding 1930–1954*, pp. 66–68. See Benhabib, *Reluctant Modernism*, p. 30 n.1.
56 See Ramin Johanbegloo, *Conversations with Isaiah Berlin* (London: Peter Halban, 1992), pp. 82–83. Benhabib, I believe, incorrectly characterises Berlin's view of Arendt as "gender stereotyping"; see *Reluctant Modernism*, p. xxxvii n.6.
57 Stuart Hampshire, "Metaphysical Mists", *London Observer*, 30 July 1978, p. 26 (quoted in Young-Bruhl, p. 471).
58 See for example the criticism of McPherson, in "Hannah Arendt on Hannah Arendt", in Hill, ed., *Hannah Arendt. The Recovery of the Public World*, op. cit., p. 322.
59 See Annette C. Baier, "Ethics in Many Voices", in Larry May and Jerome Kohn, eds, *Hannah Arendt. Twenty Years Later*, op. cit., pp. 325–346.

10 EMMANUEL LEVINAS: THE PHENOMENOLOGY OF ALTERITY

1 E. Husserl, *Méditations cartésiennes: introduction à la phénoménologie*, trans. G. Peiffer and E. Levinas (Paris: Almand Colin, 1931).
2 E. Levinas, *La Théorie de l'intuition dans la phénoménologie de Husserl* (Paris: Félix Alcan, 1930), trans. A. Orianne, *The Theory of Intuition in Husserl's Phenomenology* (Evanston, IL: Northwestern University Press, 1973). Hereafter THI and page number of English translation.
3 E. Levinas, *Totalité et infini: Essai sur l'extériorité* (The Hague: Nijhoff, 1961), trans. A. Lingis, *Totality and Infinity. An Essay on Exteriority* (Pittsburgh:

Duquesne University Press, 1969). Hereafter TI followed by page number of the English translation, followed by the page number of the French edition. Though Levinas spells his name as both 'Lévinas' and 'Levinas', we shall adopt the usage 'Levinas' throughout.

4 Florian Rötzer, *Conversations with French Philosophers*, trans. Gary E. Aylesworth (Atlantic Highlands, NJ: Humanities Press, 1995), p. 58.

5 E. Levinas, *Éthique et infini, Dialogues avec Philippe Nemo* (Paris: Fayard, 1982), p. 95, trans. Richard A. Cohen, *Ethics and Infinity* (Pittsburgh: Duquesne University Press, 1985), p. 90. Hereafter EI and pagination of English edition followed by the French pagination.

6 For a clear account of Levinas's approach to the Talmud, see Colin Davis, *Levinas. An Introduction* (Cambridge: Polity Press, 1996), pp. 93–119.

7 E. Levinas, "The Understanding of Spirituality in French and German Culture", originally published in 1933 in a Lithuanian journal *Vairas* and trans. Andrius Valevicius, *Continental Philosophy Review* 31 (1998), pp. 1–10.

8 R. Mortley, *French Philosophers in Conversation* (London: Routledge, 1991), p. 11.

9 See also Levinas, "Signature", *Difficile liberté. Essais sur le Judaisme* (Paris: Albin Michel, 1976), trans. by S. Hand, *Difficult Freedom. Essays on Judaism* (London: Athlone Press, 1990). Hereafter 'Difficult Freedom' followed by pagination of English translation.

10 See E. Levinas, *Sur Maurice Blanchot* (Montpellier: Fata Morgana, 1975), trans. by Michael B. Smith, "On Maurice Blanchot", in *Proper Names* (London: Athlone Press, 1996), pp. 127–170.

11 See Levinas's autobiographical remarks in "Signature", *Difficult Freedom*, op. cit., p. 291.

12 R. Mortley, "Levinas", *French Philosophers in Conversation*, op. cit., p. 11.

13 E. Levinas, *Proper Names*, p. 3; *Noms propres*, op. cit., p. 7. See also EI 38; 34.

14 E. Levinas, "Sur les *Ideen* de M.E. Husserl", *Revue Philosophique de la France et de l'Etranger* 108(3/4) (1929), pp. 230–265, trans. Richard A. Cohen and Michael B. Smith "On Ideas", in *Discovering Existence with Husserl* (Evanston, IL: Northwestern University Press, 1998), pp. 3–31.

15 G. Marcel, *Journal Métaphysique*, p. 207; *Metaphysical Journal*, pp. 210–211.

16 J. Wahl, *Le Malheur de la conscience dans la philosophie de Hegel* (Paris, 1929).

17 Levinas, *Hors sujet* (Montpellier: Fata Morgana, 1987), trans. Michael B. Smith, *Outside the Subject* (London: Athlone Press, 1993). Hereafter 'Outside' and page number of the English translation.

18 See his essay on Jean Wahl, *Noms propres*, op. cit., pp. 131–140, trans. *Proper Names*, op. cit., pp. 110–118.

19 E. Levinas, "Martin Heidegger et l'ontologie", *Revue Philosophique de la France et de l'Etranger* 108(5/6) (1932), pp. 395–431, reprinted in *En decouvrant l'existence avec Husserl et Heidegger* (Paris: Vrin, 1988), pp. 7–52.

20 E. Levinas, "As If Consenting to a Horror", trans. Paula Wissig, *Critical Inquiry* 15(2) (1989), pp. 485–488. Here Levinas addresses the issue of Heidegger's post-war silence on the issue of the Holocaust.

21 E. Levinas, "Quelques réflexions sur la philosophie de L'Hitlérism", *Esprit* 2(26) (1934), pp. 199–208, reprinted in E. Levinas, *Les Imprévus de l'histoire* (Montpellier: Fata Morgana, 1994), trans. by S. Hand as "Reflections on the Philosophy of Hitlerism", *Critical Inquiry* 17(1) (Autumn, 1990), pp. 62–71. Hereafter *Hitlerism* and page number of English translation.

22 E. Levinas, *De l'évasion* (Montpellier: Fata Morgana, 1982). Hereafter *Evasion* followed by the page number of the French edition.

23 E. Levinas, *De l'existence à l'existant* (Paris: Fontaine, 1947; reprinted Vrin, 1973), trans. by Alfonso Lingis as *Existence and Existents* (Dordrecht: Kluwer,

1988). Hereafter EE and pagination of English translation followed by French pagination.

24 The lectures were originally published in a collection, *Le Choix – le monde – l'existence* (Paris: Arthaud, 1948), and then as a separate volume as *Temps et l'autre* (Montpellier: Fata Morgana, 1979), trans. by Richard A. Cohen with additional essay as *Time and the Other* (Pittsburgh: Duquesne University Press, 1987). Hereafter TO followed by page number of the English translation and then the French original.

25 For the influence on Levinas of Jean Wahl's analysis of transcendence, see Levinas's essay, "Sur l'idée de la transcendance", *Existence humaine et transcendance* (Neuchatel: Editions de la Baconnière, 1944).

26 E. Levinas, *Autrement qu'être ou au-delà de l'essence* (The Hague: Nijhoff, 1974), trans. Alfonso Lingis, *Otherwise Than Being or Beyond Essence* (The Hague: Nijhoff, 1981). Hereafter OBBE and page number of English translation.

27 Levinas, *De Dieu qui vient à l'idée* (Paris: Vrin, 1982), trans. *Of God Who Comes to Thought* (Stanford, CA: Meridian, 1998).

28 See E. Levinas, "Ethics and Politics", in Sean Hand, ed., *The Levinas Reader* (Oxford: Blackwell, 1989), pp. 289–297, originally published in *Les nouveaux cahiers* 18 (1982–3), pp. 1–8.

29 J. Derrida, *Adieu à Emmanuel Levinas* (Paris: Galilée, 1997). A shorter essay by Derrida, "Adieu", is translated in *Philosophy Today*, 40(3) (Fall 1996), pp. 334–340.

30 Levinas, *De Dieu qui vient à l'idée,* op. cit., p. 140.

31 See Raoul Mortley, "Levinas", in *French Philosophers in Conversation* (London: Routledge, 1991), p. 14.

32 E. Levinas, "Beyond Intentionality", in A. Montefiore, ed., *Philosophy in France Today* (Cambridge: Cambridge University Press, 1983), pp. 100–115.

33 R. Bernasconi and D. Wood, eds, *The Provocation of Levinas: Rethinking the Other* (London: Routledge, 1988), p. 175.

34 Rötzer, *Conversations with French Philosophers*, op. cit., p. 60.

35 See David Michael Levin, "Tracework: Myself and Others in the Moral Phenomenology of Merleau-Ponty and Levinas", *International Journal for Philosophical Studies* 6(3) (October, 1998), pp. 345–392.

36 Levinas, "Meaning and Sense", *Collected Philosophical Papers* (Dordrecht: Nijhoff, 1987), p. 105. Hereafter CPP and page number.

37 "Signature", *Difficult Freedom*, op. cit., p. 292; see also Preface to French Second Edition of EE 10 (not translated in the English edition).

38 S. de Beauvoir, *The Second Sex*, trans. H. M. Parshley (London: Picador, 1988), p. 16 n. 1.

39 Levinas, "La ruine de la représentation", in *Edmund Husserl 1859–1959* (The Hague: Nijhoff, 1959), pp. 73–85, reprinted in *En decouvrant l'existence avec Husserl et Heidegger*, pp. 125–135, trans. *Discovering Existence with Husserl*, op. cit., pp. 111–121; and Levinas, "La philosophie et l'idée de l'infini", *Revue de Métaphysique et de morale* 62 (1957), pp. 241–253, reprinted in *En decouvrant l'existence avec Husserl et Heidegger*, pp. 165–178, trans. in A. Peperzak, *To the Other. An Introduction to the Philosophy of Emmanuel Levinas* (West Lafayette, IN: Purdue University Press, 1993), pp. 88–119.

40 E. Levinas, "A propos de 'Kierkegaard vivant' ", *Noms propres*, op. cit., pp. 88–92, trans. "A Propos of *Kierkegaard Vivant*", *Proper Names*, op. cit., pp. 75–79.

41 J. Derrida, "From Adieu agrave; Emmanuel Levinas", trans. Michael Naas and Pascale-Ann Brauet, *Research in Phenomenology* XXVIII (1998), p. 20.

Derrida writes on the theme of welcome in Levinas in his essay "Le mot d'accueil", in *Adieu à Emmanuel Levinas* (Paris: Galilée, 1997).

42 Levinas, "Ethics and Spirit", in *Difficult Freedom. Essays on Judaism*, op. cit., p. 10.

43 Interview with Schlomo Malka in *The Levinas Reader*, op. cit., p. 290.

44 Levinas, "Ethics and Spirit", *Difficult Freedom*, op. cit., p. 8.

45 See "The Paradox of Morality: an Interview with Emmanuel Levinas", in *The Provocation of Levinas*, op. cit., p. 168.

46 *The Provocation of Levinas*, op. cit., p. 169.

47 *The Provocation of Levinas*, op. cit., p. 171.

48 L. Irigaray, *L'Ethique de la différence sexuelle* (Paris, 1984), trans. as *An Ethics of Sexual Difference* by Carolyn Burke and Gillian Gill (Ithaca, NY: Cornell University Press, 1993). For a discussion of Levinas's conception of the feminine see Tina Chanter, *Ethics of Eros. Irigaray's Rewriting of the Philosophers* (London: Routledge, 1995), pp. 196–224.

11 JEAN-PAUL SARTRE: PASSIONATE DESCRIPTION

1 J.-P. Sartre, "Interview with Sartre", in Paul Arthur Schilpp, ed., *The Philosophy of Jean-Paul Sartre*, Library of Living Philosophers (La Salle, IL: Open Court, 1981), p. 12. Hereafter cited as Schilpp followed by the page number.

2 J.-P. Sartre, *L'Être et le néant. Essai d'ontologie phénoménologique* (Paris: Gallimard, 1943), p. 692, trans. Hazel E. Barnes, *Being and Nothingness. An Essay on Phenomenological Ontology* (London: Routledge, 1995), p. 628. Hereafter BN followed by English pagination and then pagination of French original.

3 J.-P. Sartre, *Critique de la raison dialectique* (Paris: Gallimard, 1960), trans. Alan Sheridan-Smith, *Critique of Dialectic Reason* (London: New Left Books, 1976). The second unfinished part has been published as *Critique de la raison dialectique. Tome 2. L'intelligibilité de l'histoire* (Paris: Gallimard, 1985), trans. *Critique of Dialectic Reason. Volume 2. Intelligibility of History* (London: Verso, 1991).

4 J.-P. Sartre, *Search for a Method*, trans. Hazel Barnes (New York: Vintage Books, 1968), p. 19.

5 See Sartre's interview with Leo Fretz, in Hugh Silverman and Frederick A. Elliston, eds, *Jean-Paul Sartre. Contemporary Approaches to His Philosophy* (Pittsburgh: Duquesne University Press, 1980), p. 226.

6 J.-P. Sartre, *Les Carnets de la drôle de guerre: Novembre 1939 – Mars 1940* (Paris: Gallimard, 1983), trans. Quintin Hoare, *The War Diaries* (London: Verso, 1984), p. 86. Hereafter *War Diaries* and page number of English translation.

7 Gregory McCulloch, *Using Sartre. An Analytical Introduction to Early Sartrean Themes* (London: Routledge, 1994), p. 3.

8 J.-P. Sartre, "La liberté cartésien", *Situations* I (Paris: Gallimard, 1947), pp. 289–308, trans. "Cartesian Freedom", in J.-P. Sartre, *Literary and Philosophical Essays* (London: Rider, 1955), p. 172.

9 Annie Cohen-Solal, *Sartre 1905–1980* (Paris: Gallimard, 1985), trans. Anna Cancogni, ed. Norman MacAfee, *Sartre. A Life* (New York: Pantheon Books, 1987), p. 92. Hereafter cited as Cohen-Solal, followed by pagination of the English translation.

10 J.-P. Sartre, "Une idée fondamentale de la phénoménologie de Husserl: l'intentionnalité", *Situations* I (Paris: Gallimard, 1947), p. 32, trans. Joseph P.

Fell, "Intentionality: A Fundamental Idea in Husserl's Philosophy", *Journal of the British Society for Phenomenology* 1(2) (May, 1970), p. 5. Hereafter *Intentionality* and pagination of the English followed by the French edition.

11 J.-P. Sartre, "La Transcendance de l'égo. Esquisse d'une déscription phénoménologique", *Recherches philosophiques* 6 (1936/7), pp. 85–123, reprinted as a separate book, *La Transcendance de l'égo* (Paris: Vrin, 1966), trans. Forrest Williams and Robert Kirkpatrick, *The Transcendence of the Ego* (New York: Farrar, Straus and Giroux, 1957; reprinted 1972). Hereafter TE followed by English page number and then French page number of the 1936 article. Here the reference is TE 35; 87.

12 Sartre, "La Légende de la vérité", reprinted in Michel Contat and Michel Rybalka, *Les Écrits de Sartre* (Paris: Gallimard, 1970), Appendix II, pp. 531–545.

13 See R. Wolin's introduction to Karl Löwith, *Martin Heidegger and European Nihilism* (New York: Columbia University Press, 1995), p. 13.

14 J.-P. Sartre, *Les mots* (Paris: Gallimard, 1964), trans. Irene Clephane, *Words* (Harmondsworth: Penguin, 1967), p. 14. Hereafter *Words* and page number of English translation.

15 S. de Beauvoir, *La Force de l'âge* (Paris: Gallimard, 1960), p. 27.

16 S. de Beauvoir, *La Force de l'âge*, op. cit., pp. 141–142.

17 Sartre, *L'Imagination* (Paris: Alcan, 1936), trans. Forrest Williams as *Imagination. A Psychological Critique* (Ann Arbor, MI: University of Michigan Press, 1962).

18 Sartre, *La Nausée* (Paris: Gallimard, 1938), trans. Robert Baldick, *Nausea* (Harmondsworth: Penguin, 1965). Hereafter *Nausea* and page number of the English translation.

19 Kate Fullbrook and Edward Fullbrook, *Simone de Beauvoir and Jean-Paul Sartre. The Remaking of a Twentieth-Century Legend* (London: Harvester, 1993), p. 53.

20 Reviews and reactions to *Nausea* are collected in Jacques Deguy, *Jacques Deguy commente La nausée de Jean-Paul Sartre* (Paris: Gallimard, 1993), pp. 204–209.

21 Ronald Hayman, *Writing Against. A Biography of Sartre* (London: Weidenfeld and Nicolson, 1986), p. 108.

22 See *Witness to my Life: The Letters of J.-P. Sartre to Simone de Beauvoir, 1926–1939*, ed. S. de Beauvoir, trans. L. Fahnestock and N. MacAfee (London: Hamish Hamilton, 1992), pp. 36–37.

23 J.-P. Sartre, *Esquisse d'une théorie des émotions* (Paris: Hermann, 1939), trans. Philip Mairet, *Sketch for a Theory of the Emotions* (London: Methuen, 1971). Hereafter *Sketch* and page number of English translation.

24 J.-P. Sartre, *L'Imaginaire* (Paris: Editions Gallimard, 1940), trans. Bernard Frechtman as *The Psychology of Imagination* (London: Methuen, 1972). Hereafter PI and page number of the English translation followed by the French original.

25 Sartre, *Les Mouches* (Paris: Gallimard, 1943), trans. Stuart Gilbert, *The Flies*, in J.-P. Sartre, *Altona, Men Without Shadows, The Flies* (Harmondsworth: Penguin, 1962).

26 J.-P. Sartre, *L'Existentialisme est un humanisme* (Paris: Nagel, 1946), trans. P. Mairet, *Existentialism and Humanism* (London: Methuen, 1973).

27 J.-P. Sartre, *Cahiers pour une morale* (Paris: Gallimard, 1983), trans. David Pellauer, *Notebooks for an Ethics* (Chicago: University of Chicago Press, 1992).

28 S. de Beauvoir, *The Ethics of Ambiguity*, trans. B. Frechtmann (New York: Citadel Press, 1948; reprinted 1970).

29 J.-P. Sartre, *Réflexions sur la question Juive* (Paris: Paul Morihien, 1946), trans.

George J. Becker, *Anti-Semite and Jew* (New York: Schocken Books, 1965). Hereafter *Anti-Semite* and page number of the English translation.

30 J.-P. Sartre, *Baudelaire* (Paris: Gallimard, 1947), trans. M. Turnell, *Baudelaire* (London: Hamish Hamilton, 1964).

31 J.-P. Sartre, *What is Literature?*, trans. Bernard Frechtman (London: Methuen, 1967).

32 J.-P. Sartre, *Saint Genet. Actor and Martyr*, trans. Bernard Frechtman (New York: Braziller, 1963).

33 See Peter Royle, *The Sartre-Camus Controversy. A Literary and Philosophical Critique* (Ottawa: University of Ottawa Press, 1982).

34 J.-P. Sartre, *Le Scenario Freud*, ed. J.-B. Pontalis (Paris: Gallimard, 1984), trans. Quintin Hoare, *The Freud Scenario* (London: Verso, 1985).

35 J.-P. Sartre, *Questions de méthode* (Paris: Gallimard, 1967), trans. Hazel Barnes, *Search for a Method*, op. cit.

36 As Sartre says in an interview with Leo Fretz, in Hugh Silverman and Frederick A. Elliston, eds, *Jean-Paul Sartre. Contemporary Approaches to His Philosophy*, op. cit., p. 225.

37 Sartre, *L'Idiot de la famille* (Paris Gallimard, 1971–2), trans. by Carol Cosman, *The Idiot of the Family. Gustave Flaubert* (Chicago: University of Chicago Press, Vol. 1, 1981; Vol. 2, 1987, Vol. 3, 1989).

38 See Ronald Hayman, *Writing Against. A Biography of Sartre*, op. cit., p. 6.

39 Daniel C. Dennett, *Consciousness Explained* (Harmondsworth: Penguin, 1993), makes much the same point about the nature of hallucinations and illusions. It is an essential feature of an illusion that it can be seen only from one side.

40 J.-P. Sartre, *Situations* IV (Paris: Gallimard, 1964), p. 196.

41 I owe this formulation to Phyllis Sutton Morris, "Sartre on Self-Deception", in Hugh Silverman and Frederick A. Elliston, eds, *Jean-Paul Sartre. Contemporary Approaches to His Philosophy*, op. cit., p. 35.

42 Simone de Beauvoir, *La Cérémonie des Adieux suivi de entretiens aven Jean-Paul Sartre* (Paris: Gallimard, 1981), trans. Patrick O'Brian, *Adieux. A Farewell to Sartre* (New York: Pantheon, 1984).

43 See Gregory McCulloch, *Using Sartre. An Analytical Introduction to Early Sartrean Themes*, op. cit., and Kathleen V. Wider, *The Bodily Nature of Consciousness. Sartre and Contemporary Philosophy of Mind* (Ithaca, NY: Cornell University Press, 1997).

12 MAURICE MERLEAU-PONTY:
THE PHENOMENOLOGY OF PERCEPTION

1 M. Merleau-Ponty, *Phénoménologie de la perception* (Paris: Gallimard, 1945), trans. C. Smith as *Phenomenology of Perception* (London: Routledge & Kegan Paul, 1962). Henceforth PP followed by page number of English translation then pagination of French edition.

2 Merleau-Ponty records the episode in his essay, "Un auteur scandaleux", *Sens et non-sens* (Paris: Nagel, 1966), p. 73, trans. as "A Scandalous Author", *Sense and Non-Sense* by Hubert Dreyfus and Patricia Allen Dreyfus (Evanston, IL: Northwestern University Press, 1964), p. 41. Henceforth SNS followed by page number of English translation; then page number of the French edition.

3 Simone de Beauvoir, *Memoirs of a Dutiful Daughter*, quoted in Jon Stewart, ed., *The Relation Between Sartre and Merleau-Ponty* (Evanston, IL: Northwestern University Press, 1998), p. xxx.

4 M. Merleau-Ponty, "The Philosophy of Existence", originally a radio broadcast in 1959, now in Jon Stewart, ed., *The Relation Between Sartre and Merleau-Ponty*, op. cit.

5 M. Merleau-Ponty, *The Primacy of Perception*, ed. James Edie (Evanston, IL: Northwestern University Press, 1964), p. 35. Hereafter *Primacy* and page number of English translation.

6 Conforming to a similarly traditional academic training, both Albert Camus and Hannah Arendt wrote dissertations on St Augustine.

7 Merleau-Ponty's review of Scheler was published as "Christianisme et ressentiment", *La Vie Intellectuelle* 7(36) (1935), pp. 278–306; his review of Marcel is published in *La Vie Intellectuelle* 8 (1936), pp. 98–109.

8 Alexandre Kojève, *Introduction to the Reading of Hegel. Lectures on the Phenomenology of Spirit*, assembled by Raymond Queneau, trans. James H. Nichols, Jr (Ithaca, NY: Cornell University Press, 1980).

9 See T. F. Geraets, *Vers une nouvelle philosophie transcendentale. La genèse de la philosophie de Merleau-Ponty jusqu'à la "Phénoménologie de la perception"* (The Hague: Nijhoff, 1971), appendix.

10 M. Merleau-Ponty, *La Structure du comportement* (Paris: PUF, 1942), trans. A. L. Fisher, *The Structure of Behavior* (Boston: Beacon Press, 1963). Hereafter SB and page number of English translation.

11 Both Hannah Arendt and Emmanuel Levinas will emphasise the manner in which being born is a form of conditioning into a ready-made world.

12 For a good discussion of this period, see David Archard, *Marxism and Existentialism. The Political Philosophy of Sartre and Merleau-Ponty* (Belfast: Blackstaff Press, 1980).

13 M. Merleau-Ponty, *Les Aventures de la dialectique* (Paris: Gallimard, 1955), trans. Joseph Bien, *Adventures of the Dialectic* (Evanston, IL: Northwestern University Press, 1973). For Simone de Beauvoir's response, see her "Merleau-Ponty and Pseudo-Sartreanism", reprinted in Jon Stewart, ed., *The Relation Between Sartre and Merleau-Ponty*, op. cit., pp. 448–491.

14 M. Merleau-Ponty, *Éloge de la philosophie* (Paris: Gallimard, 1953), trans. J. Wild and J. M. Edie, *In Praise of Philosophy* (Evanston, IL: Northwestern University Press, 1963), p. 4. Hereafter *Praise* and page number of English translation.

15 See Claude Lévi-Strauss, "On Merleau-Ponty", trans. C. Gross, *Graduate Faculty Philosophy Journal* 7(2) (1978), pp. 179–188.

16 M. Merleau-Ponty, *L'Oeil et l'esprit* (Paris: Gallimard, 1964), trans. Carleton Dallery, *Primacy* pp. 159–190.

17 M. Merleau-Ponty, *La Prose du monde, texte établi et présenté par Claude Lefort* (Paris: Gallimard, 1969), trans. J. O'Neill, *The Prose of the World* (Evanston, IL: Northwestern University Press, 1973). Hereafter *Prose* and page number of English translation, followed by page number of French original.

18 M. Merleau-Ponty, *Le Visible et l'invisible*, texte établi par Claude Lefort (Paris: Gallimard, 1964), trans. A. Lingis, *The Visible and the Invisible* (Evanston, IL: Northwestern University Press, 1968). Henceforth VI and page number of English translation followed by page number of French edition.

19 M. Merleau-Ponty, *Signes* (Paris: Gallimard, 1960), trans. R. McCleary, *Signs* (Evanston, IL: Northwestern University Press, 1964), p. 125. Hereafter *Signs* followed by English translation page number and then page number of French original.

20 Gabriel Marcel, *Journal métaphysique* (Paris: Gallimard, 1927), pp. 236–237, trans. Bernard Wall, *Metaphysical Journal* (Chicago: Regnery, 1952), pp. 242–243.

21 For Merleau-Ponty's 1947–1948 lectures on Bergson at the Ecole Normale, see

M. Merleau-Ponty, *L'Union de l'âme et du corps chez Malebranche, Biran et Bergson*, recueillies et redigées par Jean Deprun (Paris: Vrin, 1968), pp. 79–114.

22 Henri Bergson, *Matière et mémoire. Essay sur les relations du corps à l'esprit* (Paris, 1896), trans. Nancy Mar, *Matter and Memory* (London: G. Allen, 1913).

23 See Georges Gurvitch, *Les Tendences actuelles de la philosophie allemande* (Paris: Vrin, 1930).

24 M. Merleau-Ponty, "Husserl aux limites de la phénoménologie", *Annuaire du Collège de France* (Paris: Imprimerie Nationale, 1960), pp. 169–173, trans. John O'Neill, "Husserl at the Limits of Phenomenology", in M. Merleau-Ponty, *Themes from the Lectures at the Collège de France 1952–1960* (Evanston, IL: Northwestern University Press, 1970), pp. 113–123.

25 Husserl, *Crisis*, § 50, 172; Hua VI 175. See Herbert Spiegelberg with Karl Schuhmann, *The Phenomenological Movement. A Historical Introduction*, 3rd edition (Dordrecht: Kluwer, 1994), pp. 580–581 n. 2.

26 Jean Wahl, *Le Malheur de la conscience dans la philosophie de Hegel* (Paris: Editions Rieder, 1929).

27 M. Merleau-Ponty, "L'Existentialisme chez Hegel", *Les Temps modernes* No. 7 (April 1946), reprinted SNS 63–70; 109–122.

28 Aron Gurwitsch was born in Vilnius, Lithuania, and studied in Berlin with Carl Stumpf, who sent him to study with Husserl in Freiburg in 1922, before going to Frankfurt to study with the psychiatrist Kurt Goldstein who worked with war veterans with brain injuries. In 1929 Gurwitsch wrote his dissertation under Moritz Geiger, entitled "Phänomenologie der Thematik und des reinen Ich". As a Jew in Nazi Germany, he was refused permission to habilitate and left for France in 1933 where he lectured at the Sorbonne. In 1939 he left France for the USA.

29 E. Cassirer, *Philosophy of Symbolic Forms*, Vol. 3, *The Phenomenology of Knowledge*, trans. Ralph Manheim (New Haven, CT: Yale University Press, 1957). See especially Part Two Chapter Six, "Towards a Pathology of the Symbolic Consciousness", pp. 205–278. I would like to thank Rudolf Bernet for drawing my attention to Merleau-Ponty's dependence on Cassirer.

30 J.-P. Sartre, "Merleau-Ponty vivant", *Les Temps modernes* 17 nos. 184–185 (1961), trans. Benita Eisler, "Merleau-Ponty", in Jean-Paul Sartre, *Situations* (New York: Fawcett World Library, 1966), p. 217. Hereafter *Situations* and page number of English translation.

31 It is clear from passages such as this one in the *Structure of Behaviour* that Merleau-Ponty already held a notion of the face, similar to that which unfolded in Levinas's lectures of the 1940s.

32 But see Howard Gardner, *The Shattered Mind. The Person After Brain Damage* (London: Routledge & Kegan Paul, 1977), pp. 143–151, who recounts how two German neurologists, Richard Jung and Eberhard Bay, tracked down Schneider in the 1940s and discovered that he was completely normal, except when undergoing tests, when he appeared to revert to the symptoms earlier recorded by Gelb and Goldstein. Both Jung and Bay concluded that Schneider was unreliable and might indeed have been feigning the symptoms for Gelb and Goldstein.

33 M. Merleau-Ponty, "The Philosophy of Existence", originally a radio broadcast in 1959, now in Jon Stewart, ed., *The Relation Between Sartre and Merleau-Ponty*, op. cit., p. 495: "As Husserl said, through the perception we have of them, things are given to us in the flesh – carnally, *leibhaftig.*"

34 For a criticism of Merleau-Ponty's direct realism, see Aron Gurwitsch, *The Field of Consciousness* (Pittsburgh: Duquesne University Press, 1964), p. 299.

35 See Stephen Priest, *Merleau-Ponty* (London: Routledge, 1998), pp. 119–137.

36 C. Lévi-Strauss, *La Pensée sauvage* (Paris, 1962), trans. *The Savage Mind* (Chicago: University of Chicago Press, 1966). Lévi-Strauss dedicated *The Savage Mind* to the memory of Merleau-Ponty.

37 E. Levinas, "On Intersubjectivity: Notes on Merleau-Ponty", in *Outside the Subject*, op. cit., p. 98.

38 Merleau-Ponty is entirely absent from John Sturrock, ed., *Structuralism and Since. From Lévi-Strauss to Derrida* (Oxford: Oxford University Press, 1979) and from Peter Caws, *Structuralism. The Art of the Intelligible* (Atlantic Highlands, NJ: Humanities Press, 1988).

39 See James Schmidt, *Merleau-Ponty. Between Phenomenology and Structuralism* (London: Routledge, 1987).

40 Oliver Sacks, *The Man Who Mistook His Wife for a Hat* (London: Duckworth, 1985).

41 See A. J. Ayer's autobiography, *Part of My Life* (London: Collins, 1977), p. 285, for a positive assessment of Merleau-Ponty.

13 JACQUES DERRIDA: FROM PHENOMENOLOGY TO DECONSTRUCTION

1 For a discussion of this controversy, see Geoffrey Bennington and Jacques Derrida, *Derrida* (Chicago: University of Chicago, 1993).

2 J. Derrida, *Apories: Mourir – s'attendre aux limités de la vérité* (Paris: Galilée, 1996), trans. Thomas Dutoit, *Aporias* (Stanford, CA: Stanford University Press, 1993).

3 J. Derrida, *La Voix et le phénomène* (Paris: Presses Universitaires de France, 1967), p. 9, trans. David B. Allison, with additional essays, *Speech and Phenomena and other Essays on Husserl's Theory of Signs* (Evanston, IL: Northwestern University Press, 1973), p. 10. Hereafter SP and page number of translation; followed by page number of French original.

4 J. Derrida, *Le problème de la genèse dans la philosophie de Husserl* (Paris: PUF, 1990).

5 J. Derrida, *Le problème de la genèse dans la philosophie de Husserl*, op. cit., p. vii.

6 J. Derrida, "The Time of a Thesis: Punctuations", trans. K. McLaughlin, in Alan Montefiore, ed., *Philosophy in France Today* (Cambridge: Cambridge University Press, 1983), pp. 34–50.

7 John D. Caputo, ed., *Deconstruction in a Nutshell. A Conversation with Jacques Derrida* (New York: Fordham University Press, 1997), p. 26.

8 J. Derrida, *L'Origine de la géometrie de Edmund Husserl* (Paris: Epiméthée, 1962), trans. John P. Leavey Jr and D. B. Allison, *Origin of Geometry: An Introduction* (Brighton: Harvester, 1978). Hereafter OG and pagination of English translation.

9 I owe these details to Jacques Derrida, personal communication, during his visit to University College Dublin in February 1997.

10 See F. Rötzer, *Conversations with French Philosophers*, trans. Gary E. Aylesworth (Atlantic Highlands, NJ: Humanities Press, 1995), p. 45.

11 J. Derrida, *Positions* (Paris: Éditions de Minuit, 1972), trans. A. Bass, *Positions* (London: Athlone Press, 1981), p. 24. Hereafter *Pos.* and page number of English translation.

12 J. Derrida, *La Dissémination* (Paris: Editions du Seuil, 1972), trans. by Barbara Johnson as *Dissemination* (London: Athlone Press, 1981).

13 J. Derrida, *Marges de la philosophie* (Paris: Éditions de Minuit, 1972), trans. Alan Bass, *Margins of Philosophy* (Brighton: Harvester, 1982). Hereafter *Margins* and page number of translation, followed by pagination of French original.

14 For a summary review of Derrida's output, see Tim Mooney, "Derrida: Philosophical Roots and Bibliographical History", in R. Kearney, ed., *Continental Philosophy in the 20th Century* (London: Routledge, 1994), pp. 449–473. See also *Jacques Derrida. An Annotated Primary and Secondary Bibliography*, compiled by William Schultz and Lewis Fried (New York & London: Garland, 1992).

15 J. Derrida, *La Carte postale: de Socrate à Freud et au-delà* (Paris: Aubier-Flammarion, 1980), trans. Alan Bass, *The Postcard: From Socrates to Freud and Beyond* (Chicago: University of Chicago Press, 1987); see p. 18 for Plato's erection.

16 J. Derrida, *Glas* (Paris: Éditions Galilée, 1974), trans. John P. Leavey Jr and Richard Rand, *Glas* (Lincoln, NE: University of Nebraska Press, 1986). Hereafter *Glas* followed by pagination in English and French. The word '*glas*' has several senses in French: it is an onomatopoeic noun for the 'glug glug' sound made in the throat; it is also the tolling sound of a bell in French, and hence the book's title could be translated 'knell'.

17 J. R. Searle, "Reiterating the Differences: A Reply to Derrida", *Glyph* I (1977), pp. 198–208.

18 See J. Derrida, *Limited Inc* (Baltimore, MD: Johns Hopkins University Press, 1977); hereafter *Limited Inc* and page number of English translation. See also R. Rorty, *Contingency, Irony and Solidarity* (Cambridge: Cambridge University Press, 1989), Chapter V.

19 For a good discussion of the Searle–Derrida–Austin debate, see Christopher Norris, *Derrida* (London: Fontana, 1987), pp. 172–193.

20 J. R. Searle, "The World Turned Upside Down", in Gary B. Madison, ed., *Working Through Derrida* (Evanston, IL: Northwestern University Press, 1993), p. 178.

21 J. Derrida, *L'Autre Cap; suivi de la démocratie ajournée* (Paris: Éditions de Minuit, 1991), trans. P. A. Brault and M. G. Naas, *The Other Heading: Reflections on Today's Europe* (Bloomington, IN: Indiana University Press, 1992).

22 See J. Derrida, *Du droit à la philosophie* (Paris: Galilée, 1990), pp. 146–153.

23 J. Derrida, "The Politics of Friendship", *The Journal of Philosophy* 85 (1988), pp. 632–644. See also *Politiques de l'amitié* (Paris: Galilée, 1994), trans. George Collins, *The Politics of Friendship* (London: Verso, 1997), based on seminars first given in 1988–1989. This text opens with a paradoxical statement attributed to Aristotle by Diogenes Laertius, "O my friends, there is no friend".

24 C. Schmitt, *Der Begriff des Politischen* (Berlin: Duncker und Humblot, 1932; reprinted 1974), trans. George Schwab, *The Concept of the Political* (New Brunswick, NJ: Rutgers University Press, 1976).

25 J. Derrida, *De l'esprit. Heidegger et la question* (Paris: Galilée, 1987), trans. G. Bennington and Rachel Bowlby, *Of Spirit: Heidegger and the Question* (Chicago: University of Chicago Press, 1990).

26 For de Man's controversial essays, see Paul de Man, *Wartime Journalism, 1939–43* (Lincoln, NE: University of Nebraska Press, 1988). See J. Derrida's essay, "Like the Sound of the Sea Deep within a Shell: Paul de Man's War", in W. Hamacher *et al.*, *Responses: On Paul de Man's Wartime Journalism* (Lincoln, NE: University of Nebraska Press, 1989).

27 J. Derrida, *Mémoires: pour Paul de Man* (Paris: Éditions Galilée, 1988), trans. C. Lindsay *et al.*, *Memoires for Paul de Man* (New York: Columbia University Press, 1986).

28 J. Derrida, *Spectres de Marx* (Paris: Éditions Galilée, 1993), trans. by Peggy Kamuf as *Specters of Marx: The State of the Debt, the Work of Mourning and the New International* (London: Routledge, 1994).

29 R. Kearney, *Dialogues with Contemporary Continental Thinkers* (Manchester: Manchester University Press, 1984), p. 109. Hereafter '*Dialogues*' and page number.

30 J. Derrida, "Hospitality, Justice and Responsibility", in R. Kearney and M. Dooley, eds, *Questioning Ethics. Contemporary Debates in Philosophy* (London: Routledge, 1998), p. 81.

31 J. Derrida, *L'Écriture et la différence* (Paris: Éditions du Seuil, 1967), trans. Alan Bass, *Writing and Difference* (London: Routledge & Kegan Paul, 1978). Hereafter WD and page no. of translation.

32 Richard Rorty, "Two Meanings of 'Logocentrism' ", *Essays on Heidegger and Others*, Philosophical Papers, Vol. 2 (Cambridge: Cambridge University Press, 1991), p. 111.

33 J. Derrida, "Letter to a Japanese Friend", in Peggy Kamuf, ed., *A Derrida Reader. Between the Blinds* (London: Harvester Wheatsheaf, 1991), p. 271.

34 J. Derrida, "But beyond... (Open Letter to Anne McClintock and Rob Nixon)", *Critical Inquiry* 12 (Autumn, 1986), p. 167.

35 See Derrida's seminar, "Hospitality, Justice and Responsibility", in R. Kearney and M. Dooley, eds, *Questioning Ethics*, op. cit., pp. 65–83, esp. p. 74.

36 Florian Rötzer, *Conversations with French Philosophers*, op. cit., p. 55.

37 Richard Rorty, "Is Derrida a Transcendental Philosopher?", *Essays on Heidegger and Others*, op. cit., p. 125.

38 J. Derrida, "But beyond... (Open Letter to Anne McClintock and Rob Nixon)", *Critical Inquiry* 12 (Autumn, 1986), p. 167.

39 Derrida, "Hospitality, Justice and Responsibility", in Kearney and Dooley, eds, *Questioning Ethics*, op. cit., p. 81.

40 Derrida, "Hospitality, Justice and Responsibility", *Questioning Ethics*, op. cit., p. 81.

41 The most notable criticisms are by J. Claude Evans, *Strategies of Deconstruction. Derrida and the Myth of the Voice* (Minneapolis: University of Minnesota Press, 1991).

42 Ferdinand de Saussure, *Cours de linguistique générale* (1916, 3rd edition, Paris: Payot, 1931), trans. Wade Baskin, *Course in General Linguistics* (London: Fontana, 1974).

43 P. Ricoeur, *Husserl. An Analysis of His Phenomenology* (Evanston, IL: Northwestern University Press, 1967), pp. 4–6.

44 John Searle, "The World Turned Upside Down", in Madison, ed., *Working Through Derrida*, op. cit., pp. 170–188.

45 Derrida: "The notion of 'differance'...is a non-concept in that it cannot be defined in terms of oppositional predicates, it is neither *this* nor *that*; but rather this *and* that (e.g. the act of differing and of deferring) without being reducible to a dialectical logic either" (*Dialogues*, p. 110).

46 M. Heidegger, *Identität und Differenz* (Pfullingen: Neske, 1957).

47 J. Habermas, *The Philosophical Discourse of Modernity*, trans. Frederick Lawrence (Cambridge: Polity Press, 1987), p. 165.

48 J. Habermas, *The Philosophical Discourse of Modernity*, op. cit., p. 193.

49 J. Derrida, *D'un ton apocalyptique adopté naguère en philosophie* (Paris: Galilée, 1983).

50 See, especially, Paul de Man, *Blindness and Insight. Essays in the Rhetoric of Contemporary Criticism* (New York: Oxford University Press, 1971).

51 David Wood and Robert Bernasconi, eds, *Derrida and Différance* (Warwick: Parousia Press, 1985), p. 93.

BIBLIOGRAPHY

General

Adorno, Theodor. *Musikalische Schriften* VI, *Gesammelte Schriften* Band 19. Frankfurt: Suhrkamp, 1984.

Ariew, R. and D. Garber. Eds. *G.W. Leibniz. Philosophical Essays*. Indianapolis: Hackett, 1989.

Ayer, A. J. *Part of My Life*. London: Collins, 1977.

Barnes, Jonathan. *The Toils of Scepticism*. Cambridge: Cambridge University Press, 1990.

Bergson, Henri. *Matière et mémoire. Essay sur les relations du corps à l'esprit*. Paris, 1896.

Bergson, Henri. *Matter and Memory*. Trans. Nancy Mar. London: G. Allen, 1913.

Blumenberg, Hans. *The Legitimacy of the Modern Age*. Trans. Robert M. Wallace. Cambridge, MA: MIT Press, 1985.

Bolzano, B. *Paradoxes of the Infinite*. Trans. Donald A. Steele. London: Routledge & Kegan Paul, 1950.

Bolzano, B. *Theory of Science*. Ed. and Trans. Rolf George. Oxford: Blackwell, 1972.

Bolzano, B. *Wissenschaftslehre. Gesamtausgabe*, Reihe I, Band 11–13. Hrsg. von Jan Berg. Stuttgart, 1985–1992.

Carr, David. "Phenomenology and Fiction in Dennett", *International Journal of Philosophical Studies* 6(3) (October, 1998), pp. 331–344.

Cassirer, E. *Philosophy of Symbolic Forms*, Vol. 3, *The Phenomenology of Knowledge*. Trans. Ralph Manheim. New Haven, CT: Yale University Press, 1957.

Caws, Peter. *Structuralism. The Art of the Intelligible*. Atlantic Highlands, NJ: Humanities Press, 1988.

Chanter, Tina. *Ethics of Eros. Irigaray's Rewriting of the Philosophers*. London: Routledge, 1995.

Chisholm, Roderick. M. *Perceiving: A Philosophical Study*. Ithaca, NY: Cornell University Press, 1957.

Cleary, John J. and W. Wians. Eds. *Proceedings of the Boston Area Colloquium in Ancient Philosophy Volume IX, 1993*. New York: University Press of America, 1995.

Copi, Irving. *Introduction to Logic*, 7th Edition. New York: Macmillan, 1986.

Craig, Edward. Ed. *The Routledge Encyclopedia of Philosophy*, 10 vols. London: Routledge, 1998.

Danzinger, K. "The History of Introspection Reconsidered", *Journal of the History of the Behavioral Sciences* 16 (1980), pp. 241–262.

de Beauvoir, Simone. *Le Deuxième Sexe*. Paris: Gallimard, 1949.

de Beauvoir, Simone. *La Force de l'âge*. Paris: Gallimard, 1960.

de Beauvoir, Simone. *The Ethics of Ambiguity*. Trans. B. Frechtmann. New York: Citadel Press, 1948. Reprinted 1970.

de Beauvoir, Simone. *The Second Sex*. Trans. H. M. Parshley. London: Picador, 1988.

de Man, Paul. *Blindness and Insight. Essays in the Rhetoric of Contemporary Criticism*. New York: Oxford University Press, 1971.

de Man, Paul. *Wartime Journalism, 1939–43*. Lincoln, NE: University of Nebraska Press, 1988.

de Saussure, Ferdinand. *Cours de linguistique générale*. Paris: Payot, 1931.

Dennett, Daniel C. *The Intentional Stance*. Cambridge, MA: MIT Press, 1987.

Dennett, Daniel C. *Consciousness Explained*. London: Penguin, 1993.

Dilthey, Wilhelm. *Hermeneutics and the Study of History*. Selected Works IV. Ed. Rudolf Makkreel and Fritjhof Rodi. Princeton, NJ: Princeton University Press, 1996.

Embree, Lester. Ed. *Encyclopedia of Phenomenology*. Kluwer: Dordrecht, 1997.

Fechner, G. T. *Elements of Psychophysics*. 1860.

Findlay, J. N. *Meinong's Theory of Objects and Values*. Oxford: Clarendon, 1963.

Frege, Gottlob. *Foundations of Arithmetic*. Trans. J. L. Austin. Oxford: Blackwell, 1953.

Frege, Gottlob. *Kleine Schriften*. Ed. I. Angelelli. Hildesheim: Georg Olms, 1967.

Gardner, Howard. *The Shattered Mind. The Person After Brain Damage*. London: Routledge & Kegan Paul, 1977.

Glendinning, Simon. Ed. *Edinburgh Encyclopedia of Continental Philosophy*. Edinburgh: Edinburgh University Press, 1998.

Gödeckemeyer, Albert. *Geschichte der grieschen Skeptizismus*. 1905.

Grossmann, Reinhardt. *Meinong*. London: Routledge, 1974.

Grossmann, Reinhardt. *Phenomenology and Existentialism. An Introduction*. London: Routledge & Kegan Paul, 1984.

Gurvitch, Georges. *Les Tendences actuelles de la philosophie allemande*. Paris: Vrin, 1930.

Gurwitsch, Aron. *The Field of Consciousness*. Pittsburgh: Duquesne University Press, 1964.

Gurwitsch, Aron. *Studies in Phenomenology and Psychology*. Evanston, IL: Northwestern University Press, 1966.

Habermas, Jürgen. *Philosophical-Political Profiles*. Trans. F. G. Lawrence. Cambridge, MA: MIT Press, 1983.

Habermas, Jürgen. *The Philosophical Discourse of Modernity*. Trans. F. Lawrence. Cambridge: Polity Press, 1987.

Haller, Rudolf. Ed. *Jenseits von Sein und Nichtsein*. Graz: Academische Druck- und Verlagsanstalt, 1972.

Hamacher, W. *et al.* Eds. *Responses: On Paul de Man's Wartime Journalism*. Lincoln, NE: University of Nebraska Press, 1989.

Heinemann, Fritz. "Goethe's Phenomenological Method", *Philosophy* IX (1934), pp. 67–81.

Höfler, A. and A. Meinong. *Philosophische Propädeutik*, I, *Logik*. Leipzig, 1890.

Irigary, L. *L'Ethique de la différence sexuelle*. Paris: Editions de Minuit, 1984.

Irigary, L. *An Ethics of Sexual Difference*. Trans. Carolyn Burke and Gillian Gill. Ithaca, NY: Cornell University Press, 1993.

Jacquette, Dale. *Meinongian Logic: The Semantics of Existence and Non-Existence*. Berlin: De Gruyter, 1996.

James, William. *Principles of Psychology*, 2 vols, 1890. Reprinted Cambridge, MA: Harvard University Press, 1983.

Jaspers, Karl. *Die Schuldfrage*. Heidelberg, 1946.

Jaspers, Karl. *The Question of German Guilt*. Trans. E. B. Ashton. New York: Dial Press, 1947.

Jaspers, Karl. *Rechenhalt und Ausblick. Reden und Aufsätze*. Munich: Piper, 1958.

Jaspers, Karl. *Philosophische Autobiographie*. Munich, 1977.

Johanbegloo, Ramin. *Conversations with Isaiah Berlin*. London: Peter Halban, 1992.

Jonas, Hans. "Philosophy at the End of the Century: A Survey of its Past and Future", *Social Research* 61(4) (Winter, 1994).

Kalsi, Marie-Luise Schubert. *Meinong's Theory of Knowledge*. Dordrecht: Nijhoff, 1987.

Kearney, Richard. *Dialogues with Contemporary Continental Thinkers*. Manchester: Manchester University Press, 1984.

Kearney, Richard. *Modern Movements in European Philosophy*. Manchester: Manchester University Press, 1986.

Kearney, Richard. Ed. *Continental Philosophy in the Twentieth Century*. London: Routledge, 1994.

Kearney, R. and M. Dooley. Eds. *Questioning Ethics. Contemporary Debates in Philosophy*. London: Routledge, 1998.

Kojève, Alexandre. *Introduction to the Reading of Hegel. Lectures on the Phenomenology of Spirit*. Assembled by Raymond Queneau. Trans. James H. Nichols, Jr. Ithaca, NY: Cornell University Press, 1980.

Koyré, Alexandre. *From the Closed World to the Infinite Universe*. Baltimore, MD: Johns Hopkins University Press, 1957.

Kusch, Martin. *Psychologism. A Case Study in the Sociology of Philosophical Knowledge*. London: Routledge, 1995.

Lesniewski, S. *Collected Works*, 2 vols. Dordrecht: Kluwer, 1992.

Lévi-Strauss, C. *La Pensée sauvage*. Paris, 1962.

Lévi-Strauss, C. *The Savage Mind*. Chicago: University of Chicago Press, 1966.

Lyons, William. *The Disappearance of Introspection*. Cambridge, MA: MIT Press, 1986.

Mach, Ernst. *Die Mechanik in ihrer Entwicklung historisch-kritisch dargestellt*. Prague, 1883.

Mach, Ernst. *Die Analyse der Empfindungen*. 1906.

Mach, Ernst. *The Analysis of Sensations*. Trans. C. M. Williams and S. Waterlow. Chicago, 1914.

Mach, Ernst. *The Science of Mechanics*. Trans. T. J. McCormack. La Salle, IL: Open Court, 1960.

Marcel, Gabriel. *Journal métaphysique*. Paris: Gallimard, 1927.

Marcel, Gabriel. *Metaphysical Journal*. Trans. Bernard Wall. Chicago: Regnery, 1952.

Meinong, Alexius. *On Assumptions*. Trans. James Heanue. Berkeley, CA: University of California Press, 1983.

Mill, J. S. *A System of Logic, Ratiocinative and Inductive, Being a Connected View of the Principles of Evidence, and the Methods of Scientific Investigation*. London: Parker, 1843.

Mill, J. S. *The Later Letters of John Stuart Mill 1849–1873*. Ed. F. E. Mineka and D. N. Lindley, J. S. Mill, Collected Works Vol. XVII. Toronto and London: University of Toronto Press, 1972.

Mortley, Raoul. *French Philosophers in Conversation*. London: Routledge, 1991.

Moser, Paul K. and J. D. Trout. Eds. *Contemporary Materialism. A Reader*. London: Routledge, 1995.

Novák, Josef. Ed. *On Masaryk*. Amsterdam: Rodopi, 1988. pp. 27–38.

Peirce, Charles Sanders. *Collected Papers*. Ed. C. Hartshorne and Paul Weiss. Cambridge, MA: Harvard University Press, 1931–1935.

Pfänder, A. *Phenomenology of Willing and Other Phaenomenologica*. Trans. Herbert Spiegelberg. Evanston, IL: Northwestern University Press, 1967.

Quine, W. V. *Ontological Relativity and Other Essays*. New York: Columbia University Press, 1969.

Reinach, Adolf. "Concerning Phenomenology", trans. Dallas Willard. *The Personalist* 50 (1969), pp. 194–221.

Rich, Adrienne. *On Lies, Secrets and Silence*. New York: Norton, 1979.

Richter, Raoul. *Der Skeptizimus in der Philosophie*, Vol. I. Leipzig, 1904.

Ritter, J. Ed. *Historisches Wörterbuch der Philosophie*. Darmstadt: Wissenschaftliche Buchgesellschaft, 1974– .

Rötzer, F. *Conversations with French Philosophers*. Trans. G. E. Aylesworth. Atlantic Highlands, NJ: Humanities Press, 1995.

Russell, B. *The Principles of Mathematics*. London: Allen & Unwin, reprinted 1956.

Sacks, Oliver. *The Man Who Mistook His Wife for a Hat*. London: Duckworth, 1985.

Sajama, Seppo and Matti Kamppinen. *A Historical Introduction to Phenomenology*. London and New York: Croom Helm, 1987.

Schilpp, Paul Arthur. Ed. *The Philosophy of Karl Jaspers*. New York: Tudor Books, 1957.

Schleiermacher, F. D. E. *Hermeneutics: The Handwritten Manuscripts*. Trans. J. Duke and J. Forstman. Atlanta, GA: Scholar's Press, 1977.

Schmitt, C. *Der Begriff des Politischen*. Berlin: Duncker und Humblot, 1932. Reprinted 1974.

Schmitt, C. *The Concept of the Political*. Trans. George Schwab. New Brunswick, NJ: Rutgers University Press, 1976.

Searle, John R. *Intentionality*. Cambridge: Cambridge University Press, 1983.

Searle, John R. *The Construction of Social Reality*. London: Allen Lane, 1995.

Searle, John R. *The Rediscovery of the Mind*. Cambridge, MA: MIT Press, 1992.

Solomon, Robert. Ed. *Phenomenology and Existentialism*. New York: Harper and Row, 1972.

Spengler, O. *Der Untergang des Abendlandes*, 2 vols (1918, 1922). Reprinted Munich: Beck, 1927.

Spengler, O. *The Decline of the West*, 2 vols. Trans. C. F. Atkinson. New York: Knopf, 1947.

Spiegelberg, Herbert. *The Context of the Phenomenological Movement*. The Hague: Nijhoff, 1981.

Spiegelberg, Herbert, with Karl Schuhmann. *The Phenomenological Movement. A Historical Introduction*, 3rd edition. Dordrecht: Kluwer, 1994.

St Augustine, *On Christian Doctrine*. Trans. D. W. Robertson, Jr. Indianapolis: Bobbs-Merrill, 1958.

Stein, Edith. *On the Problem of Empathy*. Trans. Waltraut Stein. *Collected Works of Edith Stein*, Vol. 3. Washington, DC: ICS Publications, 1989.

Straus, Erwin W. Ed. *Phenomenology: Pure and Applied*. Pittsburgh: Duquesne University Press, 1964.

Stumpf, Carl. *Über den psychologischen Ursprung der Raumvorstellung*. Leipzig, 1873.

Stumpf, Carl. *Tonpsychologie*, 2 vols. Leipzig: Hirzel, 1883/1890.

Thévenaz, Pierre. *What is Phenomenology?*. Trans. J. M. Edie. Chicago: Quadrangle Books, 1966.

Trendelenburg, Adolf. *Geschichte der Kategorienlehre*. Berlin, 1846. Reprinted Hildesheim: Olms, 1963.

Twardowski, Kazimir. *Zur Lehre vom Inhalt und Gegenstand der Vorstellungen. Eine psychologische Untersuchung*. Vienna, 1894.

Twardowski, Kazimir. *On the Content and Object of Presentations. A Psychological Investigation*. Trans. R. Grossmann. The Hague: Nijhoff, 1977.

Tylor, E. B. *Primitive Culture*. 1871.

Tymieniecka, A.-T. Ed. *Ingardiana*. Analecta Husserliana IV. Dordrecht: Reidel, 1976.

Wahl, Jean. *Le Malheur de la conscience dans la philosophie de Hegel*. Paris: Editions Rieder, 1929.

Waldenfels, Bernhard. *Phänomenologie in Frankreich*. Frankfurt: Suhrkamp, 1983.

Waldenfels, Bernhard. *Einführung in die Phänomenologie*. Munich: Wilhelm Fink, 1992.

Wundt, W. "Selbstbeobachtung und innere Wahrnehmung", *Philosophische Studien* 4 (1888), pp. 292–309.

Wundt, W. *Principles of Physiological Psychology*. Translated from the 5th edition by E. B. Titchener. London: Sonnenshein, 1902.

Zaner, Richard. M. *The Way of Phenomenology: Criticism as a Philosophical Discipline*. New York: Pegasus, 1970.

Zaner, Richard M. and Don Ihde. Eds. *Phenomenology and Existentialism*. New York: Putnam's Sons, 1973.

Franz Brentano

Primary sources

Brentano, Franz. *Aenigmatias. Rätsel*. 1878. Reprinted Berne: A. Francke Verlag, 1962.

Brentano, Franz. *Aristoteles und seine Weltanschauung*. 1911. Reprinted Hamburg: Meiner, 1977.

Brentano, Franz. *Deskriptive Psychologie*. Ed. R. Chisholm and W. Baumgartner. Hamburg: Meiner, 1982.

Brentano, Franz. *Die Abkehr vom Nichtrealen*. Hrsg. F. Mayer-Hillebrand. Berne, 1952. Reprinted Hamburg: Meiner, 1977.

Brentano, Franz. *Die Lehre vom richtigen Urteil*. Berne: A. Francke Verlag, 1956.

Brentano, Franz. *Die Psychologie des Aristoteles insbesondere seine Lehre vom Nous*

Poietikos. Mainz, 1867. Reprinted Darmstadt: Wissenschaftliche Buchgesellschaft, 1967.

Brentano, Franz. *Die vier Phasen der Philosophie und ihr augenblicklicher Status.* Leipzig: Meiner, 1926. Reprinted Hamburg: Meiner, 1968.

Brentano, Franz. *Geschichte der Philosophie der Neuzeit.* Ed. Klaus Hedwig. Hamburg: Meiner, 1987.

Brentano, Franz. *Kategorienlehre.* Ed. A. Kastil. Leipzig: Meiner, 1933. Reprinted Hamburg: Meiner, 1974.

Brentano, Franz. *Meine letzten Wünsche für Österreich.* Vienna, 1894.

Brentano, Franz. *Psychologie vom empirischen Standpunkt,* 3 vols. Hamburg: Meiner, 1973.

Brentano, Franz. *Über die Zukunft der Philosophie.* Hamburg: Meiner, 1968.

Brentano, Franz. *Untersuchungen zur Sinnespsychologie.* Ed. R. M. Chisholm and R. Fabian. Hamburg: Meiner, 1979.

Brentano, Franz. *Versuch über die Erkenntnis.* Hamburg: Meiner, 1970.

Brentano, Franz. *Vom Ursprung sittlicher Erkenntnis.* Leipzig, 1889.

Brentano, Franz. *Von der mannigfachen Bedeutung des Seienden nach Aristoteles.* Freiburg, 1862. Reprinted Darmstadt: Wissenschaftliche Buchgesellschaft, 1960.

Brentano, Franz. *Wahrheit und Evidenz.* Hrsg. Oskar Kraus. Leipzig: Meiner, 1930. Reprinted Hamburg: Meiner, 1974.

Brentano: primary sources in translation

Brentano, Franz. *Aristotle and His World View.* Ed. and Trans. R. George. Berkeley, CA: University of California Press, 1978.

Brentano, Franz. *Descriptive Psychology.* Trans. B. Müller. London: Routledge, 1995.

Brentano, Franz. *On the Existence of God: Lectures Given at the Universities of Würzburg and Vienna.* Trans. S. F. Krantz. Dordrecht: Nijhoff, 1987.

Brentano, Franz. *On the Several Senses of Being in Aristotle.* Trans. R. George. Berkeley, CA: University of California Press, 1975.

Brentano, Franz. *Philosophical Investigations of Time, Space and the Continuum.* Trans. Barry Smith. New York: Croom Helm, 1988.

Brentano, Franz. *Psychology from an Empirical Standpoint.* Trans. A. C. Rancurello, D. B. Terrell, and L. L. McAlister, 2nd edition. New Introduction by Peter Simons. London: Routledge, 1995.

Brentano, Franz. *Sensory and Noetic Consciousness, Psychology from an Empirical Standpoint III.* Trans. U. McAlister and M. Scattle. London: Routledge & Kegan Paul, 1981.

Brentano, Franz. *The Foundation and Construction of Ethics.* Trans. E. H. Schneewind. London: Routledge & Kegan Paul, 1973.

Brentano, Franz. "The Four Phases of Philosophy and its Present Condition", trans. Stephen Satris, *Philosophy Today* 43(1) (Spring, 1999), pp. 14–28.

Brentano, Franz. *The Origin of Our Knowledge of Right and Wrong.* Trans. R. M. Chisholm and E. H. Schneewind. London: Routledge & Kegan Paul, 1969.

Brentano, Franz. *The Psychology of Aristotle.* Trans. R. George. London: University of California Press, 1977.

Brentano, Franz. *The Theory of the Categories.* Trans. R. M. Chisholm and N. Guterman. The Hague: Nijhoff, 1981.

Brentano, Franz. *The True and the Evident*. Trans. R. Chisholm. London: Routledge & Kegan Paul, 1966.

Brentano: further reading

Albertazzi, Liliana, Massimo Libardi, and Roberto Poli. Eds. *The School of Franz Brentano*. Dordrecht: Kluwer, 1996.

Baumgartner, W. and F.-P. Burkard. "Franz Brentano: Eine Skizze seines Lebens und seiner Werke", *International Bibliography of Austrian Philosophy*. Amsterdam: Rodopi, 1990.

Baumgartner, W. and P. M. Simons. "Brentano's Mereology", *Axiomathes* 5(1) (April, 1994), pp. 55–76.

Bergmann, Gustav. *Realism. A Critique of Brentano and Meinong*. Milwaukee, WI: University of Wisconsin Press, 1967.

Brentano, J. C. M. "The Manuscripts of Franz Brentano", *Revue Internationale de Philosophie* 20 (1966), pp. 477–482.

Campos, Eliam. *Die Kantkritik Brentanos*. Bonn: Bouvier Verlag Herbert Grundmann, 1979.

Chisholm, Roderick. M. *Brentano and Meinong Studies*. Amsterdam: Rodopi, 1982.

Chisholm, Roderick. M. *Brentano and Intrinsic Value*. Cambridge: Cambridge University Press, 1986.

Chisholm, Roderick. M. and R. Haller. Eds. *Die Philosophie Brentanos*. Amsterdam: Rodopi, 1978.

Gilson, Lucie. *La Psychologie descriptive selon Franz Brentano*. Paris: Vrin, 1955.

Gilson, Lucie. *Méthode et métaphysique selon Franz Brentano*. Paris: Vrin, 1955.

Kastil, A. *Die Philosophie Franz Brentanos*. Munich: Lehnen, 1951.

Körner, Stephan. "On Brentano's Objections to Kant's Theory of Knowledge", *Topoi* 6 (1987), pp. 11–19.

McAlister, Linda L. Ed. *The Philosophy of Franz Brentano*. London: Duckworth, 1976.

Moran, Dermot. "The Inaugural Address: Brentano's Thesis", *Proceedings of the Aristotelian Society* Supplementary Vol. LXX (1996), pp. 1–27.

Mulligan, K. Ed. *Mind, Meaning and Metaphysics*. Dordrecht: Kluwer, 1990. pp. 11–27.

Münch, Dieter. "Brentano and Comte", *Grazer Philosophische Studien* 35 (1989), pp. 33–54.

Poli, Roberto. Ed. *The Brentano Puzzle*. London: Ashgate, 1998.

Rollinger, Robin. "Husserl and Brentano on Imagination", *Archiv für Geschichte der Philosophie* 75 (1993), pp. 195–210.

Rollinger, Robin. *Husserl's Position in the School of Brentano*. Utrecht: Dept of Philosophy, Utrecht University, 1996.

Simons, Peter M. "Brentano's Reform of Logic", *Topoi* 6 (1987), pp. 25–38.

Smith, Barry. "The Substance of Brentano's Ontology", *Topoi* 6 (1987), pp. 39–49.

Smith, Barry. *Austrian Philosophy. The Legacy of Franz Brentano*. Chicago: Open Court, 1994.

Srzednicki, Jan. *Franz Brentano's Analysis of Truth*. The Hague: Nijhoff, 1965.

Stegmüller, Wolfgang. "The Philosophy of Self-Evidence: Franz Brentano", in *Main Currents in Contemporary German, British and American Philosophy*. Dordrecht: Reidel, 1969.

Edmund Husserl

Primary sources

Husserl, Edmund. *Gesammelte Werke*. Husserliana. Dordrecht: Kluwer, 1950.

——Volume I: Edmund Husserl, *Cartesianische Meditationen und Pariser Vorträge*. Hrsg. Stephan Strasser. 1991.

——Volume II: Edmund Husserl, *Die Idee der Phänomenologie. Fünf Vorlesungen*. Nachdruck der 2. erg. Auflage. Hrsg. W. Biemel. 1973.

——Volume III/1: Edmund Husserl, *Ideen zu einer reinen Phänomenologie und phänomenologischen Philosophie*. Erstes Buch: *Allgemeine Einführung in die reine Phänomenologie* 1. Halbband: *Text der 1–3. Auflage*. Hrsg. K. Schuhmann. 1977.

——Volume III/2: Edmund Husserl, *Ideen zu einer reinen Phänomenologie und phänomenologischen Philosophie*. Erstes Buch: *Allgemeine Einführung in die reine Phänomenologie*. 2. Halbband: *Ergänzende Texte (1912–1929)*. Hrsg. K. Schuhmann. 1977.

——Volume IV: Edmund Husserl, *Ideen zu einer reinen Phänomenologie und phänomenologischen Philosophie*. Zweites Buch: *Phänomenologische Untersuchungen zur Konstitution*. Hrsg. Marly Biemel. 1991.

——Volume V: Edmund Husserl, *Ideen zu einer reinen Phänomenologie und phänomenologischen Philosophie*. Drittes Buch: *Die Phänomenologie und die Fundamente der Wissenschaften*. Hrsg. Marly Biemel. 1971.

——Volume VI: Edmund Husserl, *Die Krisis der europäischen Wissenschaften und die transzendentale Phänomenologie. Eine Einleitung in die phänomenologische Philosophie*. Hrsg. W. Biemel. The Hague: Nijhoff, 1962. Reprinted 1976.

——Volume VII: Edmund Husserl, *Erste Philosophie (1923/24)*. Erster Teil: *Kritische Ideengeschichte*. Hrsg. R. Boehm. 1965.

——Volume VIII: Edmund Husserl, *Erste Philosophie (1923/24)*. Zweiter Teil: *Theorie der phänomenologischen Reduktion*. Hrsg. R. Boehm. 1965.

——Volume IX: Edmund Husserl, *Phänomenologische Psychologie. Vorlesungen Sommersemester 1925*. Hrsg. W. Biemel. The Hague: Nijhoff, 1968.

——Volume X: Edmund Husserl, *Zur Phänomenologie des inneren Zeinbewußtseins (1893–1917)*. Hrsg. R. Boehm. The Hague: Nijhoff, 1966. Second Edition 1969.

——Volume XI: Edmund Husserl, *Analysen zur passiven Synthesis. Aus Vorlesungs- und Forschungsmanuskripten (1918–1926)*. Hrsg. M. Fleischer. 1988.

——Volume XII: Edmund Husserl, *Philosophie der Arithmetik. Mit ergänzenden Texten (1890–1901)*. Hrsg. L. Eley. The Hague: Nijhoff, 1970.

——Volume XIII: Edmund Husserl, *Zur Phänomenologie der Intersubjektivität. Texte aus dem Nachlaß. Erster Teil. 1905–1920*. Hrsg. I. Kern. 1973.

——Volume XIV: Edmund Husserl, *Zur Phänomenologie der Intersubjektivität. Texte aus dem Nachlaß. Zweiter Teil. 1921–1928*. Hrsg. I. Kern. 1973.

—— VolumeXV: Edmund Husserl, *Zur Phänomenologie der Intersubjektivität. Texte aus dem Nachlaß. Dritter Teil. 1929–1935*. Hrsg. I. Kern. 1973.

——Volume XVI: Edmund Husserl, *Ding und Raum. Vorlesungen 1907*. Hrsg. U. Claesges. The Hague: Nijhoff, 1973.

——Volume XVII: Edmund Husserl, *Formale und transzendentale Logik. Versuch einer Kritik der logischen Vernunft. Mit ergänzenden Texten*. Hrsg. Paul Janssen. 1974.

——Volume XVIII: Edmund Husserl, *Logische Untersuchungen*. Erster Band: *Prolegomena zur reinen Logik*. Text der 1. und der 2. Auflage. Hrsg. E. Holenstein. 1975.

——Volume XIX: Edmund Husserl, *Logische Untersuchungen*. Zweiter Band: *Untersuchungen zur Phänomenologie und Theorie der Erkenntnis*. In zwei Bänden. Hrsg. Ursula Panzer. 1984.

——Volume XXI: Edmund Husserl, *Studien zur Arithmetik und Geometrie. Texte aus dem Nachlaß (1886–1901)*. Hrsg. I. Strohmeyer. 1983.

——Volume XXII: Edmund Husserl, *Aufsätze und Rezensionen (1890–1910)*. Hrsg. B. Rang. 1979.

——Volume XXIII: Edmund Husserl, *Phantasie, Bildbewusstsein, Erinnerung. Zur Phänomenologie der anschaulichen Vergegenwärtigungen. Texte aus dem Nachlaß (1898–1925)*. Hrsg. Eduard Marbach. 1980.

——Volume XXIV: Edmund Husserl, *Einleitung in die Logik und Erkenntnistheorie. Vorlesungen 1906/07*. Hrsg. Ullrich Melle. Dordrecht: Kluwer, 1985.

——Volume XXV: Edmund Husserl, *Aufsätze und Vorträge 1911–1921*. Hrsg. H. R. Sepp, Thomas Nenon. Dordrecht: Kluwer, 1986.

——Volume XXVI: Edmund Husserl, *Vorlesungen über Bedeutungslehre. Sommersemester 1908*. Hrsg. Ursula Panzer. 1986.

——Volume XXVII: Edmund Husserl, *Aufsätze und Vorträge 1922–1937*. Hrsg. Thomas Nenon, H. R. Sepp. Dordrecht: Kluwer, 1989.

——Volume XXVIII: Edmund Husserl, *Vorlesungen über Ethik und Wertlehre (1908–1914)*. Hrsg. Ullrich Melle. Dordrecht: Kluwer, 1988.

——Volume XXIX: Edmund Husserl, *Die Krisis der europäischen Wissenschaften und die transzendentale Phänomenologie. Ergänzungsband. Texte aus dem Nachlaß 1934–1937*. Hrsg. Reinhold N. Smid. 1992.

——Volume XXX: Edmund Husserl, *Logik und allgemeine Wissenschaftstheorie. Vorlesungen 1917/18, mit ergänzenden Texten aus der ersten Fassung 1910/11*. Hrsg. Ursula Panzer. 1996

Husserl, Edmund. *Arbeit an den Phänomenen. Ausgewählte Schriften*. Hrsg. Bernhard Waldenfels. Frankfurt: Fischer, 1993.

Husserl, Edmund. *Briefwechsel*. Ed. Karl Schuhmann in collaboration with Elizabeth Schuhmann, 10 vols. Dordrecht: Kluwer, 1994.

Husserl, Edmund. *Gesammelte Schriften*. Hamburg: Meiner, 1996.

Husserl, Edmund. *Erfahrung und Urteil. Untersuchungen zur Genealogie der Logik*. Hrsg. Ludwig Landgrebe, Hamburg: Felix Meiner Verlag, 1999.

Husserl, Edmund. *Méditations cartésiennes: introduction à la phénoménologie*. Trans. G. Peiffer and E. Levinas. Paris: Almand Colin, 1931.

Husserl: primary sources in translation

Husserl, Edmund. *Cartesian Meditations*. Trans. D. Cairns. The Hague: Nijhoff, 1967.

Husserl, Edmund. *Early Writings in the Philosophy of Logic and Mathematics*. Trans. Dallas Willard. Collected Works V. Dordrecht: Kluwer, 1994.

Husserl, Edmund. *Experience and Judgment: Investigations in a Genealogy of Logic*. Rev. and Ed. L. Landgrebe. Trans. J. S. Churchill and K. Ameriks. Evanston, IL: Northwestern University Press, 1973.

Husserl, Edmund. "Fichte's Ideal of Humanity [Three Lectures]", trans. James G. Hart, *Husserl Studies* 12 (1995), pp. 111–133.

Husserl, Edmund. *Formal and Transcendental Logic.* Trans. D. Cairns. The Hague: Nijhoff, 1969.

Husserl, Edmund. *Husserl. Shorter Works.* Trans. and Ed. Frederick Elliston and Peter McCormick. Notre Dame, IN: University of Notre Dame Press, 1981. pp. 9–17.

Husserl, Edmund. *Ideas. A General Introduction to Pure Phenomenology.* Trans. W. R. Boyce Gibson. London: Allen and Unwin, 1931.

Husserl, Edmund. *Ideas pertaining to a Pure Phenomenology and to a Phenomenological Philosophy, First Book.* Trans. F. Kersten. Dordrecht: Kluwer, 1983.

Husserl, Edmund. *Ideas pertaining to a Pure Phenomenology and to a Phenomenological Philosophy, Second Book.* Trans. R. Rojcewicz and A. Schuwer. Dordrecht: Kluwer, 1989.

Husserl, Edmund. *Ideas pertaining to a Pure Phenomenology and to a Phenomenological Philosophy, Third Book.* Trans. Ted E. Klein and W. E. Pohl. Collected Works Vol. 1. The Hague: Nijhoff, 1980.

Husserl, Edmund. *Introduction to the Logical Investigations. Draft of a Preface to the Logical Investigations.* Ed. E. Fink. Trans. P. J. Bossert and C. H. Peters. The Hague, Nijhoff, 1975.

Husserl, Edmund. "Kant and the Idea of Transcendental Philosophy", trans. Ted E. Klein and William E. Pohl in *Southwestern Journal of Philosophy* 5 (Fall, 1974).

Husserl, Edmund. *Logical Investigations,* 2 vols. Trans. J. N. Findlay. New York: Humanities Press, 1970.

Husserl, Edmund. *On the Phenomenology of the Consciousness of Internal Time.* Trans. J. B. Brough. Dordrecht: Kluwer, 1990.

Husserl, Edmund. *Phenomenological Psychology. Lectures, Summer Semester 1925.* Trans. J. Scanlon. The Hague: Nijhoff, 1977.

Husserl, Edmund. *Philosophy as a Rigorous Science,* 1911, in Lauer, Quentin. *Edmund Husserl. Phenomenology and the Crisis of Philosophy.* New York: Harper and Row, 1964.

Husserl, Edmund. *Psychological and Transcendental Phenomenology and the Confrontation with Heidegger (1927–1931), The Encyclopaedia Britannica Article, The Amsterdam Lectures "Phenomenology and Anthropology" and Husserl's Marginal Notes in Being and Time, and Kant on the Problem of Metaphysics.* Trans. T. Sheehan and R. E. Palmer. Dordrecht: Kluwer, 1997.

Husserl, Edmund. "Syllabus of a Course of Four Lectures on 'Phenomenological Method and Phenomenological Philosophy', Delivered at University College, London, June 6, 8, 9, 12, 1922", *Journal of the British Society for Phenomenology* 1(1) (1970), pp. 18–23.

Husserl, Edmund. *The Crisis of European Sciences and Transcendental Phenomenology. An Introduction to Phenomenological Philosophy.* Trans. David Carr. Evanston, IL: Northwestern University Press, 1970.

Husserl, Edmund. *The Idea of Phenomenology.* Trans. W. P. Alston and G. Nakhnikian. The Hague: Nijhoff, 1964.

Husserl, Edmund. *The Paris Lectures.* Trans. P. Koestenaum. The Hague: Nijhoff, 1970.

Husserl, Edmund. *The Phenomenology of Internal Time Consciousness.* Ed. M. Heidegger. Trans. J. S. Churchill. London: Indiana University Press, 1964.

Husserl, Edmund. *Thing and Space: Lectures of 1907.* Trans. R. Rojcewicz. Collected Works VII. Dordrecht: Kluwer, 1997.

Husserl: further reading

Adorno, T. *Against Epistemology: A Metacritique*. Trans. Willis Domingo. Oxford: Blackwell, 1982.

Bell, David. *Husserl*. London: Routledge, 1991.

Bernet, Rudolf. *La Vie du sujet. Recherches sur l'interprétation de Husserl dans la phénoménologie*. Paris: PUF, 1994.

Bernet, Rudolf. "Edmund Husserl", in *The Blackwell Companion to Continental Philosophy*. Ed. Simon Critchley. Oxford: Blackwell, 1998.

Bernet, Rudolf, Iso Kern, and Eduard Marbach. *An Introduction to Husserlian Phenomenology*. Evanston, IL: Northwestern University Press, 1993.

Bossert, Philip J. *The Origins and Early Development of Edmund Husserl's Method of Phenomenological Reduction*, PhD thesis, Washington University, St Louis, 1973.

Cairns, Dorion. *Conversations with Husserl and Fink*, Phaenomenologica 66. The Hague: Nijhoff, 1975.

Cavallin, Jans. *Content and Object. Husserl, Twardowski, and Psychologism*. Dordrecht: Kluwer, 1997.

Chisholm, Roderick. Ed. *Realism and the Background of Phenomenology*. Atascadero, CA: Ridgeview, 1960.

Cho, Kah Kyung. "Phenomenology as Cooperative Task: Husserl-Farber Correspondence during 1936–37", *Philosophy and Phenomenological Research* 50, Supplement (Fall, 1990), pp. 27–43.

Cobb-Stevens, Richard. "The Beginnings of Phenomenology: Husserl and his Predecessors", in *Twentieth-Century Continental Philosophy. Routledge History of Philosophy*, Vol. VIII. Ed. R. Kearney. London: Routledge, 1994. pp. 5–37.

de Boer, Theodor. *The Development of Husserl's Thought*. The Hague: Nijhoff, 1978.

Dreyfus, Hubert. "*Sinn* and the Intentional Object", in *Phenomenology and Existentialism*. Ed. Robert Solomon. New York: Harper and Row, 1972.

Dreyfus, Hubert. Ed. *Husserl, Intentionality and Cognitive Science*. Cambridge, MA: MIT Press, 1982.

Elliston, F. and P. McCormick. Eds. *Husserl. Expositions and Appraisals*. Notre Dame, IN: University of Notre Dame Press, 1977.

Elveton, R. O. Ed. *The Phenomenology of Edmund Husserl. Selected Critical Readings*. Chicago: Quadrangle, 1970.

Farber, Marvin. *Philosophical Essays in Memory of Edmund Husserl*. Cambridge, MA: Harvard University Press, 1940.

Farber, Marvin. *The Foundation of Phenomenology*. Albany, NY: SUNY Press, 1943.

Frege, Gottlob. "Rezension von: E.G. Husserl, *Philosophie der Arithmetik I*", *Zeitschrift für Philosophie und philosophische Kritik* (1894), pp. 313–332.

Føllesdal, Dagfinn. "Husserl on Evidence and Justification", *Edmund Husserl and the Phénomenological Tradition* (1969), pp. 107–129.

Føllesdal, Dagfinn. "Husserl's Notion of Noema", *Journal of Philosophy* 66 (1969), pp. 680–687.

Føllesdal, Dagfinn. "Noema and Meaning in Husserl", *Philosophy and Phenomenological Research* 50, Supplement (Fall, 1990), pp. 263–271.

Haaparanta, Leila. Ed. *Mind, Meaning and Mathematics. Essays on the Philosophical Views of Husserl and Frege*. Dordrecht: Kluwer, 1994.

Harney, Maurita. *Intentionality, Sense and Mind*. The Hague: Nijhoff, 1984.

Hart, James G. *The Person and the Common Life. Studies in a Husserlian Social Ethics.* Dordrecht: Kluwer, 1992.

Hill, Claire Ortiz. *Word and Object in Husserl, Frege and Russell.* Athens, OH: Ohio University Press, 1991.

Hill, Claire Ortiz. "Frege's Attack on Husserl and Cantor", *The Monist* 77(3) (1994), pp. 345–357.

Hill, Claire Ortiz. "Husserl and Hilbert on Completeness", in *Essays on the Development of the Foundations of Mathematics.* Ed. J. Hintikka. Dordrecht: Kluwer, 1995. pp. 143–163.

Hill, Claire Ortiz. "Did George Cantor Influence Edmund Husserl", *Synthese* 113(1) (October, 1997), pp. 145–170.

Hill, Claire Ortiz. "Abstraction and Idealization in Edmund Husserl and Georg Cantor Prior to 1895", *Poznan Studies in the Philosophy of the Sciences and the Humanities* XX (1998), pp. 1–27.

Hopkins, Burt C. Ed. *Husserl in Contemporary Context.* Dordrecht: Kluwer, 1997.

Huertas-Jourda, José. *On the Threshold of Phenomenology: A Study of Edmund Husserl's Philosophie der Arithmetik.* New York University, February 1969.

Husserl, Malvine. *"Skizze eines Lebensbildes von Edmund Husserl".* Ed. Karl Schuhmann. *Husserl Studies* 5 (1988), pp. 105–125.

Ingarden, Roman. *On the Motives which led Husserl to Transcendental Idealism.* Dordrecht: Kluwer, 1975.

Janssen, Paul. *Edmund Husserl. Einführung in seine Phänomenologie.* Freiburg: Karl Alber, 1976.

Kolakowski, Leszek. *Husserl and the Search for Certitude.* New Haven, CT: Yale University Press, 1975.

Landgrebe, Ludwig. *The Phenomenology of Edmund Husserl. Six Essays.* Ed. D. Welton. Ithaca, NY: Cornell University Press, 1981.

Lapointe, François. *Edmund Husserl and His Critics. An International Bibliography (1894–1979).* Bowling Green, OH: Philosophy Documentation Center, 1980.

McKenna, William, R. M. Harlan, and L. E. Winters. Eds. *Apriori and World. European Contributions to Husserlian Phenomenology.* The Hague: Nijhoff, 1981.

McKenna, William. *Husserl's "Introductions" to Phenomenology. Interpretation and Critique.* Dordrecht: Kluwer, 1982.

Marbach, Eduard. *Das Problem des Ich in der Phänomenologie Husserls.* The Hague: Nijhoff, 1974.

Marion, Jean-Luc. *Réduction et donation. Recherches sur Husserl, Heidegger et la phénoménologie.* Paris: PUF, 1989.

Marx, Werner. *Die Phänomenologie Edmund Husserls. Eine Einführung.* Munich: Wilhelm Fink, 1987.

Miller, Izchak. *Husserl: Perception and Temporal Awareness.* Cambridge, MA: MIT Press, 1984.

Mohanty, J. N. *Edmund Husserl's Theory of Meaning.* The Hague: Nijhoff, 1976.

Mohanty, J. N. Ed. *Readings on Edmund Husserl's Logical Investigations.* The Hague: Nijhoff, 1977.

Mohanty, J. N. *Husserl and Frege.* Bloomington, IN: Indiana University Press, 1982.

Mohanty, J. N. and William R. McKenna. Eds. *Husserl's Phenomenology: A Textbook.* Washington, DC: Center for Advanced Research in Phenomenology & University Press of America, 1989.

Mulligan, K. Ed. *Speech Act and Sachverhalt. Reinach and the Foundations of Realist Phenomenology*. Dordrecht: Nijhoff, 1987.

Mulligan, K. "Husserl on States of Affairs in the *Logical Investigations*", *Epistemologia* XII (1989), Special Issue, pp. 207–234.

Mulligan, K. and B. Smith. "A Husserlian Theory of Indexicality", *Grazer Philosophische Studien* 28(1996), pp. 133–163.

Münsterberg, Hugo. *The Peace and America*. New York: Appleton, 1915.

Osborn, Andrew. *The Philosophy of Edmund Husserl in its Development from his Mathematical Interests to his First Conception of Phenomenology in the Logical Investigations*. New York: International Press, 1934.

Palmer, Richard. "Husserl's Debate with Heidegger in the Margin of *Kant and the Problem of Metaphysics*", *Man and World* 30 (1997), pp. 5–33.

Patočka, Jan. *An Introduction to Husserl's Phenomenology*. Trans. Erazim Kohák. La Salle, IL: Open Court, 1996.

Philipse, Herman. "The Concept of Intentionality: Husserl's Development from the Brentano Period to the *Logical Investigations*", *Philosophy Research Archives* XII (March, 1987), pp. 293–328.

Prechtl, Peter. *Husserl. Zur Einführung*. Hamburg: Junius, 1991.

Ricoeur, Paul. *Husserl. An Analysis of his Phenomenology*. Trans. Edward G. Ballard and Lester E. Embree. Evanston, IL: Northwestern University Press, 1967.

Schuhmann, Karl. *Husserl-Chronik. Denk- und Lebensweg Edmund Husserls*. The Hague: Nijhoff, 1977.

Schuhmann, Karl. "Husserl and Masaryk", in J. Novak, Ed. *On Masaryk*. Amsterdam: Rodopi, 1988. pp. 129–156.

Schuhmann, Karl. "Husserl's Yearbook", *Philosophy and Phenomenological Research* 50, Supplement (Fall, 1990), pp. 1–25.

Schuhmann, Karl. *Husserls Staatsphilosophie*. Freiburg/Munich: Alber, 1998.

Schuhmann, Karl and B. Smith. "Questions: An Essay in Daubertian Phenomenology", *Philosophy and Phenomenological Research* 47 (March, 1987), 353–384.

Seebohm, Thomas. "Psychologism Revisited", *Phenomenology and the Formal Sciences*. Ed. T. Seebohm, D. Føllesdal and J. N. Moriarty. Dordrecht: Kluwer, 1991. pp. 149–182.

Sepp, Hans Reiner. Ed. *Edmund Husserl und die phänomenologische Bewegung. Zeugnisse in Text und Bild*. Freiburg/München: Karl Alber Verlag, 1988.

Skousgaard, Stephen. Ed. *Phenomenology and the Understanding of Human Destiny*. Washington, DC: Center for Advanced Research in Phenomenology & University Press of America, 1981.

Smid, Reinhold. "An Early Interpretation of Husserl's Phenomenology: Johannes Daubert and the *Logical Investigations*", *Husserl Studies* 2 (1985), pp. 267–290.

Smith, Barry. Ed. *Parts and Moments: Studies in Logic and Formal Ontology*. Munich: Philosophia Verlag, 1982.

Smith, Barry and David Woodruff Smith. Eds. *The Cambridge Companion to Husserl*. Cambridge: Cambridge University Press, 1995.

Smith, David Woodruff and Ronald McIntyre. *Husserl and Intentionality. A Study of Mind, Meaning and Language*. Dordrecht: Reidel, 1982.

Sokolowski, Robert. *The Formation of Husserl's Concept of Constitution*. The Hague: Nijhoff, 1964.

Sokolowski, Robert. "The Husserl Archives and the Edition of Husserl's Works", *New Scholasticism* 38 (1964), pp. 473–482.

Sokolowski, Robert. "Intentional Analysis and the Noema", *Dialectica* 38(2–3) (1984), pp. 113–129.

Spiegelberg, Herbert. "Husserl in England: Facts and Lessons", *Journal of the British Society for Phenomenology* 1(1) (1970), pp. 4–17.

Ströker, Elizabeth. *The Husserlian Foundations of Science.* Ed. Lee Hardy. Washington, DC: Center for Advanced Research in Phenomenology & University Press of America, 1987.

Ströker, Elizabeth. *Husserl's Transcendental Phenomenology.* Stanford, CA: Stanford University Press, 1993.

Szilasi, W. *Einführung in die Phänomenologie Edmund Husserls.* Tübingen, 1959.

Taminiaux, J. "Heidegger and Husserl's *Logical Investigations*", in *Dialectic and Difference.* Atlantic Highlands, NJ: Humanities Press, 1985. pp. 91–114.

Van Breda, H. L. and J. Taminiaux. Eds. *Edmund Husserl 1859–1959. Recueil commémoratif publié à l'occasion du centenaire de la naissance du philosophe.* Phaenomenologica 4. The Hague: Nijhoff, 1959.

Van Breda, H. L. and J. Taminiaux. Eds. *Husserl et la pensée moderne.* Actes du deuxième Colloque International de Phénoménologie, Knefeld, 1–3 novembre 1956. The Hague: Nijhoff, 1959.

Welton, Donn. "Husserl and Frege", *The Journal of Philosophy* 69(10) (October, 1987).

Welton, Donn. Ed. *The Essential Husserl.* Bloomington, IN: Indiana University Press, 1999.

Wetz, Franz Josef. *Edmund Husserl.* Frankfurt/New York: Campus Verlag, 1995.

Martin Heidegger

Primary sources

Heidegger, Martin. *Gesamtausgabe.* Frankfurt am Main: Vittorio Klostermann, 1973–.

Heidegger, Martin. *Auf der Erfahrung des Denkens.* Pfullingen: Neske, 1954.

Heidegger, Martin. *Beiträge zur Philosophie (Vom Ereignis)*, GA 65. Hrsg. Freidrich-Wilhelm von Herrmann. Frankfurt: Klostermann, 1994.

Heidegger, Martin. *Der Begriff der Zeit.* Tübingen: Neimeyer, 1989.

Heidegger, Martin. *Der Ursprung des Kunstwerkes.* Stuttgart: Reclam, 1960.

Heidegger, Martin. *Die Grundbegriffe der Metaphysik. Welt–Endlichkeit–Einsamkeit*, GA 29/30. Hrsg. Friedrich-Wilhelm von Herrmann. Frankfurt: Klostermann, 1992.

Heidegger, Martin. *Die Grundprobleme der Phänomenologie*, GA 24. Hrsg. Friedrich-Wilhelm von Herrmann. Frankfurt: Klostermann, 1989.

Heidegger, Martin. *Einführung in die Metaphysik.* Tübingen: Max Niemeyer Verlag, 1953.

Heidegger, Martin. *Frühe Schriften*, GA 1. Hrsg. Friedrich-Wilhelm von Herrmann. Frankfurt: Klostermann, 1978.

Heidegger, Martin. *Holzwege.* Frankfurt: Klostermann, 1950.

Heidegger, Martin. *Identität und Differenz.* Pfullingen: Neske, 1957.

Heidegger, Martin. *Platon: Sophistes*, GA 19. Hrsg. Ingeborg Schüßler. Frankfurt, Klostermann, 1992.

Heidegger, Martin. *Prolegomena zur Geschichte des Zeitbegriffs*, GA 20. Hrsg. Petra Jaeger. Frankfurt: Klostermann, 1994.

Heidegger, Martin. *Unterwegs zur Sprache*. Pfullingen: Neske, 1959.

Heidegger, Martin. *Wegmarken*, GA 9. Hrsg. Friedrich-Wilhelm von Herrmann. Frankfurt: Klostermann, 1996.

Heidegger, Martin and Karl Jaspers. *Briefwechsel 1920–1926*. Hrsg. Walter Biemel and Hans Saner. Frankfurt: Klostermann, 1990.

Heidegger: primary sources in translation

Heidegger, Martin. *An Introduction to Metaphysics*. Trans. R. Manheim. New York: Doubleday, 1961.

Heidegger, Martin. *Aristotle's Metaphysics, 1–3*. Trans. W. Brogan and P. Warneck. Bloomington, IN: Indiana University Press, 1955.

Heidegger, Martin. *Basic Concepts*. Trans. G. E. Aylesworth. Bloomington, IN: Indiana University Press, 1993.

Heidegger, Martin. *Basic Questions in Philosophy*. Trans. R. Rojcewicz and A. Schuwer. Bloomington, IN: Indiana University Press, 1994.

Heidegger, Martin. *Basic Writings*. Ed. D. F. Krell. London: Routledge & Kegan Paul, 1978.

Heidegger, Martin. *Being and Time*. Trans. John Macquarrie and E. Robinson. New York: Harper and Row, 1962.

Heidegger, Martin. *Being and Time*. Trans. Joan Stambaugh. Albany, NY: SUNY Press, 1996.

Heidegger, Martin. *Discourse on Thinking*. Trans. J. M. Anderson and E. H. Freund. London: Harper and Row, 1969.

Heidegger, Martin. *Early Greek Thinking*. Trans. D. F. Krell and F. A. Capuzzi. London: Harper and Row, 1975.

Heidegger, Martin. *Existence and Being*. Introduction by W. Brock. London: Vision, 1968.

Heidegger, Martin. *German Existentialism*. Trans. D. D. Runes. New York: Wisdom Library, 1965.

Heidegger, Martin. *Hegel's Concept of Experience*. London: Harper and Row, 1970.

Heidegger, Martin (with Eugen Fink). *Heraclitus Seminar*. Trans. C. H. Seibert. Tuscaloosa, AL: University of Alabama Press, 1979.

Heidegger, Martin. *History of the Concept of Time: Prolegomena*. Trans. T. Kisiel. Bloomington, IN: Indiana University Press, 1985.

Heidegger, Martin. *Hölderlin's Hymn "The Ister"*. Trans. W. McNeill and J. Davis. Bloomington, IN: Indiana University Press, 1996.

Heidegger, Martin. *Kant and the Problem of Metaphysics*. Trans. J. S. Churchill. Bloomington, IN: Indiana University Press, 1962.

Heidegger, Martin. *Nietzsche*, 2 vols. Trans. D. F. Krell. San Francisco: Harper, 1991.

Heidegger, Martin. *Pathmarks*. Ed. William McNeill. Cambridge: Cambridge University Press, 1998, pp. 97–135.

Heidegger, Martin. *On the Way to Language*. Trans. P. D. Hertz. New York: Harper and Row, 1971.

Heidegger, Martin. *On Time and Being*. Trans J. Stambaugh. New York: Harper and Row, 1962.

Heidegger, Martin. *Parmenides*. Trans. A. Schuwer and R. Rojcewicz. Bloomington, IN: Indiana University Press, 1992.

Heidegger, Martin. *Phenomenological Interpretation of Kant's "Critique of Pure Reason"*. Trans. P. Emad and K. Maly. Bloomington, IN: Indiana University Press, 1997.

Heidegger, Martin. "Phenomenological Interpretations with Respect to Aristotle", trans. Michael Baur, *Man and World* 25 (1992), pp. 355–393.

Heidegger, Martin. *Plato's Sophist*. Trans. R. Rojcewicz and A. Schuwer. Bloomington, IN: Indiana University Press, 1997.

Heidegger, Martin. *Poetry, Language and Thought*. Trans. A. Hofstadter. New York: Harper and Row, 1975.

Heidegger, Martin. *The Basic Problems of Phenomenology*. Trans. A. Hofstadter. Bloomington, IN: Indiana University Press, 1982.

Heidegger, Martin. *The Concept of Time*. Trans. W. McNeill. Oxford: Blackwell, 1992.

Heidegger, Martin. *The End of Philosophy*. Trans. J. Stambaugh. London: Souvenir Press, 1975.

Heidegger, Martin. *The Fundamental Concepts of Metaphysics: World, Finitude, Solitude*. Trans. W. McNeill and N. Walker. Bloomington, IN: Indiana University Press, 1995.

Heidegger, Martin. *The Metaphysical Foundations of Logic*. Trans. M. Heim. Bloomington, IN: Indiana University Press, 1984.

Heidegger, Martin. *The Piety of Thinking: Essays*. Trans. J. G. Hart and J. C. Maraldo. Bloomington, IN: Indiana University Press, 1976.

Heidegger, Martin. *The Principle of Reason*. Trans. R. Lilly. Bloomington, IN: Indiana University Press, 1991.

Heidegger, Martin. *The Question Concerning Technology and Other Essays*. Trans. W. Lovitt. New York: Harper and Row, 1977.

Heidegger, Martin. "The Rectorate 1933/4: Facts and Thoughts", trans. K. Harries, *Review of Metaphysics* 38 (March, 1985), pp. 481–502.

Heidegger, Martin. *What is Philosophy?*. Trans. W. Kluback and J. T. Wilde. New York: Twayne, 1958.

Heidegger: further reading

Adorno, T. *The Jargon of Authenticity*. Trans. J. Tarnwoski and F. Will. Evanston, IL: Northwestern University Press, 1973.

Caputo, John. D. *Heidegger and Aquinas*. New York: Fordham University Press, 1982.

Courtine, Jean-François. *Heidegger et la phénoménologie*. Paris: Vrin, 1990.

Dreyfus, Hubert L. *Being-In-the-World. A Commentary on Heidegger's Being and Time, Division I*. Cambridge, MA: MIT Press, 1991.

Dreyfus, Hubert L. and Harrison Hall. Eds. *Heidegger: A Critical Reader*. Oxford: Blackwell, 1992.

Farias, Victor. *Heidegger et le nazisme*. Paris: Editions Verdier, 1987.

Farias, Victor. *Heidegger and Nazism*. Trans. J. Margolis and T. Rockmore. Philadelphia: Temple University Press, 1989.

Friedman, Michael. "Overcoming Metaphysics: Carnap and Heidegger", in *The Origins of Logical Empiricism, Minnesota Studies* XVI (1996), pp. 45–79.

Guignon, C. Ed. *The Cambridge Companion to Heidegger*. Cambridge: Cambridge University Press, 1993.

Habermas, J. "Martin Heidegger, On the Publication of the Lectures from 1935", in R. Wolin, ed., *The Heidegger Controversy. A Critical Reader*. Cambridge, MA: MIT Press, 1993. p. 191.

Harries, K. and C. Jamme. Eds. *Martin Heidegger. Politics, Art and Technology*. New York: Holmes and Meier, 1994.

Heidegger, Hermann. "Der Wirtschaftshistoriker und die Wahrheit. Notwendige Bemerkungen zu den Veröffentlichungen Hugo Otts über Martin Heidegger", *Heidegger Studies* 13 (1997), pp. 177–192.

Hemming, Laurence Paul. "Speaking Out of Turn: Heidegger and *die Kehre*", *International Journal of Philosophical Studies* 6(3) (October, 1998), pp. 331–344.

Kisiel, Theodore. *The Genesis of Heidegger's Being and Time*. Berkeley, CA: University of California Press, 1993.

Kisiel, Theodore. "Why Students of Heidegger Will Have to Read Emil Lask", in Deborah G. Chaffin, ed., *Emil Lask and the Search for Concreteness*. Athens, OH: Ohio University Press, 1993.

Kisiel, Theodore and John Van Buren. Eds. *Reading Heidegger from the Start: Essays in his Earliest Thought*. Albany, NY: SUNY Press, 1994.

Kockelmans, J. J. Ed. *A Companion to Martin Heidegger's Being and Time*. Washington, DC: Catholic University of America Press, 1986.

Löwith, Karl. *Martin Heidegger and European Nihilism*. Ed. R. Wolin. New York: Columbia University Press, 1995.

Milchman, Alan and Alan Rosenberg. Eds. *Martin Heidegger and the Holocaust*. Atlantic Highlands, NJ: Humanities Press, 1997.

Murray, Michael. Ed. *Heidegger and Modern Philosophy*. New Haven, CT: Yale University Press, 1978.

Neske, G. and E. Kettering. Eds. *Martin Heidegger and National Socialism. Questions and Answers*. Trans. L. Harries. New York: Paragon House, 1990.

Ott, Hugo. *Martin Heidegger. A Political Life*. Trans. Allan Blunden. London: Harper Collins, 1993.

Petzet, Heinrich. *Auf einem Stern zugehen: Begegungen und Gespräche mit Martin Heidegger, 1929–1976*. Frankfurt: Societäts-Verlag, 1983.

Petzet, Heinrich. *Encounters and Dialogues with Martin Heidegger 1929–1976*. Trans. P. Emad and K. Maly. Chicago: University of Chicago Press, 1993.

Philipse, Herman. *Heidegger's Philosophy of Being*. Princeton, NJ: Princeton University Press, 1998.

Pöggeler, Otto. *Martin Heidegger's Path of Thinking*. Atlantic Highlands, NJ: Humanities Press, 1989.

Richardson, William. *Heidegger: Through Phenomenology to Thought*. The Hague: Nijhoff, 1963.

Rockmore, Tom. *Heidegger's Nazism and Philosophy*. London: Harvester, 1992.

Rorty, Richard. *Essays on Heidegger and Others. Philosophical Papers*, Vol. 2. Cambridge: Cambridge University Press, 1991.

Safranski, R. *Martin Heidegger. Between Good and Evil*. Cambridge, MA: Harvard University Press, 1998.

Schneeberger, Guido. *Nachlese zu Heidegger: Dokumente zu seinem Leben und Denken*. Bern: Suhr, 1962.

Sheehan, Thomas. "Heidegger's Early Years; Fragments for a Philosophical Biography", *Listening* 12 (1977), pp. 5–8.

Sheehan, Thomas. "Heidegger's Introduction to the Phenomenology of Religion, 1920–21", *The Personalist* LX(3) (1979), pp. 312–324.

Sheehan, Thomas. "Caveat Lector: The New Heidegger", *New York Review of Books* 4 December 1980. pp. 39–41.

Sheehan, Thomas. Ed. *Heidegger: The Man and the Thinker*. Chicago: Precedent, 1981.

Stern, Günther. "On the Pseudo-Concreteness of Heidegger's Philosophy", *Philosophy and Phenomenological Research* 8(3) (1947–8), pp. 337–370.

Taminiaux, Jacques. *Heidegger and the Project of Fundamental Ontology*. Albany, NY: SUNY Press, 1991.

Van Buren, John. *The Young Heidegger. Rumor of the Hidden King*. Bloomington, IN: Indiana University Press, 1994.

Hans-Georg Gadamer

Primary sources

Gadamer, Hans-Georg. *Gesammelte Werke*, 10 vols. Tübingen. J.C.B.Mohr. 1985–1995.

Gadamer, Hans-Georg. *Platos dialektische Ethik*. Hamburg: Meiner, 1968.

Gadamer, Hans-Georg. *Wahrheit und Methode*, Band 1, *Grundzüge einer philosophischen Hermeneutik*. Tübingen: Lohr, 1960; 2nd edition, 1965.

Gadamer, Hans-Georg. *Wahrheit und Methode*, Band 2, *Ergänzungen*, Register. 2. Auflage. 1993.

Gadamer: primary sources in translation

Gadamer, Hans-Georg. "Back from Syracuse", trans. J. McCumber. *Critical Inquiry* 15 (Winter, 1989), p. 428.

Gadamer, Hans-Georg. *Dialogue and Dialectic. Eight Hermeneutical Studies on Plato*. Trans. P. Christopher Smith. New Haven, CT: Yale University Press, 1980.

Gadamer, Hans-Georg. *Hegel's Dialectic. Five Hermeneutical Studies*. Trans. P. Christopher Smith. New Haven, CT: Yale University Press, 1976.

Gadamer, Hans-Georg. *Heidegger Ways*. Trans. J. W. Stanley. Albany, NY: SUNY Press, 1994.

Gadamer, Hans-Georg. *Literature and Philosophy in Dialogue*. Trans. R. H. Paslick. Albany, NY: SUNY Press, 1994.

Gadamer, Hans-Georg. *Philosophical Apprenticeships*. Trans. Robert R. Sullivan. Cambridge, MA: MIT Press, 1990.

Gadamer, Hans-Georg. *Philosophical Hermeneutics*. Trans. and Ed. David E. Linge. Berkeley, CA: University of California Press, 1977.

Gadamer, Hans-Georg. *Plato's Dialectical Ethics*. Trans. Robert M. Wallace. New Haven, CT: Yale University Press, 1991.

Gadamer, Hans-Georg. *Reason in the Age of Science*. Trans. F. G. Lawrence. Cambridge, MA: MIT Press, 1981.

Gadamer, Hans-Georg. *The Enigma of Health*. Trans. J. Gaiger and N. Walker. Cambridge: Polity Press, 1996.

Gadamer, Hans-Georg. *The Idea of the Good in Platonic-Aristotelian Philosophy*. New Haven, CT: Yale University Press, 1986.

Gadamer, Hans-Georg. *The Relevance of the Beautiful and Other Essays*. Trans. N. Walker. Cambridge: Cambridge University Press, 1986.

Gadamer, Hans-Georg. *Truth and Method*, 2nd edition. Trans. Joel Weimsheimer and Donald G. Marshall. London: Sheed & Ward, 1989.

Gadamer: further reading

Barnes, J. "Review of Gadamer's *Philosophical Apprenticeships*", *London Review of Books* 8(19) (1986).

Betti, E. "Hermeneutics as the General Methodology of the *Geisteswissenschaften*", in J. Bleicher, ed., *Contemporary Hermeneutics*. London: Routledge & Kegan Paul, 1980. pp. 51–94.

Dostal, Robert. "The World We Never Lost: The Hermeneutics of Trust", *Philosophy and Phenomenological Research* 47 (1987), pp. 414–434.

Dreyfus, Hubert L. "Hermeneutics and Holism", *Review of Metaphysics* 34 (1980).

Dunne, Joseph. *Back to the Rough Ground. 'Phronesis' and 'Techne' in Modern Philosophy and in Aristotle*. Notre Dame, IN: University of Notre Dame Press, 1993.

Grondin, Jean. "On the Sources of *Truth and Method*", *Sources of Hermeneutics*. Albany, NY: SUNY Press, 1995.

Hahn, Lewis E. Ed. *The Philosophy of Hans-Georg Gadamer*, Library of the Living Philosophers. La Salle, IL: Open Court, 1997.

Hirsch, E. D. *Validity in Interpretation*. New Haven, CT: Yale University Press, 1967.

Kögler, Hans-Herbert. *Die Macht des Dialogs. Kritische Hermeneutik nach Gadamer, Foucault, und Rorty*. Stuttgart: Metzler, 1992.

Michelfelder, Diane P. and Richard E. Palmer. Eds. *Dialogue and Deconstruction. The Gadamer-Derrida Encounter*. Albany, NY: SUNY Press, 1989.

Misgeld, Dieter and Graeme Nicholson. Eds. *Hans-Georg Gadamer on Education, Poetry and History. Applied Hermeneutics*. Albany, NY: SUNY Press, 1992.

Mueller-Vollmer, K. Ed. *The Hermeneutics Reader*. Oxford: Basil Blackwell, 1986.

Orozco, Teresa. *Platonische Gewalt. Gadamers politische Hermeneutik der NS-Zeit*. Hamburg: Argument Verlag, 1995.

Palmer, Richard O. *Hermeneutics. Interpretation Theory in Schleiermacher, Dilthey, Heidegger, and Gadamer*. Evanston, IL: Northwestern University Press, 1969.

Silverman, H. J. Ed. *Gadamer and Hermeneuitics*. London: Routledge, 1991.

Wachterhauser, Brice R. *Hermeneutics and Modern Philosophy*. Albany, NY: SUNY Press, 1986.

Warnke, G. *Gadamer: Hermeneutics, Tradition and Reason*. Cambridge: Polity Press, 1987.

Weinsheimer, J. *Gadamer's Hermeneutics: A Reading of Truth and Method*. New Haven, CT: Yale University Press, 1985.

Hannah Arendt

Primary sources

Arendt, Hannah. *Between Past and Future: Eight Exercises in Political Thought*, 1961. Reprinted New York: Penguin, 1977.

Arendt, Hannah. *Crises of the Republic*. New York: Harcourt Brace Jovanovich, 1972.

Arendt, Hannah. *Der Liebesbegriff bei Augustin. Versuch einer philosophischen Interpretation*. Berlin: Springer-Verlag, 1929.

Arendt, Hannah. *Eichmann in Jerusalem. A Report on the Banality of Evil*, 2nd rev. edition. New York: Penguin, 1964.

Arendt, Hannah. *Essays in Understanding, 1930–1954*. Ed. Jerome Kohn. New York: Harcourt Brace Jovanovich, 1994.

Arendt, Hannah. "Foreword", to Karl Jaspers, *The Future of Germany*. Trans. E. B. Ashton. Chicago: University of Chicago Press, 1967.

Arendt, Hannah. Ed. *Illuminations*. Walter Benjamin. New York: Schocken Books, 1969.

Arendt, Hannah. *Lectures on Kant's Political Philosophy*. Ed. Ronald Beiner. Chicago: University of Chicago Press, 1982.

Arendt, Hannah. *Love and St. Augustine*. Ed. Joanna V. Scott and Judith C. Stark. Chicago: University of Chicago Press, 1996.

Arendt, Hannah. "Martin Heidegger at Eighty", *New York Review of Books* 21 October 1971, pp. 50–54.

Arendt, Hannah. *Men in Dark Times*. New York: Harcourt Brace Jovanovich, 1968.

Arendt, Hannah. *Rahel Varnhagen. The Life of a Jewish Woman*. Trans. Richard and Clara Winston, rev. edition. New York: Harcourt Brace Jovanovich, 1974.

Arendt, Hannah. "Reflections on Little Rock", *Dissent* VI(1) (Winter, 1959), pp. 45–56.

Arendt, Hannah. "Rejoinder to Eric Voegelin's Review of *The Origins of Totalitarianism*", *Review of Politics* 15 (January, 1953), pp. 76–85.

Arendt, Hannah. "Review of Alice Ruehle-Gerstel's *Das Frauenproblem der Gegenwart*", *Die Gesellschaft* 10 (1932).

Arendt, Hannah. *The Human Condition. A Study of the Central Dilemmas Facing Modern Man*. Chicago: University of Chicago Press, 1958. (Reprint: Anchor Books, 1959).

Arendt, Hannah. *The Jew as Pariah*. Ed. Ron Feldman. New York: Grove Press, 1978.

Arendt, Hannah. *The Life of the Mind. Vol. One: Thinking*. New York: Harcourt Brace, 1971.

Arendt, Hannah. *The Life of the Mind. Vol. Two: Willing*. New York: Harcourt Brace, 1978.

Arendt, Hannah. *The Origins of Totalitarianism*. New York: Harcourt Brace Jovanovich, 1951.

Arendt, Hannah. *Vita activa oder Vom tätigen Leben*. Stuttgart: Kohlhammer, 1960.

Arendt, Hannah. "What is *Existenz* philosophy?", *Partisan Review* 13(1) (1946), pp. 34–56.

Arendt, Hannah und Martin Heidegger. *Briefe 1925 bis 1975 und andere Zeugnisse aus den Nachlässen*. Hrsg. Ursula Ludz. Frankfurt: Klostermann, 1998.

Arendt, Hannah and Karl Jaspers. *Hannah Arendt and Karl Jaspers Correspondence 1926–1969*. Ed. Lotte Köhler and Hans Saner. Trans. Robert and Rita Kimber. New York: Harcourt Brace, 1992.

Arendt, Hannah and Mary McCarthy. *Between Friends: The Correspondence of*

Hannah Arendt and Mary McCarthy 1949–1975. Ed. Carol Brightman. New York: Harcourt Brace Jovanovich, 1995.

Arendt: further reading

Barnouw, Dagmar. *Visible Spaces: Hannah Arendt and the German-Jewish Experience*. Baltimore, MD: Johns Hopkins University Press, 1990.

Benhabib, Seyla. *The Reluctant Modernism of Hannah Arendt*. London: Sage, 1996.

Bernauer, James W. Ed. *Amor Mundi. Explorations in the Faith and Thought of Hannah Arendt*. Dordrecht: Nijhoff, 1987.

Bowen-Moore, Patricia. *Hannah Arendt's Philosophy of Natality*. Basingstoke: Macmillan, 1989.

Bradshaw, Leah. *Acting and Thinking: The Political Thought of Hannah Arendt*. Toronto: University of Toronto Press, 1989.

Canovan, Margaret. *The Political Thought of Hannah Arendt*. London: Dent, 1979.

Dossa, Shiraz.*The Public Realm and the Public Self: The Political Theory of Hannah Arendt*. Waterloo, Ontario: Wilfrid Laurier University Press, 1989.

Ellison, Ralph. *Who Speak for the Negro?*. Ed. R. Penn Warren. New York: Random House, 1965.

Ettinger, Elizbieta. *Hannah Arendt/Martin Heidegger*. New Haven, CT: Yale University Press, 1995.

Gottsegen, Michael. *The Political Thought of Hannah Arendt*. Albany, NY: SUNY Press, 1993.

Hansen, Philip. *Hannah Arendt. Politics, History, Citizenship*. Cambridge: Polity Press, 1993.

Hill, Melvyn A. Ed. *Hannah Arendt. The Recovery of the Public World*. New York: St Martin's Press, 1979.

Hinchman, Lewis P. and Sandra K. Hinchman. Eds. *Hannah Arendt. Critical Essays*. Albany, NY: SUNY Press, 1993.

Honig, Bonnie. Ed. *Feminist Interpretations of Hannah Arendt*. University Park, PA: University of Pennsylvania Press, 1995.

Kateb, George. *Hannah Arendt. Politics, Conscience, Evil*. Totowa, NJ: Rowman and Allanheld, 1984.

Lazare, Bernard. *Job's Dung Heap*. New York: Schocken Books, 1948.

McCarthy, Mary. "Saying Good-by to Hannah", *New York Review of Books* 22 January 1976, pp. 8–10.

Passerin d'Entreves, Maurizio. *The Political Philosophy of Hannah Arendt*. London: Routledge, 1994.

Taminiaux, Jacques. *La Fille de Thrace et le penseur professionnel: Arendt et Heidegger*. Paris: Editions Payot, 1992.

Taminiaux, Jacques. *The Thracian Maid and the Professional Thinker*. Trans. Michael Gendre. Albany, NY: SUNY Press, 1997.

Villa, Dana R. *Arendt and Heidegger. The Fate of the Political*. Princeton, NJ: Princeton University Press, 1996.

Young-Bruehl, Elisabeth. *Hannah Arendt. For Love of the World*. New Haven, CT: Yale University Press, 1982.

Young-Bruehl, Elisabeth. "Hannah Arendt Among Feminists", *Hannah Arendt. Twenty Years Later*. Cambridge, MA: MIT Press, 1997.

Emmanuel Levinas

Primary Sources

Levinas, E. *A l'heure des nations*. Paris: Editions de Minuit, 1988.

Levinas, E. *Autrement qu'être ou au-delà de l'essence*. Phaenomenologica Vol. 54. The Hague: Nijhoff, 1974.

Levinas, E. *De Dieu qui vient a l'idée*. Paris: Vrin, 1982.

Levinas, E. *De l'évasion*. Montpellier: Fata Morgana, 1982.

Levinas, E. *De l'existence à l'existant*. Paris: Fontaine, 1947. Reprinted Vrin, 1973.

Levinas, E. *Difficile liberté. Essais sur le Judaisme*. Paris: Albin Michel, 1963.

Levinas, E. *Du sacré au saint*. Paris: Minuit, 1977.

Levinas, E. *En découvrant l'existence avec Husserl et Heidegger*. Paris: Vrin, 1949; reprinted 1974, 1988.

Levinas, E. *Entre nous: Essais sur le penser-à-l'autre*. Paris: Grasset, 1991.

Levinas, E. *Éthique et infini*. Paris: Fayard, 1982.

Levinas, E. *Existence humaine et transcendance*. Neuchatel: Editions de la Baconnière, 1944.

Levinas, E. *Hors sujet*. Montpellier: Fata Morgana, 1987.

Levinas, E. *Humanisme de l'autre homme*. Montpellier. Fata Morgana, 1973.

Levinas, E. *L'Au delà du verset. Lectures et discours talmudiques*. Paris: Editions de Minuit, 1981.

Levinas, E. *Le Temps et l'autre*. Paris: Arthaud, 1948. Reprinted Montpellier: Fata Morgana, 1979.

Levinas, E. *La Mort et le temps*. Paris: L'Herne, 1991.

Levinas, E. *La Théorie de l'intuition dans la phénoménologie de Husserl*. Paris: Félix Alcan, 1930. Reprinted Paris: Vrin, 1963.

Levinas, E. *Les Imprévus de l'histoire*. Montpellier: Fata Morgana, 1994.

Levinas, E. *Liberté et commandement*. Montpellier: Fata Morgana, 1994.

Levinas, E. *Noms propres*. Montpellier: Fata Morgana, 1975.

Levinas, E. *Nouvelles lectures talmudiques*. Paris: Editions de Minuit, 1996.

Levinas, E. *Quatre lectures talmudiques*. Paris: Editions de Minuit, 1968.

Levinas, E. "Sur les *Ideen* de M.E. Husserl", *Revue Philosophique de la France et de l'Etranger* 108(3–4) (1929).

Levinas, E. *Sur Maurice Blanchot*. Montpellier: Fata Morgana, 1975.

Levinas, E. *Totalité et infini. Essai sur l'extériorité*. The Hague: Nijhoff, 1961.

Levinas, E. *Transcendance et intelligibilité*. Geneva: Labor et Fides, 1984.

Levinas: primary sources in translation

Levinas, E. "*As if consenting to a Horror*", trans. Paula Wissig. *Critical Inquiry* 15(2) (Winter, 1989) pp. 485–488.

Levinas, E. *Basic Philosophical Writings*. Ed. Adriaan Peperzak, Simon Critchley, and Robert Bernasconi. Bloomington, IN: Indiana University Press, 1996.

Levinas, E. *Between Us*. London: Athlone Press, 1997.

Levinas, E. *Beyond the Verse*. Trans. Gary D. Mole. London: Athlone Press, 1994.

Levinas, E. *Collected Philosophical Papers*. Trans. A. Lingis. Dordrecht: Kluwer, 1987.

Levinas, E. *Difficult Freedom. Essays on Judaism.* Trans. S. Hand. London: Athlone Press, 1990.

Levinas, E. *Discovering Existence with Husserl.* Trans. R. Cohen and Michael B. Smith. Evanston, IL: Northwestern University Press, 1998.

Levinas, E. *Emmanuel Levinas: Basic Writings.* Ed. R. Bernasconi, S. Critchley, and A. Peperzak. Bloomington, IN: Indiana University Press, 1996.

Levinas, E. *Ethics and Infinity.* Trans. R. Cohen. Pittsburgh: Duquesne University Press, 1985.

Levinas, E. *Existence and Existents.* Trans. A. Lingis. Dordrecht: Kluwer, 1988.

Levinas, E. *In the Time of Nations.* Trans. Michael B. Smith. London: Athlone Press, 1994.

Levinas, E. *Nine Talmudic Readings.* Trans. A. Aronowicz. Bloomington, IN: Indiana University Press, 1990.

Levinas, E. *Of God Who Comes to Thought.* Stanford, Ca: Meridian, 1998.

Levinas, E. *Otherwise Than Being or Beyond Essence.* Trans. A. Lingis. The Hague: Nijhoff, 1981.

Levinas, E. *Outside the Subject.* Trans. Michael B. Smith. London: Athlone Press, 1993.

Levinas, E. *Proper Names.* Trans. Michael B. Smith. London: Athlone Press, 1996.

Levinas, E. "Reflections on the Philosophy of Hitlerism", trans. S. Hand, *Critical Inquiry* 17(1) (Autumn, 1990).

Levinas, E. *The Levinas Reader.* Ed. Sean Hand. Oxford: Blackwell, 1989.

Levinas, E. *The Theory of Intuition in Husserl's Phenomenology.* Trans. A. Orianne. Evanston, IL: Northwestern University Press, 1973.

Levinas, E. "The Understanding of Spirituality in French and German Culture", trans. Andrius Valevicius, *Continental Philosophy Review* 31 (1998).

Levinas, E. *Time and the Other.* Trans. R. Cohen. Pittsburgh: Duquesne University Press, 1987.

Levinas, E. *Totality and Infinity.* Trans. A. Lingis. Pittsburgh: Duquesne University Press, 1969.

Levinas: further reading

Bernasconi, Robert and Simon Critchley. Eds. *Re-Reading Levinas.* London: Athlone Press, 1991.

Bernasconi, Robert and David Wood. Eds. *The Provocation of Levinas: Rethinking the Other.* London: Routledge, 1988.

Burggraeve, Roger. *Emmanuel Levinas: Une bibliographie primaire et secondaire (1929–1985).* Leuven: Peeters, 1986.

Caputo, J. *Against Ethics.* Bloomington, IN: Indiana University Press, 1993.

Chalier, Catherine. *Levinas: L'Utopie de l'humain.* Paris: Albin Michel, 1993.

Cohen, R. A. *Elevations. The Height of the Good in Levinas and Rosenzweig.* Chicago: University of Chicago Press, 1994.

Cohen, Robert. Ed. *Face to Face with Levinas.* Albany, NY: SUNY Press, 1986.

Critchley, Simon. *The Ethics of Deconstruction: Derrida and Levinas.* Oxford: Blackwell, 1992.

Davis, Colin. *Levinas. An Introduction.* Cambridge: Polity Press, 1996.

Gibbs, R. *Correlations in Rosenzweig and Levinas.* Princeton, NJ: Princeton University Press, 1992.

Greisch, Jean and Jacques Rolland. Eds. *Emmanuel Levinas: L'Éthique comme philosophie première*. Paris: Editions du Cerf, 1993.

Kearney, R. "Ethics of the Infinite", Interview with Levinas, in *Dialogues with Contemporary Continental Thinkers*. Manchester: Manchester University Press, 1984.

Laruelle, François. Ed. *Textes pour Emmanuel Levinas*. Paris: Éditions Jean-Michel Place, 1980.

Llewelyn, J. *Emmanuel Levinas: The Genealogy of Ethics*. London: Routledge, 1995.

Peperzak, Adriaan Theodoor. *To the Other: An Introduction to the Philosophy of Emmanuel Levinas*. West Lafayette, IN: Purdue University Press, 1993.

Peperzak, Adriaan Theodoor. Ed. *Ethics as First Philosophy. The Significance of Emmanuel Levinas*. London: Routledge, 1995.

Peperzak, Adriaan Theodoor. *Beyond. The Philosophy of Emmanuel Levinas*. Evanston, IL: Northwestern University Press, 1997.

Poirié, François. *Emmanuel Levinas. Qui êtes-vous?*. Lyons: La Manufacture, 1987.

Rötzer, Florian. "Emmanuel Levinas", *Conversations with French Philosophers*. Atlantic Highlands, NJ: Humanities Press, 1995. pp. 57–66.

Wyschogrod, Edith. *Emmanuel Levinas: The Problem of Ethical Metaphysics*. The Hague: Nijhoff, 1974.

Jean-Paul Sartre

Primary sources

Sartre, Jean-Paul. *Baudelaire*. Paris: Gallimard, 1947.

Sartre, Jean-Paul. *Cahiers pour une morale*. Paris: Gallimard, 1983.

Sartre, Jean-Paul. *Critique de la raison dialectique*. Paris: Gallimard, 1960.

Sartre, Jean-Paul. *Critique de la raison dialectique. Tome 2. L'intelligibilité de l'histoire*. Paris: Gallimard, 1985.

Sartre, Jean-Paul. *Esquisse d'une théorie des émotions*. Paris: Hermann, 1939.

Sartre, Jean-Paul. *L'Être et le néant. Essai d'ontologie phénoménologique*. Paris: Gallimard, 1943.

Sartre, Jean-Paul. *L'Existentialisme est un humanisme*. Paris: Nagel, 1946.

Sartre, Jean-Paul. *L'Idiot de la famille*, 3 vols. Paris: Gallimard, 1971–1972.

Sartre, Jean-Paul. *L'Imaginaire. Psychologie phénoménologique de l'imagination*. Paris: Editions Gallimard, 1940.

Sartre, Jean-Paul. *L'Imagination*. Paris: Alcan, 1936.

Sartre, Jean-Paul. *Le Scenario Freud*. Paris: Gallimard, 1984.

Sartre, Jean-Paul. *La Nausée*. Paris: Gallimard, 1938.

Sartre, Jean-Paul. *La Transcendance de l'égo. Esquisse d'une déscription phénoménologique. Recherches philosophiques* 6 (1936/7), pp. 85–123.

Sartre, Jean-Paul. *Les Carnets de la drôle de guerre: Novembre 1939 – Mars 1940*. Paris: Gallimard, 1983.

Sartre, Jean-Paul. *Les mots*. Paris: Gallimard, 1964.

Sartre, Jean-Paul. *Les Mouches*. Paris: Gallimard, 1943.

Sartre, Jean-Paul. *Questions de méthode*. Paris: Gallimard, 1967.

Sartre, Jean-Paul. *Réflexions sur la question Juive*. Paris: Gallimard, Paul Morihien, 1946.

Sartre, Jean-Paul. *Saint Genet, comédien et martyre*. Paris: Gallimard, 1952.

Sartre, Jean-Paul. *Situations*, I–X. Paris: Gallimard, 1947–1976.

Sartre: primary sources in translation

Sartre, Jean-Paul. *Anti-Semite and Jew*. Trans. George J. Becker. New York: Schocken Books, 1965.

Sartre, Jean-Paul. *Baudelaire*. Trans. M. Turnell. London: Hamish Hamilton, 1964.

Sartre, Jean-Paul. *Being and Nothingness. An Essay on Phenomenological Ontology*. Trans. Hazel Barnes. London: Routledge, 1995.

Sartre, Jean-Paul. *Critique of Dialectic Reason*. Trans. Alan Sheridan-Smith. London: New Left Books, 1976.

Sartre, Jean-Paul. *Critique of Dialectic Reason. Volume 2. Intelligibility of History*. London: Verso, 1991.

Sartre, Jean-Paul. *Existentialism and Humanism*. Trans. P. Mairet. London: Methuen, 1973.

Sartre, Jean-Paul. *Imagination. A Psychological Critique*. Trans. Forrest Williams. Ann Arbor, MI: University of Michigan Press, 1962.

Sartre, Jean-Paul. "Intentionality: A Fundamental Idea in Husserl's Philosophy", *Journal of the British Society for Phenomenology* 1(2) (May, 1970), pp. 4–5.

Sartre, Jean-Paul. *Literary and Philosophical Essays*. London: Rider, 1955.

Sartre, Jean-Paul. *Nausea*. Trans. Robert Baldick. Harmondsworth: Penguin, 1965.

Sartre, Jean-Paul. *Notebook for an Ethics*. Chicago: University of Chicago Press, 1992.

Sartre, Jean-Paul. *Search for a Method*. Trans. Hazel Barnes. New York: Vintage Books, 1968.

Sartre, Jean-Paul. *Sketch for a Theory of the Emotions*. London: Methuen, 1971

Sartre, Jean-Paul. *The Idiot of the Family. Gustav Flaubert*. Trans. Carol Cosman. Chicago: University of Chicago Press, Vol. 1, 1981; Vol. 2, 1987; Vol. 3, 1989.

Sartre, Jean-Paul. *The Flies*. Trans. Stuart Gilbert. In J.-P. Sartre, *Altona, Men Without Shadows, The Flies*. Harmondsworth: Penguin, 1962.

Sartre, Jean-Paul. *The Freud Scenario*. London: Verso, 1985.

Sartre, Jean-Paul. *The Psychology of Imagination*. Trans. Bernard Frechtman. London: Methuen, 1972.

Sartre, Jean-Paul. *The War Diaries*. Trans. Quintin Hoare. London: Verso, 1984.

Sartre, Jean-Paul. *Transcendence of the Ego*. Trans. Forrest Williams and Robert Kirkpatrick. New York: Farrar, Straus and Giroux, 1957.

Sartre, Jean-Paul. *What is Literature?*. London: Methuen, 1967.

Sartre, Jean-Paul. *Witness to my Life: The Letters of J.-P. Sartre to Simone de Beauvoir, 1926–1939*. Ed. S. de Beauvoir. Trans. L. Fahnestock and N. MacAfee. London: Hamish Hamilton, 1992.

Sartre, Jean-Paul. *Words*. Trans. Irene Clephane. Harmondsworth: Penguin, 1967.

Sartre: further reading

Bair, Deirdre. *Simone de Beauvoir. A Biography*. New York: Simon and Schuster, 1990.

Caws, Peter. *Sartre*. London: Routledge & Kegan Paul, 1979.

Cohen-Solal, Annie. *Sartre. A Life*. Trans. A Cancogni. Ed. Norman McAfee. New York: Pantheon Books, 1987.

Contat, Michel and Michel Rybalka, *Les Écrits de Sartre*. Paris: Gallimard, 1970.

Danto, Arthur. *Sartre*. London: Fontana & Collins, 1975.

Deguy, Jacques. *Jacques Deguy commente La nausée de Jean-Paul Sartre*. Paris: Gallimard, 1993.

de Beauvoir, Simone. *The Ethics of Ambiguity*. Trans. B. Frechtmann. New York: Citadel Press, 1948; reprinted 1970.

de Beauvoir, Simone. *La Cérémonie des Adieux suivi de entretiens aven Jean-Paul Sartre*. Paris: Gallimard, 1981.

de Beauvoir, Simone. *Adieux. A Farewell to Sartre*, Trans. Patrick O'Brian. New York: Pantheon, 1984.

Fullbrook, Kate and Edward Fullbrook, *Simone de Beauvoir and Jean-Paul Sartre. The Remaking of a Twentieth-Century Legend*. London: Harvester, 1993.

Hayman, Ronald. *Writing Against. A Biography of Sartre*. London: Weidenfeld and Nicolson, 1986.

McCulloch, Gregory. *Using Sartre. An Analytical Introduction to Early Sartrean Themes*. London: Routledge, 1994.

Natanson, M. *A Critique of J.-P. Sartre's Ontology*. The Hague: Nijhoff, 1973.

Royle, Peter. *The Sartre-Camus Controversy. A Literary and Philosophical Critique*. Ottowa: University of Ottowa Press, 1982.

Schilpp, P. A. Ed. *The Philosophy of Jean-Paul Sartre*. La Salle, IL: Open Court, 1981.

Silverman, Hugh and Frederick A. Elliston. Eds. *Jean-Paul Sartre. Contemporary Approaches to His Philosophy*. Pittsburgh: Duquesne University Press, 1980.

Warnock, Mary. *The Philosophy of Sartre*. London: Hutchinson, 1965.

Wider, Kathleen V. *The Bodily Nature of Consciousness. Sartre and Contemporary Philosophy of Mind*. Ithaca, NY: Cornell University Press, 1997.

Wilcocks, R. *J-P. Sartre. A Bibliography of International Criticism*. Edmonton: University of Alberta Press, 1975.

Maurice Merleau-Ponty

Primary sources

Merleau-Ponty, M. "Christianisme et ressentiment", *La Vie Intellectuelle* 7(36) (1935).

Merleau-Ponty, M. *Éloge de la philosophie*. Paris: Gallimard, 1953.

Merleau-Ponty, M. "Husserl aux limites de la phénoménologie", *Annuaire du Collège de France*. Paris: Imprimerie Nationale, 1960.

Merleau-Ponty, M. *L'Oeil et l'esprit*. Paris: Gallimard, 1964.

Merleau-Ponty, M. *L'Union de l'âme et du corps chez Malebranche, Biran et Bergson*. Recueillies et redigées par Jean Deprun. Paris: Vrin, 1968.

Merleau-Ponty, M. *Le Visible et l'invisible*. Paris: Gallimard, 1964.

Merleau-Ponty, M. *La Nature. Notes cours du Collège de France*. Établi et annoté par Dominique Séglard. Paris: Seuil, 1995.

Merleau-Ponty, M. *La Prose du monde, texte établi et présenté par Claude Lefort* Paris: Gallimard, 1969.

Merleau-Ponty, M. *La Structure du comportement*. Paris: PUF, 1942.

Merleau-Ponty, M. *Les Aventures de la dialectique*. Paris: Gallimard, 1955.

Merleau-Ponty, M. *Phénoménologie de la perception*. Paris: Gallimard, 1945.

Merleau-Ponty, M. *Sens et non-sens*. Paris: Nagel, 1966.

Merleau-Ponty, M. *Signes*. Paris: Gallimard, 1960.

BIBLIOGRAPHY

Merleau-Ponty: primary sources in translation

Merleau-Ponty,. M. *Adventures of the Dialectic.* Trans. J. Bien. Evanston, IL: Northwestern University Press, 1973.

Merleau-Ponty, M. *Humanism and Terror.* Trans. J. O'Neill. Boston: Beacon Press, 1969.

Merleau-Ponty, M. *In Praise of Philosophy.* Trans. J. Wild and J. M. Edie. Evanston, IL: Northwestern University Press, 1963.

Merleau-Ponty, M. *Phenomenology of Perception.* Trans. C. Smith. London: Routledge & Kegan Paul, 1962.

Merleau-Ponty, M. *Sense and Non-Sense.* Trans. H. Dreyfus. Evanston, IL: Northwestern University Press, 1964.

Merleau-Ponty, M. *Signs.* Trans. R. McCleary. Evanston, IL: Northwestern University Press, 1964.

Merleau-Ponty, M. *The Primacy of Perception.* Ed. James Edie. Evanston, IL: Northwestern University Press, 1964.

Merleau-Ponty, M. *The Prose of the World.* Ed. Claude Lefort. Trans. J. O'Neill. Evanston, IL: Northwestern University Press, 1973.

Merleau-Ponty, M. *The Structure of Behavior.* Trans. A. L. Fisher. Boston: Beacon Press, 1963.

Merleau-Ponty, M. *Themes from the Lectures at the Collège de France 1952–1960.* Trans. J. O'Neill. Evanston, IL: Northwestern University Press, 1970.

Merleau-Ponty: further reading

Archard, David. *Marxism and Existentialism. The Political Philosophy of Sartre and Merleau-Ponty.* Belfast: Blackstaff, 1980.

Bannan, J. F. *The Philosophy of Merleau-Ponty.* New York: Harcourt, Brace and World, 1967.

Cataldi, Sue L. *Emotion, Depth and Flesh. A Study of Sensitive Space. Reflections on Merleau-Ponty's Philosophy of Embodiment.* Albany, NY: SUNY Press, 1993.

Cooper, B. *Merleau-Ponty and Marxism: From Terror to Reform.* Toronto: University of Toronto Press, 1979.

Edie, James M. "Was Merleau-Ponty a Structuralist?", *Semiotica* (1972), pp. 297–323.

Geraets, T. F. *Vers une nouvelle philosophie transcendentale. La genèse de la philosophie de Merleau-Ponty jusqu'à la "Phénoménologie de la perception".* The Hague: Nijhoff, 1971.

Gillan, G. Ed. *The Horizons of the Flesh: Critical Perspectives on the Thought of Merleau-Ponty.* Carbondale, IL: Southern Illinois University Press, 1973.

Hadreas, Peter. *In Place of the Flawed Diamond. An Investigation of Merleau-Ponty's Philosophy.* New York: Peter Lang, 1986.

Johnson, Galen A. and Michael B. Smith. Eds. *Ontology and Alterity in Merleau-Ponty.* Evanston, IL: Northwestern University Press, 1990.

Kearney, Richard. "Maurice Merleau-Ponty", in *Modern Movements in European Philosophy.* Manchester: Manchester University Press, 1986.

Knuks, Sonia. *The Political Philosophy of Merleau-Ponty.* Brighton: Harvester, 1981.

Kwant, Remi. *The Phenomenological Philosophy of Merleau-Ponty*. Pittsburgh: Duquesne University Press, 1963.

Kwant, Remi. *From Phenomenology to Metaphysics: An Inquiry into the Last Period of Merleau-Ponty's Philosophical Life*. Pittsburgh: Duquesne University Press, 1966.

Langer, Monika. *Merleau-Ponty's Phenomenology of Perception: A Guide and Commentary*. London: Macmillan, 1989.

Lévi-Strauss, Claude. "On Merleau-Ponty", Trans. C. Gross, *Graduate Faculty Philosophy Journal* 7(2) (1978).

Levinas, E. "On Intersubjectivity: Notes on Merleau-Ponty", *Outside the Subject*. Trans. Michael Smith. London: The Athlone Press, 1993. pp. 96–103.

Madison, Gary. *The Phenomenology of Merleau-Ponty*. Athens, OH: Ohio University Press, 1981.

Mallin, Samuel. *Merleau-Ponty's Philosophy*. New Haven, CT: Yale University Press, 1979.

O'Neill, John. *Perception, Expression and History: The Social Phenomenology of Maurice Merleau-Ponty*. Evanston, IL: Northwestern University Press, 1970.

Priest, Stephen. *Merleau-Ponty*. London: Routledge, 1998.

Rabil, A. *Merleau-Ponty: Existentialist of the Social World*. New York: Columbia University Press, 1967.

Sallis, J. Ed. *Merleau-Ponty: Perception, Structure and Language*. Atlantic Highlands, NJ: Humanities Press, 1981.

Sartre, Jean-Paul. "Merleau-Ponty", *Situations*. Trans. B. Eisler. New York: Fawcett World Library, 1966.

Schmidt, J. *Maurice Merleau-Ponty: Between Phenomenology and Structuralism*. London: Routledge, 1987.

Stewart, Jon. Ed. *The Relation Between Sartre and Merleau-Ponty*. Evanston, IL: Northwestern University Press, 1998.

Whiteside, K. "The Merleau-Ponty Bibliography: Additions and Corrections", *Journal of the History of Philosophy* 21 (1983), pp. 195–201.

Whiteside, K. *Merleau-Ponty and the Foundation of an Existential Politics*. Princeton, NJ: Princeton University Press, 1988.

Jacques Derrida

Primary Sources

Derrida, J. *Adieux: à Emmanuel Levinas*. Paris: Galilée, 1997.

Derrida, J. *Apories: Mourir – s'attendre aux limités de la vérité*. Paris: Éditions Galilée, 1996.

Derrida, J. *Cosmopolites de tous les pays, encore un effort!*. Paris: Galilée, 1997.

Derrida, J. *De l'esprit: Heidegger et la question*. Paris: Galilée, 1987.

Derrida, J. *De la grammatologie*. Paris: Éditions de Minuit, 1967.

Derrida, J. *Donner le temps*, 1, *La fausse monnaie*. Paris: Galilée, 1991.

Derrida, J. *Du droit à la philosophie*. Paris: Galilée, 1990.

Derrida, J. *D'un ton apocalyptique adopté naguère en philosophie*. Paris: Éditions Galilée, 1983.

Derrida, J. *Éperons. Les styles de Nietzsche*. Paris: Flammarion, 1978.

Derrida, J. *Force de loi: le fondement mystique de l'autorité*. Paris: Galilée, 1994.

Derrida, J. *Glas*. Paris: Éditions Galilée, 1974.

Derrida, J. *L'Archéologie du frivole: lire Condillac*. Paris: Éditions Galilée, 1973.

Derrida, J. *L'Autre Cap; suivi de la démocratie ajournée*. Paris: Éditions de Minuit, 1991.

Derrida, J. *L'Écriture et la différence*. Paris: Éditions du Seuil, 1967.

Derrida, J. *L'Origine de la géometrie de Husserl*. Introduction et traduction. Paris: Epiméthée, 1962.

Derrida, J. *Le Problème de la genèse dans la philosophie de Husserl*. Paris: PUF, 1990.

Derrida, J. *La Carte postale: de Socrate à Freud et au-delà*. Paris: Aubier-Flammarion, 1980.

Derrida, J. *La Dissémination*. Paris: Éditions du Seuil, 1972.

Derrida, J. *La Faculté de juger*. Paris: Éditions de Minuit, 1985.

Derrida, J. *La Verité en peinture*. Paris: Aubier-Flammarion, 1978.

Derrida, J. *La Voix et le phénomène*. Paris: Presses Universitaires de France, 1967.

Derrida, J. *Limited Inc*. Présentations et traductions par Elisabeth Weber. Paris: Galilée, 1990.

Derrida, J. *Mal d'archive: une impression freudienne*. Paris: Galilée, 1995.

Derrida, J. *Marges de la philosophie*. Paris: Éditions de Minuit, 1972.

Derrida, J. *Mémoires: pour Paul de Man*. Paris: Galilée, 1988.

Derrida, J. *Mémoires d'aveugle: l'autoportrait et autre ruines*. Paris: Louvre, 1990.

Derrida, J. *Parages*. Paris: Galilée, 1986.

Derrida, J. *Passions*. Paris: Galilée, 1993.

Derrida, J. *Points de suspensions. Entetiens*. Paris: Galilée, 1992.

Derrida, J. *Politiques de l'amitié; suivi de l'oreille de Heidegger*. Paris: Galilée, 1994.

Derrida, J. *Positions*. Paris: Éditions de Minuit, 1972.

Derrida, J. *Psyché: inventions de l'autre*. Paris: Galilée, 1987.

Derrida, J. *Résistances: de la psychoanalyse*. Paris: Galilée, 1996.

Derrida, J. *Shibboleth: pour Paul Celan*. Paris: Galilée, 1986.

Derrida, J. *Signéponge*. Paris: Éditions du Seuil, 1988.

Derrida, J. *Spectres de Marx: l'état de la dette, le travail du deuil et la nouvelle Internationale*. Paris: Galilée, 1993.

Derrida: primary sources in translation

Derrida, J. *Acts of Literature*. Ed. D. Attridge. London: Routledge, 1992.

Derrida, J. *Aporias*. Trans. T. Dutoit. Stanford, CA: Stanford University Press, 1993.

Derrida, J. "But beyond...(Open Letter to Anne McClintock and Rob Nixon)", *Critical Inquiry* 12 (Autumn, 1986), p. 167.

Derrida, J. *Cinders*. Trans. N. Lukacher. Lincoln, NE: University of Nebraska Press, 1991.

Derrida, J. *Dissemination*. Trans. B. Johnson. London: Athlone Press, 1981.

Derrida, J. *Edmund Husserl's Origin of Geometry. An Introduction*. Trans. J. P. Leavey and D. B. Allison. Sussex: Harvester Press, 1978.

Derrida, J. *Given Time 1: Counterfeit Money*. Trans. P. Kamuf. Chicago: Chicago University Press, 1993.

Derrida, J. *Glas*. Trans. J. P. Leavey Jr. and Richard Rand. Lincoln, NE: University of Nebraska Press, 1986.

Derrida, J. "Adieu", trans. Pascale-Anne Brault and Michael Naas, *Philosophy Today* 40(3) (1996), pp. 334–340.

Derrida, J. *Limited Inc., abc...(Supplement to "Glyph" 2)*. London: Johns Hopkins University Press, 1977.

Derrida, J. *Margins of Philosophy*. Trans. A. Bass. Brighton: Harvester, 1982.

Derrida, J. *Memoires for Paul de Man*. Trans. C. Lindsay *et al*. New York: Columbia University Press, 1986.

Derrida, J. *Of Grammatology*. Trans. G. Spivak. Baltimore, MD: Johns Hopkins University Press, 1976.

Derrida, J. *Of Spirit: Heidegger and the Question*. Trans. G. Bennington and R. Bowlby. Chicago: Chicago University Press, 1990.

Derrida, J. *Points of Suspension*. Trans. P. Kamuf *et al*. Stanford, CA: Stanford University Press, 1995.

Derrida, J. *Positions*. Trans. A. Bass. London: Athlone Press, 1981.

Derrida, J. *Signsponge*. Trans. R. Rand. New York: Columbia University Press, 1984.

Derrida, J. *Specters of Marx: The State of the Debt, the Work of Mourning and the New International*. Trans. P. Kamuf. London: Routledge, 1994.

Derrida, J. *Speech and Phenomena and other Essays on Husserl's Theory of Signs*. Ed. and Trans. David Allison. Evanston, IL: Northwestern University Press, 1973.

Derrida, J. *Spurs*. Trans. B. Harlow. Chicago: Chicago University Press, 1979.

Derrida, J. *The Ear of the Other*. Trans. P. Kamuf and A. Ronell. New York: Schocken Books, 1985.

Derrida, J. *The Gift of Death*. Trans. D. Wills. Chicago: Chicago University Press, 1995.

Derrida, J. *The Other Heading: Reflections on Today's Europe*. Trans. P. A. Brault and M. G. Naas. Bloomington, IN: Indiana University Press, 1992.

Derrida, J. "The Politics of Friendship", *The Journal of Philosophy* 85 (1988), pp. 632–644.

Derrida, J. *The Politics of Friendship*. Trans. George Collins. London: Verso, 1997.

Derrida, J. *The Postcard: From Socrates to Freud and Beyond*. Trans. A. Bass. Chicago: Chicago University Press, 1987.

Derrida, J. "The Time of a Thesis: Punctuations", in A. Monteriore, ed., *Philosophy in France Today*. Cambridge: Cambridge University Press, 1983. pp. 34–50.

Derrida, J. *The Truth in Painting*. Trans. G. Bennington and I. McLeod. Chicago: Chicago University Press, 1987.

Derrida, J. *Writing and Difference*. Trans. A. Bass. London: Routledge & Kegan Paul, 1978.

Derrida: further reading

Bennington, G. and J. Derrida. *Derrida*. Chicago: University of Chicago Press, 1993.

Caputo, J. *Radical Hermeneutics: Deconstruction and the Hermeneutical Project*. Bloomington, IN: Indiana University Press, 1987.

Caputo, J. *Deconstruction in a Nutshell. A Conversation with Jacques Derrida*. New York: Fordham University Press, 1997.

Caputo, J. *The Prayers and Tears of Jacques Derrida*. Bloomington, IN: Indiana University Press, 1997.

Cavell, S. "What did Derrida want of Austin?", in *Philosophical Passages: Wittgenstein, Emerson, Austin, Derrida*. Oxford, Blackwell, 1995. pp. 42–90.

Collins, J. and B. Mayblin. *Derrida for Beginners*. Cambridge: Icon Books, 1996.

Culler, J. *On Deconstruction: Theory and Criticism after Structuralism*. Ithaca, NY: Cornell University Press, 1982.

Evans, J. Claude. *Strategies of Deconstruction. Derrida and the Myth of the Voice*. Minneapolis: University of Minnesota Press, 1991.

Gasché, R. *The Tain of the Mirror: Derrida and the Philosophy of Reflection*. Cambridge, MA: Harvard University Press, 1986.

Hopkins, Burt. "Derrida's Reading of Husserl in *Speech and Phenomena*: Ontologism and the Metaphysics of Presence", *Husserl Studies* 2 (1985), pp. 193–214.

Kamuf, Peggy. Ed. *A Derrida Reader. Between the Blinds*. London: Harvester, 1991.

Kofman, Sarah. *Lectures de Derrida*. Paris: Galilée, 1984.

Montefiore, A. Ed. *Philosophy in France Today*. Cambridge: Cambridge University Press, 1983.

Norris, C. *Deconstruction: Theory and Practice*. London: Methuen, 1982.

Norris, C. *Derrida*. London. Fontana, 1987.

Rorty, Richard. *Contingency, Irony and Solidarity*. Cambridge: Cambridge University Press, 1989.

Rorty, Richard. *Essays on Heidegger and Others. Philosophical Papers*, Vol. 2. Cambridge: Cambridge University Press, 1991.

Schultz, William and Lewis Fried. Eds. *Jacques Derrida. An Annotated Primary and Secondary Bibliography*. New York & London: Garland, 1992.

Searle, J. R. "The World Turned Upside Down", *Working Through Derrida*. Evanston, IL: Northwestern University Press, 1993.

Searle, J. R. "Reiterating the Differences: A Reply to Derrida", *Glyph* I (1977), pp. 198–208.

Sturrock, John. Ed. *Structuralism and Since. From Lévi-Strauss to Derrida*. Oxford: Oxford University Press, 1979.

Taylor, Mark. Ed. *Deconstruction in Context*. Chicago: University of Chicago Press, 1986.

Wood, David. Ed. *Derrida. A Critical Reader*. Oxford: Blackwell, 1992.

Wood, David and Robert Bernasconi, Eds. *Derrida and Différance*. Warwick: Parousia Press, 1985.

INDEX

phenomenology x, 5, 18–19, 322–3, 327–9; philosophy 329–30; public/private spheres 340; reason/violence 352; religious element 330–2; response/responsibility 349; on Sartre 334–5, 345; 'Some Reflections on the Philosophy of Hitlerism' 324–5; speech 348; subjectivity 341–3, 344–5; survivor guilt 325; Talmud 323–4; *The Theory of Intuition in Husserl's Phenomenology* 359; *Time and the Other* lectures 325, 338–40; trace 331–2, 469; war 17, 330, 333–5, 343–4; Zionism 326; *see also Totality and Infinity*
Lévy-Bruhl, Lucien 87, 182
life, biological/human 315
The Life of the Mind (Arendt) 289, 304, 306
life philosophy 168
life-world, Husserl ix, 181–6, 233; consciousness 66–7; *The Crisis of European Sciences and Transcendental Phenomenology* (Husserl) 147; horizon 162–3; Husserl 181–6; idealisation 12–14, 147
Lipps, Theodor 76, 79, 102
Locke, John 140, 311
logic: Brentano 26, 37–8; Husserl 70, 102–3, 104, 105, 123
Logical Investigations (Husserl) 63, 74–5, 80, 189; Brentano 26, 37, 70; composition 91–4; constitution 164; Derrida on 456, 460; descriptive psychology 7–8, 9–10, 137; *Erlebnisse* 138; expression 109–10, 110–13; and Frege 73; Heidegger 201; individual/universal 109–10; inner/outer perceptions 130; intentionality 76, 113–18; other 175; phenomenology 1–2, 5, 7–8, 9–10, 60, 66, 106–9; pole of identity 171; presentation 113–18; presuppositions 125, 126; realism/idealism 121–3; science as idea 94–6; truth/judgements 118–19
logocentrism 185, 437, 447, 448–50
logos 229–30, 235, 448
Lotze, Hermann 29, 75, 137

Löwith, Karl 245
Lukács, Georg 397
Lukasiewicz, Jan 37
Lycée Louis-le-Grand 437

McCarthy, Mary 303
McCulloch, Gregory 15, 358, 390
McGinn, Colin 14
Mach, Ernst 1, 7, 24, 34, 42, 69
Mannheim, Karl 295
Marcel, Gabriel 19, 324, 389
Marcuse, Herbert 4, 218, 245
Marty, Anton 24, 49–50, 51
Marxism: Arendt 307; class struggle 398; Derrida 444; and Heidegger 245; labour 307; Merleau-Ponty 393, 397, 399; phenomenology x, 21; Sartre 375
Masaryk, Thomas 24, 25, 67–8
master–slave dialectic 343–4, 409–10
mathematics 71
matter of the act 116, 118
Mauss, Marcel 443
meanings: deconstruction 450–1; Derrida 435–6, 447–8, 453, 471, 472; expression 111–12, 175; Heidegger 202–3; Husserl 234, 454; language 435–6; Levinas 327; multiple 472; noematic 158; phenomenology 101; readers 472; slippage of 471
Meinong, Alexius 24, 45, 49, 56, 100
memory 117
Men in Dark Times (Arendt) 288
mental acts 8–9, 45; Brentano 35, 55; Husserl 25, 93; intentions 52; naturalism 136; *see also Erlebnisse*
mental processes 130, 165
mental states 23, 41
mereology 36
Merleau-Ponty, Maurice 391–3, 397–9; *Adventures of the Dialectic* 398–9; art 401, 405–6; 'The Battle Over Existentialism' 396; behaviourism 393–4, 413–14, 416–17; *Being and Time* (Heidegger) 412; Bergson 393, 406–7; body 17, 391, 403–4, 409, 418–19, 423–5, 427; *Cartesian Meditations* (Husserl) 404; chiasm 429; child psychology 400; 'The